JAWAHARLAL
NEHRU

The Discovery of India

JAWAHARLAL NEHRU

The Discovery of India

DELHI
OXFORD UNIVERSITY PRESS
CALCUTTA CHENNAI MUMBAI

Oxford University Press, Great Clarendon Street, Oxford OX2 6DP

Oxford   New York
Athens   Auckland   Bangkok   Calcutta
Cape Town   Chennai   Dar es Salaam   Delhi
Florence   Hong Kong   Istanbul   Karachi
Kuala Lumpur   Madrid   Melbourne   Mexico City
Mumbai   Nairobi   Paris   Singapore
Taipei   Tokyo   Toronto

and associates in
Berlin   Ibadan

First published 1946 by
The Signet Press, Calcutta
Centenary Edition 1989
Eighth impression 1997

Printed at Rekha Printers Pvt. Ltd., New Delhi 110020
and published by Manzar Khan, Oxford University Press
YMCA Library Building, Jai Singh Road, New Delhi 110001

To my colleagues and co-prisoners in
the Ahmadnagar Fort Prison Camp
from 9 August 1942 to 28 March 1945

FOREWORD

My father's three books — *Glimpses of World History, An Autobiograpy* and *The Discovery of India* — have been my companions through life. It is difficult to be detached about them.

Indeed *Glimpses* was written for me. It remains the best introduction to the story of man for young and growing people in India and all over the world. The *Autobiography* has been acclaimed as not merely the quest of one individual for freedom, but as an insight into the making of the mind of new India. I had to correct the proofs of *Discovery* while my father was away, I think in Calcutta, and I was in Allahabad ill with mumps! The *Discovery* delves deep into the sources of India's national personality. Together, these books have moulded a whole generation of Indians and inspired persons from many other countries.

Books fascinated Jawaharlal Nehru. He sought out ideas. He was extraordinarily sensitive to literary beauty. In his writings he aimed at describing his motives and appraisals as meticulously as possible. The purpose was not self-justification or rationalization, but to show the rightness and inevitability of the actions and events in which he was a prime participant. He was a luminous man and his writings reflected the radiance of his spirit.

The decision of the Jawaharlal Nehru Memorial Fund to bring out a uniform edition of these three classics will be widely welcomed.

Indira Gandhi

New Delhi
4 November 1980

PREFACE

This book was written by me in Ahmadnagar Fort prison during the five months, April to September 1944. Some of my colleagues in prison were good enough to read the manuscript and make a number of valuable suggestions. On revising the book in prison I took advantage of these suggestions and made some additions. No one, I need hardly add, is responsible for what I have written or necessarily agrees with it. But I must express my deep gratitude to my fellow-prisoners in Ahmadnagar Fort for the innumerable talks and discussions we had, which helped me greatly to clear my own mind about various aspects of Indian history and culture. Prison is not a pleasant place to live in even for a short period, much less for long years. But it was a privilege for me to live in close contact with men of outstanding ability and culture and a wide human outlook which even the passions of the moment did not obscure.

My eleven companions in Ahmadnagar Fort were an interesting cross-section of India and represented in their several ways not only politics but Indian scholarship, old and new, and various aspects of present-day India. Nearly all the principal living Indian languages, as well as the classical languages which have powerfully influenced India in the past and present, were represented and the standard was often that of high scholarship. Among the classical languages were Sanskrit and Pali, Arabic and Persian; the modern languages were Hindi, Urdu, Bengali, Gujarati, Marathi, Telugu, Sindhi and Oriya. I had all this wealth to draw upon and the only limitation was my own capacity to profit by it. Though I am grateful to all my companions, I should like to mention especially Maulana Abul Kalam Azad, whose vast erudition invariably delighted me but sometimes also rather overwhelmed me, Govind Ballabh Pant, Narendra Deva and M. Asaf Ali.

It is a year and a quarter since I finished writing this book and some parts of it are already somewhat out of date, and much has happened since I wrote it. I have felt tempted to add and revise, but I have resisted the temptation. Indeed I could not have done otherwise for life outside prison is of a different texture and there is no leisure for thought or writing. It has been difficult enough for me to read again what I have written. I wrote originally in long-hand; this was typed after my release. I was unable to find time to read the typescript and the publication of the book was being delayed when my daughter, Indira, came to my rescue and took this burden off my shoulders. The book remains as written in prison with no additions or changes, except for the postscript at the end.

I do not know how other authors feel about their writings, but always I have a strange sensation when I read something that I had written some time previously. That sensation is heightened when the writing had been done in the close and abnormal atmosphere of prison and the subsequent reading has taken place outside. I recognize it of course, but not wholly; it seems almost that I was reading some familiar piece written by another, who was near to me and yet who was different. Perhaps that is the measure of the change that has taken place in me.

So I have felt about this book also. It is mine and not wholly mine, as I am constituted today; it represents rather some past self of mine which has already joined that long succession of other selves that existed for a while and faded away, leaving only a memory behind.

Jawaharlal Nehru

Anand Bhawan, Allahabad
29 December 1945

CONTENTS

CHAPTER SEVEN: THE LAST PHASE (1): CONSOLIDATION OF BRITISH RULE AND RISE OF NATIONALIST MOVEMENT

CHAPTER EIGHT: THE LAST PHASE (2): NATIONALISM VERSUS IMPERIALISM

CHAPTER ONE

AHMADNAGAR FORT

Twenty Months

Ahmadnagar Fort, 13th April 1944

IT IS MORE THAN TWENTY MONTHS SINCE WE WERE BROUGHT HERE, more than twenty months of my ninth term of imprisonment. The new moon, a shimmering crescent in the darkening sky, greeted us on our arrival here. The bright fortnight of the waxing moon had begun. Ever since then each coming of the new moon has been a reminder to me that another month of my imprisonment is over. So it was with my last term of imprisonment which began with the new moon, just after the *Deepavali*, the festival of light. The moon, ever a companion to me in prison, has grown more friendly with closer acquaintance, a reminder of the loveliness of this world, of the waxing and waning of life, of light following darkness, of death and resurrection following each other in interminable succession. Ever changing, yet ever the same, I have watched it in its different phases and its many moods in the evening, as the shadows lengthen, in the still hours of the night, and when the breath and whisper of dawn bring promise of the coming day. How helpful is the moon in counting the days and the months, for the size and shape of the moon, when it is visible, indicate the day of the month with a fair measure of exactitude. It is an easy calendar (though it must be adjusted from time to time), and for the peasant in the field the most convenient one to indicate the passage of the days and the gradual changing of the seasons.

Three weeks we spent here cut off completely from all news of the outside world. There were no contacts of any kind, no interviews, no letters, no newspapers, no radio. Even our presence here was supposed to be a state secret unknown to any except to the officials in charge of us, a poor secret, for all India knew where we were.

Then newspapers were allowed and, some weeks later, letters from near relatives dealing with domestic affairs. But no interviews during these 20 months, no other contacts.

The newspapers contained heavily censored news. Yet they gave us some idea of the war that was consuming more than half the world, and of how it fared with our people in India. Little we knew about these people of ours except that scores of thousands lay in prison or internment camp without trial, that thousands had been shot to death, that tens of thousands had been driven out of schools and colleges, that something indistinguishable from martial law prevailed over the whole country, that terror and frightfulness darkened the land. They were worse off, far worse than us, those scores of thousands in prison, like us, without trial, for there were not only no interviews but also no letters or newspapers for them, and even books were seldom allowed. Many sickened for lack of healthy food, some of our dear ones died for lack of proper care and treatment.

There were many thousands of prisoners of war kept in India, mostly from Italy. We compared their lot with the lot of our own people. We were told that they were governed by the Geneva Convention. But there was no convention or law or rule to govern the conditions under which Indian prisoners and detenus had to exist, except such ordinances which it pleased our British rulers to issue from time to time.

Famine

Famine came, ghastly, staggering, horrible beyond words. In Malabar, in Bijapur, in Orissa, and, above all, in the rich and fertile province of Bengal, men and women and little children died in their thousands daily for lack of food. They dropped down dead before the palaces of Calcutta, their corpses lay in the mud-huts of Bengal's innumerable villages and covered the roads and fields of its rural areas. Men were dying all over the world and killing each other in battle; usually a quick death, often a brave death, death for a cause, death with a purpose, death which seemed in this mad world of ours an inexorable logic of events, a sudden end to the life we could not mould or control. Death was common enough everywhere.

But here death had no purpose, no logic, no necessity; it was the result of man's incompetence and callousness, man-made, a slow creeping thing of horror with nothing to redeem it, life merging and fading into death, with death looking out of the shrunken eyes and withered frame while life still lingered for a while. And so it was not considered right or proper to mention it; it was not good form to talk or write of unsavoury topics. To do so was to 'dramatize' an unfortunate situation. False reports were issued by those in authority in India and in England. But corpses cannot easily be overlooked; they come in the way.

While the fires of hell were consuming the people of Bengal and elsewhere, we were first told by high authority that owing to wartime prosperity the peasantry in many parts of India had too much to eat. Then it was said that the fault lay with provincial autonomy, and that the British Government in India, or the India Office in London, sticklers for constitutional propriety, could not interfere with provincial affairs. That constitution was suspended, violated, ignored, or changed daily by hundreds of decrees and ordinances issued by the Viceroy under his sole and unlimited authority. That constitution meant ultimately the unchecked authoritarian rule of a single individual who was responsible to no one in India, and who had greater power than any dictator anywhere in the world. That constitution was worked by the permanent services, chiefly the Indian Civil Service and the police, who were mainly responsible to the Governor, who was the agent of the Viceroy, and who could well ignore the ministers when such existed. The ministers, good or bad, lived on sufferance and dared not disobey the orders from above or even interfere with the discretion of the services supposed to be subordinate to them.

Something was done at last. Some relief was given. But a million had died, or two millions, or three; no one knows how many starved to death or died of disease during those months of horror. No one knows of the many more millions of emaciated boys and girls and little children who just escaped death then, but are stunted and broken in body and spirit. And still the fear of widespread famine and disease hovers over the land.

President Roosevelt's Four Freedoms. The Freedom from Want. Yet rich England, and richer America, paid little heed to the hunger of the body that was killing millions in India, as they had paid little heed to the fiery thirst of the spirit that is consuming the people of India. Money was not needed it was said, and ships to carry food were scarce owing to war-time requirements. But in spite of governmental obstruction and desire to minimize the overwhelming tragedy of Bengal, sensitive and warm-hearted men and women in England and America and elsewhere came to our help. Above all, the Governments of China and Eire, poor in their own resources, full of their own difficulties, yet having had bitter experience themselves of famine and misery and sensing what ailed the body and spirit of India, gave generous help. India has a long memory, but whatever else she remembers or forgets, she will not forget these gracious and friendly acts.

The War for Democracy

In Asia and Europe and Africa, and over the vast stretches of the Pacific and Atlantic and Indian Oceans, war has raged in all its dreadful aspects. Nearly seven years of war in China, over four and a half years of war in Europe and Africa, and two years and four months of World War. War against fascism and nazism and attempts to gain world dominion. Of these years of war I have so far spent nearly three years in prison, here and elsewhere in India.

I remember how I reacted to fascism and nazism in their early days, and not I only, but many in India. How Japanese agression in China had moved India deeply and revived the age-old friendship for China; how Italy's rape of Abyssinia had sickened us; how the betrayal of Czechoslovakia had hurt and embittered us; how the fall of Republican Spain, after a struggle full of heroic endurance, had been a tragedy and a personal sorrow for me and others.

It was not merely the physical acts of aggression in which fascism and nazism indulged, not only the vulgarity and brutality that accompanied them, terrible as they were, that affected us, but the principles on which they stood and which they proclaimed so loudly and blatantly, the theories of life on which they tried to fashion themselves; for these went counter to what we believed in the present, and what we had held from ages past. And even if our racial memory had forsaken us and we had lost our moorings, our own experiences, even though they came to us in different garb, and somewhat disguised for the sake of decency, were enough to teach us to what these nazi principles and theories of life and the state ultimately led. For our people had been the victims for long of those very principles and methods of government. So we reacted immediately and intensely against fascism and nazism.

I remember how I refused a pressing invitation from Signor Mussolini to see him in the early days of March, 1936. Many of Britain's leading statesmen, who spoke harshly of the fascist Duce in later years when Italy became a belligerent, referred to him tenderly and admiringly in those days, and praised his regime and methods.

Two years later, in the summer before Munich, I was invited on behalf of the Nazi government, to visit Germany, an invitation to which was added the remark that they knew my opposition to nazism and yet they wanted me to see Germany for myself. I could go as their guest or privately, in my own name or incognito, as I desired, and I would have perfect freedom to go where I liked. Again I declined with thanks. Instead I went to Czechoslovakia, that 'far-away country' about which England's then Prime Minister knew so little.

Before Munich I met some of the members of the British Cabinet and other prominent politicians of England, and ventured to express my anti-fascist and anti-nazi views before them. I found that my views were not welcomed and I was told that there were many other considerations to be borne in mind.

During the Czechoslovak crisis, what I saw of Franco-British statesmanship in Prague and in the Sudetenland, in London and Paris, and in Geneva where the League Assembly was then sitting, amazed and disgusted me. Appeasement seemed to be a feeble word for it. There was behind it not only a fear of Hitler, but a sneaking admiration for him.

And now, it is a curious turn of fate's wheel that I, and people like me, should spend our days in prison while war against fascism and nazism is raging, and many of those who used to bow to Hitler and Mussolini, and approve of Japanese aggression in China, should hold aloft the banner of freedom and democracy and anti-fascism.

In India the change is equally remarkable. There are those here, as elsewhere, 'governmentarians', who hover round the skirts of government and echo the views which they think will be approved by those whose favour they continually seek. There was a time, not so long ago, when they praised Hitler and Mussolini, and held them up as models, and when they cursed the Soviet Union with bell, book, and candle. Not so now, for the weather has changed. They are high government and state officials, and loudly they proclaim their anti-fascism and anti-nazism and even talk of democracy, though with bated breath, as something desirable but distant. I often wonder what they would have done if events had taken a different turn, and yet there is little reason for conjecture, for they would welcome with garlands and addresses of welcome whoever happened to wield authority.

For long years before the war my mind was full of the war that was coming. I thought of it, and spoke of it, and wrote about it, and prepared myself mentally for it. I wanted India to take an eager and active part in the mighty conflict, for I felt that high principles would be at stake, and out of this conflict would come great and revolutionary changes in India and the world. At that time I did not envisage an immediate threat to India: any probability of actual invasion. Yet I wanted India to take her full share. But I was convinced that only as a free country and an equal could she function in this way.

That was the attitude of the National Congress, the one great organization in India which consistently for all these years had been anti-fascist and anti-nazi, as it had been anti-imperialist. It had stood for Republican Spain, for Czechoslovakia, and throughout for China.

And now for nearly two years the Congress has been declared illegal—outlawed and prevented from functioning in any way. The Congress is in prison. Its elected members of the provincial parliaments, its speakers of these parliaments, its ex-ministers, its mayors and presidents of municipal corporations, are in prison.

Meanwhile the war goes on for democracy and the Atlantic Charter and the Four Freedoms.

Time in Prison : The Urge to Action

Time seems to change its nature in prison. The present hardly exists, for there is an absence of feeling and sensation which might separate it from the dead past. Even news of the active, living and dying world outside has a certain dream-like unreality, an immobility and an unchangeableness as of the past. The outer objective time ceases to be, the inner and subjective sense remains, but at a lower level, except when thought pulls it out of the present and experiences a kind of reality in the past or in the future. We live, as Auguste Comte said, dead men's lives, encased in our pasts, but this is especially so in prison where we try to find some sustenance for our starved and locked-up emotions in memory of the past or fancies of the future.

There is a stillness and everlastingness about the past; it changes not and has a touch of eternity, like a painted picture or a statue in bronze or marble. Unaffected by the storms and upheavals of the present, it maintains its dignity and repose and tempts the troubled spirit and the tortured mind to seek shelter in its vaulted catacombs. There is peace there and security, and one may even sense a spiritual quality.

But it is not life, unless we can find the vital links between it and the present with all its conflicts and problems. It is a kind of art for art's sake, without the passion and the urge to action which are the very stuff of life. Without that passion and urge, there is a gradual oozing out of hope and vitality, a settling down on lower levels of existence, a slow merging into non-existence. We become prisoners of the past and some part of its immobility sticks to us.

This passage of the mind is all the easier in prison where action is denied and we become slaves to the routine of jail-life.

Yet the past is ever with us and all that we are and that we have comes from the past. We are its products and we live immersed in it. Not to understand it and feel it as something living within us is not to understand the present. To combine it with the present and extend it to the future, to break from it where it cannot be so united, to make of all this the pulsating and vibrating material for thought and action—that is life.

Any vital action springs from the depths of the being. All the long past of the individual and even of the race has prepared the background for that psychological moment of action. All the racial memories, influences of heredity and environment and training, subconscious urges, thoughts and dreams and actions from infancy and childhood onwards, in their curious and tremendous mix-up, inevitably drive to that new action, which again becomes yet another factor influencing the future. Influencing the future, partly determining it, possibly even largely determining it, and yet, surely, it is not all determinism.

Aurobindo Ghose writes somewhere of the present as 'the pure and virgin moment,' that razor's edge of time and existence which divides the past from the future, and is, and yet, instantaneously is not. The phrase is attractive and yet what does it mean? The virgin moment emerging from the veil of the future in all its naked purity, coming into contact with us, and immediately becoming the soiled and stale past. Is it we that soil it and violate it? Or is the moment not so virgin after all, for it is bound up with all the harlotry of the past?

Whether there is any such thing as human freedom in the philosophic sense or whether there is only an automatic determinism, I do not know. A very great deal appears certainly to be determined by the past complex of events which bear down and often overwhelm the individual. Possibly even the inner urge that he experiences, that apparent exercise of free will, is itself conditioned. As Schopenhauer says, 'a man can do what he will, but not will as he will.' A belief in an absolute determinism seems to me to lead inevitably to complete inaction, to death in life. All my sense of life rebels against it, though of course that very rebellion may itself have been conditioned by previous events.

I do not usually burden my mind with such philosophical or metaphysical problems, which escape solution. Sometimes they come to me almost unawares in the long silences of prison, or even in the midst of an intensity of action, bringing with them a sense of detachment or consolation in the face of some painful experience. But usually it is action and the thought of action that fill me, and when action is denied, I imagine that I am preparing for action.

The call of action has long been with me; not action divorced from thought, but rather flowing from it in one continuous sequence. And when, rarely, there has been full harmony between the two, thought leading to action and finding its fulfilment in it, action leading back to thought and a fuller understanding— then I have sensed a certain fullness of life and a vivid intensity in that moment of existence. But such moments are rare, very rare, and usually one outstrips the other and there is a lack of harmony, and vain effort to bring the two in line. There was a time, many years ago, when I lived for considerable periods in a state of emotional exaltation, wrapped up in the action which absorbed me. Those days of my youth seem far away now, not merely because of the passage of years but far more so because of the ocean of experience and painful thought that separates them from to-day. The old exuberance is much less now, the almost uncontrollable impulses have toned down, and passion and feeling are more in check. The burden of thought is often a hindrance, and in the mind where there was once certainty, doubt creeps in. Perhaps it is just age, or the common temper of our day.

And yet, even now, the call of action stirs strange depths within me, and often a brief tussle with thought. I want to experience again 'that lonely impulse of delight' which turns to risk and danger and faces and mocks at death. I am not enamoured of death, though I do not think it frightens me. I do not believe in the negation of or abstention from life. I have loved life and it attracts me still and, in my own way, I seek to experience it, though many invisible barriers have grown up which surround me; but that very desire leads me to play with life, to peep over its edges, not to be a slave to it, so that we may value each other all the more. Perhaps I ought to have been an aviator, so that when the slowness and dullness of life overcame me I could have rushed into the tumult of the clouds and said to myself:

> *'I balanced all, brought all to mind,*
> *The years to come seemed waste of breath,*
> *A waste of breath the years behind,*
> *In balance with this life, this death.'*

The Past in its Relation to the Present

This urge to action, this desire to experience life through action, has influenced all my thought and activity. Even sustained thinking, apart from being itself a kind of action, becomes part of the action to come. It is not something entirely abstract, in the void, unrelated to action and life. The past becomes something that leads up to the present, the moment of action, the future something that flows from it; and all three are inextricably intertwined and interrelated.

Even my seemingly actionless life in prison is tacked on somehow, by some process of thought and feeling, to coming or imagined action, and so it gains for me a certain content without which it would be a vacuum in which existence would become intolerable. When actual action has been denied me I have sought some such approach to the past and to history. Because my own personal experiences have often touched historic events and sometimes I have even had something to do with the influencing of such events in my own sphere, it has not been difficult for me to envisage history as a living process with which I could identify myself to some extent.

I came late to history and, even then, not through the usual direct road of learning a mass of facts and dates and drawing conclusions and inferences from them, unrelated to my life's course. So long as I did this, history had little significance for me. I was still less interested in the supernatural or problems of a future life. Science and the problems of to-day and of our present life attracted me far more.

Some mixture of thought and emotion and urges, of which I was only dimly conscious, led me to action, and action, in its turn, sent me back to thought and a desire to understand the present.

The roots of that present lay in the past and so I made voyages of discovery into the past, ever seeking a clue in it, if any such existed, to the understanding of the present. The domination of the present never left me even when I lost myself in musings of past, events and of persons far away and long ago, forgetting where or what I was. If I felt occasionally that I belonged to the past. I felt also that the whole of the past belonged to me in the present. Past history merged into contemporary history: it became a living reality tied up with sensations of pain and pleasure.

If the past had a tendency to become the present, the present also sometimes receded into the distant past and assumed its immobile, statuesque appearance. In the midst of an intensity of action itself, there would suddenly come a feeling as if it was some past event and one was looking at it, as it were, in retrospect.

It was this attempt to discover the past in its relation to the present that led me twelve years ago to write *Glimpses of World History* in the form of letters to my daughter. I wrote rather superficially and as simply as I could, for I was writing for a girl in her early teens, but behind that writing lay that quest and voyage of discovery. A sense of adventure filled me and I lived successively different ages and periods and had for companions men and women who had lived long ago. I had leisure in jail, there was no sense of hurry or of completing a task within an allotted period of time, so I let my mind wander or take root for a while, keeping in tune with my mood, allowing impression to sink in and fill the dry bones of the past with flesh and blood.

It was a similar quest, though limited to recent and more intimate times and persons, that led me later to write my autobiography.

I suppose I have changed a good deal during these twelve years. I have grown more contemplative. There is perhaps a little more poise and equilibrium, some sense of detachment, a greater calmness of spirit. I am not overcome now to the same extent as I used to be by tragedy or what I conceived to be tragedy. The turmoil and disturbance are less and are more temporary, even though the tragedies have been on a far greater scale.

Is this, I have wondered, the growth of a spirit of resignation, or is it a toughening of the texture? Is it just age and a lessening of vitality and of the passion of life? Or is it due to long periods in prison and life slowly ebbing away, and the thoughts that fill the mind passing through, after a brief stay, leaving only ripples behind? The tortured mind seeks some mechanism of escape, the senses get dulled from repeated shocks, and a feeling comes over one that so much evil and misfortune shadow the world that a little more or less does not make much difference. There is only one thing that remains to us that cannot be taken away: to act with courage and dignity and to stick to the ideals that have given meaning to life; but that is not the politician's way.

Someone said the other day: death is the birthright of every person born —a curious way of putting an obvious thing. It is a birthright which nobody has denied or can deny, and which all of us seek to forget and escape so long as we may. And yet there was something novel and attractive about the phrase. Those who complain so bitterly of life have always a way out of it, if they so choose. That is always in our power to achieve. If we cannot master life we can at least master death. A pleasing thought lessening the feeling of helplessness.

Life's Philosophy

Six or seven years ago an American publisher asked me to write an essay on my philosophy of life for a symposium he was preparing. I was attracted to the idea but I hesitated, and the more

24

I thought over it, the more reluctant I grew. Ultimately, I did not write that essay.

What was my philosophy of life? I did not know. Some years earlier I would not have been so hesitant. There was a definiteness about my thinking and objectives then which has faded away since. The events of the past few years in India, China, Europe, and all over the world have been confusing, upsetting and distressing, and the future has become vague and shadowy and has lost that clearness of outline which it once possessed in my mind.

This doubt and difficulty about fundamental matters did not come in my way in regard to immediate action, except that it blunted somewhat the sharp edge of that activity. No longer could I function, as I did in my younger days, as an arrow flying automatically to the target of my choice ignoring all else but that target. Yet I functioned, for the urge to action was there and a real or imagined co-ordination of that action with the ideals I held. But a growing distaste for politics as I saw them seized me and gradually my whole attitude to life seemed to undergo a transformation.

The ideals and objectives of yesterday were still the ideals of to-day, but they had lost some of their lustre and, even as one seemed to go towards them, they lost the shining beauty which had warmed the heart and vitalized the body. Evil triumphed often enough, but what was far worse was the coarsening and distortion of what had seemed so right. Was human nature so essentially bad that it would take ages of training, through suffering and misfortune, before it could behave reasonably and raise man above that creature of lust and violence and deceit that he now was? And, meanwhile, was every effort to change it radically in the present or the near future doomed to failure?

Ends and means: were they tied up inseparably, acting and reacting on each other, the wrong means distorting and sometimes even destroying the end in view? But the right means might well be beyond the capacity of infirm and selfish human nature.

What then was one to do? Not to act was a complete confession of failure and a submission to evil; to act meant often enough a compromise with some form of that evil, with all the untoward consequences that such compromises result in.

My early approach to life's problems had been more or less scientific, with something of the easy optimism of the science of the nineteenth and early twentieth century. A secure and comfortable existence and the energy and self-confidence I possessed increased that feeling of optimism. A kind of vague humanism appealed to me.

Religion, as I saw it practised, and accepted even by thinking minds, whether it was Hinduism or Islam or Buddhism or Christianity, did not attract me. It seemed to be closely associated with superstitious practices and dogmatic beliefs, and behind it lay a method of approach to life's problems which was certainly not that of science. There was an element of magic about it, an uncritical credulousness, a reliance on the supernatural.

Yet it was obvious that religion had supplied some deeply felt inner need of human nature, and that the vast majority of people all over the world could not do without some form of religious belief. It had produced many fine types of men and women, as well as bigoted, narrow-minded, cruel tyrants. It had given a set of values to human life, and though some of these values had no application to-day, or were even harmful, others were still the foundation of morality and ethics.

In the wider sense of the word, religion dealt with the uncharted regions of human experience, uncharted, that is, by the scientific positive knowledge of the day. In a sense it might be considered an extension of the known and charted region, though the methods of science and religion were utterly unlike each other, and to a large extent they had to deal with different kinds of media. It was obvious that there was a vast unknown region all around us, and science, with its magnificent achievements, knew little enough about it, though it was making tentative approaches in that direction. Probably also, the normal methods of science, its dealings with the visible world and the processes of life, were not wholly adapted to the physical, the artistic, the spiritual, and other elements of the invisible world. Life does not consist entirely of what we see and hear and feel, the visible world which is undergoing change in time and space; it is continually touching an invisible world of other, and possibly more stable or equally changeable elements, and no thinking person can ignore this invisible world.

Science does not tell us much, or for the matter of that anything about the purpose of life. It is now widening its boundaries and it may invade the so-called invisible world before long and help us to understand this purpose of life in its widest sense, or at least give us some glimpses which illumine the problem of human existence. The old controversy between science and religion takes a new form—the application of the scientific method to emotional and religious experiences.

Religion merges into mysticism and metaphysics and philosophy. There have been great mystics, attractive figures, who cannot easily be disposed of as self-deluded fools. Yet mysticism (in the narrow sense of the word) irritates me; it appears to be vague and soft and flabby, not a rigorous discipline of the mind but a surrender of mental faculties and a living in a sea of emotional experience. · The experience may lead occasionally to some insight into inner and less obvious processes, but it is also likely to lead to self-delusion.

Metaphysics and philosophy, or a metaphysical philosophy, have a greater appeal to the mind. They require hard thinking and the application of logic and reasoning, though all this is necessarily based on some premises, which are presumed to be self-evident, and yet which may or may not be true. All thinking persons, to a greater or less degree, dabble in metaphysics and philosophy, for not to do so is to ignore many of the aspects of this universe of ours. Some may feel more attracted to them than others, and the emphasis on them may vary in different ages. In the ancient world, both in Asia and Europe, all the emphasis was laid on the supremacy of the inward life over things external, and this inevitably led to metaphysics and philosophy. The modern man is wrapped up much more in these things external, and yet even he, in moments of crisis and mental trouble often turns to philosophy and metaphysical speculations.

Some vague or more precise philosophy of life we all have, though most of us accept unthinkingly the general attitude which is characteristic of our generation and environment. Most of us accept also certain metaphysical conceptions as part of the faith in which we have grown up. I have not been attracted towards metaphysics; in fact, I have had a certain distaste for vague speculation. And yet I have sometimes found a certain intellectual fascination in trying to follow the rigid lines of metaphysical and philosophic thought of the ancients or the moderns. But I have never felt at ease there and have escaped from their spell with a feeling of relief.

Essentially, I am interested in this world, in this life, not in some other world or a future life. Whether there is such a thing as a soul, or whether there is a survival after death or not, I do not know; and, important as these questions are, they do not trouble me in the least. The environment in which I have grown up takes the soul (or rather the *ātma*) and a future life, the *Karma* theory of cause and effect, and reincarnation for granted. I have been affected by this and so, in a sense, I am favourably disposed towards these assumptions. There might be a soul which survives the physical death of the body, and a theory of cause and effect governing life's actions seems reasonable, though it leads to obvious difficulties when one thinks of the ultimate cause. Presuming a soul, there appears to be some logic also in the theory of reincarnation.

But I do not believe in any of these or other theories and assumptions as a matter of religious faith. They are just intellectual speculations in an unknown region about which we know next to nothing. They do not affect my life, and whether they were proved right or wrong subsequently, they would make little difference to me.

Spiritualism with its séances and its so-called manifestations of spirits and the like has always seemed to me a rather absurd and impertinent way of investigating psychic phenomena and the mysteries of the after-life. Usually it is something worse, and is an exploitation of the emotions of some over-credulous people who seek relief or escape from mental trouble. I do not deny the possibility of some of these psychic phenomena having a basis of truth, but the approach appears to me to be all wrong and the conclusions drawn from scraps and odd bits of evidence to be unjustified.

Often, as I look at this world, I have a sense of mysteries, of unknown depths. The urge to understand it, in so far as I can, comes to me: to be in tune with it and to experience it in its fullness. But the way to that understanding seems to me essentially the way of science, the way of objective approach, though I realise that there can be no such thing as true objectiveness. If the subjective element is unavoidable and inevitable, it should be conditioned as far as possible by the scientific method.

What the mysterious is I do not know. I do not call it God because God has come to mean much that I do not believe in. I find myself incapable of thinking of a deity or of any unknown supreme power in anthropomorphic terms, and the fact that many people think so is continually a source of surprise to me. Any idea of a personal God seems very odd to me. Intellectually, I can appreciate to some extent the conception of monism, and I have been attracted towards the *Advaita* (non-dualist) philosophy of the Vedanta, though I do not presume to understand it in all its depth and intricacy, and I realise that merely an intellectual appreciation of such matters does not carry one far. At the same time the Vedanta, as well as other similar approaches, rather frighten me with their vague, formless incursions into infinity. The diversity and fullness of nature stir me and produce a harmony of the spirit, and I can imagine myself feeling at home in the old Indian or Greek pagan and pantheistic atmosphere, but minus the conception of God or Gods that was attached to it.

Some kind of ethical approach to life has a strong appeal for me, though it would be difficult for me to justify it logically. I have been attracted by Gandhiji's stress on right means and I think one of his greatest contributions to our public life has been this emphasis. The idea is by no means new, but this application of an ethical doctrine to large-scale public activity was certainly novel. It is full of difficulty, and perhaps ends and means are not really separable but form together one organic whole. In a world which thinks almost exclusively of ends and ignores means, this emphasis on means seems odd and remarkable. How far it has succeeded in India I cannot say. But there is no doubt that it has created a deep and abiding impression on the minds of large numbers of people.

A study of Marx and Lenin produced a powerful effect on my mind and helped me to see history and current affairs in a new light. The long chain of history and of social development appeared to have some meaning, some sequence, and the future lost some of its obscurity. The practical achievements of the Soviet Union were also tremendously impressive. Often I disliked or did not understand some development there and it seemed to me to be too closely concerned with the opportunism of the moment or the power politics of the day. But despite all these developments and possible distortions of the original passion for human betterment, I had no doubt that the Soviet Revolution had advanced human society by a great leap and had lit a bright flame which could not be smothered, and that it had laid the foundations for that new civilization towards which the world could advance. I am too much of an individualist and believer in personal freedom to like overmuch regimentation. Yet it seemed to me obvious that in a complex social structure individual freedom had to be limited, and perhaps the only way to read personal freedom was through some such limitation in the social sphere. The lesser liberties may often need limitation in the interest of the larger freedom.

Much in the Marxist philosophical outlook I could accept without difficulty: its monism and non-duality of mind and matter, the dynamics of matter and the dialectic of continuous change by evolution as well as leap, through action and interaction, cause and effect, thesis, antithesis and synthesis. It did not satisfy me completely, nor did it answer all the questions in my mind, and, almost unawares, a vague idealist approach would creep into my mind, something rather akin to the Vedanta approach. It was not a difference between mind and matter, but rather of something that lay beyond the mind. Also there was the background of ethics. I realised that the moral approach is a changing one and depends upon the growing mind and an advancing civilization; it is conditioned by the mental climate of the age. Yet there was something more to it than that, certain basic urges which had greater permanence. I did not like the frequent divorce in communist, as in other, practice between action and these basic urges or principles. So there was an odd mixture in my mind which I could not rationally explain or resolve. There was a general tendency not to think too much of those fundamental questions which appear to be beyond reach, but rather to concentrate on the problems of life—to understand in the narrower and more immediate sense what should be done and how. Whatever ultimate reality may be, and whether we can ever grasp it in whole or in part, there certainly appear to be vast possibilities of increasing human knowledge, even though this may be partly or largely subjective, and of applying this to the advancement and betterment of human living and social organization.

There has been in the past, and there is to a lesser extent even to-day among some people, an absorption in finding an answer to the riddle of the universe. This leads them away from the individual and social problems of the day, and when they are unable to solve that riddle they despair and turn to inaction and triviality, or find comfort in some dogmatic creed. Social evils, most of which are certainly capable of removal, are attributed to original sin, to the unalterableness of human nature, or the social structure, or (in India) to the inevitable legacy of previous births. Thus one drifts away from even the attempt to think rationally and scientifically and takes refuge in irrationalism, superstition, and unreasonable and inequitable social prejudices and practices. It is true that even rational and scientific thought does not always take us as far as we would like to go. There is an infinite number of factors and relations all of which influence and determine events in varying degrees. It is impossible to grasp all of them, but we can try to pick out the dominating forces at work and by observing external material reality, and by experiment and practice, trial and error, grope our way to ever-widening knowledge and truth.

For this purpose, and within these limitations, the general Marxist approach, fitting in as it more or less does with the present state of scientific knowledge, seemed to me to offer considerable help. But even accepting that approach, the consequences that flow from it and the interpretation on past and present happenings were by no means always clear. Marx's general analysis of social development seems to have been remarkably correct, and yet many developments took place later which did not fit in with his outlook for the immediate future. Lenin successfully adapted the Marxian thesis to some of these subsequent developments, and again since then further remarkable changes have taken place—the rise of fascism and nazism and all that lay behind them. The very rapid growth of technology and the practical application of vast developments in scientific knowledge are now changing the world picture with an amazing rapidity, leading to new problems.

And so while I accepted the fundamentals of the socialist theory, I did not trouble myself about its numerous inner controversies. I had little patience with leftist groups in India, spending much of their energy in mutual conflict and recrimination over fine points of doctrine which did not interest me at all. Life is too complicated and, as far as we can understand it in our present state of knowledge, too illogical, for it to be confined within the four corners of a fixed doctrine.

The real problems for me remain problems of individual and social life, of harmonious living, of a proper balancing of an individual's inner and outer life, of an adjustment of the relations between individuals and between groups, of a continuous becoming something better and higher of social development, of the ceaseless adventure of man. In the solution of these problems the way of observation and precise knowledge and deliberate reasoning, according to the method of science, must be followed. This method may not always be applicable in our quest of truth, for art and poetry and certain psychic experiences seem to belong to a different order of things and to elude the objective methods of science. Let us, therefore, not rule out intuition and other methods of sensing truth and reality. They are necessary even for the purposes of science. But always we must hold to our anchor of precise objective knowledge tested by reason, and even more so by experiment and practice, and always we must beware of losing ourselves in a sea of speculation unconnected with the day-to-day problems of life and the needs of men and women. A living philosophy must answer the problems of to-day.

It may be that we of this modern age, who so pride ourselves on the achievements of our times, are prisoners of our age, just as the ancients and the men and women of medieval times were prisoners of their respective ages. We may delude ourselves, as others have done before us, that our way of looking at things is the only right way, leading to truth. We cannot escape from that prison or get rid entirely of that illusion, if illusion it is.

Yet I am convinced that the methods and approach of science have revolutionized human life more than anything else in the long course of history, and have opened doors and avenues of further and even more radical change, leading up to the very portals of what has long been considered the unknown. The technical achievements of science are obvious enough: its capacity to transform an economy of scarcity into one of abundance is evident, its invasion of many problems which have so far been the monopoly of philosophy is becoming more pronounced.

Space-time and the quantum theory utterly changed the picture of the physical world. More recent researches into the nature of matter, the structure of the atom, the transmutation of the elements, and the transformation of electricity and light, either into the other, have carried human knowledge much further. Man no longer sees nature as something apart and distinct from himself. Human destiny appears to become a part of nature's rhythmic energy.

All this upheaval of thought, due to the advance of science, has led scientists into a new region, verging on the metaphysical. They draw different and often contradictory conclusions. Some see in it a new unity, the antithesis of chance. Others, like Bertrand Russell, say, 'Academic philosophers ever since the time of Parmenides have believed the world is unity. The most fundamental of my beliefs is that this is rubbish.' Or again, 'Man is the product of causes which had no prevision of the end they were achieving; his origin, his growth, his hopes and fears, his loves and beliefs are but the outcome of accidental collocations of atoms.' And yet the latest developments in physics have gone a long way to demonstrate a fundamental unity in nature. 'The belief that all things are made of a single substance is as old as thought itself; but ours is the generation which, first of all in history, is able to receive the unity of nature, not as a baseless dogma or a hopeless aspiration, but a principle of science based on proof as sharp and clear as anything which is known.'*

Old as this belief is in Asia and Europe, it is interesting to compare some of the latest conclusions of science with the fundamental ideas underlying the Advaita Vedantic theory. These ideas were that the universe is made of one substance whose form is perpetually changing, and further that the sum-total of energies remains always the same. Also that 'the explanations of things are to be found within their own nature, and that no external beings or existences are required to explain what is going on in the universe,' with its corollary of a self-evolving universe.

It does not very much matter to science what these vague speculations lead to, for meanwhile it forges ahead in a hundred directions, in its own precise experimental way of observation, widening the bounds of the charted region of knowledge, and changing human life in the process. Science may be on the verge of discovering vital mysteries, which yet may elude it. Still it will go on along its appointed path, for there is no end to its journeying. Ignoring for the moment the 'why?' of philosophy, science will go on asking 'how?', and as it finds this out it gives greater content and meaning to life, and perhaps takes us some way to answering the 'why?'.

*Karl K. Darrow. 'The Renaissance of Physics' (New York, 1936), p. 301.

Or, perhaps, we cannot cross that barrier, and the mysterious will continue to remain the mysterious, and life with all its changes will still remain a bundle of good and evil, a succession of conflicts, a curious combination of incompatible and mutually hostile urges.

Or again, perhaps, the very progress of science, unconnected with and isolated from moral discipline and ethical considerations, will lead to the concentration of power and the terrible instruments of destruction which it has made, in the hands of evil and selfish men, seeking the domination of others—and thus to the destruction of its own great achievements. Something of this kind we see happening now, and behind this war there lies this internal conflict of the spirit of man.

How amazing is this spirit of man! In spite of innumerable failings, man, throughout the ages, has sacrificed his life and all he held dear for an ideal, for truth, for faith, for country and honour. That ideal may change, but that capacity for self-sacrifice continues, and, because of that, much may be forgiven to man, and it is impossible to lose hope for him. In the midst of disaster, he has not lost his dignity or his faith in the values he cherished. Plaything of nature's mighty forces, less than a speck of dust in this vast universe, he has hurled defiance at the elemental powers, and with his mind, cradle of revolution, sought to master them. Whatever gods there be, there is something godlike in man, as there is also something of the devil in him.

The future is dark, uncertain. But we can see part of the way leading to it and can tread it with firm steps, remembering that nothing that can happen is likely to overcome the spirit of man which has survived so many perils; remembering also that life, for all its ills, has joy and beauty, and that we can always wander, if we know how to, in the enchanted woods of nature.

> 'What else is wisdom? What of man's endeavour
> Or God's high grace, so lovely and so great?
> To stand from fear set free, to breathe and wait;
> To hold a hand uplifted over Hate;
> And shall not Loveliness be loved for ever?*

The Burden of the Past

The twenty-first month of my imprisonment is well on its way; the moon waxes and wanes and soon two years will have been completed. Another birthday will come round to remind me that I am getting older; my last four birthdays I have spent in prison, here and in Dehra Dun Jail, and many others in the

*Chorus from 'The Bacchae of Euripides. Gilbert Murray's translation.

course of my previous terms of imprisonment. I have lost count of their number.

During all these months I have often thought of writing, felt the urge to it and at the same time a reluctance. My friends took it for granted that I would write and produce another book, as I had done during previous terms of imprisonment. It had almost become a habit.

Yet I did not write. There was a certain distaste for just throwing out a book which had no particular significance. It was easy enough to write, but to write something that was worth while was another matter, something that would not grow stale while I sat in prison with my manuscript and the world went on changing. I would not be writing for to-day or to-morrow but for an unknown and possibly distant future. For whom would I write? and for when? Perhaps what I wrote would never be published, for the years I would spend in prison were likely to witness even greater convulsions and conflicts than the years of war that are already over. India herself might be a battle-ground or there might be civil commotion.

And, even if we escaped all these possible developments, it was a risky adventure to write now for a future date, when the problems of to-day might be dead and buried and new problems arisen in their place. I could not think of this World War as just another war, only bigger and greater. From the day it broke out, and even earlier, I was full of premonitions of vast and cataclysmic changes, of a new world arising for better or for worse. What would my poor writing of a past and vanished age be worth then?

All these thoughts troubled and restrained me, and behind them lay deeper questions in the recesses of my mind, to which I could find no easy answer.

Similar thoughts and difficulties came to me during my last term of imprisonment, from October, 1940, to December, 1941, mostly spent in my old cell of Dehra Dun Jail, where six years earlier I had begun writing my autobiography. For ten months there I could not develop the mood for writing, and, I spent my time in reading or in digging and playing about with soil and flowers. Ultimately I did write: it was meant to be a continuation of my autobiography. For a few weeks I wrote rapidly and continuously, but before my task was finished I was suddenly discharged, long before the end of my four-year term of imprisonment.

It was fortunate that I had not finished what I had undertaken, for if I had done so I might have been induced to send it to a publisher. Looking at it now, I realise its little worth;

how stale and uninteresting much of it seems. The incidents it deals with have lost all importance and have become the debris of a half-forgotten past, covered over by the lava of subsequent volcanic eruptions. I have lost interest in them. What stand out in my mind are personal experiences which had left their impress upon me; contacts with certain individuals and certain events; contacts with the crowd—the mass of the Indian people, in their infinite diversity and yet their amazing unity; some adventures of the mind; waves of unhappiness and the relief and joy that came from overcoming them; the exhilaration of the moment of action. About much of this one may not write. There is an intimacy about one's inner life, one's feelings and thoughts, which may not and cannot be conveyed to others. Yet those contacts, personal and impersonal, mean much; they affect the individual and mould him and change his reactions to life, to his own country, to other nations.

As in other prisons, here also in Ahmadnager Fort, I took to gardening and spent many hours daily, even when the sun was hot, in digging and preparing beds for flowers. The soil was very bad, stony, full of debris and remains of previous building operations, and even the ruins of ancient monuments. For this is a place of history, of many a battle and palace intrigue in the past. That history is not very old, as Indian history goes, nor is it very important in the larger scheme of things. But one incident stands out and is still remembered: the courage of a beautiful woman, Chand Bibi, who defended this fort and led her forces, sword in hand, against the imperial armies of Akbar. She was murdered by one of her own men.

Digging in this unfortunate soil, we have come across parts of ancient walls and the tops of domes and buildings buried far underneath the surface of the ground. We could not go far, as deep digging and archæological explorations were not approved by authority, nor did we have the wherewithal to carry this on. Once we came across a lovely lotus carved in stone on the side of a wall, probably over a doorway.

I remembered another and a less happy discovery in Dehra Dun Jail. In the course of digging in my little yard, three years ago, I came across a curious relic of past days. Deep under the surface of the ground, the remains of two ancient piles were uncovered and we viewed them with some excitement. They were part of the old gallows that had functioned there thirty or forty years earlier. The jail had long ceased to be a place of execution and all visible signs of the old gallows-tree had been removed. We had discovered and uprooted its foundations, and all my fellow-prisoners, who had helped in this process, rejoiced that we had put away at last this thing of ill omen.

Now I have put away my spade and taken to the pen instead. Possibly what I write now will meet the same fate as my unfinished manuscript of Dehra Dun Jail. I cannot write about the present so long as I am not free to experience it through action. It is the need for action in the present that brings it vividly to me, and then I can write about it with ease and a certain facility. In prison it is something vague, shadowy, something I cannot come to grips with, or experience as the sensation of the moment. It ceases to be the present for me in any real sense of the word, and yet it is not the past either, with the past's immobility and statuesque calm.

Nor can I assume the role of a prophet and write about the future. My mind often thinks of it and tries to pierce its veil and clothe it in the garments of my choice. But these are vain imaginings and the future remains uncertain, unknown, and there is no assurance that it will not betray again our hopes and prove false to humanity's dreams.

The past remains; but I cannot write academically of past events in the manner of a historian or scholar. I have not that knowledge or equipment or training; nor do I possess the mood for that kind of work. The past oppresses me or fills me sometimes with its warmth when it touches on the present, and becomes, as it were, an aspect of that living present. If it does not do so, then it is cold, barren, lifeless, uninteresting. I can only write about it, as I have previously done, by bringing it in some relation to my present-day thoughts and activities, and then this writing of history, as Goethe once said, brings some relief from the weight and burden of the past. It is, I suppose, a process similar to that of psychoanalysis, but applied to a race or to humanity itself instead of to an individual.

The burden of the past, the burden of both good and ill, is over-powering, and sometimes suffocating, more especially for those of us who belong to very ancient civilizations like those of India and China. As Nietzsche says: 'Not only the wisdom of centuries—also their madness breaketh out in us. Dangerous is it to be an heir.'

What is my inheritance? To what am I an heir? To all that humanity has achieved during tens of thousands of years, to all that it has thought and felt and suffered and taken pleasure in, to its cries of triumph and its bitter agony of defeat, to that astonishing adventure of man which began so long ago and yet continues and beckons to us. To all this and more, in common with all men. But there is a special heritage for those of us of India, not an exclusive one, for none is exclusive and all are common to the race of man, one more especially applicable to us, something that is in our flesh and blood and bones, that has gone to make us what we are and what we are likely to be.

It is the thought of this particular heritage and its application to the present that has long filled my mind, and it is about this that I should like to write, though the difficulty and complexity of the subject appal me and I can only touch the surface of it. I cannot do justice to it, but in attempting it I might be able to do some justice to myself by clearing my own mind and preparing it for the next stages of thought and action.

Inevitably, my approach will often be a personal one; how the idea grew in my mind, what shapes it took, how it influenced me and affected my action. There will also be some entirely personal experiences which have nothing to do with the subject in its wider aspects, but which coloured my mind and influenced my approach to the whole problem. Our judgments of countries and peoples are based on many factors; among them our personal contacts, if there have been any, have a marked influence. If we do not personally know the people of a country we are apt to misjudge them even more than otherwise, and to consider them entirely alien and different.

In the case of our own country our personal contacts are innumerable, and through such contacts many pictures or some kind of composite picture of our countrymen form in our mind. So I have filled the picture gallery of my mind. There are some portraits, vivid, life-like, looking down upon me and reminding me of some of life's high points—and yet it all seems so long ago and like some story I have read. There are many other pictures round which are wrapped memories of old comradeship and the friendship that sweetens life. And there are innumerable pictures of the mass—Indian men and women and children, all crowded together, looking up at me, and I trying to fathom what lie behind those thousands of eyes of theirs.

I shall begin this story with an entirely personal chapter, for this gives the clue to my mood in the month immediately following the period I have written about towards the end of my autobiography. But this is not going to be another autobiography, though I am afraid the personal element will often be present.

The World War goes on. Sitting here in Ahmadnagar Fort, a prisoner perforce inactive when a fierce activity consumes the world, I fret a little sometimes and I think of the big things and brave ventures which have filled my mind these many years. I try to view the war impersonally as one would look at some elemental phenomenon, some catastrophe of nature, a great earthquake or a flood. I do not succeed of course. But there seems no other way if I am to protect myself from too much hurt and hatred and excitement. And in this mighty manifestation of savage and destructive nature my own troubles and self sink into insignificance.

I remember the words that Gandhiji said on that fateful evening of August 8th, 1942: 'We must look the world in the face with calm and clear eyes even though the eyes of the world are bloodshot to-day.'

CHAPTER TWO

BADENWEILER, LAUSANNE

Kamala

ON SEPTEMBER 4TH, 1935, I WAS SUDDENLY RELEASED FROM THE
mountain jail of Almora, for news had come that my wife was
in a critical condition. She was far away in a sanatorium at
Badenweiler in the Black Forest of Germany. I hurried by
automobile and train to Allahabad, reaching there the next day,
and the same afternoon I started on the air journey to Europe.
The air liner took me to Karachi and Baghdad and Cairo, and
from Alexandria a seaplane carried me to Brindisi. From Brindisi
I went by train to Basle in Switzerland. I reached Badenweiler
on the evening of September 9th, four days after I had left Allahabad and five days after my release from Almora jail.

There was the same old brave smile on Kamala's face when I
saw her, but she was too weak and too much in the grip of pain
to say much. Perhaps my arrival made a difference, for she was
a little better the next day and for some days after. But the crisis
continued and slowly drained the life out of her. Unable to
accustom myself to the thought of her death, I imagined that
she was improving and that if she could only survive that crisis
she might get well. The doctors, as is their way, gave me hope.
The immediate crisis seemed to pass and she held her ground.
She was never well enough for a long conversation. We talked
briefly and I would stop as soon as I noticed that she was getting
tired. Sometimes I read to her. One of the books I remember
reading out to her in this way was Pearl Buck's 'The Good Earth'.
She liked my doing this, but our progress was slow.

Morning and afternoon I trudged from my *pension* in the
little town to the sanatorium and spent a few hours with her.
I was full of the many things I wanted to tell her and yet I had
to restrain myself. Sometimes we talked a little of old times,
old memories, of common friends in India; sometimes, a little
wistfully, of the future and what we would do then. In spite
of her serious condition she clung to the future. Her eyes were
bright and vital, her face usually cheerful. Odd friends who
came to visit her were pleasantly surprised to find her looking

39

better than they had imagined. They were misled by those bright eyes and that smiling face.

In the long autumn evenings I sat by myself in my room in the *pension*, where I was staying, or sometimes went out for a walk across the fields or through the forest. A hundred pictures of Kamala succeeded each other in my mind, a hundred aspects of her rich and deep personality. We had been married for nearly twenty years, and yet how many times she had surprised me by something new in her mental or spiritual make-up. I had known her in so many ways and, in later years, I had tried my utmost to understand her. That understanding had not been denied to me, but I often wondered if I really knew her or understood her. There was something elusive about her, something fay-like, real but unsubstantial, difficult to grasp. Sometimes, looking into her eyes, I would find a stranger peeping out at me.

Except for a little schooling, she had had no formal education; her mind had not gone through the educational process. She came to us as an unsophisticated girl, apparently with hardly any of the complexes which are said to be so common now. She never entirely lost that girlish look, but as she grew into a woman her eyes acquired a depth and a fire, giving the impression of still pools behind which storms raged. She was not the type of modern girl, with the modern girl's habits and lack of poise; yet she took easily enough to modern ways. But essentially she was an Indian girl and, more particularly, a Kashmiri girl, sensitive and proud, childlike and grown-up, foolish and wise. She was reserved to those she did not know or did not like, but bubbling over with gaiety and frankness before those she knew and liked. She was quick in her judgment and not always fair or right, but she stuck to her instinctive likes and dislikes. There was no guile in her. If she disliked a person, it was obvious, and she made no attempt to hide the fact. Even if she had tried to do so, she would probably not have succeeded. I have come across few persons who have produced such an impression of sincerity upon me as she did.

Our Marriage and After

I thought of the early years of our marriage when, with all my tremendous liking for Kamala, I almost forgot her and denied her, in so many ways, that comradeship which was her due. For I was then like a person possessed, giving myself utterly to the cause I had espoused, living in a dream-world of my own, and looking at the real people who surrounded me as unsubstantial shadows. I worked to the utmost of my capacity and my mind was filled to the brim with the subject that engrossed me. I gave all my energy to that cause and had little left to spare.

And yet I was very far from forgetting her, and I came back to her again and again as to a sure haven. If I was away for a number of days the thought of her cooled my mind and I looked forward eagerly to my return home. What indeed could I have done if she had not been there to comfort me and give me strength, and thus enable me to re-charge the exhausted battery of my mind and body?

I had taken from her what she gave me. What had I given to her in exchange during these early years? I had failed evidently and, possibly, she carried the deep impress of those days upon her. With her inordinate pride and sensitiveness she did not want to come to me to ask for help, although I could have given her that help more than anyone else. She wanted to play her own part in the national struggle and not be merely a hanger-on and a shadow of her husband. She wanted to justify herself to her own self as well as to the world. Nothing in the world could have pleased me more than this, but I was far too busy to see beneath the surface, and I was blind to what she looked for and so ardently desired. And then prison claimed me so often and I was away from her, or else she was ill. Like Chitra in Tagore's play, she seemed to say to me: 'I am Chitra. No goddess to be worshipped, nor yet the object of common pity to be brushed aside like a moth with indifference. If you deign to keep me by your side in the path of danger and daring, if you allow me to share the great duties of your life, then you will know my true self.'

But she did not say this to me in words and it was only gradually that I read the message of her eyes.

In the early months of 1930 I sensed her desire and we worked together, and I found in this experience a new delight. We lived for a while on the edge of life, as it were, for the clouds were gathering and a national upheaval was coming. Those were pleasant months for us, but they ended too soon, and, early in April, the country was in the grip of civil disobedience and governmental repression, and I was in prison again.

Most of us menfolk were in prison. And then a remarkable thing happened. Our women came to the front and took charge of the struggle. Women had always been there of course, but now there was an avalanche of them, which took not only the British Government but their own menfolk by surprise. Here were these women, women of the upper or middle classes, leading sheltered lives in their homes—peasant women, working-class women, rich women—pouring out in their tens of thousands in defiance of government order and police *lathi*. It was not only that display of courage and daring, but what was even more surprising was the organizational power they showed.

Never can I forget the thrill that came to us in Naini Prison when news of this reached us, the enormous pride in the women of India that filled us. We could hardly talk about all this among ourselves, for our hearts were full and our eyes were dim with tears.

My father had joined us later in Naini Prison, and he told us much that we did not know. He had been functioning outside as the leader of the civil disobedience movement, and he had encouraged in no way these aggressive activities of the women all over the country. He disliked, in his paternal and somewhat old-fashioned way, young women and old messing about in the streets under the hot sun of summer and coming into conflict with the police. But he realised the temper of the people and did not discourage any one, not even his wife and daughters and daughter-in-law. He told us how he had been agreeably surprised to see the energy, courage, and ability displayed by women all over the country; of the girls of his own household he spoke with affectionate pride.

At father's instance, a 'Resolution of Remembrance' was passed at thousands of public meetings all over India on January 26th, 1931, the anniversary of India's Independence Day. These meetings were banned by the police and many of them were forcibly broken up. Father had organized this from his sickbed and it was a triumph of organization, for we could not use the newspapers, or the mails, or the telegraph, or the telephone, or any of the established printing presses. And yet at a fixed time on an identical day all over this vast country, even in remote villages, the resolution was read out in the language of the province and adopted. Ten days after the resolution was so adopted, father died.

The resolution was a long one. But a part of it related to the women of India: 'We record our homage and deep admiration for the womanhood of India, who, in the hour of peril for the motherland, forsook the shelter of their homes and, with unfailing courage and endurance, stood shoulder to shoulder with their menfolk in the front line of India's national army to share with them the sacrifices and triumphs of the struggle....'

In this upheaval Kamala had played a brave and notable part and on her inexperienced shoulders fell the task of organizing our work in the city of Allahabad when every known worker was in prison. She made up for that inexperience by her fire and energy and, within a few months, she became the pride of Allahabad.

We met again under the shadow of my father's last illness and his death. We met on a new footing of comradeship and understanding. A few months later when we went with our daughter to Ceylon for our first brief holiday, and our last, we seemed to have discovered each other anew. All the past years that we had passed together had been but a preparation for this new and more intimate relationship.

We came back all too soon and work claimed me and, later, prison. There was to be no more holidaying, no working together, not even being together, except for a brief while between two long prison terms of two years each which followed each other. Before the second of these was over, Kamala lay dying.

When I was arrested in February, 1934, on a Calcutta warrant, Kamala went up to our rooms to collect some clothes for me. I followed her to say good-bye to her. Suddenly she clung to me and, fainting, collapsed. This was unusual for her as we had trained ourselves to take this jail-going lightly and cheerfully and to make as little fuss about it as possible. Was it some premonition she had that this was our last more or less normal meeting?

Two long prison terms of two years each had come between me and her just when our need for each other was greatest, just when we had come so near to each other. I thought of this during the long days in jail, and yet I hoped that the time would surely come when we would be together again. How did she fare during these years? I can guess but even I do not know, for during jail interviews, or during a brief interval outside there was little normality. We had to be always on our best behaviour lest we might cause pain to the other by showing our own distress. But it was obvious that she was greatly troubled and distressed over many things and there was no peace in her mind. I might have been of some help, but not from jail.

The Problem of Human Relationships

All these and many other thoughts, came to my mind during my long solitary hours in Badenweiler. I did not shed the atmosphere of jail easily; I had long got used to it and the new environment did not make any great change. I was living in the nazi domain with all its strange happenings which I disliked so much, but nazism did not interfere with me. There were few evidences of it in that quiet village in a corner of the Black Forest.

Or perhaps my mind was full of other matters. My past life unrolled itself before me and there was always Kamala standing by. She became a symbol of Indian women, or of woman herself. Sometimes she grew curiously mixed up with my ideas of India, that land of ours so dear to us, with all her faults and weaknesses, so elusive and so full of mystery. What was Kamala? Did I know her? understand her real self? Did she know or understand me? For I too was an abnormal person with mystery and unplumbed depths within me, which I could not myself fathom.

43

Sometimes I had thought that she was a little frightened of me because of this. I had been, and was, a most unsatisfactory person to marry. Kamala and I were unlike each other in some ways, and yet in some other ways very alike; we did not complement each other. Our very strength became a weakness in our relations to each other. There could either be complete understanding, a perfect union of minds, or difficulties. Neither of us could live a humdrum domestic life, accepting things as they were.

Among the many pictures that were displayed in the bazaars in India, there was one containing two separate pictures of Kamala and me, side by side, with the inscription at the top, *adarsha jori*, the model or ideal couple, as so many people imagined us to be. But the ideal is terribly difficult to grasp or to hold. Yet I remember telling Kamala, during our holiday in Ceylon, how fortunate we had been in spite of difficulties and differences, in spite of all the tricks life had played upon us, that marriage was an odd affair, and it had not ceased to be so even after thousands of years of experience. We saw around us the wrecks of many a marriage or, what was no better, the conversion of what was bright and golden into dross. How fortunate we were, I told her, and she agreed, for though we had sometimes quarrelled and grown angry with each other we kept that vital spark alight, and for each one of us life was always unfolding new adventure and giving fresh insight into each other.

The problem of human relationships, how fundamental it is, and how often ignored in our fierce arguments about politics and economics. It was not so ignored in the old and wise civilizations of India and China, where they developed patterns of social behaviour which, with all their faults, certainly gave poise to the individual. That poise is not in evidence in India to-day. But where is it in the countries of the West which have progressed so much in other directions? Or is poise essentially static and opposed to progressive change? Must we sacrifice one for the other? Surely it should be possible to have a union of poise and inner and outer progress, of the wisdom of the old with the science and the vigour of the new. Indeed we appear to have arrived at a stage in the world's history when the only alternative to such a union is likely to be the destruction and undoing of both.

Christmas 1935

Kamala's condition took a turn for the better. It was not very marked, but after the strain of the past weeks we experienced great relief. She had got over that crisis and stabilized her condition, and that in itself was a gain. This continued for another month and I took advantage of it to pay a brief visit to England with our daughter, Indira. I had not been there for eight years and many friends pressed me to visit them.

I came back to Badenweiler and resumed the old routine. Winter had come and the landscape was white with snow. As Christmas approached there was a marked deterioration in Kamala's condition. Another crisis had come, and it seemed that her life hung by a mere thread. During those last days of 1935 I ploughed my way through snow and slush not knowing how many days or hours she would live. The calm winter scene with its mantle of white snow seemed so like the peace of cold death to me, and I lost all my past hopeful optimism.

But Kamala fought this crisis also and with amazing vitality survived it. She grew better and more cheerful and wanted us to take her away from Badenweiler. She was weary of the place, and another factor which made a difference was the death of another patient in the sanatorium, who had sometimes sent flowers to her, and once or twice visited her. That patient—he was an Irish boy—had been much better than Kamala and was even allowed to go out for walks. We tried to keep the news of his sudden death from her, but we did not succeed. Those who are ill, and especially those who have the misfortune to stay in a sanatorium, seem to develop a sixth sense which tells them much that is sought to be hid from them.

In January I went to Paris for a few days and paid another brief visit to London. Life was pulling at me again and news reached me, in London, that I had been elected for a second time president of the Indian National Congress, which was to meet in April. I had been expecting this as friends had forewarned me, and I had even discussed it with Kamala. It was a dilemma for me: to leave her as she was or to resign from the presidentship. She would not have me resign. She was just a little better and we thought that I could come back to her later.

At the end of January, 1936, Kamala left Badenweiler and was taken to a sanatorium near Lausanne in Switzerland.

Death

Both Kamala and I liked the change to Switzerland. She was more cheerful and I felt a little more at home in that part of Switzerland which I knew fairly well. There was no marked change in her condition and it seemed that there was no crisis ahead. She was likely to continue as she was for a considerable period, making perhaps slow progress.

Meanwhile the call of India was insistent and friends there were pressing me to return. My mind grew restless and ever more occupied with the problems of my country. For some years I had

45

been cut off by prison or otherwise from active participation in public affairs, and I was straining at the leash. My visits to London and Paris and news from India had drawn me out of my shell and I could not go back into it.

I discussed the matter with Kamala and consulted the doctor. They agreed that I should return to India and I booked my passage by the Dutch K.L.M. air line. I was to leave Lausanne on February 28th. After all this had been fixed up, I found that Kamala did not at all like the idea of my leaving her. And yet she would not ask me to change my plans. I told her that I would not make a long stay in India and hoped to return after two or three months. I could return even earlier if she wanted me to. A cable would bring me by air to her within a week.

Four or five days remained before the date fixed for my departure. Indira, who was at school at Bex nearby, was coming over to spend those last days with us. The doctor came to me and suggested that I should postpone my return by a week or ten days. More he would not say. I agreed immediately and made another reservation in a subsequent K.L.M. plane.

As these last days went by a subtle change seemed to come over Kamala. The physical condition was much the same, so far as we could see, but her mind appeared to pay less attention to her physical environment. She would tell me that someone was calling her, or that she saw some figure or shape enter the room when I saw none.

Early on the morning of February 28th, she breathed her last. Indira was there, and so was our faithful friend and constant companion during these months, Dr. M. Atal.

A few other friends came from neighbouring towns in Switzerland, and we took her to the crematorium in Lausanne. Within a few minutes that fair body and that lovely face, which used to smile so often and so well, were reduced to ashes. A small urn contained the mortal remains of one who had been vital, so bright and so full of life.

Mussolini Return

The bond that kept me in Lausanne and Europe was broken and there was no need for me to remain there any longer. Indeed, something else within me was also broken, the realization of which only came gradually to me, for those days were black days for me and my mind did not function properly. Indira and I went to Montreux to spend a few quiet days together.

During our stay at Montreux I had a visit from the Italian Consul at Lausanne, who came over especially to convey to me Signor Mussolini's deep sympathy at my loss. I was a little surprised, for I had not met Signor Mussolini or had any other contacts with him. I asked the Consul to convey my gratitude to him.

Some weeks earlier a friend in Rome had written to me to say that Signor Mussolini would like to meet me. There was no question of my going to Rome then, and I said so. Later, when I was thinking of returning to India by air, that message was repeated and there was a touch of eagerness and insistence about it. I wanted to avoid this interview and yet I had no desire to be discourteous. Normally I might have got over my distaste for meeting him, for I was curious also to know what kind of man the Duce was. But the Abyssinian campaign was being carried on then and my meeting him would inevitably have led to all manner of inferences, and would be used for fascist propaganda. No denial from me would go far. I knew of several recent instances when Indian students and others visiting Italy had been utilized, against their wishes and sometimes even without their knowledge, for fascist propaganda. And then there had been the bogus interview with Mr. Gandhi which the *Giornale d'Italia* had published in 1931.

I conveyed my regrets, therefore, to my friend, and later wrote again and telephoned to him to avoid any possibility of misunderstanding. All this was before Kamala's death. After her death I sent another message pointing out that, even apart from other reasons, I was in no mood then for an interview with anyone.

All this insistence on my part became necessary, as I was passing through Rome by the K.L.M. and would have to spend an evening and night there. I could not avoid this passing visit and brief stay.

After a few days at Montreux I proceeded to Geneva and Marseilles, where I boarded the K.L.M. air liner for the East. On arrival in Rome in the late afternoon, I was met by a high official who handed me a letter from the *Chef de Cabinet* of Signor Mussolini. The Duce, it stated, would be glad to meet me and he had fixed six o'clock that evening for the interview. I was surprised and reminded him of my previous messages. But he insisted that it had now all been fixed up and the arrangement could not be upset. Indeed if the interview did not take place there was every likelihood of his being dismissed from his office. I was assured that nothing would appear in the press, and that I need only see the Duce, for a few minutes. All that he wanted to do was to shake hands with me and to convey personally his condolences at my wife's death. So we argued for a full hour with all courtesy on both sides but with increasing strain; it was a most exhausting hour for me and probably more so for the other party. The time fixed for the interview was at last upon us and I had my way. A telephone message was sent to the Duce's palace that I could not come.

That evening I sent a letter to Signor Mussolini expressing my regret that I could not take advantage of his kind invitation to me to see him and thanking him for his message of sympathy.

I continued my journey. At Cairo there were some old friends to meet me, and then further east, over the deserts of Western Asia. Various incidents, and the arrangements necessary for my journey, had so far kept my mind occupied. But after leaving Cairo and flying, hour after hour, over this desolate desert area, a terrible loneliness gripped me and I felt empty and purposeless. I was going back alone to my home, which was no longer home for me, and there by my side was a basket and that basket contained an urn. That was all that remained of Kamala, and all our bright dreams were also dead and turned to ashes. She is no more, Kamala is no more, my mind kept on repeating.

I thought of my autobiography, that record of my life, which I had discussed with her as she lay in Bhowali Sanatorium. And, as I was writing it, sometimes I would take a chapter or two and read it out to her. She had only seen or heard a part of it: she would never see the rest; nor would we write any more chapters together in the book of life.

When I reached Baghdad I sent a cable to my publishers in London, who were bringing out my autobiography, giving them the dedication for the book: 'To Kamala, who is no more.'

Karachi came, and crowds and many familiar faces. And then Allahabad, where we carried the precious urn to the swift-flowing Ganges and poured the ashes into the bosom of that noble river. How many of our forebears she had carried thus to the sea, how many of those who follow us will take that last journey in the embrace of her water.

CHAPTER THREE

THE QUEST

The Panorama of India's Past

DURING THESE YEARS OF THOUGHT AND ACTIVITY MY MIND HAS BEEN
full of India, trying to understand her and to analyse my own
reactions towards her. I went back to my childhood days and
tried to remember what I felt like then, what vague shape this
conception took in my growing mind, and how it was moulded
by fresh experience. Sometimes it receded into the background,
but it was always there, slowly changing, a queer mixture derived from old story and legend and modern fact. It produced a
sensation of pride in me as well as that of shame, for I was
ashamed of much that I saw around me, of superstitious practices, of outworn ideas, and, above all, our subject and poverty-
stricken state.

As I grew up and became engaged in activities which promised to lead to India's freedom, I became obsessed with the
thought of India. What was this India that possessed me and
beckoned to me continually, urging me to action so that we
might realize some vague but deeply-felt desire of our hearts?
The initial urge came to me, I suppose, through pride, both
individual and national, and the desire, common to all men,
to resist another's domination and have freedom to live the life
of our choice. It seemed monstrous to me that a great country
like India, with a rich and immemorial past, should be bound
hand and foot to a far-away island which imposed its will upon
her. It was still more monstrous that this forcible union had
resulted in poverty and degradation beyond measure. That was
reason enough for me and for others to act.

But it was not enough to satisfy the questioning that arose
within me. What is this India, apart from her physical and
geographical aspects? What did she represent in the past? What
gave strength to her then? How did she lose that old strength?
And has she lost it completely? Does she represent anything
vital now, apart from being the home of a vast number of human
beings? How does she fit into the modern world?

This wider international aspect of the problem grew upon

49

me as I realized more and more how isolation was both undesirable and impossible. The future that took shape in my mind was one of intimate co-operation, politically, economically, and culturally, between India and the other countries of the world. But before the future came there was the present, and behind the present lay the long and tangled past, out of which the present had grown. So to the past I looked for understanding. India was in my blood and there was much in her that instinctively thrilled me. And yet I approached her almost as an alien critic, full of dislike for the present as well as for many of the relics of the past that I saw. To some extent I came to her via the West, and looked at her as a friendly westerner might have done. I was eager and anxious to change her outlook and appearance and give her the garb of modernity. And yet doubts arose within me. Did I know India?—I who presumed to scrap much of her past heritage? There was a great deal that had to be scrapped, that must be scrapped; but surely India could not have been what she undoubtedly was, and could not have continued a cultured existence for thousands of years, if she had not possessed something very vital and enduring, something that was worthwhile. What was this something?

I stood on a mound of Mohenjo-daro in the Indus Valley in the north-west of India, and all around me lay the houses and streets of this ancient city that is said to have existed over five thousand years ago; and even then it was an old and well-developed civilization. 'The Indus civilization,' writes Professor Childe, 'represents a very prefect adjustment of human life to a specific environment that can only have resulted from years of patient effort. And it has endured; it is already specifically Indian and forms the basis of modern Indian culture.' Astonishing thought: that any culture or civilization should have this continuity for five or six thousand years or more; and not in a static, unchanging sense, for India was changing and progressing all the time. She was coming into intimate contact with the Persians, the Egyptians, the Greeks, the Chinese, the Arabs, the Central Asians, and the peoples of the Mediterranean. But though she influenced them and was influenced by them, her cultural basis was strong enough to endure. What was the secret of this strength? Where did it come from?

I read her history and read also a part of her abundant ancient literature, and was powerfully impressed by the vigour of the thought, the clarity of the language, and the richness of the mind that lay behind it. I journeyed through India in the company of mighty travellers from China and Western and Central Asia who came here in the remote past and left records of their travels. I thought of what India had accomplished in Eastern Asia, in

Angkor, Borobudur, and many other places. I wandered over the Himalayas, which are closely connected with old myth and legend, and which have influenced so much our thought and literature. My love of the mountains and my kinship with Kashmir especially drew me to them, and I saw there not only the life and vigour and beauty of the present, but also the memoried loveliness of ages past. The mighty rivers of India that flow from this great mountain barrier into the plains of India attracted me and reminded me of innumerable phases of our history. The Indus or *Sindhu*, from which our country came to be called India and Hindustan, and across which races and tribes and caravans and armies have come for thousands of years; the Brahmaputra, rather cut off from the main current of history, but living in old story, forcing its way into India through deep chasms cut in the heart of the northeastern mountains, and then flowing calmly in a gracious sweep between mountain and wooded plain; the Jumna, round which cluster so many legends of dance and fun and play; and the Ganges, above all the river of India, which has held India's heart captive and drawn uncounted millions to her banks since the dawn of history. The story of the Ganges, from her source to the sea, from old times to new, is the story of India's civilization and culture, of the rise and fall of empires, of great and proud cities, of the adventure of man and the quest of the mind which has so occupied India's thinkers, of the richness and fulfilment of life as well as its denial and renunciation, of ups and downs, of growth and decay, of life and death.

I visited old monuments and ruins and ancient sculptures and frescoes—Ajanta, Ellora, the Elephanta Caves, and other places —and I also saw the lovely buildings of a later age in Agra and Delhi, where every stone told its story of India's past.

In my own city of Allahabad or in Hardwar I would go to the great bathing festivals, the *Kumbh Mela*, and see hundreds of thousands of people come, as their forebears had come for thousands of years from all over India, to bathe in the Ganges. I would remember descriptions of these festivals written thirteen hundred years ago by Chinese pilgrims and others, and even then these *melas* were ancient and lost in an unknown antiquity. What was the tremendous faith, I wondered, that had drawn our people for untold generations to this famous river of India?

These journeys and visits of mine, with the background of my reading, gave me an insight into the past. To a somewhat bare intellectual understanding was added an emotional appreciation, and gradually a sense of reality began to creep into my mental picture of India, and the land of my forefathers became peopled with living beings, who laughed and wept, loved and suffered; and among them were men who seemed to know life and understand it, and out of their wisdom they had built a structure which gave India a cultural stability which lasted for thousands of years. Hundreds of vivid pictures of this past filled my mind, and they would stand out as soon as I visited a particular place associated with them. At Sarnath, near Benares, I would almost see the Buddha preaching his first sermon, and some of his recorded words would come like a distant echo to me through two thousand five hundred years. Ashoka's pillars of stone with their inscriptions would speak to me in their magnificent language and tell me of a man who, though an emperor, was greater than any king or emperor. At Fatehpur-Sikri, Akbar, forgetful of his empire, was seated holding converse and debate with the learned of all faiths, curious to learn something new and seeking an answer to the eternal problem of man.

Thus slowly the long panorama of India's history unfolded itself before me, with its ups and downs, its triumphs and defeats. There seemed to me something unique about the continuity of a cultural tradition through five thousand years of history, of invasion and upheaval, a tradition which was widespread among the masses and powerfully influenced them. Only China has had such a continuity of tradition and cultural life. And this panorama of the past gradually merged into the unhappy present, when India, for all her past greatness and stability, was a slave country, an appendage of Britain, and all over the world terrible and devastating war was raging and brutalizing humanity. But that vision of five thousand years gave me a new perspective, and the burden of the present seemed to grow lighter.

The hundred and eighty years of British rule in India were just one of the unhappy interludes in her long story; she would find herself again; already the last page of this chapter was being written. The world also will survive the horror of to-day and build itself anew on fresh foundations.

Nationalism and Internationalism

My reaction to India thus was often an emotional one, conditioned and limited in many ways. It took the form of nationalism. In the case of many people the conditioning and limiting factors are absent. But nationalism was and is inevitable in the India of my day; it is a natural and healthy growth. For any subject country national freedom must be the first and dominant urge; for India, with her intense sense of individuality and a past heritage, it was doubly so.

Recent events all over the world have demonstrated that the notion that nationalism is fading away before the impact of internationalism and proletarian movements has little truth. It is still one of the most powerful urges that move a people, and round it cluster sentiments and traditions and a sense of common living and common purpose. While the intellectual strata of the middle classes were gradually moving away from nationalism, or so they thought, labour and proletarian movements, deliberately based on internationalism, were drifting towards nationalism. The coming of war swept everybody everywhere into the net of nationalism. This remarkable resurgence of nationalism, or rather a re-discovery of it and a new realization of its vital significance, has raised new problems and altered the form and shape of old problems. Old established traditions cannot be easily scrapped or dispensed with; in moments of crisis they rise and dominate the minds of men, and often, as we have seen, a deliberate attempt is made to use those traditions to rouse a people to a high pitch of effort and sacrifice. Traditions have to be accepted to a large extent and adapted and transformed to meet new conditions and ways of thought, and at the same time new traditions have to be built up. The nationalist ideal is deep and strong; it is not a thing of the past with no future significance. But other ideals, more based on the ineluctable facts of to-day, have arisen, the international ideal and the proletarian ideal, and there must be some kind of fusion between these various ideals if we are to have a world equilibrium and a lessening of conflict. The abiding appeal of nationalism to the spirit of man has to be recognized and provided for, but its sway limited to a narrower sphere.

If nationalism is still so universal in its influence, even in countries powerfully affected by new ideas and international forces, how much more must it dominate the mind of India. Sometimes we are told that our nationalism is a sign of our backwardness and even our demand for independence indicates our narrowmindedness. Those who tell us so seem to imagine that true internationalism would triumph if we agreed to remain as junior partners in the British Empire or Commonwealth of Nations. They do not appear to realize that this particular type of so-called internationalism is only an extension of a narrow British nationalism, which could not have appealed to us even if the logical consequences of Anglo-Indian history had not utterly rooted out its possibility from our minds. Nevertheless, India, for all her intense nationalistic fervour, has gone further than many nations in her acceptance of real internationalism and the co-ordination, and even to some extent the subordination, of the independent nation state to a world organization.

India's Strength and Weakness

The search for the sources of India's strength and for her deterioration and decay is long and intricate. Yet the recent causes of that decay are obvious enough. She fell behind in the march of technique, and Europe, which had long been backward in many matters, took the lead in technical progress. Behind this technical progress was the spirit of science and a bubling life and spirit which displayed itself in many activities and in adventurous voyages of discovery. New techniques gave military strength to the countries of western Europe, and it was easy for them to spread out and dominate the East. That is the story not only of India, but of almost the whole of Asia.

Why this should have happened so is more difficult to unravel, for India was not lacking in mental alertness and technical skill in earlier times. One senses a progressive deterioration during centuries. The urge to life and endeavour becomes less, the creative spirit fades away and gives place to the imitative. Where triumphant and rebellious thought had tried to pierce the mysteries of nature and the universe, the wordy commentator comes with his glosses and long explanations. Magnificent art and sculpture give way to meticulous carving of intricate detail without nobility of conception or design. The vigour and richness of language, powerful yet simple, are followed by highly ornate and complex literary forms. The urge to adventure and the overflowing life which led to vast schemes of distant colonization and the transplantation of Indian culture in far lands: all these fade away and a narrow orthodoxy taboos even the crossing of the high seas. A rational spirit of inquiry, so evident in earlier times, which might well have led to the further growth of science, is replaced by irrationalism and a blind idolatory of the past. Indian life becomes a sluggish stream, living in the past, moving slowly through the accumulations of dead centuries. The heavy burden of the past crushes it and a kind of coma seizes it. It is not surprising that in this condition of mental stupor and physical weariness India should have deteriorated and remained rigid and immobile, while other parts of the world marched ahead.

Yet this is not a complete or wholly correct survey. If there had only been a long and unrelieved period of rigidity and stagnation, this might well have resulted in a complete break with the past, the death of an era, and the erection of something new on its ruins. There has not been such a break and there is a definite continuity. Also, from time to time, vivid periods of renascence have occurred, and some of them have been long and brilliant. Always there is visible an attempt to understand and adapt the new and harmonize it with the old, or at any rate with parts of the old which were considered worth preserving. Often that old retains an external form only, as a kind of symbol, and changes its inner content. But something vital and living continues, some urge driving the people in a direction not wholly realized, and always a desire for synthesis between the old and the new. It was this urge and desire that kept them going and enabled them to absorb new ideas while retaining much of the old. Whether there was such a thing as an Indian dream through the ages, vivid and full of life or sometimes reduced to the murmurings of troubled sleep, I do not know. Every people and every nation has some such belief or myth of national destiny and perhaps it is partly true in each case. Being an Indian I am myself influenced by this reality or myth about India, and I feel that anything that had the power to mould hundreds of generations, without a break, must have drawn its enduring vitality from some deep well of strength, and have had the capacity to renew that vitality from age to age.

Was there some such well of strength? And if so, did it dry up, or did it have hidden springs to replenish it? What of today? Are there any springs still functioning from which we can refresh and strengthen ourselves? We are an old race, or rather an odd mixture of many races, and our racial memories go back to the dawn of history. Have we had our day and are we now living in the late afternoon or evening of our existence, just carrying on after the manner of the aged, quiescent, devitalized, uncreative, desiring peace and sleep above all else?

No people, no races remain unchanged. Continually they are mixing with others and slowly changing; they may appear to die almost and then rise again as a new people or just a variation of the old. There may be a definite break between the old people and the new, or vital links of thought and ideals may join them.

History has numerous instances of old and well-established civilizations fading away or being ended suddenly, and vigorous new cultures taking their place. Is it some vital energy, some inner source of strength that gives life to a civilization or a people, without which all effort is ineffective, like the vain attempt of an aged person to play the part of a youth?

Among the peoples of the world to-day I have sensed this vital energy chiefly in three—Americans, Russians, and the Chinese; a queer combination! Americans, in spite of having their roots in the old world, are a new people, uninhibited and without the burdens and complexes of old races, and it is easy to understand their abounding vitality. So also are the Canadians, Australians, and New Zealanders, all of them largely cut off from the old world and facing life in all its newness.

Russians are not a new people, and yet there has been a complete break from the old, like that of death, and they have been reincarnated anew, in a manner for which there is no example in history. They have become youthful again with an energy and vitality that are amazing. They are searching for some of their old roots again, but for all practical purposes they are a new people, a new race and a new civilization.

The Russian example shows how a people can revitalize itself, become youthful again, if it is prepared to pay the price for it, and tap the springs of suppressed strength and energy among the masses. Perhaps this war, with all its horror and frightfulness, might result in the rejuvenation of other peoples also, such as survive from the holocaust.

The Chinese stand apart from all these. They are not a new race, nor have they gone through that shock of change, from top to bottom, which came to Russia. Undoubtedly, seven years of cruel war has changed them, as it must. How far this change is due to the war or to more abiding causes, or whether it is a mixture of the two, I do not know, but the vitality of the Chinese people astonishes me. I cannot imagine a people endowed with such bed-rock strength going under.

Something of that vitality which I saw in China I have sensed at times in the Indian people also. Not always, and anyway it is difficult for me to take an objective view. Perhaps my wishes distort my thinking. But always I was in search for this in my wanderings among the Indian people. If they had this vitality, then it was well with them and they would make good. If they lacked it completely, then our political efforts and shouting were all make-believe and would not carry us far. I was not interested in making some political arrangement which would enable our people to carry on more or less as before, only a little better. I felt they had vast stores of suppressed energy and ability, and I wanted to release these and make them feel young and vital again. India, constituted as she is, cannot play a secondary part in the world. She will either count for a great deal or not count at all. No middle position attracted me. Nor did I think any intermediate position feasible.

Behind the past quarter of a century's struggle for India's independence and all our conflicts with British authority, lay in my mind, and that of many others, the desire to revitalize India. We felt that through action and self-imposed suffering and sacrifice, through voluntarily facing risk and danger, through refusal to submit to what we considered evil and wrong, would we re-charge the battery of India's spirit and waken her from her long slumber. Though we came into conflict continually with the British Government in India, our eyes were always turned towards our own people. Political advantage had value only in so far as it helped in that fundamental purpose of ours. Because of this governing motive, frequently we acted as no politician, moving in the narrow sphere of politics only, would have done, and foreign and Indian critics expressed surprise at the folly and intransigence of our ways. Whether we were foolish or not, the historians of the future will judge. We aimed high and looked far. Probably we were often foolish, from the point of view of opportunist politics, but at no time did we forget that our main purpose was to raise the whole level of the Indian people, psychologically and spiritually and also, of course, politically and economically. It was the building up of that real inner strength of the people that we were after, knowing that the rest would inevitably follow. We had to wipe out some generations of shameful subservience and timid submission to an arrogant alien authority.

The Search for India

Though books and old monuments and past cultural achievements helped to produce some understanding of India, they did not satisfy me or give me the answer I was looking for. Nor could they, for they dealt with a past age, and I wanted to know if there was any real connection between that past and the present. The present for me, and for many others like me, was an odd mixture of medi-ævalism, appalling poverty and misery and a somewhat super-ficial modernism of the middle classes. I was not an admirer of my own class or kind, and yet inevitably I looked to it for leader-ship in the struggle for India's salvation; that middle class felt caged and circumscribed and wanted to grow and develop itself. Unable to do so within the framework of British rule, a spirit of revolt grew against this rule, and yet this spirit was not directed against the structure that crushed us. It sought to retain it and control it by displacing the British. These middle classes were too much the product of that structure to challenge it and seek to uproot it.

New forces arose that drove us to the masses in the villages, and for the first time, a new and different India rose up before the young intellectuals who had almost forgotten its existence or attached little importance to it. It was a disturbing sight, not only because of its stark misery and the magnitude of its problems, but because it began to upset some of our values and conclusions. So began for us the discovery of India as it was, and it produced both understanding and conflict within us. Our reactions varied and depended on our previous environment and experience. Some were already sufficiently acquainted with these village masses not to experience any new sensation; they took them for granted. But for me it was a real voyage of discovery, and, while I was always painfully conscious of the failings and weaknesses of my people, I found in India's countryfolk something, difficult to define, which attracted me. That something I had missed in our middle classes.

I do not idealise the conception of the masses and, as far as possible, I try to avoid thinking of them as a theoretical abstraction. The people of India are very real to me in their great variety and, in spite of their vast numbers, I try to think of them as individuals rather than as vague groups. Perhaps it was because I did not expect much from them that I was not disappointed; I found more than I had expected. It struck me that perhaps the reason for this, and for a certain stability and potential strength that they possessed, was the old Indian cultural tradition which was still retained by them in a small measure. Much had gone in the battering they had received during the past 200 years. Yet something remained that was worth while, and with it so much that was worthless and evil.

During the 'twenties my work was largely confined to my own province and I travelled extensively and intensively through the towns and villages of the forty-eight districts of the United Provinces of Agra and Oudh, that heart of Hindustan as it has so long been considered, the seat and centre of both ancient and mediæval civilization, the melting pot of so many races and cultures, the area where the great revolt of 1857 blazed up and was later ruthlessly crushed. I grew to know the sturdy Jat of the northern and western districts, that typical son of the soil, brave and independent looking, relatively more prosperous; the Rajput peasant and petty landholder, still proud of his race and ancestry, even though he might have changed his faith and adopted Islam; the deft and skilful artisans and cottage workers, both Hindu and Moslem; the poorer peasantry and tenants in their vast numbers, especially in Oudh and the eastern districts, crushed and ground down by generations of oppression and poverty, hardly daring to hope that a change would come to better their lot, and yet hoping and full of faith.

During the 'thirties, in the intervals of my life out of prison, and especially during the election campaign of 1936-37, I travelled more extensively throughout India, in towns and cities and villages alike. Except for rural Bengal, which unhappily I have only rarely visited, I toured in every province and went deep into villages. I spoke of political and economic issues and judging from my speech I was full of politics and elections. But all this while, in a corner of my mind, lay something deeper and more vivid, and elections or the other excitements of the passing day meant little to it. Another and a major excitement had seized me, and I was again on a great voyage of discovery and the land of India and the people of India lay spread out before me. India with all her infinite charm and variety began to grow upon me more and more, and yet the more I saw of her, the more I realized how very difficult it was for me or for anyone else to grasp the ideas she had embodied. It was not her wide spaces that eluded me, or even her diversity, but some depth of soul which I could not fathom, though I had occasional and tantalizing glimpses of it. She was like some ancient palimpsest on which layer upon layer of thought and reverie had been inscribed, and yet no succeeding layer had completely hidden or erased what had been written previously. All of these existed in our conscious or subconscious selves, though we may not have been aware of them, and they had gone to build up the complex and mysterious personality of India. That sphinx-like face with its elusive and sometimes mocking smile was to be seen throughout the length and breadth of the land. Though outwardly there was diversity and infinite variety among our people, everywhere there was that tremendous impress of oneness, which had held all of us together for ages past, whatever political fate or misfortune had befallen us. The unity of India was no longer merely an intellectual conception for me: it was an emotional experience which overpowered me. That essential unity had been so powerful that no political division, no disaster or catastrophe, had been able to overcome it.

It was absurd, of course, to think of India or any country as a kind of anthropomorphic entity. I did not do so. I was also fully aware of the diversities and divisions of Indian life, of classes, castes, religions, races, different degrees of cultural development. Yet I think that a country with a long cultural background and a common outlook on life develops a spirit that is peculiar to it and that is impressed on all its children, however much they may differ among themselves. Can anyone fail to see this in China, whether he meets an old-fashioned mandarin or a Communist who has apparently broken with the past? It was this spirit of India that I was after, not through idle curiosity, though I was curious enough, but because I felt that it might give me some key to the understanding of my country and people, some guidance to thought and action. Politics and elections were day to day affairs when we grew excited over trumpery matters. But if we were going to build the house of India's future, strong and secure and beautiful, we would have to dig deep for the foundations.

'Bharat Mata'

Often, as I wandered from meeting to meeting, I spoke to my audience of this India of ours, of Hindustan and of *Bharata*, the old Sanskrit name derived from the mythical founder of the race. I seldom did so in the cities, for there the audiences were more sophisticated and wanted stronger fare. But to the peasant, with his limited outlook, I spoke of this great country for whose freedom we were struggling, of how each part differed from the other

59

and yet was India, of common problems of the peasants from north to south and east to west, of the *Swaraj* that could only be for all and every part and not for some. I told them of my journeying from the Khyber Pass in the far north-west to *Kanya Kumari* or Cape Comorin in the distant south, and how everywhere the peasants put me identical questions, for their troubles were the same—poverty, debt, vested interests, landlords, moneylenders, heavy rents and taxes, police harassment, and all these wrapped up in the structure that the foreign government had imposed upon us—and relief must also come for all. I tried to make them think of India as a whole, and even to some little extent of this wide world of which we were a part. I brought in the struggle in China, in Spain, in Abyssinia, in Central Europe, in Egypt and the countries of Western Asia. I told them of the wonderful changes in the Soviet Union and of the great progress made in America. The task was not easy; yet it was not so difficult as I had imagined, for our ancient epics and myths and legends, which they knew so well, had made them familiar with the conception of their country, and some there were always who had travelled far and wide to the great places of pilgrimage situated at the four corners of India. Or there were old soldiers who had served in foreign parts in World War I or other expeditions. Even my references to foreign countries were brought home to them by the consequences of the great depression of the 'thirties.

Sometimes as I reached a gathering, a great roar of welcome would greet me: *Bharat Mata kī Jai*—'Victory to Mother India.' I would ask them unexpectedly what they meant by that cry, who was this *Bharat Mata*, Mother India, whose victory they wanted? My question would amuse them and surprise them, and then, not knowing exactly what to answer, they would look at each other and at me. I persisted in my questioning. At last a vigorous Jat, wedded to the soil from immemorial generations, would say that it was the *dharti*, the good earth of India, that they meant. What earth? Their particular village patch, or all the patches in the district or province, or in the whole of India? And so question and answer went on, till they would ask me impatiently to tell them all about it. I would endeavour to do so and explain that India was all this that they had thought, but it was much more. The mountains and the rivers of India, and the forests and the broad fields, which gave us food, were all dear to us, but what counted ultimately were the people of India, people like them and me, who were spread out all over this vast land. *Bharat Mata*, Mother India, was essentially these millions of people, and victory to her meant victory to these people. You are parts of this *Bharat Mata*, I told them, you are in a manner yourselves *Bharat Mata*, and as this idea slowly

soaked into their brains, their eyes would light up as if they
had made a great discovery.

The Variety and Unity of India

The diversity of India is tremendous; it is obvious; it lies on
the surface and anybody can see it. It concerns itself with physical appearances as well as with certain mental habits and traits.
There is little in common, to outward seeming, between the
Pathan of the North-West and the Tamil in the far South. Their
racial stocks are not the same, though there may be common
strands running through them; they differ in face and figure,
food and clothing, and, of course, language. In the North-
Western Frontier Province there is already the breath of Central
Asia, and many a custom there, as in Kashmir, reminds one of
the countries on the other side of the Himalayas. Pathan popular dances are singularly like Russian Cossack dancing. Yet,
with all these differences, there is no mistaking the impress of
India on the Pathan, as this is obvious on the Tamil. This is
not surprising, for these border lands, and indeed Afghanistan
also, were united with India for thousands of years. The old
Turkish and other races who inhabited Afghanistan and parts
of Central Asia before the advent of Islam were largely Buddhists, and earlier still, during the period of the Epics,
Hindus. The frontier area was one of the principal centres of
old Indian culture and it abounds still with ruins of monuments and monasteries and, especially, of the great university
of Taxila, which was at the height of its fame two thousand
years ago, attracting students from all over India as well as
different parts of Asia. Changes of religion made a difference,
but could not change entirely the mental backgrounds which
the people of those areas had developed.

The Pathan and the Tamil are two extreme examples; the
others lie somewhere in between. All of them have their distinctive features, all of them have still more the distinguishing
mark of India. It is fascinating to find how the Bengalis, the
Marathas, the Gujratis, the Tamils, the Andhras, the Oriyas,
the Assamese, the Canarese, the Malayalis, the Sindhis, the
Punjabis, the Pathans, the Kashmiris, the Rajputs, and the great
central block comprising the Hindustani-speaking people, have
retained their peculiar characteristics for hundreds of years,
have still more or less the same virtues and failings of which
old tradition or record tells us, and yet have been throughout
these ages distinctively Indian, with the same national heritage
and the same set of moral and mental qualities. There was
something living and dynamic about this heritage which showed

61

itself in ways of living and a philosophical attitude to life and its problems. Ancient India, like ancient China, was a world in itself, a culture and a civilization which gave shape to all things. Foreign influences poured in and often influenced that culture and were absorbed. Disruptive tendencies gave rise immediately to an attempt to find a synthesis. Some kind of a dream of unity has occupied the mind of India since the dawn of civilization. That unity was not conceived as something imposed from outside, a standardization of externals or even of beliefs. It was something deeper and, within its fold, the widest tolerance of belief and custom was practised and every variety acknowledged and even encouraged.

Differences, big or small, can always be noticed even within a national group, however closely bound together it may be. The essential unity of that group becomes apparent when it is compared to another national group, though often the differences between two adjoining groups fade out or intermingle near the frontiers, and modern developments are tending to produce a certain uniformity everywhere. In ancient and mediaeval times, the idea of the modern nation was non-existent, and feudal, religious, racial, or cultural bonds had more importance. Yet I think that at almost any time in recorded history an Indian would have felt more or less at home in any part of India, and would have felt as a stranger and alien in any other country. He would certainly have felt less of a stranger in countries which had partly adopted his culture or religion. Those who professed a religion of non-Indian origin or, coming to India, settled down there, became distinctively Indian in the course of a few generations, such as Christians, Jews, Parsees, Moslems. Indian converts to some of these religions never ceased to be Indians on account of a change of their faith. They were looked upon in other countries as Indians and foreigners, even though there might have been a community of faith between them.

To-day, when the conception of nationalism has developed much more, Indians in foreign countries inevitably form a national group and hang together for various purposes, in spite of their internal differences. An Indian Christian is looked upon as an Indian wherever he may go. An Indian Moslem is considered an Indian in Turkey or Arabia or Iran, or any other country where Islam is the dominant religion.

All of us, I suppose, have varying pictures of our native land and no two persons will think exactly alike. When I think of India, I think of many things: of broad fields dotted with innumerable small villages; of towns and cities I have visited; of the magic of the rainy season which pours life into the dry parched-up land and converts it suddenly into a glistening expanse of beauty and greenery, of great rivers and flowing water; of the Khyber Pass in all its bleak surroundings; of the southern tip of India; of people, individually and in the mass; and, above all, of the Himalayas, snow-capped, or some mountain valley in Kashmir in the spring, covered with new flowers, and with a brook bubbling and gurgling through it. We make and preserve the pictures of our choice, and so I have chosen this mountain background rather than the more normal picture of a hot, sub-tropical country. Both pictures would be correct, for India stretches from the tropics right up to the temperate regions, from near the equator to the cold heart of Asia.

Travelling through India

Towards the end of 1936 and in the early months of 1937 my touring progressively gathered speed and became frantic. I passed through this vast country like some hurricane, travelling night and day, always on the move, hardly staying anywhere, hardly resting. There were urgent demands for me from all parts and time was limited, for the general elections were approaching and I was supposed to be an election-winner for others. I travelled mostly by automobile, partly by aeroplane and railway. Occasionally I had to use, for short distances, an elephant, a camel, or a horse; or travel by steamer, paddle-boat, or canoe; or use a bicycle; or go on foot. These odd and varied methods of transport sometimes became necessary in the interior, far from the beaten track. I carried a double set of microphones and loud speakers with me, for it was not possible to deal with the vast gatherings in any other way; nor indeed could I otherwise retain my voice. Those microphones went with me to all manner of strange places, from the frontiers of Tibet to the border of Baluchistan, where no such thing had ever been seen or heard of previously.

From early morning till late at night I travelled from place to place where great gatherings awaited me, and in between these there were numerous stops where patient villagers stood to greet me. These were impromptu affairs, which upset my heavy programme and delayed all subsequent engagements; and yet how was it possible for me to rush by, unheeding and careless of these humble folk? Delay was added to delay and, at the big open-air gatherings, it took many minutes for me to pass through the crowds to the platform, and later to come away. Every minute counted, and the minutes piled up on top of each other and became hours; so that by the time evening came I was several hours late. But the crowd was waiting patiently, though it was winter and they sat and shivered in the open, insufficiently

63

clad as they were. My day's programme would thus prolong itself to eighteen hours and we would reach our journey's end for the day at midnight or after. Once in the Karnatak, in mid-February, we passed all bounds and broke our own records. The day's programme was a terribly heavy one and we had to pass through a very beautiful mountain forest with winding and none-too-good roads, which could only be tackled slowly. There were half-a-dozen monster meetings and many smaller ones. We began the day by a function at eight in the morning; our last engagement was at 4 a.m. (it should have been seven hours earlier), and then we had to cover another seventy miles before we reached our resting place for the night. We arrived at 7 a.m., having covered 415 miles that day and night, apart from numerous meetings. It had been a twenty-three-hour day and an hour later I had to begin my next day's programme.

Someone took the trouble to estimate that during these months some ten million persons actually attended the meetings I addressed, while some additional millions were brought into some kind of touch with me during my journeys by road. The biggest gatherings would consist of about one hundred thousand persons, while audiences of twenty thousand were fairly common. Occasionally in passing through a small town I would be surprised to notice that it was almost deserted and the shops were closed. The explanation came to me when I saw that almost the entire population of the town, men, women, and even children, had gathered at the meeting-place, on the other side of the town, and were waiting patiently for my arrival.

How I managed to carry on in this way without physical collapse, I cannot understand now, for it was a prodigious feat of physical endurance. Gradually, I suppose, my system adapted itself to this vagrant life. I would sleep heavily in the automobile for half an hour between two meetings and find it hard to wake up. Yet I had to get up and the sight of a great cheering crowd would finally wake me. I reduced my meals to a minimum and often dropped a meal, especially in the evenings, feeling the better for it. But what kept me up and filled me with vitality was the vast enthusiasm and affection that surrounded me and met me everywhere I went. I was used to it, and yet I could never get quite used to it, and every new day brought its surprises.

General Elections

My tour was especially concerned with the general elections all over India that were approaching. But I did not take kindly to the usual methods and devices that accompany electioneering. Elections were an essential and inseparable part of the democratic process and there was no way of doing away with them. Yet, often enough, elections brought out the evil side of man, and it was obvious that they did not always lead to the success of the better man. Sensitive persons, and those who were not prepared to adopt rough-and-ready methods to push themselves forward, were at a disadvantage and preferred to avoid these contests. Was democracy then to be a close preserve of those possessing thick skins and loud voices and accommodating consciences?

Especially were these election evils most prevalent where the electorate was small; many of them vanished, or at any rate were not so obvious, when the electorate was a big one. It was possible for the biggest electorate to be swept off its feet on a false issue, or in the name of religion (as we saw later), but there were usually some balancing factors which helped to prevent the grosser evils. My experience in this matter confirmed my faith in the widest possible franchise. I was prepared to trust that wide electorate far more than a restricted one, based on a property qualification or even an educational test. The property qualification was anyhow bad; as for education it was obviously desirable and necessary. But I have not discovered any special qualities in a literate or slightly educated person which would entitle his opinion to greater respect than that of a sturdy peasant, illiterate but full of a limited kind of common sense. In any event, where the chief problem is that of the peasant, his opinion is far more important. I am a convinced believer in adult franchise, for men and women, and, though I realize the difficulties in the way, I am sure that the objections raised to its adoption in India have no great force and are based on the fears of privileged classes and interests.

The general elections in 1937 for the provincial assemblies were based on a restricted franchise affecting about twelve per cent of the population. But even this was a great improvement on the previous franchise, and nearly thirty millions all over India, apart from the Indian States, were now entitled to vote. The scope of these elections was vast and comprised the whole of India, minus the States. Every province had to elect its Provincial Assembly, and in most provinces there were two Houses, and there were thus two sets of elections. The number of candidates ran into many thousands.

My approach to these elections, and to some extent the approach of most Congressmen, was different from the usual one. I did not trouble myself about the individual candidates, but wanted rather to create a country-wide atmosphere in favour of our national movement for freedom as represented by the Congress, and for the programme contained in our election manifesto. I felt that if we succeeded in this, all would be well; if not, then it did not matter much if an odd candidate won or lost.

My appeal was an ideological one and I hardly referred to the candidates, except as standard-bearers of our cause. I knew many of them, but there were many I did not know at all, and I saw no reason why I should burden my mind with hundreds of names. I asked for votes for the Congress, for the independence of India, and for the struggle for independence. I made no promises, except to promise unceasing struggle till freedom was attained. I told people to vote for us only if they understood and accepted our objective and our programme, and were prepared to live up to them; not otherwise. I charged them not to vote for the Congress if they disagreed with this objective or programme. We wanted no false votes, no votes for particular persons because they liked them. Votes and elections would not take us far; they were just small steps in a long journey, and to delude us with votes, without intelligent acceptance of what they signified or willingness for subsequent action, was to play us false and be untrue to our country. Individuals did not count, though we wanted good and true individuals to represent us; it was the cause that counted, the organization that represented it, and the nation to whose freedom we were pledged. I analysed that freedom and what it should mean to the hundreds of millions of our people. We wanted no change of masters from white to brown, but a real people's rule, by the people and for the people, and an ending of our poverty and misery.

That was the burden of my speeches, and only in that impersonal way could I fit myself into the election campaign. I was not greatly concerned with the prospects of particular candidates. My concern was with a much bigger issue. As a matter of fact that approach was the right one even from the narrower point of view of a particular candidate's success. For thus he and his election were lifted up to a higher and more elemental level of a great nation's fight for freedom, and millions of poverty-stricken people striving to put an end to their ancient curse of poverty. These ideas, expressed by scores of leading Congressmen, came and spread like a mighty wind fresh from the sea, sweeping away all petty ideas and electioneering stunts. I knew my people and liked them, and their million eyes had taught me much of mass psychology.

I was talking about the elections front day to day, and yet the elections seldom occupied my mind; they floated about superficially on the surface. Nor was I particularly concerned with the voters only. I was getting into touch with something much bigger: the people of India in their millions; and such message as I had was meant for them all, whether they were voters or not; for every Indian, man, woman, and child. The excitement of this adventure held me, this physical and emotional communion with vast numbers of people. It was not the feeling of being in a crowd, one among many, and being swayed by the impulses of the crowd. My eyes held those thousands of eyes: we looked at each other, not as strangers meeting for the first time, but with recognition, though of what this was none could say. As I saluted them with a *namaskar*, the palms of my hands joined together in front of me, a forest of hands went up in salutation, and a friendly, personal smile appeared on their faces, and a murmur of greeting rose from that assembled multitude and enveloped me in its warm embrace. I spoke to them and my voice carried the message I had brought, and I wondered how far they understood my words or the ideas that lay behind them. Whether they understood all I said or not, I could not say, but there was a light of a deeper understanding in their eyes, which seemed to go beyond spoken words.

The Culture of the Masses

Thus I saw the moving drama of the Indian people in the present, and could often trace the threads which bound their lives to the past, even while their eyes were turned towards the future. Everywhere I found a cultural background which had exerted a powerful influence on their lives. This background was a mixture of popular philosophy, tradition, history, myth, and legend, and it was not possible to draw a line between any of these. Even the entirely uneducated and illiterate shared this background. The old epics of India, the *Ramayana* and the *Mahabharata* and other books, in popular translations and paraphrases, were widely known among the masses, and every incident and story and moral in them was engraved on the popular mind and gave a richness and content to it. Illiterate villagers would know hundreds of verses by heart and their conversation would be full of references to them or to some story with a moral, enshrined in some old classic. Often I was surprised by some such literary turn given by a group of villagers to a simple talk about present-day affairs. If my mind was full of pictures from recorded history and more-or-less ascertained fact, I realised that even the illiterate peasant had a picture gallery in his mind, though this was largely drawn from myth and tradition and epic heroes and heroines, and only very little from history. Nevertheless, it was vivid enough.

I looked at their faces and their figures and watched their movements. There was many a sensitive face and many a sturdy body, straight and clean-limbed; and among the women there was grace and suppleness and dignity and poise and, very often, a look that was full of melancholy. Usually the finer physical types were among the upper castes, who were just a little better off in the economic sense. Sometimes, as I was passing along a country road, or through a village, I would start with surprise on seeing a fine type of man, or a beautiful woman, who reminded me of some fresco of ancient times. And I wondered how the type endured and continued through ages, in spite of all the horror and misery that India had gone through. What could we not do with these people under better conditions and with greater opportunities opening out to them?

There was poverty and the innumerable progeny of poverty everywhere, and the mark of this beast was on every forehead. Life had been crushed and distorted and made into a thing of evil, and many vices had flowed from this distortion and continuous lack and ever-present insecurity. All this was not pleasant to see; yet that was the basic reality in India. There was far too much of the spirit of resignation and acceptance of things as they were. But there was also a mellowness and a gentleness, the cultural heritage of thousands of years, which no amount of misfortune had been able to rub off.

Two Lives

In this and other ways I tried to discover India, the India of the past and of the present, and I made my mood receptive to impressions and to the waves of thought and feeling that came to me from living beings as well as those who had long ceased to be. I tried to identify myself for a while with this unending procession, at the tail end of which I, too, was struggling along. And then I would separate myself and as from a hill-top, apart, look down at the valley below.

To what purpose was all this long journeying? To what end these unending processions? A feeling of tiredness and disillusion would sometimes invade my being, and then I would seek escape from it in cultivating a certain detachment. Slowly my mind had prepared itself for this, and I had ceased to attach much value to myself or to what happened to me. Or so I thought, and to some extent I succeeded, though not much, I fear, as there is too much of a volcano within me for real detachment. Unexpectedly all my defences are hurled away and all my detachment goes.

But even the partial success I achieved was very helpful and, in the midst of activity, I could separate myself from it and look at it as a thing apart. Sometimes, I would steal an hour or two, and forgetting my usual preoccupations, retire into that cloistered chamber of my mind and live, for a while, another life. And so, in a way, these two lives marched together, inseparably tied up with one another, and yet apart.

CHAPTER FOUR

THE DISCOVERY OF INDIA

The Indus Valley Civilization

THE INDUS VALLEY CIVILIZATION, OF WHICH IMPRESSIVE REMAINS
have been discovered at Mohenjo-daro in Sind and at Harappa
in the Western Punjab, is the earliest picture that we have of
India's past. These excavations have revolutionised the conception of ancient history. Unfortunately, a few years after this work
of excavation began in these areas, it was stopped, and for the
last thirteen years or so nothing significant has been done. The
stoppage was initially due to the great depression of the early
'thirties. Lack of funds was pleaded, although there was never
any lack for the display of imperial pomp and splendour. The
coming of World War II effectively stopped all activity, and
even the work of preservation of all that has been dug out has
been rather neglected. Twice I have visited Mohenjo-daro, in
1931 and 1936. During my second visit I found that the rain and
the dry sandy air had already injured many of the buildings that
had been dug out. After being preserved for over five thousand
years under a covering of sand and soil, they were rapidly
disintegrating owing to exposure, and very little was being done
to preserve these priceless relics of ancient times. The officer of
the archaeological department in charge of the place complained
that he was allowed practically no funds or other help or material
to enable him to keep the excavated buildings as they were.
What has happened during these last eight years I do not know,
but I imagine that the wearing away has continued, and within
another few years many of the characteristic features of Mohenjo-
daro will have disappeared.

That is a tragedy for which there is no excuse, and something
that can never be replaced will have gone, leaving only pictures
and written descriptions to remind us of what it was.

Mohenjo-daro and Harappa are far apart. It was sheer chance
that led to the discovery of these ruins in these two places. There
can be little doubt that there lie many such buried cities and
other remains of the handiwork of ancient man in between these
two areas; that, in fact, this civlization was widespread over large

parts of India, certainly of North India. A time may come when this work of uncovering the distant past of India is again taken in hand and far-reaching discoveries are made. Already remains of this civilization have been found as far apart as Kathiawar in the west and the Ambala district of the Punjab, and there is reason for believing that it spread to the Gangetic Valley. Thus it was something much more than an Indus Valley civilization. The inscriptions found at Mohenjo-daro have so far not been fully deciphered.

But what we know, even thus far, is of the utmost significance. The Indus Valley civilization, as we find it, was highly developed and must have taken thousands of years to reach that stage. It was, surprisingly enough, a predominantly secular civilization, and the religious element, though present, did not dominate the scene. It was clearly also the precursor of later cultural periods in India.

Sir John Marshall tells us: 'One thing that stands out clear and unmistakable both at Mohenjo-daro and Harappa is that the civilization hitherto revealed at these two places is not an incipient civilization, but one already age-old and stereotyped on Indian soil, with many millenniums of human endeavour behind it. Thus India must henceforth be recognised, along with Persia, Mesopotamia, and Egypt, as one of the most important areas where the civilizing processes were initiated and developed.' And, again, he says that 'the Punjab and Sind, if not other parts of India as well, were enjoying an advanced and singularly uniform civilization of their own, closely akin, but in some respects even superior, to that of contemporary Mesopotamia and Egypt.'

These people of the Indus Valley had many contacts with the Sumerian civilization of that period, and there is even some evidence of an Indian colony, probably of merchants, at Akkad. 'Manufactures from the Indus cities reached even the markets on the Tigris and Euphrates. Conversely, a few Sumerian devices in art, Mesopotamia toilet sets, and a cylinder seal were copied on the Indus. Trade was not confined to raw materials and luxury articles; fish, regularly imported from the Arabian Sea coasts, augmented the food supplies of Mohenjo-daro.'*

Cotton was used for textiles even at that remote period in India. Marshall compares and contrasts the Indus Valley civilization with those of contemporary Egypt and Mesopotamia: 'Thus, to mention only a few salient points, the use of cotton for textiles was exclusively restricted at this period to India and was not extended to the western world until 2,000 or 3,000 years later. Again, there is nothing that we know of in prehistoric Egypt or

*Gordon Childe. 'What Happened in History', p. 112 (Pelican Books, 1943).

Mesopotamia or anywhere else in western Asia to compare with the well-built baths and commodious houses of the citizens of Mohenjo-daro. In these countries much money and thought were lavished on the building of magnificent temples for the gods and on the palaces and tombs of kings, but the rest of the people seemingly had to content themselves with insignificant dwellings of mud. In the Indus Valley the picture is reversed and the finest structures are those erected for the convenience of the citizens.' These public and private baths, as well as the excellent drainage system we find at Mohenjo-daro, are the first of their kind yet discovered anywhere. There are also two-storied private houses, made of baked bricks, with bath-rooms and a porter's lodge, as well as tenements.

Yet another quotation from Marshall, the acknowledged authority on the Indus Valley civilization, who was himself responsible for the excavations. He says that 'equally peculiar to the Indus Valley and stamped with an individual character of their own are its art and its religion. Nothing that we know of in other countries at this period bears any resemblance, in point of style, to the faience models of rams, dogs, and other animals, or to the intaglio engravings on the seals, the best of which—notably the humped and shorthorn bulls—are distinguished by a breadth of treatment and a feeling for a line and plastic form that have rarely been surpassed in glyptic art; nor would it be possible, until the classic age of Greece, to match the exquisitely supple modelling of the two human statuettes from Harappa.... In the religion of the Indus people there is much, of course, that might be paralleled in other countries. This is true of every prehistoric and most historic religions as well. But, taken as a whole, their religion is so characteristically Indian as hardly to be distinguished from still living Hinduism.'

We find thus this Indus Valley civilization connected and trading with its sister civilizations of Persia, Mesopotamia, and Egypt, and superior to them in some ways. It was an urban civilization, where the merchant class was wealthy and evidently played an important role. The streets, lined with stalls and what were probably small shops, give the impression of an Indian bazaar of to-day. Professor Childe says: 'It would seem to follow that the craftsmen of the Indus cities were, to a large extent, producing "for the market." What, if any, form of currency and standard of value had been accepted by society to facilitate the exchange of commodities is, however, uncertain. Magazines attached to many spacious and commodious private houses mark their owners as merchants. Their number and size indicate a strong and prosperous merchant community.' 'A surprising wealth of ornaments of gold, silver, precious stones and faience, of vessels of beaten copper and of metal implements and weapons, has been collected from the ruins.' Childe adds that 'well-planned streets and a magnificent system of drains, regularly cleared out, reflect the vigilance of some regular municipal government. Its authority was strong enough to secure the observance of town-planning by-laws and the maintenance of approved lines for streets and lanes over several reconstructions rendered necessary by floods.'*

Between this Indus Valley civilization and to-day in India there are many gaps and periods about which we know little. The links joining one period to another are not always evident, and a very great deal has of course happened and innumerable changes have taken place. But there is always an underlying sense of continuity, of an unbroken chain which joins modern India to the far distant period of six or seven thousand years ago when the Indus Valley civilization probably began. It is surprising how much there is in Mohenjo-daro and Harappa which reminds one of persisting traditions and habits—popular ritual, craftsmanship, even some fashions in dress. Much of this influenced Western Asia.

It is interesting to note that at this dawn of India's story, she does not appear as a puling infant, but already grown up in many ways. She is not oblivious of life's ways, lost in dreams of a vague and unrealizable supernatural world, but has made considerable technical progress in the arts and amenities of life, creating not only things of beauty, but also the utilitarian and more typical emblems of modern civilization—good baths and drainage systems.

The Coming of the Aryans

Who were these people of the Indus Valley civilization and whence had they come? We do not know yet. It is quite possible, and even probable, that their culture was an indigenous culture and its roots and offshoots may be found even in southern India. Some scholars find an essential similarity between these people and the Dravidian races and culture of south India. Even if there was some ancient migration to India, this could only have taken place some thousands of years before the date assigned to Mohenjo-daro. For all practical purposes we can treat them as the indigenous inhabitants of India.

What happened to the Indus Valley civilization and how did it end? Some people (among them, Gordon Childe) say that there was a sudden end to it due to an unexplained catastrophe. The river Indus is well-known for its mighty floods which overwhelm and wash away cities and villages. Or a changing climate

Gordon Childe. 'What Happened in History,' p. 113, 114.

might lead to a progressive desiccation of the land and the encroachment of the desert over cultivated areas. The ruins of Mohenjo-daro are themselves evidence of layer upon layer of sand being deposited, raising the ground level of the city and compelling the inhabitants to build higher on the old foundations. Some excavated houses have the appearance of two- or three-storied structures, and yet they represent a periodic raising of the walls to keep pace with the rising level. The province of Sind we know was rich and fertile in ancient times, but from mediæval times onwards it has been largely desert.

It is probable, therefore, that these climatic changes had a marked effect on the people of those areas and their ways of living. And in any event climatic changes must have only affected a relatively small part of the area of this widespread urban civilization, which, as we have now reason to believe, spread right up to the Gangetic Valley, and possibly even beyond. We have really not sufficient data to judge. Sand, which probably overwhelmed and covered some of these ancient cities, also preserved them; while other cities and evidences of the old civilization gradually decayed and went to pieces in the course of ages. Perhaps future archæological discoveries might disclose more links with later ages.

While there is a definite sense of continuity between the Indus Valley civilization and later periods, there is also a kind of break or a gap, not only in point of time but also in the kind of civilization that came next. This latter was probably more agricultural to begin with, though towns existed and there was some kind of city life also. This emphasis on the agricultural aspect may have been given to it by the newcomers, the Aryans who poured into India in successive waves from the north-west.

The Aryan migrations are supposed to have taken place about a thousand years after the Indus Valley period; and yet it is possible that there was no considerable gap and tribes and peoples came to India from the north-west from time to time, as they did in later ages, and became absorbed in India. We might say that the first great cultural synthesis and fusion took place between the incoming Aryans and the Dravidians, who were probably the representatives of the Indus Valley civilization. Out of this synthesis and fusion grew the Indian races and the basic Indian culture, which had distinctive elements of both. In the ages that followed there came many other races: Iranians, Greeks, Parthians, Bactrians, Scythians, Huns, Turks (before Islam), early Christians, Jews, Zoroastrians; they came, made a difference, and were absorbed. India was, according to Dodwell, 'infinitely absorbent like the ocean.' It is odd to think of India, with her caste system and exclusiveness, having this astonishing inclusive capacity to absorb foreign races and cultures. Perhaps it was due to this that she retained her vitality and rejuvenated herself from time to time. The Moslems, when they came, were also powerfully affected by her. 'The foreigners (Muslim Turks),' says Vincent Smith, 'like their forerunners the Sakas and the Yueh-chi, universally yielded to the wonderful assimilative power of Hinduism, and rapidly became Hinduised.'

What is Hinduism?

In this quotation Vincent Smith has used the words 'Hinduism' and 'Hinduised'. I do not think it is correct to use them in this way unless they are used in the widest sense of Indian culture. They are apt to mislead to-day when they are associated with a much narrower, and specifically religious, concept. The word 'Hindu' does not occur at all in our ancient literature. The first reference to it in an Indian book is, I am told, in a *Tantrik* work of the eighth century A.C., where 'Hindu' means a people and not the followers of a particular religion. But it is clear that the word is a very old one, as it occurs in the Avesta and in old Persian. It was used then and for a thousand years or more later by the peoples of western and central Asia for India, or rather for the people living on the other side of the Indus river. The word is clearly derived from Sindhu, the old, as well as the present, Indian name for the Indus. From this Sindhu came the words Hindu and Hindustan, as well as Indus and India.

The famous Chinese pilgrim I-tsing, who came to India in the seventh century A.C., writes in his record of travels that the 'northern tribes', that is the people of Central Asia, called India 'Hindu' (Hsin-tu) but, he adds, 'this is not at all a common name...and the most suitable name for India is the Noble Land (Aryadesha).' The use of the word 'Hindu' in connection with a particular religion is of very late occurrence.

The old inclusive term for religion in India was *Arya dharma*. Dharma really means something more than religion. It is from a root word which means to hold together; it is the inmost consti- tution of a thing, the law of its inner being. It is an ethical concept which includes the moral code, righteousness, and the whole range of man's duties and responsibilities. Arya dharma would include all the faiths (Vedic and non-Vedic) that originated in India; it was used by Buddhists and Jains as well as by those who accepted the Vedas. Buddha always called his way to salvation the 'Aryan Path'.

The expression *Vedic dharma* was also used in ancient times to signify more particularly and exclusively all those philosophies, moral teachings, ritual and practices, which were supposed to derive from the Vedas. Thus all those who acknowledged the general authority of the Vedas could be said to belong to the Vedic dharma.

Sanatana dharma, meaning the ancient religion, could be applied to any of the ancient Indian faiths (including Buddhism and Jainism), but the expression has been more or less monopolized to-day by some orthodox sections among the Hindus who claim to follow the ancient faith.

Buddhism and Jainism were certainly not Hinduism or even the Vedic dharma. Yet they arose in India and were integral parts of Indian life, culture and philosophy. A Buddhist or Jain in India is a hundred per cent product of Indian thought and culture, yet neither is a Hindu by faith. It is, therefore, entirely misleading to refer to Indian culture as Hindu culture. In later ages this culture was greatly influenced by the impact of Islam, and yet it remained basically and distinctively Indian. To-day it is experiencing in a hundred ways the powerful effect of the industrial civilization, which rose in the west, and it is difficult to say with any precision what the outcome will be.

Hinduism, as a faith, is vague, amorphous, many-sided, all things to all men. It is hardly possible to define it, or indeed to say definitely whether it is a religion or not, in the usual sense of the word. In its present form, and even in the past, it embraces many beliefs and practices, from the highest to the lowest, often opposed to or contradicting each other. Its essential spirit seems to be to live and let live. Mahatma Gandhi has attempted to define it: 'If I were asked to define the Hindu creed, I should simply say: Search after truth through nonviolent means. A man may not believe in God and still call himself a Hindu. Hinduism is a relentless pursuit after truth...Hinduism is the religion of truth. Truth is God. Denial of God we have known. Denial of truth we have not known.' Truth and non-violence, so says Gandhi: but many eminent and undoubted Hindus say that non-violence, as Gandhi understands it, is no essential part of the Hindu creed. We thus have truth left by itself as the distinguishing mark of Hinduism. That, of course, is no definition at all.

It is, therefore, incorrect and undesirable to use 'Hindu' or 'Hinduism' for Indian culture, even with reference to the distant past, although the various aspects of thought, as embodied in ancient writings, were the dominant expression of that culture. Much more is it incorrect to use those terms, in that sense, to-day. So long as the old faith and philosophy were chiefly a way of life and an outlook on the world, they were largely synonymous with Indian culture; but when a more rigid religion developed, with all manner of ritual and ceremonial, it became something more and at the same time something much less than that composite culture. A Christian or a Moslem could, and often did, adapt himself to the Indian way of life and culture, and yet remained in faith an orthodox Christian or Moslem. He had Indianized himself and become an Indian without changing his religion.

The correct word for 'Indian', as applied to country or culture or the historical continuity of our varying traditions, is 'Hindi', from 'Hind', a shortened form of Hindustan. Hind is still commonly used for India. In the countries of Western Asia, in Iran and Turkey, in Iraq, Afghanistan, Egypt, and elsewhere, India has always been referred to, and is still called, Hind; and everything Indian is called 'Hindi'. 'Hindi' has nothing to do with religion, and a Moslem or Christian Indian is as much a Hindi as a person who follows Hinduism as a religion. Americans who call all Indians Hindus are not far wrong; they would be perfectly correct if they used the word 'Hindi'. Unfortunately, the word 'Hindi' has become associated in India with a particular script—the *devanagri* script of Sanskrit—and so it has become difficult to use it in its larger and more natural significance. Perhaps when present-day controversies subside we may revert to its original and more satisfying use. To-day, the word 'Hindustani' is used for Indian; it is, of course, derived from Hindustan. But this is too much of a mouthful and it has no such historical and cultural associations as 'Hindi' has. It would certainly appear odd to refer to ancient periods of Indian culture as 'Hindustani'.

Whatever the word we may use, Indian or Hindi or Hindustani, for our cultural tradition, we see in the past that some inner urge towards synthesis, derived essentially from the Indian philosophic outlook, was the dominant feature of Indian cultural, and even racial, development. Each incursion of foreign elements was a challenge to this culture, but it was met successfully by a new synthesis and a process of absorption. This was also a process of rejuvenation and new blooms of culture arose out of it, the background and essential basis, however, remaining much the same.

The Earliest Records, Scripture and Mythology

Before the discovery of the Indus Valley civilization, the Vedas were supposed to be the earliest records we possess of Indian culture. There was much dispute about the chronology of the Vedic period, European scholars usually giving later dates and Indian scholars much earlier ones. It was curious, this desire on the part of Indians to go as far back as possible and thus enhance the importance of our ancient culture. Professor Winternitz thinks that the beginnings of Vedic literature go back to 2,000

B.C., or even 2,500 B.C. This brings us very near the Mohenjo-daro period.

The usual date accepted by most scholars to-day for the hymns of the Rig Veda is 1,500 B.C., but there is a tendency, ever since the Mohenjo-daro excavations, to date further back these early Indian scriptures. Whatever the exact date may be, it is probable that this literature is earlier than that of either Greece or Israel, that, in fact, it represents some of the earliest documents of the human mind that we possess. Max Müller has called it: 'The first word spoken by the Aryan man.'

The Vedas were the outpourings of the Aryans as they streamed into the rich land of India. They brought their ideas with them from that common stock out of which grew the Avesta in Iran, and elaborated them in the soil of India. Even the language of the Vedas bears a striking resemblance to that of the Avesta, and it has been remarked that the Avesta is nearer the Veda than the Veda is to its own epic Sanskrit.

How are we to consider the scripture of various religions, much of it believed by its votaries to be revealed scripture? To analyse it and criticize it and look upon it as a human document is often to offend the true believers. Yet there is no other way to consider it.

I have always hesitated to read books of religion. The totalitarian claims made on their behalf did not appeal to me. The outward evidences of the practice of religion that I saw did not encourage me to go to the original sources. Yet I had to drift to these books, for ignorance of them was not a virtue and was often a severe drawback. I knew that some of them had powerfully influenced humanity and anything that could have done so must have some inherent power and virtue in it, some vital source of energy. I found great difficulty in reading through many parts of them, for try as I would, I could not arouse sufficient interest; but the sheer beauty of some passages would hold me. And then a phrase or a sentence would suddenly leap up and electrify me and make me feel the presence of the really great. Some words of the Buddha or of Christ would shine out with deep meaning and seem to me applicable as much to-day as when they were uttered 2,000 or more years ago. There was a compelling reality about them, a permanence which time and space could not touch. So I felt sometimes when I read about Socrates or the Chinese philosophers, and also when I read the Upanishads and the Bhagavad Gita. I was not interested in the metaphysics, or the description of ritual, or the many other things which apparently had no relation to the problems that faced me. Perhaps I did not understand the inner significance of much that I read, and sometimes, indeed, a second reading threw more light.

I made no real effort to understand mysterious passages and I passed by those which had no particular significance for me. Nor was I interested in long commentaries and glossaries. I could not approach these books, or any book, as Holy Writ which must be accepted in their totality without challenge or demur. Indeed, this approach of Holy Writ usually resulted in my mind being closed to what they contained. I was much more friendly and open to them when I could consider them as having been written by human beings, very wise and far-seeing, but nevertheless ordinary mortals, and not incarnations or mouthpieces of a divinity, about whom I had no knowledge or surety whatever.

It has always seemed to me a much more magnificent and impressive thing that a human being should rise to great heights, mentally and spiritually, and should then seek to raise others up, rather than that he should be the mouthpiece of a divine or superior power. Some of the founders of religions were astonishing individuals, but all their glory vanishes in my eyes when I cease to think of them as human beings. What impresses me and gives me hope is the growth of the mind and spirit of man, and not his being used as an agent to convey a message.

Mythology affected me in much the same way. If people believed in the factual content of these stories, the whole thing was absurd and ridiculous. But as soon as one ceased believing in them, they appeared in a new light, a new beauty, a wonderful flowering of a richly endowed imagination, full of human lessons. No one believes now in the stories of Greek gods and goddesses and so, without any difficulty, we can admire them and they become part of our mental heritage. But if we had to believe in them, what a burden it would be, and how, oppressed by this weight of belief, we would often miss their beauty. Indian mythology is richer, vaster, very beautiful, and full of meaning. I have often wondered what manner of men and women they were who gave shape to these bright dreams and lovely fancies, and out of what gold mine of thought and imagination they dug them.

Looking at scripture then as a product of the human mind, we have to remember the age in which it was written, the environment and mental climate in which it grew, the vast distance in time and thought and experience that separates it from us. We have to forget the trappings of ritual and religious usage in which it is wrapped, and remember the social background in which it expanded. Many of the problems of human life have a permanence and a touch of eternity about them, and hence the abiding interest in these ancient books. But they dealt with other problems also, limited to their particular age, which have no living interest for us now.

The Vedas

Many Hindus look upon the Vedas as revealed scripture. This seems to me to be peculiarly unfortunate, for thus we miss their real significance — the unfolding of the human mind in the earliest stages of thought. And what a wonderful mind it was! The Vedas (from the root *vid*, to know) were simply meant to be a collection of the existing knowledge of the day; they are a jumble of many things: hymns, prayers, ritual for sacrifice, magic, magnificent nature poetry. There is no idolatory in them; no temples for the gods. The vitality and affirmation of life pervading them are extraordinary. The early Vedic Aryans were so full of the zest for life that they paid little attention to the soul. In a vague way they believed in some kind of existence after death.

Gradually the conception of God grows: there are the Olympian type of gods, and then monotheism, and later, rather mixed with it, the conception of monism. Thought carries them to strange realms, and brooding on nature's mystery comes, and the spirit of inquiry. These developments take place in the course of hundreds of years, and by the time we reach the end of the Veda, the *Vedanta* (*anta*, meaning end), we have the philosophy of the Upanishads.

The Rig Veda, the first of the Vedas, is probably the earliest book that humanity possesses. In it we can find the first outpourings of the human mind, the glow of poetry, the rapture at nature's loveliness and mystery. And in these early hymns there are, as Dr. Macnicol says, the beginnings of 'the brave adventures made so long ago and recorded here, of those who seek to discover the significance of our world and of man's life within it....India here set out on a quest which she has never ceased to follow.'

Yet behind the Rig Veda itself lay ages of civilized existence and thought, during which the Indus Valley and the Mesopotamian and other civilizations had grown. It is appropriate, therefore, that there should be this dedication in the Rig Veda: 'To the Seers, our ancestors, the first path-finders!'

These Vedic hymns have been described by Rabindranath Tagore as 'a poetic testament of a people's collective reaction to the wonder and awe of existence. A people of vigorous and unsophisticated imagination awakened at the very dawn of civilization to a sense of the inexhaustible mystery that is implicit in life. It was a simple faith of theirs that attributed divinity to every element and force of nature, but it was a brave and joyous one, in which the sense of mystery only gave enchantment to life, without weighing it down with bafflement—the faith of a race unburdened with intellectual brooding on the conflicting diversity of the objective universe, though now and again illumined by intuitive experience as: "Truth is one: (though) the wise call it by various names." '

But that brooding spirit crept in gradually till the author of the Veda cried out: 'O Faith, endow us with belief,' and raised deeper questions in a hymn called the 'The Song of Creation', to which Max Müller gave the title: 'To the Unknown God':

1. Then there was not non-existent nor existent: there was no realm of air, no sky beyond it.
   What covered in, and where? and what gave shelter? was water there, unfathomed depth of water?

2. Death was not then, nor was there aught immortal: no sign was there, the day's and night's divider.
   That one thing, breathless, breathed by its own nature: apart from it was nothing whatsoever.

3. Darkness there was: at first concealed in darkness, this all was undiscriminated chaos.
   All that existed then was void and formless: by the great power of warmth was born that unit.

4. Thereafter rose desire in the beginning, desire the primal seed and germ of spirit.
   Sages who searched with their heart's thought discovered the existent's kinship in the non-existent.

5. Transversely was their severing line extended: what was above it then, and what below it?
   There were begetters, there were mighty forces, free action here and energy of yonder.

6. Who verily knows and who can here declare it, whence it was born and whence comes this creation?
   The gods are later than this world's production.
   Who knows, then, whence it first came into being.

7. He, the first origin of this creation, whether he formed it all or did not form it.
   Whose eye controls this world in highest heaven, he verily knows it, or perhaps he knows it not.*

The Acceptance and the Negation of Life

From these dim beginnings of long ago flow out the rivers of Indian thought and philosophy, of Indian life and culture and

*'Hindu Scriptures.' Everyman's Library. Dent, London.

literature, ever widening and increasing in volume, and sometimes flooding the land with their rich deposits. During this enormous span of years they changed their courses sometimes, and even appeared to shrivel up, yet they preserved their essential identity. They could not have done so if they had not possessed a sound instinct for life. That staying power need not necessarily be a virtue; it may well mean, as I think it has meant in India for a long time past, stagnation and decay. But it is a major fact to be reckoned with, especially in these days when we seem to be witnessing an undermining, in repeated wars and crises, of a proud and advanced civilization. Out of this crucible of war, wherein so much is melting, we hope that something finer will emerge for the west as well as the east, something that will retain all the great achievements of humanity and add to them what they lacked. But this repeated and widespread destruction not only of material resources and human lives, but of essential values that have given meaning to life, is significant. Was it that in spite of astonishing progress in numerous directions and the higher standards, undreamed of in previous ages, that came in its train, our modern highly industrialized civilization did not possess some essential ingredient, and that the seeds of self-destruction lay within it?

A country under foreign domination seeks escape from the present in dreams of a vanished age, and finds consolation in visions of past greatness. That is a foolish and dangerous pastime in which many of us indulge. An equally questionable practice for us in India is to imagine that we are still spiritually great though we have come down in the world in other respects. Spiritual or any other greatness cannot be founded on lack of freedom and opportunity, or on starvation and misery. Many western writers have encouraged the notion that Indians are other-worldly. I suppose the poor and unfortunate in every country become to some extent other-worldly, unless they become revolutionaries, for this world is evidently not meant for them. So also subject peoples.

As a man grows to maturity he is not entirely engrossed in, or satisfied with, the external objective world. He seeks also some inner meaning, some psychological and physical satisfactions. So also with peoples and civilizations as they mature and grow adult. Every civilization and every people exhibit these parallel streams of an external life and an internal life. Where they meet or keep close to each other, there is an equilibrium and stability. When they diverge conflict arises and the crises that torture the mind and spirit.

We see from the period of the Rig Veda hymns onwards the development of both these streams of life and thought. The early ones are full of the external world, of the beauty and mystery of nature, of joy in life and an overflowing vitality. The gods and goddesses, like those of Olympus, are very human; they are supposed to come down and mix with men and women; there is no hard and fast line dividing the two. Then thought comes and the spirit of inquiry and the mystery of a transcendental world deepens. Life still continues in abundant measure, but there is also a turning away from its outward manifestations and a spirit of detachment grows as the eyes are turned to things invisible, which cannot be seen or heard or felt in the ordinary way. What is the object of it all? Is there a purpose in the universe? And, if so, how can man's life be put in harmony with it? Can we bring about a harmonious relation between the visible and invisible worlds, and thus find out the right conduct of life?

So we find in India, as elsewhere, these two streams of thought and action—the acceptance of life and the abstention from it—developing side by side, with the emphasis on the one or the other varying in different periods. Yet the basic background of that culture was not one of other-worldliness or world-worthlessness. Even when, in philosophical language, it discussed the world as *maya*, or what is popularly believed to be illusion, that very conception was not an absolute one but relative to what was thought of as ultimate reality (something like Plato's shadow of reality), and it took the world as it is and tried to live its life and enjoy its manifold beauty. Probably semitic culture, as exemplified in many religions that emerged from it, and certainly early Christianity, was far more other-worldly. T. E. Lawrence says that 'the common base of all semitic creeds, winners or losers, was the ever present idea of world-worthlessness.' And this often led to an alternation of self-indulgence and self-denial.

In India we find during every period when her civilization bloomed an intense joy in life and nature, a pleasure in the act of living, the development of art and music and literature and song and dancing and painting and the theatre, and even a highly sophisticated inquiry into sex relations. It is inconceivable that a culture or view of life based on other-worldliness or world-worthlessness could have produced all these manifestations of vigorous and varied life. Indeed it should be obvious that any culture that was basically other-worldly could not have carried on for thousands of years.

Yet some people have thought that Indian thought and culture represent essentially the principle of life negation and not of life affirmation. Both principles are, I suppose, present in varying degrees in all the old religions and cultures. But I should have thought that Indian culture, taken as a whole, never emphasized the negation of life, though some of its philosophies did so;

it seems to have done so much less than Christianity. Buddhism and Jainism rather emphasized the abstention from life, and in certain periods of Indian history there was a running away from life on a big scale, as, for instance, when large numbers of people joined the Buddhist *Viharas* or monasteries. What the reason for this was I do not know. Equally, or more, significant instances can be found during the Middle Ages in Europe when a widespread belief existed that the world was coming to an end. Perhaps the ideas of renunciation and life-negation are caused or emphasized by a feeling of frustration due to political and economic factors.

Buddhism, in spite of its theoretical approach, or rather approaches, for there are several, as a matter of fact avoids extremes; its is the doctrine of the golden mean, the middle path. Even the idea of *Nirvana* was very far from being a kind of nothingness, as it is sometimes supposed to be; it was a positive condition, but because it was beyond the range of human thought negative terms were used to describe it. If Buddhism, a typical product of Indian thought and culture, had merely been a doctrine of life negation or denial, it would surely have had some such effect on the hundreds of millions who profess it. Yet, as a matter of fact, the Buddhist countries are full of evidence to the contrary, and the Chinese people are an outstanding example of what affirmation of life can be.

The confusion seems to have arisen from the fact that Indian thought was always laying stress on the ultimate purpose of life. It could never forget the transcendent element in its makeup; and so, while affirming life to the full, it refused to become a victim and a slave of life. Indulge in right action with all your strength and energy, it said, but keep above it, and do not worry much about the results of such action. Thus it taught detachment in life and action, not abstention from them. This idea of detachment runs through Indian thought and philosophy, as it does through most other philosophies. It is another way of saying that a right balance and equilibrium should be kept between the visible and invisible worlds, for if there is too much attachment to action in the visible world, the other world is forgotten and fades away, and action itself becomes without ultimate purpose.

There is an emphasis on truth, a dependence on it, a passion for it, in these early adventures of the Indian mind. Dogma or revelation are passed by as something for lesser minds which cannot rise above them. The approach was one of experiment based on personal experience. That experience, when it dealt with the invisible world, was, like all emotional and psychic experiences, different from the experience of the visible, external world. It seemed to go out of the three-dimensional world we know into some different and vaster realm, and was thus difficult to describe in terms of three dimensions. What that experience was, and whether it was a vision or realization of some aspects of truth and reality, or was merely a phantasm of the imagination, I do not know. Probably it was often self-delusion. What interests me more is the approach, which was not authoritarian or dogmatic but was an attempt to discover for oneself what lay behind the external aspect of life.

It must be remembered that the business of philosophy in India was not confined to a few philosophers or highbrows. Philosophy was an essential part of the religion of the masses; it percolated to them in some attenuated form and created that philosophic outlook which became nearly as common in India as it is in China. That philosophy was for some a deep and intricate attempt to know the causes and laws of all phenomena, the search for the ultimate purpose of life, and the attempt to find an organic unity in life's many contradictions. But for the many it was a much simpler affair, which yet gave them some sense of purpose, of cause and effect, and endowed them with courage to face trial and misfortune and not lose their gaiety and composure. The ancient wisdom of China and India, the Tao or the True Path, wrote Tagore to Dr. Tai Chit-tao, was the pursuit of completeness, the blending of life's diverse work with the joy of living. Something of that wisdom impressed itself even upon the illiterate and ignorant masses, and we have seen how the Chinese people, after seven years of horrible war, have not lost the anchor of their faith or the gaiety of their minds. In India our trial has been more drawn out, and poverty and uttermost misery have long been the inseparable companions of our people. And yet they still laugh and sing and dance and do not lose hope.

Synthesis and Adjustment. The Beginnings of the Caste System

The coming of the Aryans into India raised new problems—racial and political. The conquered race, the Dravidians, had a long background of civilization behind them, but there is little doubt that the Aryans considered themselves vastly superior and a wide gulf separated the two races. Then there were also the backward aboriginal tribes, nomads or forest-dwellers. Out of this conflict and interaction of races gradually arose the caste system, which, in the course of succeeding centuries, was to affect Indian life so profoundly. Probably caste was neither Aryan nor Dravidian. It was an attempt at the social organization of different races, a rationalization of the facts as they existed at the time. It brought degradation in its train afterwards, and it is still a burden and a curse; but we can hardly judge it from subsequent standards or later developments. It was in keeping with the spirit of the times and some such grading took place in most of the ancient civilizations, though apparently China was free from it. There was a four-fold division in that other branch of the Aryans, the Iranians, during the Sassanian period, but it did not petrify into caste. Many of these old civilizations, including that of Greece, were entirely dependent on mass slavery. There was no such mass or large-scale labour slavery in India, although there were relatively small numbers of domestic slaves. Plato in his 'Republic' refers to a division similar to that of the four principal castes. Mediæval catholicism knew this division also.

Caste began with a hard and fast division between Aryans and non-Aryans, the latter again being divided into the Dravidian races and the aboriginal tribes. The Aryans, to begin with, formed one class and there was hardly any specialization. The word *Arya* comes from a root word meaning to till, and the Aryans as a whole were agriculturists and agriculture was considered a noble occupation. The tiller of the soil functioned also as priest, soldier, or trader, and there was no privileged order of priests. The caste divisions, originally intended to separate the Aryans from the non-Aryans, reacted on the Aryans themselves, and as division of functions and specialization increased, the new classes took the form of castes.

Thus at a time when it was customary for the conquerors to exterminate or enslave the conquered races, caste enabled a more peaceful solution which fitted in with the growing specialization of functions. Life was graded and out of the mass of agriculturists evolved the *Vaishyas*, the agriculturists, artisans, and merchants; the *Kshatriyas*, or rulers and warriors; and the *Brahmins*, priests and thinkers who were supposed to guide policy and preserve and maintain the ideals of the nation. Below these three were the *Shudras* or labourers and unskilled workers, other than the agriculturists. Among the indigenous tribes many were gradually assimilated and given a place at the bottom of the social scale, that is among the Shudras. This process of assimilation was a continuous one. These castes must have been in a fluid condition; rigidity came in much later. Probably the ruling class had always great latitude, and any person who by conquest or otherwise assumed power, could, if he so willed, join the hierarchy as a Kshatriya, and get the priests to manufacture an appropriate genealogy connecting him with some ancient Aryan hero.

The word *Arya* ceased to have any racial significance and came to mean 'noble', just as *unarya* meant ignoble and was usually applied to nomadic tribes, forest-dwellers, etc.

85

The Indian mind was extraordinarily analytical and had a passion for putting ideas and concepts, and even life's activities, into compartments. The Aryans not only divided society into four main groups but also divided the individual's life into four parts: the first part consisted of growth and adolescence, the student period of life, acquiring knowledge, developing self-discipline and self-control, continence; the second was that of the householder and man of the world; the third was that of the elder statesman, who had attained a certain poise and objectivity, and could devote himself to public work without the selfish desire to profit by it; and the last stage was that of the recluse, who lived a life largely cut off from the world's activities. In this way also they adjusted the two opposing tendencies which often exist side by side in man—the acceptance of life in its fullness and the rejection of it.

In India, as in China, learning and eruditions have always stood high in public esteem, for learning was supposed to imply both superior knowledge and virtue. Before the learned man the ruler and the warrior have always bowed. The old Indian theory was that those who were concerned with the exercise of power could not be completely objective. Their personal interests and inclinations would come into conflict with their public duties. Hence the task of determining values and the preservation of ethical standards was allotted to a class or group of thinkers who were freed from material cares and were, as far as possible, without obligations, so that they could consider life's problems in a spirit of detachment. This class of thinkers or philosophers was thus supposed to be at the top of the social structure, honoured and respected by all. The men of action, the rulers and warriors came after them and, however powerful they might be, did not command the same respect. The possession of wealth was still less entitled to honour and respect. The warrior class, though not at the top, held a high position, and not as in China, where it was looked upon with contempt.

This was the theory, and to some extent it may be found elsewhere, as in Christendom in mediæval Europe, when the Roman Church assumed the functions of leadership in all spiritual, ethical, and moral matters, and even in the general principles underlying the conduct of the State. In practice Rome became intensely interested in temporal power, and the princes of the Church were rulers in their own right. In India the Brahmin class, in addition to supplying the thinkers and the philosophers, became a powerful and entrenched priesthood, intent on preserving its vested interests. Yet this theory in varying degrees has influenced Indian life profoundly, and the ideal has continued to be of a man full of learning and charity, essentially good, self-disciplined, and capable of sacrificing himself for the sake of others.

The Brahmin class has shown all the vices of a privileged and entrenched class in the past, and large numbers of them have possessed neither learning nor virtue. Yet they have largely retained the esteem of the public, not because of temporal power or possession of money, but because they have produced a remarkable succession of men of intelligence, and their record of public service and personal sacrifice for the public good has been a notable one. The whole class profited by the example of its leading personalities in every age, and yet the public esteem went to the qualities rather than to any official status. The tradition was one of respecting learning and goodness in any individual who possessed them. There are innumerable examples of non-Brahmins, and even persons belonging to the depressed classes, being so respected and sometimes considered as saints. Official status and military power never commanded the same measure of respect, though it may have been feared.

Even to-day, in this money age, the influence of this tradition is marked, and because of it Gandhiji (who is not a Brahmin) can become the supreme leader of India and move the hearts of millions without force or compulsion or official position or possession of money. Perhaps this is as good a test as any of a nation's cultural background and its conscious or subconscious objective: to what kind of a leader does it give its allegiance?

The central idea of old Indian civilization, or Indo-Aryan culture, was that of *dharma*, which was something much more than religion or creed; it was a conception of obligations, of the discharge of one's duties to oneself and to others. This dharma itself was part of *Rita*, the fundamental moral law governing the functioning of the universe and all it contained. If there was such an order then man was supposed to fit into it, and he should function in such a way as to remain in harmony with it. If man did his duty and was ethically right in his action, the right consequences would inevitably follow. Rights as such were not emphasized. That, to some extent, was the old outlook everywhere. It stands out in marked contrast, with the modern assertion of rights, rights of individuals, of groups, of nations.

The Continuity of Indian Culture

Thus in these very early days we find the beginnings of the civilization and culture which were to flower so abundantly and richly in subsequent ages, and which have continued, in spite of many changes, to our own day. The basic ideals, the governing concepts are taking shape, and literature and philosophy, art and drama, and all other activities of life were conditioned by these ideals and world-view. Also we see that exclusiveness and touch-me-notism which were to grow and grow till they became unalterable, octopus-like, with their grip on everything —the caste system of modern times. Fashioned for a particular day, intended to stabilize the then organization of society and give it strength and equilibrium, it developed into a prison for that social order and for the mind of man. Security was purchased in the long run at the cost of ultimate progress.

Yet it was a very long run and, even within that framework, the vital original impetus for advancement in all directions was so great that it spread out all over India and over the eastern seas, and its stability was such that it survived repeated shock and invasion.

Professor Macdonell, in his 'History of Sanskrit Literature,' tells us that 'the importance of Indian literature as a whole consists in its originality. When the Greeks towards the end of the fourth century B.C. invaded the north-west, the Indians had already worked out a national culture of their own, unaffected by foreign influences. And in spite of successive waves of invasion and conquest by Persians, Greeks, Scythians, Mohammedans, the national development of the life and literature of the Indo-Aryan race remained practically unchecked and unmodified from without down to the era of British occupation. No other branch of the Indo-European stock has experienced an isolated evolution like this. No other country except China can trace back its language and literature, its religious beliefs and rites, its dramatic and social customs through an uninterrupted development of more than 3,000 years.'

Still India was not isolated, and throughout this long period of history she had continuous and living contacts with Iranians and Greeks, Chinese and Central Asians and others. If her basic culture survived these contacts there must have been something in that culture itself which gave it the dynamic strength to do so, some inner vitality and understanding of life. For this three or four thousand years of cultural growth and continuity is remarkable. Max Müller, the famous scholar and Orientalist, emphasizes this: "There is, in fact, an unbroken continuity between the most modern and the most ancient phases of Hindu thought, extending over more than three thousand years.' Carried away by his enthusiasm, he said (in his lectures delivered before the University of Cambridge, England, in 1882): 'If we were to look over the whole world to find out the country most richly endowed with all the wealth, power, and beauty that nature can bestow—in some parts a very paradise on earth—I should point to India. If I were asked under what sky the human mind has most fully developed some of its choicest gifts, has most deeply pondered over the greatest problems of life, and has found solutions of some of them which well deserve the attention even of those who have studied Plato and Kant—I should point to India. And if I were to ask myself from what literature we here in Europe, we who have been nurtured almost exclusively on the thoughts of Greeks and Romans, and of one Semitic race, the Jewish, may draw the corrective which is most wanted in order to make our inner life more perfect, more comprehensive, more universal, in fact more truly human a life, not for this life only, but a transfigured and eternal life—again I should point to India.'

Nearly half a century later Romain Rolland wrote in the same strain: 'If there is one place on the face of the earth where all the dreams of living men have found a home from the very earliest days when man began the dream of existence, it is India.'

The Upanishads

The Upanishads, dating from about 800 B.C., take us a step further in the development of Indo-Aryan thought, and it is a big step. The Aryans have long been settled down and a stable, prosperous civilization has grown up, a mixture of the old and the new, dominated by Aryan thought and ideals, but with a background of more primitive forms of worship. The Vedas are referred to with respect, but also in a spirit of gentle irony. The Vedic gods no longer satisfy and the ritual of the priests is made fun of. But there is no attempt to break with the past; the past is taken as a starting point for further progress.

The Upanishads are instinct with a spirit of inquiry, of mental adventure, of a passion for finding out the truth about things. The search for this truth is, of course, not by the objective methods of modern science, yet there is an element of the scientific method in the approach. No dogma is allowed to come in the way. There is much that is trivial and without any meaning or relevance for us to-day. The emphasis is essentially on self-realization, on knowledge of the individual self and the absolute self, both of which are said to be the same in essence. The objective external world is not considered unreal but real in a relative sense, an aspect of the inner reality.

There are many ambiguities in the Upanishads and different interpretations have been made. But that is a matter for the philosopher or scholar. The general tendency is towards monism and the whole approach is evidently intended to lessen the differences that must have existed then, leading to fierce debate. It is the way of synthesis. Interest in magic and such like supernatural knowledge is sternly discouraged, and ritual and ceremonies without enlightenment are said to be in vain—'those engaged in them, considering themselves men of understanding and learned, stagger along aimlessly like blind men led by the blind, and fail to reach the goal.' Even the Vedas are treated as the lower knowledge; the higher one being that of the inner mind. There is a warning given against philosophical learning without discipline of conduct. And there is a continuous attempt to harmonize social activity with spiritual adventure. The duties and obligations imposed by life were to be carried out, but in a spirit of detachment.

Probably the ethic of individual perfection was over-emphasized and hence the social outlook suffered. 'There is nothing higher than the person,' say the Upanishads. Society must have been considered as stabilized and hence the mind of man was continually thinking of individual perfection, and in quest of this it wandered about in the heavens and in the innermost recesses of the heart. This old Indian approach was not a narrow nationalistic one, though there must have been a feeling that India was the hub of the world, just as China and Greece and Rome have felt at various times. 'The whole world of mortals is an interdependent organism,' says the Mahabharata.

The metaphysical aspects of the questions considered in the Upanishads are difficult for me to grasp, but I am impressed by this approach to a problem which has so often been shrouded by dogma and blind belief. It was the philosophical approach and not the religious one. I like the vigour of the thought, the questioning, the rationalistic background. The form is terse, often of question and answer between pupil and teacher, and it has been suggested that the Upanishads were some kind of lecture notes made by the teacher or taken down by his disciples. Professor F. W. Thomas in 'The Legacy of India' says: 'What gives to the Upanishads their unique quality and unfailing human appeal is an earnest sincerity of tone, as of friends conferring upon matters of deep concern.' And C. Rajagopalachari thus eloquently speaks of them: 'The spacious imagination, the majestic sweep of thought, and the almost reckless spirit of exploration with which, urged by the compelling thirst for truth, the Upanishad teachers and pupils dig into the "open secret" of the universe, make this most ancient of the world's holy books still the most modern and most satisfying.'

The dominating characteristic of the Upanishads is the dependence on truth. 'Truth wins ever, not falsehood. With truth is paved the road to the Divine.' And the famous invocation is for light and understanding: 'Lead me from the unreal to the real! Lead me from darkness to light! Lead me from death to immortality.'

Again and again the restless mind peeps out, ever seeking, ever questioning: 'At whose behest doth mind light on its perch? At whose command doth life, the first, proceed? At whose behest do men send forth this speech? What god, indeed, directed eye and ear?' And again: 'Why cannot the wind remain still? Why has the human mind no rest? Why, and in search of what, does the water run out and cannot stop its flow even for a moment?' It is the adventure of man that is continually calling and there is no resting on the way and no end of the journey. In the *Aitereya Brahmana* there is a hymn about this long endless journey which we must undertake, and every verse ends with the refrain: *Charaiveti, charaiveti*—'Hence, O traveller, march along, march along!'

There is no humility about all this quest, the humility before an all-powerful deity, so often associated with religion. It is the triumph of mind over the environment. 'My body will be reduced to ashes and my breath will join the restless and deathless air, but not I and my deeds. O mind, remember this always, remember this.' In a morning prayer the sun is addressed thus: 'O sun of refulgent glory, I am the same person as makes thee what thou art!' What superb confidence!

What is the soul? It cannot be described or defined except negatively: 'It is not this, not this.' Or, in a way, positively: 'That thou art!' The individual soul is like a spark thrown out and reabsorbed by the blazing fire of the absolute soul. 'As fire, though one, entering the world, takes a separate form according to whatever it burns, so does the inner Self within all things become different, according to whatever it enters, yet itself is without form.' This realization that all things have that same essence removes the barriers which separate us from them and produces a sense of unity with humanity and nature, a unity which underlies the diversity and manifoldness of the external world. 'Who knoweth all things are Self; for him what grief existeth, what delusion, when (once) he gazeth on the oneness?' 'Aye, whoso seeth all things in that Self, and Self in everything; from That he'll no more hide.'

It is interesting to compare and contrast the intense individualism and exclusiveness of the Indo-Aryans with this all-embracing approach, which overrides all barriers of caste and class and every other external and internal difference. This latter is a kind of metaphysical democracy. 'He who sees the one spirit in all, and all in the one spirit, henceforth can look with contempt on no creature.' Though this was theory only, there can be no doubt that it must have affected life and produced that atmosphere of tolerance and reasonableness, that acceptance of free-thought in matters of faith, that desire and capacity to live and let live, which are dominant features of Indian culture, as they are of the Chinese. There was no totalitarianism in religion or culture, and they indicate an old and wise civilization with inexhaustible mental reserves.

There is a question in the Upanishads to which a very curious and yet significant answer is given. 'The question is: "What is this universe? From what does it arise? Into what does it go?" And the answer is: "In freedom it rises, in freedom it rests, and into freedom it melts away." ' What exactly this means I am unable to understand, except that the authors of the Upanishads were passionately attached to the idea of freedom and wanted to see everything in terms of it. Swami Vivekananda was always emphasizing this aspect.

It is not easy for us, even imaginatively, to transplant our-selves to this distant period and enter the mental climate of that day. The form of writing itself is something that we are unused to, odd looking, difficult to translate, and the background of life is utterly different. We take for granted so many things to-day because we are used to them, although they are curious and un-reasonable enough. But what we are not used to at all is much more difficult to appreciate or understand. In spite of all these difficulties and almost insuperable barriers, the message of the Upanishads has found willing and eager listeners throughout Indian history and has powerfully moulded the national mind and character. 'There is no important form of Hindu thought, heterodox Buddhism included, which is not rooted in the Upa-nishads,' says Bloomfield.

Early Indian thought penetrated to Greece, through Iran, and influenced some thinkers and philosophers there. Much later, Plotinus came to the east to study Iranian and Indian philo-sophy and was especially influenced by the mystic element in the Upanishads. From Plotinus many of these ideas are said to have gone to St. Augustine, and through him influenced the Chris-tianity of the day.*

The rediscovery by Europe, during the past century and a half, of Indian philosophy created a powerful impression on European philosophers and thinkers. Schopenhauer, the pessimist, is often quoted in this connection. 'From every sentence (of the Upa-nishads) deep, original and sublime thoughts arise, and the whole is pervaded by a high and holy and earnest spirit.... In the whole world there is no study...so beneficial and so elevating as that of the Upanishads....(They) are products of the highest wisdom....It is destined sóoner or later to become the   faith

*Romain Rolland has given a long Note (as an appendix to his book on Vivekananda), 'On the Hellenic-Christian Mysticism of the First Centuries and its Relationship to Hindu Mysticism.' He points out that 'a hundred facts testify to how great an extent the East was mingled with Hellenic thought during the second century of our era.'

of the people.' And again: 'The study of the Upanishads has been the solace of my life, it will be the solace of my death.' Writing on this, Max Müller says: 'Schopenhauer was the last man to write at random, or to allow himself to go into ecstasies over so-called mystic and inarticulate thought. And I am neither afraid nor ashamed to say that I share his enthusiasm for the Vedanta, and feel indebted to it for much that has been helpful to me in my passage through life.' In another place Max Müller says: 'The Upanishads are the ...sources of...the Vedanta philosophy, a system in which human speculation seems to me to have reached its very acme.' 'I spend my happiest hours in reading Vedantic books. They are to me like the light of the morning, like the pure air of the mountains—so simple, so true, if once understood.'

But perhaps the most eloquent tribute to the Upanishads and to the later book, the Bhagavad Gita, was paid by A.E. (G. W. Russell) the Irish poet: 'Goethe, Wordsworth, Emerson and Thoreau among moderns have something of this vitality and wisdom, but we can find all they have said and much more in the grand sacred books of the East. The Bhagavad Gita and the Upanishads contain such godlike fullness of wisdom on all things that I feel the authors must have looked with calm remembrance back through a thousand passionate lives, full of feverish strife for and with shadows, ere they could have written with such certainty of things which the soul feels to be sure.'*

The Advantages and Disadvantages of an Individualistic Philosophy

There is, in the Upanishads, a continual emphasis on the fitness of the body and clarity of the mind, on the discipline of both body and mind, before effective progress can be made. The acquisition of knowledge, or any achievement, requires restraint, self-suffering, self-sacrifice. This idea of some kind of penance, *tapasya*, is inherent in Indian thought, both among the thinkers at the top and the unread masses below. It is present to-day as it was present some thousands of years ago, and it is necessary to appreciate it in order to understand the psychology underlying the mass movements which have convulsed India under Gandhiji's leadership.

*There is an odd and interesting passage in one of the Upanishads (the Chhandogya): 'The sun never sets nor rises. When people think to themselves the sun is setting he only changes about after reaching the end of the day, and makes night below and day to what is on the other side. Then when people think he rises in the morning, he only shifts himself about after reaching the end of the night, and makes day below and night to what is on the other side. In fact he never does set at all.'

It is obvious that the ideas of the authors of the Upanishads, the rarefied mental atmosphere in which they moved, were confined to a small body of the elect who were capable of understanding them. They were entirely beyond the comprehension of the vast mass of the people. A creative minority is always small in numbers but, if it is in tune with the majority, and is always trying to pull the latter up and make it advance, so that the gap between the two is lessened, a stable and progressive culture results. Without that creative minority a civilization must inevitably decay. But it may also decay if the bond between a creative minority and the majority is broken and there is a loss of social unity in society as a whole, and ultimately that minority itself loses its creativeness and becomes barren and sterile; or else it gives place to another creative or vital force which society throws up.

It is difficult for me, as for most others, to visualize the period of the Upanishads and to analyse the various forces that were at play. I imagine, however, that in spite of the vast mental and cultural difference between the small thinking minority and the unthinking masses, there was a bond between them or, at any rate, there was no obvious gulf. The graded society in which they lived had its mental gradation also and these were accepted and provided for. This led to some kind of social harmony and conflicts were avoided. Even the new thought of the Upanishads was interpreted for popular purposes so as to fit in with popular prejudices and superstitions, thereby losing much of its essential meaning. The graded social structure was not touched; it was preserved. The conception of monism became transformed into one of monotheism for religious purposes, and even lower forms of belief and worship were not only tolerated but encouraged, as suited to a particular stage of development.

Thus the ideology of the Upanishads did not permeate to any marked extent to the masses and the intellectual separation between the creative minority and the majority became more marked. In course of time this led to new movements—a powerful wave of materialistic philosophy, agnosticism, atheism. Out of this again grew Buddhism and Jainism, and the famous Sanskrit epics, the Ramayana and the Mahabharata, wherein yet another attempt was made to bring about a synthesis between rival creeds and ways of thought. The creative energy of the people, or of the creative minority, is very evident during these periods, and again there appears to be a bond between that minority and the majority. On the whole they pull together.

In this way period succeeds period with bursts of creative effort in the fields of thought and action, in literature and the drama, in sculpture and architecture, and in cultural, missionary and colonial enterprises far from India's borders. In between, there are periods of disharmony and conflict, due both to inner causes and intrusions from outside. Yet they are ultimately overcome and a fresh period of creative energy supervenes. The last great period of such activity in a variety of directions was the classical epoch which began in the fourth century after Christ. By about 1000 A.C., or earlier, signs of inner decay in India are very evident, although the old artistic impulse continued to function and produce fine work. The coming of new races with a different background brought a new driving force to India's tired mind and spirit, and out of that impact arose new problems and new attempts at solution.

It seems that the intense individualism of the Indo-Aryans led, in the long run, to both the good and the evil that their culture produced. It led to the production of very superior types, not in one particular limited period of history, but again and again, age after age. It gave a certain idealist and ethical background to the whole culture, which persisted and still persists, though it may not influence practice much. With the help of this background and by sheer force of example at the top, they help together the social fabric and repeatedly rehabilitated it when it threatened to go to pieces. They produced an astonishing flowering of civilization and culture which, though largely confined to the upper circles, inevitably spread to some extent to the masses. By their extreme tolerance of other beliefs and other ways than their own, they avoided the conflicts that have so often torn society asunder, and managed to maintain, as a rule, some kind of equilibrium. By allowing, within the larger framework, considerable freedom to people to live the life of their choice, they showed the wisdom of an old and experienced race. All these were very remarkable achievements.

But that very individualism led them to attach little importance to the social aspect of man, of man's duty to society. For each person life was divided and fixed up, a bundle of duties and responsibilities within his narrow sphere in the graded hierarchy. He had no duty to, or conception of, society as a whole, and no attempt was made to make him feel his solidarity with it. This idea is perhaps largely a modern development and cannot be found in any ancient society. It is unreasonable, therefore, to expect it in ancient India. Still, the emphasis on individualism, on exclusiveness, on graded castes is much more evident in India. In later ages it was to grow into a very prison for the mind of our people—not only for the lower castes, who suffered most from it, but for the higher ones also. Throughout our history it was a weakening factor, and one might perhaps say that along with the growth of rigidity in the caste system, grew rigidity of mind and the creative energy of the race faded away. Another curious fact seems to stand out. The extreme tolerance of every kind of belief and practice, every superstition and folly, had its injurious side also, for this perpetuated many an evil custom and prevented people from getting rid of the traditional burdens that prevented growth. The growing priesthood exploited this situation to their own advantage and built up their powerful vested interests on the foundation of the superstitions of the masses. That priesthood was probably never quite so powerful as in some branches of the Christian Church, for there were always spiritual leaders who condemned its practices, and there was a variety of beliefs to choose from, but it was strong enough to hold and exploit the masses.

So this mixture of free thought and orthodoxy lived side by side, and out of them scholasticism grew, and a puritanical ritualism. The appeal was always made to the ancient authorities, but little attempt was made to interpret their truths in terms of changing conditions. The creative and spiritual forces weakened, and only the shell of what used to be so full of life and meaning remained.

Aurobindo Ghose has written: 'If an ancient Indian of the time of the Upanishad, of the Buddha, or the later classical age were to be set down in modern India...he would see his race clinging to forms and shells and rags of the past and missing nine-tenths of its nobler meaning...he would be amazed by the extent of the mental poverty, the immobility, the static repetition, the cessation of science, the long sterility of art, the comparative feebleness of the creative intuition.'

Materialism

One of our major misfortunes is that we have lost so much of the world's ancient literature— in Greece, in India, and elsewhere. Probably this was inevitable as these books were originally written on plam-leaves or on *bhurjapatra*, the thin layers of the bark of the birch tree which peel off so easily, and later on paper. There were only a few copies of a work in existence and if they were lost or destroyed, that work disappeared, and it can only be traced by references to it, or quotations from it, in other books. Even so, about fifty or sixty thousand manuscripts in Sanskrit or its variations have already been traced and listed and fresh discoveries are being constantly made. Many old Indian books have so far not been found in India at all but their translations in Chinese or Tibetan have been discovered. Probably an organized search for old manuscripts in the libraries of religious institutions, monasteries and private persons would yield rich results. That, and the critical examination of these manuscripts and, where considered desirable, their publication and translation, are among the many things we have to do in India when we succeed in breaking through our shackles and can function for ourselves. Such study is bound to throw light on many phases of Indian history and especially on the social background behind historic events and changing ideas. The fact that in spite of repeated losses and destruction, and without any organized attempt to discover them, over fifty thousand manuscripts have been brought out, shows how extra-ordinarily abundant must have been the literary, dramatic, philosophical and other productions of old times. Many of the manuscripts discovered still await thorough examination.

Among the books that have been lost is the entire literature on materialism which followed the period of the early Upanishads. The only references to this, now found, are in criticisms of it and in elaborate attempts to disprove the materialist theories. There can be no doubt, however, that the materialist philosophy was professed in India for centuries and had, at the time, a powerful influence on the people. In the famous *Arthashāstra*, Kautilya's book on political and economic organization, written in the fourth century B.C., it is mentioned as one of the major philosophies of India.

We have then to rely on the critics and persons interested in disparaging this philosophy, and they try to pour ridicule on it and show how absurd it all is. That is an unfortunate way for us to find out what it was. Yet their very eagerness to discredit it shows how important it was in their eyes. Possibly much of the literature of materialism in India was destroyed by the priests and other believers in the orthodox religion during subsequent periods.

The materialists attacked authority and all vested interests in thought, religion and theology. They denounced the Vedas and priestcraft and traditional beliefs, and proclaimed that belief must be free and must not depend on pre-suppositions or merely on the authority of the past. They inveighed against all forms of magic and superstition. Their general spirit was comparable in many ways to the modern materialistic approach; it wanted to rid itself of the chains and burden of the past, of speculation about matters which could not be perceived, of worship of imaginary gods. Only that could be presumed to exist which could be directly perceived, every other inference or presumption was equally likely to be true or false. Hence matter in its various forms and this world could only be considered as really existing. There was no other world, no heaven or hell, no soul separate from the body. Mind and intelligence and everything else have developed from the basic elements. Natural phenomena did not concern themselves with human values and were indifferent to what we consider good or bad. Moral rules were mere conventions made by men.

We recognize all this; it seems curiously of our day and not of more than two thousand years ago. How did these thoughts arise, these doubts and conflicts, this rebellion of the mind of man against traditional authority? We do not know enough of social and political conditions then, but it seems clear that it was an age of political conflict and social turmoil, leading to a disintegration of faith and to keen intellectual inquiry and a search for some way out, satisfying to the mind. It was out of this mental turmoil and social maladjustment that new paths grew and new systems of philosophy took shape. Systematic philosophy, not the intuitional approach of the Upanishads, but based on close reasoning and argument, begins to appear in many garbs, Jain, Buddhist, and what might be called Hindu, for want of a better word. The Epics also belong to this period and the Bhagavad Gita. It is difficult to build up an accurate chronology of this age, as thought and theory overlapped and acted and reacted on each other. Buddha came in the sixth century B.C. Some of these developments preceded him, others followed, or often there was a parallel growth.

About the time of the rise of Buddhism, the Persian Empire reached the Indus. This approach of a great Power right to the borders of India proper must have influenced people's thoughts. In the fourth century B.C. Alexander's brief raid into north-west India took place. It was unimportant in itself, but it was the precursor of far-reaching changes in India. Almost immediately after Alexander's death, Chandragupta built up the great Maurya Empire. That was, historically speaking, the first strong, widespread and centralized state in India. Tradition mentions many such rulers and overlords of India and one of the epics deals with the struggle for the suzerainty of India, meaning thereby probably northern India. But, in all probability, ancient India, like ancient Greece, was a collection of small states. There were many tribal republics, some of them covering large areas; there were also petty kingdoms; and there were, as in Greece, city states with powerful guilds of merchants. In Buddha's time there were a number of these tribal republics and four principal kingdoms in Central and Northern India (including Gandhara or part of Afghanistan). Whatever the form of organization, the tradition of city or village autonomy was very strong, and even when an overlordship was acknowledged there was no interference with the internal working of the state. There was a kind of primitive democracy, though, as in Greece, it was probably confined to the upper classes.

Ancient India and Greece, so different in many ways, have so much in common that I am led to believe that their background of life was very similar. The Peloponnesian war, ending in the breakdown of Athenian democracy might in some ways be compared to the Mahabharata war,* the great war of ancient India. The failure of Hellenism and of the free city state led to a feeling of doubt and despair, to a pursuit of mysteries and revelations, a lowering of the earlier ideals of the race. The emphasis shifted from this world to the next. Later, new schools of philosophy—the Stoic and the Epicurean—developed.

It is dangerous and misleading to make historical comparisons on slender, and sometimes contradictory, data. Yet one is tempted to do so. The period in India after the Mahabharata war, with its seemingly chaotic mental atmosphere, reminds one of the post-Hellenic period of Greece. There was a vulgarization of ideals and then a groping for new philosophies. Politically and economically similar internal changes might have been taking place, such as the weakening of the tribal republic and city state and the tendency to centralize state power.

But this comparison does not take us very far. Greece never really recovered from these shocks, although Greek civilization flourished for some additional centuries in the Mediterranean and influenced Rome and Europe. In India there was a remarkable recovery and the thousand years from the Epic Period and the Buddha onwards were full of creative energy. Innumerable great names in philosophy, literature, drama, mathematics, and the arts stand out. In the early centuries of the Christian era a remarkable burst of energy resulted in the organization of colonial enterprises which took the Indian people and their culture to distant islands in the eastern seas.

The Epics. History, Tradition, and Myth

The two great epics of ancient India—the *Ramayana* and the *Mahabharata*—probably took shape in the course of several hundred years, and even subsequently additions were made to them. They deal with the early days of the Indo-Aryans, their conquests and civil wars, when they were expanding and consolidating themselves, but they were composed and compiled later. I do not know of any books anywhere which have exercised such a continuous and pervasive influence on the mass mind as these two. Dating back to a remote antiquity, they are still a living force in the life of the Indian people. Not in the original

The epic dealing with this war is also called Mahabharata.

Sanskrit, except for a few intellectuals, but in translations and adaptations, and in those innumerable ways in which tradition and legend spread and become a part of the texture of a people's life. They represent the typical Indian method of catering all together for various degrees of cultural development, from the highest intellectual to the simple unread and untaught villager. They make us understand somewhat the secret of the old Indians in holding together a variegated society divided up in many ways and graded in castes, in harmonizing their discords, and giving them a common background of heroic tradition and ethical living. Deliberately they tried to build up a unity of outlook among the people, which was to survive and overshadow all diversity.

Among the earliest memories of my childhood are the stories from these epics told to me by my mother or the older ladies of the house, just as a child in Europe or America might listen to fairy tales or stories of adventure. There was for me both adventure and the fairy element in them. And then I used to be taken every year to the popular open-air performances where the Ramayana story was enacted and vast crowds came to see it and join in the processions. It was all very crude, but that did not matter, for everyone knew the story by heart and it was carnival time.

In this way Indian mythology and old tradition crept into my mind and got mixed up with all manner of other creatures of the imagination. I do not think I ever attached very much importance to these stories as factually true, and I even criticized the magical and supernatural element in them. But they were just as imaginatively true for me as were the stories from the Arabian Nights or the *Panchatantra*, that storehouse of animal tales from which Western Asia and Europe have drawn so much.*

As I grew up other pictures crowded into my mind: fairy stories, both Indian and European, tales from Greek mythology, the story of Joan of Arc, *Alice in Wonderland*, and many stories of Akbar and Birbal, Sherlock Holmes, King Arthur and his Knights,

---

*The story of the innumerable translations and adaptations of the 'Panchatantra' into Asiatic and European languages is a long, intricate, and fascinating one. The first known translation was from Sanskrit into Pahlavi in the middle of the sixth century A.C. at the instance of Khusrau Anushirwan, Emperor of Persia. Soon after (c. 570 A.C.) a Syrian translation appeared, and later on an Arabic one. In the eleventh century new translations appeared in Syrian, Arabic, and Persian, the last named becoming famous as the story of 'Kalia Daman.' It was through these translations that the 'Panchatantra' reached Europe. There was a Greek translation from the Syrian at the end of the eleventh century, and a little later a Hebrew translation. In the fifteenth and sixteenth centuries a number of translations and adaptations appeared in Latin, Italian, Spanish, German, Swedish, Danish, Dutch Icelandic, French, English, Hungarian, Turkish, and a number of Slav languages. Thus the stories of the 'Panchatantra' merged into Asiatic and European literatures.

the Rani of Jhansi, the young heroine of the Indian Mutiny, and tales of Rajput chivalry and heroism. These and many others filled my mind in strange confusion, but always there was the background of Indian mythology which I had imbibed in my earliest years.

If it was so with me, in spite of the diverse influences that worked on my mind, I realized how much more must old mythology and tradition work on the minds of others and, especially, the unread masses of our people. That influence is a good influence both culturally and ethically, and I would hate to destroy or throw away all the beauty and imaginative symbolism that these stories and allegories contain.

Indian mythology is not confined to the epics; it goes back to the Vedic period and appears in many forms and garbs in Sanskrit literature. The poets and the dramatists take full advantage of it and build their stories and lovely fancies round it. The Ashoka tree is said to burst into flower when touched by the foot of a beautiful woman. We read of the adventures of Kāma, the god of love, and his wife, Rati (or rapture), with their friend Vasanta, the god of spring. Greatly daring, Kāma shoots his flowery arrow at Shiva himself and is reduced to ashes by the fire that flashed out of Shiva's third eye. But he survives as Ananga, the bodiless one.

Most of the myths and stories are heroic in conception and teach adherence to truth and the pledged word, whatever the consequences, faithfulness unto death and even beyond, courage, good works and sacrifice for the common good. Sometimes the story is pure myth, or else it is a mixture of fact and myth, an exaggerated account of some incident that tradition preserved. Facts and fiction are so interwoven together as to be inseparable, and this amalgam becomes an imagined history, which may not tell us exactly what happened but does tell us something that is equally important—what people believed had taken place, what they thought their heroic ancestors were capable of, and what ideals inspired them. So, whether fact or fiction, it became a living element in their lives, ever pulling them up from the drudgery and ugliness of their everyday existence to higher realms, ever pointing towards the path of endeavour and right living, even though the ideal might be far off and difficult to reach.

Goethe is reported to have condemned those who said that the old Roman stories of heroism, of Lucretia and others, were spurious and false. Anything, he said, that was essentially false and spurious could only be absurd and unfruitful and never beautiful and inspiring, and that 'if the Romans were great enough to invent things like that, we at least should be great enough to believe them.'

Thus this imagined history, mixture of fact and fiction, or sometimes only fiction, becomes symbolically true and tells us of the minds and hearts and purposes of the people of that particular epoch. It is true also in the sense that it becomes the basis for thought and action, for future history. The whole conception of history in ancient India was influenced by the speculative and ethical trends of philosophy and religion. Little importance was attached to the writing of a chronicle or the compilation of a bare record of events. What those people were more concerned with was the effect and influence of human events and actions on human conduct. Like the Greeks, they were strongly imaginative and artistic and they gave rein to this artistry and imagination in dealing with past events, intent as they were on drawing some moral and lesson from them for future behaviour.

Unlike the Greeks, and unlike the Chinese and the Arabs, Indians in the past were not historians. This was very unfortunate and it has made it difficult for us now to fix dates or make up an accurate chronology. Events run into each other, overlap and produce an enormous confusion. Only very gradually are patient scholars to-day discovering the clues to the maze of Indian history. There is really only one old book, Kalhana's 'Rajatarangini', a history of Kashmir written in the twelfth century A.C., which may be considered as history. For the rest we have to go to the imagined history of the epics and other books, to some contemporary records, to inscriptions, to artistic and architectural remains, to coins, and to the large body of Sanskrit literature, for occasional hints; also, of course, to the many records of foreign travellers who came to India, notably Greeks and Chinese, and, during a later period, Arabs.

This lack of historical sense did not affect the masses, for as elsewhere and more so than elsewhere, they built up their view of the past from the traditional accounts and myth and story that were handed to them from generation to generation. This imagined history and mixture of fact and legend became widely known and gave to the people a strong and abiding cultural background. But the ignoring of history had evil consequences which we pursue still. It produced a vagueness of outlook, a divorce from life as it is, a credulity, a woolliness of the mind where fact was concerned. That mind was not at all woolly in the far more difficult, but inevitably vaguer and more indefinite, realms of philosophy; it was both analytic and synthetic, often very critical, sometimes sceptical. But where fact was concerned, it was uncritical, because, perhaps, it did not attach much importance to fact as such.

The impact of science and the modern world have brought a greater appreciation of facts, a more critical faculty, a weighing of evidence, a refusal to accept tradition merely because it is tradition. Many competent historians are at work now, but they often err on the other side and their work is more a meticulous chronicle of facts than living history. But even to-day it is strange how we suddenly become overwhelmed by tradition, and the critical faculties of even intelligent men cease to function. This may partly be due to the nationalism that consumes us in our present subject state. Only when we are politically and economically free will the mind function normally and critically.

Very recently there has been a significant and revealing instance of this conflict between the critical outlook and nationalist tradition. In the greater part of India the *Vikram Samvat* calendar is observed; this is based on a solar reckoning, but the months are lunar. Last month, in April, 1944, according to this calendar, 2,000 years were completed and a new millennium began. This has been the occasion for celebrations throughout India, and the celebrations were justified, both because it was a big turning point in the reckoning of time and because Vikram, or Vikramāditya, with whose name the calendar is associated, has long been a great hero in popular tradition. Innumerable stories cling to his name, and many of these found their way in mediaeval times in different garbs to various parts of Asia, and later to Europe.

Vikram has long been considered a national hero, a beau ideal of a prince. He is remembered as a ruler who pushed out foreign invaders. But his fame rests on the literary and cultural brilliance of his court, where he collected some of the most famous writers, artists, and musicians—the 'nine gems' of his court as they are called. Most of the stories deal with his desire to do good to his people, and to sacrifice himself or his personal interest at the slightest provocation in order to benefit someone else. He is famous for his generosity, service for others, courage, and lack of conceit. Essentially he has been popular because he was considered a good man and a patron of the arts. The fact that he was a successful soldier or a conqueror hardly comes out in the stories. That emphasis on the goodness and self-sacrificing nature of the man is characteristic of the Indian mind and of Indian ideals. Vikramāditya's name, like that of Caesar, became a kind of symbol and title, and numerous subsequent rulers added it to their names. This has added to the confusion, as there are many Vikramādityas mentioned in history.

But who was this Vikram? And when did he exist? Historically speaking everything is vague. There is no trace of any such ruler round about 57 B.C. when the Vikram Samvat era should begin. There was, however, a Vikramāditya in North India in the fourth century A.C., and he fought against Hun invaders and pushed them out. It is he who is supposed to have kept the 'nine

103

gems' in his court and around whom all these stories gather. The problem then is this: How is this Vikramāditya who existed in the fourth century A.C. to be connected with an era which begins in 57 B.C.? The probable explanation appears to be that an era dating from 57 B.C. existed in the Malava State in Central India, and, long after Vikram, this era and calendar were connected with him and renamed after him. But all this is vague and uncertain.

What has been most surprising is the way in which quite intelligent Indians have played about with history in order somehow to connect the traditional hero, Vikram, with the beginning of the era 2,000 years ago. It has also been interesting to find how emphasis is laid on his fight against the foreigner and his desire to establish the unity of India under one national state. Vikram's realm was, in fact, confined to North and Central India.

It is not Indians only who are affected by nationalist urges and supposed national interest in the writing or consideration of history. Every nation and people seem to be affected by this desire to gild and better the past and distort it to their advantage. The histories of India that most of us have had to read, chiefly written by Englishmen, are usually long apologies for and panegyrics of British rule, and a barely veiled contemptuous account of what happened here in the millenniums preceding it. Indeed, real history for them begins with the advent of the Englishman into India; all that went before is in some mystic kind of way a preparation for this divine consummation. Even the British period is distorted with the object of glorifying British rule and British virtues. Very slowly a more correct perspective is developing. But we need not go to the past to find instances of the manipulation of history to suit particular ends and support one's own fancies and prejudices. The present is full of this, and if the present, which we have ourselves seen and experienced, can be so distorted, what of the past?

Nevertheless, it is true that Indians are peculiarly liable to accept tradition and report as history, uncritically and without sufficient examination. They will have to rid themselves of this loose thinking and easy way of arriving at conclusions.

But I have digressed and wandered away from the gods and goddesses and the days when myth and legend began. Those were the days when life was full and in harmony with nature, when man's mind gazed with wonder and delight at the mystery of the universe, when heaven and earth seemed very near to each other, and the gods and goddesses came down from Kailasa or their other Himalayan haunts, even as the gods of Olympus used to come down, to play with and sometimes punish men and women. Out of this abundant life and rich imagination grew myth and legend and strong and beautiful gods and goddesses, for the ancient Indians, like the Greeks, were lovers of beauty and of life. Professor Gilbert Murray* tells us of the sheer beauty of the Olympian system. That description might well apply to the early creations of the Indian mind also. 'They are artists' dreams, ideals, allegories; they are symbols of something beyond themselves. They are gods of half-rejected tradition, of unconscious make-believe, of aspiration. They are gods to whom doubtful philosophers can pray, with all a philosopher's due caution, as to many radiant and heart-searching hypotheses. They are not gods in whom anyone believes as a hard fact.' Equally applicable to India is what Professor Murray adds: 'As the most beautiful image carved by man was not the god, but only a symbol to help towards conceiving the god; so the god himself, when conceived, was not the reality but only a symbol to help towards conceiving the reality. . . . Meanwhile they issued no creeds that contradicted knowledge, no commands that made man sin against his own inner light.'

Gradually the days of the Vedic and other gods and goddesses receded into the background and hard and abstruse philosophy took their place. But in the minds of the people these images still floated, companions in joy and friends in distress, symbols of their own vaguely-felt ideals and aspirations. And round them poets wrapped their fancies and built the houses of their dreams, full of rich embroidery and lovely fantasy. Many of these legends and poets' fancies have been delightfully adapted by F. W. Bain in his series of little books containing stories from Indian mythology. In one of these, 'The Digit of the Moon,' we are told of the creation of woman. 'In the beginning, when Twashtri (the Divine Artificer) came to the creation of woman he found that he had exhausted his materials in the making of man and that no solid elements were left. In this dilemma, after profound meditation, he did as follows: he took the rotundity of the moon, and the curves of the creepers, and the clinging of tendrils, and the trembling of grass, and the slenderness of the reed, and the bloom of flowers, and the lightness of leaves, and the tapering of the elephant's trunk, and the glances of deer, and the clustering of rows of bees, and the joyous gaiety of sunbeams, and the weeping of clouds, and the fickleness of the winds, and the timidity of the hare, and the vanity of the peacock, and the softness of the parrot's bosom, and the hardness of adamant, and the sweetness of honey, and the cruelty of the tiger, and the warm glow of fire, and the coldnesss of snow, and the chattering of

*Gilbert Murray's 'Five Stages of Greek Religion,' p. 76. (Thinkers' Library, Watts, London.)

jays, and the cooing of the *kokila*, and the hypocrisy of the crane, and the fidelity of the *chakravaka;* and compounding all these together, he made woman and gave her to man.'

The Mahabharata

It is difficult to date the epics. They deal with remote periods when the Aryans were still in the process of settling down and consolidating themselves in India. Evidently many authors have written them or added to them in successive periods. The Ramayana is an epic poem with a certain unity of treatment; the Mahabharata is a vast and miscellaneous collection of ancient lore. Both must have taken shape in the pre-Buddhist period, though additions were no doubt made later.

Michelet, the French historian, writing in 1864, with special reference to the Ramayana, says: 'Whoever has done or willed too much let him drink from this deep cup a long draught of life and youth....Everything is narrow in the west—Greece is small and I stifle; Judea is dry and I pant. Let me look towards lofty Asia and the profound East for a little while. There lies my great poem, as vast as the Indian Ocean, blessed, gilded with the sun, the book of divine harmony wherein is no dissonance. A serene peace reigns there, and in the midst of conflict an infinite sweetness, a boundless fraternity, which spreads over all living things, an ocean (without bottom or bound) of love, of pity, of clemency.'

Great as the Ramayana is as an epic poem, and loved by the people, it is really the Mahabharata that is one of the outstanding books of the world. It is a colossal work, an encyclopaedia of tradition and legend, and political and social institutions of ancient India. For a decade or more a host of competent Indian scholars have been engaged in critically examining and collating the various available texts, with a view to publishing an authorized edition. Some parts have been issued by them but the work is still incomplete and is proceeding. It is interesting to note that even in these days of total and horrible war, Russian oriental scholars have produced a Russian translation of the Mahabharata.

Probably this was the period when foreign elements were coming into India and bringing their customs with them. Many of these customs were unlike those of the Aryans, and so a curious mixture of opposing ideas and customs is observable. There was no polyandry among the Aryans, and yet one of the leading heroines of the Mahabharata story is the common wife of five brothers. Gradually the absorption of the earlier indigenous elements as well as of newcomers was taking place, and the Vedic religion was being modified accordingly. It was beginning to take that all-inclusive form which led to modern Hinduism.

This was possible, as the basic approach seems to have been that there could be no monoply in truth, and there were many ways of seeing it and approaching it. So all kinds of different and even contradictory beliefs were tolerated.

In the Mahabharata a very definite attempt has been made to emphasize the fundamental unity of India, or Bhāratvarsha as it was called, from Bharat, the legendary founder of the race. An earlier name was Aryavarta, the land of the Aryas, but this was confined to Northern India up to the Vindhya mountains in Central India. The Aryans had probably not spread beyond that mountain range at that period. The Ramayana story is one of Aryan expansion to the south. The great civil war, which occurred later, described in the Mahabharata, is vaguely supposed to have taken place about the fourteenth century B.C. That war was for the overlordship of India (or possibly of northern India), and it marks the beginning of the conception of India as a whole, of Bhāratvarsha. In this conception a large part of modern Afghanistan, then called Gāndhāra (from which the name of the present city of Kandahar), which was considered an integral part of the country was included. Indeed the queen of the principal ruler was named Gāndhāri, the lady from Gāndhāra. Dilli or Delhi, not the modern city but ancient cities situated near the modern site, named Hastināpur and Indraprastha, becomes the metropolis of India.

Sister Nivedita (Margaret Noble), writing about the Mahabharata, has pointed out: 'The foreign reader...is at once struck by two features: in the first place its unity in complexity; and, in the second, its constant efforts to impress on its hearers the idea of a single centralized India, with a heroic tradition of her own as formative and uniting impulse.'*

The Mahabharata contains the Krishna legends and the famous poem, the Bhagavad Gita. Even apart from the philosophy of the Gita, it lays stress on ethical and moral principles in statecraft and in life generally. Without this foundation of *dharma* there is no true happiness and society cannot hold together. The aim is social welfare, not the welfare of a particular group only but of the whole world, for 'the entire world of mortals is a self-dependent organism.' Yet *dharma* itself is relative and depends on the times and the conditions prevailing, apart from some basic principles, such as adherence to truth, non-violence, etc. These principles endure and do not change, but otewise *dharma*, that

*I have taken this quotation from Sir S. Radhakrishnan's 'Indian Philosophy'. I am indebted to Radhakrishnan for other quotations and much else in this and other chapters.

amalgam of duties and responsibilities, changes with the changing age. The emphasis on non-violence, here and elsewhere, is interesting, for no obvious contradiction appears to be noticed between this and fighting for a righteous cause. The whole epic centres round a great war. Evidently the conception of *ahimsa*, non-violence, had a great deal to do with the motive, the absence of the violent mental approach, self-discipline and control of anger and hatred, rather than the physical abstention from violent action, when this became necessary and inevitable.

The Mahabharata is a rich storehouse in which we can discover all manner of precious things. It is full of a varied, abundant and bubbling life, something far removed from that other aspect of Indian thought which emphasized asceticism and negation. It is not merely a book of moral precepts though there is plenty of ethics and morality in it. The teaching of the Mahabharata has been summed up in the phrase: 'Thou shalt not do to others what is disagreeable to thyself.' There is an emphasis on social welfare and this is noteworthy, for the tendency of the Indian mind is supposed to be in favour of individual perfection rather than social welfare. It says: 'Whatever is not conducive to social welfare, or what ye are likely to be ashamed of, never do.' Again: 'Truth, self-control, asceticism, generosity, non-violence, constancy in virtue—these are the means of success, not caste or family.' 'Virtue is better than immortality and life.' 'True joy entails suffering.' There is a dig at the seeker after wealth: 'The silkworm dies of its wealth.' And, finally, the injunction so typical of a living and advancing people; 'Discontent is the spur of progress.'

There is in the Mahabharata the polytheism of the Vedas, the monism of the Upanishads, and deisms, and dualisms, and monotheism. The outlook is still creative and more or less rationalistic, and the feeling of exclusiveness is yet limited. Caste is not rigid. There was still a feeling of confidence, but as external forces invaded and challenged the security of the old order, that confidence lessened somewhat and a demand for greater uniformity arose in order to produce internal unity and strength. New taboos grew up. The eating of beef, previously countenanced, is later absolutely prohibited. In the Mahabharata there are references to beef or veal being offered to honoured guests.

The Bhagavad Gita

The Bhagavad Gita is part of the Mahabharata, an episode in the vast drama. But it stands apart and is complete in itself. It is a relatively small poem of 700 verses—'the most beautiful, perhaps

the only true philosophical song existing in any known tongue,'
so William von Humboldt described it. Its popularity and influence have not waned ever since it was composed and written in
the pre-Buddhistic age, and to-day its appeal is as strong as ever
in India. Every school of thought and philosophy looks up to it
and interprets it in its own way. In times of crisis, when the mind
of man is tortured by doubt and is torn by the conflict of duties,
it has turned all the more to the Gita for light and guidance. For
it is a poem of crisis, of political and social crisis and, even more so,
of crisis in the spirit of man. Innumerable commentaries on the
Gita have appeared in the past and they continue to come out with
unfailing regularity. Even the leaders of thought and action of the
present day—Tilak, Aurobindo Ghose, Gandhi—have written on
it, each giving his own interpretation. Gandhiji bases his firm
belief in non-violence on it, others justify violence and warfare
for a righteous cause.

The poem begins with a conversation between Arjuna and
Krishna on the very field of battle before the great war begins.
Arjuna is troubled, his conscience revolts at the thought of the war
and the mass murder that it involves, the killing of friends and
relatives—for what purpose? What conceivable gain can outweigh
this loss, this sin? All his old standards fail him, his values collapse.
Arjuna becomes the symbol of the tortured spirit of man, which,
from age to age, has been torn by conflicting obligations and mora-
lities. From this personal conversation we are taken step by step
to higher and more impersonal regions of individual duty and social
behaviour, of the application of ethics to human life, of the spiritual
outlook that should govern all. There is much that is metaphysical
in it, and an attempt to reconcile and harmonize the three ways
for human advancement: the path of the intellect or knowledge,
the path of action, and the path of faith. Probably more emphasis
is laid on faith than on the others, and even a personal god
emerges, though he is considered as a manifestation of the absolute. The Gita deals essentially with the spiritual background of
human existence and it is in this context that the practical problems of everyday life appear. It is a call to action to meet the
obligations and duties of life, but always keeping in view that
spiritual background and the larger purpose of the universe. Inaction is condemned, and action and life have to be in accordance
with the highest ideals of the age, for these ideals themselves may
vary from age to age. The *yugadharma*, the ideal of the particular
age, has always to be kept in view.

Because modern India is full of frustration and has suffered
from too much quietism, this call to action makes a special
appeal. It is also possible to interpret that action in modern
terms as action for social betterment and social service, practical,

altruistic, patriotic and humanitarian. Such action is desirable, according to the Gita, but behind it must lie the spiritual ideal. And action must be in a spirit of detachment, not much concerned with its results. The law of cause and effect holds good under all circumstances; right action must therefore necessarily yield right results, though these might not be immediately apparent.

The message of the Gita is not sectarian or addressed to any particular school of thought. It is universal in its approach for everyone, Brahmin or outcaste: "All paths lead to Me,' it says. It is because of this universality that it has found favour with all classes and schools. There is something in it which seems to be capable of being constantly renewed, which does not become out of date with the passing of time—an inner quality of earnest inquiry and search, of contemplation and action, of balance and equilibrium in spite of conflict and contradiction. There is a poise in it and a unity in the midst of disparity, and its temper is one of supremacy over the changing environment, not by seeking escape from it but fitting in with it. During the 2,500 years since it was written, Indian humanity has gone repeatedly through the processes of change and development and decay; experience has succeeded experience, thought has followed thought, but it has always found something living in the Gita, something that fitted into the developing thought and had a freshness and applicability to the spiritual problems that afflict the mind.

Life and Work in Ancient India

A great deal has been done by scholars and philosophers to trace the development of philosophic and metaphysical thought in the India of the past; much has also been done to fix the chronology of historic events and draw in broad outline political maps of those periods. But not much has so far been done to investigate the social and economic conditions of those days, how people lived, carried on their work, what they produced and how, and the way trade functioned. Greater attention is being paid to these vital questions now and some works by Indian scholars, and one by an American, have appeared. But a great deal remains to be done. The Mahabharata itself is a storehouse of sociological and other data and many more books will no doubt yield useful information. But they have to be critically examined from this particular point of view. One book of inestimable value is Kautilya's 'Arthashāstra' of the fourth century B.C., which gives details of the political, social, economic, and military organization of the Maurya Empire.

An earlier account, which definitely takes us back to the pre-Buddhist period in India, is contained in the collection of the Jātaka tales. These Jātakas were given their present shape some time after the Buddha. They are supposed to deal with the previous incarnations of the Buddha and have become an important part of Buddhist literature. But the stories are evidently much older and they deal with the pre-Buddhistic period and give us much valuable information about life in India in those days. Professor Rhys Davids has described them as the oldest, most complete and most important collection of folklore extant. Many of the subsequent collection of animal and other stories which were written in India and found their way to western Asia and Europe can be traced to the Jātakas.

The Jātakas deal with the period when the final amalgamation of the two principal races of India, the Dravidians and the Aryans, was taking place. They reveal 'a multiform and chaotic society which resists more or less every attempt at classification and about which there can be no talk of an organization according to caste in that age.'* The Jātakas may be said to represent the popular tradition as contrasted with the priestly or Brahminic tradition and the Kshatriya or ruling class tradition.

There are chronologies and genealogies of various kingdoms and their rulers. Kingship, originally elective, becomes hereditary according to the rule of primogeniture. Women are excluded from this succession, but there are exceptions. As in China, the ruler is held responsible for all misfortunes; if anything goes wrong the fault must lie with the king. There was a council of ministers and there are also references to some kind of State assembly. Nevertheless the king was an autocratic monarch though he had to function within established conventions. The high priest had an important position in court as an adviser and person in charge of religious ceremonies. There are references to popular revolts against unjust and tyrannical kings, who are sometimes put to death for their crimes.

Village assemblies enjoyed a measure of autonomy. The chief source of revenue was the land. The land-tax was supposed to represent the king's share of the produce, and it was usually, but not always, paid in kind. Probably this tax was about one-sixth of the produce. It was predominantly an agricultural civilization and the basic unit was the self-governing village. The political and economic structure was built up from these village communities which were grouped in tens and hundreds. Horticulture, rearing of livestock, and dairy farming were practised on

*Richard Fick. 'The Social Organisation in North-East India in Buddha's Time' (Calcutta, 1920), p. 286. A more recent book, chiefly based on the Jātaka stories, is Ratilal Mehta's 'Pre-Buddhist India' (Bombay, 1939). I am indebted to this latter book for most of my facts.

an extensive scale. Gardens and parks were common, and fruits and flowers were valued. The list of flowers mentioned is a long one; among the favourite fruits were the mango, fig, grape, plantain and the date. There were evidently many shops of vegetable and fruit sellers in the cities, as well as of florists. The flower-garland was then, as now, a favourite of the Indian people.

Hunting was a regular occupation chiefly for the food it provided. Flesh-eating was common and included poultry and fish; venison was highly esteemed. There were fisheries and slaughter-houses. The principal articles of diet were, however, rice, wheat, millet and corn. Sugar was extracted from sugar-cane. Milk and its various products were then, as they are now, highly prized. There were liquor shops, and liquor was apparently made from rice, fruits and sugar-cane.

There was mining for metals and precious stones. Among the metals mentioned are gold, silver, copper, iron, lead, tin, and brass. Among the precious stones were diamonds, rubies, corals, also pearls. Gold, silver and copper coins are referred to. There were partnerships for trade, and loans were advanced on interest.

Among the manufactured goods are silks, woollens and cotton textiles, rugs, blankets and carpets. Spinning, weaving and dyeing are flourishing and widespread industries. The metallurgical industry produces weapons of war. The building industry uses stone, wood, and bricks. Carpenters make a variety of furniture, etc., including carts, chariots, ships, bedsteads, chairs, benches, chests, toys, etc. Cane-workers make mattresses, baskets, fans, and sunshades. Potters function in every village. From flowers and sandalwood a number of perfumes, oils and 'beauty' products are made, including sandalwood powder. Various medicines and drugs are manufactured and dead bodies are sometimes embalmed.

Apart from the many kinds of artisans and craftsmen who are mentioned, various other professions are referred to: teachers, physicians and surgeons, merchants and traders, musicians, astrologers, greengrocers, actors, dancers, itinerant jugglers, acrobats, puppet-players, pedlars.

Domestic slavery appears to have been fairly common, but agricultural and other work was done with the help of hired labour. There were even then some untouchables—the *chandalas* as they were called, whose chief business was the disposal of dead bodies.

Trade associations and craft-guilds had already assumed importance. 'The existence of trade associations,' says Fick, 'which grew partly for economical reasons, better employment of capital, facilities of intercourse, partly for protecting the legal interest of their class, is surely to be traced to an early period of Indian culture.' The Jātakas say that there were eighteeen craft-unions but they actually mention only four: the wood-workers and the masons, the smiths, the leather workers, and the painters.

Even in the Epics there are references to trade and craft organizations. The Mahabharata says: 'the safeguard of corporations (guilds) is union.' It is said that 'the merchant-guilds were of such authority that the king was not allowed to establish any laws repugnant to these trade unions. The heads of guilds are mentioned next after priests as objects of a king's anxious concern.'* The chief of the merchants, the *shreshthi* (modern seth), was a man of very considerable importance.

One rather extraordinary development emerges from the Jātaka accounts. This is the establishment of special settlements or villages of people belonging to particular crafts. Thus there was a carpenters' village, consisting, it is said, of 1,000 families; a smiths' village, and so on. These specialized villages were usually situated near a city, which absorbed their special products and which provided them with the other necessaries of life. The whole village apparently worked on co-operative lines and undertook large orders. Probably out of this separate living and organization the caste system developed and spread out. The example set by the Brahmins and the nobility was gradually followed by the manufacturers' corporations and trade guilds.

Great roads, with travellers' rest houses and occasional hospitals, covered north India and connected distant parts of the country. Trade flourished not only in the country itself but between India and foreign countries. There was a colony of Indian merchants living at Memphis in Egypt about the fifth century B.C. as the discovery of modelled heads of Indians there has shown. Probably there was trade also between India and the islands of South-East Asia.

Overseas trade involved shipping and it is clear that ships were built in India both for the inland waterways and for ocean traffic. There are references in the Epics to shipping duties being paid by 'merchants coming from afar.'

The Jātakas are full of references to merchants' voyages. There were overland caravans across deserts going westward to the seaport of Broach and north towards Gandhara and Central Asia. From Broach ships went to the Persian Gulf for Babylon (Baveru). There was a great deal of river traffic and, according to the Jātakas, ships travelled from Benares, Patna, Champa (Bhagalpur) and other places to the sea and thence to southern ports and Ceylon and Malaya. Old Tamil poems tell us of the

*Prof. E. Washburn Hopkins in 'Cambridge History of India', Vol. I, p. 269.

flourishing port of Kaveripattinam on the Kaveri river in the South, which was a centre of international trade. These ships must have been fairly large as it is said in the Jātakas that 'hundreds' of merchants and emigrants embarked on a ship.

In the 'Milinda' (this is of the first century A.C. Milinda is the Greek Bactrian king of North India who became an ardent Buddhist) it is said: 'As a shipowner who has become wealthy by constantly levying freight in some seaport town will be able to traverse the high seas, and go to Vanga (Bengal) or Takkola, or China or Sovira, or Surat or Alexandria, or the Koromandel coast, or Further India, or any other place where ships do congregate.'*

Among the exports from India were: 'Silks, muslins, the finer sorts of cloth, cutlery and armour, brocades, embroideries and rugs, perfumes and drugs, ivory and ivory work, jewellery and gold (seldom silver); these were the main articles in which the merchant dealt.'†

India, or rather North India, was famous for her weapons of war, especially for the quality of her steel, her swords and daggers. In the fifth century B.C. a large body of Indian troops, cavalry and infantry, accompanied the Persian army to Greece. When Alexander invaded Persia, it is stated in the famous Persian epic poem, Firdusi's 'Shahnamah', that swords and other weapons were hurriedly sent for by the Persians from India. The old (pre-Islamic) Arabic word for sword is 'muhannad,' which means 'from Hind' or Indian. This word is in common use still.

Ancient India appears to have made considerable progress in the treatment of iron. There is an enormous iron pillar near Delhi which has baffled modern scientists who have been unable to discover by what process it was made, which has enabled it to withstand oxidation and other atmospheric changes. The inscription on it is in the Gupta script which was in use from the fourth to the seventh century A.C. Some scholars are, however, of opinion that the pillar itself is much older than this inscription, which was added later.

Alexander's invasion of India in the fourth century B.C. was, from a military point of view, a minor affair. It was more of a raid across the border, and not a very successful raid for him. He met with such stout resistance from a border chieftain that the contemplated advance into the heart of India had to be reconsidered. If a small ruler on the frontier could fight thus, what of the larger and more powerful kingdoms further south? Probably this was the main reason why his army refused to march further and insisted on returning.

*Mrs. C. A. F. Rhys Davids in 'Cambridge History of India', Vol. I, p. 212.
†Rhys Davids. 'Buddhist India', p. 98.

The quality of India's ·military strength was seen very soon after Alexander's return and death, when Seleucus attempted another invasion. He was defeated by Chandragupta and driven back. Indian armies then had an advantage which others lacked; this was the possession of trained war-elephants, which might be compared to the tanks of to-day. Seleucus Nikator obtained 500 of these war-elephants from India for his campaign against Antigonus in Asia Minor in 302 B.C., and military historians say that these elephants were the decisive factor in the battle which ended in the death of Antigonus and the flight of his son Demetrius.

There are books on the training of elephants, the breeding of horses, etc.; each one of these called a *shāstra*. This word has come to mean scripture or holy writ, but it was applied indiscriminately to every kind of knowledge and science, varying from mathematics to dancing. In fact the line between religious and secular knowledge was not strictly drawn. They overlapped and everything that seemed useful to life was the object of inquiry.

Writing in India goes back to the most ancient times. Old pottery belonging to the Neolithic period is inscribed with writing in the Brahmi characters. Mohenjo-daro has inscriptions which have not so far been wholly deciphered. The Brahmi inscriptions found all over India are undoubtedly the basic script from which devanagari and others have arisen in India. Some of Ashoka's inscriptions are in the Brahmi script; others, in the northwest, are in the Kharoshti script.

As early as the sixth or seventh century B.C., Panini wrote his great grammar of the Sanskrit language.* He mentions previous grammars and already in his time Sanskrit had crystallized and become the language of an ever-growing literature. Panini's book is something more than a mere grammar. It has been described by the Soviet professor Th. Stcherbatsky, of Leningrad, as 'one of the greatest productions of the human mind.' Panini is still the standard authority on Sanskrit grammar, though subsequent grammarians have added to it and interpreted it. It is interesting to note that Panini mentions the Greek script. This indicates that there were some kind of contacts between India and the Greeks long before Alexander came to the East.

The study of astronomy was especially pursued and it often merged into astrology. Medicine had its textbooks and there were hospitals. Dhanwantari is the legendary founder of the Indian science of medicine. The best known old textbooks,

---

*Keith and some others place Panini at c. 300 B.C., but the balance of authority seems to be clear that Panini lived and wrote before the commencement of the Buddhist period.

however, date from the early centuries of the Christian era. These are by Charak on medicine and Sushruta on surgery. Charak is supposed to have been the royal court physician of Kanishka who had his capital in the north-west. These textbooks enumerate a large number of diseases and give methods of diagnosis and treatment. They deal with surgery, obstetrics, baths, diet, hygiene, infant-feeding, and medical education. The approach was experimental, and dissection of dead bodies was being practised in the course of surgical training. Various surgical instruments are mentioned by Sushruta, as well as operations, including amputation of limbs, abdominal, cæsarean section, cataract, etc. Wounds were sterilized by fumigation. In the third or fourth century B.C. there were also hospitals for animals. This was probably due to the influence of Jainism and Buddhism with their emphasis on non-violence.

In mathematics the ancient Indians made some epoch-making discoveries, notably that of the zero sign, of the decimal place-value system, of the use of the minus sign, and the use in algebra of letters of the alphabet to denote unknown quantities. It is difficult to date these, as there was always a big time-lag between the discovery and its practical application. But it is clear that the beginnings of arithmetic, algebra, and geometry were laid in the earliest period. Ten formed the basis of enumeration in India even at the time of the Rig Veda. The time and number sense of the ancient Indians was extraordinary. They had a long series of number names for very high numerals. The Greeks, Romans, Persians, and Arabs had apparently no terminology for denominations above the thousand or at most the myriad ($10^4 = 10,000$). In India there were eighteen specific denominations (10^{18}), and there are even longer lists. In the story of Buddha's early education he is reported to have named denominations up to 10^{50}.

At the other end of the scale there was a minute division of time of which the smallest unit was approximately one-seventeenth of a second, and the smallest lineal measure is given as something which approximates to 1.37×7^{-10} inches. All these big and small figures were no doubt entirely theoretical and used for philosophical purposes. Nevertheless, the old Indians, unlike other ancient nations, had vast conceptions of time and space. They thought in a big way. Even their mythology deals with ages of hundreds of millions of years. To them the vast periods of modern geology or the astronomical distances of the stars would not have come as a surprise. Because of this background, Darwin's and other similar theories could not create in India the turmoil and inner conflict which they produced in Europe in the middle of the nineteenth century. The popular mind in Europe was used to a time scale which did not go beyond a few thousand years.

In the 'Arthashāstra' we are given the weights and measures which were in use in North India in the fourth century B.C. There used to be careful supervision of the weights in the market places.

In the epic period we have frequent mention of some kind of forest universities, situated not far from a town or city, where students gathered round well-known scholars for training and education, which comprised a variety of subjects, including military training. These forest abodes were preferred so as to avoid the distractions of city life and enable the students to lead a disciplined and continent life. After some years of this training they were supposed to go back and live as householders and citizens. Probably these forest schools consisted of small groups, though there are indications that a popular teacher would attract large numbers.

Benares has always been a centre of learning, and even in Buddha's day it was old and known as such. It was in the Deer Park near Benares that Buddha preached his first sermon; but Benares does not appear to have been at any time anything like a university, such as existed then and later in other parts of India. There were numerous groups there, consisting of a teacher and his disciples, and often between rival groups there was fierce debate and argument.

But in the north-west, near modern Peshawar, there was an ancient and famous university at Takshashila or Taxila. This was particularly noted for science, especially medicine, and the arts, and people went to it from distant parts of India. The Jātaka stories are full of instances of sons of nobles and Brahmins travelling, unattended and unarmed, to Taxila to be educated. Probably students came also from Central Asia and Afghanistan, as it was conveniently situated.

It was considered an honour and a distinction to be a graduate of Taxila. Physicians who had studied in the school of medicine there were highly thought of, and it is related that whenever Buddha felt unwell his admirers brought to him a famous physician who had graduated from Taxila. Panini, the great grammarian of the sixth-seventh century B.C., is said to have studied there.

Taxila was thus a pre-Buddhist university and a seat of Brahminical learning. During the Buddhist period it became also a centre of Buddhist scholarship and attracted Buddhist students from all over India and across the border. It was the headquarters of the north-western province of the Maurya Empire.

The legal position of women, according to Manu, the earliest exponent of the law, was definitely bad. They were always dependent on somebody—on the father, the husband, or the son. Almost they were treated, in law, as chattels. And yet from the numerous stories in the Epics this law was not applied very rigidly and they held an honoured place in the home and in society. The old law-giver, Manu, himself says: 'Where women are honoured the gods dwell.' There is no mention of women students at Taxila or any of the old universities; but some of them did function as students somewhere, for there is repeated mention of learned and scholarly women. In later ages also there were a number of eminent women scholars. Bad as the legal position of women was in ancient India, judged by modern standards, it was far better than in ancient Greece and Rome, in early Christianity, in the Canon Law of mediæval Europe, and indeed right up to comparatively modern times at the beginning of the nineteenth century.

The exponents of the law from Manu onwards refer to forms of partnership in business. Manu refers chiefly to priests; Yagnavalkya includes trade and agriculture. A later writer, Narada, says: 'Loss, expense, profit of each partner are equal to, more than, or less than those of other partners according as his share (invested) is equal, greater, or less. Storage, food, charges (tolls), loss, freightage, expense of keeping, must be paid by each partner in accordance with the terms of agreement.'

Manu's conception of a state was evidently that of a small kingdom. This conception was, however, growing and changing, leading to the vast Maurya Empire of the fourth century B.C. and to international contacts with the Greek world.

Megasthenes, the Greek Ambassador in India in the fourth century B.C., totally denies the existence of slavery in India. But in this he was wrong as there were certainly domestic slaves, and there are references in Indian books of the period to improving the lot of the slaves. It is clear, however, that there was no large-scale slavery and no slave gangs for labour purposes, as were common in many countries then, and this may have led Megasthenes to believe that slavery was completely absent. It was laid down that 'Never shall an Arya be subjected to slavery.' Who exactly was an Arya, and who was not, it is difficult to say, but the Aryan fold at that time had come to mean rather vaguely all the four basic castes, including the shudras, but not the untouchables.

In China also, in the days of the early Han Dynasty, slaves were used primarily in domestic service. They were unimportant in agriculture or in large-scale labour works. Both in India and China these domestic slaves formed a very small propor-

118

tion of the population, and in this important respect there was thus a vast difference between Indian and Chinese society and contemporary Greek and Roman society.

What were the Indians like in those distant days? It is difficult for us to conceive of a period so far and so different from ours, and yet some vague picture emerges from the miscellaneous data that we have. They were a light-hearted race, confident and proud of their traditions, dabbling in the search for the mysterious, full of questions addressed to nature and human life, attaching importance to the standards and values they had created, but taking life easily and joyously, and facing death without much concern.

Arrian, the Greek historian of Alexander's campaign in North India, was struck by this light-hartedness of the race. 'No nation,' he writes, 'is fonder of singing and dancing than the Indian.'

Mahāvira and Buddha : Caste

Some such background existed in North India from the time of the Epics onwards to the early Buddhist period. It was ever changing politically and economically, and the processes of synthesis and amalgamation, as well as the specialization of labour, were taking place. In the realm of ideas there was continuous growth and often conflict. The early Upanishads had been followed by the development of thought and activity in many directions; they were themselves a reaction against priest-craft and ritualism. Men's minds had rebelled against much that they saw, and out of that rebellion had grown these early Upanishads as well as, a little later, the strong current of materialism, and Jainism and Buddhism, and the attempt to synthesize various forms of belief in the Bhagavad Gita. Out of all this again grew the six systems of Indian philosophy. Yet behind all this mental conflict and rebellion lay a vivid and growing national life.

Both Jainism and Buddhism were breakaways from the Vedic religion and its offshoots, though in a sense they had grown out of it. They deny the authority of the Vedas and, most fundamental of all matters, they deny or say nothing about the existence of a first cause. Both lay emphasis on non-violence and build up organizations of celibate monks and priests. There is a certain realism and rationalism in their approach, though inevitably this does not carry us very far in our dealings with the invisible world. One of the fundamental doctrines of Jainism is that truth is relative to our standpoints. It is a rigorous ethical and non-transcendental system, laying a special emphasis on the ascetic aspect of life and thought.

119

Mahāvira, the founder of Jainism, and Buddha were contemporaries, and both came from the Kshatriya warrior class. Buddha died at the age of eighty, in 544 B.C., and the Buddhist era begins then. (This is the traditional date. Historians give a later date 487 B.C., but are now inclined to accept the traditional date as more correct.) It is an odd coincidence that I am writing this on the Buddhist New Year's Day, 2488—the day of the full moon of the month of Vaisākha—the *Vaisakhi Purnima*, as it is called. It is stated in Buddhist literature that Buddha was born on this full moon day of Vaisākha (May-June); that he attained enlightenment and finally died also on the same day of the year.

Buddha had the courage to attack popular religion, superstition, ceremonial, and priestcraft, and all the vested interests that clung to them. He condemned also the metaphysical and theological outlook, miracles, revelations, and dealings with the supernatural. His appeal was to logic, reason, and experience; his emphasis was on ethics, and his method was one of psychological analysis, a psychology without a soul. His whole approach comes like the breath of the fresh wind from the mountains after the stale air of metaphysical speculation.

Buddha did not attack caste directly, yet in his own order he did not recognize it, and there is no doubt that his whole attitude and activity weakened the caste system. Probably caste was very fluid in his day and for some centuries later. It is obvious that a caste-ridden community could not indulge in foreign trade or other foreign adventures, and yet for fifteen hundred years or more after Buddha, trade was developing between India and neighbouring countries, and Indian colonies flourished. Foreign elements continued to stream into India from the northwest and were absorbed.

It is interesting to observe this process of absorption which worked at both ends. New castes were formed at the bottom of the scale, and any successful invading element became transformed soon into Kshatriyas or the ruling class. Coins of the period just before and after the beginning of the Christian era show this rapid change in the course of two or three generations. The first ruler has a foreign name. His son or grandson appears with a Sanskrit name and is crowned according to the traditional rites meant for Kshatriyas.

Many of the Rajput Kshatriya clans date back to the Shaka or Scythian invasions which began about the second century B.C. or from the later invasion of the White Huns. All these accepted the faith and institutions of the country and then tried to affiliate themselves to the famous heroes of the Epics. Thus the Kshatriya group depended on status and occupation rather than on descent, and so it was much easier for foreigners to be incorporated into it.

It is curious and significant that throughout the long span of Indian history there have been repeated warnings given by great men against priestcraft and the rigidity of the caste system, and powerful movements have risen against them; yet slowly, imperceptibly, almost, it seems, as if it were the inevitable course of destiny, caste has grown and spread and seized every aspect of Indian life in its strangling grip. Rebels against caste have drawn many followers, and yet in course of time their group has itself become a caste. Jainism, a rebel against the parent religion and in many ways utterly different from it, was yet tolerant to caste and adapted itself to it; and so it survives and continues in India, almost as an offshoot of Hinduism. Buddhism, not adapting itself to caste, and more independent in its thought and outlook, ultimately passes away from India, though it influences India and Hinduism profoundly. Christianity comes here eighteen hundred years ago and settles down and gradually develops its own castes. The Moslem social structure in India, in spite of its vigorous denunciation of all such barriers within the community, is also partly affected.

In our own period numerous movements to break the tyranny of caste have arisen among the middle classes and they have made a difference, but not a vital one, so far as the masses are concerned. Their method was usually one of direct attack. Then Gandhi came and tackled the problem, after the immemorial Indian fashion, in an indirect way, and his eyes were on the masses. He has been direct enough, aggressive enough, persistent enough, but without challenging the original basic functional theory underlying the four main castes. He has attacked the rank undergrowth and overgrowth, knowing well that he was undermining the whole caste structure thereby.* He has already shaken the foundations and the masses have been powerfully affected. For them the whole structure holds or breaks altogether. But an even greater power than he is at work: the conditions of modern life—and it seems that at last this hoary and tenacious relic of past times must die.

But while we struggle with caste in India (which, in its origin,

*Gandhiji's references to caste have been progressively stronger and more pointed, and he has made it repeatedly clear that caste as a whole and as it exists must be eliminated. Referring to the constructive programme which he has placed before the nation, he says: 'It has undoubtedly independence, political, social and economic, as its aim. It is a moral, non-violent revolution in all the departments of life of a big nation, at the end of which caste and untouchability and such other superstitions must vanish, differences between Hindu and Muslim become things of the past, enmity against Englishmen or Europeans must be wholly forgotten...' And again quite recently: 'The caste system, as we know, is an anachronism. It must go if both Hinduism and India are to live and grow from day to day.'

was based on colour), new and overbearing castes have arisen in the west with doctrines of racial exclusiveness, sometimes clothed in political and economic terms, and even speaking in the language of democracy.

Before the Buddha, seven hundred years before Christ, a great Indian, the sage and lawgiver Yagnavalkya, is reported to have said: 'It is not our religion, still less the colour of our skin, that produces virtue; virtue must be practised. Therefore, let no one do to others what he would not have done to himself.'

Chandragupta and Chanakya. The Maurya Empire Established

Buddhism spread gradually in India. Although in origin a Kshatriya movement, and representing a conflict between the ruling class and the priests, its ethical and democratic aspect, and more especially its fight against priestcraft and ritualism, appealed to the people. It developed as a popular reform movement, attracting even some Brahmin thinkers. But generally Brahmins opposed it and called Buddhists heretics and rebels against the established faith. More important than the outward progress was the interaction of Buddhism and the older faith on each other, and the continuous undermining of Brahmins. Two and a half centuries later, the Emperor Ashoka became a convert to the faith and devoted all his energies to spreading it by peaceful missionary efforts in India and foreign countries.

These two centuries saw many changes in India. Various processes had long been going on to bring about racial fusion and to amalgamate the petty states and small kingdoms and republics; the old urge to build up a united centralized state had been working, and out of all this emerged a powerful and highly developed empire. Alexander's invasion of the north-west gave the final push to this development, and two remarkable men arose who could take advantage of the changing conditions and mould them according to their will. These men were Chandragupta Maurya and his friend and minister and counsellor, the Brahmin, Chānakya. This combination functioned well. Both had been exiled from the powerful Nanda kingdom of Magadha, which had its headquarters at Pataliputra (the modern Patna); both went to Taxila in the north-west and came in contact with the Greeks stationed there by Alexander. Chandragupta met Alexander himself; he heard of his conquests and glory and was fired by ambition to emulate him. Chandragupta and Chānakya watched and prepared themselves; they hatched great and ambitious schemes and waited for the opportunity to realize them.

Soon news came of Alexander's death at Babylon in 323 B.C., and immediately Chandragupta and Chānakya raised the old and ever-new cry of nationalism and roused the people against the foreign invader. The Greek garrison was driven away and Taxila captured. The appeal to nationalism had brought allies to Chandragupta and he marched with them across north India to Pataliputra. Within two years of Alexander's death, he was in possession of that city and kingdom and the Maurya Empire had been established.

Alexander's general, Seleucus, who had inherited after his chief's death the countries from Asia Minor to India, tried to re-establish his authority in north-west India and crossed the Indus with an army. He was defeated and had to cede a part of Afghanistan, up to Kabul and Herat, to Chandragupta, who also married the daughter of Seleucus. Except for south India, Chandragupta's empire covered the whole of India, from the Arabian Sea to the Bay of Bengal, and extended in the north to Kabul. For the first time in recorded history a vast centralized state had risen in India. The city of Pataliputra was the capital of this great empire.

What was this new state like? Fortunately we have full accounts, both Indian and Greek. Megasthenes, the ambassador sent by Seleucus, has left a record and, much more important is that contemporary account—Kautilya's 'Arthashāstra,' the 'Science of Polity,' to which reference has already been made. Kautilya is another name for Chānakya, and thus we have a book written, not only by a great scholar, but a man who played a dominating part in the establishment, growth and preservation of the empire. Chānakya has been called the Indian Machiavelli, and to some extent the comparison is justified. But he was a much bigger person in every way, greater in intellect and action. He was no mere follower of a king, a humble adviser of an all-powerful emperor. A picture of him emerges from an old Indian play—the *Mudra-Rakshasa*—which deals with this period. Bold and scheming, proud and revengeful, never forgetting a slight, never forgetting his purpose, availing himself of every device to delude and defeat the enemy, he sat with the reins of empire in his hands and looked upon the emperor more as a loved pupil than as a master. Simple and austere in his life, uninterested in the pomp and pageantry of high position, when he had redeemed his pledge and accomplished his purpose, he wanted to retire, Brahmin-like, to a life of contemplation.

There was hardly anything Chānakya would have refrained from doing to achieve his purpose; he was unscrupulous enough; yet he was also wise enough to know that this very purpose might be defeated by means unsuited to the end. Long before Clausewitz, he is reported to have said that war is only a continuance of state policy by other means. But, he adds, war must always serve the larger ends of policy and not become an end in itself; the statesman's objective must always be the betterment of the state as a result of war, not the mere defeat and destruction of the enemy. If war involves both parties in a common ruin, that is the bankruptcy of statesmanship. War must be conducted by armed forces; but much more important than the force of arms is the high strategy which saps the enemy's morale and disrupts his forces and brings about his collapse, or takes him to the verge of collapse, before armed attack. Unscrupulous and rigid as Chānakya was in the pursuit of his aim, he never forgot that it was better to win over an intelligent and high-minded enemy than to crush him. His final victory was obtained by sowing discord in the enemy's ranks, and, in the very moment of this victory, so the story goes, he induced Chandragupta to be generous to his rival chief. Chānakya himself is said to have handed over the insignia of his own high office to the minister of that rival, whose intelligence and loyalty to his old chief had impressed him greatly. So the story ends not in the bitterness of defeat and humiliation, but in reconciliation and in laying the firm and enduring foundations of a state, which had not only defeated but won over its chief enemy.

The Maurya Empire maintained diplomatic relations with the Greek world, both with Seleucus and his successors and with Ptolemy Philadelphus. These relations rested on the solid foundation of mutual commercial interest. Strabo tells us that the Oxus river in central Asia formed a link in an important chain along which Indian goods were carried to Europe by way of the Caspian and the Black Sea. This route was popular in the third century B.C. Central Asia then was rich and fertile. More than a thousand years later it began to dry up. The Arthashāstra mentions that the king's stud had 'Arabian steeds'!

The Organization of the State

What was this new state like that arose in 321 B.C. and covered far the greater part of India, right up to Kabul in the north? It was an autocracy, a dictatorship at the top, as most empires were and still are. There was a great deal of local autonomy in the towns and village units, and elective elders looked after these local affairs. This local autonomy was greatly prized and hardly any king or supreme ruler interfered with it. Nevertheless, the influence and many-sided activities of the central government were all-pervasive, and in some ways this Mauryan state reminds one of modern dictatorships. There could have been then, in a purely agricultural age, nothing like the control of the individual by the state which we see to-day. But, in spite of limitations, an effort was made to control and regulate life. The state was very far from being just a police state, interested in keeping external and internal peace and collecting revenue.

There was a widespread and rigid bureaucracy and there are frequent references to espionage. Agriculture was regulated in many ways, so were rates of interest. Regulation and periodical inspection took place of food, markets, manufacturers, slaughter-houses, cattle-raising, water rights, sports, courtesans, and drinking saloons. Weights and measures were standardized. The cornering and adulteration of foodstuffs were rigorously punished. Trade was taxed, and, so also in some respects, the practice of religion. When there was a breach of regulation or some other misdemeanour, the temple monies were confiscated. If rich people were found guilty of embezzlement or of profiting from national calamity, their property was also confiscated. Sanitation and hospitals were provided and there were medical men at the chief centres. The state gave relief to widows, orphans, the sick, and the infirm. Famine relief was a special care of the state, and half the stores in all the state warehouses were always kept in reserve for times of scarcity and famine.

All these rules and regulations were probably applied far more to the cities than to the villages; and it is also likely that practice lagged far behind theory. Nevertheless, even the theory is interesting. The village communities were practically auto-nomous.

Chānakya's Arthashāstra deals with a vast variety of subjects and covers almost every aspect of the theory and practice of government. It discusses the duties of the king, of his ministers and councillors, of council meetings, of departments of government, of diplomacy, of war and peace. It gives details of the vast army which Chandragupta had, consisting of infantry, cavalry, chariots, and elephants.* And yet Chānakya suggests that mere numbers do not count for much; without discipline and proper leaderhip they may become a burden. Defence and fortifications are also dealt with.

Among the other matters discussed in the book are trade and commerce, law and law courts, municipal government, social customs, marriage and divorce, rights of women, taxation and revenue, agriculture, the working of mines and factories, arti-sans, markets, horticulture, manufactures, irrigation, and water-

---

The game of chess, which had its origin in India, probably developed from this four-fold conception of the army. It was called 'chaturanga', four-limbed, from which came the word 'shatrang'. Alberuni gives an account of this game as played in India by four players.

ways, ships and navigation, corporations, census operations, fisheries, slaughter houses, passports, and jails. Widow remarriage is recognized; also divorce under certain circumstances.

There is a reference to *chinapatta*, silk fabrics of China manufacture, and a distinction is made between these and the silk made in India. Probably the latter was of a coarser variety. The importation of Chinese silk indicates trade contacts with China at least as early as the fourth century B.C.

The king, at the time of his coronation, had to take the oath of service to the people—'May I be deprived of heaven, of life, and of offspring if I oppress you.' 'In the happiness of his subjects lies his happiness; in their welfare, whatever pleases himself he shall consider as not good, but whatever pleases his subjects, he shall consider as good.' 'If a king is energetic, his subjects will be equally energetic.' Public work could not suffer or await the king's pleasure; he had always to be ready for it. And if the king misbehaved, his people had the right to remove him and put another in his place.

There was an irrigation department to look after the many canals, and a navigation department for the harbours, ferries, bridges, and the numerous boats and ships that went up and down the rivers and crossed the seas to Burma and beyond. There was apparently some kind of navy, too, as an adjunct of the army.

Trade flourished in the empire and great roads connected the distant parts, with frequent rest-houses for travellers. The chief road was named King's Way and this went right across the country from the capital to the north-west frontier. Foreign merchants are especially mentioned and provided for, and seem to have enjoyed a kind of extra-territoriality. It is said that the old Egyptians wrapped their mummies in Indian muslins and dyed their cloth with indigo obtained from India. Some kind of glass has also been discovered in the old remains. Megasthenes, the Greek ambassador, tells us that the Indians loved finery and beauty, and even notes the use of the shoe to add to one's height.

There was a growth of luxury in the Maurya Empire. Life becomes more complicated, specialized, and organized. 'Inns, hostelries, eating-houses, serais, and gaming-houses are evidently numerous; sects and crafts have their meeting places and the latter their public dinners. The business of entertainment provides a livelihood for various classes of dancers, singers, and actors. Even the villages are visited by them, and the author of the Arthashāstra is inclined to discourage the existence of a common hall used for their shows as too great a distraction from the life of the home and the fields. At the same time there are penalties for refusal to assist in organizing public entertainment. The king provides in amphitheatres, constructed for the occasion, dramatic, boxing, and other contests of men and animals, and also spectacles with displays of pictured objects of curiosity...not seldom the streets were lighted for festivals.'* There were also royal processions and hunts.

There were many populous cities in this vast empire, but the chief of them was the capital, Pataliputra, a magnificent city spread out along the banks of the Ganges, where the Sone river meets it (the modern Patna). Megasthenes describes it thus: 'At the junction of this river (Ganges) with another is situated Palibothra, a city of eighty stadia (9·2 miles) in length and fifteen stadia (1·7 miles) in breadth. It is of a shape of a parallelogram and is girded with a wooden wall, pierced with loopholes for the discharge of arrows. It has a ditch in front for defence and for receiving the sewage of the city. This ditch, which encompassed it all round, is 600 feet in breadth and thirty cubits in depth, and the wall is crowned with 570 towers and has four and sixty gates.'

Not only was this great wall made of wood, but most of the houses also. Apparently this was a precaution against earthquakes, as that area was peculiarly liable to them. In 1934 the great Bihar earthquake forcibly reminded us of this fact. Because the houses were of wood, very elaborate precautions against fire were taken. Every householder had to keep ladders, hooks, and vessels full of water.

Pataliputra had a municipality elected by the people. It had thirty members, divided up into six committees of five members each, dealing with industries and handicrafts, deaths and births, manufactures, arrangements for travellers and pilgrims, etc. The whole municipal council looked after finance, sanitation, water supply, public buildings, and gardens.

Buddha's Teaching

Behind these political and economic revolutions that were changing the face of India, there was the ferment of Buddhism and its impact on old-established faiths and its quarrels with vested interests in religion. Far more than the debates and arguments, of which India has always been so enamoured, the personality of a tremendous and radiant being had impressed the people and his memory was fresh in their minds. His message, old and yet very new and original for those immersed in metaphysical subtleties, captured the imagination of the intellectuals; it went deep down into the hearts of the people. 'Go unto all lands,' had said the Buddha to his disciples, 'and preach this gospel. Tell them that

*Dr. F. W. Thomas, in 'The Cambridge History of India', Vol. I, p. 480.

the poor and the lowly, the rich and the high, are all one, and that all castes unite in this religion as do the rivers in the sea.' His message was one of universal benevolence, of love for all. For 'Never in this world does hatred cease by hatred; hatred ceases by love.' And 'Let a man overcome anger by kindness, evil by good.'

It was an ideal of righteousness and self-discipline. 'One may overcome a thousand men in battle, but he who conquers himself is the greatest victor.' 'Not by birth, but by his conduct alone, does a man become a low-caste or a Brahmin.' Even a sinner is not to be condemned, for 'who would willingly use hard speech to those who have done a sinful deed, strewing salt, as it were, upon the wound of their fault?' Victory itself over another leads to unhappy consequences—'Victory breeds hatred, for the conquered is unhappy.'

All this he preached without any religious sanction or any reference to God or another world. He relies on reason and logic and experience and asks people to seek the truth in their own minds. He is reported to have said: 'One must not accept my law from reverence, but first try it as gold is tried by fire.' Ignorance of truth was the cause of all misery. Whether there is a God or an Absolute or not, he does not say. He neither affirms nor denies. Where knowledge is not possible we must suspend judgment. In answer to a question, Buddha is reported to have said: 'If by the absolute is meant something out of relation to all known things, its existence cannot be established by any known reasoning. How can we know that anything unrelated to other things exists at all? The whole universe, as we know it, is a system of relations: we know nothing that is, or can be, unrelated.' So we must limit ourselves to what we can perceive and about which we can have definite knowledge.

So also Buddha gives no clear answer about the existence of the soul. He does not deny it and he does not affirm it. He refuses to discuss this question, which is very remarkable, for the Indian mind of his day was full of the individual soul and the absolute soul, of monism and monotheism and other metaphysical hypotheses. But Buddha set his mind against all forms of metaphysics. He does, however, believe in the permanence of a natural law, of universal causation, of each successive state being determined by pre-existing conditions, of virtue and happiness and vice and suffering being organically related.

We use terms and descriptions in this world of experience and say 'it is' or 'it is not.' Yet neither may be correct when we go behind the superficial aspect of things, and our language may be inadequate to describe what is actually happening. Truth may lie somewhere in the middle of 'is' and 'is not' or beyond them.

The river flows continuously and appears to be the same from moment to moment, yet the waters are ever changing. So also fire. The flame keeps glowing and even maintains its shape and form, yet it is never the same flame and it changes every instant. So everything continually changes and life in all its forms is a stream of becoming. Reality is not something that is permanent and unchanging, but rather a kind of radiant energy, a thing of forces and movements, a succession of sequences. The idea of time is just 'a notion abstracted by mere usage from this or that event.' We cannot say that one thing is the cause of something else for there is no core of permanent being which changes. The essence of a thing is its immanent law of relation to other so-called things. Our bodies and our souls change from moment to moment; they cease to be, and something else, like them and yet different, appears and then passes off. In a sense we are dying all the time and being reborn and this succession gives the appearance of an unbroken identity. It is 'the continuity of an ever-changing identity.' Everything is flux, movement, change.

All this is difficult for our minds to grasp, used as we are to set methods of thinking and of interpreting physical phenomena. Yet it is remarkable how near this philosophy of the Buddha brings us to some of the concepts of modern physics and modern philosophic thought.

Buddha's method was one of psychological analysis and, again, it is surprising to find how deep was his insight into this latest of modern sciences. Man's life was considered and examined without any reference to a permanent self, for even if such a self exists, it is beyond our comprehension. The mind was looked upon as part of the body, a composite of mental forces. The individual thus becomes a bundle of mental states, the self is just a stream of ideas. 'All that we are is the result of what we have thought.'

There is an emphasis on the pain and suffering of life, and the 'Four Noble Truths' which Buddha enunciated deal with this suffering, its cause, the possibility of ending it, and the way to do it. Speaking to his disciples, he is reported to have said: 'and while ye experienced this (sorrow) through long ages, more tears have flowed from you and have been shed by you, while ye strayed and wandered on this pilgrimage (of life), and sorrowed and wept, because that was your portion which ye abhorred, and that which ye loved was not your portion, than all the water which is in the four great oceans.'

Through an ending of this state of suffering is reached 'Nirvana.' As to what Nirvana is, people differ, for it is impossible to describe a transcendental state in our inadequate language and in terms of the concepts of our limited minds. Some say it is just extinction, a blowing out. And yet Buddha is reported to have denied this and to have indicated that it was an intense kind of activity. It was the extinction of false desire, and not just annihilation, but it cannot be described by us except in negative terms.

Buddha's way was the middle path, between the extremes of self-indulgence and self-mortification. From his own experience of mortification of the body, he said that a person who has lost his strength cannot progress along the right path. This middle path was the Aryan eightfold path: right beliefs, right aspirations, right speech, right conduct, right mode of livelihood, right effort, right-mindedness, and right rapture. It is all a question of self-development, not grace. And if a person succeeds in developing along these lines and conquers himself, there can be no defeat for him: 'Not even a god can change into defeat the victory of a man who has vanquished himself.'

Buddha told his disciples what he thought they could understand and live up to. His teaching was not meant to be a full explanation of everything, a complete revelation of all that is. Once, it is said, he took some dry leaves in his hand and asked his favourite disciple, Ananda, to tell him whether there were any other leaves besides those in his hand. Ananda replied: 'The leaves of autumn are falling on all sides, and there are more of them than can be numbered.' Then said the Buddha: 'In like manner I have given you a handful of truths, but besides these there are many thousands of other truths, more than can be numbered.'

The Buddha Story

The Buddha story attracted me even in early boyhood, and I was drawn to the young Siddhārtha who, after many inner struggles and pain and torment, was to develop into the Buddha. Edwin Arnold's 'Light of Asia' became one of my favourite books. In later years, when I travelled about a great deal in my province, I liked to visit the many places connected with the Buddha legend, sometimes making a detour for the purpose. Most of these places lie in my province or not far from it. Here (on the Nepal frontier) Buddha was born, here he wandered, here (at Gaya in Bihar) he sat under the Bodhi tree and gained enlightenment, here he preached his first sermon, here he died.

When I visited countries where Buddhism is still a living and dominant faith, I went to see the temples and the monasteries and met monks and laymen, and tried to make out what Buddhism had done to the people. How had it influenced them, what impress had it left on their minds and faces, how did they react to modern life? There was much I did not like. The rational ethical doctrine had become overlaid with so much verbiage, so much ceremonial, canon law, so much, in spite of the Buddha, metaphysical doctrine and even magic. Despite Buddha's warning, they had deified him, and his huge images, in the temples and elsewhere, looked down upon me and I wondered what he would have thought. Many of the monks were ignorant persons, rather conceited and demanding obeisance, if not to themselves then to their vestments. In each country the national characteristics had imposed themselves on the religion and shaped it according to their distinctive customs and modes of life. All this was natural enough and perhaps an inevitable development.

But I saw much also that I liked. There was an atmosphere of peaceful study and contemplation in some of the monasteries and the schools attached to them. There was a look of peace and calm on the faces of many of the monks, a dignity, a gentleness, an air of detachment and freedom from the cares of the world. Did all this accord with life to-day, or was it a mere escape from it? Could it not be fitted into life's ceaseless struggle and tone down the vulgarity and acquisitiveness and violence that afflict us?

The pessimism of Buddhism did not fit in with my approach to life, nor did the tendency to walk away from life and its problems. I was, somewhere at the back of my mind, a pagan with a pagan's liking for the exuberance of life and nature, and not very much averse to the conflicts that life provides. All that I had experienced, all that I saw around me, painful and distressing as it was, had not dulled that instinct.

Was Buddhism passive and pessimistic? Its interpreters may say so; many of its own devotees may have drawn that meaning. I am not competent to judge of its subtleties and its subsequent complex and metaphysical development. But when I think of the Buddha no such feeling arises in me, nor can I imagine that a religion based mainly on passivity and pessimism could have had such a powerful hold on vast numbers of human beings, among them the most gifted of their kind.

The conception of the Buddha, to which innumerable loving hands have given shape in carven stone and marble and bronze, seems to symbolize the whole spirit of Indian thought, or at least one vital aspect of it. Seated on the lotus flower, calm and impassive, above passion and desire, beyond the storm and strife of this world, so far away he seems, out of reach, unattainable. Yet again we look and behind those still, unmoving features there is a passion and an emotion, strange and more powerful than the passions and emotions we have known. His eyes are closed, but some power of the spirit looks out of them and a vital energy fills the frame. The ages roll by and Buddha seems not so far away after all; his voice whispers in our ears and tells us not to run away from the struggle but, calm-eyed, to face it, and to see in life ever greater opportunities for growth and advancement.

Personality counts to-day as ever, and a person who has impressed himself on the thought of mankind as Buddha has, so that even to-day there is something living and vibrant about the thought of him, must have been a wonderful man—a man who was, as Barth says, the 'finished model of calm and sweet majesty, of infinite tenderness for all that breathes and compassion for all that suffers, of perfect moral freedom and exemption from every prejudice.' And the nation and the race which can produce such a magnificent type must have deep reserves of wisdom and inner strength.

Ashoka

The contacts between India and the western world which Chandragupta Maurya had established continued during the reign of his son, Bindusara. Ambassadors came to the court at Pataliputra from Ptolemy of Egypt and Antiochus, the son and successor of Seleucus Nikator of western Asia. Ashoka, grandson of Chandragupta, added to these contacts, and India became in his time an important international centre, chiefly because of the rapid spread of Buddhism.

Ashoka succeeded to this great empire about 273 B.C. He had previously served as viceroy in the north-western province, of which Taxila, the university centre, was the capital. Already the empire included far the greater part of India and extended right into central Asia. Only the south-east and a part of the south were beyond its sway. The old dream of uniting the whole of India under one supreme government fired Ashoka and forthwith he undertook the conquest of Kalinga on the east coast, which corresponds roughly with modern Orissa and part of Andhra. His armies triumphed in spite of the brave and obstinate resistance of the people of Kalinga. There was a terrible slaughter in this war, and when news of this reached Ashoka he was stricken with remorse and disgusted with war. Unique among the victorious monarchs and captains in history, he decided to abandon warfare in the full tide of victory. The whole of India acknowledged his sway, except for the southern tip, and that tip was his for the taking. But he refrained from any further aggression, and his mind turned, under the influence of Buddha's gospel, to conquests and adventures in other fields. What Ashoka felt and how he acted are known to us in his own words in the numerous edicts he issued, carved in rock and metal. Those edicts, spread out all over India, are still with us, and they conveyed his messages not only to his people but to posterity. In one of the edicts it is said that:

'Kalinga was conquered by His Sacred and Gracious Majesty when he had been consecrated eight years. One hundred and fifty thousand persons were thence carried away as captive, one hundred thousand were there slain, and many times that number died.

'Directly after the annexation of the Kalingas began His Sacred Majesty's zealous protection of the Law of Piety, his love of that Law, and his inculcation of that Law (*Dharma*). Thus arose His Sacred Majesty's remorse for having conquered the Kalingas, because the conquest of a country previously unconquered involves the slaughter, death, and carrying away captive of the people. That is a matter of profound sorrow and regret to His Sacred Majesty.'

No longer, goes on the edict, would Ashoka tolerate any more killing or taking into captivity, not even of a hundredth or a thousandth part of the number killed and made captive in Kalinga. True conquest consists of the conquest of men's hearts by the law of duty or piety, and, adds Ashoka, such real victories had already been won by him, not only in his own dominions, but in distant kingdoms.

The edict further says:

'Moreover, should any one do him wrong, that too must be borne with by His Sacred Majesty, so far as it can possibly be borne with. Even upon the forest folk in his dominions His Sacred Majesty looks kindly and he seeks to make them think aright, for, if he did not, repentance would come upon His Sacred Majesty. For His Sacred Majesty desires that all animate beings should have security, self-control, peace of mind, and joyousness.'

This astonishing ruler, beloved still in India and in many other parts of Asia, devoted himself to the spread of Buddha's teaching, to righteousness and goodwill, and to public works for the good of the people. He was no passive spectator of events, lost in contemplation and self-improvement. He laboured hard at public business and declared that he was always ready for it: 'at all times and at all places, whether I am dining or in the ladies' apartments, in my bedroom or in my closet, in my carriage or in my palace gardens, the official reporters should keep me informed of the people's business....At any hour and at any place work I must for the commonweal.'

His messengers and ambassadors went to Syria, Egypt, Macedonia, Cyrene, and Epirus, conveying his greeting and Buddha's message. They went to central Asia also and to Burma and Siam, and he sent his own son and daugher, Mahendra and Sanghamitra, to Ceylon in the south. Everywhere an appeal was made to the mind and the heart; there was no force or compulsion. Ardent Buddhist as he was, he showed respect and consideration for all other faiths. He prcclaimed in an edict:

'All sects deserve reverence for one reason or another. By thus acting a man exalts his own sect and at the same time does service to the sects of other people.'

Buddhism spread rapidly in India from Kashmir to Ceylon. It penetrated into Nepal and later reached Tibet and China and Mongolia. In India, one of the consequences of this was the growth of vegetarianism and abstention from alcoholic drinks. Till then both Brahmins and Kshatriyas often ate meat and took wine. Animal sacrifice was forbidden.

Because of the growth of foreign contacts and missionary enterprises, trade between India and other countries must have also grown. We have records of an Indian colony in Khotan (now Sinkiang, Central Asia). The Indian universities, especially Taxila, also attracted more students from abroad.

Ashoka was a great builder and it has been suggested that he employed foreign craftsmen to assist in building some of his huge structures. This inference is drawn from the designs of some clustered columns which remind one of Persepolis. But even in those early sculptures and other remains the characteristically Indian art tradition is visible.

Ashoka's famous many-pillared hall in his palace at Pataliputra was partly dug out by archæologists about thirty years ago. Dr. Spooner, of the Archaeological Department of India, in his official report, said that this was 'in an almost incredible state of preservation, the logs which formed it being as smooth and perfect as the day they were laid, more than two thousand years ago.' He says further that the 'marvellous preservation of the ancient wood, whose edges were so perfect that the very lines of jointure were indistinguishable, evoked admiration of all who witnessed the experiment. The whole was built with a precision and reasoned care that could not possibly be excelled to-day.... In short, the construction was absolute perfection of such work.

In other excavated buildings also in different parts of the country wooden logs and rafters have been found in an excellent state of preservation. This would be surprising anywhere, but in India it is more so, for the climate wears them away and all manner of insects eat them up. There must have been some special treatment of the wood; what this was is still, I believe, a mystery.

Between Pataliputra (Patna) and Gaya lie the impressive remains of Nālanda university, which was to become famous in later days. It is not clear when this began functioning and there are no records of it in Ashoka's time.

Ashoka died in 232 B.C., after ruling strenuously for forty-one years. Of him H. G. Wells says in his 'Outline of History': 'Amidst the tens of thousands of names of monarchs that crowd the columns of history, their majesties and graciousnesses and serenities and royal highnesses and the like, the name of Ashoka shines, and shines almost alone, a star. From the Volga to Japan his name is still honoured. China, Tibet, and even India, though it has left his doctrine, preserve the tradition of his greatness. More living men cherish his memory to-day than have ever heard the names of Constantine or Charlemagne.'

CHAPTER FIVE

THROUGH THE AGES

Nationalism and Imperialism under the Guptas

THE MAURYA EMPIRE FADED AWAY AND GAVE PLACE TO THE SUNGA dynasty, which ruled over a much smaller area. In the south great states were rising, and in the north the Bactrians, or Indo-Greeks, were spreading out from Kabul to the Punjab. Under Menander they threatened Pataliputra itself but were defeated and repelled. Menander himself succumbed to the spirit and atmosphere of India and became a Buddhist, a famous one, known as King Milinda, popular in Buddhist legend and regarded almost as a saint. From the fusion of Indian and Greek cultures rose the Græco-Buddhist art of Gandhara, the region covering Afghanistan and the frontier.

There is a granite pillar called the Heliodorus column, dating from the first century B.C., at Besnagar, near Sanchi in Central India, bearing an inscription in Sanskrit. This gives us a glimpse of the process of Indianization of the Greeks who had come to the frontier, and their absorption of Indian culture. The inscription has been translated thus: 'This Garuda column of Vasudeva (Vishnu), the God of gods, was erected by Heliodorus, a worshipper of Vishnu, the son of Dion, and an inhabitant of Taxila, who came as Greek ambassador from the great King Antialcidas to King Kashiputra Bhagabhadra, the saviour, then reigning in the fourteenth year of his kingship.'

'Three immortal precepts, when practised well, lead to heaven —self-restraint, self-sacrifice (charity), conscientiousness.'

In Central Asia the Shakas or Scythians (Seistan=Shakasthan) had established themselves in the Oxus Valley. The Yueh Chih, coming from further east, drove them out and pushed them into North India. These Shakas became converts to Buddhism and Hinduism. Among the Yueh Chih, one of the clans, the Kushans, established their supremacy and then extended their sway over Northern India. They defeated the Shakas and pushed them still further south, the Shakas going to Kathiawad and the Deccan. The Kushans thereupon established an extensive and durable empire over the whole of North India and a great part of Central Asia. Some of them became converts to the Hindu faith, but most of them became Buddhists, and their most famous king, Kanishka, is also one of the heroes of Buddhist legend, which records his great deeds and public works. Buddhist though he was, it appears that the state religion was a mixed affair to which even Zoroastrianism had contributed. This borderland state, called the Kushan Empire, with its seat near modern Peshawar, and the old university of Taxila near, by, became the meeting place of men from many nations. There the Indians met the Scythians, the Yueh Chih, the Iranians, the Bactrian Greeks, the Turks, and the Chinese, and the various cultures reacted on each other. A vigorous school of sculpture and painting arose as a result of their interactions. It was during this period that, historically, the first contacts took place between China and India, and a Chinese embassy came to India in 64 A.C. Minor but very welcome gifts of China to India at that time were the peach and the pear trees. Right on the borders of the Gobi Desert, at Turfan and Kucha, rose fascinating amalgams of Indian, Chinese, and Iranian cultures.

During the Kushan period a great schism divided Buddhism into two sections—the Mahayana and the Hinayana—and controversy raged between them and, as has been India's way, the issue was put to debate in great assemblies, to which representatives came from all over the country. Kashmir was situated near the centre of the empire and was full of this debate and of cultural activities. One name stands out in this controversy, that of Nagarjuna, who lived in the first century A.C. He was a towering personality, great in Buddhist scholarship and Indian philosophy, and it was largely because of him that Mahayana triumphed in India. It was the Mahayana doctrine that spread to China, while Ceylon and Burma adhered to Hinayana.

The Kushans had Indianized themselves and had become patrons of Indian culture; yet an undercurrent of nationalist reistance to their rule continued, and when, later, fresh tribes poured into India, this nationalist and anti-foreign movement took shape at the beginning of the fourth century A.C. Another great ruler, also named Chandragupta, drove out the new intruders and established a powerful and widespread empire.

Thus began the age of the imperial Guptas in 320 A.C. which produced a remarkable succession of great rulers, successful in war and in the arts of peace. Repeated invasions had produced a strong anti-foreign feeling and the old Brahmin-Kshatriya element in the country was forced to think in terms of defence both of their homeland and their culture. The foreign elements which had been absorbed were accepted, but all new-comers met with a vigorous resitance, and an attempt was made to build up a homogenous state based on old Brahminic ideals. But the old self-assurance was going and these ideals began to develop a rigidity which was foreign to their nature. India seemed to draw into her shell, both physically and mentally.

Yet that shell was deep enough and wide enough. Previously, in the ages since the Aryans had come down to what they called Aryavarta or Bharatvarsha, the problem that faced India was to produce a synthesis between this new race and culture and the old race and civilization of the land. To that the mind of India devoted itself and it produced an enduring solution built on the strong foundations of a joint Indo-Aryan culture. Other foreign elements came and were absorbed. They made little difference. Though India had many contacts with other countries through trade and otherwise, essentially she was absorbed in herself and paid little attention to what happened elsewhere. But now periodic invasion by strange peoples with strange customs had shaken her up and she could no longer ignore these eruptions, which not only broke up her political structure but endangered her cultural ideals and social structure also. The reaction was essentially a nationalist one, with the strength as well as the narrowness of nationalism. That mixture of religion and philosophy, history and tradition, custom and social structure, which in its wide fold included almost every aspect of the life of India, and which might be called Brahminism or (to use a later word) Hinduism, became the symbol of nationalism. It was indeed a national religion, with its appeal to all those deep instincts, racial and cultural, which form the basis everywhere of nationalism to-day. Buddhism, child of Indian thought, had its nationalist background also. India was to it the holy land where Buddha had lived and preached and died, where famous scholars and saints had spread the faith. But Buddhism was essentially international, a world religion, and as it developed and spread it became increasingly so. Thus it was natural for the old Brahminic faith to become the symbol again and again of nationalist revivals.

That faith and philosophy were tolerant and chivalrous to the various religions and racial elements in India, and they still continued to absorb them into their wide-flung structure, but they became increasingly aggressive to the outsider and sought to protect themselves against his impact. In doing so, the spirit of nationalism they had roused often took on the semblance of imperialism as it frequently does when it grows in strength. The age of the Guptas, enlightened, vigorous, highly cultured, and full of vitality as it was, rapidly developed these imperialistic tendencies. One of its great rulers, Samudragupta, has been called the Indian Napoleon. From a literary and artistic point of view it was a brilliant. period.

From early in the fourth century onwards for about a hundred and fifty years the Guptas ruled over a powerful and prosperous state in the north. For almost another century and a half their successors continued but they were on the defensive now and the empire shrank and became smaller and smaller. New invaders from Central Asia were pouring into India and attacking them. These were the White Huns, as they are called, who ravaged the land, as under Attila they were ravaging Europe. Their barbarous behaviour and fiendish cruelty at last roused the people, and a united attack by a confederacy under Yashovarman was made on them. The Hun power was broken and their chief, Mihiragula, was made a prisoner. But the descendant of the Guptas, Baladitya, in accordance with his country's customs, treated him with generosity and allowed him to leave India. Mihiragula responded to this treatment by returning later and making a treacherous attack on his benefactor.

But the Hun rule in Northern India was of brief duration— about half a century. Many of them remained, however, in the country as petty chiefs giving trouble occasionally and being absorbed into the sea of Indian humanity. Some of these chiefs became aggressive early in the seventh century A.C. They were crushed by the King of Kanauj, Harshavardhana, who thereafter built up a powerful state right across Northern and Central India. He was an ardent Buddhist but his Buddhism was of the Mahāyāna variety which was akin in many ways to Hinduism. He encouraged both Buddhism and Hinduism. It was in his time that the famous Chinese pilgrim Hsuan Tsang (or Yuan Chwang) came to India (in 629 A.C.). Harshavardhana was a poet and dramatist and he gathered round his court many artists and poets, making his capital Ujjayini, a famous centre of cultural activities. Harsha died in 648 A.C., just about the time when Islam was emerging from the deserts of Arabia, to spread out rapidly across Africa and Asia.

South India

In South India for more than 1,000 years after the Maurya Empire had shrunk and finally ceased to be, great states flourished. The Andhras had defeated the Shakas and were later the contemporaries of the Kushans; then came the Chalukyan Empire in the west to be followed by the Rashtrakutas. Further south were the Pallavas who were mainly responsible for the colonizing expeditions from India. Later came the Chola Empire which spread right across the peninsula and conquered Ceylon and Southern Burma. The last great Chola ruler, Rajendra, died in 1044 A.C.

Southern India was especially noted for its fine products and its trade by sea. They were sea-powers and their ships carried merchandise to distant countries. Colonies of Greeks lived there and Roman coins have also been found. The Chalukyan kingdom exchanged ambassadors with the Sassanid rulers of Persia.

The repeated invasions of North India did not affect the South directly. Indirectly they led to many people from the north migrating to the south and these included builders and craftsmen and artisans. The south thus became a centre of the old artistic traditions while the north was more affected by new currents which the invaders brought with them. This process was accelerated in later centuries and the south became the stronghold of Hindu orthodoxy.

Peaceful Development and Methods of Warfare

A brief account of repeated invasions and of empire succeeding empire is likely to convey a very wrong idea of what was taking place in India. It must be remembered that the period dealt with covers 1,000 years or more and the country enjoyed long stretches of peaceful and orderly government.

The Mauryas, the Kushans, the Guptas, and, in the south, the Andhras, Chalukyas, Rashtrakutas and others, each lasted for two or three hundred years—longer, as a rule, than the British Empire has so far lasted in India. Nearly all these were indigenous dynasties and even those, like the Kushans, who came from across the northern border, soon adapted themselves to this country and its cultural traditions and functioned as Indian rulers with their roots in India. There were frontier forays and occasional conflicts between adjoining states, but the general conditions of the country was one of peaceful government, and the rulers took especial pride in encouraging artistic and cultural activities. These activities crossed state boundaries, for the cultural and literary background was the same throughout India. Every religious or philosophic controversy immediately spread and was debated all over the north and south.

Even when there was war between two states, or there was an internal political revolution, there was relatively little interference with the activities of the mass of the people. Records have been found of agreements between the warring rulers and the heads of village self-governing communities, promising not to injure the harvests in any way and to give compensation for any injury unintentionally caused to the land. This could not apply, of course, to invading armies from abroad, nor probably could it apply to any real struggle for power.

The old Indo-Aryan theory of warfare strictly laid down that no illegitimate methods were to be employed and a war for a righteous cause must be righteously conducted. How far the practice fitted in with the theory is another matter. The use of poisoned arrows was forbidden, so also concealed weapons, or the killing of those who were asleep or who came as fugitives or suppliants. It was declared that there should be no destruction of fine buildings. But this view was already undergoing a change in Chānakya's time and he approves of more destructive and deceptive methods, if these are considered essential for the defeat of the enemy.

It is interesting to note that Chānakya in his Arthashāstra, in discussing weapons of warfare, mentions machines which can destroy a hundred persons at one time and also some kind of explosives. He also refers to trench warfare. What all this meant it is not possible to say now. Probably the reference is to some traditional stories of magical exploits. There is no ground for thinking that gunpowder is meant.

India has had many distressful periods in the course of her long history, when she was ravaged by fire and sword or by famine, and internal order collapsed. Yet a broad survey of this history appears to indicate that she had a far more peaceful and orderly existence for long periods of time at a stretch than Europe has had. And this applies also to the centuries following the Turkish and Afghan invasions, right up to the time when the Moghul Empire was breaking up. The notion that the Pax Britannica brought peace and order for the first time to India is one of the most extraordinary of delusions. It is true that when British rule was established in India the country was at her lowest ebb and there was a break-up of the political and economic structure. That indeed was one of the reasons why that rule was established.

India's Urge to Freedom

The East bowed low before the blast
In patient, deep disdain;
She let the legions thunder past,
And plunged in thought again.

So says the poet and his lines are often quoted. It is true that the east, or at any rate that part of it which is called India, has been enamoured of thinking, often of thinking about matters which to those who consider themselves practical men seem absurd and pointless. She has always honoured thought and the men of thought, the highbrows, and has refused to consider the

141

men of the sword or the possessors of money as superior to them. Even in her days of degradation, she has clung to thought and found some comfort in it.

But it is not true that India has ever bowed patiently before the blast or been indifferent to the passage of foreign legions. Always she has resisted them, often successfully, sometimes unsuccessfully, and even when she failed for the time being, she has remembered and prepared herself for the next attempt. Her method has been two-fold: to fight them and drive them out, and to absorb those who could not be driven away. She resisted, with considerable success, Alexander's legions, and immediately after his death drove out the Greek garrisons in the north. Later she absorbed the Indo-Greeks and the Indo-Scythians and ultimately again established a national hegemony. She fought the Huns for generations and drove them out; such as remained being absorbed. When the Arabs came they stopped near the Indus. The Turks and Afghans spread further only gradually. It took them several centuries to establish themselves firmly on the throne of Delhi. It was a continuous, long drawn-out conflict and, while this struggle was going on, the other process of absorption and Indianization was also at work, ending in the invaders becoming as much Indian as anyone else. Akbar became the great representative of the old Indian ideal of a synthesis of differing elements and their fusion into a common nationality. He indentified himself with India, and India took to him although he was a newcomer; because of this he built well and laid the foundations of a splendid empire. So long as his successors kept in line with this policy and with the genius of the nation, their empire endured. When they broke away and opposed the whole drift of national development, they weakened and their empire went to pieces. New movements arose, narrow in outlook but representing a resurgent nationalism, and though they were not strong enough to build permanently, they were capable of destroying the empire of the Moghuls. They were successful for a time, but they looked too much to the past and thought in terms of reviving it. They did not realize that much had happened which they could not ignore or pass by, that the past can never take the place of the present, that even that present in the India of their day was one of stagnation and decay. It had lost touch with the changing world and left India far behind. They did not appreciate that a new and vital world was arising in the west, based on a new outlook and on new techniques, and a new power, the British, represented that new world of which they were so ignorant. The British triumphed, but hardly had they established themselves in the north when the great mutiny broke out and developed with a war of independence, and nearly put an end to British rule.

The urge to freedom, to independence, has always been there, and the refusal to submit to alien domination.

Progress Versus Security

We have been an exclusive people, proud of our past and of our heritage and trying to build walls and barriers to preserve it. Yet in spite of our race-consciousness and the growing rigidity of caste, we have, like others who take such pride in the purity of their racial stock, developed into a strange mixture of races —Aryan, Dravidian, Turanian, Semitic, and Mongolian. The Aryans came here in repeated waves and mixed with the Dravidians; they were followed in the course of thousands of years by successive waves of other migratory peoples and tribes: the Medians, Iranians, Greeks, Bactrians, Parthians, Shakas or Scythians, Kushans or the Yueh Chih, Turks, Turco-Mongols, and others who came in large or small groups and found a home in India. 'Fierce and warlike tribes,' says Dodwell in his 'India,' 'again and again, invaded its (India's) northern plains, overthrew its princes, captured and laid waste its cities, set up new states and built new capitals of their own and then vanished into the great tide of humanity, leaving to their descendants nothing but a swiftly diluted strain of alien blood and a few shreds of alien custom that were soon transformed into something cognate with their overmastering surroundings.'

To what were these overmastering surroundings due? Partly to the influence of geography and climate, to the very air of India. But much more so, surely, to some powerful impulse, some tremendous urge, or idea of the significance of life, that was impressed upon the subconscious mind of India when she was fresh and young at the very dawn of her history. That impress was strong enough to persist and to affect all those who came into contact with her, and thus to absorb them into her fold, howsoever they differed. Was this impulse, this idea, the vital spark that lighted up the civilization that grew up in this country and, in varying degrees, continued to influence its people through historical ages?

It seems absurd and presumptuous to talk of an impulse, or an idea of life, underlying the growth of Indian civilization. Even the life of an individual draws sustenance from a hundred sources; much more complicated is the life of a nation or of a civilization. There are myriad ideas that float about like flotsam and jetsam on the surface of India, and many of them are mutually antagonistic. It is easy to pick out any group of them to justify a particular thesis; equally easy to choose another group to demolish it. This is, to some extent, possible everywhere; in

an old and big country like India, with so much of the dead clinging on to the living, it is peculiarly easy. There is also obvious
danger in simple classifications of very complex phenomena.
There are very seldom sharp contrasts in the evolution of practice
and thought; each thought runs into another, and even ideas
keeping their outer form change their inner contents; or they
frequently lag behind a changing world and become a drag
upon it.

We have been changing continually throughout the ages and
at no period were we the same as in the one preceding it. To-day,
racially and culturally, we are very different from what we
were; and all around me, in India as elsewhere, I see change marching ahead with a giant's stride. Yet I cannot get over the fact
that Indian and Chinese civilizations have shown an extraordinary staying power and adaptability and, in spite of many changes and crises, have succeeded, for an enormous span of years,
in preserving their basic identity. They could not have done so
unless they were in harmony with life and nature. Whatever it
was that kept them to a large extent to their ancient moorings,
whether it was good or bad or a mixture of the two, it was a thing
of power or it could not have survived for so long. Possibly it exhausted its utility long ago and has been a drag and a hindrance
ever since, or it may be that the accretions of later ages have
smothered the good in it and only the empty shell of the fossil
remains.

There is perhaps a certain conflict always between the idea
of progress and that of security and stability. The two do not
fit in, the former wants change, the latter a safe unchanging
haven and a continuation of things as they are. The idea of
progress is modern and relatively new even in the west; the
ancient and mediæval civilizations thought far more in terms
of a golden past and of subsequent decay. In India also the past
has always been glorified. The civilization that was built up here
was essentially based on stability and security, and from this
point of view it was far more successful than any that arose in
the west. The social structure, based on the caste system and
joint families, served this purpose and was successful in providing
social security for the group and a kind of insurance for the
individual who by reason of age, infirmity, or any other incapacity,
was unable to provide for himself. Such an arrangement, while
favouring the weak, hinders, to some extent, the strong. It
encourages the average type at the cost of the abnormal, the bad
or the gifted. It levels up or down and individualism has less play
in it. It is interesting to note that while Indian philosophy is
highly individualistic and deals almost entirely with the individual's
growth to some kind of inner perfection, the Indian social structure

144

was communal and paid attention to groups only. The individual was allowed perfect freedom to think and believe what he liked, but he had to conform strictly to social and communal usage.

With all this conformity there was a great deal of flexibility also in the group as a whole and there was no law or social rule that could not change by custom. Also new groups could have their own customs, beliefs, and practices and yet be considered members of the larger social group. It was this flexibility and adaptability that helped in the absorption of foreign elements. Behind it all were some basic ethical doctrines and a philosophic approach to life and a tolerance of other people's ways.

So long as stability and security were the chief ends in view, this structure functioned more or less successfully, and even when economic changes undermined it, there was a process of adaptation and it continued. The real challenge to it came from the new dynamic conception of social progress which could not be fitted into the old static ideas. It is this conception that is uprooting old-established systems in the east as it has done in the west. In the west while progress is still the dominant note, there is a growing demand for security. In India the very lack of security has forced people out of their old ruts and made them think in terms of a progress that will give more security.

In ancient and mediæval India, however, there was no such challenge of progress. But the necessity for change and continuous adaptation was recognized and hence grew a passion for synthesis. It was a synthesis not only of the various elements that came into India but also an attempt at a synthesis between the outer and inner life of the individual, between man and nature. There were no such wide gaps and cleavages as seem to exist to-day. This common cultural background created India and gave it an impress of unity in spite of its diversity. At the root of the political structure was the self-governing village system, which endured at the base while kings came and went. Fresh migrations from outside and invaders merely ruffled the surface of this structure without touching those roots. The power of the state, however despotic in appearance, was curbed in a hundred ways by customary and constitutional restraints, and no ruler could easily interfere with the rights and privileges of the village community. These customary rights and privileges ensured a measure of freedom both for the community and the individual.

Among the people of India to-day none are more typically Indian or prouder of Indian culture and tradition than the Rajputs. Their heroic deeds in the past have become a living part of that very tradition. Yet many of the Rajputs are said to be descended from the Indo-Scythians, and some even from the Huns who came to India. There is no sturdier or finer peasant in India than the Jat, wedded to the soil and brooking no interference with his land. He also has a Scythian origin. And so too the Kathi, the tall, handsome peasant of Kathiawad. The racial origins of some of our people can be traced back with a certain definiteness, of others it is not possible to do so. But whatever the origin might have been, all of them have become distinctively Indian, participating jointly with others in India's culture and looking back on her past traditions as their own.

It would seem that every outside element that has come to India and been absorbed by India, has given something to India and taken much from her; it has contributed to its own and to India's strength. But where it has kept apart, or been unable to become a sharer and participant in India's life, and her rich and diverse culture, it has had no lasting influence, and has ultimately faded away, sometimes injuring itself and India in the process.

India and Iran

Among the many peoples and races who have come in contact with and influenced India's life and culture, the oldest and most persistent have been the Iranians. Indeed the relationship precedes even the beginnings of Indo-Aryan civilization, for it was out of some common stock that the Indo-Aryans and the ancient Iranians diverged and took their different ways. Racially connected, their old religions and languages also had a common background. The Vedic religion had much in common with Zoroastrianism, and Vedic Sanskrit and the old Pahlavi, the language of the Avesta, closely resemble each other. Classical Sanskrit and Persian developed separately but many of their root-words were common, as some are common to all the Aryan languages. The two languages, and even more so their art and culture, were influenced by their respective environments. Persian art appears to be intimately connected with the soil and scenery of Iran, and to that probably is due the persistence of Iran's artistic tradition. So also the Indo-Aryan artistic tradition and ideals grew out of the snow-covered mountains, rich forests, and great rivers of north India.

Iran, like India, was strong enough in her cultural foundations to influence even her invaders and often to absorb them. The Arabs, who conquered Iran in the seventh century A.C., soon succumbed to this influence and, in place of their simple desert ways, adopted the sophisticated culture of Iran. The Persian language, like French in Europe, became the language of cultured people across wide stretches of Asia. Iranian art and culture spread from Constantinople in the west right up to the edge of the Gobi Desert.

In India this Iranian influence was continuous, and during

the Afghan and Moghul periods in India, Persian was the court language of the country. This lasted right up to the beginning of the British period. All the modern Indian languages are full of Persian words. This was natural enough for the languages descended from the Sanskrit, and more especially for Hindustani, which itself is a mixed product, but even the Dravidian languages of the south have been influenced by Persian. India has produced in the past some brilliant poets in the Persian language, and even to-day there are many fine scholars of Persian, both Hindu and Moslem.

There seems to be little doubt that the Indus Valley civilization had some contacts with the contemporaneous civilizations of Iran and Mesopotamia. There is a striking similarity between some of the designs and seals. There is also some evidence to show that there were contacts between Iran and India in the pre-Achæmian period. India is mentioned in the Avesta and there is also some kind of a description of north India in it. In the Rig Veda there are references to Persia—the Persians were called 'Parshavas' and later 'Parasikas,' from which the modern word 'Parsi' is derived. The Parthians were referred to as 'Parthavas.' Iran and north India were thus traditionally interested in each other from the most ancient times, prior to the Achæmian dynasty. With Cyrus the Great, king of kings, we have record of further contacts. Cyrus reached the borderlands of India, probably Kabul and Baluchistan. In the sixth century B.C. the Persian Empire under Darius stretched right up to north-west India, including Sind and probably part of western Punjab. That period is sometimes referred to as the Zoroastrian period of Indian history and its influence must have been widespread. Sun worship was encouraged.

The Indian province of Darius was the richest in his empire and the most populous. Sind then must have been very different from the desiccated desert land of recent times. Herodotus tells us of the wealth and density of the Indian population and of the tribute paid to Darius: 'The population of the Indians is by far the greatest of all the people that we know; and they paid tribute proportionately larger than all the rest—(the sum of) 360 talents of gold dust' (equivalent to over a million pounds sterling). Herodotus also mentions the Indian contingent in the Persian armies consisting of infantry, cavalry, and chariots. Later, elephants are mentioned.

From a period prior to the seventh century B.C., and for ages afterwards, there is some evidence of relations between Persia and India through trade, especially early commerce between India and Babylon, which it is believed, was largely via the Persian Gulf.* From the sixth century onwards direct contacts

*Prof. A. V. Willaims Jackson, in 'The Cambridge History of India,' Vol I, p. 329.

grew through the campaigns of Cyrus and Darius. After Alexander's conquest Iran was for many centuries under Greek rule. Contacts with India continued and Ashoka's buildings, it is said, were influenced by the architecture of Persepolis. The Græco-Buddhist art that developed in north-west India and Afghanistan has also the touch of Iran. During the Gupta period in India, in the fourth and fifth centuries A.C., which is noted for its artistic and cultural activities, contacts with Iran continued.

The borderland areas of Kabul, Kandahar, and Seistan, which were often politically parts of India, were the meeting place of Indians and Iranians. In later Parthian times they were called 'White India.' Referring to these areas, the French savant, James Darmesteler, says: 'Hindu civilization prevailed in those parts, which in fact in the two centuries before and after Christ were known as White India, and remained more Indian than Iranian till the Mussulman conquest.'

In the north, trade and travellers came overland to India. South India depended more on the sea and sea-borne trade connected it with other countries. There is record of an exchange of ambassadors between a southern kingdom and the Persia of the Sassanids.

The Turkish, Afghan, and Moghul conquests of India resulted in a rapid development of India's contacts with central and western Asia. In the fifteenth century (just about the time of the European Renaissance) the Timurid Renaissance was flowering in Samarkand and Bokhara, powerfully influenced by Iran. Babar, himself a prince of the Timurid line, came out of this *milieu* and established himself on the throne of Delhi. That was early in the sixteenth century when Iran was having, under the Safavis, a brilliant artistic revival—a period known as the golden age of Persian art. It was to the Safavi king that Babar's son, Humayun, went for refuge, and it was with his help that he came back to India. The Moghul rulers of India kept up the closest of contacts with Iran and there was a stream of scholars and artists coming over the frontier to seek fame and fortune at the brilliant court of the Great Moghul.

A new architecture developed in India, a combination of Indian ideals and Persian inspiration, and Delhi and Agra were covered with noble and beautiful buildings. Of the most famous of these, the Taj Mahal, M. Grousset, the French savant, said that it is 'the soul of Iran incarnate in the body of India.'

Few people have been more closely related in origin and throughout history than the people of India and the people of Iran. Unfortunately the last memory we have of this long, intimate and honourable association is that of Nadir Shah's invasion, a brief but terrible visitation two hundred years ago.

Then came the British and they barred all the doors and stopped all the routes that connected us with our neighbours in Asia. New routes were opened across the seas which brought us nearer to Europe, and more particularly England, but there were to be no further contacts overland between India and Iran and central Asia and China till, in the present age, the development of the airways made us renew the old companionship. This sudden isolation from the rest of Asia has been one of the most remarkable and unfortunate consequences of British rule in India.*

There has, however, been one continuing bond, not with Iran of modern times but with old Iran. Thirteen hundred years ago, when Islam came to Iran, some hundreds or thousands of the followers of the old Zoroastrian faith migrated to India. They found a welcome here and settled down on the western coast, following their faith and customs without being interferred with and without interfering with others. It is remarkable how the Parsis, as they have been called, have quietly and unostentatiously fitted into India, made it their home, and yet kept quite apart as a small community, tenaciously holding on to their old customs. Intermarriage outside the fold of the community was not allowed and there have been very few instances of it. This in itself did not occasion any surprise in India, as it was usual here for people to marry within their own caste. Their growth in numbers has been very slow and even now their total number is about one hundred thousand. They have prospered in business and many of them are the leaders of industry in India. They have had practically no contacts with Iran and are completely Indian, and yet they hold on to their old traditions and the memories of their ancient homeland.

In Iran there has recently been a strong tendency to look back to the old civilization of pre-Islamic days. This has nothing to do with religion; it is cultural and nationalistic, seeking and taking pride in the long and persistent cultural tradition of Iran.

World developments and common interests are forcing Asiatic countries to look at each other again. The period of European domination is passed over as a bad dream and memories of long ago remind them of old friendships and common adventures.

*Prof. E. J. Rapson writes: 'The power which has succeeded in welding all the subordinate ruling powers into one great system of government is essentially naval; and since it controls the sea-ways, it has been forced in the interests of security, to close the land-ways. This has been the object of British policy in regard to the countries which lie on the frontiers of the Indian Empire—Afghanistan, Baluchistan, and Burma. Political isolation has thus followed as a necessary consequence of political unity. But it must be remembered that this political isolation is a recent and an entirely novel feature in the history of India. It is the great landmark which separates the present from the past.' ('The Cambridge History of India,' Vol. I, p. 52.)

There can be no doubt that in the near future India will draw closer to Iran, as she is doing to China.

Two months ago the leader of an Iranian Cultural Mission to India said in the city of Allahadabad. 'The Iranians and Indians are like two brothers, who, according to a Persian legend, had got separated from each other, one going east and the other to the west. Their families had forgotten all about each other and the only thing that remained in common between them were the snatches of a few old tunes which they still played on their flutes. It was through these tunes that, after a lapse of centuries, the two families recognized each other and were reunited. So also we come to India to play on our flutes our age-old songs, so that, hearing them, our Indian cousins may recognize us as their own and become reunited with their Iranian cousins.'

India and Greece

Ancient Greece is supposed to be the fountain-head of European civilization and much has been written about the fundamental difference between the Orient and the Occident. I do not understand this; a great deal of it seems to me to be vague and unscientific, without much basis in fact. Till recently many European thinkers imagined that everything that was worth-while had its origin in Greece or Rome. Sir Henry Maine has said somewhere that except the blind forces of nature, nothing moves in this world which is not originally Greek. European classical scholars, deeply learned in Greek and Latin lore, knew very little about India and China. Yet Professor E. R. Dodds emphasizes the 'Oriental background against which Greek culture ro e, and from which it was never completely isolated save in the minds of classical scholars.'

Scholarship in Europe was necessarily limited for a long time to Greek, Hebrew, and Latin, and the picture of the world that grew out of it was of the Mediterranean world. The basic idea was not essentially different from that of the old Romans, though inevitably many changes and adaptations had to be made to it. That idea not only governed the conceptions of history and geopolitics and the development of culture and civilization, but also came in the way of scientific progress. Plato and Aristotle dominated the mind. Even when some knowledge of what the peoples of Asia had done in the past soaked into the European mind, it was not willingly accepted. There was an unconscious resistance to it, an attempt to fit it somehow into the previous picture. If scholars believed so, much more so did the unread crowd believe in some essential difference between the east and the west. The industrialization of Europe and the consequent material progress impressed this difference still further on the popular mind, and by an odd process of rationalization ancient Greece became the father or mother of modern Europe and America. Additional knowledge of the past of the world shook these conclusions in the minds of a few thinkers, but so far as the mass of the people were concerned, intellectuals and non-intellectuals, the centuries-old ideas continued, phantoms floating about in the upper layer of their consciousness and fading away into the landscape they had fashioned for themselves.

I do not understand the use of the words Orient and Occident, except in the sense that Europe and America are highly industrialized and Asia is backward in this respect. This industrialization is something new in the world's history, and it has changed and continues to change the world more than anything else has done. There is no organic connection between Hellenic civilization and modern European and American civilization. The modern notion that the really important thing is to be comfortable is entirely foreign to the ideas underlying Greek or any other ancient literature. Greeks and Indians and Chinese and Iranians were always seeking a religion and a philosophy of life which affected all their activities and which were intended to produce an equilibrium and a sense of harmony. This ideal emerges in every aspect of life—in literature, art, and institutions—and it produces a sense of proportion and completeness. Probably these impressions are not wholly justified and the actual conditions of life may have been very different. But even so, it is important to remember how far removed are modern Europe and America from the whole approach and outlook of the Greeks, whom they praise so much in their leisure moments, and with whom they seek some distant contacts, in order to satisfy some inner yearning of their hearts, or find some oasis in the harsh and fiery deserts of modern existence.

Every country and people in the East and the West has had an individuality, a message, and has attempted to solve life's problems each in its own way. Greece is something definite, superb in its own way; so is India, so is China, so is Iran. Ancient India and ancient Greece were different from each other and yet they were akin, just as ancient India and ancient China had kinship in thought, in spite of great differences. They all had the same broad, tolerant, pagan outlook, joy in life and in the surprising beauty and infinite variety of nature, love of art, and the wisdom that comes from the accumulated experience of an old race. Each of them developed in accordance with its racial genius, influenced by its natural environment, and emphasized some one aspect of life more than others. This emphasis varied. The Greeks, as a race, may have lived more in the present and found joy and harmony in the beauty they saw around them or which they themselves created. The Indians found this joy and harmony also in the present, but, at the same time, their eyes were turned towards deeper knowledge and their minds trafficked with strange questions. The Chinese, fully aware of these questions and their mystery, in their wisdom avoided entanglement with them. In their different ways each tried to express the fullness and beauty of life. History has shown that India and China had stronger foundations and greater staying power; they have thus far survived, though they have been badly shaken and have greatly deteriorated, and the future is obscure.

Old Greece, for all its brilliance, had a short life; it did not survive except in its splendid achievements, its influence on succeeding cultures, and the memory of that short bright day of abundant life. Perhaps because it was too much engrossed in the present, it became the past.

India is far nearer in spirit and outlook to the old Greece than the nations of Europe are to-day, although they call themselves children of the Hellenic spirit. We are apt to forget this because we have inherited fixed concepts which prevent reasoned thought. India, it is said, is religious, philosophical, speculative, metaphysical, unconcerned with this world, and lost in dreams of the beyond and the hereafter. So we are told, and perhaps those who tell us so would like India to remain plunged in thought and entangled in speculation, so that they might possess this world and the fullness thereof, unhindered by these thinkers, and take their joy of it. Yes, India has been all this but also much more than this. She has known the innocence and insouciance of childhood, the passion and abandon of youth, and the ripe wisdom of maturity that comes from long experience of pain and pleasure; and over and over again she has renewed her childhood and youth and age. The tremendous inertia of age and size have weighed her down, degrading custom and evil practice have eaten into her, many a parasite has clung to her and sucked her blood, but behind all this lie the strength of ages and the sub-conscious wisdom of an ancient race. For we are very old, and trackless centuries whisper in our ears; yet we have known how to regain our youth again and again, though the memory and dreams of those past ages endure with us.

It is not some secret doctrine or esoteric knowledge that has kept India vital and going through these long ages, but a tender humanity, a varied and tolerant culture, and a deep understanding of life and its mysterious ways. Her abundant vitality flows out from age to age in her magnificent literature and art, though we have only a small part of this with us and much lies hidden still or has been destroyed by nature or man's vandalism. The *Trimurti*, in the Elephanta caves, might well be the many-faced statue of India herself, powerful, with compelling eyes, full of deep knowledge and understanding, looking down upon us. The Ajanta frescoes are full of a tenderness and love of beauty and life, and yet always with a suspicion of something deeper, something beyond.

Geographically and climatically Greece is different from India. There are no real rivers there, no forests, no big trees, which abound in India. The sea with its immensity and changing moods affected the Greeks far more than it did the Indians, except perhaps those who lived near India's coastline. India's life was more continental, of vast plains and huge mountains, of mighty rivers and great forests. There were some mountains in Greece also, and the Greeks chose Olympus as the abode of the gods, just as the Indians placed their gods and even their sages on the Himalayan heights. Both developed a mythology which was indivisibly mixed up with history, and it was not possible to separate fact from fiction. The old Greeks are said to have been neither pleasure-seekers nor ascetics; they did not avoid pleasure as something evil and immoral, nor did they go out deliberately to amuse themselves as modern people are apt to do. Without the inhibitions which afflict so many of us, they took life in their stride, applying themselves wholly to whatever they did, and thus somehow they appear to have been more alive than we are. Some such impression one gathers of life in India also from our old literature. There was an ascetic aspect of life in India, as there was later in Greece, but it was confined to a limited number of people and did not affect life generally. That aspect was to grow more important under the influence of Jainism and Buddhism, but even so it did not change materially the background of life.

Life was accepted as it was and lived fully both in India and Greece; nevertheless, there was a belief in the supremacy of some kind of inner life. This led to curiosity and speculation, but the spirit of inquiry was not so much directed towards objective experience as to logical reasoning fixed on certain concepts which were accepted as obviously true. That indeed was the general attitude everywhere before the advent of the scientific method. Probably this speculation was confined to a small number of intellectuals, yet even the ordinary citizens were influenced by it and discussed philosophical problems, as they did everything else, in their public meeting places. Life was communal, as it is even now in India, especially in the rural areas, where people meet in the market place, in the enclosure of the temple or mosque, at the well-head, or at the *panchayat ghar* or common assembly house, where such exists, to discuss the news of the day and their common needs. Thus public opinion was formed and found expression. There was plenty of leisure for these discussions.

And yet Hellenism has among its many splendid achievements one that is even more unique than others, the early beginnings of experimental science. This was developed far more in the Hellenic world of Alexandria than in Greece itself, and the two centuries from 330 to 130 B.C. stand out in the record of scientific development and mechanical invention. There is nothing to compare with this in India, or, for the matter of that, anywhere else till science again took a big stride from the seventeenth century onwards. Even Rome for all its empire and the Pax Romana over a considerable area, its close contacts with Hellenic civilization, its opportunities to draw upon the learning and experiences of many peoples, made no significant contribution to science, invention, or mechanical development. After the collapse of classical civilization in Europe it was the Arabs who kept the flame of scientific knowledge alight through the Middle Ages.

This burst of scientific activity and invention in Alexandria was no doubt the social product of the time, called forth by the needs of a growing society and of seafaring, just as the advance in arithmetic and algebraic methods, the use of the zero sign and the place-value system in India were also due to social needs, advancing trade and more complex organization. But it is doubtful how far the scientific spirit was present in the old Greeks as a whole and their life must have followed traditional patterns, based on their old philosophic approach seeking an integration and harmony in man and with nature. It is that approach which is common to old Greece and India. In Greece, as in India, the year was divided up by popular festivals which heralded the changing seasons and kept man in tune with nature's moods. We have still these festivals in India for spring and harvest-time and *deepavali*, the festival of light at the end of autumn, and the *holi* carnival in early summer, and celebrations of the heroes of epic tradition. There is still singing and dancing at some of these festivals, folk-songs and folk-dances like the *rasa-lila*, the dance of Krishna with the gopis (cowherdesses).

There is no seclusion of women in ancient India except to some extent among royalty and the nobility. Probably there was more segregation of the sexes in Greece than in India then. Women of note and learning are frequently mentioned in the old Indian books, and often they took part in public debates. Marriage, in Greece, was apparently wholly a contractual affair; but in India it has always been considered a sacramental union, though other forms are mentioned.

Greek women were apparently especially welcome in India. Often the maids-in-waiting at royal courts mentioned in the old plays are Greek. Among the noted imports from Greece into India at the port of Barygaza (Broach in Western India) were, it is said, 'singing boys and pretty maidens.' Megasthenes describing the life of the Maurya king Chandragupta, tells us: 'the king's food was prepared by women who also served him with wine which is much used by all Indians.' Some of the wine certainly came from Grecian lands or colonies, for an old Tamil poet refers to 'the cool and fragrant wine brought by the Yavanas (Ionians or Greeks) in their good ships.' A Greek account relates that the king of Pataliputra (probably Ashoka's father, Bindusara) wrote to Antiochus asking him to buy and send him sweet wine, dried figs, and a Sophist philosopher. Antiochus replied: 'We shall send you the figs and wine, but in Greece the laws forbid a Sophist to be sold.'

It is clear from Greek literature that homosexual relations were not looked upon with disfavour. Indeed there was a romantic approval of them. Possibly this was due to the segregation of the sexes in youth. A similar attitude is found in Iran, and Persian literature is full of such references. It appears to have become an established literary form and convention to represent the beloved as a male companion. There is no such thing in Sanskrit literature and homosexuality was evidently neither approved nor at all common in India.

Greece and India were in contact with each other from the earliest recorded times, and in a later period there were close contacts between India and Hellenized western Asia. The great astronomical observatory at Ujjayini (now Ujjain) in central India was linked with Alexandria in Egypt. During this long period of contact there must have been many exchanges in the world of thought and culture between these two ancient civilizations. There is a tradition recorded in some Greek book that learned Indians visited Socrates and put questions to him. Pythagoras was particularly influenced by Indian philosophy and Professor H. G. Rawlinson remarks that 'almost all the theories, religious, philosophical, and mathematical, taught by the Pythagorians were known in India in the sixth century B.C.' A European classical scholar, Urwick, has based his interpretation of the 'Republic' of Plato upon Indian thought.* Gnosticism is supposed to be a definite attempt to fuse together Greek Platonic and Indian elements. The philosopher, Apollonius of Tyana probably visited the university of Taxila in north-west India about the beginning of the Christian era.

*Zimmern in his 'The Green Commonwealth' refers to Urwick's book, 'The Message of Plato' (1920). I have not seen this book.

The famous traveller and scholar, Alberuni, a Persian born in Khorasan in Central Asia, came to India in the eleventh century A.C. He had already studied Greek philosophy which was popular in the early days of Islam in Baghdad. In India he took the trouble to learn Sanskrit in order to study Indian philosophy. He was struck by many common features and he has compared the two in his book on India. He refers to Sanskrit books dealing with Greek astronomy and Roman astronomy.

Though inevitably influencing each other Greek and Indian civilizations were each strong enough to hold their own and develop on their distinctive lines. In recent years there has been a reaction from the old tendency to ascribe everything to Greece and Rome, and Asia's, and especially India's role has been emphasized. 'Considered broadly,' says Professor Tarn, 'what the Asiatic took from Greek was usually externals only, matters of form; he rarely took the substance—civic institutions may have been an exception—and never spirit. For in matters of spirit Asia was quite confident that she could outstay the Greeks, and she did.' Again: 'Indian civilization was strong enough to hold its own against Greek civilization, but except in the religious sphere, was seemingly not strong enough to influence it as Babylonia did; nevertheless, we may find reason for thinking that in certain respects India was the dominant partner.' 'Except for the Buddha statue the history of India would in all essentials have been precisely what it has been had the Greeks never existed.'

It is an interesting thought that image worship came to India from Greece. The Vedic religion was opposed to all forms of idol and image worship. There were not even any temples for the gods. There probably were some traces of image worship in the older faiths in India, though this was certainly not widely prevalent. Early Buddhism was strongly opposed to it and there was a special prohibition against the making of images and statues of the Buddha. But Greek artistic influence in Afghanistan and round about the frontier was strong and gradually it had its way. Even so, no statues of the Buddha were made to begin with, but Apollo—like staues of the Bodhisattvas (supposed to be the previous incarnations of the Buddha) appeared. These were followed by statues and images of the Buddha himself. This encouraged image-worship in some forms of Hinduism though not in the Vedic religion which continued to be free of it. The word for an image or statue in Persian and in Hindustani still is *But* (like put) derived from Buddha.

The human mind appears to have a passion for finding out some kind of unity in life, in nature and the universe. That desire, whether it is justified or not, must fulfil some essential need of the mind. The old philosophers were ever seeking this, and even modern scientists are impelled by this urge. All our schemes and planning, our ideas of education and social and political organization, have at their back the search for unity and harmony.

We are told now by some able thinkers and philosophers that this basic conception is false and there is no such thing as order or unity in this accidental universe. That may be so, but there can be little doubt that even this mistaken belief, if such it was, and the search for unity in India, Greece, and elsewhere, yielded positive results and produced a harmony, a balance, and a richness in life.

The Old Indian Theatre

The discovery by Europe of the old Indian drama led immediately to suggestions that it had its origin in, or had been greatly influenced by, Greek drama. There was some plausibility in the theory, for till then no other ancient drama had been known to exist, and after Alexander's raid Hellenized states were established on the frontiers of India. These states continued to function for several centuries and Greek theatrical representations must have been known there. This question was closely scrutinized and debated by European scholars throughout the nineteenth century. It is now generally admitted that the Indian theatre was entirely independent in its origins, in the ideas which governed it, and in its development. Its earliest beginnings can be traced back to the hymns and dialogues of the Rig Veda which have a certain dramatic character. There are references to *Nataka* or the drama in the Ramayana and the Mahabharata. It began to take shape in the song and music and dances of the Krishna legends. Panini, the great grammarian of the sixth or seventh century B.C., mentions some dramatic forms.

A treatise on the Art of the Theatre—the *Natya-Shāstra*—is said to date from the third century A.C. but this was evidently based or previous books on the subject. Such a book could only be written when the dramatic art was fully developed and public representations were common. A considerable literature must have preceded it, and behind it must lie many centuries of gradual progress. Recently an ancient playhouse, dating from the second century B.C., has been unearthed in the Ramgarh Hills in Chota Nagpur. It is significant that this playhouse fits in with the general description of theatres given in the Natya-Shāstra.

It is now believed that the regular Sanskrit drama was fully established by the third century B.C., though some scholars take the date back to the fifth century. In the plays that we have, mention is often made of earlier authors and plays which have not so far been found. One such lost author was Bhāsa, highly praised by many subsequent dramatists. Early in this century a bunch of thirteen of his plays was discovered. Probably the earliest Sanskrit plays so far discovered, are those of Ashvaghosa, who lived just before or after the beginning of the Christian era. These are really fragments only of manuscripts on palm leaves, and they were discovered, strangely enough, at Turfan on the borders of the Gobi desert. Ashvaghosa was a pious Buddhist and wrote also the *Buddha Charita*, a life of the Buddha, which was well known and had long been popular in India and China and Tibet. The Chinese translation, made in a past age, was by an Indian scholar.

These discoveries have given a new perspective to the history of the old Indian drama and it may be that further discoveries and finds will throw more light on this fascinating development of Indian culture. For, as Sylvain Lévi has written in his 'Le Théâtre Indien': 'Le théâtre est la plus haute expression de la civilisation qui l'enfante. Qu'il traduise ou qu'il interprète la vie réelle, il est tenu de la résumer sous une forme frappante, dégagée des accessoires insignifiants, généralisée dans un symbole. L'originalité de l'Inde s'est exprimée tout entière dans son art dramatique; elle y a combiné et condensé ses dogmes, ses doctrines, ses institutions....'

Europe first learned of the old Indian drama from Sir William Jones's translation of Kālidāsa's 'Shakuntala', published in 1789. Something in the nature of a commotion was created among European intellectuals by this discovery and several editions of the book followed. Translations also appeared (made from Sir William Jones's translation) in German, French, Danish, and Italian. Goethe was powerfully impressed and he paid a magnificent tribute to 'Shakuntala'. The idea of giving a prologue to Faust is said to have originated from Kālidāsa's prologue, which was in accordance with the usual tradition of the Sanskrit drama.*

*There is a tendency on the part of Indian writers, to which I have also partly succumbed, to give selected extracts and quotations from the writings of European scholars in praise of old Indian literature and philosophy. It would be equally easy, and indeed much easier, to give other extracts giving an exactly opposite viewpoint. The discovery by the European scholars of the eighteenth and nineteenth centuries of Indian thought and philosophy led to an outburst of admiration and enthusiasm. There was a feeling that these filled a need, something that European culture had been unable to do. Then there was a reaction away from this attitude and criticism and scepticism grew. This was caused by a feeling that the philosophy was formless and diffuse and a dislike of the rigid caste structure of Indian society. Both these reactions in favour and against, were based on very incomplete knowledge of old Indian literature. Goethe himself moved from one opinion to the other, and while he acknowledged the tremendous stimulus of Indian thought on western civilization, he refused to submit to its far reaching influence. This dual and conflicting approach has been characteristic of

Kalidasa is acknowledged to be the greatest poet and dramatist of Sanskrit literature. 'Le nom de Kālidāsa,' says Professor Sylvain Levi, 'domine la poésie indienne et la résume brillamment. Le drame, l'épopée savante. l'élégie attestent aujourd'hui encore la puissance et la souplesse de ce magnifique génie; seul entre les disciples de Sarasvati (the goddess of learning and the arts), il a eu le bonheur de produire un chef dœ'uvre vraiment classique, où l'Inde s'admire et où l'humanité se reconnait. Les applaudissements qui saluèrent la naissance de Cakuntala à Ujjayini ont après de long siècles éclaté d'un bout du monde à l'autre, quand William Jones l'eut révélé à l'Occident. Kâlidâsa a marqué sa place dans cette pléiade entincelante où chaque nom résume une période de l'esprit humain. La série de ces noms forme l'histoire, ou plutôt elle est l'histoire même.'

Kālidāsa wrote other plays also and some long poems. His date is uncertain but very probably he lived towards the end of the fourth century A.C. at Ujjayini during the reign of Chandragupta II, Vikramaditya of the Gupta dynasty. Tradition says that he was one of the nine gems of the court, and there is no doubt that his genius was appreciated and he met with full recognition during his life. He was among the fortunate whom life treated as a cherished son and who experienced its beauty and tenderness more than its harsh and rough edges. His writings betray this love of life and a passion for nature's beauty.

One of Kālidāsa's long poems is the *Meghaduta*, the Cloud Messenger. A lover, made captive and separated from his beloved, asks a cloud, during the rainy season, to carry his message of desperate longing to her. To this poem and to Kālidāsa, the American scholar, Ryder, has paid a splendid tribute. He refers to the two parts of the poem and says: 'The former half is a description of external nature, yet interwoven with human feeling; the latter half is a picture of a human heart, yet the picture is framed in natural beauty. So exquisitely is the thing done that none can say which half is superior. Of those who read this perfect poem in the original text, some are moved by the one, some by the other. Kālidāsa understood in the fifth century what Europe did not learn until the nineteenth, and even now comprehends only imperfectly, that the world was not made for man, that man reaches his full stature only as he realizes the dignity and worth of life that is not human. That Kālidāsa seized

the European mind in regard to India. In recent years that great European and typical product of the best European culture, Romain Rolland, made a more synthetic and very friendly approach to the basic foundations of Indian tought: For him East and West represented different phases of the eternal struggle of the human soul. On this subject— Western reaction to Indian thought—Mr. Alex Aronson, of Santiniketan University, has written with learning and ability.

this truth is a magnificent tribute to his intellectual power, a quality quite as necessary to great poetry as perfection of form. Poetical fluency is not rare; intellectual grasp is not very uncommon; but the combination of the two has not been found perhaps more than a dozen times since the world began. Because he possessed this harmonious combination, Kālidāsa ranks not with Anacreon and Horace and Shelley, but with Sophocles, Virgil, and Milton.'

Probably long before Kālidāsa, another famous play was produced—Shudraka's 'Mrichhkatika' or the Clay Cart, a tender rather artificial play, and yet with a reality which moves us and gives us a glimpse into the mind and civilization of the day.

About 400 A.C., also during the reign of Chandragupta II, yet another notable play was produced, Vishāka-datta's 'Mudra-Rākshasa' or the signet ring. This is a purely political play with no love motive or story from mythology. It deals with the times of Chandragupta Maurya, and his chief minister, Chanakya, the author of the Arthashāstra, is the hero. In some ways it is a remarkably topical play to-day.

Harsha, the king, who established a new empire early in the seventh century A.C., was also a playwright and we have three plays written by him. About 700 A.C. there lived Bhavabhuti, another shining star in Sanskrit literature. He does not yield himself easily to translation for his beauty is chiefly of language, but he is very popular in India, and only Kālidāsa has precedence over him. Wilson, who used to be professor of Sanskrit at Oxford University, has said of these two: 'It is impossible to conceive language so beautifully musical, or so magnificently grand, as that of the verses of Bhavabhuti and Kālidāsa.'

The stream of Sanskrit drama continued to flow for centuries, but after Murari, early in the ninth century, there is a marked delcine in the quality. That decline, and a progressive decay were becoming visible also in other forms of life's activities. It has been suggested that this decline of the drama may be partly due to the lack of royal patronage during the Indo-Afghan and Moghul periods and the Islamic disapproval of the drama as an art-form, chiefly because of its intimate association with the national religion. For this literary drama, apart from the popular aspects which continued, was highbrow and sophisticated and dependent on aristocratic patronage. But there is little substance in this argument though it is possible that political changes at the top had some indirect effect. As a matter of fact the decline of the Sanskrit drama was obvious long before those political changes took place. And even those changes were confined for some centuries to north India, and if this drama had any vitality left it could have continued its creative career in the south.

The record of the Indo-Afghan, Turkish, and Moghul rulers, apart from some brief puritanical periods, is one of definite encouragement of Indian culture, occasionally with variations and additions to it. Indian music was adopted as a whole and with enthusiasm by the Moslem Courts and the nobility and some of its greatest masters have been Moslems. Literature and poetry were also encouraged and among the noted poets in Hindi are Moslems. Ibrahim Adil Shah, the ruler of Bijapur, wrote a treatise in Hindi on Indian music.

Both Indian poetry and music were full of references to the Hindu gods and goddesses and yet they were accepted and the old allegories and metaphors continued. It might be said that except in regard to actual image-making no attempt was made by Moslem rulers, apart from a few exceptions, to suppress any art-form.

The Sanskrit drama declined because much in India was declining in those days and the creative spirit was lessening. It declined long before the Afghans and Turks established themselves on the throne of Delhi. Subsequently Sanskrit had to compete to some extent as the learned language of the nobility with Persian. But one obvious reason appears to have been the ever-widening gap between the language of the Sanskrit drama and the languages of day-to-day life. By 1000 A.C. the popular spoken languages, out of which our modern languages have grown, were beginning to take literary forms.

Yet, in spite of all this, it is astonishing how the Sanskrit drama continued to be produced right through the medieval period and up to recent times. In 1892 appeared a Sanskrit adaptation of Shakespeare's 'Midsummer Night's Dream.' Manuscripts of old plays are continually being discovered. A list of these prepared by Professor Sylvain Lévi in 1890 contained 377 plays by 189 authors. A more recent list contains 650 plays.

The language of the old plays (of Kālidāsa and others) is mixed—Sanskrit and one or more *Prākrits*, that is, popular variations of Sanskrit. In the same play educated people speak in Sanskrit and ordinary uneducated folk, usually women, though there are exceptions, in Prakrit. The poetical and lyrical passages, which abound, are in Sanskrit. This mixture probably brought the plays nearer to the average audience· It was a compromise between the literary language and the demands of a popular art.

Yet, essentially, the old drama represents an aristocratic art meant for sophisticated audiences, usually royal courts and the like. Sylvain Lévi compares it, in some ways, to French tragedy, which was cut off from the crowd by the choice of its subjects and, turning away from real life, created a conventional society.

161

But apart from this high-class literary theatre, there has always been a popular theatre based on stories from Indian mythology and the epics, themes well known to the audience, and concerned more with display than with any dramatic element. This was in the language of the people in each particular area and was therefore confined to that area. Sanskrit plays, on the other hand, being in the all-India language of the educated, had an all-India vogue.

These Sanskrit plays were undoubtedly meant for acting and elaborate stage-directions are given, and rules for seating the audience. Unlike the practice in ancient Greece, actresses took part in the presentation. In both Greek and Sanskrit there is a sensitive awareness of nature and a feeling of being a part of that nature. There is a strong lyric element and poetry seems to be an integral part of life, full of meaning and significance. It was frequently recited. Reading the Greek drama one comes across many customs and ways of thought and life which suddenly remind one of old Indian customs. Nevertheless Greek drama is essentially different from the Sanskrit.

The essential basis of the Greek drama is tragedy, the problem of evil. Why does man suffer? Why is there evil in the world? The enigma of religion, of God. What a pitiful thing is man, child of a day, with his blind and aimless strivings against all-powerful fate—'The Law that abides and changes not, ages long.' Man must learn by suffering and, if he is fortunate, he will rise above his striving:

> *Happy he, on the weary sea*
> *Who hath fled the tempest and won the haven.*
> *Happy whoso has risen, free,*
> *Above his striving. For strangely graven*
> *Is the art of life that one and another*
> *In gold and power may outpass his brother.*
> *And men in their millions float and flow,*
> *And seethe with a million hopes as leaven;*
> *And they win their Will, or they miss their Will,*
> *And the hopes are dead or are pined for still;*
> *But whoever can know,*
> *As the long days go,*
> *That to Live is happy, hath found his Heaven!*

Man learns by suffering, he learns how to face life, but he learns also that the ultimate mystery remains and he cannot find an answer to his questions or solve the riddle of good and evil.

> *There be many shapes of mystery;*
> *And many things God brings to be,*
> *Past hope or fear.*

And the end men looked for cometh not,
And a path is there where no man thought.*

There is nothing comparable to the power and majesty of
Greek tragedy in Sanskrit. Indeed there is no tragedy at all for
a tragic ending was not permitted. No such fundamental questions are discussed for the commonly held patterns of religious
faith were accepted by the dramatists. Among these were the
doctrines of rebirth and cause and effect. Accident or evil without cause was ruled out, for what happens now is the necessary
result of some previous happening in a former life. There is no
intervention of blind forces against which man has to fight,
though his struggles are of no avail. The philosophers and the
thinkers were not satisfied by these simple explanations and they
were continually going behind them in their search for final
causes and fuller explanations. But life was generally governed
by these beliefs and the dramatists did not challenge them. The
plays and Sanskrit poetry in general were in full accord with
the Indian spirit and there are few traces of any rebellion
against it.

The rules laid down for dramatic writing were strict and it
was not easy to break them. Yet there is no meek submission to
fate; the hero is always a man of courage who faces all hazards.
'The ignorant rely on Providence', says Chānakya contemptuously
in the 'Mudra-Rākshasa,' they look to the stars for help instead
of relying on themselves. Some artificiality creeps in: the hero is
always the hero, the villain almost always acts villainously;
there are few intermediate shades.

Yet there are powerful dramatic situations and moving scenes
and a background of life which seems like a picture in a dream,
real and yet unreal, all woven together by a poet's fancy in
magnificent language. It almost seems, though it may not have
been so, that life in India was more peaceful, more stable then;
as if it had discovered its roots and found answer to its questions.
It flows along serenely and even strong winds and passing storms
ruffle its surface only. There is nothing like the fierce tempests
of Greek tragedy. But it is very human and there is an æsthetic
harmony and a logical unity about it. The Nataka, the Indian
drama, says Sylvain Lévi, still remains the happiest invention
of the Indian genius.

Professor A. Berriedale Keith† says also that 'The Sanskrit

---

*These two quotations are from Professor Gilbert Murray's translations from Euripides.
The first one is from 'The Bacchae,' and the second from 'Alcestis.'
†I have frequently consulted Sylvain Lévi's 'Le Théâtre Indien' (Paris, 1890), and A.
Berriedale Keith's, 'Sanskrit Drama' (Oxford, 1924), and some quotations have been taken
from these two books.

drama may legitimately be regarded as the highest product of Indian poetry, and as summing up in itself the final conception of literary art achieved by the very self-conscious creators of Indian literature....The Brahmin, in fact, much abused as he has been in this as in other matters, was the source of the intellectual distinction of India. As he produced Indian philosophy, so by another effort of his intellect he evolved the subtle and effective form of the drama.'

An English translation of Shudraka's 'Mrichhkatika' was staged in New York in 1924. Mr. Joseph Wood Krutch, the dramatic critic of the *Nation*, wrote of it as follows: 'Here, if anywhere, the spectator will be able to see a genuine example of that pure art theatre of which theorists talk, and here, too, he will be led to meditate upon that real wisdom of the East which lies not in esoteric doctrine but in a tenderness far deeper and truer than that of the traditional Christianity which has been so thoroughly corrupted by the hard righteousness of Hebraism.... A play wholly artificial yet profoundly moving because it is not realistic but real....Whoever the author may have been, and whether he lived in the fourth century or the eighth, he was a man good and wise with the goodness and wisdom which come not from the lips or the smoothly flowing pen of the moralist but from the heart. An exquisite sympathy with the fresh beauty of youth and love tempered his serenity, and he was old enough to understand that a light-hearted story of ingenious complication could be made the vehicle of tender humanity and confident goodness....Such a play can be produced only by a civilization which has reached stability; when a civilization has thought its way through all the problems it faces, it must come to rest upon something calm and naive like this. Macbeth and Othello, however great and stirring they might be, are barbarous heroes because the passionate tumult of Shakespeare is the tumult produced by the conflict between a newly awakened sensibility and a series of ethical concepts inherited from the savage age. The realistic drama of our own time is a product of a like confusion; but when problems are settled, and when passions are reconciled with the decisions of an intellect, then form alone remains.... Nowhere in our European past do we find, this side the classics, a work more completely civilized.'

Vitality and Persistence of Sanskrit

Sanskrit is a language amazingly rich, efflorescent, full of luxuriant growth of all kinds, and yet precise and strictly keeping within the framework of grammar which Panini laid down two thousand six hundred years ago. It spread out, added to its richness, became fuller and more ornate, but always it stuck to its original roots.

In the years of the decline of Sanskrit literature, it lost some of its power and simplicity of style and became involved in highly complex forms and elaborate similes and metaphors. The grammatical rule which enable words to be joined together, became in the hands of the epigones a mere device to show off their cleverness by combining whole strings of words running into many lines.

Sir William Jones observed as long ago as 1784: 'The Sanskrit language, whatever be its antiquity, is of a wonderful structure; more perfect than the Greek, more copious than the Latin and more exquisitely refined than either: yet bearing to both of them a stronger affinity, both in the roots of verbs, and in the forms of grammar, than could possibly have been produced by accident; so strong indeed, that no philologer could examine them all without believing them to have sprung from *some common source* which perhaps no longer exists....'

William Jones was followed by many other European scholars, English, French, German, and others, who studied Sanskrit and laid the foundations of a new science—comparative philology. German scholarship forged ahead in this new domain and it is to these German scholars of the nineteenth century that the greatest credit must go for research in Sanskrit. Practically every German university had a Sanskrit department, with one or two professors in charge of it.

Indian scholarship, which was considerable, was of the old style, uncritical and seldom acquainted with foreign classical languages, except Arabic and Persian. A new type of scholarship arose in India under European inspiration, and many Indians went to Europe (usually to Germany) to train themselves in the new methods of research and critical and comparative study. These Indians had an advantage over the Europeans, and yet there was a disadvantage also. The disadvantage was due to certain preconceived notions, inherited beliefs and tradition, which came in the way of dispassionate criticism. The advantage, and it was great, was the capacity to enter into the spirit of the writing, to picture the environment in which it grew and thus to be more in tune with it.

A language is something infinitely greater than grammar and philology. It is the poetic testament of the genius of a race and a culture, and the living embodiment of the thoughts and fancies that have moulded them. Words change their meanings from age to age and old ideas transform themselves into new, often keeping their old attire. It is difficult to capture the meaning, much less the spirit, of an old word or phrase. Some kind of a romantic and poetical approach is necessary if we are to have a glimpse into that old meaning and into the minds of those who used the language in former days. The richer and more abundant the language, the greater the difficulty. Sanskrit, like other classical languages, is full of words which have not only poetic beauty but a deep significance, a host of associated ideas, which cannot be translated into a language foreign in spirit and outlook. Even its grammar, its philosophy, have a strong poetic content; one of its old dictionaries is in poetic form.

It is no easy matter, even for those of us who have studied Sanskrit, to enter into the spirit of this ancient tongue and to live again in its world of long ago. Yet we may do so to a small extent, for we are the inheritors of old traditions and that old world still clings to our fancies. Our modern languages in India are children of Sanskrit, and to it owe most of their vocabularly and their forms of expression. Many rich and significant words in Sanskrit poetry and philosophy, untranslatable in foreign languages, are still living parts of our popular languages. And Sanskrit itself, though long dead as a language of the people, has still an astonishing vitality. But for foreigners, however learned, the difficulties become greater. Unfortunately, scholars and learned men are seldom poets, and it is the scholar poet who is required to interpret a language. From these scholars we usually get, as M. Barth has pointed out, 'traductions infidèles à force d'être littérales.'

So while the study of comparative philology has progressed and much research work has been done in Sanskrit, it is rather barren and sterile from the point of view of a poetic and romantic approach to this language. There is hardly any translation in English or any other foreign language from the Sanskrit which can be called worthy of or just to the original. Both Indians and foreigners have failed in this work for different reasons. That is a great pity and the world misses something that is full of beauty and imagination and deep thinking, something that is not merely the heritage of India but should be the heritage of the human race.

The hard discipline, reverent approach, and insight of the English translation of the Authorized Version of the Bible, not only produced a noble book, but gave to the English language strength and dignity. Generations of European scholars and poets have laboured lovingly over Greek and Latin classics and produced fine translations in various European languages. And so even common folk can share to some extent in those cultures and, in their drab lives, have glimpses of truth and loveliness. Unfortunately, this work has yet to be done with the Sanskrit classics. When it will be done, or whether it will be done at all, I do not know. Our scholars grow in numbers and grow in scholarship, and we have our poets too, but between the two there is a wide and ever-growing gap. Our creative tendencies are turned in a different direction, and the many demands that the world of to-day makes upon us hardly give us time for the leisured study of the classics. Especially in India we have to look another way and make up for long lost time; we have been too much immersed in the classics in the past, and because we lost our own creative instincts we ceased to be inspired even by those classics which we claimed to cherish so much. Translations, I suppose, from the Indian classics will continue to appear, and scholars will see to it that the Sanskrit words and names are properly spelt and have all the necessary diacritical marks, and that there are plenty of notes and explanations and comparisons. There will be everything, in fact, literally and conscientiously rendered, only the living spirit will be missing. What was a thing of life and joy, so lovely and musical and full of imaginative daring, will become old and flat and stale, with neither youth nor beauty, but with only the dust of the scholar's study and the smell of midnight oil.

For how long Sanskrit has been a dead language, in the sense of not being popularly spoken, I do not know. Even in the days of Kālidāsa it was not the people's language, though it was the language of educated people throughout India. So it continued for centuries, and even spread to the Indian colonies in south-east Asia and central Asia. There are records of regular Sanskrit recitations, and possibly plays also, in Cambodia in the seventh century A.C. Sanskrit is still used for some ceremonial purposes in Thailand (Siam). In India the vitality of Sanskirt has been amazing. When the Afghan rulers had established themselves on the throne of Delhi, about the beginning of the thirteenth century, Persian became the court language over the greater part of India and, gradually, many educated people took to it in preference to Sanskrit. The popular languages also grew and developed literary forms. Yet in spite of all this Sanskrit continued, though it declined in quality. Speaking at the Oriental Conference held in 1937 at Trivandrum, over which he presided, Dr. F. F. Thomas pointed out what a great unifying force Sanskrit had been in India and how widespread its use still was. He actually suggested that a simple form of Sanskrit, a kind of basic Sanskrit, should be encouraged as a common all-India language to-day! He quoted, agreeing with him, what Max Müller had said previously: 'Such is the marvellous continuity between the past and the present in India, that in spite of repeated social convulsions, religious reforms, and foreign invasions, Sanskrit may be said to be still the only language spoken over the whole extent of that vast country ... Even at the present moment, after a century of English rule and English teaching, I believe that Sanskrit is more widely understood in India than Latin was in Europe at the time of Dante.'

I have no idea of the number of people who understood Latin in the Europe of Dante's time; nor do I know how many understand Sanskrit in India to-day; but the number of these latter is still large, especially in the south. Simple spoken Sanskrit is not very difficult to follow for those who know well any of the present-day Indo-Aryan languages—Hindi, Bengali, Marathi, Gujrati, etc. Even present-day Urdu, itself wholly an Indo-Aryan language, probably contains 80 per cent words derived from Sanskrit. It is often difficult to say whether a word has come from Persian or Sanskrit, as the root words in both these languages are alike. Curiously enough, the Dravidian languages of the south, though entirely different in origin, have borrowed and adopted such masses of words from the Sanskrit that nearly half their vocabulary is very nearly allied to Sanskrit.

Books in Sanskrit on a variety of subjects, including dramatic works, continued to be written throughout the medieval period and right up to modern times. Indeed, such books still appear from time to time, and so do Sanskrit magazines. The standard is not high and they do not add anything of value to Sanskrit literature. But the surprising thing is that this hold of Sanskrit should continue in this way throughout this long period. Sometimes public gatherings are still addressed in Sanskrit, though naturally the audiences are more or less select.

This continuing use of Sanskrit has undoubtedly prevented the normal growth of the modern Indian languages. The educated intellectuals looked upon them as vulgar tongues not suited to any creative or learned work, which was written in Sanskrit, or later not infrequently in Persian. In spite of this handicap the great provincial languages gradually took shape in the course of centuries, developed literary forms, and built up their literatures.

It is interesting to note that in modern Thailand when the need arose for new technical, scientific, and governmental terms, many of these were adapted from Sanskrit.

The ancient Indians attached a great deal of importance to sound, and hence their writing, poetry or prose, had a rhythmic and musical quality. Special efforts were made to ensure the correct enunciation of words and elaborate rules were laid down for this purpose. This became all the more necessary as, in the old days, teaching was oral, and whole books were committed to memory and thus handed down from generation to generation. The significance attached to the sound of words led to attempts to co-ordinate the sense with the sound, resulting sometimes in delightful combinations, and at other times in crude and artificial mixtures. E. H. Johnstone has written about this: 'The classical poets of India have a sensitiveness to variations of sound, to which the literature of other countries afford few parallels, and their delicate combinations are a source of never-failing joy. Some of them, however, are inclined to attempt to match the sense with the sound in a way that is decidedly lacking in subtlety, and they have perpetrated real atrocities in the manufacture of verses with a limited number of consonants or even only one.'*

Recitations from the Vedas, even in the present day, are done according to the precise rules for enunciation laid down in ancient times.

The modern Indian languages descended from the Sanskrit, and therefore called Indo-Aryan languages, are: Hindi-Urdu, Bengali, Marathi, Gujrati, Oriya, Assamese, Rajasthani (a variation of Hindi), Punjabi, Sindhi, Pashto, and Kashmiri. The Dravidian languages are: Tamil, Telugu, Kanarese, and Malayalam. These fifteen languages cover the whole of India, and of these, Hindi, with its variation Urdu, is far the most widespread and is understood even where it is not spoken. Apart from these, there are only some dialects and some undeveloped languages spoken, in very limited areas, by some backward hill and forest tribes. The oft-repeated story of India having five hundred or more languages is a fiction of the mind of the philologist and the census commissioner who notes down every variation in dialect and every petty hill-tongue on the Assam-Bengal frontier with Burma as a separate language, although sometimes it is spoken only by a few hundred or a few thousand persons. Most of these so-called hundreds of languages are confined to this eastern frontier of India and to the eastern border tracts of Burma. According to the method adopted by census commissioners, Europe has hundreds of languages and Germany was, I think, listed as having about sixty.

The real language question in India has nothing to do with this variety. It is practically confined to Hindi-Urdu, one language with two literary forms and two scripts. As spoken there is hardly any difference; as written, especially in literary style, the gap widens. Attempts have been, and are being, made to lessen this gap and develop a common form, which is usually styled Hindustani. This is developing into a common language understood all over India.

Pashto, one of the Indo-Aryan languages derived from Sanskrit, is the popular language in the North West Frontier Province as well as in Afghanistan. It has been influenced, more than any of our other languages, by Persian. This frontier area has in the past produced a succession of brilliant thinkers, scholars, and grammarians in Sanskrit.

The language of Ceylon is Singhalese. This is also an Indo-

*From E. H. Johnstone's translation of 'Asvaghosa's Buddhacarita' (Lahore, 1936).

Aryan language derived directly from Sanskrit. The Singhalese people have not only got their religion, Buddhism, from India, but are racially and linguistically akin to Indians. Sanskrit, it is now well recognized, is allied to the European classical and modern languages. Even the Slavonic languages have many common forms and roots with Sanskrit. The nearest approach to Sanskrit in Europe is made by the Lithuanian language.

Buddhist Philosophy

Buddha, it is said, used the popular language of the area he lived in, which was a Prākrit, a derivative of Sanskrit. He must have known Sanskrit, of course, but he preferred to speak in the popular tongue so as to reach the people. From this Prākrit developed the Pali language of the early Buddhist scriptures. Buddha's dialogues and other accounts and discussions were recorded in Pali long after his death, and these form the basis of Buddhism in Ceylon, Burma, and Siam, where the Hinayana form of Buddhism prevails.

Some hundreds of years after Buddha there was a revival of Sanskrit in India, and Buddhist scholars wrote their philosophical and other works in Sanskrit. Ashvaghosha's writings and plays (the earliest plays we have), which are meant to be propaganda for Buddhism, are in Sanskrit. These Sanskrit writings of Buddhist scholars in India went to China, Japan, Tibet, and Central Asia, where the Mahāyāna form of Buddhism prevailed.

The age which gave birth to the Buddha had been one of tremendous mental ferment and philosophic inquiry in India. And not in India only for that was the age of Lao-tze and Confucius, of Zoroaster and Pythagoras. In India it gave rise to materialism as well as to the Bhagavad Gita, to Buddhism and Jainism, and to many other currents of thought which were subsequently to consolidate themselves in the various systems of Indian philosophy. There were different strata of thought, one leading to another, and sometimes overlapping each other.

Different schools of philosophy developed side by side with Buddhism, and Buddhism itself had schisms leading to the formation of different schools of thought. The philosophic spirit gradually declined giving place to scholasticism and polemical controversy.

Buddha had repeatedly warned his people against learned controversy over metaphysical problems. 'Whereof one cannot speak thereof one must be silent,' he is reported to have said. Truth was to be found in life itself and not in argument about matters outside the scope of life and therefore beyond the ken of the human intellect. He emphasized the ethical aspects of life and evidently felt that these suffered and were neglected because of a preoccupation with metaphysical subtleties. Early Buddhism reflected to some extent this philosophic and rational spirit of the Buddha, and its inquiries were based on experience. In the world of experience the concept of pure being could not be grasped and was therefore put aside; so also the idea of a creator God, which was a presumption not capable of logical proof. Nevertheless the experience remained and was real enough in a sense; what could this be except a mere flux of becoming, ever changing into something else? So these intermediate degrees of reality were recognized and further inquiry proceeded on these lines on a psychological basis.

Buddha, rebel as he was, hardly cut himself off from the ancient faith of the land. Mrs. Rhys Davids says that 'Gautama was born and brought up and lived and died as a Hindu.... There was not much in the metaphysics and principles of Gautama which cannot be found in one or other of the orthodox systems, and a great deal of his morality could be matched from earlier or later Hindu books. Such originality as Gautama possessed lay in the way in which he adapted, enlarged, ennobled, and systematized that which had already been well said by others; in the way in which he carried out to their logical conclusion principles of equity and justice already acknowledged by some of the most prominent Hindu thinkers. The difference between him and other teachers lay chiefly in his deep earnestness and in his broad public spirit of philanthropy.'*

Yet Buddha had sown the seeds of revolt against the conventional practice of the religion of his day. It was not his theory or philosophy that was objected to—for every conceivable philosophy could be advocated within the fold of orthodox belief so long as it remained a theory—but the interference with the social life and organization of the people. The old system was free and flexible in thought, allowing for every variety of opinion, but in practice it was rigid, and non-conformity with practice was not approved. So, inevitably, Buddhism tended to break away from the old faith, and, after Buddha's death, the breach widened.

With the decline of early Buddhism, the *Mahāyāna* form developed, the older form being known as the *Hinayāna*. It was in this Mahāyāna that Buddha was made into a god and devotion to him as a personal god developed. The Buddha image also appeared from the Grecian north-west. About the same time there was a revival of Brahminism in India and of Sanskrit scholarship.

Between the Hināyana and the Mahāyāna there was bitter controversy and the debate and opposition to each other has continued throughout subsequent history. The Hināyāna countries

---

* *This quotation, as well as much else, is taken from Sir S. Radhakrishnan's 'Indian Philosophy' (George Allen and Unwin, London, 1940).*

(Ceylon, Burma, Siam) even now rather look down upon the Buddhism that prevails in China and Japan, and I suppose this feeling is reciprocated.

While the Hinayāna adhered, in some measure, to the ancient purity of doctrine and circumscribed it in a Pali Canon, the Mahāyāna spread out in every direction, tolerating almost everything and adapting itself to each country's distinctinve outlook. In India it began to approach the popular religion; in each of the other countries—China and Japan and Tibet—it had a separate development. Some of the greatest of the early Buddhist thinkers moved away from the agnostic attitude which Buddha had taken up in regard to the existence of the soul and rejected it completely.

Among a galaxy of men of remarkable intellect, Nāgārjuna stands out as one of the greatest minds that India has produced. He lived during Kanishka's reign, about the beginning of the Christian era, and he was chiefly responsible for formulating the Mahāyāna doctrines. The power and daring of his thought are remarkable and he is not afraid of arriving at conclusions which to most people must have appeared as scandalous and shocking. With a ruthless logic he pursues his argument till it leads him to deny even what he believed in. Thought cannot know itself and cannot go outside itself or know another. There is no God apart from the universe, and no universe apart from God, and both are epually appearances.

And so he goes on till there is nothing left, no distinction between truth and error, no possibility of understanding or misunderstanding anything, for how can anyone misunderstand the unreal? Nothing is real. The world has only a phenomenal existence; it is just an ideal system of qualities and relations, in which we believe but which we cannot intelligibly explain. Yet behind all this experience he hints at something—the Absolute—which is beyond the capacity of our thinking, for in the very process of thought it becomes something relative.*

This absolute is often referred to in Buddhist philosophy as *Shunyata* or nothingness (Shunya is the word for the zero mark)

*Professor Th. Stcherbatsky of the Academy of Sciences of the U.S.S.R., in his book 'The Conception of Buddhist Nirvana' (Leningrad, 1927) suggests that Nāgārjuna should be placed 'among the great philosophers of humanity.' He refers to his 'wonderful style' which never ceases to be interesting, bold, baffling, sometimes seemingly arrogant. He compares Nāgārjuna's views with those of Bradley and Hegel: 'Very remarkable are then the coincidences between Nāgārjuna's negativism and the condemnation by Mr. Bradley of almost every conception of the everyday world: things and qualities, relations, space and time, change, causation, motion, the self. From the Indian standpoint Bradley can be characterised as a genuine Madhyamika. But above all these parallelisms we may perhaps find a still greater family likeness between the dialectical method of Hegel and Nāgārjuna's dialectics.'

Stcherbatsky points out certain resemblances between some of the Buddhist schools of philosophy and the outlook of modern science, especially the conception of the final condition of the universe according to the law of entropy. He gives an interesting story. When the yet it is something very different from our conception of vacancy or nothingness.* In our world of experience we have to call it nothingness for there is no other word for it, but in terms of metaphysical reality it means something transcendent and immanent in all things.

Says a famous Buddhist scholar: 'It is on account of *Shunyata* that everything becomes possible, without it nothing in the world is possible.'

All this shows where metaphysics leads to and how wise was Buddha's warning against such speculations. Yet the human mind refuses to imprison itself and continues to reach out for that fruit of knowledge which it well knows is beyond reach. Metaphysics developed in Buddhist philosophy but the method was based on a psychological approach. Again, it is surprising to find the insight into the psychological states of the mind. The subconscious self of modern psychology is clearly envisaged and discussed. An extraordinary passage in one of the old books has been pointed out to me. This reminds one in a way of the Oedipus Complex theory, though the approach is wholly different.†

Four definite schools of philosophy developed in Buddhism, two of these belonged to the Hinayāna branch, and two to the Mahāyāna. All these Buddhist systems of philosophy have their origin in the Upanishads, but they do not accept the authority of the Vedas. It is this denial of the Vedas that distinguishes them from the so-called Hindu systems of philosophy which developed about the same time. These latter, while accepting the Vedas generally and, in a sense, paying formal obeisance to them, do not consider them as infallible, and indeed go their own way without much regard for them. As the Vedas and the Upanishads spoke

educational authorities of newly founded republic of Buriats in Transbaikalia in the U.S.S.R. started an anti-religious propaganda, they emphasized that modern science takes a materialistic view of the universe. The Buddhist monks of that republic, who were Mahāyānists, retorted in a pamphlet, pointing out that materialism was not unknown to them and that, in fact, one of their schools had developed a materialistic theory.

Professor Stcherbatsky who is an authority on the subject, having personally examined the original texts in various languages, including Tibetan, says that 'shunyata' is relativity. Everything being relative and interdependent has no absoluteness by itself. Hence it is 'shunyā.' On the other hand, there is something entirely beyond the phenomenal world, but comprising it, which might be considered the absolute. This cannot be conceived or described in terms of the finite and phenomenal world and hence it is referred to as 'tathata' or thatness, suchness. This absolute has also been called 'shunyata'.

† *This occurs in Vaṣubandhu's 'Abhidharmakosa', which was written in the early fifth century* A.C., *collecting previous views and traditions. The original in Sanskrit has been lost. But Chinese and Tibetan translations exist. The Chinese translation is by the famous Chinese pilgrim to India, Hsuan Tsang. From this Chinese translation a French translation has been made (Paris-Louvain, 1926). My colleague and companion in detention, Acharya Narendra Dev, has been translating this book from the French into Hindi and English, and he pointed out this passage to me. It is in the third chapter.*

with many voices, it was always possible for subsequent thinkers to emphasize one aspect rather than another, and to build their system on this foundation.

Professor Radhakrishnan thus describes the logical movement of Buddhist thought as it found expression in the four schools. It begins with a dualistic metaphysics looking upon knowledge as a direct awareness of objects. In the next stage ideas are made the media through which reality is apprehended, thus raising a screen between mind and things. These two stages represent the Hinayāna schools. The Mahāyāna schools went further and abolished the things behind the images and reduced all experience to a series of ideas in their mind. The ideas of relativity and the sub-conscious self come in. In the last stage—this was Nāgārjuna's Madhyamika philosophy or the middle way—mind itself is dissolved into mere ideas, leaving us with loose units of ideas and perceptions about which we can say nothing definite.

Thus we arrive finally at airy nothing, or something that is so difficult to grasp for our finite minds that it cannot be described or defined. The most we can say is that it is some kind of conscious-ness—*vijyana* as it is called.

In spite of this conclusion arrived at by psychological and metaphysical analysis which ultimately reduces the conception of the invisible world or the absolute to pure consciousness, and thus to nothing, so far as we can use or comprehend words, it is emphasized that ethical relations have a definite value in our finite world. So in our lives and in our human relations we have to con-form to ethics and live the good life. To that life and to this pheno-menal world we can and should apply reason and knowledge and experience. The infinite, or whatever it may be called, lies some-where in the beyond and to it therefore these cannot be applied.

Effect of Buddhism on Hinduism

What was the effect of Buddha's teachings on the old Aryan reli-gion and the popular beliefs that prevailed in India? There can be no doubt that they produced powerful and permanent effects on many aspects of religious and national life. Buddha may not have thought of himself as the founder of a new religion; probably he looked upon himself as a reformer only. But his dynamic perso-nality and his forceful messages attacking many social and religious practices inevitably led to conflict with the entrenched priesthood. He did not claim to be an uprooter of the existing social order or economic system; he accepted their basic premises and only at-tacked the evils that had grown under them. Nevertheless he functioned, to some extent, as a social revolutionary and it was because of this that he angered the Brahmin class who were inter-ested in the continuance of the existing social practices. There is

174

nothing in Buddha's teachings that cannot be reconciled with the wide-flung range of Hindu thought. But when Brahmin supremacy was attacked it was a different matter.

It is interesting to note that Buddhism first took root in Magadha, that part of northern India where Brahminism was weak. It spread gradually west and north and many Brahmins also joined it. To begin with, it was essentially a Kshatriya movement but with a popular appeal. Probably it was due to the Brahmins, who later joined it, that it developed more along philosophical and metaphysical lines. It may have been due also chiefly to the Brahmin Buddhists that the Mahāyāna form developed; for, in some ways, and notably in its catholic variety, this was more akin to the varied form of the existing Aryan faith.

Buddhism influenced Indian life in a hundred ways, as it was bound to, for it must be remembered that it was a living, dynamic, and widespread religion in India for over a thousand years. Even in the long years of its decline in India, and when later it practically ceased to count as a separate religion here, much of it remained as a part of the Hindu faith and in national ways of life and thought. Even though the religion as such was ultimately rejected by the people, the ineffaceable imprint of it remained and powerfully influenced the development of the race. This permanent effect had little to do with dogma or philosophic theory or religious belief. It was the ethical and social and practical idealism of Buddha and his religion that influenced our people and left their imperishable marks upon them, even as the ethical ideals of Christianity affected Europe though it may not pay much attention to its dogmas, and as Islam's human, social, and practical approach influenced many people who were not attracted by its religious forms and beliefs.

The Aryan faith in India was essentially a national religion restricted to the land, and the social caste structure it was developing emphasized this aspect of it. There were no missionary enterprises, no proselytization, no looking outside the frontiers of India. Within India it proceeded on its own unobtrusive and subconscious way and absorbed new-comers and old, often forming new castes out of them. This attitude to the outside world was natural for those days, for communications were difficult and the need for foreign contacts hardly arose. There were no doubt such contacts for trade and other purposes but they made no difference to India's life and ways. The ocean of Indian life was a self-contained one, big and diverse enough to allow full play for its many currents, self-conscious and absorbed in itself, caring little for what happened beyond its boundaries. In the very heart of this ocean burst forth a new spring, pouring out a fountain of fresh and limpid water, which ruffled the old surface and overflowed, not caring at all for those old boundaries and barriers that man and nature had erected. In this fountain of Buddha's teaching the appeal was to the nation but it was also to more than the nation. It was a universal call for the good life and it recognized no barriers of class or caste or nation.

This was a novel approach for the India of his day. Ashoka was the first person to act upon it in a big way with his embassies to, and missionary activities in, foreign countries. India thus began to develop an awareness of the world, and probably it was largely this that led, in the early centuries of the Christian era, to vast colonial enterprises. These expeditions across the seas were organized by Hindu rulers and they carried the Brahminical system and Aryan culture with them. This was an extraordinary development for a self-contained faith and culture which were gradually building up a mutually exclusive caste system. Only a powerful urge and something changing their basic outlook could have brought this about. That urge may have been due to many reasons, and most of all to trade and the needs of an expanding society, but the change of outlook was partly due to Buddhism and the foreign contacts it had brought about. Hinduism was dynamic enough and full of an overflowing energy at the time but it had previously not paid much attention to foreign countries. One of the effects of the universalism of the new faith was to encourage this dynamic energy to flow out to distant countries.

Much of the ritualism and ceremonial associated with the Vedic, as well as more popular forms of religion, disappeared, particularly animal sacrifices. The idea of non-violence, already present in the Vedas and Upanishads, were emphasized by Buddhism and and even more so by Jainism. There was a new respect for life and a kindness to animals. And always behind all this was the endeavour to lead the good life, the higher life.

Buddha had denied the moral value of austere asceticism. But the whole effect of his teaching was one of pessimism towards life. This was especially the Hinayāna view and even more so that of Jainism. There was an emphasis on other-worldliness, a desire for liberation, of freedom from the burdens of the world. Sexual continence was encouraged and vegetarianism increased. All these ideas were present in India before the Buddha but the emphasis was different. The emphasis of the old Aryan ideal was on a full and all-rounded life. The student stage was one of continence and discipline, the householder participated fully in life's activities and took sex as part of them. Then came a gradual withdrawal and a greater concentration on public service and individual improvement. Only the last stage of life, when old age had come, was that of sanyāsa or full withdrawal from life's normal work and attachments.

Previously small groups of ascetically inclined people lived in forest settlements, usually attracting students. With the coming of Buddhism huge monasteries and nunneries grew up everywhere and there was a regular flow of population towards them. The very name of the province of Bihar to-day is derived from *Vihara*, monastery, which indicates how full that huge area must have been of monasteries Such monasteries were educational establishments also or were connected with schools and sometimes with universities.

Not only India but the whole of Central Asia had large numbers of huge Buddhist monasteries. There was a famous one in Balkh, accommodating 1,000 monks, of which we have many records. This was called *Nava-vihara*, the new monastery, which was Persianized into *Naubahar*.

Why was it that Buddhism resulted in the growth of other-worldliness in India far more than in some other countries where it has flourished for long periods—in China, Japan and Burma? I do not know, but I imagine that the national background of each country was strong enough to mould the religion according to its shape. China, for instance, had the powerful traditions derived from Confucius and Lao-tze and other philosophers. Then again, China and Japan adopted the Mahāyāna form of Buddhism which was less pessimistic in its approach than the Hinayāna. India was also influenced by Jainism which was the most otherworldly and life-negating of all these doctrines and philosophies.

Yet another very curious effect of Buddhism in India and on its social structure appears to have been one that was entirely opposed to its whole outlook. This was in relation to caste, which it did not approve of though it accepted its original basis. The caste system in the time of the Buddha was flexible and had not developed the rigidity of later periods. More importance was attached to capacity, character, and occupation, than to birth. Buddha himself often uses the term Brahmin as equivalent to an able, earnest, and disciplined person. There is a famous story in the Chhandogya Upanishad which shows us how caste and sex relations were viewed then.

This is the story of Satyakāma whose mother was Jābala. Satyakāma wanted to become a student of the sage Gautama (not the Buddha) and, as he was leaving his home, he asked his mother: 'Of what gotra (family or clan) am I?' His mother said to him: 'I do not know, my child, of what family thou art. In my youth when I had to move about much as a servant (waiting on the guests in my father's house), I conceived thee. I do not know of what family thou art. I was Jābala by name, thou art Satyakāma. Say that thou art Satyakāma Jābala (that is, Satyakāma, the son of Jābala).'

Satyakāma then went to Gautama and the sage asked him about his family. He replied in the words of his mother. Thereupon the teacher said: 'No one but a true Brahmin would thus speak out. Go and fetch fuel, friend. I shall initiate you. You have not swerved from the truth.' Probably at the time of the Buddha the Brahmins were the only more or less rigid caste. The Kshatriyas or the ruling class were proud of their group and family traditions but, as a class, their doors were open for the incorporation of individuals or families who became rulers. For the rest most people were Vaishyas, the agriculturists, an honoured calling. There were other occupational castes also. The so-called caste-less people, the untouchables, appear to have been very few, probably some forest folk and some whose occupation was the disposal of dead bodies, etc.

The emphasis of Jainism and Buddhism on non-violence led to the tilling of the soil being considered a lowly occupation, for it often resulted in the destruction of animal life. This occupation, which had been the pride of the Indo-Aryans, went down in the scale of values in some parts of the country, in spite of its fundamental importance, and those who actually tilled the land descended in the social scale.

Thus Buddhism, which was a revolt against priestcraft and ritualism and against the degradation of any human being and his deprivation of the opportunities of growth and leading a higher life, unconsciously led to the degradation of vast numbers of tillers of the soil. It would be wrong to make Buddhism responsible for this, for it had no such effect elsewhere. There was something inherent in the caste system which took it in this direction. Jainism pushed it along that way because of its passionate attachment to non-violence—Buddhism also inadvertently helped in the process.

How did Hinduism Absorb Buddhism in India?

Eight or nine years ago, when I was in Paris, André Malraux put me a strange question at the very beginning of our conversation. What was it, he asked me, that enabled Hinduism, to push away organized Buddhism from India, without any major conflict, over a thousand years ago? How did Hinduism succeed in absorbing, as it were, a great and widespread popular religion, without the usual wars of religion which disfigure the history of so many countires? What inner vitality or strength did Hinduism possess then which enabled it to perform this remarkable feat? And did India possess this inner vitality and strength to-day? If so, then her freedom and greatness were assured.

The question was perhaps typical of a French intellectual who was also a man of action. And yet few persons in Europe or America would trouble themselves over such matters; they would be much too full of the problems of to-day. Those present-day world problems filled and troubled Malraux also, and with his powerful and analytical mind he sought light wherever he could find it in the past or in the present—in thought, speech, writing, or, best of all, in action, in the game of life and death.

For Malraux the question was obviously not just an academic one. He was full of it and he burst out with it as soon as we met. It was a question after my own heart, or rather the kind of question that my own mind was frequently framing. But I had no satisfactory answer to it for him or for myself. There are answers and explanations enough, but they seem to miss the core of the problem.

It is clear that there was no widespread or violent extermination of Buddhism in India. Occasionally there were local troubles or conflicts between a Hindu ruler and the Buddhist *Sangha*, or organization of monks, which had grown powerful. These had usually a political origin and they did not make any essential difference. It must also be remembered that Hinduism was at no time wholly displaced by Buddhism. Even when Buddhism was at its height in India, Hinduism was widely prevalent. Buddhism died a natural death in India, or rather it was a fading out and a transformation into something else. 'India,' says Keith, 'has a strange genius for converting what it borrows and assimilating it.' If that is true of borrowings from abroad or from alien sources, still more is it applicable to something that came out of its own mind and thought. Buddhism was not only entirely a product of India; its philosophy was in line with previous Indian thought and the philosophy of the Vedanta (the Upanishads). The Upanishads had even ridiculed priestcraft and ritualism and minimised the importance of caste.

Brahminism and Buddhism acted and reacted on each other, and in spite of their dialectical conflicts or because of them, approached nearer to each other, both in the realm of philosophy and that of popular belief. The Mahāyāna especially approached the Brahminical system and forms. It was prepared to compromise with almost anything, so long as its ethical background remained. Brahminism made of Buddha an *avatar*, a God. So did Buddhism. The Mahāyāna doctrine spread rapidly but it lost in quality and distinctiveness what it gained in extent. The monasteries became rich, centres of vested interests, and their discipline became lax. Magic and superstition crept into the popular forms of worship. There was a progressive degeneration of Buddhism in India after the first millenium of its existence. Mrs. Rhys Davids points out its diseased state during that period: 'under the overpowering influence of these sickly imaginations the moral teachings of Gautama have been almost hid from view. The theories grew and flourished, each new step, each new hypothesis demanded another; until the whole sky was filled with forgeries of the brain, and the nobler and simpler lessons of the founder of the religion were smothered beneath the glittering mass of metaphysical subtleties.'*

This description might well apply to many of the 'sickly imaginings' and 'forgeries of the brain' which were afflicting Brahminism and its offshoots at that time.

Buddhism had started at a time of social and spiritual revival and reform in India. It infused the breath of new life in the people, it tapped new sources of popular strength and released new talent and capacity for leadership. Under the imperial patronage of Ashoka it spread rapidly and became the dominant religion of India. It spread also to other countries and there was a constant stream of learned Buddhist scholars going abroad from India and coming to India. This stream continued for many centuries. When the Chinese pilgrim Fa-hien came to India in the fifth century A.C., a thousand years after Buddha, he saw that Buddhism was flourishing in its parent country. In the seventh century A.C. the still more famous pilgrim Hsuan Tsang (or Yuan-Chwang) came to India and witnessed signs of decay, although even then it was strong in some areas. Quite a large number of Buddhist scholars and monks gradually drifted from India to China.

Meanwhile there had been a revival of Brahminism and a great cultural renaissance under the Imperial Guptas in the fourth and fifth centuries A.C. This was not anti-Buddhist in any way but it certainly increased the importance and power of Brahminism, and it was also a reaction against the otherworldliness of Buddhism. The later Guptas contended for long against Hun invasions and, though they drove them off ultimately, the country was weakened and a process of decay set in. There were several bright periods subsequently and many remarkable men arose. But both Brahminism and Buddhism deteriorated and degrading practices grew up in them. It became difficult to distinguish the two. If Brahminism absorbed Buddhism, this process changed Brahminism also in many ways.

In the eighth century Shankarāchārya, one of the greatest of India's philosophers, started religious orders or maths for Hindu sanyasins or monks. This was an adoption of the old Buddhist practice of the *sangha*. Previously there had been no such organizations of sanyasins in Brahminism, although small groups of them existed.

Some degraded forms of Buddhism continued in East Bengal and in Sind in the north-west. Otherwise Buddhism gradually vanished from India as a widespread religion.

The Indian Philosophical Approach

Though one thought leads to another, each usually related to life's changing texture, and a logical movement of the human

*S. Radhakrishnan, 'Indian Philosophy,' Allen & Unwin, London, 1927.

mind is sometimes discrenible, yet thoughts overlap and the new and the old run side by side, irreconcilable and often contradicting each other. Even an individual's mind is a bundle of contradictions and it is difficult to recocnile his action one with another. A people, comprising all stages of cultural development, represent in themselves and in their thoughts, beliefs, and activities, different ages of the past leading up to the present. Probably their activities may conform more to the social and cultural pattern of the present day, or else they would be stranded and isolated from life's moving stream, but behind these activities lie primitive beliefs and unreasoned convictions. It is astonishing to find in countries industrially advanced, where every person automatically uses or takes advantage of the latest modern discovery or device, beliefs and set ideas which reason denies and intelligence cannot accept. A politician may of course succeed in his business without being a shining example of reason or intelligence. A lawyer may be a brilliant advocate and jurist and yet be singularly ignorant of other matters. Even a scientist, that typical representative of the modern age, often forgets the method and outlook of science when he goes out of his study or laboratory.

This is so even in regard to the problems that affect our daily lives in their material aspects. In philosophy and metaphysics the problems are more remote, less transient and less connected with our day's routine. For most of us they are entirely beyond our grasp unless we undergo a rigid discipline and training of the mind. And yet all of us have some kind of philosophy of life, conscious or unconscious, if not thought out then inherited or accepted from others and considered as self-evident. Or we may seek refuge from the perils of thought in faith in some religious creed or dogma, or in national destiny, or in a vague and comforting humanitarianism. Often all these and others are present together, though with little to connect them, and we develop split personalities, each functioning in its separate compartment.

Probably there was more unity and harmony in the human personality in the old days, though this was at a lower level than to-day except for certain individuals who were obviously of a very high type. During this long age of transition, through which humanity has been passing, we have managed to break up that unity, but have not so far succeeded in finding another. We cling still to the ways of dogmatic religion, adhere to outworn practices and beliefs, and yet talk and presume to live in terms of the scientific method. Perhaps science has been too narrow in its approach to life and has ignored many vital aspects of it, and hence it could not provide a suitable basis for a new unity and harmony. Perhaps it is gradually broadening this basis now, and we shall achieve a new harmony for the human personality on a much higher level than the previous one. But the problem is a more difficult and complex one now, for it has grown beyond the limits of the human personality. It was perhaps easier to develop some kind of a harmonious personality in the restricted spheres of ancient and medieval times. In that little world of town and village, with fixed concepts of social organization and behaviour, the individual and the group lived their self-contained lives, protected, as a rule, from outer storms. To-day the sphere of even the individual has grown world-wide, and different concepts of social organization conflict with each other and behind them are different philosophies of life. A strong wind arising somewhere creates a cyclone in one place and an anti-cyclone in another. So if harmony is to be achieved by the individual, it has to be supported by some kind of social harmony throughout the world.

In India, far more so than elsewhere, the old concept of social organization and the philosophy of life underlying it, have persisted, to some extent, to the present day. They could not have done so unless they had some virtue which stabilized society and made it conform to life's conditions. And they would not have failed ultimately and become a drag and a hindrance, divorced from life, if the evil in them had not overcome that virtue. But, in any event, they cannot be considered to-day as isolated phenomena; they must be viewed in that world context and made to harmonize with it.

'In India,' says Havell, 'religion is hardly a dogma, but a working hypothesis of human conduct, adapted to different stages of spiritual development and different conditions of life. A dogma might continue to be believed in, isolated from life, but a working hypothesis of human conduct must work and conform to life, or it obstructs life. The very *raison d'être* of such a hypothesis is its workableness, its conformity to life, and its capacity to adapt itself to changing conditions. So long as it can do so it serves its purpose and performs its allotted function. When it goes off at a tangent from the curve of life, loses contact with social needs, and the distance between it and life grows, it loses all its vitality and significance.'

Metaphysical theories and speculations deal not with the everchanging stuff of life but with the permanent reality behind it, if such exists. Hence they have a certain permanence which is not affected by external changes. But, inevitably, they are the products of the environment in which they grow and of the state of development of the human minds that conceived them. If their influence spreads they affect the general philosophy of life of a people. In India, philosophy, though in its higher reaches confined to the elect, has been more pervasive than elsewhere and has had a strong influence in moulding the national outlook and in developing a certain distinctive attitude of mind.

Buddhist philosophy played an important part in this process and, during the medieval period, Islam left its impress upon the national outlook, directly as well as indirectly, through the evolution of new sects which sought to bridge the gap between Hinduism and the Islamic social and religious structure. But, in the main, the dominating influence has been that of the six systems of Indian philosophy, or *darshanas*, as they are called. Some of these systems were themselves greatly affected by Buddhist thought. All of them are considered orthodox and yet they vary in their approach and their conclusions, though they have many common ideas. There is polytheism, and theism with a personal God, and pure monism, and a system which ignores God altogether and bases itself on a theory of evolution. There is both idealism and realism. The various facets of the complex and inclusive Indian mind are shown in their unity and diversity. Max Müller drew attention to both these factors: '...the more have I become impressed with the truth...that there is behind the variety of the six systems a common fund of what may be called national and popular philosophy...from which each thinker was allowed to draw for his own purposes.'

There is a common presumption in all of them: that the universe is orderly and functions according to law, that there is a mighty rhythm about it. Some such presumption becomes necessary, for otherwise there could hardly be any system to explain it. Though the law of causality, of cause and effect, functions, yet there is a measure of freedom to the individual to shape his own destiny. There is belief in rebirth and an emphasis on unselfish love and disinterested activity. Logic and reason are relied upon and used effectively for argument, but it is recognised that often intuition is greater than either. The general argument proceeds on a rational basis, in so far as reason can be applied to matters often outside its scope. Professor Keith has pointed out that 'The systems are indeed orthodox and admit the authority of the sacred scriptures, but they attack the problems of existence with human means, and scripture serves for all practical purposes but to lend sanctity to results which are achieved not only without its aid, but often in very dubious harmony with its tenets.'

The Six Systems of Philosophy

The early beginnings of the Indian systems of philosophy take us back to the pre-Buddhist era. They develop gradually, the Brahminical systems side by side with the Buddhist, often criticizing each other, often borrowing from one another. Before the beginning of the Christian era, six Brahminical systems had taken shape and crystallized themselves, out of the welter of many such systems. Each one of them represents an independent approach, a separate argument, and yet they were not isolated from each other but rather parts of a larger plan.

The six systems are known as: (1) *Nyāya*, (2) *Vaishesika*, (3) *Sāmkhya*, (4) *Yoga*, (5) *Mimāmsa*, and (6) *Vedānta*.

The *Nyāya* method is analytic and logical. In fact Nyāya means logic or the science of right reasoning. It is similar in many ways to Aristotle's syllogisms, though there are also fundamental differences between the two. The principles underlying Nyāya logic were accepted by all the other systems, and, as a kind of mental discipline, Nyāya has been taught throughout the ancient and medieval periods and up to to-day in India's schools and universities. Modern education in India has discarded it, but wherever Sanskrit is taught in the old way, Nyāya is still an essential part of the curriculum. It was not only considered an indispensable preparation for the study of philosophy, but a necessary mental training for every educated person. It has had at least as important a place in the old scheme of Indian education as Aristotle's logic has had in European education.

The method was, of course, very different from the modern scientific method of objective investigation. Nevertheless, it was critical and scientific in its own way, and, instead of relying on faith, tried to examine the objects of knowledge critically and to proceed step by step by methods of logical proof. There was some faith behind it, certain presumptions which were not capable of logical treatment. Having accepted some hypotheses the system was built up on those foundations. It was presumed that there is a rhythm and unity in life and nature. There was belief in a personal God, in individual souls, and an atomic universe. The individual was neither the soul alone nor the body, but the product of their union. Reality was supposed to be a complex of souls and nature.

The *Vaishesika* system resembles the Nyāya in many ways. It emphasizes the separateness of individual selves and objects, and develops the atomic theory of the universe. The principle of *dharma*, the moral law, is said to govern the universe, and round this the whole system revolves. The hypothesis of a God is not clearly admitted. Between the Nyāya and Vaisheshika systems and early Buddhist philosophy there are many points of contact. On the whole they adopt a realistic approach.

The *Sāmkhya* system, which Kapila (*c*. seventh century B.C.) is said to have shaped out of many early and pre-Buddhist currents of thought, is remarkable. According to Richard Garbe: 'In Kapila's doctrine, for the first time in the history of the world, the complete independence and freedom of the human mind, its full confidence in its own powers, were exhibited.'

The Sāmkhya became a well-co-ordinated system after the rise of Buddhism. The theory is a purely philosophical and metaphysical conception arising out of the mind of man and having little to do with objective observation. Indeed, such observation was not possible in matters beyond its reach. Like Buddhism, Sāmkhya proceeded along rationalistic lines of inquiry and met the challenge of Buddhism on the latter's own ground of reasoned argument without support of authority. Because of this rationalistic approach, God had to be ruled out. In Sāmkhya thus there is neither a personal God nor an impersonal one, neither monotheism nor monism. Its approach was atheistic and it undermined the foundations of a supernatural religion. There is no creation of the universe by a god, but rather a constant evolution, the product of interaction between spirit, or rather spirits, and matter, though that matter itself is of the nature of energy. This evolution is a continuous process.

The Sāmkhya is called *dvaita*, or a dualistic philosophy, because it builds its structure on two primary causes: *prakriti*, or an ever-active and changing nature or energy, and *purusha*, the spirit which does not change. There is an infinite number of purushas or souls, or something in the nature of consciousness. Under the influence of purusha, which itself is inactive, prakriti evolves and leads to the world of continuous becoming. Causality is accepted, but it is said that the effect really exists hidden in the cause. Cause and effect become the undeveloped and developed states of one and the same thing. From our practical point of view, however, cause and effect are different and distinct, but basically there is an identity between them. And so the argument goes on, showing how from the unmanifested prakriti or energy, through the influence of purusha or consciousness, and the principle of causality, nature with its immense complexity and variety of elements has developed and is ever changing and developing. Between the lowest and the highest in the universe there is a continuity and a unity. The whole conception is metaphysical, and the argument, based on certain hypotheses, is long, intricate, and reasoned.

The *Yoga* system of Patanjali is essentially a method for the discipline of the body and the mind leading up to psychic and spiritual training. Patanjali not only crystallized this old system but also wrote a famous commentary on Panini's Sanskrit grammar. This commentary, called the 'Mahābhāshya' is as much of a classic as Panini's work. Professor Stcherbatsky, of Leningrad, has written that 'the ideal scientific wrok for India is the grammar of Panini with the Mahābhāshya of Patanjali.'*

Yoga is a word well known now in Europe and America, though little understood, and it is associated with quaint practices, more especially with sitting Buddha-like and gazing on one's navel or

It is not established that Patanjali, the grammarian, was the same person as Patanjali, the author of the 'Yoga Sutras.' The grammarian's date is definitely known—second century B.C. Some people are of opinion that the author of the 'Yoga Sutras' was a different person and lived two or three hundred years later.

the tip of one's nose.* Some people learning odd tricks of the body presume to become authorities on the subject in the West, and impress and exploit the credulous and the seekers after the sensational. The system is much more than these devices and is based on the psychological conception that by proper training of the mind certain higher levels of consciousness can be reached. It is meant to be a method for finding out things for oneself rather than a preconceived metaphysical theory of reality or of the universe. It is thus experimental and the most suitable conditions for carrying out the experiment are pointed out. As such a method it can be adopted and used by any system of philosophy, whatever its theoretical approach may be. Thus the adherents of the atheistic Sāmkhya philosophy may use this method. Buddhism developed its own forms of Yoga training, partly similar, partly different. The theoretical parts of Patanjali's Yoga system are therefore of relatively small importance; it is the method that counts. Belief in God is no integral part of the system, but it is suggested that such belief in a personal God, and devotion to him, helps in concentrating the mind and thus serves a practical purpose.

The later stages of Yoga are supposed to lead to some kind of intuitive insight or to a condition of ecstasy, such as the mystics speak of. Whether this is some kind of higher mental state, opening the door to further knowledge, or is merely a kind of self-hypnosis, I do not know. Even if the former is possible, the latter certainly also happens, and it is well-known that unregulated Yoga has sometimes led to unfortunate consequences so far as the mind of the person is concerned.

But before these final stages of meditation and contemplation are reached, there is the discipline of the body and mind to be practised. The body should be fit and healthy, supple and graceful, hard and strong. A number of bodily exercises are prescribed, as also ways of breathing, in order to have some control over it and normally to take deep and long breaths. 'Exercises' is the wrong word, for they involve no strenuous movement. They are rather postures—*asanas* as they are called—and, properly done, they relax and tone up the body and do not tire it at all. This old and typical Indian method of preserving bodily fitness is rather remarkable when one compares it with the more usual methods involving rushing about, jerks, hops, and jumps which leave one panting, out of breath, and tired out. These other methods have also been common enough in India, as have wrestling, swimming, riding, fencing, archery, Indian clubs, something in the nature of ju-jitsu, and many other pastimes and games. But the old *asana* method is perhaps more typical of India and seems to fit in with the spirit of her philosophy. There is a poise in it and an unruffled

* *The word 'Yoga' means union. Possibly it is derived from the same root as the English word 'yoke'—joining.*

calm even while it exercises the body. Strength and fitness are gained without any waste of energy or disturbance of the mind. And because of this the *asanas* are suited to any age and some of them can be performed even by the old.

There are a large number of these *asanas*. For many years now I have practised a few simple selected ones, whenever I have had the chance, and I have no doubt that I have profited greatly by them, living as I often did in environments unfavourable to the mind and body. These and some breathing exercises are the extent of my practice of the physical exercises of the Yoga system. I have not gone beyond the elementary stages of the body, and my mind continues to be an unruly member, misbehaving far too often.

The discipline of the body, which includes eating and drinking the right things and avoiding the wrong ones, is to be accompanied by what the Yoga system describes as ethical preparation. This includes non-violence, truthfulness, continence, etc. Non-violence or *ahimsa* is something much more than abstention from physical violence. It is an avoidance of malice and hatred.

All this is supposed to lead to a control of the senses; then comes contemplation and meditation, and finally intense concentration, which should lead to various kinds of intuition.

Vivekananda, one of the greatest of the modern exponents of Yoga and the Vedanta, has laid repeated stress on the experimental character of Yoga and on basing it on reason. 'No one of these Yogas gives up reason, no one asks you to be hood-winked or to deliver your reason into the hands of priests of any type whatsoever.... Each one of them tells you to cling to your reason, to hold fast to it.' Though the spirit of Yoga and the Vedanta may be akin to the spirit of science, it is true that they deal with different media, and hence vital differences creep in. According to the Yoga, the spirit is not limited to the intelligence, and also 'thought is action, and only action can make thought of any value.' Inspiration and intuition are recognized but may they not lead to deception? Vivekananda answers that inspiration must not contradict reason: 'What we call inspiration is the development of reason. The way to intuition is through reason....No genuine inspiration ever contradicts reason. Where it does it is no inspiration.' Also 'inspiration must be for the good of one and all; and not for name or fame or personal gain. It should always be for the good of the world, and perfectly unselfish.'

Again, 'Experience is the only source of knowledge.' The same methods of investigation which we apply to the sciences and to exterior knowledge should be applied to religion. 'If a religion is destroyed by such investigation it was nothing but a useless and unworthy superstition; the sooner it disappeared the better.' 'Why religions should claim that they are not bound to abide by the standpoint of reason no one knows....For it is better that mankind should become atheist by following reason than blindly believe in two hundred million gods on the authority of anybody....Perhaps there are prophets, who have passed the limits of sense and obtained a glimpse of the beyond. We shall believe it only when we can do the same ourselves; not before.' It is said that reason is not strong enough, that often it makes mistakes. If reason is weak why should a body of priests be considered any better guides? 'I will abide by my reason,' continues Vivekananda, 'because with all its weakness there is some chance of my getting at truth through it....We should therefore follow reason, and also sympathise with those who do not come to any sort of belief, following reason.' 'In the study of this Raja Yoga no faith or belief is necessary. Believe nothing until you find it out for yourself.'*

Vivekananda's unceasing stress on reason and his refusal to take anything on trust derived from his passionate belief in the freedom of the mind and also because he had seen the evils of authority in his own country: 'for I was born in a country where they have gone to the extreme of authority.' He interpreted—and he had the right to interpret—the old Yoga systems and the Vedānta accordingly. But, however much experiment and reason may be at the back of them, they deal with regions which are beyond the reach or even the understanding of the average man—a realm of psychical and psychological experiences entirely different from the world we know and are used to. Those experiments and experiences have certainly not been confined to India, and there is abundant evidence of them in the records of Christian mystics, Persian Sufis, and others. It is extraordinary how these experiences resemble each other, demonstrating, as Romain Rolland says, 'the universality and perennial occurrence of the great facts of religious experience, their close resemblance under the diverse costumes of race and time, attesting to the persistent unity of the human spirit—or rather, for it goes deeper than the spirit, which is itself obliged to delve for it—to the identity of the materials constituting humanity.'

Yoga, then, is an experimental system of probing into the psychical background of the individual and thus developing certain perceptions and control of the mind. How far this can be utilised to advantage by modern psychology, I do not know; but some attempt to do so seems worth while. Aurobindo Ghose has defined Yoga as follows: 'All Raja-Yoga depends on this perception and experience—that our inner elements, combinations, functions, forces, can be separated or dissolved, can be newly combined and set to novel and formerly impossible uses,

*Most of the extracts from Vivekananda's writings have been taken from Romain Rolland's 'Life of Vivekananda.'

or can be transformed and resolved into a new general synthesis by fixed internal processes.'

The next system of philosophy is known as the *Mimāmsa*. This is ritualistic and tends towards polytheism. Modern popular Hinduism as well as Hindu Law have been largely influenced by this system and its rules which lay down the *dharma* or the scheme of right living as conceived by it. It might be noted that the polytheism of the Hindus is of a curious variety, for the *devas*, the shining ones or gods, for all their special powers are supposed to be of a lower order of creation than man. Both the Hindus and Buddhists believe that human birth is the highest stage that the Being has reached on the road to self-realization. Even the *devas* can only achieve this freedom and realization through human birth. This conception is evidently far removed from normal polytheism. Buddhists say that only man can attain the supreme consummation of Buddhahood.

Sixthly and lastly in this series comes the *Vedānta* system, which, arising out of the Upanishads, developed and took many shapes and forms, but was always based on a monistic philosophy of the universe. The *purusha* and *prakriti* of the Sāmkhya are not considered as independent substances but as modifications of a single reality—the absolute. On the foundation of the early Vedānta, Shankara (or Shankarāchārya) built a system which is called the *Advaita Vedānta* or non-dualist Vedānta. It is this philosophy which represents the dominant philosophic outlook of Hinduism to-day. It is based on pure monism, the only ultimate reality in the metaphysical sense being the *Atman*, the Absolute Soul. That is the subject, all else is objective. How that Absolute Soul pervades everything, how the one appears as the many, and yet retains its wholeness, for the Absolute is indivisible and cannot be divided, all this cannot be accounted for by the processes of logical reasoning, for our minds are limited by the finite world. The Upanishad had described this *Atman*, if this can be called a description thus: 'Whole is that, whole (too) is this; from whole, whole cometh; take whole from whole, (yet) whole remains.'

Shankara builds a subtle and intricate theory of knowledge and proceeding from certain assumptions, step by step, by logical argument, leads up to the complete system of advaitism or non-dualism. The individual soul is not a separate entity but that Absolute Soul itself though limited in some ways. It is compared to the space enclosed in a jar, the *Atman* being universal space. For practical purposes they may be treated as distinct from one another but this distinction is apparent only, not real. Freedom consists in realizing this unity, this oneness of the individual with the Absolute Soul.

The phenomenal world we see about us thus becomes a mere reflection of that reality, or a shadow cast by it on the empirical plane. It has been called Mâyâ, which has been mistranslated as 'illusion.' But it is not non-existence. It is an intermediate form between Being and non-Being. It is a kind of relative existence, and so perhaps the conception of relativity brings us nearer to the meaning of Mâyâ. What is good and evil then in this world? Are they also mere reflections and shadows with no substance? Whatever they may be in the ultimate analysis in this empirical world of ours there is a validity and importance in these ethical distinctions. They are relevant where individuals function as such. These finite individuals cannot imagine the infinite without limiting it; they can only form limited and objective conceptions of it. Yet even these finite forms and concepts rest ultimately in the infinite and Absolute. Hence the form of religion becomes a relative affair and each individual has liberty to form such conceptions as he is capable of.

Shankara accepted the Brahminical organization of social life on the caste basis, as representing the collective experience and wisdom of the race. But he held that any person belonging to any caste could attain the highest knowledge.

There is about Shankara's attitude and philosophy a sense of world negation and withdrawal from the normal activities of the world in search for that freedom of the self which was to him the final goal for every person. There is also a continual insistence on self-sacrifice and detachment.

And yet Shankara was a man of amazing energy and vast activity. He was no escapist retiring into his shell or into a corner of the forest, seeking his own individual perfection and oblivious of what happened to others. Born in Malabar in the far south of India, he travelled incessantly all over India, meeting innumerable people, arguing, debating, reasoning, convincing, and filling them with a part of his own passion and tremendous vitality. He was evidently a man who was intensely conscious of his mission, a man who looked upon the whole of India from Cape Comorin to the Himalayas as his field of action and as something that held together culturally and was infused by the same spirit, though this might take many external forms. He strove hard to synthesize the diverse currents that were troubling the mind of India of his day and to build a unity of outlook out of that diversity. In a brief life of thirty-two years he did the work of many long lives and left such an impress of his powerful mind and rich personality on India that it is very evident to-day. He was a curious mixture of a philosopher and a scholar, an agnostic and a mystic, a poet and a saint, and in addition to all this, a practical reformer and an able organizer. He built up, for the first time within the Brahminical fold, ten religious orders and of these four are very much alive to-day. He established four great *maths* or monasteries, locating them far from each other, almost at the four corners of India.

One of these was in the south at Sringeri in Mysore, another at Puri on the east coast, the third at Dvaraka in Kathiawad on the west coast, and the fourth at Badrinath in the heart of the Himalayas. At the age of thirty-two this Brahmin from the tropical south died at Kedarnath in the upper snow-covered reaches of the Himalayas.

There is a significance about these long journeys of Shankara throughout this vast land at a time when travel was difficult and the means of transport very slow and primitive. The very conception of these journeys, and his meeting kindred souls everywhere and speaking to them in Sanskrit, the common language of the learned throughout India, brings out the essential unity of India even in those far-off days. Such journeys could not have been uncommon then or earlier; people went to and fro in spite of political divisions, new books travelled, and every new thought or fresh theory spread rapidly over the entire country and became the subject of interested talk and often of heated debate. There was not only a common intellectual and cultural life among the educated people, but vast numbers of common folk were continually travelling to the numerous places of pilgrimage, spread out all over the land and famous from epic times.

All this going to and fro and meeting people from different parts of the country must have intensified the conception of a common land and a common culture. This travelling was not confined to the upper castes; among the pilgrims were men and women of all castes and classes. Whatever the religious significance of these pilgrimages in the minds of the people might have been, they were looked upon also, as they are to-day, as holiday-time and opportunities for merry-making and seeing different parts of the country. Every place of pilgrimage contained a cross-section of the people of India in all their great variety of custom, dress, and language, and yet very conscious of their common features and the bonds that held them together and brought all of them to meet in one place. Even the difference of language between the north and the south did not prove a formidable barrier to this intercourse.

All this was so then and Shankara was doubtless fully aware of it. It would seem that Shankara wanted to add to this sense of national unity and common consciousness. He functioned on the intellectual, philosophical and religious plane and tried to bring about a greater unity of thought all over the country. He functioned also on the popular plane in many ways, destroying many a dogma and opening the door of his philosophic sanctuary to every one who was capable of entering it. By locating his four great monasteries in the north, south, east, and west, he evidently wanted to encourage the conception of a culturally united India. These four places had been previously places of pilgrimage from

191

all parts of the country, and now became more so.

How well the ancient Indians chose their sacred places of pilgrimage! Almost always they are lovely spots with beautiful natural surroundings. There is the icy cave of Amaranath in Kashmir, and there is the temple of the Virgin Goddess right at the southern tip of India at Rameshwaram, near Cape Comorin. There is Benares, of course, and Hardwar, nestling at the foot of the Himalayas, where the Ganges flows out of its tortuous mountain valleys into the plains below, and Prayaga (or Allahabad) where the Ganges meets the Jumna, and Mathura and Brindaban by the Jumna, round which the Krishna legends cluster, and Budh Gaya where Buddha is said to have attained enlightenment, and so many places in the south. Many of the old temples, especially in the south, contain famous sculptures and other artistic remains. A visit to many of the places of pilgrimage thus gives an insight into old Indian art.

Shankara is said to have helped in putting an end to Buddhism in India as a widespread religion, and that thereafter Brahminism absorbed it in a fraternal embrace. But Buddhism had shrunk in India even before Shankara's time. Some of Shankara's Brahmin opponents called him a disguised Buddhist. It is true that Buddhism influenced him considerably.

India and China

It was through Buddhism that China and India came near to each other and developed many contacts. Whether there were any such contacts before Ashoka's reign we do not know; probably there was some sea-borne trade, for silk used to come from China. Yet there must have been overland contacts and migrations of peoples in far earlier periods, for Mongoloid features are common in the eastern border areas of India. In Nepal these are very marked. In Assam (Kamarupa of old) and Bengal they are often evident. Historically speaking, however, Ashoka's missionaries blazed the trail and, as Buddhism spread in China, there began that long succession of pilgrims and scholars who journeyed between India and China for 1,000 years. They travelled overland across the Gobi Desert and the plains and mountains of Central Asia and over the Himalayas—a long, hard journey full of peril. Many Indians and Chinese perished on the way, and one account says that as many as 90 per cent of these pilgrims perished. Many having managed to reach the end of their journey did not return and settled in the land of their adoption. There was another route also, not much safer, though probably shorter: this was by sea via Indo-China, Java, and Sumatra, Malaya and the Nicobar Islands. This was also frequently used, and sometimes a pilgrim travelled overland and returned by sea. Buddhism and Indian culture had spread all over Central Asia and in parts of Indonesia, and there were large numbers of monasteries and study centres dotted all over these vast areas. Travellers from India or China thus found a welcome and shelter along these routes by land and sea. Sometimes scholars from China would break journey for a few months at some Indian colony in Indonesia in order to learn Sanskrit before they came to India.

The first record of an Indian scholar's visit to China is that of Kashyapa Matanga who reached China in 67 A.D. in the reign of the Emperor Ming Ti and probably at his invitation. He settled down at Lo Yang by the Lo river. Dharmaraksha accompanied him and, in later years, among the noted scholars who went were Buddhabhadra, Jinabhadra, Kumarajiva, Paramartha, Jinagupta, and Bodhidharma. Each one of these took a group of monks or disciples with him. It is said that at one time (sixth century A.C.) there were more than 3,000 Indian Buddhist monks and 10,000 Indian families in the Lo Yang province alone.

These Indian scholars who went to China not only carried many Sanskrit manuscripts with them, which they translated into Chinese, but some of them also wrote original books in the Chinese language. They made quite a considerable contribution to Chinese literature, including poetry. Kumarajiva who went to China in 401 A.C., was a prolific writer and as many as forty-seven different books written by him have come down to us. His Chinese style is supposed to be very good. He translated the life of the great Indian scholar Nāgārjuna into Chinese. Jinagupta went to China in the second half of the sixty century A.C. He translated thirty-seven original Sanskrit works into Chinese. His great knowledge was so much admired that an emperor of the T'ang dynasty became his disciple.

There was two-way traffic between India and China and many Chinese scholars came here. Among the best known who have left records of their journeys are Fa Hien (or Fa Hsien), Sung Yun, Hsuan-Tsang (or Chwen Chuang), and I-Tsing (or Yi-Tsing). Fa Hien came to India in the fifth century; he was a disciple of Kumarajiva in China. There is an interesting account of what Kumarajiva told him on the eve of his departure for India, when he went to take leave of his teacher. Kumarajiva charged him not to spend all his time in gathering religious knowledge only but to study in some detail the life and habits of the people of India, so that China might understand them and their country as a whole. Fa Hien studied at Pataliputra university.

The most famous of the Chinese travellers to India was Hsuan-Tsang who came in the seventh century when the great T'ang dynasty flourished in China and Harshavardhana ruled over an empire in North India. Hsuan-Tsang came overland across the Gobi Desert and passing Turfan and Kucha, Taskhand and

Samarkand, Balkh, Khotan and Yarkand, crossed the Himalayas into India. He tells us of his many adventures, of the perils he overcame, of the Buddhist rulers and monasteries in Central Asia, and of the Turks there who were ardent Buddhists. In India he travelled all over the country, greatly honoured and respected everywhere, making accurate observations of places and peoples, and noting down some delightful and some fantastic stories that he heard. Many years he spent at the great Nalanda University, not far from Pataliputra, which was famous for its many-sided learning and attracted students from far corners of the country. It is said that as many as 10,000 students and monks were in residence there. Hsuan-Tsang took the degree of Master of the Law there and finally became vice-principal of the university.

Hsuan-Tsang's book the Si-Yu-Ki or the Record of the Western Kingdom (meaning India), makes fascinating reading. Coming from a highly civilized and sophisticated country, at a time when China's capital Si-an-fu was a centre of art and learning, his comments on and descriptions of conditions in India are valuable. He tells us of the system of education which began early and proceeded by stages to the university where the five branches of knowledge taught were: (1) Grammar, (2) Science of Arts and Crafts, (3) Medicine, (4) Logic, and (5) Philosophy. He was particularly struck by the love of learning of the Indian people. Some kind of primary education was fairly widespread as all the monks and priests were teachers, Of the people he says: 'With respect to the ordinary people, although they are naturally light-minded, yet they are upright and honourable. In money matters they are without craft, and in administering justice they are considerate.... They are not deceitful or treacherous in their conduct, and are faithful in their oaths and promises. In their rules of government there is remarkable rectitude, whilst in their behaviour there is much gentleness and sweetness. With respect to criminals or rebels, these are few in number, and only occasionally troublesome.' He says further: 'As the administration of the government is founded on benign principles, the executive is simple....People are not subject to forced labour....In this way taxes on people are light....The merchants who engage in commerce come and go in carrying out their transactions.'

Hsuan-Tsang returned the way he came, via Central Asia, carrying a large number of manuscripts with him. From his account one gathers a vivid impression of the wide sway of Buddhism in Khorasan, Iraq, Mosul, and right up to the frontiers of Syria. And yet this was a time when Buddhism was in decay there and Islam, already beginning in Arabia, was soon to spread out over all these lands. About the Iranian people, Hsuan-Tsang makes an interesting observation: they 'care not for learning, but give themselves entirely to works of art. All they make the neighbouring countries value very much.'

Iran then, as before and after, concentrated on adding to the beauty and grace of life, and its influence spread far in Asia. Of the strange little kingdom of Turfan, on the edge of the Gobi Desert, Hsuan-Tsang tells us, and we have learned more about it in recent years from the work of archæologists. Here many cultures came and mixed and coalesced, producing a rich combination which drew its inspiration from China and India and Persia and even Hellenic sources. The language was Indo-European, derived from India and Iran, and resembling in some ways the Celtic languages of Europe; the religion came from India; the ways of life were Chinese; many of the artistic wares they had were from Iran. The statues and frescoes of the Buddhas and gods and goddesses, beautifully made, have often Indian draperies and Grecian headdresses. These goddesses, says Monsieur Grousset, represent 'the happiest combination of Hindu suppleness, Hellenic eloquence, and Chinese charm.'

Hsuan-Tsang went back to his homeland, welcomed by his Emperor and his people, and settled down to write his book and translate the many manuscripts he had brought. When he had started on his journey, many years earlier, there is a story that the Emperor T'ang mixed a handful of dust in a drink and offered this to him, saying: 'You would do well to drink this cup, for are we not told that a handful of one's country's soil is worth more than ten thousand pounds of foreign gold?'

Hsuan-Tsang's visit to India and the great respect in which he was held both in China and India led to the establishment of political contacts between the rulers of the two countries. Harshavardhana of Kanauj and the T'ang Emperor exchanged embassies. Hsuan-Tsang himself remained in touch with India, exchanging letters with friends there and receiving manuscripts. Two interesting letters, originally written in Sanskrit, have been preserved in China. One of these was written in 654 A.C. by an Indian Buddhist scholar, Sthavira Prajnādeva, to Hsuan-Tsang. After greeting and news about common friends and their literary work, he proceeds to say: 'We are sending you a pair of white cloths to show that we are not forgetful. The road is long, so do not mind the smallness of the present. We wish you may accept it. As regards the Sutras and Shastras which you may require please send us a list. We will copy them and send them to you.' Hsuan-Tsang in his reply says: 'I learnt from an ambassador who recently came back from India that the great teacher Shilabhadra was no more. This news overwhelmed me with grief that knew no bounds....Among the Sutras and Shastras that I, Hsuan-Tsang, had brought with me I have already translated the **Yogacharyabhumi-Shastra** and other works, in all thirty

volumes. I should humbly let you know that while crossing the
Indus I had lost a load of sacred texts. I now send you a list of the
texts annexed to this letter. I request you to send them to me if
you get the chance. I am sending some small articles as presents.
Please accept them.'*

Hsuan-Tsang has told us much of Nalanda university, and
there are other accounts of it also. Yet when I went, some years
ago, and saw the excavated ruins of Nalanda I was amazed at
their extent and the huge scale on which it was planned. Only
a part of it has so far been uncovered, and over the rest there
are inhabited localities, but even this part consisted of huge
courts surrounded by stately buildings in stone.

Soon after Hsuan-Tsang's death in China, yet another famous
Chinese pilgrim made the journey to India—I-tsing (or Yi-tsing).
He started in 671 A.C., and it took him nearly two years to reach
the Indian port of Tamralipti, at the mouth of the Hooghly.
For he came by sea and stopped for many months at Shribhoga
(modern Palembang in Sumatra) to study Sanskrit. This journey
of his by sea has a certain significance, for it is probable that
there were disturbed conditions in Central Asia then and political
changes were taking place. Many of the friendly Buddhist monasteries that dotted the land route may have ceased to exist. It is
also likely that the sea route was more convenient with the growth
of Indian colonies in Indonesia, and constant trade and other
contacts between India and these countries. It appears from his
and other accounts that there was at that time regular navigation
between Persia (Iran), India, Malaya, Sumatra, and China.
I-tsing sailed in a Persian ship from Kwangtung, and went first
to Sumatra.

I-tsing also studied at Nalanda university for a long time and
carried back with him several hundred Sanskrit texts. He was
chiefly interested in the fine points of Buddhist ritual and ceremonial and has written in detail about them. But he tells us
much also about customs, clothes, and food. Wheat was the
staple diet in North India, as now, and rice in the south and the
east. Meat was sometimes eaten, but this was rare. (I-tsing probably tells us more about the Buddhist monks than about others).
Ghee (clarified butter), oil, milk, and cream were found everywhere, and cakes and fruits were abundant. I-tsing noted the
importance that Indians have always attached to a certain ceremonial purity. 'Now the first and chief difference between India
of the five regions and other nations is the peculiar distinction
between purity and impurity.' Also: 'To preserve what has been
left from the meal, as is done in China, is not at all in accordance
with Indian rules.'

I-tsing refers to India generally as the West (Si-fang), but he

*Quoted in 'India and China' by Dr. P. C. Bagchi (Calcutta, 1944).

tells us that it was known as Aryadesha – 'the Aryadesha'; 'arya' means noble, 'desha' region—the noble region, a name for the west. It is so called because men of noble character appear there successively, and people all praise the land by that name. It is also called Madhyadesha, i.e., the middle land, for it is the centre of a hundred myriads of countries. The people are all familiar with this name. The northern tribes (Hu or Mongols or Turks) alone call the Noble Land 'Hindu' (Hsin-tu), but this is not at all a common name; it is only a vernacular name, and has no special significance. The people of India do not know this designation, and the most suitable name for India is the 'Noble Land.'

I-tsing's reference to 'Hindu' is interesting. He goes on to say: 'Some say that Indu means the moon, and the Chinese name for India, i.e., Indu (Yin-tu), is derived from it. Although it might mean this, it is nevertheless not the common name. As for the Indian name for the Great Chou (China), i.e., Cheena, it is a name and has no special meaning.' He also mentions the Sanskrit names for Korea and other countries.

For all his admiration for India and many things Indian, I-tsing made it clear that he gave first place to his native land, China. India might be the 'noble region,' but China was the 'divine land.' 'The people of the five parts of India are proud of their own purity and excellence. But high refinement, literary elegance, propriety, moderation, ceremonies of welcoming and parting, the delicious taste of food, and the richness of benevolence and righteousness are found in China only, and no other country can excel her.' 'In the healing arts of acupuncture and cautery and the skill of feeling the pulse, China has never been superseded by any part of India; the medicament for prolonging life is only found in China....From the character of men and the quality of things China is called the "divine land". Is there anyone in the five parts of India who does not admire China?'

The word used in the old Sanskrit for the Chinese Emperor is *deva-putra*, which is an exact translation of 'Son of Heaven'.

I-tsing, himself a fine scholar in Sanskrit, praises the language and says it is respected in far countries in the north and south. ... 'How much more then should people of the divine land (China), as well as the celestial store house (India), teach the real rules of the language!'*

Sanskrit scholarship must have been fairly widespread in China. It is interesting to find that some Chinese scholars tried to introduce Sanskrit phonetics into the Chinese language. A well-known example of this is that of the monk Shon Wen, who lived at the time of the T'ang dynasty. He tried to develop an alphabetical system along these lines in Chinese.

* These extracts have been taken from J. Takakusu's translation of I-Tsing's: 'A record of the Buddhist Religions as practised in India and Malay Archipelago' (Oxford, 1896).

With the decay of Buddhism in India this Indo-Chinese commerce of scholars practically ceased, though pilgrims from China occasionally came to visit the holy places of Buddhism in India. During the political revolutions from the eleventh century A.C. onwards, crowds of Buddhist monks, carrying bundles of manuscripts, went to Nepal or crossed the Himalayas, into Tibet. A considerable part of old Indian literature thus and previously, found its way to China and Tibet and in recent years it has been discovered afresh there in the original or more frequently, in translations. Many Indian classics have been preserved in Chinese and Tibetan translations relating not only to Buddhism but also to Brahminism, astronomy, mathematics, medicine, etc. There are supposed to be 8,000 such works in the Sung-pao collection in China. Tibet is full of them. There used to be frequent co-operation between Indian, Chinese, and Tibetan scholars. A notable instance of this co-operation, still extant, is a Sanskrit-Tibetan-Chinese dictionary of Buddhist technical terms. This dates from the ninth or tenth century A.C. and is named the 'Mahavyutpatti.'

Among the most ancient printed books discovered in China, dating from the eighth century A.C., are books in Sanskrit. These were printed from wooden blocks. In the tenth century the Imperial Printing Commission was organized in China and as a result of this, and right up to the Sung era, the art of printing developed rapidly. It is surprising and difficult to account for that, in spite of the close contacts between Indian and Chinese scholars and their exchanges of books and manuscripts for hundreds of years, there is no evidence whatever of the printing of books in India during that period. Block printing went to Tibet from China at some early period and, I believe, it is still practised there. Chinese printing was introduced into Europe during the Mongol or Yuan dynasty (1260-1368). First known in Germany, it spread to other countries during the fifteenth century.

Even during the Indo-Afghan and Mughal periods in India there was occasional diplomatic intercourse between India and China. Mohammed bin Tughlak, Sultan of Delhi (1326-51) sent the famous Arab traveller, Ibn Batuta, as ambassador to the Chinese court. Bengal had at that time shaken off the suzerainty of Delhi and became an independent sultanate. In the middle of the fourteenth century the Chinese court sent two ambassadors, Hu-Shien and Fin-Shien, to the Bengal Sultan. This led to a succession of ambassadors being sent from Bengal to China during Sultan Ghias-ud Din's reign. This was the period of the Ming Emperors in China. One of the later embassies, sent in 1414 by Saif-ud Din, carried valuable presents, among them a live giraffe. How a giraffe managed to reach India is a mystery: probably it it came as a gift from Africa and was sent on to the Ming Emperor as a rarity which would be appreciated. It was indeed greatly appreciated in China where a giraffe is considered an auspicious symbol by the followers of Confucius. There is no doubt that the animal was a giraffe for, apart from a long account of it, there is also a Chinese picture of it on silk. The court artist, who made this picture, has written a long account in praise of it and of the good fortune that flows from it. 'The ministers and the people all gathered to gaze at it and their joy knows no end.'

Trade between India and China, which had flourished during the Buddhist period, was continued throughout the Indo-Afghan and Mughal periods, and there was a continuous exchange of commodities. The trade went overland across the northern Himalayan passes and along the old caravan routes of central Asia. There was also a considerable sea-borne trade, via the islands of south-east Asia, chiefly to south Indian ports.

During these thousand years and more of intercourse between India and China, each country learned something from the other, not only in the regions of thought and philosophy, but also in the arts and sciences of life. Probably China was more influenced by India than India by China, which is a pity, for India could well have received, with profit to herself, some of the sound commonsense of the Chinese, and with its aid checked her own extravagant fancies. China took much from India but she was always strong and self-confident enough to take it in her own way and fit it in somewhere in her own texture of life.* Even Buddhism and its intricate philosophy became tinged with the doctrines of Confucius and Lao-tze. The somewhat pessimistic outlook of Buddhist philosophy could not change or suppress the love of life and gaiety of the Chinese. There is an old Chinese proverb which says: 'If the government gets hold of you, they'll flog you to death; if the Buddhists get hold of you, they'll starve you to death!'

A famous Chinese novel of the sixteenth century—'Monkey' by Wu Ch'en-en (translated into English by Arthur Waley)— deals with the mythical and fantastic adventures of Hsuan-Tsang on his way to India. The book ends with a dedication to India: 'I dedicate this work to Buddha's pure land. May it repay the kindness of patron and preceptor, may it mitigate the sufferings of the lost and damned....'

After being cut off from each other for many centuries, India and China were brought by some strange fate under the influence of the British East India Company. India had to endure this for long; in China the contact was brief, but even so it brought opium and war.

And now the wheel of fate has turned full circle and again

*Professor Hu Shih, the leader of the new Chinese renaissance movement, has written on the past 'Indianization of China.'

199

India and China look towards each other and past memories crowd in their minds; again pilgrims of a new kind cross or fly over the mountains that separate them, bringing their messages of cheer and goodwill and creating fresh bonds of a friendship that will endure.

Indian Colonies and Culture in South-East Asia

To know and understand India one has to travel far in time and space, to forget for a while her present condition with all its misery and narrowness and horror, and to have glimpses of what she was and what she did. 'To know my country', wrote Rabindranath Tagore, 'one has to travel to that age, when she realized her soul and thus transcended her physical boundaries, when she revealed her being in a radiant magnanimity which illumined the eastern horizon, making her recognized as their own by those in alien shores who were awakened into a surprise of life; and not now when she has withdrawn herself into a narrow barrier of obscurity, into a miserly pride of exclusiveness, into a poverty of mind that dumbly revolves around itself in an unmeaning repetition of a past that has lost its light and has no message for the pilgrims of the future.'

One has not only to go back in time but to travel, in mind if not in body, to various countries of Asia, where India spread out in many ways, leaving immortal testimony of her spirit, her power, and her love of beauty. How few of us know of these great achievements of our past, how few realize that if India was great in thought and philosophy, she was equally great in action. The history that men and women from India made far from their homeland has still to be written. Most westerners still imagine that ancient history is largely concerned with the Mediterranean countries, and medieval and modern history is dominated by the quarrelsome little continent of Europe. And still they make plans for the future as if Europe only counted and the rest could be fitted in anywhere.

Sir Charles Eliot has written that 'Scant justice is done to India's position in the world by those European histories which recount the exploits of her invaders and leave the impression that her own people were a feeble dreamy folk, sundered from the rest of mankind by their seas and mountain frontiers. Such a picture takes no account of the intellectual conquests of the Hindus. Even their political conquests were not contemptible, and are remarkable for the distance, if not the extent, of the territories occupied....But such military or commercial invasions are insignificant compared with the spread of Indian thought.'[*]

*Eliot: 'Hinduism and Buddhism', Vol. I., p. xii.

Eliot was probably unaware, when he wrote, of many recent discoveries in south-east Asia, which have revolutionized the conception of India's and Asia's past. The knowledge of those discoveries would have strengthened his argument and shown that Indian activities abroad, even apart from the spread of her thought, were very far from being insignificant. I remember when I first read, about fifteen years ago, some kind of a detailed account of the history of South-East Asia, how amazed I was and how excited I became. New panoramas opened out before me, new perspectives of history, new conceptions of India's past, and I had to adjust all my thinking and previous notions to them. Champa, Cambodia and Angkor, Srivijaya and Majapahit suddenly rose out of the void, took living shape, vibrant with that instinctive feeling which makes the past touch the present.

Of Sailendra, the mighty man of war and conquest and other achievements, Dr. H. G. Quaritch Wales has written: 'This great conqueror, whose achievements can only be compared with those of the greatest soldiers known to western history, and whose fame in his time sounded from Persia to China, in a decade or two built up a vast maritime empire which endured for five centuries, and made possible the marvellous flowering of Indian art and culture in Java and Cambodia. Yet in our encyclopædias and histories...one will search in vain for a reference to this far-flung empire or to its noble founder....The very fact of such an empire ever having existed is scarcely known, except by a handful of Oriental scholars.'* The military exploits of these early Indian colonists are important as throwing light on certain aspects of the Indian character and genius which have hitherto not been appreciated. But far more important is the rich civilization they built up in their colonies and settlements and which endured for over a thousand years.

During the past quarter of a century a great deal of light has been thrown on the history of this widespread area in south-east Asia, which is sometimes referred to as Greater India. There are many gaps still, many contradictions, and scholars continue to put forward their rival theories, but the general outline is clear enough, and sometimes there is an abundance of detail. There is no lack of material, for there are references in Indian books, and accounts of Arab travellers and, most important of all, Chinese historical accounts. There are also many old inscriptions, coperplates, etc., and in Java and Bali there is a rich literature based on Indian sources, and often paraphrasing Indian epics and myths. Greek and Latin sources have also supplied some information. But, above all, there are the magnificent ruins of ancient monuments, especially at Angkor and Borobudur†.

*In 'Towards Angkor', Harrap, 1937.
†Reference might be made to Dr. R. C. Majumdar's 'Ancient Indian Colonies in the Far

From the first century of the Christian era onwards wave after wave of Indian colonists spread east and south-east reaching Ceylon, Burma, Malaya, Java, Sumatra, Borneo, Siam, Cambodia, and Indo-China. Some of them managed to reach Formosa, the Philippine Islands and Celebes. Even as far as Madagascar the current language is Indonesian with a mixture of Sanskrit words. It must have taken them several hundred years to spread out in this way, and possibly all of these places were not reached directly from India but from some intermediate settlement. There appear to have been four principal waves of colonization from the first century A.C. to about 900 A.C., and in between there must have been a stream of people going eastwards. But the most remarkable feature of these ventures was that they were evidently organized by the state. Widely scattered colonies were started almost simultaneously and almost always the settlements were situated on strategic points and on important trade routes. The names that were given to these settlements were old Indian names. Thus Cambodia, as it is known now, was called Kamboja, which was a well-known town in ancient India, in Gandhara or the Kabul valley. This itself indicates roughly the period of this colonization, for at that time Gandhara (Afghanistan) must have been an important part of Aryan India.

What led to these extraordinary expeditions across perilous seas and what was the tremendous urge behind them? They could not have been thought of or organized unless they had been preceded for many generations or centuries by individuals or small groups intent on trade. In the most ancient Sanskrit books there are vague references to these countries of the east. It is not always easy to identify the names given in them but sometimes there is no difficulty. Java is clearly from 'Yavadvipa' or the Island of Millet. Even to-day java means barley or millet in India. The other names given in the old books are also usually associated with minerals, metals, or some industrial or agricultural product. This nomenclature itself makes one think of trade.

Dr. R. C. Majumdar has pointed out that 'If literature can be regarded as a fair reflex of the popular mind, trade and commerce must have been a supreme passion in India in the centuries immediately preceding and following the Christian era.' All this indicates an expanding economy and a constant search for distant markets.

This trade gradually increased in the third and second centuries B.C. and then these adventurous traders and merchants may have been followed by missionaries, for this was just the period after Ashoka. The old stories in Sanskrit contain many accounts of perilous sea voyages and of shipwrecks. Both Greek and Arab

East' (Calcutta, 1927), and his 'Svarnadvipa' (Calcutta, 1937). Also to the publications of the Greater India Society (Calcutta).

accounts show that there was regular maritime intercourse between India and the Far East at least as early as the first century A.C. The Malay Peninsula and the Indonesian Islands lay on the direct trade route between China and India, Persia, Arabia, and the Mediterranean. Apart from their geographical importance these countries contained valuable minerals. metals, spices, and timber. Malaya was then, as now, famous for its tin mines. Probably the earliest voyages were along the east coast of India-Kalinga (Orissa), Bengal, Burma and then down the Malay Peninsula. Later the direct sea routes from east and south India were developed. It was along this sea route that many Chinese pilgrims came to India. Fa Hsien in the fifth century passed Java and complains that there were many heretics then, meaning people following the Brahminical faith and not Buddhism.

It is clear that shipbuilding was a well-developed and flourishing industry in ancient India. We have some details and particulars of the ships built in those days. Many Indian ports are mentioned. South Indian (Andhra) coins of the second and third centuries A.C. bear the device of a two-masted ship. The Ajanta Frescoes depict the conquest of Ceylon and ships carrying elephants are shown.

The huge states and empires that developed from the original Indian settlements were essentially naval powers interested in trade and, therefore, in the control of the sea-routes. They came into conflict with each other on the seas, and at least once one of them challenged the Chola State of South India. But the Cholas were also strong on the seas and they sent a naval expedition which subdued for a while the Sailendra Empire.

There is an interesting Tamil inscription of 1088 A.C. which refers to a 'Corporation of the Fifteen Hundred.' This was apparently a union of traders who were described in it as 'brave men, born to wander over many countries ever since the beginning of the Krita age, penetrating the regions of the six continents by land and water routes, and dealing in various articles such as horses, elephants, precious stones, perfumes, and drugs, either wholesale or in retail.'

This was the background of the early colonizing ventures of the Indian people. Trade and adventure and the urge for expansion drew them to these eastern lands which were comprehensively described in old Sanskrit books as the Svarnabhumi, the Land of Gold or as Svarnadvipa, the Island of Gold. The very name had a lure about it. The early colonists settled down, more followed and thus a peaceful penetration went on. There was a fusion of the Indians with the races they found there, and also the evolution of a mixed culture. It was only then, probably, that the political element came from India, some Kshatriya princes, cadets of the noble families, in search of adventure and dominion.

It is suggested, from a similarity of names, that many of these people who came were from the wide-spread Malva tribe in India—hence the Malay race which has played such an important part in the whole of Indonesia. A part of central India is still known as Malwa. The early colonists are supposed to have gone from Kalinga on the east coast (Orissa) but it was the Hindu Pallava Kingdom of the south that made an organized effort at colonization. The Sailendra dynasty, which became so famous in south-east Asia, is believed to have come from Orissa. At that time Orissa was a stronghold of Buddhism but the ruling dynasty was Brahminical.

All these Indian colonies were situated between two great countries and two great civilizations—India and China. Some of them, on the Asiatic mainland, actually touched the frontiers of the Chinese Empire, the others were on the direct trade route between China and India. Thus they were influenced by both these countries and a mixed Indo-Chinese civilization grew up but such was the nature of these two cultures that there was no conflict between the two and mixed patterns of different shapes and varying contents emerged. The countries of the mainland—Burma, Siam, Indo-China—were more influenced by China, the islands and the Malay Peninsula had more of the impress of India. As a rule the methods of government and the general philosophy of life came from China, religion and art from India. The mainland countries depended for their trade largely on China and there were frequent exchanges of ambassadors. But even in Cambodia and in the mighty remains of Angkor the only artistic influence that has been so far detected came from India. But Indian art was flexible and adaptable and in each country it flowered afresh and in many new ways, always retaining that basic impress which it derived from India. Sir John Marshall has referred to 'the amazingly vital and flexible character of Indian art' and he points out how both Indian and Greek art had the common capacity to 'adapt themselves to suit the needs of every country, race, and religion with which they came into contact.'

Indian art derives its basic character from certain ideals associated with the religious and philosophic outlook of India. As religion went from India to all these eastern lands, so also went this basic conception of art. Probably the early colonies were definitely Brahminical and Buddhism spread later. The two existed side by side as friends and mixed forms of popular worship grew up. This Buddhism was chiefly of the Mahāyāna type, easily adaptable, and both Brahminism and Buddhism, under the influence of local habits and traditions, had probably moved away from the purity of their original doctrines. In later years there were mighty conflicts between a Buddhist state and a

Brahminical state but these were essentially political and economic wars for control of trade and sea routes.

The history of these Indian colonies covers a period of about thirteen hundred years or more, from the early beginnings in the first or second century A.C. to the end of the fifteenth century. The early centuries are vague and not much is known except that many small states existed. Gradually they consolidate themselves and by the fifth century great cities take shape. By the eighth century seafaring empires have arisen, partly centralized but also exercising a vague suzerainty over many lands. Sometimes these dependencies became independent and even presumed to attack the central power and this has led to some confusion in our understanding of those periods.

The greatest of these states was the Sailendra Empire, or the empire of Sri Vijaya, which became the dominant power both on sea and land in the whole of Malaysia by the eighth century. This was till recently supposed to have its origin and capital in Sumatra but later researches indicate that it began in the Malay Peninsula. At the height of its power it included Malaya, Ceylon, Sumatra, part of Java, Borneo, Celebes, the Philippines, and part of Formosa, and probably exercised suzerainty over Cambodia and Champa (Annam). It was a Buddhist Empire.

But long before the Sailendra dynasty had established and consolidated this empire, powerful states had grown up in Malaya, Cambodia, and Java. In the northern part of the Malay Peninsula, near the borders of Siam, extensive ruins, says R. J. Wilkinson, 'point to the past existence of powerful states and a high standard of wealth and luxury.' In Champa (Annam) there was the city of Pandurangam in the third century and in the fifth century Kamboja became a great city. A great ruler, Jayavarman, united the smaller states in the ninth century and built up the Cambodian Empire with its capital at Angkor. Cambodia was probably under the suzerainty of the Sailendras from time to time, but this must have been nominal, and it reasserted its independence in the ninth century. This Cambodian state lasted for nearly four hundred years under a succession of great rulers and great builders, Jayavarman, Yashovarman, Indravarman, Suryavarman. The capital became famous in Asia and was known as 'Angkor the Magnificent,' a city of a million inhabitants, larger and more splendid than the Rome of the Cæsars. Near the city stood the vast temple of Angkor Vat. The empire of Cambodia flourished till the end of the thirteenth century, and the account of a Chinese envoy who visited it in 1297 describes the wealth and splendour of its capital. But suddenly it collapsed, so suddenly that some buildings were left unfinished. There were external attacks and internal troubles, but the major disaster seems to have been the silting up of the Mekong river, which converted the approaches to the city into marshlands and led to its abandonment.

Java also broke away from the Sailendra Empire in the ninth century, but even so the Sailendras continued as the leading power in Indonesia till the eleventh century, when they came into conflict with the Chola power of South India. The Cholas were victorious and held sway over large parts of Indonesia for over fifty years. On the withdrawal of the Cholas the Sailendras recovered and continued as an independent state for nearly three hundred years more. But it was no longer the dominant power in the eastern seas and in the thirteenth century began the disruption of its empire. Java grew at its expense as also did the Thais (Siam). In the second half of the fourteenth century Java completely conquered the Sailendra Empire of Srivijaya.

This Javan state which now rose into prominence had a long history behind it. It was a Brahminical state which had continued its attachment to the older faith in spite of the spread of Buddhism. It had resisted the political and economic sway of the Sailendra Empire of Srivijaya even when more than half of Java itself was occupied by the latter. It consisted of a community of sea faring folk intent on trade and passionately fond of building great structures in stone. Originally it was called the Kingdom of Singhasari, but in 1292 a new city, Majapahit, was founded and from this grew the empire of Majapahit which succeeded Srivijaya as the dominant power in south-east Asia. Majapahit insulted some Chinese envoys sent by Kublai Khan and was punished for this by a Chinese expedition. Probably the Javanese learnt from the Chinese the use of gunpowder and this helped them finally to defeat the Sailendras.

Majapahit was a highly centralized, expanding empire. Its system of taxation is said to have been very well organized and special attention was paid to trade and its colonies. There was a commerce department of government, a colonial department, and departments for public health, war, the interior, etc. There was also a supreme court of justice consisting of a number of judges. It is astonishing how well this imperialist state was organized. Its chief business was trade from India to China. One of its well-known rulers was the Queen Suhita.

The war between Majapahit and Srivijaya was a very cruel one and though it ended in the complete victory of the former, it sowed the seeds of fresh conflict. From the ruins of the Sailendra power, allied to other elements, notably Arabs and Moslem converts, rose the Malaya power in Sumatra and Malacca. The command of the eastern seas, which had so long been held by South India or the Indian colonies, now passed to the Arabs. Malacca rose into prominence as a great centre of trade and seat of political power, and Islam spread over the Malay Peninsula and the islands. It was this new power that finally put and end to

Majapahit towards the end of the fifteenth century. But within a few years, in 1511, the Portuguese, under Albuquerque, came and took possession of Malacca. Europe had reached the Far East through her newly developing sea power.

The Influence of Indian Art Abroad

These records of ancient empires and dynasties have an interest for the antiquarian, but they have a large interest in the history of civilization and art. From the point of view of India they are particularly important, for it was India that functioned there and exhibited her vitality and genius in a variety of ways. We see her bubbling over with energy and spreading out far and wide, carrying not only her thought but her other ideals, her art, her trade, her language and literature, and her methods of government. She was not stagnant, or standing aloof, or isolated and cut off by mountain and sea. Her people crossed those high mountain barriers and perilous seas and built up, as M. Réné Grousset says, 'a Greater India politically as little organized as Greater Greece, but morally equally harmonious.' As a matter of fact even the political organization of these Malayasian states was of a high order, though it was not part of the Indian political structure. But M. Grousset refers to the wider areas where Indian culture spread: 'In the high plateau of eastern Iran, in the oases of Serindia, in the arid wastes of Tibet, Mongolia, and Manchuria, in the ancient civilized lands of China and Japan, in the lands of the primitive Mons and Khmers and other tribes in Indo-China, in the countries of the Malayo-Polynesians, in Indonesia and Malay, India left the indelible impress of her high culture, not only upon religion, but also upon art and literature, in a word, all the higher things of spirit.'*

Indian civilization took root especially in the countries of south-east Asia and the evidence for this can be found all over the place to-day. There were great centres of Sanskrit learning in Champa, Angkor, Srivijaya, Majapahit, and other places. The names of the rulers of the various states and empires that arose are purely Indian and Sanskrit. This does not mean that they were pure Indian, but it does mean that they were Indianized. State ceremonies were Indian and conducted in Sanskrit. All the officers of the state bear old Sanskrit titles and some of these titles and designations have been continued up till now, not only in Thailand but in the Moslem states of Malaya. The old literatures of these places in Indonesia are full of Indian myth and legend. The famous dances of Java and Bali derive from India. The little island of Bali has indeed largely maintained its old

*'Civilizations of the East' by Réné Grousset, Volume II, p. 276.

Indian culture down to modern times and even Hinduism has persisted there. The art of writing went to the Philippines from India.

In Cambodia the alphabet is derived from South India and numerous Sanskrit words have been taken over with minor variations. The civil and criminal law is based on the Laws of Manu, the ancient law-giver of India, and this has been codified, with variations due to Buddhist influence, in modern Cambodian legislation.*

But above all else it is in the magnificent art and architecture of these old Indian colonies that the Indian influence is most marked. The original impulse was modified, adapted, and fused with the genius of the place and out of this fusion arose the monuments and wonderful temples of Angkor and Borobudur. At Borobudur in Java the whole life story of Buddha is carved in stone. At other places bas-reliefs reproduce the legends of Vishnu and Rama and Krishna. Of Angkor, Mr. Osbert Sitwell has written: 'Let it be said immediately that Angkor, as it stands, ranks as chief wonder of the world to-day, one of the summits to which human genius has aspired in stone, infinitely more impressive, lovely and, as well, romantic, than anything that can be seen in China.... The material remains of a civilization that flashed its wings, of the utmost brilliance, for six centuries, and then perished so utterly that even his name has died from the lips of man.'

Round the great temple of Angkor Vat is a vast area of mighty ruins with artificial lakes and pools, and canals and bridges over them, and a great gate dominated by 'a vast sculptured head, a lovely, smiling but enigmatic Cambodian face, though one raised to the power and beauty of a god.' The face with its strangely fascinating and disturbing smile—the 'Angkor smile'—is repeated again and again. This gate leads to the temple: 'the neighbouring Bayon can be said to be the most imaginative and singular in the world, more lovely than Angkor Vat, because more unearthly in its conception, a temple from a city in some other distant planet.... imbued with the same elusive beauty that often lives between the lines of a great poem.'†

The inspiration for Angkor came from India but it was the Khmer genius that developed it, or the two fused together and produced this wonder. The Cambodian king who is said to have built this great temple is named Jayavarman VII, a typical Indian name.

Dr. Quaritch Wales says that 'when the guiding hand of India was removed, her inspiration was not forgotten, but the Khmer

*A. Lecléro, 'Recherches sur les origines brahmaniques des lois Cambodgiennes' quoted in B. R. Chatterji's 'Indian Cultural Influence in Cambodia' (Calcutta, 1928).

† These extracts have been taken from Osbert Sitwell's 'Escape with Me—An Oriental Sketch Book' (1941).

genius was released to mould from it vast new conceptions of amazing vitality different from, and hence not properly to be compared with anything matured in a purely Indian environment....It is true that Khmer culture is essentially based on the inspiration of India, without which the Khmers at best might have produced nothing greater than the barbaric splendour of the Central American Mayas; but it must be admitted that here, more than anywhere else in Greater India, this inspiration fell on fertile soil'*

This leads one to think that in India itself that original inspiration gradually faded because the mind and the soil became overworked and undernourished for lack of fresh currents and ideas. So long as India kept her mind open and gave of her riches to others, and received from them what she lacked, she remained fresh and strong and vital. But the more she withdrew into her shell, intent on preserving herself, uncontaminated by external influececs, the more she lost that inspiration and her life became increasingly a dull round of meaningless activities all centred in the dead past. Losing the art of creating beauty, her children lost even the capacity to recognize it.

It is to European scholars and archæologists that the excavations and discoveries in Java, Angkor and elsewhere in Greater India are due, more especially to French and Dutch scholars. Great cities and monuments probably still lie buried there awaiting discovery. Meanwhile it is said that important sites in Malaya containing ancient ruins have been destroyed by mining operations or for obtaining material for building roads. The war will no doubt add to this destruction.

Some years ago I had a letter from a Thai (Siamese) student who had come to Tagore's Santiniketan and was returning to Thailand. He wrote: 'I always consider myself exceptionally fortunate in being able to come to this great and ancient land of Aryavarta and to pay my humble homage at the feet of grandmother India in whose affectionate arms my mother country was so lovingly brought up and taught to appreciate and love what was sublime and beautiful in culture and religion.' This may not be typical, but it does convey some idea of the general feeling towards India which, though vague and overladen with much else, still continues in many of the countries of South-East Asia. Everywhere an intense and narrow nationalism has grown, looking to itself and distrustful of others; there is fear and hatred of European domination and yet a desire to emulate Europe and America; there is often some contempt for India because of her dependent condition; and yet behind all this there is a feeling of respect and friendship for India, for old memories endure and people have not forgotten that there was a time when India was

*From 'Towards Angkor' by Dr. H. G. Quaritch Wales (Harrap, 1933).

a mother country to these and nourished them with rich fare from her own treasure-house. Just as Hellenism spread from Greece to the countries of the Mediterranean and in Western Asia, India's cultural influence spread to many countries and left its powerful impress upon them.

'From Persia to the Chinese Sea,' writes Sylvain Lévi, 'from the icy regions of Siberia to the islands of Java and Borneo, from Oceania to Socotra, India has propagated her beliefs, her tales and her civilization. She has left indelible imprints on one-fourth of the human race in the course of a long succession of centuries. She has the right to reclaim in universal history the rank that ignorance has refused her for a long time and to hold her place amongst the great nations summarising and symbolising the spirit of Humanity.'*

Old Indian Art

The amazing expansion of Indian culture and art to other countries has led to some of the finest expressions of this art being found outside India. Unfortunately many of our old monuments and sculptures, especially in northern India, have been destroyed in the course of ages. 'To know Indian art in India alone,' says Sir John Marshall, 'is to know but half its story. To apprehend it to the full, we must follow it in the wake of Buddhism, to central Asia, China, and Japan; we must watch it assuming new forms and breaking into new beauties as it spreads over Tibet and Burma and Siam; we must gaze in awe at the unexampled grandeur of its creations in Cambodia and Java. In each of these countries, Indian art encounters a different racial genius, a different local environment, and under their modifying influence it takes on a different garb.'†

Indian art is so intimatly associated with Indian religion and philosophy that it is difficult to appreciate it fully unless one has some knowledge of the ideals that governed the Indian mind. In art, as in music, there is a gulf which separates eastern from western conceptions. Probably the great artists and builders of the middle ages in Europe would have felt more in tune with Indian art and sculpture than modern European artists who derive part of their inspiration at least from the Renaissance period and after. For in Indian art there is always a religious urge, a looking beyond, such as probably inspired the builders of the great cathedrals of Europe. Beauty is conceived as subjective, not objective; it is a thing of the spirit, though it may also take lovely shape in form or matter. The Greeks loved beauty for its

*Quoted in U. N. Ghosal's 'Progress of Greater Indian Research, 1917-1942' (Calcutta, 1943).

†From Foreword to Reginald Le May's 'Buddhist Art in Siam' (Cambridge, 1938), quoted by Ghosal in 'Progress of Greater Indian Research' (Calcutta, 1943).

own sake and found not only joy but truth in it; the ancient Indians loved beauty also but always they sought to put some deeper significance in their work, some vision of the inner truth as they saw it. In the supreme examples of their creative work they extort admiration, even though one may not understand what they were aiming at or the ideas that governed them. In lesser examples, this lack of understanding, of not being in tune with the artist's mind, becomes a bar to appreciation. There is a vague feeling of discomfort, even of irritation, at something one cannot grasp, and this leads to the conclusion that the artist did not know his job and has failed. Sometimes there is even a feeling of repulsion.

I know nothing about art, eastern or western, and am not competent to say anything about it. I react to it as any untutored layman might do. Some painting or sculpture or building fills me with delight, or moves me and makes me feel a strange emotion; or it just pleases me a little; or it does not affect me at all and I pass it by almost unnoticed; or it repels me. I cannot explain these reactions or speak learnedly about the merits or demerits of works of art. The Buddha statue at Anuradhapura in Ceylon moved me greatly and a picture of it has been my companion for many years. On the other hand some famous temples in South India, heavy with carving and detail, disturb me and fill me with unease.

Europeans, trained in the Greek tradition, at first examined Indian art from the Grecian point of view. They recognized something they knew in the Græco-Buddhist art of Gandhara and the Frontier and considered other forms in India as degraded types of this. Gradually a new approach was made and it was pointed out that Indian art was something original and vital and in no way derived from this Græco-Buddhist art, which was a pale reflection of it. This new aproach came more from the Continent of Europe than from England. It is curious that Indian art, and this applies to Sanskrit literature also, has been more appreciated on the Continent than in England. I have often wondered how far this has been conditioned by the unfortunate political relationship existing between India and England. Probably there is something in that, though there must be other and more basic causes of difference also. There are of course many Englishmen, artists and scholars and others, who have come near to the spirit and outlook of India and helped to discover our old treasures and interpret them to the world. There are many also to whom India is grateful for their warm friendship and service. Yet the fact remains that there is a gulf, and an ever-widening gulf, between Indians and Englishmen. On the Indian side this is easier to understand, at any rate for me, for a great deal has happened in recent years that has cut deep into our souls. On the other side perhaps some similar reactions have taken place for different reasons; among them, anger at being put in the wrong before the world when, according to them, the fault was not theirs. But the feeling is deeper than politics and it comes out unawares, and most of all it seems to affect English intellectuals. The Indian, to them, appears to be a special manifestation of original sin and all his works bear this mark. A popular English author, though hardly representative of English thought or intelligence, has recently written a book which is full of a malicious hatred and disgust for almost everything Indian. A more eminent and representative English author, Mr. Osbert Sitwell says in his book 'Escape With Me' (1941) that 'the idea of India, despite its manifold and diverse marvels, continued to be repellent.' He refers also to 'that repulsive, greasy quality that so often mars Hindu works of art.'

Mr. Sitwell is perfectly justified in holding those opinions about Indian art or India generally. I am sure he feels that way. I am myself repelled by much in India but I do not feel that way about India as a whole. Naturally, for I am an Indian and I cannot easily hate myself, however unworthy I may be. But it is not a question of opinions or views on art; it is much more a conscious and subconscious dislike and unfriendliness to a whole people. Is it true that those whom we have injured, we dislike and hate?

Among the Englishmen who have appreciated Indian art and applied new standards of judgment to it have been Lawrence Binyon and E. B. Havell. Havell is particularly enthusiastic about the ideals of Indian art and the spirit underlying them. He emphasizes that a great national art affords an intimate revelation of national thought and character, but it is only to be appreciated if the ideals behind it are understood. An alien governing race misapprehending and depreciating those ideals sows the seeds of intellectual antipathy. Indian art, he says, was not addressed to a narrow coterie of literati. Its intention was to make the central ideas of religion and philosophy intelligible to the masses. 'That Hindu art was successful in its educational purpose may be inferred from the fact, known to all who have intimate acquaintance with Indian life, that the Indian peasantry, though illiterate in the western sense, are among the most cultured of their class anywhere in the world.'*

In art, as in Sanskrit poetry and Indian music, the artist was supposed to identify himself with nature in all her moods, to express the essential harmony of man with nature and the universe. That has been the keynote of all Asiatic art and it is because of this that there is a certain unity about the art of Asia, in spite of its great variety and the national differences that are so evident. There is not much of old painting in India, except for the

*E. B. Havell: 'The Ideals of Indian Art' (1920), p. xix.

lovely frescoes of Ajanta. Perhaps much of it has perished. It was in her sculpture and architecture that India stood out, just as China and Japan excelled in painting.

Indian music, which is so different from European music, was highly developed in its own way and India stood out in this respect and influenced Asiatic music considerably, except for China and the Far East. Music thus became another link with Persia, Afghanistan, Arabia, Turkestan and, to some extent, in other areas where Arab civilization flourished, for instance, North Africa. Indian classical music will probably be appreciated in all these countries.

An important influence in the development of art in India, as elsewhere in Asia, was the religious prejudice against graven images. The Vedas were against image worship and it was only at a comparatively late period in Buddhism that Buddha's person was represented in sculpture and painting. In the Mathura museum there is a huge stone figure of the Bodhisattva which is full of strength and power. This belongs to the Kushan period about the beginning of the Christian era.

The early period of Indian art is full of a naturalism which may partly be due to Chinese influences. Chinese influence is visible at various stages of Indian art history, chiefly in the development of this naturalism, just as Indian idealism went to China and Japan and powerfully influenced them during some of their great periods.

During the Gupta period, fourth to sixth centuries A.C., the Golden Age of India as it is called, the caves of Ajanta were dug out and the frescoes painted. Bagh and Badami are also of this period. The Ajanta frescoes, very beautiful though they are, have, ever since their discovery, exercised a powerful influence on our present-day artists, who have turned away from life and sought to model their style on that of Ajanta, with unhappy results.

Ajanta takes one back into some distant dream-like and yet very real world. These frescoes were painted by the Buddhist monks. Keep away from women, do not even look at them, for they are dangerous, has said their Master long ago. And yet we have here women in plenty, beautiful women, princesses, singers, dancers, seated and standing, beautifying themselves, or in procession. The women of Ajanta had become famous. How well those painter-monks must have known the world and the moving drama of life, how lovingly they have painted it, just as they have painted the Boddhisattva in his calm and other-worldly majesty.

In the seventh and eighth centuries the mighty caves of Ellora were carved out of solid rock with the stupendous Kailasa temple in the centre; it is difficult to imagine how human beings conceived this or, having conceived it, gave body and shape to their conception. The caves of Elephanta, with the powerful and subtle Trimurti, date also from this period. Also the group of monuments at Mâmallapuram in South India.

In the Elephanta caves there is a broken statue of Shiva Natarâja, Shiva dancing. Even in its mutilated condition, Havell says that it is a majestic conception and an embodiment of titanic power. 'Though the rock itself seems to vibrate with the rhythmic movement of the dance, the noble head bears the same look of serene calm and dispassion which illuminate the face of the Buddha.'

There is another Shiva Natarâja in the British Museum and of this Epstein has written: 'Shiva dances, creating the world and destroying it, his large rhythms conjure up vast æons of time, and his movements have a relentless magical power of incantation. A small group of the British Museum is the most tragic summing up of the death in love motive ever seen, and it epitomises, as no other work, the fatal element in human passion. Our European allegories are banal and pointless by comparison with these profound works, devoid of the trappings of symbolism, concentrating on the essential, the essentially plastic.'*

There is a head of a Bodhisattva from Borobudur in Java which has been taken to the Glyptotek in Copenhagen. It is beautiful, in the sense of formal beauty, but, as Havell says, there is something deeper in it revealing, as in a mirror, the pure soul of the Bodhisattva. 'It is a face which incarnates the stillness of the depths of the ocean; the serenity of an azure, cloudless sky; a beatitude beyond moral ken.'

'Indian art in Java,' adds Havell, 'has a character of its own which distinguishes it from that of the continent from whence it came. There runs through both the same strain of deep serenity, but in the divine ideal of Java we lose the austere feeling which characterises the Hindu sculpture of Elephanta and Mâmallapuram. There is more of human contentment and joy in Indo-Javanese art, an expression of that peaceful security which the Indian colonists enjoyed in their happy island home, after the centuries of storm and struggle which their forefathers had experienced on the mainland.'†

India's Foreign Trade

Throughout the first millennium of the Christian era, India's trade was widespread and Indian merchants controlled many

---

Epstein: 'Let There be Sculpture' (1942), p. 193.

†*Havell: 'The Ideals of Indian Art' (1920), p. 169.*

214

foreign markets. It was dominant in the eastern seas and it reached out also to the Mediterranean. Pepper and other spices went from India or via India to the west, often on Indian and Chinese bottoms, and it is said that Alaric the Goth took away 3,000 pounds of pepper from Rome. Roman writers bemoaned the fact that gold flowed from Rome to India and the east in exchange for various luxury articles.

This trade was largely, in India as elsewhere at the time, one of give and take of materials found and developed locally. India was a fertile land and rich in some of the materials that other countries lacked, and the seas being open to her she sent these materials abroad. She also obtained them from the eastern islands and profited as a merchant carrier. But she had further advantages. She had been manufacturing cloth from the earliest ages, long before other countries did so, and a textile industry had developed. Indian textiles went to far countries. Silk was also made from very early times though probably it was not nearly as good as Chinese silk, which began to be imported as early as the fourth century B.C. The Indian silk industry may have developed subsequently, though it does not seem to have gone far. An important advance was made in the dyeing of cloth and special methods were discovered for the preparation of fast dyes. Among these was indigo, a word derived from India through Greece. It was probably this knowledge of dyeing that gave a great impetus to India's trade with foreign countries.

Chemistry in India in the early centuries A.C. was probably more advanced than in other countries. I do not know much about it but there is a 'History of Hindu Chemistry' written by the doyen of Indian chemists and scientists, Sir P. C. Ray, who trained several generations of Indian scientists. Chemistry then was closely allied to alchemy and metallurgy. A famous Indian chemist and metallurgist was named Nāgārjuna, and the similarity of the names has led some people to suggest that he was the same person as the great philosopher of the first century A.C. But this is very doubtful.

The tempering of steel was known early in India, and Indian steel and iron were valued abroad, especially for warlike purposes. Many other metals were known and used and preparations of metallic compounds were made for medicinal purposes. Distillation and calcination were well-known. The science of medicine was fairly well developed. Though based mainly on the old text books, considerable experimental progress was made right up to the medieval period. Anatomy and physiology were studied and the circulation of the blood was suggested long before Harvey.

Astronomy, oldest of sciences, was a regular subject of the university curriculum and with it was mixed up astrology. A very accurate calendar was worked out and this calendar is still in popular use. It is a solar calendar having lunar months, which leads to periodical adjustments. As elsewhere, the priests, or Brahmins, were especially concerned with this calendar and they fixed the seasonal festivals as well as indicated the exact time of the eclipses of the sun and moon, which were also in the nature of festivals. They took advantage of this knowledge to encourage among the masses beliefs and observances, which they must have known to be superstitious, and thus added to their own prestige. A knowledge of astronomy, in its practical aspects, was of great help to the people who went on the seas. The ancient Indians were rather proud of the advances they had made in astronomical knowledge. They had contacts with Arab astronomy, which was largely based on Alexandria.

It is difficult to say how far mechanical appliances had developed then, but shipbuilding was a flourishing industry and there is frequent reference to various kinds of 'machines,' especially for purposes of war. This has led some enthusiastic and rather credulous Indians to imagine all kinds of complicated machines. It does seem, however, that India at that time was not behind any country in the making and use of tools and in the knowledge of chemistry and metallurgy. It was this that gave her an advantage in trade and enabled her for several centuries to control a number of foreign markets.

Possibly she had one other advantage also—the absence of slave-labour, which handicapped Greek and other early civilizations and came in the way of their progress. The caste system, with all its evils, which progressively increased, was infinitely better than slavery even for those lowest in the scale. Within each caste there was equality and a measure of freedom; each caste was occupational and applied itself to its own particular work. This led to a high degree of specialization and skill in handicrafts and craftsmanship.

Mathematics in Ancient India

Highly intellectual and given to abstract thinking as they were, one would expect the ancient Indians to excel in mathematics. Europe got its early arithmetic and algebra from the Arabs— hence the 'Arabic numerals'—but the Arabs themselves had previously taken them from India. The astonishing progress that the Indians had made in mathematics is now well known and it is recognized that the foundations of modern arithmetic and algebra were laid long ago in India. The clumsy method of using a counting frame and the use of Roman and such like numerals had long retarded progress when the ten Indian numerals, including the zero sign, liberated the human mind from these restrictions and threw a flood of light on the behaviour of numbers. These number symbols were unique and entirely diffrent from all other symbols that had been in use in other countries. They are common enough to-day and we take them for granted, yet they contained the germs of revolutionary progress in them. It took many centuries for them to travel from India, via Baghdad, to the western world.

A hundred and fifty years ago, during Napoleon's time, La Place wrote: 'It is India that gave us the ingenious method of expressing all numbers by means of ten symbols, each symbol receiving a value of position, as well as an absolute value; a profound and important idea which appears so simple to us now that we ignore its true merit, but its very simplicity, the great ease which it has lent to all computations, puts our arithmetic in the first rank of useful inventions; and we shall appreciate the grandeur of this achievement when we remember that it escaped the genius of Archimedes and Apollonius, two of the greatest men produced by antiquity.'*

The origins of geometry, arithmetic, and algebra in India go back to remote periods. Probably to begin with there was some kind of geometrical algebra used for making figures for Vedic altars. Mention is made in the most ancient books of the geometrical method for the transformation of a square into a rectangle having a given side: $ax = c$. Geometrical figures are even now commonly used in Hindu ceremonies. Geometry made progress in India but in this respect Greece and Alexandria went ahead. It was in arithmetic and algebra that India kept the lead. The inventor or inventors of the decimal place-value system and the zero mark are not known. The earliest use of the zero symbol, so far discovered, is in one of the scriptural books dated about 200 B.C. It is considered probable that the place-value system was invented about the beginning of the Christian era. The zero, called *shunya* or nothing, was orignally a dot and later it became a small circle. It was considered a number like any other. Professor Halsted thus emphasizes the vital significance of this invention: 'The importance of the creation of the zero mark can never be exaggerated. This giving to airy nothing, not merely a local habitation and a name, a picture, a symbol but helpful power, is the characteristic of the Hindu race from whence it sprang. It is like coining the Nirvana into dynamos. No single mathematical creation has been more potent for the general on-go of intelligence and power.'†

Yet another modern mathematician has grown eloquent over this historic event. Dantzig in his 'Number' writes: 'This long

*Quoted in Hogben's 'Mathematics for the Million', (London, 1942).

†G. B. Halsted: 'On the Foundation and Technique of Arithmetic', p. 20 (Chicago, 1912), quoted in 'History of Hindu Mathematics' by B. Datta and A. N. Singh (1935).

period of nearly five thousand years saw the rise and fall of many a civilization, each leaving behind it a heritage of literature, art, philosophy, and religion. But what was the net achievement in the field of reckoning, the earliest art practised by man? An inflexible numeration so crude as to make progress well nigh impossible, and a calculating device so limited in scope that even elementary calculations called for the services of an expert.... Man used these devices for thousands of years without making a single worthwhile improvement in the instrument, without contributing a single important idea to the system....Even when compared with the slow growth of ideas during the dark ages, the history of reckoning presents a peculiar picture of desolate stagnation. When viewed in this light the achievements of the unknown Hindu, who sometime in the first centuries of our era discovered the principle of position, assumes the importance of a world event.'*

Dantzig is puzzled at the fact that the great mathematicians of Greece did not stumble on this discovery. 'Is it that the Greeks had such a marked contempt for applied science, leaving even the instruction of their children to slaves? But if so, how is it that the nation that gave us geometry and carried this science so far did not create even a rudimentary algebra? Is it not equally strange that algebra, that corner-stone of modern mathematics, also originated in India, and at about the same time that positional numeration did?'

The answer to this question is suggested by Professor Hogben: 'The difficulty of understanding why it should have been the Hindus who took this step, why it was not taken by the mathematicians of antiquity, why it should first have been taken by practical man, is only insuperable if we seek for the explanation of intellectual progress in the genius of a few gifted individuals, instead of in the whole social framework of custom thought which circumscribes the greatest individual genius. What happened in India about A.D. 100 had happened before. May be it is happening now in Soviet Russia....To accept it (this truth) is to recognise that every culture contains within itself its own doom, unless it pays as much attention to the education of the mass of mankind as to the education of the exceptionally gifted people.'†

We must assume then that these momentous inventions were not just due to the momentary illumination of an erratic genius, much in advance of his time, but that they were essentialy the product of the social *milieu* and that they answered some insistent demand of the times. Genius of a high order was certainly

*Quoted in L. Hogben's 'Mathematics for the Million', (London, 1942).

†Hogben: 'Mathematics for the Million', (London, 1942), p. 285.

necessary to find this out and fulfil the demand, but if the demand had not been there the urge to find some way out would have been absent, and even if the invention had been made it would have been forgotten or put aside till circumstances more propitious for its use arose. It seems clear from the early Sanskrit works on mathematics that the demand was there, for these books are full of problems of trade and social relationship involving complicated calculations. There are problems dealing with taxation, debt, and interest; problems of partnership, barter and exchange, and the calculation of the fineness of gold. Society had grown complex and large numbers of people were engaged in governmental operations and in an extensive trade. It was impossible to carry on without simple methods of calculation.

The adoption of zero and the decimal place-value system in India unbarred the gates of the mind to rapid progress in arithmetic and algebra. Fractions come in, and the multiplication and division of fractions; the rule of three is discovered and perfected; squares and square-roots (together with the sign of the square-root, $\sqrt{}$); cubes and cube-roots; the minus sign; tables of sines; π is evaluated as $3 \cdot 1416$; letters of the alphabet are used in algebra to denote unknowns; simple and quadratic equations are considered; the mathematics of zero are investigated. Zero is defined as $a - a = 0$; $a + 0 = a$; $a - 0 = a$; $a \times 0 = 0$; $a \div 0$ becomes infinity. The conception of negative quantities also comes in, thus: $\sqrt{4} = \pm 2$.

These and other advances in mathematics are contained in books written by a succession of eminent mathematicians from the fifth to the twelfth century A.C. There are earlier books also (Baudhayana, c. eighth century B.C.; Apastamba and Katyayana, both c. fifth century B.C.) which deal with geometrical problems, especially with triangles, rectangles, and squares. But the earliest extant book on algebra is by the famous astronomer, Aryabhata, who was born in A.C. 476. He wrote this book on astronomy and mathematics when he was only twenty-three years old. Aryabhata, who is sometimes called the inventor of algebra, must have relied, partly at least, on the work of his predecessors. The next great name in Indian mathematics is that of Bhaskara I (A.C. 522), and he was followd by Brahmagupta (A.C. 628), who was also a famous astronomer, and who stated the laws applying to *shunya* or zero and made other notable advances. There follow a succession of mathematicians who have written on arithmetic or algebra. The last great name is that of Bhaskara II, who was born in A.C. 1114. He wrote three books, on astronomy, algebra, and arithmetic. His book on arithmetic is known as 'Lilavati', which is an odd name for a treatise on mathematics, as it is the name of a woman. There are frequent references in the book to a young girl who is addressed as 'O Lilavati' and is then instructed on the problems stated. It is believed, without any definite proof, that Lilavati was Bhaskara's daughter. The style of the book is clear and simple and suitable for young persons to understand. The book is still used, partly for its style, in Sanskrit schools.

Books on mathematics continued to appear (Narayana 1150, Ganesha 1545), but these are mere repetitions of what had been done. Very little original work on mathematics was done in India after the twelfth century till we reach the modern age.

In the eighth century, during the reign of the Khalif Al-Mansur (753-774), a number of Indian scholars went to Baghdad, and among the books they took with them were works on mathematics and astronomy. Probably even earlier than this, Indian numerals had reached Baghdad, but this was the first systematic approach, and Aryabhata's and other books were translated into Arabic. They influenced the development of mathematics and astronomy in the Arab world, and Indian numerals were introduced. Baghdad was then a great centre of learning and Greek and Jewish scholars had gathered there bringing with them Greek philosophy, geometry, and science. The cultural influence of Baghdad was felt throughout the Moslem world from central Asia to Spain, and a knowledge of Indian mathematics in their Arabic translations spread all over this vast area. The numerals were called by the Arabs 'figures of Hind' (or India), and the Arabic word for a number is 'Hindsah', meaning 'from Hind'.

From this Arab world the new mathematics travelled to European countries, probably through the Moorish universities of Spain, and became the foundation for European mathematics. There was opposition in Europe to the use of the new numbers, as they were considered infidel symbols, and it took several hundred years before they were in common use. The earliest known use is in a Sicilian coin of 1134; in Britain the first use is in 1490.

It seems clear that some knowledge of Indian mathematics, and especially of the place-value system of numbers, had penetrated into western Asia even before the formal embassy carried books to Baghdad. There is an interesting passage in a complaint made by a Syrin scholar-monk who was hurt at the arrogance of some Greek scholars who looked down on Syrians. Severus Sebokht was his name, and he lived in a convent situated on the Eupharates. He writes in A.C. 662 and tries to show that the Syrians were in no way inferior to the Greeks. By way of illustration he refers to the Indians: 'I will omit all discussion of the science of the Hindus, a people not the same as the Syrians; their subtle discoveries in the science of astonomy, discoveries that are more ingenious than those of the Greeks and the Babylonians; their computing that surpasses description. I wish only to say that this computation is done by means of nine signs. If those who believe, because they speak Greek, that they have reached the limits of science, should know of these things, they would be convinced that there are also others who know something.'*

Mathematics in India inevitably makes one think of one extraordinary figure of recent times. This was Srinivasa Ramanujam. Born in a poor Brahmin family in south India, having no opportunities for a proper education, he became a clerk in the Madras Port Trust. But he was bubbling over with some irrepressible quality of instinctive genius and played about with numbers and equations in his spare time. By a lucky chance he attracted the attention of a mathematician who sent some of his amateur work to Cambridge in England. People there were impressed and a scholarship was arranged for him. So he left his clerk's job and went to Cambridge and during a very brief period there did work of profound value and amazing originality. The Royal Society of England went rather out of their way and made him a Fellow, but he died two years later, probably of tuberculosis, at the age of thirty-three. Professor Julian Huxley has, I believe, referred to him somewhere as the greatest mathematician of the century.

Ramanujam's brief life and death are symbolic of conditions in India. Of our millions how few get any education at all, how many live on the verge of starvation; of even those who get some education how many have nothing to look forward to but a clerkship in some office on a pay that is usually far less than the unemployment dole in England. If life opened its gates to them and offered them food and healthy conditions of living and education and opportunities of growth, how many among these millions would be eminent scientists, educationists, technicians, industrialists, writers and artists, helping to build a new India and a new world?

Growth and Decay

During the first thousand years of the Christian era, there are many ups and downs in India, many conflicts with invading elements and internal troubles. Yet it is a period of a vigorous national life, bubbling over with energy and spreading out in all directions. Culture develops into a rich civilization flowering out in philosophy, literature, drama, art, science, and mathematics. India's economy expands, the Indian horizon widens and other countries come within its scope. Contacts grow with Iran, China, the Hellenic world, central Asia, and above all, there is a powerful urge towards the eastern seas which leads to the establishment of Indian colonies and the spread of Indian culture far beyond India's boundaries. During the middle period of this millennium, from

*Quoted in 'History of Hindu Mathematics' by B. Datta and A. N. Singh (1933). I am indebted to this book for much information on this subject.

early in the fourth to the sixth century, the Gupta Empire flourishes and becomes the patron and symbol of this widespread intellectual and artistic activity. It is called the Golden or Classical Age of India and the writings of that period, which are classics in Sanskrit literature, reveal a serenity, a quiet confidence of the people in themselves, and a glow of pride at being privileged to be alive in that high noon of civilization, and with it the urge to use their great intellectual and artistic powers to the utmost.

Yet even before that Golden Age had come to a close, signs of weakness and decay become visible. The White Huns come from the north-west in successive hordes and are repeatedly pushed back. But they come again and again and eat their way slowly into North India. For a half-century they even establish themselves as a ruling power all over the north. But then, with a great effort, the last of the great Guptas, joining up in a confederacy with Yashovarman, a ruler of Central India, drives out the Huns.

This long-drawn-out conflict weakened India politically and militarily, and probably the settlement of large numbers of these Huns all over northern India gradually produced an inner change in the people. They were absorbed as all foreign elements had so far been absorbed, but they left their impress and weakened the old ideals of the Indo-Aryan races. Old accounts of the Huns are full of their excessive cruelty and barbarous behaviour which were so foreign to Indian standards of warfare and government.

In the seventh century there was a revival and renascence under Harsha, both political and cultural. Ujjayini (modern Ujjain), which had been the brilliant capital of the Guptas, again became a centre of art and culture and the seat of a powerful kingdom. But in the centuries that followed, this too weakens and fades off. In the ninth century Mihira Bhoja, of Gujrat, consolidates a unified state in North and Central India with his capital at Kanauj. There is another literary revival of which the central figure is Rajashekhara. Again, at the beginning of the eleventh century, another Bhoja stands out as a powerful and attractive figure, and Ujjayini again becomes a great capital. This Bhoja was a remarkable man who distinguished himself in many fields. He was a grammarian and a lexicographer, and interested in medicine and astronomy. He was a builder and a patron of art and literature, and was himself a poet and a writer to whom many works are attributed. His name has become a part of popular fable and legend as a symbol of greatness, learning, and generosity.

And yet for all these bright patches, an inner weakness seems to seize India, which affects not only her political status but her creative activities. There is no date for this, for the process was a slow and creeping one, and it affected north India earlier than the south. The south indeed becomes more important both politically and culturally. Perhaps this was due to the south having escaped the continuous strain of fighting waves of invaders; perhaps many of the writers and artists and master-builders migrated to the south to escape from the unsettled conditions in the north. The powerful kingdoms of the south, with their brilliant courts, must have attracted these people and given them opportunities for creative work which they lacked elsewhere.

But though the north did not dominate India, as it had often done in the past, and was split up into small states, life was still rich there and there were many centres of cultural and philosophic activity. Benares, as ever, was the heart of religious and philosophical thought, and every person who advanced a new theory or a new interpretation of an old theory, had to come there to justify himself. Kashmir was for long a great Sanskrit centre of Buddhist and Brahminical learning. The great universities flourished; of these, Nalanda, the most famous of all, was respected for its scholarship all over India. To have been to Nalanda was a hall-mark of culture. It was not easy to enter that university, for admission was restricted to those who had already attained a certain standard. It specialized in postgraduate study and attracted students from China, Japan, and Tibet, and even it is said, from Korea and Mongolia and Bokhara. Apart from religious and philosophical subjects (both Buddhist and Brahminical), secular and practical subjects were also taught. There was a school of art and a department for architecture; a medical school; an agricultural department; dairy farms and cattle. The intellectual life of the university is said to have been one of animated debates and discussions. The spread of Indian culture abroad was largely the work of scholars from Nalanda.

Then there was the Vikramshila university, near modern Bhagalpur in Bihar, and Vallabhi in Kathiawar. During the period of the Guptas, the Ujjayini university rose into prominence. In the south there was the Amravati university.

Yet, as the millennium approached its end, all this appears to be the afternoon of a civilization; the glow of the morning had long faded away, high noon was past. In the south there was still vitality and vigour and this lasted for some centuries more; in the Indian colonies abroad there was aggressive and full-blooded life right up to the middle of the next millennium. But the heart seems to petrify, its beats are slower, and gradually this petrification and decay spread to the limbs. There is no great figure in philosophy after Shankara in the eighth century, though there is a long succession of commentators and dialecticians. Even Shankara came from the south. The sense of curiosity and the spirit of mental adventure give place to a hard and formal logic and a sterile dialectic. Both Brahminism and Buddhism deteriorate and degraded forms of worship grow up, especially some varieties of Tantric worship and perversions of the Yoga system.

In literature, Bhavabhuti (eighth century) is the last great figure. Many books continued to be written, but their style becomes more and more involved and intricate; there is neither freshness of thought nor of expression. In mathematics, Bhaskara II (twelfth century) is the last great name. In art, E. B. Havell takes us rather beyond this period. He says that the form of expression was not artistically perfected until about the seventh and eighth centuries, when most of the great sculpture and painting in India was produced. From the seventh or eighth to the fourteenth century, according to him, was the great period of Indian art, corresponding to the highest development of Gothic art in Europe. He adds that it was in the sixteenth century that the creative impulse of the old Indian art began markedly to diminish. How far this judgment is correct I do not know, but I imagine that even in the field of art it was South India that carried on the old tradition for a longer period than the north.

The last of the major emigrations for colonial settlement took place from South India in the ninth century, but the Cholas in the south continued to be a great sea power till the eleventh century, when they defeated and conquered Srivijaya.

We thus see that India was drying up and losing her creative genius and vitality. The process was a slow one and lasted several centuries, beginning in the north and finally reaching the south. What were the causes of this political decline and cultural stagnation? Was this due to age alone, that seems to attack civilizations as it does individuals, or to a kind of tidal wave with its forward and backward motion? or were external causes and invasions responsible for it? Radhakrishnan says that Indian philosophy lost its vigour with the loss of political freedom. Sylvain Lévi writes: 'La culture sanscrite a fini avec la liberté de l'Inde; des langues nouvelles, des littératures nouvelles ont envahi la territoire aryenne et l'en ont chassé; elle s'est réfugiée dans les colléges et y a pris un air pédantesque.'

All this is true, for the loss of political freedom lead inevitably to cultural decay. But why should political freedom be lost unless some kind of decay has preceded it? A small country might easily be overwhelmed by superior power, but a huge, well-developed and highly civilized country like India cannot succumb to external attack unless there is internal decay, or the invader possesses a higher technique of warfare. That internal decay is clearly evident in India at the close of these thousand years.

There are repeatedly periods of decay and disruption in the life of every civilization, and there had been such periods in Indian history previously; but India had survived them and rejuvenated herself afresh, sometimes retiring into her shell for a while and emerging again with fresh vigour. There always remained a dynamic core which could renew itself with fresh contacts and develop again, something different from the past and yet intimately connected with it. Had that capacity for adaptation, that flexibility of mind which had saved India so often in the past left her now? Had her fixed beliefs and the growing rigidity of her social structure made her mind also rigid? For if life ceases to grow and evolve, the evolution of thought also ceases. India had all along been a curious combination of conservatism in practice and explosive thought. Inevitably that thought affected the practice, though it did so in its own way without irreverence for the past. 'Mais si leurs yeux suivaient les mots anciens, leur intelligence y voyait des idées nouvelles. L'Inde s'est transformée á son insu.' But when thought lost its explosiveness and creative power and became a tame attendant on an outworn and meaningless practice, mumbling old phrases and fearful of everything new, then life became stagnant and tied and constrained in a prison of its own making.

We have many examples of the collapse of a civilization, and perhaps the most notable of these is that of the European classical civilization which ended with the fall of Rome. Long before Rome fell to the invaders from the north, it had been on the verge of collapse from its own internal weaknesses. Its economy, once expanding, had shrunk and brought all manner of difficulties in its train. Urban industries decayed, flourishing cities grew progressively smaller and impoverished, and even fertility rapidly declined. The Emperors tried many expedients to overcome their ever-increasing difficulties. There was compulsory state regulation of merchants, craftsmen, and workers, who were tied down to particular employments. Many kinds of employment were forbidden to those outside certain groups of workers. Thus some occupations were practically converted into castes. The peasantry became serfs. But all these superficial attempts to check the decline failed and even worsened conditions; and the Roman Empire collapsed.

There was and has been no such dramatic collapse of Indian civilization, and it has shown an amazing staying power despite all that has happened; but a progressive decline is visible. It is difficult to specify in any detail what the social conditions in India were at the end of the first millennium after Christ; but it may be said with some assurance that the expanding economy of India had ended and there was a strong tendency to shrink. Probably this was the inevitable result of the growing rigidity and exclusiveness of the Indian social structure as represented chiefly by the caste system. Where Indians had gone abroad, as in south-east Asia, they were not so rigid in mind or customs or in their economy, and they had opportunities for growth and expansion. For another four or five hundred years they flourished in these colonies and displayed energy and creative vigour; but in India herself the spirit of exclusiveness sapped the creative faculty and developed a narrow, small-group, and parochial outlook. Life became cut up into set frames, where each man's job was fixed and permanent and he had little concern with others. It was the Kshatriya's business to fight in defence of the country, and others were not interested or were not even allowed to do so. The Brahmin and the Kshatriya looked down on trade and commerce. Education and opportunities of growth were withheld from the lower castes, who were taught to be submissive to those higher up in the scale. In spite of a well-developed urban economy and industries, the structure of the state was in many ways feudal. Probably even in the technique of warfare India had fallen behind. No marked progress was possible under these conditions without changing that structure and releasing fresh sources of talent and energy. The caste system was a barrier to such a change. For all its virtues and the stability it had given to Indian society, it carried within it the seeds of destruction.

The Indian social structure (and I shall consider this more fully later) had given amazing stability to Indian civilization. It had given strength and cohesion to the group, but this came in the way of expansion and a larger cohesion. It developed crafts and skill and trade and commerce, but always within each group separately. Thus particular types of activity became hereditary and there was a tendency to avoid new types of work and activity and to confine oneself to the old groove, to restrict initiative and the spirit of innovation. It gave a measure of freedom within a certain limited sphere, but at the expense of the growth of a larger freedom and at the heavy price of keeping large numbers of people permanently at the bottom of the social ladder, deprived of the opportunities of growth. So long as that structure afforded avenues for growth and expansion, it was progressive; when it reached the limits of expansion open to it, it became stationary, unprogressive, and, later, inevitably regressive.

Because of this there was decline all along the line—intellectual, philosophical, political, in technique and methods of warfare, in knowledge of and contacts with the outside world, and there was a growth of local sentiments and feudal, small-group feeling at the expense of the larger conception of India as a whole, and a shrinking economy. Yet, as later ages were to show, there was yet vitality in the old structure and an amazing tenacity, as well as some flexibility and capacity for adaptation. Because of this it managed to survive and to profit by new contacts and waves of thought, and even progress in some ways. But that progress was always tied down to and hampered by far too many relics of the past.

226

CHAPTER SIX

NEW PROBLEMS

The Arabs and the Mongols

WHILE HARSHA WAS REIGNING OVER A POWERFUL KINGDOM IN north India and Hsuan-Tsang, the Chinese scholar-pilgrim, was studying at Nalanda University, Islam was taking shape in Arabia. Islam was to come to India both as a religious and a political force and create many new problems, but it is well to remember that it took a long time before it made much difference to the Indian scene. It was nearly 600 years before it reached the heart of India and when it came to the accompaniment of political conquest, it had already changed much and its standard-bearers were different. The Arabs who, in a fine frenzy of enthusiasm and with a dynamic energy, had spread out and conquered from Spain to the borders of Mongolia carrying with them a brilliant culture, did not come to India proper. They stopped at its north-western fringe and remained there. Arab civilization gradually decayed and various Turkish tribes came into prominence in central and western Asia. It was these Turkish and Afghans from the Indian borderland who brought Islam as a political force to India.

Some dates might help to bring these facts home to us. Islam may be said to begin with the Hijrat, the departure of the Prophet Mohammed from Mecca to Medina, in 622 A.C. Mohammed died ten years latter. Some time was spent in consolidating the position in Arabia, and then those astounding series of events took place which carried the Arabs, with the banner of Islam, right across central Asia in the east and across the whole north African continent to Spain and France in the west. In the seventh century and by the beginning of the eighth, they had spread over Iraq, Iran, and central Asia. In 712 A.C. they reached and occupied Sind in the north-west of India and stopped there. A great desert separated this area from the more fertile parts of India. In the west the Arabs crossed the narrow straits between Africa and Europe (since called the Straits of Gibraltar) and entered Spain in 711 A.C. They occupied the whole of Spain and crossed the Pyrenees into France. In 732 they were defeated and checked by Charles Martel at Tours in France.

This triumphant career of a people, whose homelands were the deserts of Arabia and who had thus far played no notable

227

part in history, is most remarkable. They must have derived their vast energy from the dynamic and revolutionary character of their Prophet and his message of human brotherhood. And yet it is wrong to imagine that Arab civilization suddenly rose out of oblivion and took shape after the advent of Islam. There has been a tendency on the part of Islamic scholars to decry the pre-Islamic past of the Arab people and to refer to it as the period of *jahilīyat*, a kind of dark age of ignorance and supersition. Arab civilization, like others, had a long past, intimately connected with the development of the Semitic race, the Phœnicians, Cretans, Chaldeans, Hebrews. The Israelites became more exclusive and separated themselves from the more catholic Chaldeans and others. Between them and other Semitic races there were conflicts. Nevertheless all over the Semitic area there were contacts and interchanges and to some extent a common background. Pre-Islamic Arab civilization grew up especially in Yemen. Arabic was a highly developed language at the time of the Prophet, with a mixture of Persian and even some Indian words. Like the Phœnicians, the Arabs went far across the seas in search of trade. There was an Arab colony in south China, near Canton, in pre-Islamic days.

Nevertheless it is true that the Prophet of Islam vitalized his people and filled them with faith and enthusiasm. Considering themselves the standard-bearers of a new cause, they developed the zeal and self-confidence which sometimes fills a whole people and changes history. Their success was also undoubtedly due to the decay of the states in western and central Asia and in north Africa. North Africa was torn by internecine conflicts between rival Christian factions, leading often to bloody struggles for mastery. The Christianity that was practised there at the time was narrow and intolerant and the contrast between this and the general toleration of the Moslem Arabs, with their message of human brotherhood, was marked. It was this that brought whole peoples, weary of Christian strife, to their side.

The culture that the Arabs carried with them to distant countries was itself continuously changing and developing. It bore the strong impress of the new ideas of Islam, and yet to call it Islamic civilization is confusing and probably incorrect. With their capital at Damascus, they soon left their simple ways of living and developed a more sophisticated culture. That period might be called one of Arab-Syrian civilization. Byzantine influences came to them, but most of all, when they moved to Baghdad, the traditions of old Iran affected them and they developed the Arab-Persian civilization which became dominant over all the vast areas they controlled.

Widespread and apparently easy as the Arab conquests were, they did not go far beyond Sind in India, then or later. Was this due to the fact that India was still strong enough to resist effectively the invader? Probably so, for it is difficult to explain otherwise the lapse of several centuries before a real invasion took place. Partly it may have been due to the internal troubles of the Arabs. Sind fell away from the central authority at Baghdad and became a small independent Moslem state. But though there was no invasion, contacts between India and the Arab world grew, travellers came to and from, embassies were exchanged, Indian books, especially on mathematics and astronomy, were taken to Baghdad and were translated into Arabic. Many Indian physicians went to Baghdad. These trade and cultural relations were not confined to north India. The southern states of India also participated in them, especially the Rāshtra-kutas, on the west coast of India, for purposes of trade.

This frequent intercourse inevitably led to Indians getting to know the new religion, Islam. Missionaries also came to spread this new faith and they were welcomed. Mosques were built. There was no objection raised either by the state or the people, nor were there any religious conflics. It was the old tradition of India to be tolerant to all faiths and forms of worship. Thus Islam came as a religion to India several centuries before it came as a political force.

The new Arab Empire under the Ommeya Khalifās (Ommeyade Caliphs) had its seat and capital at Damascus where a splendid city grew up. But soon, about 750 A.C. the Abbasiyā (Abbaside) Khalifās took the capital to Baghdad. Internal conflicts followed and Spain fell away from the central empire, but continued for long as an independent Arab state. Gradually the Baghdad Empire also weakened and split up into several states, and the Seljuk Turks came from central Asia and became politically all-powerful at Baghdad, though the Khalifā still funcioned at their pleasure. Sultan Mahmud of Ghazni, a Turk, arose in Afghanistan, a great warrior and a brilliant captain, and he ignored and even taunted the Khalifā. But still Baghdad continued as the cultural centre of the Islamic world and even far-way Spain looked to it for inspiration. Europe was backward then in learning and science and art and the amenities of life. It was Arab Spain, and especially the university of Cordoba, that kept the lamp of learning and intellectual curiosity burning throughout those dark ages of Europe and some of its light pierced the European gloom.

The Crusades beginning in 1095 A.C. went on for over a century and a half. These did not merely represent a struggle between two aggressive religions, a conflict between the Cross and the Crescent. 'The Crusades,' says Professor G. M. Trevelyan, the eminent historian, 'were the military and religious aspect of a general urge towards the east on the part of the reviving energies of Europe. The prize that Europe brought back from the Crusades was not the permanent liberation of the holy Sepulchre or the potential unity of Christendom, of which the story of the Crusades was one long negation. She brought back instead the finer arts and crafts, luxury, science, and intellectual curiosity—everything that Peter the Hermit would most have despised.'

Before the last of the Crusades had ingloriously petered out, something cyclonic and cataclysmic had taken place in the heart of Asia. Chengiz (or Jenghiz) Khan had begun his devastating march westward. Born in Mongolia in 1155 A.C., he started on this great march, which was to convert central Asia into a heap of smoking ruins, in 1219. He was no youngster then. Bokhara, Samarkand, Herat, and Balkh, all great cities, each having more than a million inhabitants, were reduced to ashes. Chengiz went on to Kiev in Russia and then returned; Baghdad somehow escaped as it did not lie on his route. He died in 1227 at the age of seventy-two. His successors went further into Europe and, in 1258, Hulagu captured Baghdad and put an end to that famous centre of art and learning, where for over 500 years treasures from all parts of the world had come and accumulated. That gave a great shock to the distinctive Arab-Persian civilization in Asia, though this survived even under the Mongols; it continued especially in parts of North Africa and especially in Spain. Crowds of scholars with their books fled from Baghdad to Cairo and Spain and a renaissance of art and learning took place there. But Spain itself was slipping from the Arab grasp and Corodoba had fallen in 1236 A.C. For another two centuries and a half the kingdom of Granada continued as a bright centre of Arab culture. In 1492 A.C. Granada also fell to Ferdinand and Isabella, and Arab dominion in Spain ended. Thenceforward Cairo became the chief Arab centre, though it came under Turkish domination. The Ottoman Turks had captured Constantinople in 1453, thereby releasing those forces which gave birth to the European Renaissance.

The Mongol conquests in Asia and Europe represented something new in the art of warfare. 'In scale and in quality,' says Liddell Hart, 'in surprise and in mobility, in the strategic and in the tactical indirect approach their (the Mongols') campaigns surpass any in history.' Chengiz Khan was undoubtedly one of the greatest, if not the greatest, military leaders that the world has produced. The chivalry of Asia and Europe was matchwood before him and his brilliant successors, and it was pure chance that central and western Europe escaped conquest. From these Mongols Europe learnt new lessons in strategy and the art of warfare. The use of gunpowder also came to Europe, through these Mongols, from China.

The Mongols did not come to India. They stopped at the Indus river and pursued their conquests elsewhere. When their great empires faded away a number of smaller states rose in Asia, and then in 1369 Timur, a Turk, claiming to be a descendant of Chengiz Khan through his mother, tried to repeat the exploits of Chengiz. Samarkand, his capital, again became a seat of empire, brief-lived though this was. After Timur's death his successors were more interested in a quiet life and in cultivating the arts than in military exploits. A Timurid renaissance, as it is called, took place in central Asia and it was in this environment that Babar, a descendant of Timur, was born and grew up. Babar was the founder of the Mughal dynasty in India; he was the first of the Grand Mughals. He captured Delhi in 1526.

Chengiz Khan was not a Moslem, as some people seem to imagine because of his name which is now associated with Islam. He is said to have believed in Shamaism, a religion of the sky. What this was I do not know but the word inevitably makes one think of the Arab word for Buddhists—Samani, which was derived from the Sanskrit Shravana. Debased forms of Buddhism flourished then in various parts of Asia, including Mongolia and it is probable that Chengiz grew up under their influence.

It is odd to think that the greatest military conqueror in history was probably some kind of a Buddhist.*

In Central Asia, even to-day four legendary figures of great conquerors are remembered—Sikander (Alexander), Sultan Mahmud, Chengiz Khan and Timur. To these four must be added now a fifth, another type of person, not a warrior, but a conqueror in a different realm, round whose name legend has already gathered — Lenin.

The Flowering of Arab Culture and Contacts with India

Having rapidly conquered large parts of Asia, Africa, and a bit of Europe, the Arabs turned their minds to conquests in other fields. The empire was being consolidated, many new countries had come within their ken and they were eager to find out about this world and its ways. The intellectual curiosity, the adventures in rationalist speculation, the spirit of scientific inquiry among the Arabs of the eighth and ninth centuries are very striking.

Normally, in the early days of a religion based on fixed concepts and beliefs, faith is dominant and variations are not approved or encouraged. That faith had carried the Arabs far and that trium-

*A kind of Shamanism or Shamaism still lingers in Arctic Siberia, Mongolia, and in Tanna Tuva in Soviet Central Asia. This appears to be based entirely on a belief in spirits and has apparently no connection whatever with Buddhism. Yet it may have been influenced long ago by some degraded forms of Buddhism which were gradually submerged in local primitive superstitions. Tibet, which is patently a Buddhist country, has developed its own avriety of Buddhism called Lamaism. Mongolia with its Shamanism has also the Living Buddha tradition. Thus there seem to be various gradations in northern and central Asia of Buddhism fading off into primitive beliefs.

phant success itself must have deepened that faith. And yet we find them going beyond the limits of dogma and creed, dabbling with agnosticism, and turning their zeal and energy towards adventures of the mind. Arab travellers, among the greatest of their kind, go to far countries to find out what other peoples were doing and thinking, to study and understand their philosophies and sciences and ways of life, and then to develop their own thought. Scholars and books from abroad were brought to Baghdad and the Khalif al-Mansur (middle eighth century) established a research and translation bureau where translations were made from Greek, Syriac, Zend, Latin, and Sanskrit. Old monasteries in Syria, Asia Minor, and the Levant were ransacked for manuscripts. The old Alexandrian schools had been closed by Christian bishops and their scholars had been driven out. Many of these exiles had drifted to Persia and elsewhere. They now found a welcome and a safe haven in Baghdad and they brought Greek philosophy and science and mathematics with them—Plato and Aristotle, Ptolemy and Euclid. There were Nestorian and Jewish scholars and Indian physicians; philosophers and mathematicians.

All this continued and developed during the reigns of the Khalifs Harun-al-Rashid and al-Mamun (eighth and ninth centuries) and Baghdad became the biggest intellectual centre of the civilized world.

There were many contacts with India during this period and the Arabs learnt much of Indian mathematics, astronomy, and medicine. And yet, it would appear, that the initiative for all these contacts came chiefly from the Arabs and though the Arabs learned much from India, the Indians did not learn much from the Arabs.

The Indians remained aloof, wrapped up in their own conceits, and keeping as far as possible within their own shells. This was unfortunate, for the intellectual ferment of Baghdad and the Arab renaissance movement would have shaken up the Indian mind just when it was losing much of its creative vigour. In that spirit of intellectual inquiry the Indians of an older days would have found kinship in thought.

The study of Indian learning and science in Baghdad was greatly encouraged by the powerful Barmak family (the Barmecides) which gave viziers to Harun-al-Rashid. This family had probably been converted from Buddhism. During an illness of Harun-al-Rashid, a physician named Manak was sent for from India. Manak settled down in Baghdad and was appointed the head of a large hospital there. Arab writers mention six other Indian physicians living in Baghdad at the time, besides Manak. In astronomy the Arabs improved on both the Indians and the Alexandrians and two famous names stand out: Al Khwarismi, a mathematician and astronomer of the ninth century, and the poet-astronomer Omar Khayyam of the twelfth century. In medicine,

Arab physicians and surgeons were famous in Asia and Europe. Most famous of them was Ibn Sina (Avicenna) of Bokhara, who was called the Prince of Physicians. He died in 1037 A.C. One of the great Arab thinkers and philosophers was Abu Nasr Farabi.

In philosophy the influence of India does not seem to have been marked. Both for philosophy and science the Arabs looked to Greece and the old Alexandrian schools. Plato and, more especially, Aristotle exercised a powerful influence on the Arab mind and since then, and up to the present day, they have become more in Arabic commentaries than in the original versions, standard subjects for study in Islamic schools. Neo-Platonism from Alexandria also influenced the Arab mind. The materialist school of Greek Philosophy reached the Arabs and led to the rise of rationalism and materialism. The rationalists tried to interpret religious tenets and injunctions in terms of reason; the materialists almost rejected religion altogether. What is noteworthy is the full freedom of discussion allowed in Baghdad for all these rival and conflicting theories. This controversy and conflict between faith and reason spread from Baghdad all over the Arab world and reached Spain. The nature of God was discussed and it was stated that He cannot have any qualities, such as were commonly attributed to Him. These qualities were human. To call God benevolent or righteous was, it was suggested, just as pagan and degraded as to say that He has a beard.

Rationalism led to agnosticism and scepticism. Gradually with the decline of Baghdad and the growth of the Turkish power, this spirit of rationalist inquiry lessened. But in Arab Spain it still continued and one of the most famous of Arab philosophers in Spain went to the limits of irreligion. This was Ibn Rushd (Averroes) who lived in the twelfth century. He is reported to have said of the various religions of his time that they were meant for children or for fools or they could not be acted upon. Whether he actually said so or not is doubtful, but even the tradition shows the kind of man he was, and he suffered for his opinions. In many ways he was remarkable. He wrote strongly in favour of giving women a chance to play a part in public activities and held that they were fully capable of justifying themselves. He also suggested that incurables and such-like persons should be liquidated as they were a burden on society.

Spain was then far in advance of the other centres of European learning and Arab and Jewish scholars from Cordoba were greatly respected in Paris and elsewhere. These Arabs evidently had no high opinion of the other Europeans. An Arab writer named Said, of Toledo, described the Europeans living north of the Pyrenees thus: 'They are of a cold temperament and never reach maturity. They are of a great stature and of a white colour. But they lack all sharpness of wit and penetration of intellect.'

The flowering of Arab culture and civilization in western and central Asia derived its inspiration from two main sources—Arab and Iranian. The two mixed inextricably, producing a vigour of thought as well as a high standard of living conditions for the upper classes. From the Arabs came the vigour and the spirit of inquiry; from the Iranians, the graces of life, art, and luxury.

As Baghdad waned under Turkish domination, the spirit of rationalism and inquiry also declined. Chengiz Khan and the Mongols put an end to all this. A hundred years later central Asia woke up again and Samarkand and Herat became centres for painting and architecture, reviving somewhat the old traditions of Arab-Persian civilization. But there was no revival of Arab rationalism and interest in science. Islam had become a more rigid faith suited more to military conquests rather than the conquests of the mind. Its chief representatives in Asia were no longer the Arabs, but the Turks* and the Mongols (later called Mughals in India), and to some extent the Afghans. These Mongols in western Asia had become Moslems; in the Far East and in the middle regions many took to Buddhism.

Mahmud of Ghazni and the Afghans

Early in the eighth century, in 712, the Arabs had reached Sind and occupied it. They stopped there. Even Sind fell away from the Arab Empire within half a century or so, though it continued as a small independent Moselm state. For nearly 300 years there was no further invasion of or incursion into India. About 1000 A.C. Sultan Mahmud of Ghazni in Afghanistan, a Turk who had risen to power in central Asia, began his raids into India. There were many such raids and they were bloody and ruthless, and on every occasion Mahmud carried away with him a vast quantity of treasure. A scholar contemporary, Alberuni, of Khiva, describes these raids: 'The Hindus became like the atoms of dust scattered in all directions and like a tale of old in the mouths of people. Their scattered remains cherish of course the most inveterate aversion towards all Moslems.'

This poetic description gives us some idea of the devastation caused by Mahmud, and yet it is well to remember that Mahmud touched and despoiled only a part of north India, chiefly along the lines of his marches. The whole of central, eastern, and south India escaped from him completely.

South India at that time and later, was dominated by the powerful Chola Empire which controlled the sea routes and had

*I have often used the word 'Turk' or 'Turki'. This may confuse, as 'Turk' is associated now with the people of Turkey, who are descended from the Osmanli or Ottoman Turks. Bnt there were other kinds of Turks also—Seljuks, etc. All the Turanian races of Central Asia, Chinese Turkestan, etc., may be called Turks or Turkis.

reached as far as Srivijaya in Java and Sumatra. The Indian colonies in the eastern seas were also flourishing and strong. Sea power was shared between them and south India. But this did not save north India from a land invasion.

Mahmud annexed the Punjab and Sind to his dominions and returned to Ghazni after each raid. He was unable to conquer Kashmir. This mountain country succeeded in checking and repulsing him. He met with a severe defeat also in the Rajputana desert regions on his way back from Somnath in Kathiawar.* This was his last raid and he did not return.

Mahmud was far more a warrior than a man of faith and like many other conquerors he used and exploited the name of religion for his conquests. India was to him just a place from which he could carry off treasure and material to his homeland. He enrolled an army in India and placed it under one of his noted generals, Tilak by name, who was an Indian and a Hindu. This army he used against his own co-religionists in central Asia.

Mahmud was anxious to make his own city of Ghazni rival the great cities of central and western Asia and he carried off from India large numbers of artisans and master builders. Building interested him and he was much impressed by the city of Mathura (modern Muttra) near Delhi. About this he wrote: 'There are here a thousand edifices as firm as the faith of the faithful; nor is it likely that this city has attained its present condition but at the expense of many millions of dinars, nor could such another be constructed under a period of 200 years.'

In the intervals of his fighting Mahmud was interested in encouraging cultural activities in his own homeland and he gathered together a number of eminent men. Among these was the famous Persian poet Firdausi, author of the 'Shahnamah', who later fell out with Mahmud. Alberuni, a scholar and traveller, was a contemporary, and in his books he gives us a glimpse into other aspects of life in central Asia then. Born near Khiva, but of Persian descent, he came to India and travelled a great deal. He tells us of the great irrigation works in the Chola kingdom in the south,

* *There is a curious passage relating to this defeat in an old chronicle in Persian, the Tarikh -i- Sorath (translated by Ranchodji Amarji, Bombay, 1882) p. 112: 'Shah Mahmud took to his heels in dismay and saved his life, but many of his followers of both sexes were captured.. Turk, Afghan, and Mughal female prisoners, if they happened to be virgins, were accepted as wives by the Indian soldiers.... The bowels of the others, however, were cleaned by means of emetics and purgatives, and thereafter the captives were married to men of similar rank.' 'Low females were joined to low men. Respectable men were compelled to shave off their beards, and were enrolled among the Shekhavat and the Wadhel tribes of Rajputs; whilst the lower kinds were allotted to the castes of Kolis, Khantas, Babrias, and Mers.' I am not myself acquainted with the Tarikh-i-Sorath and do not know how far it can be considered as reliable. I have taken this quotation from K. M. Munshi's 'The Glory that was Gurjardesa' Part III, p. 140. What is especially interesting is the way foreigners are said to have been absorbed into the Rajput clans and even marriages having taken place. The cleansing process mentioned is novel.*

though it is doubtful if he visited them himself or went to south India. He learnt Sanskrit in Kashmir and studied the religion, philosophy, science, and arts of India. He had previously learnt Greek in order to study Greek philosophy. His books are not only a storehouse of information, but tell us how, behind war and pillage and massacre, patient scholarship continued, and how the people of one country tried to understand those of another even when passion and anger had embittered their relations. That passion and anger no doubt clouded judgments on either side, and each considered his own people superior to the other. Of the Indians, Alberuni says that they are 'haughty, foolishly vain, self-contained, and stolid,' and that they believe 'that there is no country like theirs, no nation like theirs, no kings like theirs, no science like theirs.' Probably a correct enough description of the temper of the people.

Mahmud's raids are a big event in Indian history, though politically India as a whole was not greatly affected by them and the heart of India remained untouched. They demonstrated the weakness and decay of north India, and Alberuni's accounts throw further light on the political disintegration of the north and west.

These repeated incursions from the north-west brought many new elements into India's closed thought and economy. Above all they brought Islam, for the first time, to the accompaniment of ruthless military conquest. So far, for over 300 years, Islam had come peacefully as a religion and taken its place among the many religions of India without trouble or conflict. The new approach produced powerful psychological reactions among the people and filled them with bitterness. There was no objection to a new religion but there was strong objection to anything which forcibly interfered with and upset their way of life.

India was, it must be remembered, a country of many religions, in spite of the dominance of the Hindu faith in its various shapes and forms. Apart from Jainism and Buddhism, which had largely faded away and been absorbed by Hinduism, there were Christianity and the Hebrew religion. Both of these had reached India probably during the first century after Christ, and both had found a place in the country. There were large numbers of Syrian Christians and Nestorians in south India and they were as much part of the country as anyone else. So were the Jews. And so too was the small community of the Zoroastrians who had come to India from Iran in the seventh century. So also were many Moslems on the west coast and in the north-west.

Mahmud came as a conqueror and the Punjab became just an outlying province of his dominions. Yet when he had established himself as a ruler there, an attempt was made to tone down his previous methods in order to win over the people of the province to some extent. There was less of interference with their ways and

Hindus were appointed to high office in the army and the administration. Only the beginnings of this process are noticeable in Mahmud's time; it was to grow later.

Mahmud died in 1030. More than 160 years passed after his death without any other invasion of India or an extension of Turkish rule beyond the Punjab. Then an Afghan, Shahab-ud-Din Ghuri, captured Ghazni and put an end to the Ghaznavite Empire. He marched to Lahore and then to Delhi. But the king of Delhi, Prithvi Raj Chauhan, defeated him utterly. Shahab-ud-Din retired to Afghanistan and came back next year with another army. This time he triumphed and in 1192 he sat on the throne of Delhi.

Prithvi Raj is a popular hero, still famous in song and legend, for reckless lovers are always popular. He had carried away the girl he loved and who loved him from the very palace of her father, Jaichandra, King of Kanauj, defying an assembled host of princelings who had come to offer court to her. He won his bride for a brief while, but at the cost of a bitter feud with a powerful ruler and the lives of the bravest on both sides. The chivalry of Delhi and central India engaged in internecine conflict and there was much mutual slaughter. And so, all for the love of a woman, Prithvi Raj lost his life and throne, and Delhi, that seat of empire, passed into the hands of an invader from outside. But his love story is sung still and he is a hero, while Jaichandra is looked upon almost as a traitor.

This conquest of Delhi did not mean the subjugation of the rest of India. The Cholas were still powerful in the south, and there were other independent states. It took another century and a half for Afghan rule to spread over the greater part of the south. But Delhi was significant and symbolic of the new order.

The Indo-Afghans. South India. Vijayanagar. Babar Sea Power

Indian history has usually been divided by English as well as some Indian historians into three major periods: Ancient or Hindu, Moslem, and the British period. This division is neither intelligent nor correct; it is deceptive and gives a wrong perspective. It deals more with the superficial changes at the top than with the essential changes in the political, economic, and cultural development of the Indian people. The so-called ancient period is vast and full of change, of growth and decay, and then growth again. What is called the Moslem or medieval period brought another change, and an important one, and yet it was more or less confined to the top and did not vitally affect the essential continuity of Indian life. The invaders who came to India from the north-west, like so many of their predecessors in more ancient times, became absorbed into India and part of her life. Their dynasties became Indian dynasties and there was a great deal of racial fusion by intermarriage. A deliberate effort was made, apart from a few exceptions, not to interfere with the ways and customs of the people. They looked to India as their home country and had no other affiliations. India continued to be an independent country.

The coming of the British made a vital difference and the old system was uprooted in many ways. They brought an entirely different impulse from the west, which had slowly developed in Europe from the times of the Renaissance, Reformation, and political revolution in England, and was taking shape in the beginnings of the industrial revolution. The American and French Revolutions were to carry this further. The British remained outsiders, aliens and misfits in India, and made no attempt to be otherwise. Above all, for the first time in India's history, her political control was exercised from outside and her economy was centered in a distant place. They made India a typical colony of the modern age, a subject country for the first time in her long history.

Mahmud of Ghazni's invasion of India was certainly a foreign Turkish invasion and resulted in the Punjab being separated from the rest of India for a while. The Afghans who came at the end of the twelfth century were different. They were an Indo-Aryan race closely allied to the people of India. Indeed, for long stretches of time Afghanistan had been, and was destined to be, a part of India. Their language, Pashto, was basically derived from Sanskrit. There are few places in India or outside which are so full of ancient monuments and remains of Indian culture, chiefly of the Buddhist period, as Afghanistan. More correctly, the Afghans should be called the Indo-Afghans. They differed in many ways from the people of the Indian plains, just as the people of the mountain valleys of Kashmir differed from the dwellers of the warmer and flatter regions below. But in spite of this difference Kashmir had always been and continued to be an important seat of Indian learning and culture. The Afghans differed also from the more highly cultured and sophisticated Arabs and Persians. They were hard and fierce like their mountain fastnesses, rigid in their faith, warriors not inclined towards intellectual pursuits or adventures of the mind. They behaved to begin with as conquerors over a rebellious people and were cruel and harsh.

But soon they toned down. India became their home and Delhi was their capital, not distant Ghazni as in Mahmud's time. Afghanistan, where they came from, was just an outlying part of their kingdom. The process of Indianization was rapid, and many of them married women of the country. One of their great rulers, Alauddin Khilji, himself married a Hindu lady, and so did his son. Some of the subsequent rulers were racially Turks, such as Qutb-ud-Din Aibak, the Sultana Razia, and Iltutmish; but the nobility and army continued to be mainly Afghan. Delhi flourished as an imperial capital. Ibn Batuta, a famous Arab traveller from Morocco, who visited many countries and saw many cities from Cairo and Constantinople to China, described it in the fourteenth century, perhaps with some exaggeration, as 'one of the greatest cities in the universe.'

The Delhi Sultanate spread southwards. The Chola kingdom was declining, but in its place a new sea faring power had grown. This was the Pandya kingdom, with its capital at Madura and its port at Kayal on the east coast. It was a small kingdom but a great centre of trade. Marco Polo twice visited this port on his way from China, in 1288 and 1293, and described it 'as a great and noble city,' full of ships from Arabia and China. He also mentions the very fine muslins, which 'look like tissues of a spider's web' and which were made on the east coast of India. Marco Polo tells us also an interesting fact. Large numbers of horses were imported by sea from Arabia and Persia into south India. The climate of south India was not suited to horse-breeding, and horses, apart from their other uses, were necessary for military purposes. The best breeding-grounds for horses were in central and western Asia, and this may well explain, to some extent, the superiority of the central Asian races in warfare. Chengiz Khan's Mongols were magnificent horsemen and were devoted to their horses. The Turks were also fine horsemen, and the love of the Arab for his horse is well-known. In north and west India there are some good breeding-grounds for horses, especially in Kathiawar, and the Rajputs are very fond of their horses. Many a petty war was waged for a famous charger. There is a story of a Delhi Sultan admiring the charger of a Rajput chief and asking him for it. The Hara chief replied to the Lodi king: 'There are three things you must not ask of a Rajput: his horse, his mistress, or his sword,' and he galloped away. There was trouble afterwards.

Late in the fourteenth century, Timur, the Turk or Turco-Mongol, came down from the north and smashed up the Delhi Sultanate. He was only a few months in India; he came to Delhi and went back . But all along his route he created a wilderness adorned with pyramids of skulls of those he had slain; and Delhi itself became a city of the dead. Fortunately, he did not go far and only some parts of the Punjab and Delhi had to suffer this terrible affliction.

It took many years for Delhi to wake up from this sleep of death, and even when it woke up it was no longer the capital of a great empire. Timur's visit had broken that empire and out of it had arisen a number of states in the south. Long before this, early in the fourteenth century, two gerat states had risen—Gulbarga, called the Bahmani kingdom,* and the Hindu kingdom of Vijaya-

*The name and origin of the Bahmani Kingdom of the South is interesting. The founder

nagar. Gulbarga now split up into five states, one of these being Ahmadnagar. Ahmad Nizam Shah, the founder of Ahmadnagar in 1490, was the son of Nizam-ul-Mulk Bhairi, a minister of the Bahmani kings. This Nizam-ul-Mulk was the son of a Brahmin accountant named Bhairu (from which his name Bhairi). Thus the Ahmednagar dynasty was of indigenous origin, and Chand Bibi, the heroine of Ahmednagar, had mixed blood. All the Moslem states in the south were indigenous and Indianized.

After Timur's sack of Delhi, north India remained weak and divided up. South India was better off and the largest and most powerful of the southern kingdoms was Vijayanagar. This state and city attracted many of the Hindu refugees from the north. From contemporary accounts it appears that the city was rich and very beautiful. 'The city is such that eye has note seen nor ear heard of any place resembling it upon the whole earth,' says Abdur-Razzak, from central Asia. There were arcades and magnificent galleries for the bazaars, and rising above them all was the palace of the king, surrounded by 'many rivulets and streams flowing through channels of cut stone, polished and even.' The whole city was full of gardens and because of them, as an Italian visitor in 1420, Nicolo Conti, writes, the circumference of the city was sixty miles. A later visitor was Paes, a Portuguese who came in 1522 after having visited the Italian cities of the Renaissance. The city of Vijayanagar, he says, is as 'large as Rome and very beautiful to the sight'; it is full of charm and wonder with its innumerable lakes and waterways and fruit gardens. It is 'the best-provided city in the world' and 'everything abounds.' The chambers of the palace were a mass of ivory, with roses and lotuses carved in ivory at the top—'it is so rich and beautiful that you would hardly find anywhere another such.' Of the ruler, Krishna Deva Raya, Paes writes: 'He is the most feared and perfect king that could possibly be, cheerful of disposition and very merry; he is one that seek to honour foreigners, and receives them kindly, asking about all their affairs whatever their condition may be.'

While Vijayanagar was flourishing in the south, the petty sultanate of Delhi had to meet a new foe. Yet another invader came down from the northern mountains and on the famous battlefield of Panipat, near Delhi, where so often India's fate has been decided, he won the throne of Delhi in 1526. This was Babar, a Turco-Mongol and a prince of the Timurid line in central Asia. With him begins the Mughal Empire of India.

Babar's success was probably due not only to the weakness of the Delhi Sultanate but to his possessing a new and improved type of artillery which was not in use in India then. From this period

of this state was an Afghan Moslem who had a Hindu patron in his early days—Gangu Brahmin. In gratitude to him he even took his name and his dynasty was called the Bahmani (from Brahmin) dynasty.

onwards India seems to lag behind in the developing science of warfare. It would be more correct to say that the whole of Asia remained where it was while Europe was advancing in this science. The great Mughal Empire, powerful as it was in India for 200 years, probably could not compete on equal terms with European armies from the seventeenth century onwards. But no European army could come to India unless it had control over the sea routes. The major change that was taking place during these centuries was the development of European sea power. With the fall of the Chola kingdom in the south in the thirteenth century, Indian sea power declined rapidly. The small Pandya state, though intimately connected with the sea, was not strong enough. The Indian colonies, however, still continued to hold command over the Indian Ocean till the fifteenth century, when they were ousted by the Arabs, who were soon to be followed by the Portuguese.

Synthesis and Growth of Mixed Culture
Purdah. Kabir. Guru Nanak. Amir Khusrau

It is thus wrong and misleading to talk of a Moslem invasion of India or of the Moslem period in India, just as it would be wrong to refer to the coming of the British to India as a Christian invasion, or to call the British period in India a Christian period. Islam did not invade India; it had come to India some centuries earlier. There was a Turkish invasion (Mahmud's), and an Afghan invasion, and then a Turco-Mongol or Mughal invasion, and of these the two latter were important. The Afghans might well be considered a border Indian group, hardly strangers to India, and the period of their political dominance should be called the Indo-Afghan period. The Mughals were outsiders and strangers to India and yet they fitted into the Indian structure with remarkable speed and began the Indo-Mughal period.

Through choice or circumstances or both, the Afghan rulers and those who had come with them, merged into India. Their dynasties became completely Indianized with their roots in India, looking upon India as their homeland, and the rest of the word as foreign. In spite of political conflict, they were generally considered as such and many even of the Rajput princes accepted them as their over-lords. But there were other Rajput chiefs who refused to submit and there were fierce conflicts. Feroze Shah, one of the well-known Sultans of Delhi, had a Hindu mother; so had Ghyas-ud-Din Tughlak. Such marriages between the Afghans, Turkish, and the Hindu nobility were not frequent, but they did take place. In the south the Moslem ruler of Gulbarga married a Hindu princess of Vijayanagar with great pomp and ceremony.

It appears that in the Moslem countries of central and western Asia Indians had a good reputation. As early as the eleventh century, that is, before the Afghan conquest, a Moslem geographer, Idrisi, wrote: 'The Indians are naturally inclined to justice, and never depart from it in their actions. Their good faith, honesty, and fidelity to their engagements are well-known, and they are so famous for these qualities that people flock to their country from every side.'[*]

An efficient administration grew up and communications were especially improved, chiefly for military reasons. Government was more centralized now though it took care not to interfere with local customs. Sher Shah (who intervened during the early Mughal period) was the ablest among the Afghan rulers. He laid the foundations of a revenue system which was later to be expanded by Akbar. Raja Todar Mal, Akbar's famous revenue minister, was first employed by Sher Shah. Hindu talent was increasingly used by the Afghan rulers.

The effect of the Afghan conquest on India and Hinduism was two-fold, each development contradicting the other. The immediate reaction was an exodus of people to the south, away from the areas under Afghan rule. Those who remained became more rigid and exclusive, retired into their shells, and tried to protect themselves from foreign ways and influences by hardening the caste system. On the other hand, there was a gradual and hardly conscious approach towards these foreign ways both in thought and life. A synthesis worked itself out: new styles of architecture arose; food and clothing changed; and life was affected and varied in many other ways. This synthesis was especially marked in music, which, following its old Indian classical pattern, developed in many directions. The Pesrian language became the official court language and many Persian words crept into popular use. At the same time the popular languages were developed.

Among the unfortunate developments that took place in India was the growth of *purdah* or the seclusion of women. Why this should have been so is not clear but somehow it did result from the inter-action of the new elements on the old. In India there had been previously some segregation of the sexes among the aristocracy, as in many other countries and notably in ancient Greece. Some such segregation existed in ancient Iran also and to some extent all over western Asia. But nowhere was there any strict seclusion of women. Probably this started in the Byzantine court circles where eunuchs were employed to guard the women's apartments. Byzantine influence travelled to Russia where there was a fairly strict seclusion of women right up to Peter the Great's time. This had nothing to do with the Tartars who, it is well established, did not segregate their women-folk. The mixed Arab-Persian civilization was affected in many ways by Byzantine customs and possibly the segregation of upper-class women grew to some

*From Sir H. M. Elliot's 'History of India', Vol. 1, p. 88.

extent. Yet, even so, there was no strict seclusion of women in Arabia or in other parts of western or central Asia. The Afghans, who crowded into northern India after the capture of Delhi, had no strict purdah. Turkish and Afghan princesses and ladies of the court often went riding, hunting, and paying visits. It is an old Islamic custom, still to be observed, that women must keep their faces unveiled during the Haj pilgrimage to Mecca. Purdah seems to have grown in India during Mughal times, when it became a mark of status and prestige among both Hindus and Moslems. This custom of seclusion of women spread especially among the upper classes of those areas where Moslem influence had been most marked—in the great central and eastern block comprising Delhi, the United Provinces, Rajputana, Bihar, and Bengal. And yet it is odd that purdah has not been very strict in the Punjab and in the Frontier Province, which are predominantly Moslem. In the south and west of India there has been no such seclusion of women, except to some extent among the Moslems.

I have no doubt at all that among the causes of India's decay in recent centuries, purdah, or the seclusion of women, holds an important place. I am even more convinced that the complete ending of this barbarous custom is essential before India can have a progressive social life. That it injures women is obvious enough, but the injury to man, to the growing child who has to spend much of its time among women in purdah, and to social life generally is equally great. Fortunately this evil practice is fast disappearing among the Hindus, more slowly among the Moslems.

The strongest factor in this liquidation of purdah has been the Congress political and social movements which have drawn tens of thousands of middle-class women into some kind of public activity. Gandhiji has been, and is, a fierce opponent of purdah and has called it a 'vicious and brutal custom' which has kept women backward and undeveloped. 'I thought of the wrong being done by men to the women of India by clinging to a barbarous custom which, whatever use it might have had when it was first introduced, had now become totally useless and was doing incalculable harm to the country.' Gandhiji urged that woman should have the same liberty and opportunity of self-development as man. 'Good sense must govern the relations between the two sexes. There should be no barrier erected between them. Their mutual behaviour should be natural and spontaneous.' Gandhiji has indeed written and spoken with passion in favour of women's equality and freedom, and has bitterly condemned their domestic slavery.

I have digressed and made a sudden jump to modern times, and must go back to the medieval period after the Afghans had established themselves in Delhi and a synthesis was working

243

itself out between old ways and new. Most of these changes took place at the top, among the nobility and upper classes, and did not affect the mass of the population, especially the rural masses. They originated in court circles and spread in the cities and urban areas. Thus began a process which was to continue for several centuries, of developing a mixed culture in north India. Delhi, and what are known now as the United Provinces, became the centre of this, just as they had been, and still continued to be, the centre of the old Aryan culture. But much of this Aryan culture drifted to the south, which became a stronghold of Hindu orthodoxy.

After the Delhi Sultanate had weakened owing to Timur's incursion, a small Moslem state grew up in Jaunpur (in the United Provinces). Right through the fifteenth century this was a centre of art and culture and toleration in religion. The growing popular language, Hindi, was encouraged, and an attempt was even made to bring about a synthesis between the religious faiths of the Hindus and the Moslems. About this time in far Kashmir in the north an independent Moslem King, Zainul-abdin, also became famous for his toleration and his encouragement of Sanskrit learning and the old culture.

All over India this new ferment was working and new ideas were troubling people's minds. As of old, India was sub-consciously reacting to the new situation, trying to absorb the foreign element and herself changing somewhat in the process. Out of this ferment arose new types of reformers who deliberately preached this synthesis and often condemned or ignored the caste system. There was the Hindu Ramanand in the south, in the fifteenth century, and his still more famous disciple Kabir, a Moslem weaver of Benares. Kabir's poems and songs became, and still are, very popular. In the north there was Guru Nanak, who is considered the founder of Sikhism. The influence of these reformers went far beyond the limits of the particular sects that grew up after them. Hinduism as a whole felt the impact of the new ideas, and Islam in India also became somewhat different from what it was elsewhere. The fierce monotheism of Islam influenced Hinduism and the vague pantheistic attitude of the Hindu had its effect on the Indian Moslem. Most of these Indian Moslems were converts bred up in and surrounded by the old traditions; only a comparatively small number of them had come from outside. Moslem mysticism, and Sufism, which probably had had it beginnings in neo-Platonism, grew.

Perhaps the most significant indication of the growing absorption of the foreign element in India was its use of the popular language of the country, even though Persian continued to be the court language. There are many notable books written by the early Moslems in Hindi. The most famous of these writers was Amir Khusrau, a Turk whose family had settled in the United Provinces for two or three generations and who lived in the fourteenth century during the reigns of several Afghan Sultans. He was a poet of the first rank in Persian, and he knew Sanskrit also. He was a great musician and introduced many innovations in Indian music. He is also said to have invented the *sitar*, the popular stringed instrument of India. He wrote on many subjects and, in particular, in praise of India, enumerating the various things in which India excelled. Among these were religion, philosophy, logic, language, and grammar (Sanskrit), music, mathematics, science and the mango fruit!

But his fame in India rests, above all, on his popular songs, written in the ordinary spoken dialect of Hindi. Wisely he did not choose the literary medium which would have been understood by a small coterie only; he went to the villager not only for his language but for his customs and ways of living. He sang of the different seasons and each season, according to the old classical style of India, had its own appropriate tune and words; he sang of life in its various phases, of the coming of the bride, of separation from the beloved, of the rains when life springs anew from the parched earth. Those songs are still widely sung and may be heard in any village or town in northern or central India. Especially when the rainy season begins and in every village big swings are hung from the branches of the mango or the peepul trees, and all the village girls and boys gather together to celebrate the occasion.

Amir Khusrau was the author also of innumerable riddles and conundrums which are very popular with children as well as grown-ups. Even during his long life Khusrau's songs and riddles had made him famous. That reputation has continued and grown. I do not know if there is any other instance anywhere of songs written 600 years go maintaining their popularity and their mass appeal and being still sung without any change of words.

The Indian Social Structure. Importance of the Group

Almost everyone who knows anything at all about India has heard of the caste system; almost every outsider and many people in India condemn it or criticize it as a whole. Probably there is hardly anyone left even in India who approves of it in all its present ramifications and developments, though there are undoubtedly many still who accept its basic theory and large numbers of Hindus adhere to it in their lives. Some confusion arises in the use of the word caste for different people attach different meaning to it. The average European, or an Indian who is allied to him in thought and approach, thinks of it as just a petrification of classes, an ingenious method to preserve a certain hierarchy of classes, to keep the upper classes permanently at the top and the lower ones permanently at the bottom of the scale. There is truth in that and in its origin it was probably a device to keep the Aryan conquerors apart from and above the conquered peoples. Undoubtedly in its growth it has acted in that way, though originally there may have been a good deal of flexibility about it. Yet that is only a part of the truth and it does not explain its power and cohesiveness and the way it has lasted down to our present day. It survived not only the powerful impact of Buddhism and many centuries of Afghan and Mughal rule and the spread of Islam, but also the strenuous efforts of innumerable Hindu reformers who raised their voices against it. It is only to-day that it is seriously threatened and its very basis has been attacked. That is not chiefly because of some powerful urge to reform itself which has arisen in Hindu society, though such urge is undoubtedly present, nor is it because of ideas from the west, though such ideas have certainly exerted their influence. The change that is taking place before our eyes is due essentially to basic economic changes which have shaken up the whole fabric of Indian society and are likely to upset it completely. Conditions of life have changed and thought-patterns are changing so much that it seems impossible for the caste system to endure. What will take its place is more than I can say, for something much more than the caste system is at stake. The conflict is between two approaches to t   problem of social organisation, which are diametrically   d to each other: the old Hindu conception of the group being the basic unit of organisation, and the excessive individualism of the west, emphasizing the individual above the group.

That conflict is not of India only; it is of the west also and of the entire world, though it takes different forms there. The nineteenth century civilization of Europe, taking shape in democratic liberalism and its extensions in the economic and social fields, represented the high-water mark of that individualism. That nineteenth century ideology with its social and political organization has extended itself and flowed into the twentieth century, but it seems wholly out of date now and is cracking under stress of crisis and war. The importance of the group and the community is emphasized more now, and the problem is to reconcile the respective claims of the individual and the group. The solution of that problem may take different forms in different countries, yet there will be an ever-increasing tendency for one basic solution to apply to all.

The caste system does not stand by itself; it is a part, and an integral part, of a much larger scheme of social organization. It may be possible to remove some of its obvious abuses and to lessen its rigidity, and yet to leave the system intact. But that

246

is highly unlikely, as the social and economic forces at play are not much concerned with this superstructure; they are attacking it at the base and undermining the other supports which held it up. Indeed, great parts of these are already gone or are rapidly going, and more and more the caste system is left stranded by itself. It has ceased to be a question of whether we like caste or dislike it. Changes are taking place in spite of our likes and dislikes. But it is certainly in our power to mould those changes and direct them, so that we can take full advantage of the character and genius of the Indian people as a whole, which have been so evident in the cohesiveness and stability of the social organization they built up.

Sir George Birdwood has said somewhere: 'So long as the Hindus hold to the caste system, India will be India; but from the day they break from it, there will be no more India. That glorious peninsula will be degraded to the position of a bitter "East End" of the Anglo-Saxon Empire.' With caste or without it, we have long been degraded to that position in the British Empire; and, in any event, whatever our future position is likely to be, it will not be confined within the bounds of that empire. But there is some truth in what Sir George Birdwood said, though probably he did not look at it from this point of view. The break-up of a huge and long standing social organization may well lead to a complete disruption of social life, resulting in absence of cohesion, mass suffering and the development on a vast scale of abnormalities in individual behaviour, unless some other social structure, more suited to the times and to the genius of the people, takes its place. Perhaps disruption is inevitable during the transition period; there is enough of this disruption all over the world to-day. Perhaps it is only through the pain and suffering that accompany such disruption that a people grow and learn the lessons of life and adapt themselves anew to changing conditions.

Nevertheless, we cannot just disrupt and hope for something better without having some vision of the future we are working for, however vague that vision may be. We cannot just create a vacuum, or else that vacuum will fill itself up in a way that we may have to deplore. In the constructive schemes that we may make, we have to pay attention to the human material we have to deal with, to the background of its thought and urges, and to the environment in which we have to function. To ignore all this and to fashion some idealistic scheme in the air, or merely to think in terms of imitating what others have done elsewhere, would be folly. It becomes desirable therefore to examine and understand the old Indian social structure which has so powerfully influenced our people.

This structure was based on three concepts: the autonomous village community, caste, and the joint family system. In all these three it is the group that counts; the individual has a secondary place. There is nothing very unique about all this separately and it is easy to find something equivalent to any of these three in other countries, especially in mediæval times. Like the old Indian republics, there were primitive republics elsewhere. There was also a kind of primitive communism. The old Russian *mir* might be comparable in some way to the Indian village community. Caste has been essentially functional and similar to the medieval trade guilds of Europe. The Chinese family system bears a strong resemblance to the Hindu joint family. I do not know enough of all these to carry the comparison far, and, in any case, it is not important for my purpose. Taken as a whole the entire Indian structure was certainly unique and, as it developed, it became more so.

Village Self-Government. The Shukra Nitisara

There is an old book of the tenth century which gives us some idea of Indian polity as it was conceived prior to the Turkish and Afghan invasions. This is the *Nītisāra*, the Science of Polity, by Shukracharya. It deals with the organization of the central government as well as of town and village life; of the king's council of state and various departments of government. The village *panchayat* or elected council has large powers, both executive and judicial, and its members were treated with the greatest respect by the king's officers. Land was distributed by this *panchayat*, which also collected taxes out of the produce and paid the government's share on behalf of the village. Over a number of these village councils there was a larger *panchayat* or council to supervise and interfere if necessary.

Some old inscriptions further tell us how the members of the village councils were elected and what their qualifications and disqualifications were. Various committees were formed, elected annually, and women could serve on them. In case of misbehaviour, a member could be removed. A member could be disqualified if he failed to render accounts of public funds. An interesting rule to prevent nepotism is mentioned: near relatives of members were not to be appointed to public office.

These village councils were very jealous of their liberties and it was laid down that no soldier could enter the village unless he had a royal permit. If the people complained of an official, the *Nītisāra* says that the king 'should take the side, not of his officers, but of his subjects.' If many complained then the official was to be dismissed, 'for who does not get intoxicated by drinking of the vanity of office.' The king was to act in accordance with the opinion of the majority of the people. 'Public opinion is more powerful than the king as the rope made of many fibres is strong enough to drag a lion.' 'In making official appointments work, character and merit are to be regarded neither caste nor family,' and 'neither through colour nor through ancestors can the spirit worthy of a Brahmin be generated.'

In the larger towns there were many artisans and merchants, and craft guilds, mercantile associations, and banking corporations were formed. Each of these controlled its own domestic affairs.

All this information is very fragmentary but it does appear from this and many other sources that there was a widespread system of self-government in towns and villages and the central government seldom interfered, so long as its quota of taxes was paid. Customary law was strong and the political or military power seldom interfered with rights based on custom. Originally the agrarian system was based on a co-operative or collective village. Individuals and families had certain rights as well as certain obligations, both of which were determined and protected by customary law.

There was no theocratic monarchy in India. In Indian polity if the king is unjust or tyrannical, the right to rebel against him is admitted. What the Chinese philosopher, Mencius, said 2,000 years ago might apply to India: 'When a ruler treats his subjects like grass and dirt, then subjects should treat him as a bandit and an enemy.' The whole conception of monarchical power differed from that of European feudalism, where the king had authority over all persons and things in his domain. This authority he delegated to lords and barons who vowed allegiance to him. Thus a hierarchy of authority was built up. Both the land and the people connected with it belonged to the feudal lord and, through him, to the king. This was the development of the Roman conception of dominium. In India there was nothing of this kind. The king had the right to collect certain taxes from the land and this revenue-collecting power was all he could delegate to others. The peasant in India was not the lord's serf. There was plenty of land available and there was no advantage in dispossessing the peasant. Thus in India there was no landlord system, as known in the west, nor was the individual peasant the full owner of his patch of land. Both these concepts were introduced much later by the British with disastrous results.

Foreign conquests brought war and destructon, revolts and their ruthless suppression, and new ruling classes relying chiefly on armed force. This ruling class could often ignore the numerous constitutional restraints which had always been part of the customary law of the country. Important consequences followed and the power of the self-governing village communities decreased and later various changes were introduced in the land-revenue system. Nevertheless the Afghan and Mughal rulers took special care not to interfere with old customs and conventions and no fundamental changes were introduced, and the economic and social structure of Indian life continued as before. Ghyas-ud-Din Tughlak issued definite instructions to his officials to preserve customary law and to keep the affairs of the state apart from religion, which was a personal matter of individual preference. But changing times and conflicts, as well as the increasing centralization of government, slowly but progressively lessened the respect given to customary law. The village self-governing community, however, continued. Its break-up began only under British rule.

The Theory and Practice of Caste. The Joint Family

'In India', says Havell, 'religion is hardly a dogma, but a working hypothesis of human conduct adapted to different stages of spiritual development and different conditions of life.' In the ancient days when Indo-Aryan culture first took shape, religion had to provide for the needs of men who were as far removed from each other in civilization and intellectual and spiritual development as it is possible to conceive. There were primitive forest-dwellers, fetishists, totem-worshippers and believers in every kind of superstition, and there were those who had attained the highest flights of spiritual thought. In between, there was every shade and gradation of belief and practice. While the highest forms of thought were pursued by some, these were wholly beyond the reach of many. As social life grew, certain uniformities of belief spread, but, even so, many differences, cultural and temperamental, remained. The Indo-Aryan approach was to avoid the forcible suppression of any belief or the destruction of any claim. Each group was left free to work out its ideals along the plane of its mental development and understanding. Assimilation was attempted but there was no denial or suppression.

A similar and even more difficult problem had to be faced in social organization. How to combine these utterly different groups in one social system, each group co-operating with the whole and yet retaining its own freedom to live its own life and develop itself. In a sense—though the comparison is farfetched—this may be compared to the numerous minority problems of to-day which afflict so many countries and are still far from solution. The United States of America solve their minority problems, more or less, by trying to make every citizen a 100 per cent American. They make everyone conform to a certain type. Other countries, with a longer and more complicated past, are not so favourably situated. Even Canada has its strong race, religion and language-conscious French group. In Europe the barriers are higher and deeper. And yet all this applies to Europeans, or those who have spread from Europe; people who have a certain common background and similarity of culture. Where non-Europeans come in, they do not fit this pattern. In the United States, negroes, though they may be 100 per cent American, are a race apart, deprived of many opportunities and privileges, which others have as a matter of course. There are innumerable worse examples elsewhere. Only Soviet Russia is said to have solved its problem of nationalities and minorities by creating what is called a multi-national state.

If these difficulties and problems pursue us even to-day with all our knowledge and progress, how much harder they must have been in the ancient days when the Indo-Aryans were evolving their civilization and social structure in a land full of variety and different types of human beings. The normal way to deal with these problems then and later was to exterminate or enslave the conquered populations. This way was not followed in India, but it is clear that every precaution was taken to perpetuate the superior position of the upper groups. Having ensured that superiority, a kind of multiple-community state was built up, in which, within certain limits and subject to some general rules, freedom was given to each group to follow its avocation and live its own life in accordance with its own customs or desires. The only real restriction was that it must not interfere or come into conflict with another group. This was a flexible and expanding system, for new groups could always be formed either by newcomers or by dissident members of an old group, provided they were numerous enough to do so. Within each group there was equality and democracy and the elected leaders guided it and frequently consulted the entire group whenever any important question arose.

These groups were almost always functional, each specializing in a particular trade or craft. They became thus some kind of trade unions or craft-guilds. There was a strong sense of solidarity within each, which not only protected the group but sheltered and helped an individual member who got into trouble or was in economic distress. The functions of each group or caste were related to the functions of other castes, and the idea was that if each group functioned successfully within its own framework, then society as a whole worked harmoniously. Over and above this, a strong and fairly successful attempt was made to create, a common national bond which would hold all these groups together—the sense of a common culture, common traditions, common heroes and saints, and a common land to the four corners of which people went on pilgrimage. This national bond was of course very different from present-day nationalism; it was weak politically but, socially and culturally, it was strong. Because of its political lack of cohesiveness it facilitated foreign conquest; because of its social strength it made recovery easy, as well as assimilation of new elements. It had so many heads that they could not be cut off and they survived conquest and disaster.

Thus caste was a group system based on services and functions. It was meant to be an all-inclusive order without any common dogma and allowing the fullest latitude to each group. Within its wide fold there was monogamy, polygamy, and celibacy; they were all tolerated, just as other customs, beliefs, and practices were tolerated. Life was to be maintained at all levels. No minority need submit to a majority, for it could always form a separate autonomous group, the only test being: is it a distinctive group large enough to function as such? Between two groups there could be any amount of variation of race, religion, colour, culture, and intellectual development.

An individual was only considered as a member of a group; he could do anything he liked so long as he did not interfere with the functioning of the group. He had no right to upset that functioning, but if he was strong enough and could gather enough supporters, it was open to him to form another group. If he could not fit in with any group, that meant that he was out of joint so far as the social activities of the world were concerned. He could then become a *sanyasi* who had renounced caste, every group and the world of activity, and could wander about and do what he liked.

It must be remembered that while the Indian social tendency was to subordinate the individual to the claims of the group and society, religious thought and spiritual seeking have always emphasized the individual. Salvation and knowledge of the ultimate truth were open to all, to the member of every caste, high or low. This salvation or enlightenment could not be a group affair; it was highly individualistic. In the search for this salvation also there were no inflexible dogmas and all doors were supposed to lead to it.

Though the group system was dominant in the organization of society, leading to caste, there has always been an individualistic tendency in India. A conflict between the two approaches is often in evidence. Partly that individualism was the result of the religious doctrine which laid emphasis on the individual. Social reformers who criticized or condemned the caste system were usually religious reformers and their main argument was that the divisions of the caste system came in the way of spiritual development and that intense individualism to which religion pointed. Buddhism was a breakaway from the group-caste ideal towards some kind of individualism as well as universalism. But this individualism became associated with a withdrawal from normal social activites. It offered no effective alternative social structure to caste, and so caste continued then and later.

What were the main castes? If we leave out for a moment those who were considered outside the pale of caste, the untouchables, there were the Brahmins, the priests, teachers, intellectuals; the Kshatriyas or the rulers and warriors; the Vaishyas or merchants, traders, bankers, etc.; and the Shudras, who were the agricultural and other workers. Probably the only closely knit and exclusive caste was that of the Brahmins. The Kshatriyas were frequently adding to their numbers both from foreign incoming elements and others in the country who rose to power and authority. The Vaishyas were chiefly traders and bankers and also engaged in a number of other professions. The main occupations of the Shudras were cultivation and domestic service.

There was always a continuous process of new castes being formed as new occupations developed, and for other reasons the older castes were always trying to get up in the social scale. These processes have continued to our day. Some of the lower castes suddenly take to wearing the sacred thread which is supposed to be reserved for the upper castes. All this really made little difference, as each caste continued to function in its own ambit and pursued its own trade or occupation. It was merely a question of prestige. Occasionally men of the lower classes, by sheer ability, attained to positions of power and authority in the state, but this was very exceptional.

The organization of society being, generally speaking, non-competitive and non-acquisitive, these divisions into castes did not make as much difference as they might otherwise have done. The Brahmin at the top, proud of his intellect and learning and respected by others, seldom had much in the way of worldly possessions. The merchant, prosperous and rich, had no very high standing in society as a whole.

The vast majority of the population consisted of the agriculturists. There was no landlord system, nor was there any peasant proprietorship. It is difficult to say who owned the land in law; there was nothing like the present doctrine of ownership. The cultivator had the right to till his land and the only real question was as to the distribution of the produce of the land. The major share went to the cultivator, the king or the state took a share (usually one-sixth), and every functional group in the village, which served the people in any way, had its share— the Brahmin priest and teacher, the merchant, the blacksmith, the carpenter, the cobbler, the potter, the builder, the barber, the scavenger, etc. Thus, in a sense, every group from the state to the scavenger was a shareholder in the produce.

Who were the depressed classes and the untouchables? The 'depressed classes' is a new designation applying rather vaguely to a number of castes near the bottom of the scale. There is no hard and fast line to separate them from the others. The untouchables are more definite. In north India only a very small number, engaged in scavenging or unclean work, are considered untouchable. Fa-Hsien tells us that when he came the persons who removed human fæces were untouchable. In south India the numbers are much larger. How they began and grew to such numbers it is difficult to say. Probably those who were engaged in occupations considered unclean were so treated; later landless agricultural labour may have been added.

The idea of ceremonial purity has been extraordinarily strong among the Hindus. This has led to one good consequence and many bad ones. The good one is bodily cleanliness. A daily bath has always been a essential feature of a Hindu's life, including most of the depressed classes. It was from India that this habit spread to England and elsewhere. The average Hindu, and even the poorest peasant, takes some pride in his shining pots and pans. This sense of cleanliness is not scientific and the man who bathes twice a day will unhesitatingly drink water that is unclean and full of germs. Nor is it corporate, at any rate now. The individual will keep his own hut fairly clean but throw all the rubbish in the village street in front of his neighbour's house. The village is usually very dirty and full of garbage heaps. It is also noticeable that cleanliness is not thought of as such but as a consequence of some religious sanction. When that religious sanction goes, there is marked deterioration in the standards of cleanliness.

The evil consequence of ceremonial purity was a growth of exclusiveness, touch-me-notism, and of not eating and drinking with people of other castes. This grew to fantastic lengths unknown in any other part of the world. It led also to certain classes being considered untouchable because they had the misfortune to do some kinds of essential work which were considered unclean. The practice of normally feeding with one's own caste people spread to all castes. It became a sign of social status and the lower castes stuck to it even more rigidly than some of the higher ones. This practice is breaking up now among the higher castes but it still continues among the lower castes, including the depressed classes.

If interdining was taboo, much more so was intermarriage between castes. Some mixed marriages inevitably took place but on the whole it is extraordinary how much each caste kept to itself and propagated its own kind. The continuation of racial identity through long ages is an illusion and yet the caste system in India has to some extent managed to preserve distinctive types, epescially among the higher castes.

Some groups at the bottom of the scale are sometimes referred to as outside the caste groups. As a matter of fact, no group not even the untouchables, are outside the framework of the caste system. The depressed classes and the untouchables form their own castes and have their *panchayats* or caste councils for settling their own affairs. But many of them have been made to suffer cruelly by being excluded from the common life of the village.

The autonomous village community and the caste system were thus two of the special features of the old Indian social structure. The third was the joint family where all the members were joint sharers in the common property and inheritance went by survivorship. The father or some other elder was the head but he functioned as a manager, and not as the old Roman paterfamilias. A division of property was permitted under certain circumstances and if the parties concerned so desired. The joint property was supposed to provide for the needs of all the members of the family, workers or non-workers. Inevitably this meant a guaranteed minimum for all of them, rather than high rewards for some. It was a kind of insurance for all including even the subnormal and the physically or mentally deficient. Thus while there was security for all, there was a certain levelling down of the standard of service demanded as well as of the recompense given. Emphasis was not laid on personal advantage or ambition but on that of the group, that is the family. The fact of growing up and living in a large family minimized the egocentric attitude of the child and tended to develop an aptitude for socialization.

All this is the very opposite of what happens in the highly individualistic civilization of the west and more especially of America, where personal ambition is encouraged and personal advantage is the almost universal aim, where all the plums go to the bright and pushing, and the weak, timid or second rate go to the wall.

The joint family system is rapidly breaking up in India and individualistic attitudes are developing, leading not only to far-reaching changes in the economic background of life but also to new problems of behaviour.

All the three pillars of the Indian social structure were thus based on the group and not on the individual. The aim was social security, stability and continuance of the group, that is of society. Progress was not the aim and progress therefore had to suffer. Within each group, whether this was the village community, the particular caste, or the large joint family, there was a communal life shared together, a sense of equality, and democractic methods. Even now caste *panchayats* function democratically. It surprised me at one time to see the eagerness of a villager, sometimes illiterate, to serve on elected committees for political or other purposes. He soon got into the way of it and was a helpful member whenever any question relating to his life came up, and was not easily subdued. But there was an unfortunate tendency for small groups to split up and quarrel among themselves.

The democratic way was not only well-known but was a common method of functioning in social life, in local government, trade-guilds, religious assemblies, etc. Caste, with all its evils, kept up the democratic habit in each group. There used to be elaborate rules of procedure, election and debate. The Marquis of Zetland has referred to some of these in writing about the early Buddhist assemblies: 'And it may come as a surprise to many to learn that in the Assemblies of the Buddhists in India 2,000 or more years ago are to be found the rudiments of our own parliamentary practice of the present day. The dignity of the Assembly was preserved by the appointment of a special officer—the embryo of "Mr. Speaker" in the House of Commons. A second officer was appointed whose duty it was to see that when necessary a quorum was secured—the prototype of the parliamentary chief whip in our own system. A member initiating business did so in the form of a motion which was then open to discussion. In some cases this was done once only, in others three times, thus anticipating the practice of parliament in requiring that a Bill be read a third time before it becomes law. If discussion disclosed a difference of opinion the matter was decided by the vote of the majority, the voting being by ballot.'*

The old Indian social structure had thus some virtues, and indeed it could not have lasted so long without them. Behind it lay the philosophical ideal of Indian culture—the integration of man and the stress of goodness, beauty and truth rather than acquisitiveness. An attempt was made to prevent the joining together and concentration of honour, power, and wealth. The duties of the individual and the group were emphasized, not their rights.

The *Smritis* (Hindu religious books) give lists of dharmas, functions and duties of various castes but none of them contains an inventory of rights. Self-sufficiency was aimed at in the group, especially in the village and, in a different sense, in the caste. It was a closed system, allowing a certain adaptability, change, and freedom within its outer framework, but inevitably growing more and more exclusive and rigid. Progressively it lost its power to expand and tap new sources of talent. Powerful vested interests prevented any radical change and kept education from spreading to other classes. The old superstitions, known to be such by many among the upper classes, were preserved and new ones were added to them. Not only the national economy but thought itself became stationary, traditional, rigid, unexpansive and unprogressive.

The conception and practice of caste embodied the aristo-

*Quoted by G. T. Garratt in 'The Legacy of India' (1937), p. xi.

cratic ideal and was obviously opposed to democratic conceptions. It had its strong sense of *noblesse oblige*, provided people kept to their hereditary stations and did not challenge the established order. India's success and achievements were on the whole confined to the upper classes; those lower down in the scale had very few chances and their opportunities were strictly limited. These upper classes were not small limited groups but large in numbers and there was a diffusion of power, authority and influence. Hence they carried on successfully for a very long period. But the ultimate weakness and failing of the caste system and the Indian social structure were that they degraded a mass of human beings and gave them no opportunities to get out of that condition—educationally, culturally, or economically. That degradation brought deterioration, all along the line including in its scope even the upper classes. It led to the petrification which became a dominant feature of India's economy and life. The contrasts between this social structure and those existing elsewhere in the past were not great, but with the changes that have taken place all over the world during the past few generations they have become far more pronounced. In the context of society to-day, the caste system and much that goes with it are wholly incompatible, reactionary, restrictive, and barriers to progress. There can be no equality in status and opportunity within its framework, nor can there be political democracy and much less economic democracy. Between these two conceptions conflict is inherent and only one of them can survive.

Babar and Akbar: The Process of Indianization

To go back. The Afghans had settled down in India and had become Indianized. Their rulers had to face first the problem of lessening the hostility of the people and then of winning them over. So, as a deliberate policy, they toned down their early ruthless methods, became more tolerant, invited co-operation, and tried to function not as conquerors from outside but as Indians born and bred in the land. What was at first a policy gradually became an inevitable trend as the Indian environment influenced these people from the north-west and absorbed them. While the process continued at the top, more powerful currents arose spontaneously among the people, aiming at a synthesis of thought and ways of living. The beginnings of a mixed culture began to appear and foundations were laid on which Akbar was to build.

Akbar was the third of the Mughal dynasty in India, yet it was in effect by him that the empire was consolidated. His grandfather, Babar, had won the throne of Delhi in 1526, but he was a stranger to India and continued to feel so. He had come from the north, where the Timurid Renaissance was flourishing in his homelands in central Asia and the influence of the art and culture of Iran was strong. He missed the friendly society he was used to, the delights of conversation, the amenities and refinements of life which had spread from Baghdad and Iran. He longed for the snow and ice of the northern highlands, for the good flesh and flowers and fruits of Ferghana. Yet, with all his disappointment at what he saw, he says that Hindustan is a remarkably fine country.

Babar died within four years of his coming to India, and much of his time was spent in fighting and in laying out a splendid capital at Agra, for which he obtained the services of a famous architect from Constantinople. Those were the days of Suleiman the Magnificent in Constantinople, when fine buidings were rising up in that city.

Babar saw little of India and, surrounded as he was by a hostile people, missed much. Yet his account tells us of the cultural poverty that had descended on north India. Partly this was due to Timur's destruction, partly to the exodus of many learned men and artists and noted craftsmen to the south. But it was also due to the drying up of the creative genius of the Indian people. Babar says that there was no lack of skilled workers and artisans, but there was no ingenuity or skill in mechanical invention. Also, it would appear that in the amenities and luxuries of life India was considerably behind Iran. Whether this was due to some inherent want of interest in this aspect of life in the Indian mind or to later developments, I do not know. Perhaps, as compared with the Iranians, the Indians of those days were not so much attracted to these refinements and luxuries. If they had cared for them sufficiently they could have easily got them from Iran, as there was frequent intercourse between the two countries. But it is more likely that this was a later development, another sign of the cultural rigidity and decline of India.

In earlier periods, as can be seen from classical literature and paintings, there was refinement enough and, for those times, a high and complicated standard of living. Even when Babar came to north India, Vijayanagar in the south had been spoken of by many European travellers as representing a very high standard of art and culture, refinement and luxury.

But in north India cultural decay was very evident. Fixed beliefs and a rigid social structure prevented social effort and advance. The coming of Islam and of a considerable number of people from outside, with different ways of living and thought, affected existing beliefs and structure. A foreign conquest, with all its evils, has one advantage: it widens the mental horizon of the people and compels them to look out of their shells. They realise that the world is a much bigger and more variegated place than they had imagined. So the Afghan conquest had affected India and many changes had taken place. Even more so the Mughals, who were far more cultured and advanced in ways of living than the Afghans, brought changes to India. In particular, they introduced the refinements for which Iran was famous, even to the extent of the highly artificial and strictly prescribed court life, which influenced the ways of living of the nobility. The Bahmani kingdom in the south had direct contacts with Iran via Calicut.

There were many changes in India and new impulses brought freshness and life to art and architecture and other cultural patterns. And yet all this was the result of two old-world patterns coming into contact, both of which had lost their initial vitality and creative vigour and were set in rigid frames. Indian culture was very old and tired, the Arab-Persian culture had long passed its zenith and the old curiosity and sense of mental adventure which distinguished the Arabs were no more in evidence.

Babar is an attractive person, a typical Renaissance prince, bold and adventurous, fond of art and literature and good living. His giandson, Akbar, is even more attractive and has greater qualities. Daring and reckless, an able general, and yet gentle and full of compassion, an idealist and a dreamer, but also a man of action and a leader of men who roused the passionate loyalty of his followers. As a warrior he conquered large parts of India, but his eyes were set on another and more enduring conquest, the conquest of the minds and hearts of the people. Those compelling eyes of his were 'vibrant like the sea in sunshine,' as Portuguese Jesuits of his court have told us. In him the old dream of a united India again took shape, united not only politically in one state but organically fused into one people.

Throughout his long reign of nearly fifty years from 1556 onwards he laboured to this end. Many a proud Rajput chief, who would not have submitted to any other person, he won over to his side. He married a Rajput princess, and his son and successor, Jehangir, was thus a half Mughal and half Rajput Hindu. Jehangir's son, Shah Jehan, was also the son of a Rajput mother. Thus racially this Turko-Mongol dynasty became far more Indian than Turk or Mongol.

Akbar was an admirer of and felt a kinship with the Rajputs, and by his matrimonial and other policy he formed an alliance with the Rajput ruling classes which strengthened his empire greatly. This Mughal-Rajput co-operation, which continued in subsequent reigns, affected not only government and the administration and army, but also art, culture, and ways of living. The Mughal nobility became progressively Indianized and the Rajputs and others were influenced by Persian culture.

Akbar won many people to his side and kept them there, but he failed to subdue the proud and indomitable spirit of Rana Pratap of Mewar in Rajputana, who preferred to lead a hunted life in the jungle rather than give even formal allegiance to one he considered a foreign conqueror.

Round himself Akbar collected a brilliant group of men, devoted to him and to his ideals. Among these were the two famous brothers Fyzee and Abul Fazl, Birbal, Raja Man Singh, and Abdul Rahim Khankhana. His court became a meeting place for men of all faiths and all who had some new idea or new invention. His toleration of views and his encouragement of all kinds of beliefs and opinions went so far as to anger some of the more orthodox Moslems. He even tried to start a new synthetic faith to suit everybody. It was in his reign that the cultural amalgamation of Hindu and Moslem in north India took a long step forward. Akbar himself was certainly as popular with the Hindus as with the Moslems. The Mughal dynasty became firmly established as India's own.

The Contrast between Asia and Europe in Mechanical Advance and Creative Energy

Akbar was full of curiosity, ever seeking to find out about things, both spiritual and temporal. He was interested in mechanical contrivances and in the science of war. He prized war-elephants especially, and they formed an important part of his army. The Portuguese Jesuits of his court tell us that 'he was interested in and curious to learn about many things, and possessed an intimate knowledge not only of military and political matters, but many of the mechanical arts.' In 'his eagerness for knowledge' he 'tried to learn everything at once, like a hungry man trying to swallow his food at a single gulp'.

And yet it is very odd how his curiosity stopped at a point and did not lead him to explore certain obvious avenues which lay open before him. With all his great prestige as the Great Mughal and the strength of his empire as a land power, he was powerless at sea. Vasco de Gama had reached Calicut, via the Cape, in 1498; Albuquerque had seized Malacca in 1511 and established Portuguese sea power in the Indian Ocean. Goa on the western coast of India had become a Portuguese possession. All this did not bring the Portuguese into direct conflict with Akbar. But Indian pilgrims going to Mecca by sea, and these sometimes included members of the imperial family, or of the nobility, were often held up for ransom by the Portuguese. It was obvious that however powerful Akbar might be on land, the Portuguese were masters of the sea. It is not difficult to understand that a continental power did not attach much importance to sea power, although, as a matter of fact, India's greatness and importance in the past had been partly due to her control of the sea routes. Akbar had a vast continent to conquer and had little time to spare for the Portuguese, to whom he attached no importance even though they stung him occasionally. He did think of building ships once, but this was looked upon more as a pastime than a serious naval development.

Again, in the matter of artillery the Mughal armies, as well as those of other states in India at the time, chiefly relied on foreign experts, who were usually Turks from the Ottoman dominions. The Master of the Artillery came to be known by the title of Rumi Khan—Rum being eastern Rome, that is, Constantinople. These foreign experts trained local men, but why did not Akbar or anyone else send his own men abroad for training or interest himself in improvement by encouraging research work?

Yet another very significant thing. The Jesuits presented Akbar with a printed Bible and perhaps one or two other printed books. Why did he not get curious about printing, which would have been of tremendous advantage to him in his governmental activities as well as in his vast enterprises?

Again, clocks. These were very popular with the Mughal nobility, and they were brought by the Portuguese and later by the English from Europe. They were regarded as luxuries for the rich, the ordinary people being content with sundials and sand- and water-clocks. No attempt was made to understand how these spring clocks were made or to get them made in India. This lack of mechanical bent is remarkable, especially as there were very fine craftsmen and artisans in India.

It is not in India alone that this paralysis of creative energy and inventive faculty is visible during this period. The whole of western and central Asia suffered from it even more. I do not know about China but I imagine that some such stagnation affected her also. It must be remembered that both in India and China, during earlier periods, there was considerable progress in various departments of science. Shipbuilding and an extensive sea-trade acted as a constant spur even to mechanical improvements. It is true that no major mechanical development took place in either of these countries or in any other country at the time. The world of the fifteenth century was, from this point of view, not very different from what it had been a thousand or two thousand years earlier.

The Arabs, who had developed to some extent the early beginnings of practical science and had advanced knowledge in many ways during the dark period of the middle ages in Europe, became unimportant and backward. It is said that some of the earliest clocks were made by the Arabs in the seventh century. Damascus had a famous clock and so did the Baghdad of Harun-al-Rashid's day. But with the decline of the Arabs the art of making clocks also disappeared from these countries, although it was progressing in some of the European countries where clocks were not rarities.

Long before Caxton, the Moorish Arabs of Spain used to print from wooden blocks.* This was done by the state for duplication of official orders. Printing there does not seem to have advanced beyond the block stage and even that faded away later. The Ottoman Turks, who for long were the dominant Moslem power in Europe and western Asia, completely ignored printing for many centuries, although printed books were being produced in large numbers in Europe, right at their very threshold. They must have known about them, but the incentive to utilize this great invention was totally lacking. Partly also religious sentiment was opposed to it, as it was considered that it was sacrilegious to print their holy book, the Koran. The printed sheets might be put to improper use or stepped upon or thrown into the rubbish heap. It was Napoleon who first introduced the printing press into Egypt and from there it spread very gradually and slowly into the other Arab countries.

While Asia had become dormant, exhausted, as it were, by its past efforts, Europe, backward in many ways, was on the threshold of vast changes. A new spirit, a new ferment, was at work sending her adventurers across the oceans and turning the minds of her thinkers in novel directions. The Renaissance had done little for the advancement of science; to some extent it turned people away from science, and the humanistic conservative education which it introduced in the universities prevented the spread of even well-known scientific ideas. It is stated that the majority of educated English people, as late as the middle of the eighteenth century, declined to believe that the earth rotated or that it revolved round the sun, in spite of Copernicus, Galileo, and Newton, and the manufacture of good telescopes. Bred up in the Greek and Latin classics, they still clung to Ptolemy's earth-centred universe. That eminent English statesman of the nineteenth century, Mr. W. E. Gladstone, in spite of his deep erudition, neither understood nor was attracted to science. Even to-day probably there are many statesmen and public men (and not in India only) who know little of science or the scientific method, though they live in a world governed by the applications of science and themselves use it for large-scale slaughter and destruction.

The Renaissance had, however, released the mind of Europe from many of its old fetters and destroyed many an idol that it had cherished. Whether it was partly and indirectly due to the Renaissance or whether it was in spite of it, a new spirit of objective inquiry was making itself felt, a spirit which not only challenged old-established authority, but also abstractions and vague

*I do not know how this kind of printing reached the Arabs in Spain. Probably it came to them via the Mongols from China, long before it reached northern and western Europe. The Arab world from Cordoba to Cairo, Damascus and Baghdad, had frequent contacts with China even before the Mongols appeared upon the scene.

speculations. Francis Bacon has written that 'the roads to human power and to human knowledge lie close together, and are nearly the same, nevertheless on account of the pernicious and inveterate habit of dwelling on abstractions it is safer to begin and raise the sciences from those foundations which have relation to practice and let the active part be as a seal which prints and determines the contemplative counterpart.' And later in the seventeenth century, Sir Thomas Browne has said: 'But the mortallest enemy unto knowedge, and that which hath done the greatest execution upon truth, hath been a peremptory adhesion to authority; and more especially, the establishing of our belief upon the dictates of antiquity. For (as every capacity may observe) most men, of ages present, so superstitiously do look upon ages past, that the authorities of the one exceed the reasons of the other. Whose persons indeed far removed from our times, their works, which seldom with us pass uncontrolled, either by contemporaries, or immediate successors, are now become out of the distance of envies; and the further removed from present times, are conceived to approach the nearer unto truth itself. Now hereby me thinks we manifestly delude ourselves, and widely walk out of the track of truth.'

Akbar's century was the sixteenth, which saw in Europe the birth of dynamics, a revolutionary advance in the life of humanity. With that discovery Europe forged ahead, slowly at first, but with an ever-increasing momentum, till in the nineteenth century it shot forward and built a new world. While Europe was taking advantage of, and exploiting the powers of nature, Asia, static and dormant, still carried on in the old traditional way, relying on man's toil and labour.

Why was this so? Asia is too big and varied a place for a single answer. Each country, especially such vast countries as China and India, must be judged separately. China was certainly then and later more cultured and her people led a more civilized life than any in Europe. India, to all outward seeming, also presented the spectacle, not only of a brilliant court, but of thriving trade, commerce, manufactures, and crafts. In many respects the countries of Europe would have seemed backward and rather crude to an Indian visitor then. And yet the dynamic quality which was becoming evident in Europe was almost wholly absent in India.

A civilization decays much more from inner failure than from an external attack. It may fail because in a sense it has worked itself out and has nothing more to offer in a changing world, or because the people who represent it deteriorate in quality and can no longer support the burden worthily. It may be that the social culture is such that it becomes a bar to advance beyond a certain point, and further advance can only take place after

that bar has been removed or some essential qualitative variation in that culture has been introduced. The decay of Indian
civilization is evident enough even before the Turkish and Afghan
invasions. Did the impact of these invaders and their new ideas
with the old India produce a new social context, thus unbinding
the fetters of the intellect and releasing fresh energy?

To some extent this happened, and art and architecture,
painting, and music, and the ways of life were affected. But those
consequences did not go deep enough; they were more or less
superficial, and the social culture remained much the same as
it used to be. In some respects indeed it became more rigid.
The Afghans brought no new element of progress; they represented a backward feudal and tribal order. India was not feudal
in the European sense, but the Rajput clans, who were the
backbone of Indian defence, were organized in some kind of a
feudal way. The Mughals were also semi-feudal but with a strong
monarchical centre. This monarchy triumphed over the vague
feudalism of Rajputana.

Akbar might have laid. the foundations of social change if his
eager, inquisitive mind had turned in that direction and sought
to find out what was happening in other parts of the world. But
he was too busy consolidating his empire and the big problem that
faced him was how to reconcile a proselytizing religion like Islam
with the national religion and customs of the people, and thus to
build up national unity. He tried to interpret religion in a rational
spirit and for the moment he appeared to have brought about a
remarkable transformation of the Indian scene. But this direct
approach did not succeed, as it has seldom succeeded elsewhere.

So not even Akbar made any basic difference to that social
context of India, and after him the air of change and mental
adventure which he had introduced subsided, and India resumed
her static and unchanging life.*

---

*Abul Fazl tells us that Akbar had heard of the discovery of America by Columbus. In the
next reign, Jehangir's, tobacco from America reached India, via Europe. It had an immediate and amazing vogue in spite of Jehangir's efforts to suppress it. Throughout the Mughal
period India had intimate contacts with central Asia. These contacts extended to Russia
and there are references to diplomatic and trade missions. A Russian friend has drawn my
attention to such refrences in Russian chronicles. In 1532 an envoy of the Emperor Babar,
named Khoja Husain, arrived in Moscow to conclude a treaty of friendship. During the
reign of Tsar Michael Fedorovitch (1613-1645) Indian traders settled on the Volga. In
1625 an Indian serai was built in Astrakhan by order of the military governor. Indian
craftsmen and especially weavers were invited to Moscow. In 1695 Semean Melenky, a
Russian trade-agent, visited Delhi and was received by Aurangzeb. In 1722 Peter the Great
visited Astrakhan and granted interviews to Indian traders. In 1745 a party of Indian
sadhus, described as hermits, arrived in Astrakhan. Two of these sadhus settled in Russia
and became Russian subjects.

Development of a Common Culture

Akbar had built so well that the edifice he had erected lasted for another 100 years in spite of inadequate successors. After almost every Mughal reign there were wars between the princes for the throne, thus weakening the central power. But the court continued to be brilliant and the fame of the Grand Mughal spread all over Asia and Europe. Beautiful buildings combining the old Indian ideals in architecture with a new simplicity and a nobility of line grew up in Agra and Delhi. This Indo-Mughal art was in marked contrast with the decadent, over-elaborate and heavily ornamented temples and other buildings of the north and south. Inspired architects and builders put up with loving hands the Taj Mahal at Agra.

The last of the so-called 'Grand Mughals,' Aurungzeb, tried to put back the clock, and in this attempt stopped it and broke it up. The Mughal rulers were strong so long as they put themselves in line with the genius of the nation and tried to work for a common nationality and a synthesis of the various elements in the country. When Aurungzeb began to oppose this movement and suppress it and to function more as a Moslem than an Indian ruler, the Mughal Empire began to break up. The work of Akbar, and to some extent his successors, was undone and the various forces that had been kept in check by Akbar's policy broke loose and challenged that empire. New movements arose, narrow in outlook but representing a resurgent nationalism, and though they were not strong enough to build permanently, and circumstances were against them, they were capable of destroying the Empire of the Mughals.

The impact of the invaders from the north-west and of Islam on India had been considerable. It had pointed out and shown up the abuses that had crept into Hindu society—the petrifaction of caste, untouchability, exclusiveness carried to fantastic lengths. The idea of the brotherhood of Islam and of the theoretical equality of its adherents made a powerful appeal, especially to those in the Hindu fold who were denied any semblance of equal treatment. From this ideological impact grew up various movements aiming at a religious synthesis. Many conversions also took place but the great majority of these were from the lower castes, especially in Bengal. Some individuals belonging to the higher castes also adopted the new faith, either because of a real change of belief, or, more often, for political and economic reasons. There were obvious advantages in accepting the religion of the ruling power.

In spite of these widespread conversions, Hinduism, in all its varieties, continued as the dominant faith of the land, solid, exclusive, self-sufficient, and sure of itself. The upper castes had no doubt about their own superiority in the realm of ideas and thought and considered Islam as a rather crude approach to the problems of philosophy and metaphysics. Even the mono-theism of Islam they found in their own religion, together with monism which was the basis of much of their philosophy. Each person could take his choice of these or of more popular and simpler forms of worship. He could be a Vaishnavite and believe in a personal God and pour out his faith to him. Or more philosophically inclined, he could wander in the tenuous realms of metaphysics and high philosophy. Though all their social structure was based on the group, in matters of religion they were highly individualistic, not believing in proselytization them-selves and caring little if some people were converted to another faith. What was objected to was in interference with their own social structure and ways of living. If another group wanted to function in its own way, it was at liberty to do so. It is worth noting that, as a rule, conversions to Islam were group conversions, so powerful was the influence of the group. Among the upper castes individuals might change their religion, but lower down the scale a particular caste in a locality, or almost an entire village would be converted. Thus their group life as well as their functions continued as before with only minor variations as regards worship, etc. Because of this we find to-day particular occupations and crafts almost entirely monopolized by Moslems. Thus the class of weavers is predominantly, and in large areas wholly Moslem. So also used to be shoe-merchants and butchers. Tailors are almost always Moslems. Various kinds of artisans and craftsmen are Moslems. Owing to the breaking up of the group system, many individuals have taken to other occupations and this has somewhat obliterated the line dividing the various occupational groups. The destruction of crafts and village industries, originally delibe-rately undertaken under early British rule and later resulting from the development of a new colonial economy, led to vast numbers of these artisans and craftsmen, more especially the weavers, being deprived of their occupations and livelihood. Those who survived this catastrophe drifted to the land and became landless labourers or shared a tiny patch of land with their relations.

Conversions to Islam in those days, whether individual or group, probably aroused no particular opposition, except when force or some kind of compulsion was used. Friends and rela-tives or neighbours might disapprove, but the Hindu commu-nity as such apparently attached little importance to this. In contrast with this indifferent attitude, conversions to-day attract widespread attention and are resented, whether they are to Islam or Christianity. This is largely due to political factors and especially to the introduction of separate religious electo-rates. Each convert is supposed to be a gain to the communal group leading ultimately to greater representation and more political power. Attempts are even made to manipulate the census to this end. Apart from political reasons, there has also been a growth in Hinduism of a tendency to proselytize and convert non-Hindus to Hinduism. This is one of the direct effects of Islam on Hinduism, though in practice it brings it into conflict with Islam in India. Orthodox Hindus still do not approve of it.

In Kashmir a long-continued process of conversion to Islam had resulted in 95 per cent of the population becoming Moslems, though they retained many of their old Hindu customs. In the middle nineteenth century the Hindu ruler of the state found that very large numbers of these people were anxious or willing to return *en bloc* to Hinduism. He sent a deputation to the pundits of Benares inquiring if this could be done. The pundits refused to countenance any such change of faith and there the matter ended.

The Moslems who came to India from outside brought no new technique or political and economic structure. In spite of a religious belief in the brotherhood of Islam, they were class bound and feudal in outlook. In technique and in the methods of production and industrial organization, they were inferior to what prevailed then in India. Thus their influence on the economic life of India and the social structure was very little. This life continued as of old and all the people, Hindu or Moslem or others, fitted into it.

The position of women deteriorated. Even the ancient laws had been unfair to them in regard to inheritance and their position in the household—though even so they were fairer than nineteenth-century English law. Those laws of inheritance derived from the Hindu joint family system and sought to protect joint property from transfer to another family. A woman by marriage changed her family. In an economic sense she was looked upon as a dependant of her father or husband or son, but she could and did hold property in her own right. In many ways she was honoured and respected and had a fair measure of freedom, taking part in social and cultural activities. Indian history is full of the names of famous women, including thinkers and philosophers, rulers and warriors. This freedom grew progressively less. Islam had a fairer law of inheritance but this did not affect Hindu women. What did affect many of them to their great disadvantage, as it affected Moslem women to a much greater degree, was the intensification of the custom of seclusion of women. This spread among the upper classes all over the north and in Bengal, but the south and west of India escaped this degrading custom. Even in the north, only the upper classes indulged in it and the masses were happily free from it. Women now had less chances of education and their activities were largely confined to the household.* Lacking most other ways of distinguishing themselves, living a confined and restricted life, they were told that their supreme virtue lay in chastity and the supreme sin in a loss of it. Such was the man-made doctrine, but man did not apply it to himself. Tulsidas in his deservedly famous poems, the Hindi Ramayana, written during Jehangir's time, painted a picture of woman which is grossly unfair and prejudiced.

Partly because the great majority of Moslems in India were converts from Hinduism, partly because of long contact, Hindus and Moslems in India developed numerous common traits, habits, ways of living and artistic tastes, especially in northern India—in music, painting, architecture, food, clothes, and common traditions. They lived together peacefully as one people, joined each other's festivals and celebrations, spoke the same language, lived in more or less the same way, and faced identical economic problems. The nobility and the landed gentry and their numerous hangers-on took their cue from the court. (These people were not landlords or owners of the land. They did not take rent but were allowed to collect and retain the state revenue for a particular area. These grants were usually for life.) They developed a highly intricate, and sophisticated common culture. They wore the same kind of clothes, ate the same type of food, had common artistic pursuits, military pastimes, hunting, chivalry, and games. Polo was a favourite game and elephant fights were popular.

All this intercourse and common living took place in spite of the caste system which prevented fusion. There were no inter-marriages except in rare instances and even then it was not fusion but usually the transfer of a Hindu woman to the Moslem fold. Nor was there inter-dining but this was not so strict. The seclusion of women prevented the development of social life. This applied even more to Moslems *inter se* for *purdah* among them was stricter. Though Hindu and Moslem men met each other frequently, such opportunities were lacking to the women of both groups. These women of the nobility and upper classes were thus far more cut off from each other and developed much more marked separate ideological groups, each largely ignorant of the other.

Among the common people in the villages, and that means the vast majority of the population, life had a much more corporate and joint basis. Within the limited circle of the village there was an intimate relationship between the Hindus and Moslems. Caste did not come in the way and the Hindus looked

And yet many instances of notable women, scholars as well as rulers, occur even during this period and later. In the eighteenth century Lakshmi Devi wrote a great legal commentary on the Mitakshara, a famous law book of the medieval period.

upon the Moslems as belonging to another caste. Most of the Moslems were converts who were still full of their old traditions. They were well acquainted with the Hindu background, mythology, and epic stories. They did the same kind of work, lived similar lives, wore the same kind of clothes, spoke the same language. They joined each other's festivals, and some semireligious festivals were common to both. They had common folk-songs. Mostly these people were peasants and artisans and craftsmen.

The third large group, in between the nobility and the peasantry and artisans, was the merchant and trader class. This was predominantly Hindu and though it had no political power, the economic structure was largely under its control. This class had fewer intimate contacts with the Moslems than any other class, above it or below. The Moslems who had come from outside India were feudal in outlook and did not take kindly to trade. The Islamic prohibition against the taking of interest also came in the way of trade. They considered themselves the ruling class, the nobility and functioned as state officials, holders of grants of land or as officers in the army. There were also many scholars attached to the court or in charge of theological and other academies.

During the Mughal period large numbers of Hindus wrote books in Persian which was the official court language. Some of these books have become classics of their kind. At the same time Moslem scholars translated Sanskrit books into Persian and wrote in Hindi. Two of the best-known Hindi poets are Malik Mohammad Jaisi who wrote the 'Padmavat' and Abdul Rahim Khānkhāna, one of the premier nobles of Akbar's court and son of his guardian. Khānkhāna was a scholar in Arabic, Persian, and Sanskrit, and his Hindi poetry is of a high quality. For sometime he was the commander-in-chief of the imperial army, and yet he has written in praise and admiration of Rana Pratap of Mewar, who was continually fighting Akbar and never submitted to him. Khānkhāna admires and commends the patriotism and high sense of honour and chivalry of his enemy on the battlefield.

It was this chivalrous and friendly approach on which Akbar based his policy and which many of his counsellors and ministers learned from him. He was particularly attached to the Rajputs, for he admired in them qualities which he himself possessed— reckless courage, a sense of honour and chivalry, and an adherence to the pledged word. He won over the Rajputs, but the Rajputs for all their admirable qualities, represented a medieval type of society which was already becoming out of date as new forces were arising. Akbar was not conscious of these new forces, for he himself was a prisoner of his own social inheritance.

Akbar's success is astonishing, for he created a sense of oneness among the diverse elements of north and central India. There was the barrier of a ruling class, mainly of foreign origin, and there were the barriers of religion and caste, a proselytizing religion opposed to the static but highly resistant system. These barriers did not disappear, but in spite of them that feeling of oneness grew. It was not merely an attachment to his person; it was an attachment to the structure he had built. His son and grandson, Jehangir and Shah Jehan, accepted that structure and functioned within its framework. They were men of no outstanding ability, but their reigns were successful because they continued on the lines so firmly laid down by Akbar. The next comer, Aurungzeb, much abler but of a different mould, swerved and left that beaten track, undoing Akbar's work. Yet not entirely, for it is extraordinary how, in spite of him and his feeble and pitiful successors, the feeling of reverence for that structure continued. That feeling was largely confined to the north and centre; it did not extend to the south or west. And it was from western India, therefore, that the challenge to it came.

Aurangzeb puts the Clock Back
Growth of Hindu Nationalism. Shivaji

Shah Jehan was a contemporary of Louis XIV of France, *le Grand Monarque*, and the Thirty Years War was then ravaging central Europe. As Versailles took shape, the Taj Mahal and the Pearl Mosque grew up in Agra, and the Jame Masjid of Delhi and the Diwan-i-Am and the Diwan-i-Khas in the imperial palace. These lovely buildings with a fairy-like beauty represent the height of Mughal splendour. The Delhi court, with its Peacock Throne, was more magnificent and luxurious than Versailles, but, like Versailles, it rested on a poverty-stricken and exploited people. There was a terrible famine in Gujarat and the Dekhan.

Meanwhile the naval power of England was rising and spreading. The only Europeans that Akbar knew were the Portuguese. During his son Jehangir's time the British navy defeated the Portuguese in Indian seas and Sir Thomas Roe, an ambassador of James I of England, presented himself at Jehangir's court in 1615. He succeeded in getting permission to start factories. The Surat factory was started, and Madras was founded in 1639. For over 100 years no one in India attached any importance to the British. The fact that the British now controlled the sea routes and had practically driven away the Portuguese had no significance for the Mughal rulers or their advisers. When the Mughal Empire was visibly weakening during Aurungzeb's reign, the British made an organized attempt to increase their possessions in India by war. This was in 1685. Aurungzeb, weak as he was growing and beset by enemies, succeeded in defeating the British. Even before this the French had established footholds in India. The overflowing energies of Europe were spreading out in India and the east just when India's political and economic condition was rapidly declining.

In France, Louis XIV was still continuing his long reign, laying the seeds of future revolution. In England, the rising middle classes had cut off the head of their king, Cromwell's brief-lived republic had flourished, Charles II had come and gone, and James II had run away. Parilament, representing to a large extent a new mercantile class, had curbed the king and established its supremacy.

It was during this period that Aurungzeb succeeded to the throne of the Mughals after a civil war, having imprisoned his own father, Shah Jehan. Only an Akbar might have understood the situation and controlled the new forces that were rising. Perhaps even he could have only postponed the dissolution of his empire unless his curiosity and thirst for knowledge led him to understand the significance of the new techniques that were arising, and of the shift in economic conditions that was taking place. Aurungzeb, far from understanding the present, failed even to appreciate the immediate past; he was a throw-back and, for all his ability and earnestness, he tried to undo what his predecessors had done. A bigot and an austere puritan, he was no lover of art or literature. He infuriated the great majority of his subjects by imposing the old hated *jeziya* poll-tax on the Hindus and destroying many of their temples. He offended the proud Rajputs who had been the props and pillars of the Mughal Empire. In the north he roused the Sikhs, who, from being a peaceful sect representing some kind of synthesis of Hindu and Islamic ideas, were converted by repression and persecution into a military brotherhood. Near the west coast of India, he angered the warlike Marathas, descendants of the ancient Rashtrakutas, just when a brilliant captain had risen amongst them.

All over the widespread domains of the Mughal Empire there was a ferment and a growth of revivalist sentiment, which was a mixture of religion and nationalism. That nationalism was certainly not of the modern secular type, nor did it, as a rule, embrace the whole of India in its scope. It was coloured by feudalism, by local sentiment and sectarian feeling. The Rajputs, more feudal than the rest, thought of their clan loyalties; the Sikhs, a comparatively small group in the Punjab, were absorbed in their own self-defence and could hardly look beyond the Punjab. Yet the religion itself had a strong national background and all its traditions were connected with India. 'The Indians,' writes Professor Macdonell, 'are the only division of the Indo-European family which has created a great national religion—Brahmanism—and a great world religion—Buddhism; while all the rest far from displaying originality in this sphere have long since adopted a foreign faith.' That combination of religion and nationalism gained strength and cohesiveness from both elements, and yet its ultimate weakness and insufficiency were also derived from that mixture. For it could only be an exclusive and partial nationalism, not including the many elements in India that lay outside that religious sphere. Hindu nationalism was a natural growth from the soil of India, but inevitably it comes in the way of the larger nationalism which rises above differences of religion or creed.

It is true that during this period of disruption, when a great empire was breaking up and many adventurers, Indian and foreign, were trying to carve out principalities for themselves, nationalism, in its present sense, was hardly in evidence at all. Each individual adventurer sought to augment his own power; each group fended for itself. Such history as we have only tells us of these adventurers, attaching more importance to them than to more significant happenings below the surface of events. Yet there are glimpses to show that it was not all adventurism, though many adventurers held the field. The Marathas, especially, had a wider conception and as they grew in power this conception also grew. Warren Hastings wrote in 1784: 'The Marathas possess, alone of all the people of Hindostan and Deccan, a principle of national attachment, which is strongly impressed on the minds of all individulals of the nation, and would probably unite their chiefs, as in one common cause, if any great danger were to threaten the general state.' Probably this national sentiment of their was largely confined to the Marathi-speaking area. Nevertheless the Marathas were catholic in their political and military system as well as their habits, and there was a certain internal democracy among them. All this gave strength to them. Shivaji, though he fought Aurungzeb, freely employed Moslems.

An equally important factor in the break-up of the Mughal Empire was the cracking up of the economic structure. There were repeated peasant risings, some of them on a big scale. From 1669 onwards the Jat peasantry, not far fram the capital itself, rose again and again against the Delhi Government. Yet another revolt of poor people was that of the Satnamis who were described by a Mughal noble as 'a gang of bloody miserable rebels, goldsmiths, carpenters, sweepers, tanners, and other ignoble beings.' Thus far revolts had been confined to princes and nobles and others of high degree. Quite another class was now experimenting with them.

While the empire was rent by strife and revolt, the new Maratha power was growing and consolidating itself in western India. Shivaji, born in 1627, was the ideal guerilla leader of hardened mountaineers and his cavalry went far and wide, sacking the city of Surat, where the English had their factory, and enforcing the *chowth* tax payment over distant parts of the Mughal dominions.

Shivaji was the symbol of a resurgent Hindu nationalism, drawing inspiration from the old classics, courageous, and possessing high qualities of leadership. He built up the Marathas as a strong unified fighting group, gave them a nationalist background, and made them a formidable power which broke up the Mughal Empire. He died in 1680, but the Maratha power continued to grow till it dominated India.

The Marathas and the British Struggle for Supremacy. Triumph of the British

The 100 years that followed the death of Aurungzeb in 1707 saw a complicated and many-sided struggle for mastery over India. The Mughal Empire rapidly fell to pieces and the imperial viceroys and governors began to function as semi-independent rulers, though so great was the prestige of the descendant of the Mughals in Delhi that a formal allegiance was paid to him even when he was powerless and a prisoner of others. These satrapies had no real power or importance, except in so far as they helped or hindered the main protagonists for power. The Nizam of Hydrabad, by virtue of the strategic position of his state in the south, appeared to have a certain importance in the beginning. But it soon transpired that this importance was entirely fictitious and the state was 'straw-stuffed and held upright' by external forces. It showed a peculiar capacity for duplicity and for profiting by the misfortunes of others while avoiding all risk and dangers. Sir John Shore described it as 'incorrigibly depraved, devoid of energy...consequently liable to sink into vassalage.' The Marathas looked upon the Nizam as one of their subordinate chieftains paying tribute to them. An attempt by him to avoid this and to show independence met with swift retribution and the Marathas put to flight his feeble and none-too-brave army. He took refuge under the protecting wings of the growing power of the British East India Company and survived as a state because of this vassalage. Indeed the Hyderabad state enlarged its area considerably, without any remarkable effort on its part, by the British victory over Tipu Sultan of Mysore.

Warren Hastings, writing in 1784, refers to the Nizam of Hyderabad: 'His dominions are of small extent and scanty revenue; his military strength is represented to be most contemptible; nor was he at any period of his life distinguished for personal courage or the spirit of enterprise. On the contrary, it seems to have been his constant and ruling maxim to foment the incentives of war among his neighbours, to profit by their weakness and embarrassments, but to avoid being a party himself in any of their contests, and to submit even to humiliating sacrifices rather than subject himself to the chances of war.'[*]

*Quoted in Edward Thompson's 'The Making of the Indian Princes' (1943), p. 1.

The real protagonists for power in India during the eighteenth century were four: two of these were Indian and two foreign. The Indians were the Marathas and Haidar Ali and his son Tipu Sultan in the south; the foreigners were the British and the French. Of these, it appeared almost inevitable, during the first half of the century, that the Marathas were destined to establish their supremacy over India as a whole and to be the successors of the Mughal Empire. Their troops appeared at the very gates of Delhi as early as 1737 and there was no power strong enough to oppose them.

Just then (in 1739) a new eruption took place in the north-west and Nadir Shah of Persia swept down to Delhi, killing and plundering, and carrying off enormous treasure including the famous Peacock Throne. It was an easy raid for him for the Delhi rulers were effete and effeminate, wholly unused to war-fare, and Nadir Shah did not come into conflict with the Marathas. In a sense, his raid facilitated matters for the Marathas, who in subsequent years spread to the Punjab. Again Maratha supremacy of India was in sight.

Nadir Shah's raid had two consequences. He put an end completely to any pretensions that the Delhi Mughal rulers had to power and dominion; henceforth they became vague shadows enjoying a ghostly sovereignty, puppets in the hands of any one who was strong enough to hold them. To a large extent they had arrived at that stage even before Nadir Shah came; he completed the process. And yet, so strong is the hold of tradition and long-established custom, the British East India Company as well as others, continued to send humble presents to them in token of tribute right up to the eve of Plassey; and even afterwards for a long time the Company considered itself and functioned as the agent of the Delhi emperor, in whose name money was coined till 1835.

The second consequence of Nadir Shah's raid was the separation of Afghanistan from India. Afghanistan, which for long ages past had been part of India, was now cut off and became part of Nadir Shah's dominions. Sometime afterwards a local rebellion resulted in the murder of Nadir Shah by a group of his own officers and Afghanistan became an independent state.

The Marathas had in no way been weakened by Nadir Shah and they continued to spread in the Punjab. But in 1761 they met with a crushing defeat at Panipat from an Afghan invader, Ahmad Shah Durrani, who was ruling Afghanistan then. The flower of the Maratha forces perished in this disaster and, for a while, their dreams of empire faded away. They recovered gradually and the Maratha dominions were divided into a number of independent states joined together in a confederacy under the leadership of the Peshwa at Poona. The chiefs of the bigger states were Scindhia of Gwalior, Holkar of Indore, and the Gaekwar of Baroda. This confederacy still dominated a vast area in western and central India. But the Panipat defeat of the Marathas by Ahmad Shah had weakened them just when the English Company was emerging as an important territorial power of India.

In Bengal, Clive, by promoting treason and forgery and with very little fighting, had won the battle of Plassey in 1757, a date which is sometimes said to mark the beginning of the British Empire in India. It was an unsavoury beginning and something of that bitter taste has clung to it ever since. Soon the British held the whole of Bengal and Bihar and one of the early consequences of their rule was a terrible famine which ravaged these two provinces in 1770, killing over a third of the population of this rich, vast, and densely populated area.

In south India, the struggle between the English and the French, a part of the world struggle between the two, ended in the triumph of the English, and the French were almost eliminated from India.

With the elimination of the French power from India, three contestants for supremacy remained—the Maratha confederacy, Haider Ali in the south, and the British. In spite of their victory at Plasssey and their spreading out over Bengal and Bihar, few, if any, people in India then looked upon the British as a dominant power, destined to rule over the whole of India. An observer would still have given the first place to the Marathas who sprawled all over western and central India right up to Delhi and whose courage and fighting qualities were well-known. Haider Ali and Tipu Sultan were formidable adversaries who inflicted a severe defeat on the British and came near to breaking the power of the East India Company. But they were confined to the south and did not directly affect the fortunes of India as a whole. Haider Ali was a remarkable man and one of the notable figures in Indian history. He had some kind of a national ideal and possessed the qualities of a leader with vision. Continually suffering from a painful disease, his self-discipline and capacity for hard work were astonishing. He realized, long before others did so, the importance of sea power and the growing menace of the British based on naval strength. He tried to organize a joint effort to drive them out and, for this purpose, sent envoys to the Marathas, the Nizam, and Shuja-ud-Dowla of Oudh. But nothing came of this. He started building his own navy and, capturing the Maldive Islands, made them his headquarters for shipbuilding and naval activities. He died by the wayside as he was marching with his army. His son Tipu continued to strengthen his navy. Tipu also sent messages to Napoleon and to the Sultan in Constantinople.

In the north a Sikh state under Ranjit Singh was growing up

in the Punjab, to spread later to Kashmir and the North West Frontier Province; but that too was a marginal state not affecting the real struggle for supremacy. This struggle, it became clear as the eighteenth century approached its end, lay between the only two powers that counted—the Marathas and the British. All the other states and principalities were subordinate and subsidiary to these two.

Tipu Sultan of Mysore was finally defeated by the British in 1799, and that left the field clear for the final contest between the Marathas and the British East India Company. Charles Metcalfe, one of the ablest of the British Officials in India, wrote in 1806: 'India contains no more than two great powers, British and Mahratta, and every other state acknowledges the influence of one or the other. Every inch that we recede will be occupied by them.' But there was rivalry amongst the Maratha chieftains, and they fought and were defeated separately by the British. They won some notable victories and especially inflicted a severe defeat on the British near Agra in 1804, but by 1818 the Maratha power was finally crushed and the great chiefs that represented it in central India submitted and accepted the overlordship of the East India Company. The British became then the unchallenged sovereigns of a great part of India, governing the country directly or through puppet and subsidiary princes. The Punjab and some outlying parts were still beyond their control, but the British Empire in India had become an established fact, and subsequent wars with the Sikhs and Gurkhas and in Burma merely rounded it off on the map.

The Backwardness of India and the Superiority of the English in Organization and Technique

Looking back over this period, it almost seems that the British succeeded in dominating India by a succession of fortuitous circumstances and lucky flukes. With remarkably little effort, considering the glittering prize, they won a great empire and enormous wealth, which helped to make them the leading power in the world. It seems easy for a slight turn in events to have taken place which would have dashed their hopes and ended their ambitions. They were defeated on many occasions—by Haider Ali and Tipu, by the Marathas, by the Sikhs, and by the Gurkhas. A little less good fortune and they might have lost their foothold in India, or at the most held on to certain coastal territories only.

And yet a closer scrutiny reveals, in the circumstances then existing, a certain inevitability in what happened. Good fortune there certainly was, but there must be an ability to profit by good fortune. India was then in a fluid and disorganized state, following the break-up of the Mughal Empire; for many centuries it had not been so weak and helpless. Organized power having broken down, the field was left open to adventurers and new claimants for dominion. Among these adventurers and claimants, the British, and the British alone at the time, possessed many of the qualities necessary for success. Their major disadvantage was that they were foreigners coming from a far country. Yet that very disadvantage worked in their favour, for no one took them very seriously or considered them as possible contestants for the sovereignty of India. It is extraordinary how this delusion lasted till long after Plassey, and their functioning in formal matters as the agents of the shadow Emperor at Delhi helped to further this false impression. The plunder that they carried away from Bengal and their peculiar methods of trade led to the belief that these foreigners were out for money and treasure and not so much for dominion; that they were a temporary though painful infliction, rather like Timur or Nadir Shah, who came and plundered and went back to his homeland.

The East India Company had originally established itself for trading purposes, and its military establishment was meant to protect this trade. Gradually, and almost unnoticed by others, it had extended the territory under its control, chiefly by taking sides in local disputes, helping one rival against another. The company's troops were better trained and were an asset to any side, and the company extracted heavy payment for the help. So the company's power grew and its military establishment increased. People looked upon these troops as mercenaries to be hired. When it was realized that the British were playing nobody's game but their own, and were out for the political domination of India, they had already established themselves firmly in the country.

Anti-foreign sentiment there undoubtedly was, and this grew in later years; but it was far removed from any general or widespread national feeling. The background was feudal and loyalty went to the local chief. Widespread distress, as in China during the days of the war lords, compelled people to join any military leader who offered regular pay or opportunities of loot. The East India Company's armies largely consisted of Indian sepoys. Only the Marathas had some national sentiment, something much more than loyalty to a leader, behind them, but even this was narrow and limited. They managed to irritate the brave Rajputs by their treatment of them. Instead of gaining them as allies, they had to deal with them as opponents or as grumbling and dissatisfied feudatories. Among the Maratha chiefs themselves there was bitter rivalry, and occasionally civil war, in spite of a vague alliance under the Peshwa's leadership. At critical moments they failed to support each other, and were separately defeated.

Yet the Marathas produced a number of very able men, statesmen and warriors, among them being Nana Farnavis, the Peshwa Baji Rao I, Mahadaji Scindhia of Gwalior, and Yaswant Rao Holkar of Indore, as also that remarkable woman, Princess Ahalya Bai of Indore. Their rank and file was good, seldom deserting a post and often facing certain death unmoved; but behind all this courage there was often an adventurism and amateurishness. both in peace and war, which were surprising. Their ignorance of the world was appalling, and even their knowledge of India's geography was strictly limited. What is worse, they did not take the trouble to find out what was happening elsewhere and what their enemies were doing. There could be no far-sighted statesmanship or effective strategy with these limitations. Their speed of movement and mobility often surprised and unnerved the enemy, but essentially war was looked upon as a series of gallant charges and little more. They were ideal guerrilla fighters. Later they reorganized their armies on more orthodox lines, with the result that what they gained in armour they lost in speed and mobility, and they could not adjust themselves easily to these new conditions. They considered themselves clever, and so they were, but it was not difficult to overreach them in peace or war, for their thought was imprisoned in an old and out-of-date framework and could not go beyond it.

The superiority in discipline and technique of foreign-trained armies had, of course, been noticed at an early stage by Indian rulers. They employed French and English officers to train their own armies, and the rivalry between these two helped to build up Indian armies. Haider Ali and Tipu also had some conception of the importance of sea-power, and they tried, unsuccessfully and too late, to build up a fleet in order to challenge the British at sea. The Marathas also made a feeble attempt in this direction. India was then a shipbuilding country, but it was not easy to build up a navy within a short time and in the face of constant opposition. With the elimination of the French many of their officers in the armies of the Indian powers had to go. The foreign officers who remained, chiefly British, often deserted their employers at critical stages, and, on some occasions, betrayed them, surrendering and marching over to their enemies (the British) with their armies and treasure. This reliance on foreign officers not only indicates the backwardness of the army organization of the Indian powers, but was also a constant source of danger owing to their unreliability. The British often had a powerful fifth column both in the administration and in the armies of the Indian rulers.

If the Marathas, with their homogeneity and group patriotism, were backward in civil and military organization, much more so were the other Indian powers. The Rajputs, for all their courage, functioned in the old feudal way, romantic but thoroughly inefficient, and were rent among themselves by tribal feuds. Many of them, from a sense of feudal loyalty to an overlord, and partly as a consequence of Akbar's policy in the past, sided with the vanishing power of Delhi. But Delhi was too feeble to profit by this, and the Rajputs deteriorated and became the playthings of others, ultimately falling into the orbit of Scindhia, the Maratha. Some of their chiefs tried to play a careful balancing game in order to save themselves. The various Moslem rulers and chiefs in northern and central India were as feudal and backward in their ideas as the Rajput. They made no real difference, except to add to the confusion and the misery of the mass of the people. Some of them acknowledged the suzerainty of the Marathas.

The Gurkhas of Nepal were splendid and disciplined soldiers, the equals, if not the superiors, of any troops that the East India Company could produce. Although completely feudal in organization, their attachment to their homelands was great, and this sentiment made them formidable fighters in its defence. They gave a fright to the British, but made no difference to the issue of the main struggle in India.

The Marathas did not consolidate themselves in the vast areas in northern and central India where they had spread. They came and went, taking no root. Perhaps nobody could take root just then owing to the alternating fortunes of war, and indeed many territories under British control, or acknowledging British suzerainty were in a far worse condition, and the British or their administration had not taken root there.

If the Marathas (and much more so the other Indian powers) were amateurish and adventurist in their methods, the British in India were thoroughly professional. Many of the British leaders were adventurous enough but they' were in no way adventurist in the policy for which they all worked in their separate spheres. 'The East India Company's secretariat,' writes Edward Thompson, 'was served in the courts of native India by a succession and galaxy of men such as even the British Empire has hardly ever possessed together at any other time.' One of the chief duties of the British residents at these courts was to bribe and corrupt the ministers and other officials. Their spy system was perfect, says a historian. They had complete information of the courts and armies of their adversaries, while those adversaries lived in ignorance of what the British were doing or were going to do. The fifth column of the British functioned continuously and in moments of crisis and in the heat of war there would be defections in their favour which made a great difference. They won most of their batles before the actual fighting took place. That had been so at Plassey and was repeated again and again right up to the Sikh wars. A notable instance of desertion was that of a high officer in the service of Scindhia of Gwalior, who had secretly come to terms with the British and went over to them with his entire army at the moment of battle. He was awarded for this later by being made the ruler of a new Indian state carved out of the territories of Scindhia whom he had betrayed. That state still exists, but the man's name became a byword for treason and treachery, just as Quisling's in recent years.

The British thus represented a higher political and military organization, well knit together and having very able leaders. They were far better informed than their adversaries and they took full advantage of the disunity and rivalries of the Indian powers. Their command of the seas gave them safe bases and opportunities to add to their resources. Even when temporarily defeated, they could recuperate and assume the offensive again. Their possession of Bengal after Plassey gave them enormous wealth and resources to carry on their warfare with the Marathas and others, and each fresh conquest added to these resources. For the Indian powers defeat often meant a disaster which could not be remedied.

This period of war and conquest and plunder converted central India and Rajputana and some parts of the south and west into derelict areas full of violence and unhappiness and misery. Armies marched across them and in their train came highway robbers, and no one cared for the miserable human beings who lived there, except to despoil them of their money and goods. Parts of India became rather like central Europe during the Thirty Years War. Conditions were bad almost everywhere but they were worst of all in the areas under British control or suzerainty: '... nothing could be more fantastic than the picture presented by Madras or by the vassal states of Oudh and Hyderabad, a seething delirium of misery. In comparison, the regions where the Nana (Farnavis, the Maratha statesman) governed were an oasis of gentle security'—so writes Edward Thomspson.

Just prior to this period, large parts of India were singularly free from disorder, in spite of the disruption of the Mughal Empire. In Bengal during the long reign of Allawardi, the semi-independent Mughal Viceroy, peaceful and orderly government prevailed and trade and business flourished, adding to the great wealth of the province. Some little time after Allawardi's death the battle of Plassey (1757) took place and the East India Company constituted themselves the agents of the Delhi Emperor, though in reality they were completely independent and could do what they willed. Then began the pillage of Bengal on behalf of the company and their agents and factors. Some years after Plassey began the reign of Ahalya Bai, of Indore in central India, and it lasted for thiry years (1765-1795). This has become almost legendary as a period during which perfect order and good govern-

280

ment prevailed and the people prospered. She was a very able ruler and organizer, highly respected during her lifetime, and considered as a saint by a grateful people after her death. Thus during the very period when Bengal and Bihar, under the new rule of the East India Company, deteriorated and there was organized plunder and political and economic chaos, leading to terrible famines, central India as well as many other parts of the country were in a prosperous condition.

The British had power and wealth but felt no responsibility for good government or any government. The merchants of the East India Company were interested in dividends and treasure and not in the improvement or even protection of those who had come under their sway. In particular, in the vassal states there was a perfect divorce between power and responsibility.

When the British had finished with the Marathas and were secure in their conquests, they turned their minds towards civil government and some kind of order was evolved. In the subsidiary states, however, the change was very slow, for in those so-called protected areas there was a permanent divorce between responsibility and power.

We are often reminded, lest we forget, that the British rescued India from chaos and anarchy. That is true in so far as they established orderly government after this period, which the Marathas have called 'the time of terror.' But that chaos and anarchy were partly at least due to the policy of the East India Company and their representatives in India. It is also conceivable that even without the good offices of the British, so eagerly given, peace and orderly government might have been established in India after the conclusion of the struggle for supremacy. Such developments had been known to have taken place in India, as in other countries, in the course of her 5,000 years of history.

Ranjit Singh and Jai Singh

It seems clear that India became a prey to foreign conquest because of the inadequacy of her own people and because the British represented a higher and advancing social order. The contrast between the leaders on both sides is marked; the Indians, for all their ability, functioned in a narrow, limited sphere of thought and action, unaware of what was happening elsewhere and therefore unable to adapt themselves to changing conditions. Even if the curiosity of individuals was roused they could not break the shell which held them and their people prisoners. The Englishmen, on the other hand, were much more worldly wise, shaken up and forced to think by events in their own country and in France and America. Two great revolutions had taken place. The campaigns of the French revolutionary armies and of Napoleon had changed the whole science of war. Even the most ignorant Englishman who came to India saw different parts of the world in the course of his journey. In England itself great discoveries were being made, heralding the industrial revolution, though perhaps few ralised their far-reaching significance at the time. But the leaven of change was working powerfully and influencing the people. Behind it all was the expansive energy which sent the British to distant lands.

Those who had recorded the history of India are so full of wars and tumults and the political and military leaders of the day, that they tell us very little of what was happening in the mind of India and how social and economic processes were at work. Only occasional and accidental glimpses emerge from this sordid record. It appears that during this period of terror the people generally were crushed and exhausted, passively submitting to the decrees of a malevolent fate, dazed and devoid of curiosity. There must have been many individuals, however, who were curious and who tried to understand the new forces at play, but they were overwhelmed by the tide of events and could not influence them.

One of the individuals who was full of curiosity was Maharaja Ranjit Singh, a Jat Sikh, who had built up a kingdom in the Punjab, which subsequently spread to Kashmir and the Frontier Province. He had failings and vices; nevertheless he was a remarkable man. The Frenchman, Jacquemont, calls him 'extremely brave' and 'almost the first inquisitive Indian I have seen, but his curiosity makes up for the apathy of the whole nation.' 'His conversation is like a nightmare.'* It must be remembered that Indians as a rule, are a reserved people, and more so the intellectuals amongst them. Very few of these would have cared to associate then with the foreign military leaders and adventurers in India, many of whose actions filled them with horror. So these intellectuals tried to preserve their dignity by keeping as far as possible from the foreign elements and met them only on formal occasions when circumstances compelled them to do so. The Indians whom Englishmen and other foreigners usually met were of the opportunist and servile class that surrounded them or the ministers, frequently corrupt and intriguing, of the Indian courts.

Ranjit Singh was not only intellectually curious and inquisitive, he was remarkably humane at a time when India and the world seethed with callousness and inhumanity. He built up a kingdom and a powerful army and yet he disliked bloodshed. 'Never was so large an empire founded by one man with so little criminality,' says Prinsep. He abolished the death sentence for every crime, however heinous it might be, when in England even petty pilferers had to face death. 'Except in actual warfare,' writes Osborne, who visited him, 'he has never been known

*Quoted by Edward Thompson in 'The Making of Indian Princes' (1943), p. 158.

to take life, though his own has been attempted more than once, and his reign will be found freer from any striking acts of cruelty and oppression than those of many more civilized monarches.'*

Another but a different type of Indian statesman was Sawai Jai Singh, of Jaipur in Rajputana. He belongs to a somewhat earlier period and he died in 1743. He lived during the period of disruption following Aurungzeb's death. He was clever and opportunist enough to survive the many shocks and changes that followed each other in quick succession. He acknowledged the suzerainty of the Delhi Emperor. When he found that the advancing Marathas were too strong to be checked, he came to terms with them on behalf of the emperor. But it is not his political or military career that interests me. He was a brave warrior and an accomplished diplomat, but he was something much more than this. He was a mathematician and an astronomer, a scientist and a town-planner, and he was interested in the study of history.

Jai Singh built big observatories at Jaipur, Delhi, Ujjain, Benares, and Mathura. Learning through Portuguese missionaries of the progress of astronomy in Portugal, he sent his own men, with one of the missionaries, to the court of the Portuguese King Emmanuel. Emmanuel sent his envoy, Xavier de Silva, with De la Hire's tables to Jai Singh. On comparing these with his own tables, Jai Singh came to the conclusion that the Portuguese tables were less exact and had several errors. He attributed these to the 'inferior diameters' of the instruments used.

Jai Singh was of course fully acquainted with Indian mathematics; he had studied the old Greek treatises and also knew of recent European developments in mathematics. He had some of the Greek books (Euclid, etc.) as well as European works on plane and spherical trigonometry and the construction and use of logarithms translated into Sanskrit. He also had Arabic books on astronomy translated.

He founded the city of Jaipur. Interested in town planning, he collected the plans of many European cities of the time and then drew up his own plan. Many of these plans of the old European cities of the time are preserved in the Jaipur museum. The city of Jaipur was so well and wisely planned that it is still considered a model of town-planning.

Jai Singh did all this and much more in the course of a comparatively brief life and in the midst of perpetual wars and court intrigues, on which he was himself often involved. Nadir Shah's invasion took place just four years before Jai Singh's death. Jai Singh would have been a remarkable man anywhere and at any time. The fact that he rose and functioned as a scientist in the typically feudal *milieu* of Rajputana and during one of the darkest

*Quotations taken from Edward Thompson: 'The Making of Indian Princes' (1943), pp. 157, 158.

periods of Indian history, when disruption and war and tumults filled the scene, is very significant. It shows that the spirit of scientific inquiry was not dead in India and that there was some ferment at work which might have yielded rich results if only an opportunity had been given to it to fructify. Jai Singh was no anachronism or solitary thinker in an unfriendly and uncomprehending environment. He was a product of his age and he collected a number of scientific workers to work with him. Out of these he sent some in the embassy to Portugal, and social custom or taboo did not deter him from doing so. It seems probable that there was plenty of good material for scientific work in the country, both theoretical and technical, if only it was given a chance to function. That opportunity did not come for a long time. Even when the troubles and disorders were over, there was no encouragement of scientific work by those in authority.

The Economic Background of India: the two Englands

What was the economic background of India when all these far-reaching political changes were taking place? V. Anstey has written that right up to the eighteenth century, 'Indian methods of production and of industrial and commerical organization could stand comparison with those in vogue in any other part of the world.' India was a highly developed manufacturing country exporting her manufactured products to Europe and other countries. Her banking system was efficient and well organized throughout the country, and the *hundis* or bills of exchange issued by the great business or financial houses were honoured everywhere in India, as well as in Iran, and Kabul and Herat and Tashkent and other places in central Asia. Merchant capital had emerged and there was an elaborate network of agents, jobbers, brokers, and middlemen. The ship building industry was flourishing and one of the flagships of an English admiral during the Napoleonic wars had been built by an Indian firm in India. India was, in fact, as advanced industrially, commercially, and financially as any country prior to the industrial revolution. No such development could have taken place unless the country had enjoyed long periods of stable and peaceful government and the highways were safe for traffic and trade.

Foreign adventurers originally came to India because of the excellence of her manufacturers which had a big market in Europe. The chief business of the British East India Company in its early days was to trade with Indian goods in Europe, and very profitable trading it was, yielding enormous dividends. So efficient and highly organized were Indian methods of production, and such was the skill of India's artisans and craftsmen, that they could compete successfully even with the higher techniques of production which were being established in England. When the big machine age began in England, Indian goods continued to pour in and had to be stopped by very heavy duties and, in some cases, by outright prohibitions.

Clive described Murshidabad, in Bengal, in 1757, the very year of Plassey, as a city 'as extensive, populous, and rich as the city of London, with the difference that there are individuals in the first possessing infinitely greater property than in the last.' The city of Dacca, in eastern Bengal, was famous for its fine muslins. These two cities, important as they were, were near the periphery of Hindustan. All over the vast land there were greater cities and large numbers of big manufacturing and trading centres, and a very rapid and ingenious system of communicating news and market prices had been evolved. The great business houses often received news, even of the wars that were going on, long before despatches reached the officials of the East India Company. The economy of India had thus advanced to as high a stage as it could reach prior to the industrial revolution. Whether it had the seeds of further progress in it or was too much bound up with the rigid social structure, it is difficult to say. It seems quite possible, however, that under normal conditions it would have undergone that change and begun to adapt itself, in its own way, to the new industrial conditions. And yet, though it was ripe for a change, that change itself required a revolution within its own framework. Perhaps some catalytic agent was necessary to bring about that change. It is clear that however highly organized and developed its pre-industrial economy was, it could not compete for long with the products of industrialized countries. It had to industrialize itself or submit to foreign economic penetration which would have led to political interference. As it happened, foreign political domination came first and this led to a rapid destruction of the economy India had built up, without anything positive or constructive taking its place. The East India Company represented both British political power and British vested interests and economic power. It was supreme and, being a company of merchants, it was intent on making money. Just when it was making money with amazing rapidity and in fantastic quantities, Adam Smith wrote about it in 'The Wealth of Nations' in 1776: 'The government of an exclusive company of marchants is perhaps the worst of all governments for any country whatever.'

Though the Indian merchant and manufacturing classes were rich and spread out all over the country, and even controlled the economic structure, they had no political power. Government was despotic and still largely feudal. In fact, it was probably more feudal than it had been at some previous stages of Indian history. Hence there was no middle class strong enough, or even consciously thinking of seizing power, as in some western countries.

The people generally had grown apathetic and servile. There was thus a gap which had to be filled before any revolutionary change could take place. Perhaps this gap had been produced by the static nature of Indian society which refused to change in a changing world, for every civilization which resists change declines. That society, as constituted, had no more creative part to play. A change was overdue.

The British, at that time, were politically much more advanced. They had had their political revolution and had established the power of Parliament over that of the King. Their middle classes, conscious of their new power, were full of the impulse to expand. That vitality and energy, proof of a growing and progressive society, were indeed very evident in England. They showed themselves in many ways and most of all in the inventions and discoveries which heralded the industrial revolution.

And yet, what was the British ruling class then? Charles and Mary Beard, the eminent American historians, tell us how the success of the American revolution removed suddenly from the royal provinces in America the 'British ruling class—a class accustomed to a barbarous criminal code, a narrow and intolerant university system, a government conceived as a huge aggregation of jobs and privileges, a contempt of men and women who toiled in field and shop, a denial of education to the masses, an established religion forced alike on Dissenters and Catholics, a dominion of squire and parson in counties and villages, callous brutality in army and navy, a scheme of primogeniture buttressing the rule of the landed gentry, a swarm of hungry placemen offering sycophancy to the king in exchange for offices, sinecures, and pensions, and a constitution of church and state so ordered as to fasten upon the masses this immense pile of pride and plunder. From the weight of this mountain the American revolutionists delivered the colonial subjects of the British Crown. Within a decade or two after that emancipation they accomplished reforms in law and policy which required 100 years or more of persistent agitation to effect in the mother country—reforms which gave to the statesmen who led in the agitation their title to immortality in English history'.*

The American Declaration of Independence, that landmark in freedom's history, was signed in 1776, and six years later the colonies separated from England and began their real intellectual, economic, and social revolution. The land system, that had grown up under British inspiration and after the model of England, was completely transformed. Many privileges were abolished and the large estates confiscated and then distributed in small lots. A stirring period of awakening and intellectual and economic activity followed. Free America, rid of feudal relics and foreign control,

*'The Rise of American Civilization' (1928), Volume I, p. 292.

marched ahead with giant strides.

In France, the great revolution smashed the Bastille, symbol of the old order, and swept away the king and feudalism and declared the rights of man to the world.

And in England then? Frightened by these revolutionary changes in America and France, England became even more reactionary, and her fierce and barbarous penal code became even more savage. When George III came to the English throne in 1760 there were about 160 offences for which men, women, and children were put to death. By the time his long reign ended in 1820, nearly a hundred new offences, carrying the death penalty, were added to this terrible list. The ordinary soldier in the British army was treated worse than a beast of the field, with a brutality and inhumanity that horrify. Death sentences were common and commoner still was flogging, inflicted in public, flogging up to several hundred lashes, till death sometimes intervened or the mangled body of the sufferer, just surviving, told the story to his dying day.

In this matter as in many others involving humanity and respect for the individual and the group, India was far more advanced and had a higher civilization. There was more literacy in India then than in England or the rest of Europe, though the education was strictly traditional. Probably there were more civic amenities also. The general condition of the masses in Europe was very backward and deplorable and compared unfavourably with the conditions prevailing in India. But there was this vital difference: new forces and living currents were working invisibly in western Europe, bringing changes in their train; in India, conditions were far more static.

England came to India. When Queen Elizabeth gave a charter to the East India Company in 1600, Shakespeare was alive and writing. In 1611 the Authorized English edition of the Bible was issued; in 1608 Milton was born. There followed Hampden and Cromwell and the political revolution. In 1660 the Royal Society of England, which was to advance the cause of science so much, was organized. A hundred years later, in 1760, the flying shuttle was invented, and there followed in quick succession the spinning jenny, the steam engine, and the power loom.

Which of these two Englands came to India? The England of Shakespeare and Milton, of noble speech and writing and brave deed, of political revolution and the struggle for freedom, of science and technical progress, or the England of the savage penal code and brutal behaviour, of entrenched feudalism and reaction? For there were two Englands, just as in every country there are these two aspects of national character and civilization. 'The discrepancy in England,' write Edward Thompson, 'between the highest and the ordinary levels of our civilization, has always been immense; I doubt if there is anything like it in any country with which we should wish to be compared and it is a discrepancy that lessens so slowly that it often seems hardly to lessen at all.'*

The two Englands live side by side, influencing each other, and cannot be separated; nor could one of them come to India forgetting completely the other. Yet in every major action one plays the leading role, dominating the other, and it was inevitable that the wrong England should play that role in India and should come in contact with and encourage the wrong India in the process.

The independence of the United States of America is more or less contemporaneous with the loss of freedom by India. Surveying the past century and a half, an Indian looks somewhat wistfully and longingly at the vast progress made by the United States during this period, and compares it with what has been done and what has not been done in his own country. It is true no doubt that the Americans have many virtues and we have many failings, that America offered a virgin field and an almost clean slate to write upon while we were cluttered up with ancient memories and traditions. And yet perhaps it is not inconceivable that if Britain had not undertaken this great burden in India and, as she tells us, endeavoured for so long to teach us the difficult art of self-government, of which we had been so ignorant, India might not only have been freer and more prosperous, but also far more advanced in science and art and all that makes life worth living.

*'Making of Indian Princes' (1903), p. 264.

CHAPTER SEVEN

THE LAST PHASE (1)

Consolidation of British Rule and Rise of Nationalist Movement

The Ideology of Empire. The New Caste

'OUR WRITING OF INDIA'S HISTORY IS PERHAPS RESENTED MORE THAN anything else we have done'—so writes an Englishman well acquainted with India and her history. It is difficult to say what Indians have resented most in the record of British rule in India; the list is long and varied. But it is true that British accounts of India's history, more especially of what is called the British period, are bitterly resented. History is almost always written by the victors and conquerors and gives their viewpoint; or, at any rate, the victors' version is given prominence and holds the field. Very probably all the early records we have of the Aryans in India, their epics and traditions, glorify the Aryans and are unfair to the people of the country whom they subdued. No individual can wholly rid himself of his racial outlook and cultural limitations, and when there is conflict between races and countries even an attempt at impartiality is considered a betrayal of one's own people. War, which is an extreme example of this conflict, results in a deliberate throwing overboard of all fairness and impartiality so far as the enemy nation is concerned; the mind coarsens and becomes closed to almost all avenues of approach except one. The overpowering need of the moment is to justify one's own actions and condemn and blacken those of the enemy. Truth hides somewhere at the bottom of the deepest well and falsehood, naked and unashamed, reigns almost supreme.

Even when actual war is not being waged there is often potential war and conflicts between rival countries and interests. In a country dominated by an alien power that conflict is inherent and continuous and affects and perverts people's thoughts and actions; the war mentality is never wholly absent. In the old days when war and its consequences, brutality and conquest and enslavement of a people, were accepted as belonging to the natural order of events, there was no particular need to cover them or justify them from some other point of view. With the growth of higher standards the need for justification has arisen, and this leads to a perversion of facts, sometimes deliberate, often unconscious. Thus hypocrisy pays its tribute to virtue, and a false and sickening piety allies itself to evil deeds.

In any country, and especially in a huge country like India with its complicated history and mixed culture, it is always possible to find facts and trends to justify a particular thesis, and then this becomes the accepted basis for a new argument. America, it is said, is a land of contradictions, in spite of its standardization and uniformity. How much more then must India be full of contradictions and incongruities. We shall find there, as elsewhere, what we seek, and on this preconceived basis we can build up a structure of belief and opinion. And yet that structure will have untrue foundations and will give a false picture of reality.

Recent Indian history, that is the history of the British period, is so connected with present-day happenings that the passions and prejudices of to-day powerfully influence our interpretation of it. Englishmen and Indians are both likely to err, though their errors will lie in opposite directions. Far the greater part of the records and papers out of which history takes shape and is written comes from British sources and inevitably represents the British point of view. The very circumstances of defeat and disruption prevented the Indian side of the story from being properly recorded, and many of the records that existed suffered destruction during the great Revolt of 1857. The papers that survived were hidden away in family archives and could not be published for fear of consequences. They remained dispersed, little known, and many perished in the manuscript stage from the incursion of termites and other insects which abound in the country. At a later stage when some of these papers were discovered they threw a new light on many historical incidents. Even British-written Indian history had to be somewhat modified, and the Indian conception, often very different from the British, took shape. Behind this conception lay also a mass of tradition and memories, not of the remote past but of a period when our grandfathers and great-grandfathers were the living witnesses and often the victims of events. As history this tradition may have little value, but it is important as it enables us to understand the background of the Indian mind to-day. The villain of the British in India is often a hero to Indians, and those whom the British have delighted to honour and reward are often traitors and quislings in the eyes of the great majority of the Indian people. That taint clings to their descendants.

The history of the American Revolution has been differently written by Englishmen and Americans, and even to-day when old passions have subsided and there is friendship between the two peoples each version is resented by the other party. In our own day Lenin was a monster and a brigand to many English statesmen of high repute, yet millions have considered him as a saviour and the greatest man of the age. These comparisons will give us some faint idea of the resentment felt by Indians at being forced to study in their schools and colleges so-called histories which disparage India's past in every way, vilify those whose memory they cherish, and honour and glorify the achievements of British rule in India.

Gopal Krishna Gokhale once wrote in his gently ironical way of the inscrutable wisdom of Providence which had ordained the British connection for India. Whether it was due to this inscrutable wisdom or to some process of historic destiny or just chance, the coming of the British to India brought two very different races together; or, at any rate, it should have brought them together, but as it happened they seldom approached each other and their contacts were indirect. English literature and English political thought influenced a tiny fringe of those who had learned English. But this political thought, though dynamic in its context, had no reality in India then. The British who came to India were not political or social revolutionaries; they were conservatives representing the most reactionary social class in England, and England was in some ways one of the most conservative countries in Europe.

The impact of western culture on India was the impact of a dynamic society, of a 'modern' consciousness, on a static society wedded to medieval habits of thought which, however sophisticated and advanced in its own way, could not progress because of its inherent limitations. And, yet, curiously enough the agents of this historic process were not only wholly unconscious of their mission in India but, as a class, actually represented no such process. In England their class fought this historic process but the forces opposed to them were too strong and could not be held back. In India they had a free field and were successful in applying the brakes to that very change and progress which, in the larger context, they represented. They encouraged and consolidated the position of the socially reactionary groups in India, and opposed all those who worked for political and social change. If change came it was in spite of them or as an incidental and unexpected consequence of their activities. The introduction of the steam engine and the railway was a big step towards a change of the mediæval structure, but it was intended to consolidate their rule and facilitate the exploitation for their own benefit of the interior of the country. This contradiction between the deliberate policy of the British authorities in India and some of its unintended consequences produces a certain confusion and masks that policy itself. Change came to India because of this impact of the west, but it came almost in spite of the British in India. They succeeded in slowing down the pace of that change to such an extent that even to-day the transition is very far from complete.

The feudal landlords and their kind who came from England

to rule over India had the landlord's view of the world. To them India was a vast estate belonging to the East India Company, and the landlord was the best and the natural representative of his estate and his tenants. That view continued even after the East India Company handed over its estate of India to the British Crown, being paid very handsome compensation at India's cost. (Thus began the public debt of India. It was India's purchase money, paid by India.) The British Government of India then became the landlords (or landlords' agents). For all practical purposes they considered themselves 'India', just as the Duke of Devonshire might be considered 'Devonshire' by his peers. The millions of people who lived and functioned in India were just some kind of landlord's tenants who had to pay their rents and cesses and to keep their place in the natural feudal order. For them a challenge to that order was an offence against the very moral basis of the universe and a denial of a divine dispensation.

This somewhat metaphysical conception of British rule in India has not changed fundamentally, though it is expressed differently now. The old method of obvious rack-renting gave place to more subtle and devious devices. It was admitted that the landlord should be benevolent towards his tenantry and should seek to advance their interests. It was even agreed that some of the more loyal and faithful among the tenants should be promoted to the estate office and share in a subordinate way in the administration. But no challenge to the system of landlordism could be tolerated. The estate must continue to function as it used to even when it changed hands. When pressure of events made some such change inevitable, it was stipulated that all the faithful employees in the estate office should continue, all the old and new friends, followers and dependants of the landlord should be provided for, the old age pensioners should continue to draw their pensions, the old landlord himself should now function as a benevolent patron and adviser of the estate, and thus all attempts to bring about essential changes should be frustrated.

This sense of identifying India with their own interests was strongest in the higher administrative services, which were entirely British. In later years these developed in that close and well-knit corporation called the Indian Civil Service—'the world's most tenacious trade union,' as it has been called by an English writer. They ran India, they were India, and anything that was harmful to their interests must of necessity be injurious to India. From the Indian Civil Service and the kind of history and record of current events that was placed before them, this conception spread in varying degrees to the different strata of the British people. The ruling class naturally shared it in full measure, but even the worker and the farmer were influenced by it to some slight extent, and felt, in spite of their own subordinate position in their own country, the pride of possession and empire. That same worker or farmer if he came to India inevitably belonged to the ruling class here. He was totally ignorant of India's history and culture and he accepted the prevailing ideology of the British in India, for he had no other standards to judge by or apply. At the most a vague benevolence filled him, but that was strictly conditioned within that framework. For a hundred years this ideology permeated all sections of the British people, and became, as it were, a national heritage, a fixed and almost unalterable notion, which governed their outlook on India and imperceptibly affected even their domestic outlook. In our own day that curious group which has no fixed standards or principles or much knowledge of the outside world, the leaders of the British Labour Party, have usually been the staunchest supporters of the existing order in India. Sometimes a vague sense of uneasiness fills them at a seeming contradiction between their domestic and colonial policy, between their professions and practice, but, considering themselves above all as practical men of commonsense, they sternly repress all these stirrings of conscience. Practical men must necessarily base themselves on established and known practice, on existing conditions, and not take a leap into the dark unknown merely because of some principle or untested theory.

Viceroys who come to India direct from England have to fit in with and rely upon the Indian Civil Service structure. Belonging to the possessing and ruling class in England, they have no difficulty whatever in accepting the prevailing I.C.S. outlook, and their unique position of absolute authority, unparalleled elsewhere, leads to subtle changes in their ways and methods of expression. Authority corrupts and absolute authority corrupts absolutely, and no man in the wide world to-day has had or has such absolute authority over such large number of people as the British Viceroy of India. The Viceroy speaks in a manner such as no Prime Minister of England or President of the United States can adopt. The only possible parallel would be that of Hitler. And not the Viceroy only, but the British members of his Council, the Governors, and even the smaller fry who function as secretaries of departments or magistrates. They speak from a noble and unattainable height, secure not only in the conviction that what they say and do is right, but that it will have to be accepted as right whatever lesser mortals may imagine, for theirs is the power and the glory.

Some members of the Viceroy's Council are appointed direct from England and do not belong to the Indian Civil Service. There is usually a marked difference in their ways and utterances from those of the Civil Service. They function easily enough in that framework, but they cannot quite develop that superior and self-satisfied air of assured authority. Much less can the Indian members of the Council (a fairly recent addition), who are obvious supers, whatever their numbers or intelligence. Indians belonging to the Civil Service, whatever their rank in the official hierarchy, do not belong to the charmed circle. A few of them try to ape the manners of their colleagues without much success; they become rather pompous and ridiculous.

The new generation of British members of the Indian Civil Service are, I believe, somewhat different in mind and texture from their predecessors. They do not easily fit into the old framework, but all authority and policy flow from the senior members and the newcomers make no difference. They have either to accept the established order or, as has sometimes happened, resign and return to their homeland.

I remember that when I was a boy the British-owned newspapers in India were full of official news and utterances; of service news, transfers and promotions; of the doings of English society, of polo, races, dances, and amateur theatricals. There was hardly a word about the people of India, about their political, cultural, social, or economic life. Reading them one would hardly suspect that they existed.

In Bombay there used to be quadrangular cricket matches between four elevens made up respectively of Hindus, Moslems, Parsees, and Europeans. The European eleven was called Bombay Presidency; the others were just Hindus, Moslems, Parsees. Bombay was thus essentially represented by the Europeans; the others, one would imagine, were foreign elements who were recognized for this purpose. These quadrangular matches still take place, though there is much argument about them, and a demand that elevens should not be chosen on religious lines. I believe that the 'Bombay Presidency' team is now called 'European.'

English clubs in India usually have territorial names—the Bengal Club, the Allahabad Club, etc. They are confined to Britishers, or rather to Europeans. There need be no objection to territorial designation, or even to a group of persons having a club for themselves and not approving of outsiders joining it. But this designation is derived from the old British habit of considering that they are the real India that counts, the real Bengal, the real Allahabad. Others are just excrescences, useful in their own way if they know their places, but otherwise a nuisance. The exclusion of non-Europeans is far more a racial affair than a justifiable means for people with cultural affinities to meet together in their leisure moments for play and social intercourse, without the intrusion of other elements. For my part I have no objection to exclusive English or European clubs, and very few Indians would care to join them; but when this social exclusiveness is clearly based on racialism and on a ruling class always exhibiting its superiority and unapproachability, it bears another aspect. In Bombay there is a well-known club which did not allow and so far as I know, does not allow, an Indian (except as a servant) even in its visitors' room, even though he might be a ruling prince or a captain of industry.

Racialism in India is not so much English versus Indian; it is European as opposed to Asiatic. In India every European, be he German, or Pole, or Rumanian, is automatically a member of the ruling race. Railway carriages, station retiring-rooms, benches in parks, etc., are marked 'For Europeans Only.' This is bad enough in South Africa or elsewhere, but to have to put up with it in one's own country is a humiliating and exasperating reminder of one's enslaved condition.

It is true that a gradual change has been taking place in these external manifestations of racial superiority and imperial arrogance, but the process is slow and frequent instances occur to show how superficial it is. Political pressure and the rise of a militant nationalism enforce change and lead to a deliberate attempt to tone down the former racialism and aggressiveness; and yet that very political movement, when it reaches a stage of crisis and is sought to be crushed, leads to a resurgence of all the old imperialist and racial arrogance in its extremest form.

The English are a sensitive people, and yet when they go to foreign countries there is a strange lack of awareness about them. In India, where the relation of ruler and ruled makes mutual understanding difficult, this lack of awareness is peculiarly evident. Almost one would think that it is deliberate, so that they may see only what they want to see and be blind to all else; but facts do not vanish because they are ignored, and when they compel attention there is a feeling of displeasure and resentment at the unexpected happening, as of some trick having been played.

In this land of caste the British, and more especially the Indian Civil Service, have built up a caste which is rigid and exclusive. Even the Indian members of the service do not really belong to that caste, though they wear the insignia and conform to its rules. That caste has developed something in the nature of a religious faith in its own paramount importance, and round that faith has grown an appropriate mythology which helps to maintain it. A combination of faith and vested interests is a powerful one, and any challenge to it arouses the deepest passions and fierce indignation.

The Plunder of Bengal helps the Industrial Revolution in England

The East India Company had received permission from the

Mughal Emperor to start a factory at Surat early in the seventeenth century. Some years later they purchased a patch of land in the south and founded Madras. In 1662 the island of Bombay was presented to Charles II of England by way of dowry from Portugal, and he transferred it to the company. In 1690 the city of Calcutta was founded. Thus by the end of the seventeenth century the British had gained a number of footholds in India and established some bridge-heads on the Indian coastline. They spread inland slowly. The battle of Plassey in 1757 for the first time brought a vast area under their control, and within a few years Bengal, Bihar, Orissa, and the east coast were subject to them. The next big step forward was taken about forty years later, at the beginning of the nineteenth century. This brought them to the gates of Delhi. The third major advance took place after the last defeat of the Marathas in 1818; the fourth in 1849, after the Sikh wars, completed the picture.

Thus the British have been in the city of Madras a little over 300 years; they have ruled Bengal, Bihar, etc., for 187 years; they extended their domination over the south 145 years ago; they established themselves in the United Provinces (as they are now called), central and western India about 125 years ago; and they spread to the Punjab ninety-five years ago. (This is being written in June, 1944.) Leaving out the city of Madras as too small an area, there is a difference of nearly 100 years between their occupation of Bengal and that of the Punjab. During this period British policy and administrative methods changed repeatedly. These changes were dictated by new developments in England as well as the consolidation of British rule in India. The treatment of each newly acquired area varied according to these changes, and depended also on the character of the ruling group which had been defeated by the British. Thus in Bengal, where the victory had been very easy, the Moslem landed gentry were looked upon as the ruling classes and a policy was pursued to break their power. In the Punjab, on the other hand, power was seized from the Sikhs and there was no initial antagonism between the British and the Moslems. In the greater part of India the Marathas had been opponents of the British.

A significant fact which stands out is that those parts of India which have been longest under British rule are the poorest to-day. Indeed some kind of chart might be drawn up to indicate the close connection between length of British rule and progressive growth of poverty. A few large cities and some new industrial areas do not make any essential difference to this survey. What is noteworthy is the condition of the masses as a whole, and there can be no doubt that the poorest parts of India are Bengal, Bihar, Orissa, and parts of the Madras presidency; the mass level and standards of living are highest in the Punjab. Bengal certainly was a very rich and prosperous province before the British came. There may be many reasons for these contrasts and differences But it is difficult to get over the fact that Bengal, once so rich and flourishing, after 187 years of British rule, accompanied, as we are told, by strenuous attempts on the part of the British to improve its condition and to teach its people the art of self-government, is to-day, a miserable mass of poverty-stricken, starving, and dying people.

Bengal had the first full experience of British rule in India. That rule began with outright plunder, and a land revenue system which extracted the uttermost farthing not only from the living but also from the dead cultivators. The English historians of India, Edward Thompson and G. T. Garrett, tell us that 'a gold-lust unequalled since the hysteria that took hold of the Spaniards of Cortes' and Pizarro's age filled the English mind. Bengal in particular was not to know peace again until she has been bled white.' 'For the monstrous financial immorality of the English conduct in India for many a year after this, Clive was largely responsible.'* Clive, the great empire-builder, whose statue faces the India Office in London to-day. It was pure loot. The 'Pagoda tree' was shaken again and again till the most terrible famines ravaged Bengal. This process was called trade later on but that made little difference. Government was this so-called trade, and trade was plunder. There are few instances in history of anything like it. And it must be remembered that this lasted, under various names and under different forms, not for a few years but for generations. The outright plunder gradually took the shape of legalized exploitation which, though not so obvious, was in reality worse. The corruption, venality, nepotism, violence, and greed of money of these early generations of British rule in India is something which passes comprehension. It is significant that one of the Hindustani words which has become part of the English language is 'loot.' Says Edward Thompson, and this does not refer to Bengal only, 'one remembers the early history of British India which is perhaps the world's high-water mark of graft.'

The result of all this, even in its early stages, was the famine of 1770, which swept away over a third of the population of Bengal and Bihar. But it was all in the cause of progress, and Bengal can take pride in the fact that she helped greatly in giving birth to the industrial revolution in England. The American writer, Brooke Adams, tells us exactly how this happened: 'The influx of Indian treasure, by adding considerably to the nation's cash capital, not only increased its stock of energy, but added much to its flexibility and the rapidity of its movement. Very soon after Plassey, the Bengal plunder began to arrive in London,

*'Rise and Fulfilment of British Rule in India' by Edward Thompson and G. T. Garrett (London, 1935).

and the effect appears to have been instantaneous, for all authorities agree that the "industrial revolution" began with the year 1770.... Plassey was fought in 1757, and probably nothing has ever equalled the rapidity of the change that followed. In 1760 the flying shuttle appeared, and coal began to replace wood in smelting. In 1764 Hargreaves invented the spinning jenny, in 1776 Crompton contrived the mule, in 1785 Cartwright patented the power loom and in 1768 Watt matured the steam engine....But though these machines served as outlets for the accelerating movements of the time, they did not cause the acceleration. In themselves inventions are passive...waiting for a sufficient store of force to have accumulated to set them working. That store must always take the shape of money, and money not hoarded but in motion. Before the influx of the Indian treasure, and the expansion of credit which followed, no force sufficient for this purpose existed.... Possibly since the world began, no investment has ever yielded the profit reaped from the Indian plunder, because for nearly fifty years Great Britain stood without a competitor.'*

The Destruction of India's Industry and the Decay of her Agriculture

The chief business of the East India Company in its early period, the very object for which it was started, was to carry Indian manufactured goods, textiles, etc., as well as spices and the like from the east to Europe, where there was a great demand for these articles. With the developments in industrial techniques in England a new class of industrial capitalists rose there, demanding a change in this policy. The British market was to be closed to Indian products and the Indian market opened to British manufactures. The British Parliament, influenced by this new class, began to take a greater interest in India and the working of the East India Company. To begin with, Indian goods were excluded from Britain by legislation, and as the East India Company held a monopoly in the Indian export business, this exclusion influenced other foreign markets also. This was followed by vigorous attempts to restrict and crush Indian manufactures by various measures and internal duties which prevented the flow of Indian goods within the country itself. British goods meanwhile had free entry. The Indian textile industry collapsed, affecting vast numbers of weavers and artisans. The process was rapid in Bengal and Bihar, elsewhere it spread gradually with the expansion of British rule and the building of railways. It continued throughout the nineteenth century, breaking up other old industries also, ship-building, metal working, glass, paper, and many crafts.

*Brooke Adams: 'The Law of Civilization and Decay' (1928), pp. 259-60, quoted by Kate Mitchel: 'India' (1943).

To some extent this was inevitable as the older manufacturing came into conflict with the new industrial technique. But it was hastened by political and economic pressure and no attempt was made to apply the new techniques to India. Indeed every attempt was made to prevent this happening, and thus the economic development of India was arrested and the growth of the new industry prevented. Machinery could not be imported into India. A vacuum was created which could only be filled by British goods, and which led to rapidly increasing unemployment and poverty. The classic type of modern colonial economy was built up, India becoming an agricultural colony of industrial England, supplying raw materials and providing markets for England's industrial goods.

The liquidation of the artisan class led to unemployment on a prodigious scale. What were all these scores of millions, who had so far been engaged in industry and manufacture, to do now? Where were they to go? Their old profession was no longer open to them, the way to a new one was barred. They could die of course; that way of escape from an intolerable situation is always open. They did die in tens of millions. The English Governor-General of India, Lord Bentinck, reported in 1834 that 'the misery hardly finds a parallel in the history of commerce. The bones of the cotton weavers are bleaching the plains of India.'

But still vast numbers of them remained, and these increased from year to year as British policy affected remoter areas of the country and created more unemployment. All these hordes of artisans and craftsmen had no job, no work, and all their ancient skill was useless. They drifted to the land, for the land was still there. But the land was fully occupied and could not possibly absorb them profitably. So they became a burden on the land and the burden grew, and with it grew the poverty of the country, and the standard of living fell to incredibly low levels. This compulsory back-to-the-land movement of artisans and craftsmen led to an ever-growing disproportion between agriculture and industry; agriculture became more and more the sole business of the people because of the lack of occupations and wealth-producing activities.

India became progressively ruralized. In every progressive country there has been, during the past century, a shift of population from agriculture to industry; from village to town; in India this process was reversed, as a result of British policy. The figures are instructive and significant. In the middle of the nineteenth century about fifty-five per cent of the population is said to have been dependent on agriculture; recently this proportion was estimated to be seventy-four per cent. (This is a pre-war figure.) Though there has been greater industrial employment during the war, the number of those dependent on agriculture actually went up in the census of 1941 owing to increase of population. The growth of a few large cities (chiefly at the expense of the small town) is apt to mislead the superficial observer and give him a false idea of Indian conditions.

This then is the real, the fundamental, cause of the appalling poverty of the Indian people, and it is of comparatively recent origin. Other causes that contribute to it are themselves the result of this poverty and chronic starvation and under-nourishment — like disease and illiteracy. Excessive population is unfortunate, and steps should be taken to curb it wherever necessary, but it still compares favourably with the density of population of many industrialized countries. It is only excessive for a predominantly agricultural community, and under a proper economic system the entire population can be made productive and should add to the wealth of the country. As a matter of fact great density of population exists only in special areas, like Bengal and the Gangetic Valley, and vast areas are still sparsely populated. It is worth remembering that Great Britain is more than twice as densely populated as India.

The crisis in industry spread rapidly to the land and became a permanent crisis in agriculture. Holdings became smaller and smaller, and fragmentation proceeded to an absurd and fantastic degree. The burden of agricultural debt grew and ownership of the land often passed to moneylenders. The number of landless labourers increased by the million. India was under an industrial-capitalist regime, but her economy was largely that of the pre-capitalist period, minus many of the wealth-producing elements of that pre-capitalist economy. She became a passive agent of modern industrial capitalism, suffering all its ills and with hardly any of its advantages.

The transition from a pre-industrialist economy to an economy of capitalist industrialism involves great hardship and heavy cost in human suffering borne by masses of people. This was especially so in the early days when no efforts were made to plan such a transition or to lessen its evil results, and everything was left to individual initiative. There was this hardship in England during the period of transition but, taken as a whole, it was not great as the change-over was rapid and the unemployment caused was soon absorbed by the new industries. But that did not mean that the cost in human suffering was not paid. It was indeed paid, and paid in full by others, particularly by the people of India, by famine and death and vast unemployment. It may be said that a great part of the costs of transition to industrialism in western Europe were paid for by India, China, and the other colonial countries, whose economy was dominated by the European powers.

It is obvious that there has been all along abundant material in India for industrial development—managerial and technical ability, skilled workers, even some capital in spite of the continuous drain from India. The historian, Montgomery Martin, giving evidence before an Inquiry Committee of the British Parliament in 1840, said: 'India is as much a manufacturing country as an agriculturist; and he who would seek to reduce her to the position of an agricultural country, seeks to lower her in the scale of civilization.' That is exactly what the British, in India sought to do, continuously and persistently, and the measure of their success is the present condition of India, after they have held despotic sway there for a century and a half. Ever since the demand for the development of modern industry arose in India (and this, I imagine, is at least 100 years old) we have been told that India is pre-eminently an agricultural country and it is in her interest to stick to agriculture. Industrial development may upset the balance and prove harmful to her main business—agriculture. The solicitude which British industrialists and economists have shown for the Indian peasant has been truly gratifying. In view of this, as well as of the tender care lavished upon him by the British Government in India, one can only conclude that some all-powerful and malign fate, some supernatural agency, has countered their intentions and measures and made that peasant one of the poorest and most miserable beings on earth.

It is difficult now for anyone to oppose industrial development in India but, even now, when any extensive and far-reaching plan is drawn up, we are warned by our British friends, who continue to shower their advice upon us, that agriculture must not be neglected and must have first place. As if any Indian with an iota of intelligence can ignore or neglect agriculture or forget the peasant. The Indian peasant is India more than anyone else, and it is on his progress and betterment that India's progress will depend. But our crisis in agriculture, grave as it is, is interlinked with the crisis in industry, out of which it arose. The two cannot be disconnected and dealt with separately, and it is essential for the disproportion between the two to be remedied.

India's ability to develop modern industry can be seen by her success in it whenever she has had the chance to build it up. Indeed, such success has been achieved in spite of the strenuous opposition of the British Government in India and of vested interests in Britain. Her first real chance came during the war of 1914-18 when the inflow of British goods was interrupted. She profited by it, though only to a relatively small extent because of British policy. Ever since then there has been continuous pressure on the Government to facilitate the growth of Indian industry by removing the various barriers and special interests that come in the way. While apparently accepting this as its policy, the Government has obstructed all real growth, especially of basic industries. Even in the Constitution Act of 1935 it was specifically laid down that Indian legislatures could not interfere with the vested interests of British industry in India. The pre-war years witnessed repeated and vigorous attempts to build up basic and heavy industries, all scotched by official policy. But the most amazing instances of official obstruction have been during the present war, when war needs for production were paramount. Even those vital needs were not sufficient to overcome British dislike of Indian industry. That industry has grown because of the force of events, but its growth is trivial compared to what it could have been or to the growth of industry in many other countries.

The direct opposition of the earlier periods to the growth of Indian industry gave place to indirect methods, which have been equally effective, just as direct tribute gave place to manipulation of customs and excise duties and financial and currency policies, which benefited Britain at the expense of India.

Long subjection of a people and the denial of freedom bring many evils, and perhaps the greatest of these lies in the spiritual sphere—demoralization and sapping of the spirit of the people. It is hard to measure this, though it may be obvious. It is easier to trace and measure the economic decay of a nation, and as we look back on British economic policy in India, it seems that the present poverty of the Indian people is the ineluctable consequence of it. There is no mystery about this poverty; we can see the causes and follow the processes which have led to the present condition.

India Becomes for the First Time a Political and Economic Appendage of Another Country

The establishment of British rule in India was an entirely novel phenomenon for her, not comparable with any other invasion or political or economic change. 'India had been conquered before, but by invaders who settled within her frontiers and made themselves part of her life.' (Like the Normans in England or the Manchus in China.)' She had never lost her independence, never been enslaved. That is to say, she had never been drawn into a political and economic system whose centre of gravity lay outside her soil, never been subjected to a ruling class which was, and which remained, permanently alien in origin and character.'*

Every previous ruling class, whether it had originally come from outside or was indigenous, had accepted the structural unity of India's social and economic life and tried to fit into it. It had become Indianised and had struck roots in the soil of the country. The new rulers were entirely different, with their base elsewhere, and between them and the average Indian there was a vast and

*K. S. Shelvankar: 'The Problem of India' (Penguin Special, London, 1940).

unbridgeable gulf—a difference in tradition, in outlook, in income, and ways of living. The early Britishers in India, rather cut off from England, adopted many Indian ways of living. But it was a superficial approach and even this was deliberately abandoned with the improvement in communications between India and England. It was felt that the British ruling class must maintain its prestige in India by keeping aloof, exclusive, apart from Indians, living in a superior world of its own. There were two worlds: the world of British officials and the world of India's millions, and there was nothing in common between them except a common dislike for each other. Previously races had merged into one another, or at least fitted into an organically interdependent structure. Now racialism became the acknowledged creed and this was intensified by the fact that the dominant race had both political and economic power, without check or hindrance.

The world market that the new capitalism was building up would have, in any event, affected India's economic system. The self-sufficient village community, with its traditional division of labour, could not have continued in its old form. But the change that took place was not a normal development and it disintegrated the whole economic and structural basis of Indian society. A system which had social sanctions and controls behind it and was a part of the people's cultural heritage was suddenly and forcibly changed and another system, administered from outside the group, was imposed. India did not come into a world market but became a colonial and agricultural appendage of the British structure.

The village community, which had so far been the basis of Indian economy, was disintegrated, losing both its economic and administrative functions. In 1830, Sir Charles Metcalfe, one of the ablest of British officials in India, described these communities in words which have often been quoted: 'The village communities are little republics having nearly everything they want within themselves; and almost independent of foreign relations. They seem to last where nothing else lasts. This union of the village communities, each one forming a separate little state in itself...is in a high degree conducive to their happiness, and to the enjoyment of a great portion of freedom and independence.'

The destruction of village industries was a powerful blow to these communities. The balance between industry and agriculture was upset, the traditional division of labour was broken up, and numerous stray individuals could not be easily fitted into any group activity. A more direct blow came from the introduction of the landlord system, changing the whole conception of ownership of land. This conception had been one of communal ownership, not so much of the land as of the produce of the land. Possibly not fully appreciating this, but more probably taking the step deliberately for reasons of their own, the British governors, themselves representing the English landlord class, introduced something resembling the English system in India. At first they appointed revenue-farmers for short terms, that is persons who were made responsible for the collection of the revenue or land tax and payment of it to the Government. Later these revenue-farmers developed into landlords. The village community was deprived of all control over the land and its produce; what had always been considered as the chief interest and concern of that community now became the private property of the newly created landowner. This led to the breakdown of the joint life and corporate character of the community, and the co-operative system of services and functions began to disappear gradually.

The introduction of this type of property in land was not only a great economic change, but it went deeper and struck at the whole Indian conception of a co-operative group social structure. A new class, the owners of land, appeared; a class created by, and therefore to a large extent identified with, the British Government. The break-up of the old system created new problems and probably the beginnings of the new Hindu-Moslem problem can be traced to it. The landlord system was first introduced in Bengal and Bihar where big landowners were created under the system known as the Permanent Settlement. It was later realized that this was not advantageous to the state as the land revenue had been fixed and could not be enhanced. Fresh settlements in other parts of India were therefore made for a period only and enhancements in revenue took place from time to time. In some provinces a kind of peasant proprietorship was established. The extreme rigour applied to the collection of revenue resulted, especially in Bengal, in the ruin of the old landed gentry, and new people from the monied and business classes took their place. Thus Bengal became a province predominantly of Hindu landlords, while their tenants, though both Hindu and Moslem, were chiefly the latter.

Big landowners were created by the British after their own English pattern, chiefly because it was far easier to deal with a few individuals than with a vast peasantry. The objective was to collect as much money in the shape of revenue, and as speedily, as possible. If an owner failed at the stipulated time he was immediately pushed out and another took his place It was also considered necessary to create a class whose interests were identified with the British. The fear of revolt filled the minds of British officials in India and they referred to this repeatedly in their papers. Governor-General Lord William Bentinck said in 1829: 'If security was wanting against extensive popular tumult or revolution, I should say that the Permanent Settlement, though a failure in many other respects, has this great advantage at least, of having created a vast body of rich landed proprietors deeply interested in the continuance of British Dominion and having complete command over the mass of the people.'

British rule thus consolidated itself by creating new classes and vested interests which were tied up with that rule and privileges which depended on its continuance. There were the landowners and the princes, and there was a large number of subordinate members of the services in various departments of government, from the *patwari*, the village head-man, upwards. The two essential branches of government were the revenue system and the police. At the head of both of these in each district was the collector or district magistrate who was the linchpin of the administration. He functioned as an autocrat in his district, combining in himself executive, judicial, revenue, and police functions. If there were any small Indian states adjoining the area under his control, he was also the British agent for them.

Then there was the Indian Army, consisting of British and Indian troops but officered entirely by Englishmen. This was reorganized repeatedly, especially after the mutiny of 1857, and ultimately became organizationally linked up with the British Army. This was so arranged as to balance its different elements and keep the British troops in key positions. 'Next to the grand counterpoise of a sufficient European force comes the counterpoise of natives against natives,' says the official report on reorganization in 1858. The primary function of these forces was to serve as an army of occupation—'Internal Security Troops' they were called, and a majority of these was British. The Frontier Province served as a training ground for the British Army at India's expense. The Field Army (chiefly Indian) was meant for service abroad and it took part in numerous British imperial wars and expeditions, India always bearing the cost. Steps were taken to segregate Indian troops from the rest of the population.

Thus India had to bear the cost of her own conquest, and then of her transfer (or sale) from the East India Company to the British Crown, for the extension of the British Empire to Burma and elsewhere, for expeditions to Africa, Persia, etc., and for her defence against Indians themselves. She was not only used as a base for imperial purposes, without any reimbursement for this, but she had further to pay for the training of part of the British Army in England—'capitation' charges these were called. Indeed India was charged for all manner of other expenses incurred by Britain, such as the maintenance of British diplomatic and consular establishments in China and Persia, the entire cost of the telegraph line from England to India, part of the expenses of the British Mediterranean fleet, and even the receptions given to the Sultan of Turkey in London.

The building of railways in India, undoubtedly desirable and necessary, was done in an enormously wasteful way. The Government of India guaranteed 5 per cent interest on all capital invested and there was no need to check or estimate what was necessary. All purchases were made in England.

The civil establishment of government was also run on a lavish and extravagant scale, all the highly paid positions being reserved for Europeans. The process of Indianization of the administrative machine was very slow and only became noticeable in the twentieth century. This process, far from transferring any power to Indian hands, proved yet another method of strengthening British rule. The really key positions remained in British hands, and Indians in the administration could only function as the agents of British rule.

To all these methods must be added the deliberate policy, pursued throughout the period of British rule, or creating divisions among Indians, of encouraging one group at the cost of another. This policy was openly admitted in the early days of their rule, and indeed it was a natural one for an imperial power. With the growth of the nationalist movement that policy took subtler and more dangerous forms and, though denied, functioned more intensively than ever.

Nearly all our major problems to-day have grown up during British rule and as a direct result of British policy: the princes; the minority problem; various vested interests, foreign and Indian; the lack of industry and the neglect of agriculture; the extreme backwardness in the social services; and, above all, the tragic poverty of the people. The attitude to education has been significant. In Kaye's 'Life of Metcalfe' it is stated that 'this dread of the free diffusion of knowledge became a chronic disease ...continually afflicting the members of Government with all sorts of hypochondriacal day-dreams and nightmares, in which visions of the printing press and the Bible were making their flesh creep, and their hair to stand erect with horror. It was our policy in those days to keep the natives of India in the profoundest state of barbarism and darkness, and every attempt to diffuse the light of knowledge among the people, either of our own or of the independent states, was vehemently opposed and resented.'*

Imperialism must function in this way or else it ceases to be imperialism. The modern type of finance-imperialism added new kinds of economic exploitation which were unknown in earlier ages. The record of British rule in India during the nineteenth century must necessarily depress and anger an Indian, and yet it illustrates the superiority of the British in many fields, not least in their capacity to profit by our disunity and weaknesses. A people who are weak and who are left behind in the march of time invite trouble and ultimately have only themselves to

*Quoted by Edward Thompson, 'The Life of Lord Metcalfe.'

blame. If British imperialism with all its consequences was, in the circumstances, to be expected in the natural order of events, so also was the growth of opposition to it inevitable, and the final crisis between the two.

The Growth of the Indian States System

One of our major problems in India to-day is that of the Princes of the Indian states. These states are unique of their kind in the world and they vary greatly in size and political and social conditions. Their number is 601. About fifteen of these may be considered major states, the biggest of these being Hyderabad, Kashmir, Mysore, Travancore, Baroda, Gwalior, Indore, Cochin, Jaipur, Jodhpur, Bikanir, Bhopal, and Patiala. Then follow a number of middling states and, lastly, several hundreds of very small areas, some not bigger than a pin's point on the map. Most of these tiny states are in Kathiawar, western India, and the Punjab.

These states not only vary in size from that of France to almost that of an average farmer's holding, but also differ in every other way. Mysore is industrially the most advanced; Mysore, Travancore, and Cochin are educationally far ahead of British India.* Most of the states are, however, very backward and some are completely feudal. All of them are autocracies, though some have started elected councils whose powers are strictly limited. Hyderabad, the premier state, still carries on with a typical feudal régime supported by an almost complete denial of civil liberties. So also most of the states in Rajputana and the Punjab. A lack of civil liberties is a common feature of the states.

These states do not form compact blocks; they are spread out all over India, islands surrounded by non-state areas. The vast majority of them are totally unable to support even a semi-independent economy; even the largest, situated as they are, can hardly hope to do so without the full co-operation of the surrounding areas. If there was any economic conflict between a state and non-state India, the former could be easily reduced to submission by tariff barriers and other economic sanctions. It is manifest that both politically and economically these states, even the largest of them, cannot be separated and treated as independent entities. As such they would not survive and the rest of India would also suffer greatly. They would become hostile enclaves all

---

*Travancore, Cochin, Mysore, and Baroda are, from the point of view of popular education, far in advance of British India. In Travancore, it is interesting to note that popular education began to be organized in 1801. (Compare England where it started in 1870.) The literacy percentage in Travancore is now 58 for men and 41 for women; this is over four times higher than the British India percentage. Public health is also better organized in Travancore. Women play an important part in public service and activities in Travancore.

over India, and if they relied on some external power for protection, this in itself would be a continuous and serious menace to a free India. Indeed they would not have survived till to-day but for the fact that politically and economically the whole of India, including the states, is under one dominant power which protects them. Apart from the possible conflicts between a state and non-state India, it must be remembered that there is continuous pressure on the autocratic ruler of the state from his own people, who demand free institutions. Attempts to achieve this freedom are suppressed and kept back with the aid of the British power.

Even in the nineteenth century, these states, as constituted, became anachronisms. Under modern conditions it is impossible to conceive of India being split up into scores of separate independent entities. Not only would there be perpetual conflict but all planned economic and cultural progress would become impossible. We must remember that when these states took shape and entered into treaties with the East India Company, at the beginning of the nineteenth century, Europe was divided up into numerous small principalities. Many wars and revolutions have changed the face of Europe since then and are changing it to-day, but the face of India was set and petrified by external pressure imposed upon it and not allowed to change. It seems absurd to hold up some treaty drawn up 140 years ago, usually on the field of battle or immediately afterwards, between two rival commanders or their chiefs, and to say that this temporary settlement must last for ever. The people of the state of course had no say in that settlement, and the other party at the time was a commercial corporation concerned only with its own interests and profits. This commercial corporation, the East India Company, acted not as the agent of the British Crown or Parliament but, in theory, as the agent of the Delhi Emperor, from whom power and authority were supposed to flow, although he was himself quite powerless. The British Crown or Parliament had nothing whatever to do with these treaties. Parliament only considered Indian affairs when the charter of the East India Company came up for discussion from time to time. The fact that the East India Company was functioning in India under the authority conferred on it by the *Diwani* grant of the Mughal Emperor made it independent of any direct interference by the British Crown or Parliament. Indirectly Parliament could, if it so chose, cancel the charter or impose new conditions at the time of renewal. The idea that the English King or Parliament should even in theory function as agents and therefore as subordinates of the shadowy Emperor at Delhi was not liked in England and so they studiously kept aloof from the activities of the East India Company. The money spent in the Indian wars was Indian money raised and disposed of by the East India Company.

Subsequently, as the territory under the control of the East

India Company increased in area and its rule was consolidated, the British Parliament began to take greater interest in Indian affairs. In 1858, after the shock of the Indian mutiny and revolt, the East India Company transferred its domain of India (for money paid by India) to the British crown. That transfer did not involve a separate transfer of the Indian states apart from the rest of India. The whole of India was treated as a unit and the British Parliament functioned in India through the Government of India which exercised a suzerainty over the states. The states had no separate relations with the British Crown or Parliament. They were part and parcel of the system of government, direct and indirect, represented by the Government of India. This government, in later years, ignored those old treaties whenever it suited its changing policy to do so, and exercised a very effective suzerainty over the states.

Thus the British Crown was not in the picture at all so far as the Indian states were concerned. It is only in recent years that the claim to some kind of independence has been raised on behalf of the states, and it has been further claimed that they have some special relations with the British Crown, apart from the Government of India. These treaties, it should be noted, are with very few of the states; there are only forty treaty states, the rest have 'engagements and sanads.' These forty states have three-fourths of the total Indian state population, and six of them have considerably more than one-third of this population.*

In the Government of India Act of 1935, for the first time, some distinction was made between the relations of the states and the rest of India with the British Parliament. The states were removed from the supervisory authority and direction of the Government of India and placed directly under the Viceroy who, for this purpose, was called the Crown representative. The Viceroy continued to be, at the same time, the head of the Government of India. The political department of the Government of India, which used to be responsible for the states, was now placed directly under the Viceroy and was no longer under his executive council.

How did these states come into existence? Some are quite new, created by the British; others were the vice-royalties of the Mughal Emperor, and their rulers were permitted to continue as feudatory chiefs by the British; yet others, notably the Maratha chiefs, were defeated by British armies and then made into feudatories. Nearly all these can be traced back to the beginnings of British rule; they have no earlier history. If some of them functioned independently for a while, that independence was of brief duration and ended in defeat in war or threat of war. Only a few of the states,

*These six are: Hyderabad, 12-13 million; Mysore, 7½ million; Travancore, 6¼ million; Baroda, 4 million; Kashmir, 3 million; Gwalior, 3 million; totalling over 36 million. The total Indian states population is about 90 million.

and these are chiefly in Rajputana, date back to pre-Mughal times. Travancore has an ancient, 1,000-year-old historical continuity. Some of the proud Rajput clans trace back their genealogy to pre-historic times. The Maharana of Udaipur, of the *Suryavansh* or race of the sun, has a family tree comparable to that of the Mikado of Japan. But these Rajput chiefs became Mughal feudatories and then submitted to the Marathas, and finally to the British. The representatives of the East India Company, writes Edward Thompson, 'now set the princes in their positions, lifting them out of the chaos in which they were submerged. When thus picked up and re-established, "the princes" were as completely helpless and derelict as any powers since the beginning of the world. Had the British Government not intervened, nothing but exstinction lay before the Rajput states, and disintegration before the Maratha states. As for such states as Oudh and the Nizam's dominions, their very existence was bogus; they were kept in a semblance of life, only by means of the breath blown through them by the protecting power.'*

Hyderabad, the premier state to-day, was small, in area to begin with. Its boundaries were extended twice, after Tipu Sultan's defeat by the British and the Maratha wars. These additions were at the instance of the British, and on the express stipulation that the Nizam was to function in a subordinate capacity to them. Indeed, on Tipu's defeat, the offer of part of his territory was first made to the Peshwa, the Maratha leader, but he refused to accept it on those conditions.

Kashmir, the next largest state, was sold by the East India Company after the Sikh wars to the great-grandfather of the present ruler. It was subsequently taken under direct British control on a plea of misgovernment. Later the ruler's powers were restored to them. The present state of Mysore was created by the British after Tipu's wars. It was also under direct British rule for a lengthy period.

The only truly independent kingdom in India is Nepal on the north-eastern frontier, which occupies a position analogous to that of Afghanistan, though it is rather isolated. All the rest came within the scope of what was called the 'subsidiary system,' under which all real power lay with the British Government, exercised through a resident or agent. Often even the ministers of the ruler were British officials imposed upon him. But the entire responsibility for good government and reform lay with the ruler, who with the

*'*The Making of the Indian Princes*', Edward Thompson, pp. 270-1. In this book as well as Thompson's '*Life of Lord Metcalfe*,' there are vivid pictures of Hyderabad and British control and graft there; also of Delhi and Ranjit Singh's Punjab. The Butler Committee (1928-29), appointed by the British Government to consider the problem of the Indian States, said in its report: 'It is not in accordance with historical facts that when the Indian States came into contact with the British power they were independent. Some were rescued, others were created by the British.'

best will in the world (and he usually lacked that will as well as competence) could do little in the circumstances. Henry Lawrence wrote in 1846 about the Indian states system: 'If there was a device for ensuring mal-government it is that of a native ruler and minister both relying on foreign bayonets, and directed by a British Resident; even if all these were able, virtuous, and considerate, still the wheels of government could hardly move smoothly. If it be difficult to select one man, European or native, with all the requisites of a just administrator, where are three who can or will work together to be found? Each of the three may work incalculable mischief, but no one of them *can* do good if thwarted by the other.'

Earlier still, in 1817, Sir Thomas Munro wrote to the Governor-General: 'There are many weighty objections to the employment of a subsidiary force. It has a natural tendency to render the government of every country in which it exists weak and oppressive, to extinguish all honourable spirit among the higher classes of society, and to degrade and impoverish the whole people. The usual remedy of a bad government in India is a quiet revolution in the palace, or a violent one by rebellion or foreign conquests. But the presence of a British force cuts off every chance of remedy, by supporting the prince on the throne against every foreign and domestic enemy. It renders him indolent, by teaching him to trust to strangers for his security, and cruel and avaricious, by showing him that he has nothing to fear from the hatred of his subjects. Wherever the subsidiary system is introduced, unless the reigning prince be a man of great abilities, the country will soon bear the marks of it in decaying villages and decreasing population....Even if the prince himself were disposed to adhere rigidly to the (British) alliance, there will always be some amongst his principal officers who will urge him to break it. As long as there remains in the country any high-minded independence, which seeks to throw off the control of strangers, such counsellors will be found. I have a better opinion of the natives of India than to think that this spirit will ever be completely extinguished; and I can therefore have no doubt that the subsidiary system must everywhere run its full course and destroy every government which it undertakes to protect.'*

In spite of such protests the subsidiary Indian state system was built up, and it brought, inevitably, corruption and tyranny in its train. The governments of these states were often bad enough, but, in any event, they were almost powerless; a few of the British residents or agents in these states, like Metcalfe, were honest and conscientious, but more often they were neither, and they exercised the harlot's privilege of having power without responsibility. Private English adventurers, secure in the knowledge of their race and of official backing, played havoc with the funds of the state. Some of the accounts of what took place in these states during the

*Quoted by Edward Thompson in 'The Making of the Indian Princes' (1943).

311

first half of the nineteenth century, especially in Oudh and Hyderabad, are almost incredible. Oudh was annexed to British India a little before the Mutiny of 1857.

British policy was then in favour of such annexations, and every pretext was taken advantage of for a 'lapse' of the state to British authority. But the Mutiny and great Revolt of 1857 demonstrated the value of the subsidiary state system to the British Government. Except for some minor defections the Indian princes not only remained aloof from the rising, but, in some instances, actually helped the British to crush it. This brought about a change in British policy towards them, and it was decided to keep them and even to strengthen them.

The doctrine of British 'paramountcy' was proclaimed, and in practice the control of the political department of the Government of India over the states has been strict and continuous. Rulers have been removed or deprived of their powers; ministers have been imposed upon them from the British services. Quite a large number of such ministers are functioning now in the states, and they consider themselves answerable far more to British authority than to their nominal head, the prince.

Some of the princes are good, some are bad; even the good ones are thwarted and checked at every turn. As a class they are of necessity backward, feudal in outlook, and authoritarian in methods, except in their dealings with the British Government, when they show a becoming subservience. Shelvankar has rightly called the Indian states 'Britain's fifth column in India.'

Contradictions of British Rule in India
Ram Mohan Roy. The Press
Sir William Jones. English Education in Bengal

One remarkable contradiction meets us at every turn in considering the record of British rule in India. The British became dominant in India, and the foremost power in the world, because they were the heralds of the new big-machine industrial civilization. They represented a new historic force which was going to change the world, and were thus, unknown to themselves, the forerunners and representatives of change and revolution; and yet they deliberately tried to prevent change, except in so far as this was necessary to consolidate their position and help them in exploiting the country and its people to their own advantage. Their outlook and objectives were reactionary, partly because of the background of the social class that came here, but chiefly because of a deliberate desire to check changes in a progressive direction, as these might strengthen the Indian people and thus ultimately weaken the British hold on India. The fear of the people runs through all their thought and policy, for they did not want to and could not merge with them, and were destined to remain an isolated foreign ruling group, surrounded by an entirely different and hostile humanity. Changes, and some in a progressive direction, did came, but they came in spite of British policy, although their impetus was the impact of the new west through the British.

Individual Englishmen, educationists, orientalists, journalists, missionaries, and others played an important part in bringing western culture to India, and in their attempts to do so often came into conflict with their own Government. That Government feared the effects of the spread of modern education and put many obstacles in its way, and yet it was due to the pioneering efforts of able and earnest Englishmen, who gathered enthusiastic groups of Indian students around them, that English thought and literature and political tradition were introduced to India. (When I say Englishmen I include, of course, people from the whole of Great Britain and Ireland, though I know this is improper and incorrect. But I dislike the word Britisher, and even that probably does not include the Irish. My apologies to the Irish, the Scots, and the Welsh. In India they have all functioned alike and have been looked upon as one indistinguishable group.) Even the British Government, in spite of its dislike of education, was compelled by circumstances to arrange for the training and production of clerks for its growing establishment. It could not afford to bring out from England large numbers of people to serve in this subordinate capacity. So education grew slowly and, though it was a limited and perverted education, it opened the doors and windows of the mind to new ideas and dynamic thoughts.

The printing press and indeed all machinery were also considered dangerous and explosive for the Indian mind, not to be encouraged in any way lest they led to the spread of sedition and industrial growth. There is a story that the Nizam of Hyderabad once expressed a desire to see European machinery and thereupon the British Resident procured for him an airpump and a printing press. The Nizam's momentary curiosity having been satisfied, these were stored away with other gifts and curiosities. But when the Government in Calcutta heard of this they expressed their displeasure to their Resident and rebuked him especially for introducing a printing press in an Indian state. The Resident offered to get it broken up secretly if the Government so desired.

But while private printing presses were not encouraged, Government could not carry on its work without printing, and official presses were therefore started in Calcutta and Madras and elsewhere.

The first private printing press was started by the Baptist missionaries in Serampore, and the first newspaper was started by an Englishman in Calcutta in 1780.

All these and other like changes crept in gradually, influencing the Indian mind and giving rise to the 'modern' consciousness.

Only a small group was directly influenced by the thought of Europe, for India clung to her own philosophic background, considering it superior to that of the west. The real impact and influence of the west were on the practical side of life which was obviously superior to the eastern. The new techniques—the railway train, the printing press, other machinery, more efficient ways of warfare—could not be ignored, and these came up against old methods of thought almost unawares, by indirect approaches, creating a conflict in the mind of India. The most obvious and far-reaching change was the break-up of the agrarian system and the introduction of conceptions of private property and land-lordism. Money economy had crept in and 'land became a market-able commodity. What had once been held rigid by custom was dissolved by money.'

Bengal witnessed and experienced all these agrarian, technical, educational, and intellectual changes long before any other consi-derable part of India, for Bengal had a clear half-century of British rule before it spread over wider areas. During the second half of the eighteenth century and the first half of the nineteenth, Bengal therefore played a dominant role in British Indian life. Not only was Bengal the centre and heart of the British administration, but it also produced the first groups of English-educated Indians who spread out to other parts of India under the shadow of the British power. A number of very remarkable men rose in Bengal in the nineteenth century, who gave the lead to the rest of India in cultural and political matters, and out of whose efforts the new nationalist movement ultimately took shape. Bengal not only had a much longer acquaintance with British rule but it experienced it in its earliest phases when it was both harsher and more exuberant, more fluid and less set in rigid frames. It had accepted that rule, adapted itself to it, long before northern and central India submitted. The great Revolt of 1857 had little effect on Bengal, although the first spark appeared accidentally at Barrackpore near Calcutta.

Previous to British rule Bengal had been an outlying province of the Mughal Empire, important but still rather cut off from the centre. During the early mediæval period many debased forms of worship and of Tantric philosophy and practices had flourished among the Hindus there. Then came many Hindu reform move-ments affecting social customs and laws and even changing some-what the well-recognized rules of inheritance elsewhere. Chaitanya, a great scholar who became a man of faith and emotion, establish-ed a form of Vaishnavism, based on faith, and influenced greatly the people of Bengal. The Bengalis developed a curious mixture of high intellectual attainments and equally strong emotionalism. This tradition of loving faith and service of humanity was repre-sented in Bengal in the second half of the nineteenth century by another remarkable man of saintly character, Ramakrishna

Paramahansa; in his name an order of service was established which has an unequalled record in humanitarian relief and social work. Full of the ideal of the patient loving service of the Franciscans of old, and quiet unostentatious, efficient, rather like the Quakers, the members of the Ramakrishna Mission carry on their hospitals and educational establishments and engage in relief work, whenever any calamity occurs, all over India and even outside.

Ramakrishna represented the old Indian tradition. Before him, in the eighteenth century, another towering personality had risen in Bengal, Raja Ram Mohan Roy, who was a new type combining in himself the old learning and the new. Deeply versed in Indian thought and philosophy, a scholar in Sanskrit, Persian, and Arabic, he was a product of the mixed Hindu-Moslem culture that was then dominant among the cultured classes of India. The coming of the British to India and their superiority in many ways led his curious and adventurous mind to find out what their cultural roots were. He learnt English but this was not enough; he learnt Greek, Latin, and Hebrew also to discover the sources of the religion and culture of the west. He was also attracted by science and the technical aspects of western civilization, though at that time these technical changes were not so obvious as they subsequently became. Being of a philosophical and scholarly bent, Ram Mohan Roy inevitably went to the older literatures. Describing him, Monier-Williams, the Orientalist, has said that he was 'perhaps the first earnest-minded investigator of the science of Comparative Religion that the world has produced'; and yet, at the same time, he was anxious to modernize education and take it out of the grip of the old scholasticism. Even in those early days he was in favour of the scientific method, and he wrote to the Governor-General emphasizing the need for education in 'mathematics, natural philosophy, chemistry, anatomy, and other useful sciences.'

He was more than a scholar and an investigator; he was a reformer above all. Influenced in his early days by Islam and later, to some extent, by Christianity, he stuck nevertheless to the foundations of his own faith. But he tried to reform that faith and rid it of abuses and the evil practices that had become associated with it. It was largely because of his agitation for the abolition of *suttee* that the British Government prohibited it. This *suttee*, or the immolation of women on the funeral pyre of their husbands, was never widespread. But rare instances continued to occur among the upper classes. Probably the practice was brought to India originally by the Scytho-Tartars, among whom the custom prevailed of vassals and liegemen killing themselves on the death of their lord. In early Sanskrit literature the *suttee* custom is denounced. Akbar tried hard to stop it, and the Marathas also were opposed to it.

Ram Mohan Roy was one of the founders of the Indian press.

From 1780 onwards a number of newspapers had been published by Englishmen in India. These were usually very critical of the Government and led to conflict and the establishment of a strict censorship. Among the earliest champions of the freedom of the press in India were Englishmen and one of them, James Silk Buckingham, who is still remembered, was deported from the country. The first Indian owned and edited newspaper was issued (in English) in 1818, and in the same year the Baptist missionaries of Serampore brought out a Bengali monthly and a weekly, the first periodicals published in an Indian language. Newspapers and periodicals in English and the Indian languages followed in quick succession in Calcutta, Madras, and Bombay.

Meanwhile the struggle for a free press had already begun, to continue with many ups and downs till to-day. The year 1818 also saw the birth of the famous Regulation III, which provided for the first time for detention without trial. This regulation is still in force to-day, and a number of people are kept in prison under this 126-year-old decree.

Ram Mohan Roy was associated with several newspapers. He brought out a bi-lingual, Bengali-English magazine, and later, desiring an all-India circulation, he published a weekly in Persian, which was recognized then as the language of the cultured classes all over India. But this came to grief soon after the enactment in 1823 of new measures for the control of the press. Ram Mohan and others protested vigorously against these measures and even addressed a petition to the King-in-Council in England.

Ram Mohan Roy's journalist activities were intimately connected with his reform movements. His synthetic and universalist points of view were resented by orthodox sections who also opposed many of the reforms he advocated. But he also had staunch supporters, among them the Tagore family which played an outstanding part later in the renaissance in Bengal. Ram Mohan went to England on behalf of the Delhi Emperor and died in Bristol in the early thirties of the nineteenth century.

Ram Mohan Roy and others studied English privately. There were no English schools or colleges outside Calcutta and the Government's policy was definitely opposed to the teaching of English to Indians. In 1781, the Calcutta Madrasa was started by the Government in Calcutta for Arabic studies. In 1817, a group of Indians and Europeans started the Hindu College in Calcutta, now called the Presidency College. In 1791, a Sanskrit College was started in Benares. Probably in the second decade of the nineteenth century some missionary schools were teaching English. During the twenties a school of thought arose in government circles in favour of the teaching of English, but this was opposed. However, as an experimental measure some English classes were attached to the Arabic school in Delhi and to some institutions in

Calcutta. The final decision in favour of the teaching of English was embodied in Macaulay's Minute on Education of February, 1835. In 1857, the Universities of Calcutta, Madras and Bombay began their career.

If the British Government in India was reluctant to teach English to Indians, Brahmin scholars objected even more, but for different reasons, to teach Sanskrit to Englishmen. When Sir William Jones, already a linguist and a scholar, came to India as a judge of the Supreme Court, he expressed his desire to learn Sanskrit. But no Brahmin would agree to teach the sacred language to a foreigner and an intruder, even though handsome rewards were offered. Jones ultimately, with considerable difficulty, got hold of a non-Brahmin Vaidya or medical practitioner who agreed to teach, but on his own peculiar and stringent conditions. Jones agreed to every stipulation, so great was his eagerness to learn the ancient language of India. Sanskrit fascinated him and especially the discovery of the old Indian drama. It was through his writings and translations that Europe first had a glimpse of some of the treasures of Sanskrit literature. In 1784 Sir William Jones established the Bengal Asiatic Society which later became the Royal Asiatic Society. To Jones, and to the many other European scholars, India owes a deep debt of gratitude for the rediscovery of her past literature. Much of it was known of course throughout every age, but the knowledge had become more and more confined to select and exclusive groups, and the dominance of Persian, as the language of culture, had diverted people's minds from it. The search for manuscripts brought out many a little-known work and the application of modern critical methods of scholarship gave a new background to the vast literature that was revealed.

The advent and use of the printing press gave a great stimulus to the development of the popular Indian languages. Some of these languages—Hindi, Bengali, Gujrati, Marathi, Urdu, Tamil, Telugu—had not only long been in use, but had also developed literatures. Many of the books in them were widely known among the masses. Almost always these books were epic in form, poems, or collection of songs and verses, which could easily be memorized. There was practically no prose literature in them at the time. Serious writing was almost confined to Sanskrit and Persian, and every cultured person was supposed to know one of them. These two classical languages played a dominating role and prevented the growth of the popular provincial languages. The printing of books and newspapers broke the hold of the classics and immediately prose literatures in the provincial languages began to develop. The early Christian missionaries, especially of the Baptist mission at Serampore, helped in this process greatly. The first private printing presses were set up by them and their efforts to translate the Bible into prose versions of the Indian languages met with considerable success.

There was no difficulty in dealing with the well-known and established languages, but the missionaries went further and tackled some of the minor and undeveloped languages and gave them shape and form, compiling grammars and dictionaries for them. They even laboured at the dialects of the primitive hill and forest tribes and reduced them to writing. The desire of the Christian missionaries to translate the Bible into every possible language thus resulted in the development of many Indian languages. Christian mission work in India has not always been admirable or praiseworthy, but in this respect, as well as in the collection of folklore, it has undoubtedly been of great service to India.

The reluctance of the East India Company to spread education was justified, for as early as 1830 a batch of students of the Hindu College of Calcutta (where Sanskrit and English were taught) demanded certain reforms. They asked for restrictions on the political power of the company and provision for free and compulsory education. Free education was well-known in India from the most ancient times. That education was traditional, not very good or profitable, but it was available to poor students without any payment, except some personal service to the teacher. In this respect both the Hindu and Moslem traditions were similar.

While the new education was deliberately prevented from spreading, the old education had been largely liquidated in Bengal. When the British seized power in Bengal there were a very large number of *muafis*, that is tax-free grants of land. Many of these were personal, but most were in the shape of endowments for educational institutions. A vast number of elementary schools of the old type subsisted on them, as well as some institutions for higher education, which was chiefly imparted in Persian. The East India Company was anxious to make money rapidly in order to pay dividends to its shareholders in England, and the demands of its directors were continuous and pressing. A deliberate policy was therefore adopted to resume and confiscate these *muafi* lands. Strict proof was demanded of the original grant, but the old *sanads* and papers had long been lost or eaten up by termites; so the *muafis* were resumed and the old holders were ejected, and the schools and colleges lost their endowments. Huge areas were involved in this way and many old families were ruined. The educational establishments, which had been supported by these *muafis*, ceased to function, and a vast number of teachers and others connected with them were thrown out of employment.

This process helped in ruining the old feudal classes in Bengal, both Moslem and Hindu, as well as those classes who were dependent on them. Moslems were especially affected as they were, as a group, more feudal than the Hindus and were also the chief beneficiaries of the *muafis*. Among the Hindus there were far larger

318

numbers of middle class people engaged in trade and commerce and the professions. These people were more adaptable and took to English education more readily. They were also more useful to the British for their subordinate services. Moslems avoided English education and, in Bengal, they were not looked upon with favour by the British rulers, who were afraid that the remnants of the old ruling class might give trouble. Bengali Hindus thus acquired almost a monopoly in the beginning in the subordinate government service and were sent to the northern provinces. A few Moslems, relics of the old families, were later taken into this service.

English education brought a widening of the Indian horizon, an admiration for English literature and institutions, a revolt against some customs and aspects of Indian life, and a growing demand for political reform. The new professional classes took the lead in political agitation, which consisted chiefly in sending representations to Government. English-educated people in the professions and the services formed in effect a new class, which was to grow all over India, a class influenced by western thought and ways and rather cut off from the mass of the population. In 1852 the British Indian Association was started in Calcutta. This was one of the forerunners of the Indian National Congress, and yet a whole generation was to pass before the Congress was started in 1885. This gap represents the period of the Revolt of 1857-58, its suppression and its consequences. The great difference between the state of Bengal and that of northern and central India in the middle of the century is brought out by the fact that while in Bengal the new intelligentsia (chiefly Hindu) had been influenced by English thought and literature and looked to England for political constitutional reform, the other areas were seething with the spirit of revolt.

In Bengal one can see more clearly than elsewhere the early effects of British rule and western influence. The break-up of the agrarian economy was complete and the old feudal classes had almost been eliminated. In their place had come new land-owners whose organic and traditional contacts with the land were far less, and who had few of the virtues and most of the failings of the old feudal landlords. The peasantry suffered famine and spoliation in many ways and were reduced to extreme poverty. The artisan class was almost wiped out. Over these disjointed and broken-up foundations rose new groups and classes, the products of British rule and connected with it in many ways. There were the merchants who were really middlemen of British trade and industry, profiting by the leavings of that industry. There were also the English-educated classes in the subordinate services and the learned professions, both looking to the British power for advancement and both influenced in varying degrees by western thought. Among these grew up a spirit of revolt against the rigid conventions and social framework of Hindu society. They looked to English liberalism and institutions for inspiration.

This was the effect on the upper fringe of the Hindus of Bengal. The mass of the Hindus there were not directly affected and even the Hindu leaders probably seldom thought of the masses. The Moslems were not affected at all, some individuals apart, and they kept deliberately aloof from the new education. They had been previously backward economically and they became even more so. The nineteenth century produced a galaxy of brilliant Hindus in Bengal, and yet there is hardly a single Moslem Bengali leader of any note who stands out there during this period. So far as the masses were concerned there was hardly any appreciable difference between the Hindus and Moslems; they were indistinguishable in habits, ways of living, language, and in their common poverty and misery. Indeed, nowhere in India were the religious and other differences between Hindus and Moslems of all classes so little marked as in Bengal. Probably 98 per cent of the Moslems were converts from Hinduism, usually from the lowest strata of society. In population figures there was probably a slight majority of Moslems over Hindus. (To-day the proportions in Bengal are: 53 per cent Moslems, 46 per cent Hindus, 1 per cent others.)

All these early consequences of the British connection, and the various economic, social, intellectual, and political movements that they gave rise to in Bengal, are noticeable elsewhere in India, but in lesser and varying degrees. The break-up of the old feudal order and economy was less complete and more gradual elsewhere. In fact that order rose in rebellion and even when crushed, survived to some extent. The Moslems in upper India were culturally and economically far superior to their co-religionists of Bengal, but even they kept aloof from western education.

The Hindus took to this education more easily and were more influenced by western ideas. The subordinate Government services and the professions had far more Hindus than Moslems. Only in the Punjab this difference was less marked.

The Revolt of 1857-58 flared up and was crushed, but Bengal was hardly touched by it. Throughout the nineteenth century the new English-educated class, mainly Hindu, looked up with admiration towards England and hoped to advance with her help and in co-operation with her. There was a cultural renaissance and a remarkable growth of the Bengali language, and the leaders of Bengal stood out as the leaders of political India.

Some glimpse of that faith in England which filled the mind of Bengal in those days, as well as of the revolt against old-established social codes, may be had from that moving message of Rabindranath Tagore, which he gave on his eightieth birth-day (May, 1941), a few months before his death. 'As I look back,' he says, 'on the vast stretch of years that lie behind me and see in clear perspective

the history of my early development, I am struck by the change
that has taken place both in my own attitude and in the psychology
of my countrymen—a change that carries within it a cause of
profound tragedy.

'Our direct contact with the larger world of men was linked
up with the contemporary history of the English people whom
we came to know in those earlier days. It was mainly through
their mighty literature that we formed our ideas with regard to
these newcomers to our Indian shores. In those days the type of
learning that was served out to us was neither plentiful nor
diverse, nor was the spirit of scientific inquiry very much in
evidence. Thus their scope being strictly limited, the educated
of those days had recourse to English language and literature.
Their days and nights were eloquent with the stately declama-
tions of Burke, with Macaulay's long-rolling sentences; discussions centred upon Shakespeare's drama and Byron's poetry and
above all upon the large-hearted liberalism of the nineteenth
century English politics.

'At the time though tentative attempts were being made to
gain our national independence, at heart we had not lost faith
in the generosity of the English race. This belief was so firmly
rooted in the sentiments of our leaders as to lead them to hope
that the victor would of his own grace pave the path to freedom
for the vanquished. This belief was based upon the fact that
England at the time provided a shelter to all those who had to
flee from persecution in their own country. Political martyrs
who had suffered for the honour of their people were accorded
unreserved welcome at the hands of the English. I was impressed
by this evidence of liberal humanity in the character of the
English and thus I was led to set them on the pedestal of my
highest respect. This generosity in their national character had
not yet been vitiated by imperialist pride. About this time, as a
boy in England, I had the opportunity of listening to the speeches
of John Bright, both in and outside Parliament. The large-hearted
radical liberalism of those speeches, overflowing all narrow national
bounds, had made so deep an impression on my mind that something of it lingers even to-day, even in these days of graceless
disillusionment.

'Certainly that spirit of abject dependence upon the charity
of our rulers was no matter of pride. What was remarkable,
however, was the whole-hearted way in which we gave our recognition to human greatness even when it revealed itself in
the foreigner. The best and noblest gifts of humanity cannot be
the monopoly of a particular race or country; its scope may
not be limited nor may it be regarded as the miser's hoard
buried underground. That is why English literature which
nourished our minds in the past, does even now convey its deep

321

resonance to the recesses of our heart.'

Tagore proceeds to refer to the Indian ideal of proper conduct prescribed by the tradition of the race. 'Narrow in themselves these time-honoured social conventions originated and held good in a circumscribed geographical area, in that strip of land, Brahmavarta by name, bound on either side by the rivers Saraswati and Drisadvati. That is how a pharisaic formalism gradually got the upper hand of free thought and the idea "proper conduct" which Manu found established in Brahmavarta steadily degenerated into socialized tyranny.

'During my boyhood days the attitude of the cultured and educated section of Bengal, nurtured on English learning, was charged with a feeling of revolt against these rigid regulations of society....In place of these set codes of conduct we accepted the ideal of "civilization" as represented by the English term.

'In our own family this change of spirit was welcomed for the sake of its sheer rational and moral force and its influence was felt in every sphere of our life. Born in that atmosphere, which was moreover coloured by our intuitive bias for literature, I naturally set the English on the throne of my heart. Thus passed the first chapters of my life. Then came the parting of ways, accompanied with a painful feeling of disillusion, when I began increasingly to discover how easily those who accepted the highest truths of civilization disowned them with impunity whenever questions of national self-interest were involved.'

The Great Revolt of 1857. Racialism

After nearly a century of British rule, Bengal had accommodated itself to it; the peasantry devastated by famine and crushed by new economic burdens, the new intelligentsia looking to the west and hoping that progress would come through English liberalism. So also, more or less in the south and in western India, in Madras and Bombay. But in the upper provinces there was no such submission or accommodation and the spirit of revolt was growing, especially among the feudal chiefs and their followers. Even in the masses discontent and an intense anti-British feeling were widespread. The upper classes keenly resented the insulting and overbearing manners of the foreigners, the people generally suffered from the rapacity and ignorance of the officials of the East India Company, who ignored their time-honoured customs and paid no heed to what the people of the country thought. Absolute power over vast numbers of people had turned their heads and they suffered no check or hindrance. Even the new judicial system they introduced became a thing of terror because of its complications and the ignorance of the judges of both the language and customs of the country.

As early as 1817, Sir Thomas Munro, writing to the Governor-General, Lord Hastings, after pointing out the advantages of British rule, said: 'but these advantages are dearly bought. They are purchased by the sacrifice of independence, of national character, and of whatever renders a people respectable....The consequence, therefore, of the conquest of India by the British arms would be, in place of raising, to debase a whole people. There is perhaps no example of any conquest in which the natives have been so completely excluded from all share of the government of their country as in British India.'

Munro was pleading for the employment of Indians in the administration. A year later he wrote again: 'Foreign conquerors have treated the natives with violence, and often with great cruelty, but none has treated them with so much scorn as we; none has stigmatized the whole people as unworthy of trust, as incapable of honesty, and as fit to be employed only where we cannot do without them. It seems to be not only ungenerous, but impolitic, to debase the character of a people fallen under our dominion.'*

British dominion was extended to the Punjab by 1850 after two Sikh wars. Maharaja Ranjit Singh, who had held and extended the Sikh state in the Punjab, had died in 1839. In 1856 Oudh was annexed. Oudh had been virtually under British rule for half a century, for it was a vassal state, its nominal ruler being both helpless and degenerate, and the British Resident all-powerful. It had sunk to the very depths of misery and illustrated all the evils of the subsidiary state system.

In May, 1857, the Indian army at Meerut mutinied. The revolt had been secretly and well organized but a premature outburst rather upset the plans of the leaders. It was much more than a military mutiny and it spread rapidly and assumed the character of a popular rebellion and a war of Indian independence. As such a popular rebellion of the masses it was confined to Delhi, the United Provinces (as they are now called), and parts of central India and Bihar. Essentially it was a feudal outburst, headed by feudal chiefs and their followers and aided by the widespread anti-foreign sentiment. Inevitably it looked up to the relic of the Mughal dynasty, still sitting in the Delhi palace, but feeble and old and powerless. Both Hindus and Moslems took full part in the Revolt.

This Revolt strained British rule to the utmost and it was ultimately suppressed with Indian help. It brought out all the inherent weaknesses of the old regime, which was making its last despairing effort to drive out foreign rule. The feudal chiefs had the sympathy of the masses over large areas, but they were incapable, unorganized and with no constructive ideal or com-

*Quoted by Edward Thompson in 'The Making of the Indian Princes' (1943).

munity of interest. They had already played their role in history and there was no place for them in the future. Many of their number, in spite of their sympathies, thought discretion the better part of valour, and stood apart waiting to see on which side victory lay. Many played the part of quislings. The Indian princes as a whole kept aloof or helped the British, fearing to risk what they had acquired or managed to retain. There was hardly any national and unifying sentiment among the leaders and a mere anti-foreign feeling, coupled with a desire to maintain their feudal privileges, was a poor substitute for this.

The British got the support of the Gurkhas and, what is much more surprising, of the Sikhs also, for the Sikhs had been their enemies and had been defeated by them only a few years before. It is certainly to the credit of the British that they could win over the Sikhs in this way; whether it is to the credit or discredit of the Sikhs of those days depends upon one's point of view. It is clear, however, that there was a lack of nationalist feeling which might have bound the people of India together. Nationalism of the modern type was yet to come; India had still to go through much sorrow and travail before she learnt the lesson which would give her real freedom. Not by fighting for a lost cause, the feudal order, would freedom come.

The Revolt threw up some fine guerrilla leaders. Feroz Shah, a relative of Bahadur Shah, of Delhi, was one of them, but, most brilliant of all was Tantia Topi who harassed the British for many months even when defeat stared him in the face. Ultimately when he crossed the Narbada river into the Maratha regions, hoping to receive aid and welcome from his own people, there was no welcome, and he was betrayed. One name stands out above others and is revered still in popular memory, the name of Lakshmi Bai, Rani of Jhansi, a girl of twenty years of age, who died fighting. 'Best and bravest' of the rebel leaders, she was called by the English general who opposed her.

British memorials of the Mutiny have been put up in Cawnpore and elsewhere. There is no memorial for the Indians who died. The rebel Indians sometimes indulged in cruel and barbarous behaviour; they were unorganized, suppressed, and often angered by reports of British excesses. But there is another side to the picture also that impressed itself on the mind of India, and in my own province especially the memory of it persists in town and village. One would like to forget all this, for it is a ghastly and horrible picture showing man at his worst, even according to the new standards of barbarity set up by nazism and modern war. But it can only be forgotten, or remembered in a detached impersonal way, when it becomes truly the past with nothing to connect it with the present. So long as the connecting links and reminders are present, and the spirit behind those events survives and shows itself, that memory also will endure and influence our people. Attempts to suppress that picture do not destroy it but drive it deeper in the mind. Only by dealing with it normally can its effect be lessened.

A great deal of false and perverted history has been written about the Revolt and its suppression. What the Indians think about it seldom finds its way to the printed page. Savarkar wrote 'The History of the War of Indian Independence' some thirty years ago, but his book was promptly banned and is banned still. Some frank and honourable English historians have occasionally lifted the veil and allowed us a glimpse of the race mania and lynching mentality which prevailed on an enormous scale. The accounts given in Kaye and Malleson's 'History of the Mutiny' and in Thompson and Garrett's 'Rise and Fulfilment of British Rule in India' make one sick with horror. 'Every Indian who was not actually fighting for the British became a "murderer of women and children"... a general massacre of the inhabitants of Delhi, a large number of whom were known to wish us success, was openly proclaimed.' The days of Timur and Nadir Shah were remembered, but their exploits were eclipsed by the new terror, both in extent and the length of time it lasted. Looting was officially allowed for a week, but it actually lasted for a month, and it was accompanied by wholesale massacre.

In my own city and district of Allahabad and in the neighbourhood, General Neill held his 'Bloody Assizes.' 'Soldiers and civilians alike were holding Bloody Assize, or slaying natives without any assize at all, regardless of age or sex. It is on the records of our British Parliament, in papers sent home by the Governor-General in Council, that "the aged, women, and children are sacrificed as well as those guilty of rebellion." They were not deliberately hanged, but burnt to death in villages—perhaps now and then accidentally shot.' 'Volunteer hanging parties went into the districts and amateur executioners were not wanting to the occasion. One gentleman boasted of the numbers he had finished off quite "in an artistic manner," with mango trees as gibbets and elephants for drops, the victims of this wild justice being strung up, as though for pastime, in the form of figures of eight.' And so in Cawnpore and Lucknow and all over the place.

It is hateful to have to refer to this past history, but the spirit behind those events did not end with them. It survived, and whenever a crisis comes or nerves give way, it is in evidence again. The world knows about Amritsar and Jallianwala Bagh, but it does not know of much that has happened since the days of the Mutiny, much that has taken place even in recent years and in our time, which has embittered the present generation. Imperialism and the domination of one people over another is bad, and so is racialism. But imperialism plus racialism can only lead to horror and ultimately to the degradation of all concerned with them. The future historians of England will have to consider how far England's decline from her proud eminence was due to her imperialism and racialism, which corrupted her public life and made her forget the lessons of her own history and literature.

Since Hitler emerged from obscurity and became the Fuehrer of Germany, we have heard a great deal about racialism and the nazi theory of the herrenvolk. That doctrine has been condemned and is to-day condemned by the leaders of the United Nations. Biologists tell us that racialism is a myth and there is no such thing as a master race. But we in India have known racialism in all its forms ever since the commencement of British rule. The whole ideology of this rule was that of the herrenvolk and the master race, and the structure of government was based upon it; indeed the idea of a master race is inherent in imperialism. There was no subterfuge about it; it was proclaimed in unambiguous language by those in authority. More powerful than words was the practice that accompanied them and, generation after generation and year after year, India as a nation and Indians as individuals were subjected to insult, humiliation, and contemptuous treatment. The English were an imperial race, we were told, with the god-given right to govern us and keep us in subjection; if we protested we were reminded of the 'tiger qualities of an imperial race.' As an Indian, I am ashamed to write all this, for the memory of it hurts, and what hurts still more is the fact that we submitted for so long to this degradation. I would have preferred any kind of resistance to this, whatever the consequences, rather than that our people should endure this treatment. And yet it is better that both Indians and Englishmen should know it, for that is the psychological background of England's connection with India, and psychology counts and racial memories are long.

One rather typical quotation will make us realize how most of the English in India have felt and acted. At the time of the Ilbert Bill agitation in 1883, Seton Kerr, who had been Foreign Secretary to the Government of India, declared that this Bill outraged 'the cherished conviction which was shared by every Englishman in India, from the highest to the lowest, by the planter's assistant in his lowly bungalow and by the editor in the full light of the Presidency town—from those to the Chief Commissioner in charge of an important province and to the Viceroy on his throne—the conviction in every man that he belongs to a race whom God has destined to govern and subdue.'*

*Quoted in 'Rise and Fulfilment of British Rule in India', Edward Thompson and G. T. Garrett (London, 1935).

The Techniques of British Rule: Balance and Counterpoise

The Revolt of 1857-58 was essentially a feudal rising, though there were some nationalistic elements in it. Yet, at the same time, it was due to the abstention or active help of the princes and other feudal chiefs that the British succeeded in crushing it. Those who had joined the Revolt were as a rule the disinherited and those deprived of their power and privileges by the British authority, or those who feared that some such fate was in store for them. British policy after some hesitation had decided in favour of a gradual elimination of the princes and the establishment of direct British rule. The Revolt brought about a change in this policy in favour not only of the princes but of the taluqdars or big landlords. It was felt that it was easier to control the masses through these feudal or semi-feudal chiefs. These taluqdars of Oudh had been the tax-farmers of the Mughals but, owing to the weakness of the central authority, they had begun to function as feudal landlords. Nearly all of them joined the Revolt, though some took care to keep a way of escape open. In spite of their rebellion the British authority offered to reinstate them (with a few exceptions) and confirm them in their estates on conditions of 'loyalty and good service.' Thus these taluqdars, who take pride in calling themselves the 'Barons of Oudh,' became one of the pillars of British rule.

Though the Revolt had directly affected only certain parts of the country, it had shaken up the whole of India and, particularly, the British administration. The Government set about reorganizing their entire system; the British Crown, that is the Parliament, took over the country from the East India Company; the Indian army, which had begun the Revolt by its mutiny, was organized afresh. The techniques of British rule, which had already been well-established, were now clarified and confirmed and deliberately acted upon. Essentially these were: the creation and protection of vested interests bound up with British rule; a policy of balancing and counterpoise of different elements, and the encouragement of fissiparous tendencies and division amongst them.

The princes and the big landlords were the basic vested interests thus created and encouraged; but now a new class, even more tied up with British rule, grew in importance. This consisted of the Indian members of the services, usually in subordinate positions. Previously the employment of Indians had been avoided except when this could not be helped, and Munro had pleaded for such employment. Experience had now demonstrated that Indians employed were so dependent on the British administration and rule that they could be relied upon and treated as agents of that rule. In the pre-mutiny days most of the Indian members of the subordinate services had been Bengalis. These had spread out over the upper provinces wherever the British administration needed clerks and the like in its civil or military establishments. Regular colonies of Bengalis had thus grown up at the administrative or military centres in the United Provinces, Delhi, and even in the Punjab. These Bengalis accompanied the British armies and proved faithful employees to them. They became associated in the minds of the rebels with the British power and were greatly disliked by them and given uncomplimentary titles.

Thus began the process of the Indianization of the administrative machine in its subordinate ranks, all real power and initiative being, however, concentrated in the hands of the English personnel. As English education spread, the Bengalis had no longer a virtual monopoly of service and other Indians came in, both on the judicial and executive sides of the administration. This Indianization became the most effective method of strengthening British rule. It created a civil army and garrison everywhere, which was more important even than the military army of occupation. There were some members of this civil army who were able and patriotic and nationalistically inclined, but like the soldier, who also may be patriotic in his individual capacity, they were bound up by the army code and discipline, and the price of disobedience, desertion, and revolt was heavy. Not only was this civil army created but the hope and prospect of employment in it affected and demoralized a vast and growing number of others. There was a measure of prestige and security in it and a pension at the end of the term of service, and if a sufficient subservience was shown to one's superior officers, other failings did not count. These civil employees were the intermediaries between the British authorities and the people, and if they had to be obsequious to their superiors they could be arrogant to and exact obedience from their own inferiors and the people at large.

The lack of other avenues of employment, other ways of making a living, added additional importance to government service. A few could become lawyers or doctors, but even so, success was by no means assured. Industry hardly existed. Trade was largely in the hands of certain hereditary classes who had a peculiar aptitude for it and who helped each other. The new education did not fit anyone for trade or industry; its chief aim was government service. Education was so limited as to offer few openings for a professional career; other social services were almost non-existent. So government service remained and, as the colleges poured out their graduates; even the growing government services could not absorb them all, and a fierce competition arose. The unemployed graduates and others formed a pool from which government could always draw; they were a potential threat to the security of even the employed. Thus the British Government in India became, not only the biggest employer, but, for all practical purposes, the sole big employer (including railways), and a vast bureaucratic machine was built up, strictly managed and controlled at the top. This enormous patronage was exercised to strengthen the British hold on the country, to crush discordant and disagreeable elements, and to promote rivalry and discord amongst various groups anxiously looking forward to employment in government service. It led to demoralization and conflict, and the government could play one group against the other.

The policy of balance and counterpoise was deliberately furthered in the Indian army. Various groups were so arranged as to prevent any sentiment of national unity growing up amongst them, and tribal and communal loyalties and slogans were encouraged. Every effort was made to isolate the army from the people and even ordinary newspapers were not allowed to reach the Indian troops. All the key positions were kept in the hands of Englishmen and no Indian could hold the King's commission. A raw English subaltern was senior to the oldest and most experienced Indian non-commissioned officer or those holding the so-called Viceroy's commissions. No Indian could be employed at army headquarters except as a petty clerk in the accounts department. For additional protection the more effective weapons of warfare were not given to the Indian forces; they were reserved for the British troops in India. These British troops were always kept with the Indian regiments in all the vital centres of India to serve as 'Internal Security Troops' for suppression of disorder and to overawe the people. While this internal army, with a predominance of British personnel, served as an army of occupation for the country, the greater portion of the Indian troops were part of the field army organized for service abroad. The Indian troops were recruited from special classes only, chiefly in northern India, which were called martial classes.

Again we notice in India that inherent contradiction in British rule. Having brought about the political unification of the country and thus let loose new dynamic forces which thought not only in terms of that unity, but aimed at the freedom of India, the British Government tried to disrupt that very unity it had helped to create. That disruption was not thought of in political terms then as a splitting up of India; it was aimed at the weakening of nationalist elements so that British rule might continue over the whole country. But it was nonetheless an attempt at disruption, by giving greater importance to the Indian states than they had ever had before, by encouraging reactionary elements and looking to them for support, by promoting divisions and encouraging one group against another, by encouraging fissiparous tendencies due to religion or province, and by organizing quisling classes which were afraid of a change which might engulf them. All this was a natural understandable policy for a foreign imperialist power to pursue, and it is a little naive to be surprised at it, harmful from the Indian nationalist point of view though it was. But the fact that it was so must be remembered if we are to understand subsequent developments. Out of this policy arose those 'important elements in India's national life' of which we are reminded so often to-day; which were created and encouraged to disagree and disrupt, and are now called upon to agree among themselves.

Because of this natural alliance of the British power with the reactionaries in India, it became the guardian and upholder of many an evil custom and practice which it otherwise condemned. India was custom-ridden when the British came, and the tyranny of old custom is often a terrible thing. Yet customs change and are forced to adapt themselves to some extent to a changing environment. Hindu law was largely custom, and as custom changed the law also was applied in a different way. Indeed, there was no provision of Hindu law which could not be changed by custom. The British replaced this elastic customary law by judicial decisions based on the old texts, and these decisions became precedents which had to be rigidly followed. That was, in theory, an advantage, as it produced greater uniformity and certainty. But, in the manner it was done, it resulted in the perpetuation of the ancient law unmodified by subsequent customs. Thus the old law which, in some particulars and in various places, had been changed by custom and was thus out of date, was petrified, and every tendency to change it in the well-known customary way was suppressed. It was still open to a group to prove a custom overriding the law, but this was extraordinarily difficult in the law courts. Change could only come by positive legislation, but the British Government, which was the legislating authority, had no wish to antagonize the conservative elements on whose support it counted. When later some legislative powers were given to partially elected assemblies, every attempt to promote social reform legislation was frowned upon by the authorities and sternly discouraged.

Growth of Industry: Provincial Differences

Slowly India recovered from the after-effects of the revolt of 1857-58. Despite British policy, powerful forces were at work changing India, and a new social consciousness was arising. The political unity of India, contact with the west, technological advances, and even the misfortune of a common subjection, led to new currents of thought, the slow development of industry, and the rise of a new movement for national freedom. The awakening of India was two-fold: she looked to the west and,

330

at the same time, she looked at herself and her own past.

The coming of the railway to India brought the industrial age on its positive side; so far only the negative aspect, in the shape of manufactured goods from Britain, had been in evidence. In 1860 the duty on imported machinery, imposed so as to prevent the industrialization of India, was removed, and large-scale industry began to develop, chiefly with British capital. First came the jute industry of Bengal, with its nerve centre at Dundee in Scotland; much later, cotton mills grew up in Ahmedabad and Bombay, largely with Indian capital and under Indian ownership; then came mining. Obstruction from the British Government in India continued, and an excise duty was put on Indian cotton goods to prevent them from competing with Lancashire textiles, even in India. Nothing, perhaps, reveals the police-state policy of the Government of India more than the fact that they had no department of agriculture and no department of commerce and industry till the twentieth century. It was, I believe, chiefly due to the donation of an American visitor, given for agricultural improvement in India, that a department of agriculture was started in the central government. (Even now this department is a very small affair.) A department for commerce and industry followed soon after, in 1905. Even then these departments functioned in a very small way. The growth of industry was artificially restricted and India's natural economic development was arrested.

Though the masses of India were desperately poor and growing poorer, a tiny fringe at the top was prospering under the new conditions and accumulating capital. It was this fringe that demanded political reform as well as opportunities for investment. On the political side, the Indian National Congress was started in 1885. Commerce and industry grew slowly, and it is interesting to note that the classes who took to them were predominantly those whose hereditary occupations for hundreds of years had been trade and commerce. Ahmedabad, the new centre of the textile industry, had been a famous manufacturing and trade centre during the Mughal period and even earlier, exporting its products to foreign countries. The big merchants of Ahmedabad had their own ships for this seaborne trade to Africa and the Persian Gulf. Broach, the seaport near by, was well-known in Græco-Roman times.

The people of Gujrat, Kathiawar, and Cutch were traders, manufacturers, merchants, and seafaring folk from ancient times. Many changes took place in India, but they carried on with their old business, adapting them to new conditions. They are now among the most prominent leaders in industry and commerce. Religion or a change of religion made no difference. The Parsees, who originally settled in Gujrat thirteen hundred years ago, may be considered as Gujratis for this purpose. (Their language has long been Gujrati.) Among the Moslems the most prominent sects in business and industry are the Khojas, Memons, and Bohras. All of these are converts from Hinduism, and all come from Gujrat, Kathiawar, or Cutch. All these Gujratis not only dominate industry and business in India, but have spread out to Burma, Ceylon, East Africa, South Africa, and other foreign countries.

The Marwaris from Rajputana used to control internal trade and finance, and were to be found at all the nerve centres of India. They were the big financiers as well as the small village bankers; a note from a well-known Marwari financial house would be honoured anywhere in India, and even abroad. The Marwaris still represent big finance in India but have added industry to it now.

The Sindhis in the north-west have also an old commercial tradition, and with their headquarters at Shikarpur or Hyderabad they used to spread out over central and western Asia and elsewhere. To-day (that is before the war) there is hardly a port anywhere in the world where one or more Sindhi shops cannot be found. Some of the Punjabis also have been traditionally in business.

The Chettys of Madras have also been leaders in business, and banking especially, from ancient times. The word 'Chetty' is derived from the Sanskrit 'Shreshthi,' the leader of a merchant guild. The common appellation 'Seth' is also derived from 'Shreshthi.' The Madras Chettys have not only played an important part in south India, but they spread out all over Burma, even in the remoter villages.

Within each province also trade and commerce were largely in the hands of the old *vaishya* class, who had been engaged in business for untold generations. They were the retail and wholesale dealers and moneylenders. In each village there was a *bania's* shop, which dealt in the necessaries of village life and advanced loans, on very profitable terms, to the villagers. The rural credit system was almost entirely in the hands of these *banias*. They spread even to the tribal and independent territories of the north-west and performed important functions there. As poverty grew agricultural indebtedness also grew rapidly, and the moneylending establishments held mortgages on the land and eventually acquired much of it. Thus the moneylender became the landlord also.

These demarcations of commercial, trading, and banking classes from others became less clearly defined as newcomers crept into various business; but they continued and are still marked. Whether they are due to the caste system, or the hold of tradition, or inherited capacity, or all of these together, it is difficult to specify. Undoubtedly among Brahmins and Kshatriyas business was looked down upon, and even the accumulation of money, though agreeable enough, was not a sufficient recompense. The possession of land was a symbol of social position, as in feudal times, and scholarship and learning were respected, even apart from possession. Under British rule government service gave prestige, security, and status, and later, when Indians were allowed to enter the Indian Civil Service, this service, called the 'heaven-born service'—heaven being some pale shadow of Whitehall—became the Elysium of the English-educated classes. The professional classes, especially lawyers, some of whom earned large incomes in the new law courts also had prestige and high status and attracted young men. Inevitably these lawyers took the lead in political and social reform movements.

The Bengalis were the first to take to the law, and some of them flourished exceedingly and cast a glamour over their profession. They were also the political leaders. They did not fit into the growing industry, either because of lack of aptitude or other reasons. The result has been that when industry began to play an important part in the country's life and to influence politics, Bengal lost its pre-eminence in the political field. The old current, when Bengalis poured out of their province as Government servants and in other capacities, was reversed and people from other provinces poured into Bengal, especially in Calcutta, and permeated the commercial and industrial life there. Calcutta had been and continues to be the chief centre of British capital and industry, and the English and the Scotch dominate business there; but they are being caught up by Marwaris and Gujratis. Even petty trades in Calcutta are often in non-Bengali hands. All the thousands of taxi-drivers in Calcutta, almost without an exception, are Sikhs from the Punjab.

Bombay became the centre and headquarters of Indian-owned industry, commerce, banking, insurance, etc. The Parsees, the Gujratis, and Marwaris, were the leaders in all these activities, and it is significant to note that the Maharashtrians or Marathas have played very little part in them. Bombay is a huge cosmopolitan city now but its population consists mainly of Marathas and Gujratis. The Marathas have distinguished themselves in the professions and in scholarship; they make, as one would expect, good soldiers; and large numbers of them are employed as workers in the textile mills. They are hardy and wiry and, as a province, poor; they are proud of the Shivaji tradition and of the achievements of their forefathers. The Gujratis are soft in body, gentler, richer, and perfectly at home in trade and commerce. Perhaps these differences are largely due to geography, for the Maratha country is bare and hard and mountainous while Gujrat is rich and fertile.

It is interesting to observe these and other differences in

333

various parts of India which continue to persist, though they tend to grow less. Madras, highly intellectual, has produced and still produces distinguished philosophers, mathematicians, and scientists. Bombay is now almost entirely devoted to business with all its advantages and disadvantages. Bengal, rather backward in industry and business, has produced some fine scientists, and has especially distinguished itself in art and literature. The Punjab has produced no outstanding personalities but is a go-ahead province advancing in many fields; its people are hard-headed, make good mechanics, and are successful in small trades and petty industries. The United Provinces (including Delhi) are a curious amalgam, and in some ways an epitome of India. They are the seat of the old Hindu culture as well as of the Persian culture that came in Afghan and Mughal times, and hence the mixture of the two is most in evidence there, intermingled with the culture of the west. There is less of provincialism there than in any other part of India. For long they have considered themselves, and have been looked upon by others, as the heart of India. Indeed, in popular parlance, they are often referred to as Hindustan.

These differences, it must be noted, are geographical and not religious. A Bengali Moslem is far nearer to a Bengali Hindu than he is to a Punjabi Moslem; so also with others. If a number of Hindu and Moslem Bengalis happen to meet anywhere, in India or elsewhere, they will immediately congregate together and feel at home with each other. Punjabis, whether Moslem or Hindu or Sikh, will do likewise. The Moslems of the Bombay presidency (Khojas, Memons, and Bohras) have many Hindu customs; the Khojas (they are the followers of the Aga Khan) and the Bohras are not looked upon as orthodox by the Moslems of the north.

Moslems, as a whole, especially in Bengal and the north, not only kept away from English education for a long time, but also took little part in the growth of industry. Partly this was due to feudal modes of thought, partly (as in Roman Catholicism) to Islam's prohibition against usury and interest on money. But, curiously enough, among the notorious moneylenders are a particular tribe of Pathans, who come from near the frontier. Moslems were thus, in the second half of the nineteenth century, backward in English education and therefore in contacts with western thought, as also in government service and in industry.

The growth of industry in India, slow and arrested as it was, gave the impression of progress and attracted attention. And yet it made practically no difference to the problem of the poverty of the masses and the overburden on the land. A few hundred thousand workers were transferred to industry out of the scores of millions of the unemployed and partially employed. This change-over was so extremely small that it did not affect the increasing ruralization of the country. Widespread unemployment and the pressure on land led to emigration of workers on a substantial scale to foreign countries, often under humiliating conditions. They went to South Africa, Fiji, Trinidad, Jamaica, Guiana, Mauritius, Ceylon, Burma, and Malaya. The small groups or individuals who found opportunities for growth and betterment under foreign rule were divorced from the masses, whose condition continued to worsen. Some capital accumulated in the hands of these groups and conditions were gradually created for further growth. But the basic problems of poverty and unemployment remained untouched.

Reform and Other Movements among Hindus and Moslems

The real impact of the west came to India in the nineteenth century through technical changes and their dynamic consequences. In the realm of ideas also there was shock and change, a widening of the horizon which had so long been confined within a narrow shell. The first reaction, limited to the small English educated class, was one of admiration and acceptance of almost everything western. Repelled by some of the social customs and practices of Hinduism, many Hindus were attracted towards Christianity, and some notable conversions took place in Bengal. An attempt was therefore made by Raja Ram Mohan Roy to adapt Hinduism to this new environment and he started the Brahmo Samaj on a more or less rationalist and social reform basis. His successors, Keshab Chander Sen, gave it a more Christian outlook. The Brahmo Samaj influenced the rising middle classes of Bengal but as a religious faith it remained confined to few, among whom, however, were some outstanding persons and families. But even these families, though ardently interested in social and religious reform, tended to go back to the old Indian philosophic ideals of the Vedanta.

Elsewhere in India also the same tendencies were at work and dissatisfaction arose at the rigid social forms and protean character of Hinduism as practised. One of the most notable reform movements was started in the second half of the nineteenth century by a Gujarati, Swami Dayananda Saraswati, but it took root among the Hindus of the Punjab. This was the Arya Samaj and its slogan was 'Back to the Vedas.' This slogan really meant an elimination of developments of the Aryan faith since the Vedas; the Vedanta philosophy as it subsequently developed, the central conception of monism, the pantheistic outlook, as well as popular and cruder developments, were all alike severely condemned. Even the Vedas were interpreted in a particular way. The Arya Samaj was a reaction to the influence of Islam and Christianity, more especially the former. It was a crusading and reforming movement from within, as well as a defensive organization for protection against external attacks. It introduced proselytization into Hinduism and thus tended to come into conflict with other proselytizing religions. The Arya Samaj, which had been a close approach to Islam, tended to become a defender of everything Hindu, against what it considered as the encroachments of other faiths. It is significant that it spread chiefly among the middle-class Hindus of the Punjab and the United Provinces. At one time it was considered by the Government as a politically revolutionary movement, but the large numbers of Government servants in it made it thoroughly respectable. It has done very good work in the spread of education both among boys and girls, in improving the condition of women, and in raising the status and standards of the depressed classes.

About the same period as Swami Dayananda, a different type of person lived in Bengal and his life influenced many of the new English-educated classes. He was Shri Ramakrishna Paramahansa, a simple man, no scholar but a man of faith, and not interested in social reform as such. He was in a direct line with Chaitanya and other Indian saints. Essentially religious and yet broad-minded, in his search for self-realization he had even met Moslem and Christian mystics some of whom lived with him for some time. He settled down at Dakshineshwar near Calcutta, and his extraordinary personality and character gradually attracted attention. People who went to visit him, and some who were even inclined to scoff at this simple man of faith, were powerfully influenced and many who had been completely westernized felt that here was something they had missed. Stressing the essentials of religious faith, he linked up the various aspects of the Hindu religion and philosophy and seemed to represent all of them in his own person. Indeed he brought within his fold other religions also. Opposed to all sectarianism, he emphasized that all roads lead to truth. He was like some of the saints we read about in the past records of Asia and Europe. Difficult to understand in the context of modern life, and yet fitting into India's many-coloured pattern and accepted and revered by many of her people as a man with a touch of the divine fire about him. His personality impressed itself on all who saw him and many who never saw him have been influenced by the story of his life. Among these latter is Romain Rolland who has written a story of his life and that of his chief disciple, Swami Vivekananda.

Vivekananda, together with his brother disciples, founded the non-sectarian Ramakrishna Mission of service. Rooted in the past and full of pride in India's heritage, Vivekananda was yet modern in his approach to life's problems and was a kind of bridge between the past of India and her present. He was a powerful orator in Bengali and English and a graceful writer of Bengali prose and poetry. He was a fine figure of a man, imposing, full of poise and dignity, sure of himself and his mission, and at the same time full of a dynamic and fiery energy and a passion to push India forward. He came as a tonic to the depressed and demoralized Hindu mind and gave it self-reliance and some roots in the past. He attended the Parliament of Religions in Chicago in 1893, spent over a year in the U.S.A., travelled across Europe, going as far as Athens and Constantinople, and visited Egypt, China, and Japan. Wherever he went, he created a minor sensation not only by his presence but by what he said and how he said it. Having seen this Hindu Sanyasin once it was difficult to forget him or his message. In America he was called the 'cyclonic Hindu.' He was himself greatly influenced by his travels in western countries; he admired British perseverence and the vitality and spirit of equality of the American people. 'America is the best field in the world to carry on any idea,' he wrote to a friend in India. But he was not impressed by the manifestations of religion in the west and his faith in the Indian philosophical and spiritual background became firmer. India, in spite of her degradation, still represented to him the Light.

He preached the monism of the Advaita philosophy of the Vedanta and was convinced that only this could be the future religion of thinking humanity. For the Vedanta was not only spiritual but rational and in harmony with scientific investigations of external nature. 'This universe has not been created by any extra-cosmic God, nor is it the work of any outside genius. It is self-creating, self-dissolving, self-manifesting, One Infinite Existence, the Brahma.' The Vedanta ideal was of the solidarity of man and his inborn divine nature; to see God in man is the real God-vision; man is the greatest of all beings. But 'the abstract Vedanta must become living—poetic—in everyday life; out of hopelessly intricate mythology must come concrete moral forms; and out of bewildering Yogi-ism must come the most scientific and practical psychology.' India had fallen because she had narrowed herself, gone into her shell and lost touch with other nations, and thus sunk into a state of 'mummified' and 'crystallized' civilization. Caste, which was necessary and desirable in its early forms, and meant to develop individuality and freedom, had become a monstrous degradation, the opposite of what it was meant to be, and had crushed the masses. Caste was a form of social organization which was and should be kept separate from religion. Social organizations should change with the changing times. Passionately, Vivekananda condemned the meaningless metaphysical discussions and arguments about ceremonials and especially the touch-me-notism of the upper caste. 'Our religion is in the kitchen. Our God is the cooking-pot, and our religion is: "don't touch me, I am holy." '

He kept away from politics and disapproved of the politicians of his day. But again and again he laid stress on the necessity for liberty and equality and the raising of the masses. 'Liberty of thought and action is the only condition of life, of growth and well-being. Where it does not exist, the man, the race, the nation must go.' 'The only hope of India is from the masses. The upper classes are physically and morally dead.' He wanted to combine western progress with India's spiritual background. 'Make a European society with India's religion.' 'Become an occidental of occidentals in your spirit of equality, freedom, work, and energy, and at the same time a Hindu to the very backbone in religious culture, and instincts.' Progressively, Vivekananda grew more international in outlook: 'Even in politics and sociology, problems that were only national twenty years ago can no longer be solved on national grounds only. They are assuming huge proportions, gigantic shapes. They can only be solved when looked at in the broader light of international grounds. International organizations, international combinations, international laws are the cry of the day. That shows solidarity. In science, every day they are coming to a similar broad view of matter.' And again: 'There cannot be any progress without the whole world following in the wake, and it is becoming every day clearer that the solution of any problem can never be attained on racial, or national, or narrow grounds. Every idea has to become broad till it covers the whole of this world, every aspiration must go on increasing till it has engulfed the whole of humanity, nay the whole of life, within its scope.' All this fitted in with Vivekananda's view of the Vedanta philosophy, and he preached this from end to end of India. 'I am thoroughly convinced that no individual or nation can live by holding itself apart from the community of others, and wherever such an attempt has been made under false ideas of greatness, policy or holiness—the result has always been disastrous to the secluding one.' 'The fact of our isolation from all the other nations of the world is the cause of our degeneration and its only remedy is getting back into the current of the rest of the world. Motion is the sign of life.'

He once wrote: 'I am a socialist not because I think it is a perfect system, but half a loaf is better than no bread. The other systems have been tried and found wanting. Let this one be tried—if for nothing else, for the novelty of the thing.'

Vivekananda spoke of many things but the one constant refrain of his speech and writing was *abhay*—be fearless, be strong. For him man was no miserable sinner but a part of divinity; why should he be afraid of anything? 'If there is a sin in the world it is weakness; avoid all weakness, weakness is sin, weakness is death.' That had been the great lesson of the Upanishads. Fear breeds evil and weeping and wailing. There had been enough of that, enough of softness. 'What our country now wants are muscles of iron and nerves of steel, gigantic wills which nothing can resist, which can penetrate into the mysteries and the secrets of the universe, and will accomplish their purpose in any fashion, even if it meant going down to the bottom of the ocean and meeting death face to face.' He condemned 'occultism and mysticism...these creepy things; there may be great truths in them, but they have nearly destroyed us....And here is the test of truth—anything that makes you weak physically, intellectually, and spiritually, reject as poison, there is no life in it, it cannot be true. Truth is strengthening. Truth is purity, truth is all-knowledge....These mysticisms, in spite of some grains of truth in them, are generally weakening....Go back to your Upanishads, the shining, the strengthening, the bright philosophy; and part from all these mysterious things, all these weakening things. Take up this philosophy; the greatest truths are the simplest things in the world, simple as your own existence.' And beware of superstition. 'I would rather see everyone of you rank atheists than superstitious fools, for the atheist is alive, and you can make something of him. But if superstition enters, the brain is gone, the brain is softening, degradation has seized upon the life.... Mystery-mongering and superstition are always signs of weakness.'*

So Vivekananda thundered from Cape Comorin on the southern tip of India to the Himalayas, and he wore himself out in the process, dying in 1902 when he was thirty-nine years of age.

A contemporary of Vivekananda, and yet belonging much more to a later generation, was Rabindranath Tagore. The

---

*Most of these extracts have been taken from 'Lectures from Colombo to Almora' by Swami Vivekananda (1933) and 'Letters of Swami Vivekananda' (1942) both published by the Advaita Ashrama, Mayavati, Almora, Himalayas. In the 'Letters' p. 390, there is a remarkable letter written by Vivekananda to a Moslem friend. In the course of this he writes:

'Whether we call it Vedantism or any ism, the truth is that Advaitism is the last word of religion and thought and the only position from which one can look upon all religions and sects with love. We believe it is the religion of the future enlightened humanity. The Hindus may get the credit of arriving at it earlier than other races, they being an older race than either the Hebrew or the Arab; yet practical Advaitism, which looks upon and behaves to all mankind as one's own soul, is yet to be developed among the Hindus universally.

'On the other hand our experience is that if ever the followers of any religion approach to this equality in an appreciable degree in the plane of practical work-a-day life—it may be quite unconscious generally of the deeper meaning and the underlying principle of such conduct, which the Hindus as a rule so clearly perceive—it is those of Islam and Islam alone....

'For our own motherland a junction of the two great systems, Hinduism and Islam —Vedanta brain and Islam body—is the only hope.

'I see in my mind's eye the future perfect India rising out of this chaos and strife, glorious and invincible, with Vedanta brain and Islam body.' This letter is dated Almora, June 10th, 1898.

Tagore family had played a leading part in various reform movements in Bengal during the nineteenth century. There were men of spiritual stature in it and fine writers and artists, but Rabindranath towered above them all, and indeed all over India his position gradually became one of unchallenged supremacy. His long life of creative activity covered two entire generations and he seems almost of our present day. He was no politician, but he was too sensitive and devoted to the freedom of the Indian people to remain always in his ivory tower of poetry and song. Again and again he stepped out of it, when he could tolerate some development no longer, and in prophetic language warned the British Government or his own people. He played a prominent part in the Swadeshi movement that swept through Bengal in the first decade of the twentieth century, and again when he gave up his knighthood at the time of the Amritsar massacre. His constructive work in the field of education, quietly begun, has already made Santiniketan one of the focal points of Indian culture. His influence over the mind of India, and specially of successive rising generations, has been tremendous. Not Bengali only, the language in which he himself wrote, but all the modern languages of India have been moulded partly by his writings. More than any other Indian, he has helped to bring into harmony the ideals of the east and the west, and broadened the bases of Indian nationalism. He has been India's internationalist par excellence, believing and working for international co-operation, taking India's message to other countries and bringing their message to his own people. And yet with all his internationalism, his feet have always been planted firmly on India's soil and his mind has been saturated with the wisdom of the Upanishads. Contrary to the usual course of development, as he grew older he became more radical in his outlook and views. Strong individualist as he was, he became an admirer of the great achievements of the Russian Revolution, especially in the spread of education, culture, health, and the spirit of equality. Nationalism is a narrowing creed, and nationalism in conflict with a dominating imperialism produces all manner of frustrations and complexes. It was Tagore's immense service to India, as it has been Gandhi's in a different plane, that he forced the people in some measure out of their narrow grooves of thought and made them think of broader issues affecting humanity. Tagore was the great humanist of India.

Tagore and Gandhi have undoubtedly been the two outstanding and dominating figures of India in this first half of the twentieth century. It is instructive to compare and contrast them. No two persons could be so different from one another in their make up or temperaments. Tagore, the aristocractic artist, turned democrat with proletarian sympathies, represented essentially the cultural tradition of India, the tradition of accepting life in the fullness thereof and going through it with song and dance. Gandhi, more a man of the people, almost the embodiment of the Indian peasant, represented the other ancient tradition of India, that of renunciation and asceticism. And yet Tagore was primarily the man of thought, Gandhi of concentrated and ceaseless activity. Both, in their different ways had a world outlook, and both were at the same time wholly Indian. They seemed to present different but harmonious aspects of India and to complement one another.

Tagore and Gandhi bring us to our present age. But we were considering an earlier period and the effect produced on the people, and especially the Hindus, by the stress laid by Vivekananda and others on the past greatness of India and their pride in it. Vivekananda himself was careful to warn his people not to dwell too much on the past, but to look to the future. 'When, O Lord,' he wrote, 'shall our land be free from this eternal dwelling upon the past?' But he himself and others had evoked that past, and there was a glamour in it, and no getting away from it.

This looking back to the past and finding comfort and sustenance there was helped by a renewed study of ancient literature and history, and later by the story of the Indian colonies in the eastern seas, as this unfolded itself. Mrs. Annie Besant was a powerful influence in adding to the confidence of the Hindu middle classes in their spiritual and national heritage. There was a spiritual and religious element about all this, and yet there was a strong political background to it. The rising middle classes were politically inclined and were not so much in search of a religion; but they wanted some cultural roots to cling on to, something that gave them assurance of their own worth, something that would reduce the sense of frustration and humiliation that foreign conquest and rule had produced. In every country with a growing nationalism there is this search apart from religion, this tendency to go to the past. Iran, without in any way weakening in its religious faith, has deliberately gone back to its pre-Islamic days of greatness and utilized this memory to strengthen its present-day nationalism. So also in other countries. The past of India, with all its cultural variety and greatness, was a common heritage of all the Indian people, Hindu Moslem, Christian, and others, and their ancestors had helped to build it. The fact of subsequent conversion to other faiths did not deprive them of this heritage; just as the Greeks, after their conversion to Christianity, did not lose their pride in the mighty achievements of their ancestors, or the Italians in the great days of the Roman Republic and early empire. If all the people of India had been converted to Islam or Christianity, her cultural heritage would still have remained to inspire them and

341

give them that poise and dignity, which a long record of civilized existence with all its mental struggles with the problems of life gives a people.

If we had been an independent nation, all of us in this country working together in the present for a common future would no doubt have looked to our common past with equal pride. Indeed, during the Mughal period, the emperors and their chief associates, newcomers as they were, wanted to identify themselves with that past and to share it with others. But the accidents and processes of history, helped no doubt by man's policy and weaknesses, worked differently, and the changes which came prevented normal development. One would have expected that the new middle class, which was the product of the impact from the west and of technological and economic changes, would have a common background in Hindu and Moslem alike. To some extent this was so, and yet differences arose which were not present, or were present in far lesser degree, in the feudal and semi-feudal classes and the masses. The Hindu and Moslem masses were hardly distinguishable from each other, the old aristocracy had developed common ways and standards. They yet followed a common culture and had common custom and festivals. The middle classes began to diverge psychologically and later in other ways.

To begin with, the new middle classes were almost absent among the Moslems. Their avoidance of western education, their keeping away from trade and industry, and their adherence to feudal ways, gave a start to the Hindus which they profited by and retained. British policy was inclined to be pro-Hindu and anti-Moslem, except in the Punjab, where Moslems took more easily to western education than elsewhere. But the Hindus had got a big start long before the British took possession of the Punjab. Even in the Punjab, though conditions were more equal for the Hindu and Moslem, the Hindus had an economic advantage. Anti-foreign sentiment was shared alike by the Hindu and Moslem aristocracy and the masses. The Revolt of 1857 was a joint affair, but in its suppression Moslems felt strongly, and to some extent rightly, that they were the greater sufferers. This Revolt also put an end finally to any dreams or fantasies of the revival of the Delhi empire. That empire had vanished long ago, even before the British arrived upon the scene. The Marathas had smashed it and controlled Delhi itself. Ranjit Singh ruled in the Punjab. Mughal rule had ended in the north without any intervention of the British, and in the south also it had disintegrated. Yet the shadow emperor sat in the Delhi palace, and though he had become a dependant and pensioner of the Marathas and the British successively, still he was a symbol of a famous dynasty. Inevitably, during the Revolt the rebels tried to take advantage of this symbol, in spite of his weakness and unwillingness. The ending of the Revolt meant also the smashing of the symbol.

As the people recovered slowly from the horror of the Mutiny days, there was a blank in their minds, a vacuum which sought for something to fill it. Of necessity, British rule had to be accepted, but the break with the past had brought something more than a new government; it had brought doubt and confusion and a loss of faith in themselves. That break indeed had come long before the Mutiny, and had led to the many movements of thought in Bengal and elsewhere to which I have already referred. But the Moslems generally had then retired into their shells far more than the Hindus, avoided western education, and lived in day-dreams of a restoration of the old order. There could be no more dreaming now, but there had to be something to which they could cling on. They still kept away from the new education. Gradually and after much debate and difficulty, Sir Syed Ahmad Khan turned their minds towards English education and started the Aligarh College. That was the only avenue leading to government service, and the lure of that service proved powerful enough to overcome old resentments and prejudices. The fact that Hindus had gone far ahead in education and service was disliked, and proved a powerful argument to do likewise. Parsees and Hindus were also going ahead in industry, but Moslem attention was directed to government service alone.

But even this new direction to their activities, which was really confined to comparatively few, did not resolve the doubt and confusion of their minds. Hindus, in like straits, had looked back and sought consolation in ancient times. Old philosophy and literature, art and history, had brought some comfort. Ram Mohan Roy, Dayananda, Vivekananda, and others had started new movements of thought. While they drank from the rich streams of English literature their minds were also full of ancient sages and heroes of India, their thoughts and deeds, and of the myths and traditions which they had imbibed from their childhood.

Much of this was common to the Moslem masses, who were well acquainted with these traditions. But it began to be felt, especially by the Moslem upper classes, that it was not quite proper for them to associate themselves with these semi-religious traditions, that any encouragement of them would be against the spirit of Islam. They searched for their national roots elsewhere. To some extent they found them in the Afghan and Mughal periods of India, but this was not quite enough to fill the vacuum. Those periods were common for Hindus and Moslems alike, and the sense of foreign intrusion had disappeared from Hindu minds. The Mughal rulers were looked upon as Indian national rulers, though in the case of Aurungzeb there was a difference of opinion. It is significant that Akbar, whom the

343

Hindus especially admired, has not been approved of in recent years by some Moslems. Last year the 400th anniversary of his birth was celebrated in India. All classes of people, including many Moslems, joined, but the Moslem League kept aloof because Akbar was a symbol of India's unity.

This search for cultural roots led Indian Moslems (that is, some of them of the middle class) to Islamic history, and to the periods when Islam was a conquering and creative force in Baghdad, Spain, Constantinople, central Asia, and elsewhere. There had always been interest in this history and some contacts with neighbouring Islamic countries. There was also the Haj pilgrimage to Mecca, which brought Moslems from various countries together. But all such contacts were limited and superficial and did not really affect the general outlook of Indian Moslems, which was confined to India. The Afghan kings of Delhi, especially Muhammad Tughlaq, had acknowledged the Khalifa (Caliph) at Cairo. The Ottoman emperors at Constantinople subsequently became the Khalifas, but they were not recognized as such in India. The Mughal Emperors in India recognized no Khalifa or spiritual superiors outside India. It was only after the complete collapse of the Mughal power early in the nineteenth century that the name of the Turkish Sultan began to be mentioned in Indian mosques. This practice was confirmed after the Mutiny.

Thus Indian Moslems sought to derive some psychological satisfaction from a contemplation of Islam's past greatness, chiefly in other countries, and in the fact of the continuance of Turkey as an independent Moslem power, practically the only one left. This feeling was not opposed to or in conflict with Indian nationalism; indeed, many Hindus admired and were well acquainted with Islamic history. They sympathized with Turkey because they considered the Turks as Asiatic victims of European aggression. Yet the emphasis was different, and in their case that feeling did not supply a psychological need as it did in the case of the Moslems.

After the Mutiny the Indian Moslems had hesitated which way to turn. The British Government had deliberately repressed them to an even greater degree than it had repressed the Hindus, and this repression had especially affected those sections of the Moslems from which the new middle class, the bourgeoise, might have been drawn. They felt down and out and were intensely anti-British as well as conservative. British policy towards them underwent a gradual change in the seventies and became more favourable. This change was essentially due to the policy of balance and counterpoise which the British Government had consistently pursued. Still, in this process, Sir Syed Ahmad Khan played an important part. He was convinced that he could only raise the Moslems through co-operation with the British authorities. He was anxious to make them accept English education and thus to draw them out of their conservative shells. He had been much impressed by what he had seen of European civilization, and, indeed, some of his letters from Europe indicate that he was so dazed that he had rather lost his balance.

Sir Syed was an ardent reformer and he wanted to reconcile modern scientific thought with Islam. This was to be done, of course, not by attacking any basic belief, but by a rationalistic interpretation of scripture. He pointed out the basic similarities between Islam and Christianity. He attacked *purdah* (the seclusion of women) among the Moslems. He was opposed to any allegiance to the Turkish Khalifat. Above all, he was anxious to push a new type of education. The beginnings of the national movement frightened him, for he thought that any opposition to the British authorities would deprive him of their help in his educational programme. That help appeared to him to be essential, and so he tried to tone down anti-British sentiments among the Moslems and to turn them away from the National Congress which was taking shape then. One of the declared objects of the Aligarh College he founded was 'to make the Mussulmans of India worthy and useful subjects of the British crown.' He was not opposed to the National Congress because he considered it predominantly a Hindu organization; he opposed it because he thought it was politically too aggressive (though it was mild enough in those days), and he wanted British help and co-operation. He tried to show that Moslems as a whole had not rebelled during the Mutiny and that many had remained loyal to the British power. He was in no way anti-Hindu or communally separatist. Repeatedly he emphasized that religious differences should have no political or national significance. 'Do you not inhabit the same land?' he said. 'Remember that the words Hindu and Mohammedan are only meant for religious distinction; otherwise all persons, whether Hindu or Mohammedan, even the Christians who reside in this country, are all in this particular respect belonging to one and the same nation.'

Sir Syed Ahmad Khan's influence was confined to certain sections of the upper classes among the Moslems; he did not touch the urban or rural masses. These masses were almost completely cut off from their upper classes and were far nearer to the Hindu masses. While some among the Moslem upper classes were descendants of the ruling groups during Mughal times, the masses had no such background or tradition. Most of them had been converted from the lowest strata of Hindu society and were most unhappily situated, being among the poorest and the most exploited.

Sir Syed had a number of able and notable colleagues. In his rationalistic approach he was supported, among others, by Syed Chirag Ali and Nawab Mohsin-ul-Mulk. His educational activities attracted Munshi Karamat Ali, Munshi Zakaullah of Delhi, Dr. Nazir Ahmad, Maulana Shibli Nomani, and the poet Hāli, who is one of the outstanding figures of Urdu literature. Sir Syed succeeded in so far as the beginnings of English education among the Moslems were concerned, and in diverting the Moslem mind from the political movement. A Mohammedan educational conference was started and this attracted the rising Moslem middle class in the professions and services.

None the less many prominent Moslems joined the National Congress. British policy became definitely pro-Moslem, or rather in favour of those elements among the Moslems who were opposed to the national movement. But early in the twentieth century the tendency towards nationalism and political activity became more noticeable among the younger generation of Moslems. To divert this and provide a safe channel for it, the Moslem League was started in 1906 under the inspiration of the British Government and the leadership of one of its chief supporters, the Aga Khan. The League had two principal objects: loyalty to the British Government and the safeguarding of Moslem interests.

It is worth noting that during the post-Mutiny period all the leading men among Indian Moslems, including Sir Syed Ahmad Khan, were products of the old traditional education, although some of them added knowledge of English later and were influenced by new ideas. The new western education had yet produced no notable figure among them. The leading poet in Urdu and one of the outstanding literary figures of the century in India, was Ghalib, who was in his prime before the Mutiny.

In the early years of the twentieth century there were two trends among the Moslem intelligentsia: one, chiefly among the younger element, was towards nationalism, the other was a deviation from India's past and even, to some extent, her present, and a greater interest in Islamic countries, especially Turkey, the seat of the Khilafat. The Pan-Islamic movement, encouraged by Sultan Abdul Hamid of Turkey, had found some response in the upper strata of Indian Moslems, and yet Sir Syed had opposed this and written against Indians interesting themselves in Turkey and the Sultanate. The young Turk movement produced mixed reactions. It was looked upon with some suspicion by most Moslems in India to begin with, and there was general sympathy for the Sultan who was considered a bulwark against the intrigues of European powers in Turkey. But there were others, among them Abul Kalam Azad, who eagerly welcomed the young Turks and the promise of constitutional and social reform that they brought. When Italy suddenly attacked Turkey in the Tripoli War of 1911, and subsequently, during the

Balkan Wars of 1912 and 1913, an astonishing wave of sympathy for Turkey roused Indian Moslems. All Indians felt that sympathy and anxiety but in the case of Moslems this was keener and something almost personal. The last remaining Moslem power was threatened with extinction; the sheet-anchor of their faith in the future was being destroyed. Dr. M. A. Ansari led a strong medical mission to Turkey and even the poor subscribed; money came more rapidly than for any proposal for the uplift of the Indian Moslems themselves. World War I was a time of trial for the Moslems because Turkey was on the other side. They felt helpless and could do nothing. When the war ended their pent-up feelings were to break out in the Khilafat movement.

The year 1912 was notable also in the development of the Moslem mind in India because of the appearance of two new weeklies, the *Al-Hilal* in Urdu and *The Comrade* in English. The *Al-Hilal* was started by Abul Kalam Azad (the present Congress President), a brilliant young man of twenty-four, who had received his early education in Al Azhar University of Cairo and, while yet in his teens, had become well-known for his Arabic and Persian scholarship and deep learning. To this he added a knowledge of the Islamic world outside India and of the reform movements that were coursing through it, as well as of European developments. Rationalist in outlook and yet profoundly versed in Islamic lore and history, he interpreted scripture from a rationalist point of view. Soaked in Islamic tradition and with many personal contacts with prominent Moslem leaders and reformers in Egypt, Turkey, Syria, Palestine, Iraq and Iran, he was powerfully affected by political and cultural developments in these countries. Because of his writings he was known in the Islamic countries probably more than any other Indian Moslem. The wars in which Turkey became involved aroused his intense interest and sympathy; and yet his approach was different from that of the older Moslem leaders. He had a wider and more rationalist outlook which kept him away from the feudal and narrowly religious and separatist approach of these older leaders, and inevitably made him an Indian nationalist. He had himself seen nationalism growing in Turkey and the other Islamic countries and he applied that knowledge to India and saw in the Indian national movement a similar development. Other Moslems in India were hardly aware of these movements elsewhere and, wrapped up in their own feudal atmosphere, had little appreciation of what was happening there. They thought in religious terms only and if they sympathised with Turkey it was chiefly because of that religious bond. In spite of that intense sympathy, they were not in tune with the nationalist and rather secular movements in Turkey.

Abul Kalam Azad spoke in a new language to them in his

weekly *Al-Hilal*. It was not only a new language in thought and approach, even its texture was different, for Azad's style was tense and virile, though sometimes a little difficult because of its Persian background. He used new phrases for new ideas and was a definite influence in giving shape to the Urdu language, as it is to-day. The older conservative leaders among the Moslems did not react favourably to all this and criticized Azad's opinions and approach. Yet not even the most learned of them could easily meet Azad in debate and argument, even on the basis of scripture and old tradition, for Azad's knowledge of these happened to be greater than theirs. He was a strange mixture of mediæval scholasticism, eighteenth century rationalism, and the modern outlook.

There were a few among the older generation who approved of Azad's writings, among them being the learned Maulana Shibli Nomani, who had himself visited Turkey, and who had been associated with Sir Syed Ahmad Khan in Aligarh College. The tradition of Aligarh College was, however, different and conservative, both politically and socially. Its trustees came from among the princes and big landlords, typical representatives of the feudal order. Under a succession of English principals, closely associated with government circles, it had fostered separatist tendencies and an anti-nationalist and anti-Congress outlook. The chief aim kept before its students was to enter government service in the subordinate ranks. For that a pro-government attitude was necessary and no truck with nationalism and sedition. The Aligarh College group had become the leaders of the new Moslem intelligentsia and influenced sometimes openly, more often from behind the scenes, almost every Moslem movement. The Moslem League came into existence largely through their efforts.

Abul Kalam Azad attacked this stronghold of conservatism and anti-nationalism not directly but by spreading ideas which undermined the Aligarh tradition. This very youthful writer and journalist caused a sensation in Moslem intellectual circles and, though the elders frowned upon him, his words created a ferment in the minds of the younger generation. That ferment had already started because of events in Turkey, Egypt, and Iran, as well as the development of the Indian nationalist movement. Azad gave a definite trend to it by pointing out that there was no conflict between Islam and sympathy for Islamic countries and Indian nationalism. This helped in bringing the Moslem League nearer to the Congress. Azad had himself joined the League, whilst yet a boy, at its first session in 1906.

The *Al-Hilal* was not approved of by the representatives of the British Government. Securities were demanded from it under the Press Act and ultimately its press was confiscated in 1914.

Thus ended the *Al-Hilal* after a brief existence of two years. Azad thereupon brought out another weekly, the *Al-Balagh*, but this, too, ended in 1916 when Azad was interned by the British Government. For nearly four years he was kept in internment, and when he came out at last he took his place immediately among the leaders of the National Congress. Ever since then he has been continuously in the highest Congress Executive, looked upon, in spite of his youthful years, as one of the elders of the Congress, whose advice both in national and political matters as well as in regard to the communal and minority questions is highly valued. Twice he had been Congress president, and repeatedly he has spent long terms in prison.

The other weekly that was started in 1912, some months before the *Al-Hilal* was *The Comrade*. This was in English and it influenced especially the younger English-educated generation of Moslems. It was edited by Maulana Mohammad Ali, who was an odd mixture of Islamic tradition and an Oxford education. He began as an adherent of the Aligarh tradition and was opposed to any aggressive politics. But he was far too able and dynamic a personality to remain confined in that static framework, and his language was always vigorous and striking. The annulment of the Partition of Bengal in 1911 had given him a shock and his faith in the bona fides of the British Government had been shaken. The Balkan Wars moved him and he wrote passionately in favour of Turkey and the Islamic tradition it represented. Progressively he grew more anti-British and the entry of Turkey in World War I completed the process. A famous and enormously long article of his (his speeches anb writings did not err on the side of brevity or conciseness) in *The Comrade* entitled 'The Choice of the Turks' put an end to *The Comrade* which was stopped by the government. Soon after, government arrested him and his brother Shaukat Ali and interned them for the duration of the war and a year after. They were released at the end of 1919 and both immediately joined the National Congress. The Ali Brothers played a very prominent part in the Khilafat agitation and in Congress politics in the early twenties and suffered prison for it. Mohammad Ali presided over an annual session of the Congress and was for many years a member of its highest executive committee. He died in 1930.

The change that took place in Mohammad Ali was symbolic of the changing mentality of the Indian Moslems. Even the Moslem League, founded to isolate the Moslems from nationalist currents and completely controlled by reactionary and semi-feudal elements, was forced to recognize the pressure from the younger generation. It was drifting, though somewhat unwillingly, with the tide of nationalism and coming nearer to the Congress. In 1913 it changed its creed of loyalty to government to a demand for self-government for India. Maulana Abul Kalam Azad had advocated this change in his forceful writings in the *Al-Hilal*.

Kemal Pasha. Nationalism in Asia. Iqbal

Kemal Pasha was naturally popular in India with Moslems and Hindus alike. He had not only rescued Turkey from foreign domination and disruption but had foiled the machinations of European imperialist powers, especially England. But as the Ataturk's policy unfolded itself—his lack of religion, his abolition of the Sultanate and Khilafat, the building up of a secular state, and his disbandment of religious orders—that popularity waned so far as the more orthodox Moslems were concerned and a silent resentment against his modernist policy rose among them. This very policy, however, made him more popular among the younger generation of both Hindus and Moslems. The Ataturk partly destroyed the dream structure that had gradually grown up in the Indian Moslem mind ever since the days of the Mutiny. Again a kind of vacuum was created. Many Moslems filled this vacuum by joining the nationalist movement, many had of course already joined it previously; others stood aloof, hesitant and doubtful. The real conflict was between feudal modes of thought and modern tendencies. The feudal leadership had for the moment been swept away by the mass Khilafat movement, but that movement itself had no solid basis in social and economic conditions or in the needs of the masses. It had its centre elsewhere, and when the core itself was eliminated by the Ataturk the superstructure collapsed, leaving the Moslem masses bewildered and disinclined to any political action. The old feudal leaders, who had lain low, crept back into prominence, helped by British policy, which had always supported them. But they could not come back to their old position of unquestioned leadership for conditions had changed. The Moslems were also throwing up, rather belatedly, a middle class, and the very experience of a mass political movement, under the leadership of the National Congress, had made a vital difference.

Though the mentality of the Moslem masses and the new growing middle class was shaped essentially by events, Sir Mohamad Iqbal played an important part in influencing the latter and especially the younger generation. The masses were hardly affected by him. Iqbal had begun by writing powerful nationalist poems in Urdu which had become popular. During the Balkan Wars he turned to Islamic subjects. He was influenced by the circumstances then prevailing and the mass feeling among the Moslems, and he himself influenced and added to the intensity of these sentiments. Yet he was very far from being a mass leader; he was a poet, an intellectual and a philosopher with affiliations to the old feudal order; he came from Kashmiri Brahmin stock. He supplied in fine poetry, which was written both in Persian and Urdu, a philosophic background to the Moslem intelligentsia and thus diverted its mind in a separatist direction. His popularity was no doubt due to the quality of his poetry, but even more so it was due to his having fulfilled a need when the Moslem mind was searching for some anchor to hold on to. The old pan-Islamic ideal had ceased to have any meaning; there was no Khilafat and every Islamic country, Turkey most of all, was intensely nationalist, caring little for other Islamic peoples. Nationalism was in fact the dominant force in Asia as elsewhere, and in India the nationalist movement had grown powerful and challenged British rule repeatedly. That nationalism had a strong appeal to the Moslem mind in India, and large numbers of Moslems had played a leading part in the struggle for freedom. Yet Indian nationalism was dominated by Hindus and had a Hinduised look. So a conflict arose in the Moslem mind; many accepted that nationalism, trying to influence it in the direction of their choice; many sympathised with it and yet remained aloof, uncertain; and yet many others began to drift in a separatist direction for which Iqbal's poetic and philosophic approach had prepared them.

This, I imagine, was the background out of which, in recent years, arose the cry for a division of India. There were many reasons, many contributory causes, errors and mistakes on every side, and especially the deliberate separatist policy of the British Government. But behind all these was this psychological background, which itself was produced, apart from certain historical causes, by the delay in the development of a Moslem middle class in India. Essentially the internal conflict in India, apart from the nationalist struggle against foreign domination, is between the remnants of the feudal order and modernist ideas and institutions. That conflict exists on the national plane as well as within each major group, Hindu, Moslem, and others. The national movement, as represented essentially by the National Congress, undoubtedly represents the historic process of growth towards these new ideas and institutions, though it tries to adapt these to some of the old foundations. Because of this, it has attracted to its fold all manner of people, differing widely among themselves. On the Hindu side, an exclusive and rigid social order has come in the way of growth, and what is more, frightened other groups. But this social order itself has been undermined and is fast losing its rigidity and, in any event, is not strong enough to obstruct the growth of the national movement in its widest political and social sense, which has developed enough impetus to go ahead in spite of obstacles. On the Moslem side, feudal elements have continued to be strong and have usually succeeded in imposing their leadership on their masses. There has been a difference of a generation or more in the development of the Hindu and Moslem middle classes, and that difference continues to show itself in many directions, political, economic, and other. It is this lag which produces a psychology of fear among the Moslems.

Pakistan, the proposal to divide India, however much it may appeal emotionally to some, is of course no solution for this backwardness, and it is much more likely to strengthen the hold of feudal elements for some time longer and delay the economic progress of the Moslems. Iqbal was one of the early advocates of Pakistan and yet he appears to have realized its inherent danger and absurdity. Edward Thompson has written that, in the course of a conversation, Iqbal told him that he had advocated Pakistan because of his position as president of the Moslem League session, but he felt sure that it would be injurious to India as a whole and to Moslems specially. Probably he had changed his mind, or he had not given much thought to the question previously, as it had assumed no importance then. His whole outlook on life does not fit in with the subsequent developments of the idea of Pakistan or division of India.

During his last years Iqbal turned more and more towards socialism. The great progress that Soviet Russia had made attracted him. Even his poetry took a different turn. A few months before his death, as he lay on his sick bed, he sent for me and I gladly obeyed the summons. As I talked to him about many things I felt that how much we had in common, in spite of differences, and how easy it would be to get on with him. He was in reminiscent mood and wandered from one subject to another, and I listened to him, talking little myself. I admired him and his poetry, and it pleased me greatly to feel that he liked me and had a good opinion of me. A little before I left him he said to me: 'What is there in common between Jinnah and you? He is a politician, you are a patriot.' I hope there is still much in common between Mr. Jinnah and me. As for my being a patriot I do not know that this is a particular qualification in these days, at least in the limited sense of the word. Greatly attached as I am to India, I have long felt that something more than national attachment is necessary for us in order to understand and solve even our own problems, and much more so those of the world as a whole. But Iqbal was certainly right in holding that I was not much of a politician, although politics had seized me and made me their victim.

Heavy Industry Begins. Tilak and Gokhale
Separate Electorates

In my desire to explore the background of the Hindu-Moslem

problems and understand what lay behind the new demand for Pakistan and separation, I have jumped over half a century. During this period many changes came, not so much in the external apparatus of government as in the temper of the people. Some trivial constitutional developments took place and these are often paraded, but they made no difference whatsoever to the authoritarian and all-pervasive character of British rule; nor did they touch the problems of poverty and unemployment. In 1911 Jamshedji Tata laid the foundations of heavy industry in India by starting steel and iron works in what came to be known as Jamshedpur. Government looked with disfavour on this and other attempts to start industries and in no way encouraged them. It was chiefly with American expert help that the steel industry was started. It had a precarious childhood but the war of 1914-18 came to its help. Again it languished and was in danger of passing into the hands of British debenture holders, but nationalist pressure saved it.

An industrial proletariat was growing up in India; it was unorganized and helpless, and the terribly low standards of the peasantry, from which it came, prevented wage increases and improvement. So far as unskilled labour was concerned, there were millions of unemployed persons who could be drawn upon and no strike could succeed in these conditions. The first Trade Union Congress was organized round about 1920. The numbers of this new proletariat were not sufficient to make any difference to the Indian political scene; they were a bucketful in a sea of peasants and workers on the land. In the 'twenties the voice of industrial labour began to be heard, but it was feeble. It might have been ignored but for the fact that the Russian Revolution had forced people to attach importance to the industrial proletariat. Some big and well-organized strikes also compelled attention.

The peasant, though he was everywhere and his problem was the supreme problem of India, was even more silent and forgotten by the political leaders and Government alike. The early stages of the political movement were dominated by the ideological urges of the upper middle classes, chiefly the professional classes and those looking forward to a place in the administrative machine. With the coming-of-age of the National Congress, which had been founded in 1885, a new type of leadership appeared, more aggressive and defiant and representing the much larger numbers of the lower middle classes as well as students and young men. The powerful agitation against the partition of Bengal had thrown up many able and aggressive leaders there of this type, but the real symbol of the new age was Bal Gangadhar Tilak, from Maharashtra. The old leadership was represented also by a Maratha, a very able and a younger man, Gopal Krishna Gokhale. Revolutionary slogans were in the air, tempers ran high and conflict was inevitable. To avoid this the old patriarch of the Congress, Dadabhai Naoroji, universally respected and regarded as the father of the country, was brought out of his retirement. The respite was brief and in 1907 the clash came, resulting apparently in a victory for the old moderate section. But this had been won because of organizational control and the then narrow franchise of the Congress. There was no doubt that the vast majority of politically minded people in India favoured Tilak and his group. The Congress lost much of its importance and interest shifted to other activities. Terroristic activity appeared in Bengal. The example set by Russian and Irish revolutionaries was being followed.

Moslem young men were also being affected by these revolutionary ideas. The Aligarh College had tried to check this tendency and now, under Government inspiration, the Aga Khan and others started the Moslem League to provide a political platform for Moslems and thus keep them away from the Congress. More important still, and of vital significance to India's future development, it was decided to introduce separate electorates for Moslems. Henceforward Moslems could only stand for election and be elected by separate Moslem electorates. A political barrier was created round them isolating them from the rest of India and reversing the unifying and amalgamating process which had been going on for centuries, and which was inevitably being speeded up by technological developments. This barrier was a small one at first, for the electorates were very limited, but with every extension of the franchise it grew and affected the whole structure of public and social life, like some canker which corrupted the entire system. It poisoned municipal and local self-government and ultimately it led to fantastic divisions. There came into existence (much later) separate Moslem trade unions and students' organizations and merchants' chambers. Because the Moslems were backward in all these activities, these organizations were not real organic growths from below, but were artificially created from above, and their leadership was held by the old semi-feudal type of person. Thus, to some extent, the Moslem middle classes and even the masses were isolated from the currents of growth which were influencing the rest of India. There were vested interests enough in India created or preserved by the British Government. Now an additional and powerful vested interest was created by separate electorates.

It was not a temporary evil which tended to fade away with developing political consciousness. Nurtured by official policy, it grew and spread and obscured the real problems before the country, whether political, social, or economic. It created divisions and ill-feeling where there had been none previously, and it actually weakened the favoured group by increasing a tendency to depend on artificial props and not to think in terms of self-reliance.

The obvious policy in dealing with groups or minorities which were backward educationally and economically was to help them in every way to grow and make up these deficiencies, especially by a forward educational policy. Nothing of this kind was done either for the Moslems or for other backward minorities, or for the depressed classes who needed it most. The whole argument centred in petty appointments in the subordinate public services, and instead of raising standards all round, merit was often sacrificed.

Separate electorates thus weakened the groups that were already weak or backward, they encouraged separatist tendencies and prevented the growth of national unity, they were the negation of democracy, they created new vested interests of the most reactionary kind. they lowered standards, and they diverted attention from the real economic problems of the country which were common to all. These electorates, first introduced among the Moslems, spread to other minorities and groups till India became a mosaic of these separate compartments. Possibly they may have done some good for a little while, though I am unable to spot it, but undoubtedly the injury they have caused to every department of Indian life has been prodigious. Out of them have grown all manner of separatist tendencies and finally the demand for a splitting up of India.

Lord Morley was the Secretary of State for India when these separate electorates were introduced. He resisted them, but ultimately agreed under pressure from the Viceroy. He has pointed out in his diary the dangers inherent in such a method and how they would inevitably delay the development of representative institutions. Probably this was exactly what the Viceroy and his colleagues intended. In the Montague-Chelmsford Report on Indian Constitutional Reform (1918) the dangers of these communal electorates were again emphasized: 'Division by creeds and classes means the creation of political camps organized against each other, and teaches men to think as partisans and not as citizens....We regard any system of communal electorates, therefore, as a very serious hindrance to the development of the self-governing principle.'

CHAPTER EIGHT

THE LAST PHASE (2)

Nationalism Versus Imperialism

Helplessness of the Middle Classes

Gandhi Comes

WORLD WAR I CAME. POLITICS WERE AT A LOW EBB, CHIEFLY BE-
cause of the split in the Congress between the two sections, the
so-called extremists and the moderates, and because of war-time
restrictions and regulations. Yet one tendency was marked: the
rising middle class among the Moslems was growing more nationa-
ally minded and was pushing the Moslem League towards the
Congress. They even joined hands.

Industry developed during the war and produced enormous
dividends—100 to 200 per cent—from the jute mills of Bengal
and the cotton mills of Bombay, Ahmedabad, and elsewhere.
Some of these dividends flowed to the owners of foreign capital in
Dundee and London, some went to swell the riches of Indian millionaires; and yet the workers who had created these dividends lived
at an incredibly low level of existence—in 'filthy, disease-ridden
hovels,' with no window or chimney, no light or water supply,
no sanitary arrangements. This near the so-called city of palaces,
Calcutta, dominated by British capital! In Bombay, where Indian
capital was more in evidence, an inquiry commission found in one
room, fifteen feet by twelve, six families, in all, thirty adults and
children, living together. Three of these women were expecting
a confinement soon, and each family had a separate oven in that
one room. These are special cases, but they are not very exceptional.
They describe conditions in the 'twenties and thirties of this century
when some improvements had already been made. What these
conditions were like previous to these improvements staggers the
imagination.*

I remember visiting some of these slums and hovels of industrial workers, gasping for breath there, and coming out dazed and

*These quotations and facts are taken from B. Shiva Rao's 'The Industrial Worker in
India' (Allen and Unwin, London, 1939) which deals with labour problems and workers'
conditions in India.

full of horror and anger. I remember also going down a coal mine in Jharia and seeing the conditions in which our womenfolk worked there. I can never forget that picture or the shock that came to me that human beings should labour thus. Women were subsequently prohibited from working underground, but now they have been sent back there because, we are told, war needs require additional labour; and yet millions of men are starving and unemployed. There is no lack of men, but the wages are so low and the conditions of work so bad that they do not attract.

A delegation sent by the British Trade Union Congress visited India in 1928. In their report they said that 'In Assam tea the sweat, hunger, and despair of a million Indians enter year by year.' The Director of Public Health in Bengal, in his report for 1927-28, said that the peasantry of that province were 'taking to a dietary on which even rats could not live for more than five weeks.'

World War I ended at last, and the peace, instead of bringing us relief and progress, brought us repressive legislation and martial law in the Punjab. A bitter sense of humiliation and a passionate anger filled our people. All the unending talk of constitutional reform and Indianization of the services was a mockery and an insult when the manhood of our country was being crushed and the inexorable and continuous process of exploitation was deepening our poverty and sapping our vitality. We had become a derelict nation.

Yet what could we do, how change this vicious process? We seemed to be helpless in the grip of some all-powerful monster; our limbs were paralysed, our minds deadened. The peasantry were servile and fear-ridden; the industrial workers were no better. The middle classes, the intelligentsia, who might have been beacon-lights in the enveloping darkness, were themselves submerged in this all-pervading gloom. In some ways their condition was even more pitiful than that of the peasantry. Large numbers of them, *déclassé* intellectuals, cut off from the land and incapable of any kind of manual or technical work, joined the swelling army of the unemployed, and helpless, hopeless, sank ever deeper into the morass. A few successful lawyers or doctors or engineers or clerks made little difference to the mass. The peasant starved, yet centuries of an unequal struggle against his environment had taught him to endure, and even in poverty and starvation he had a certain calm dignity, a feeling of submission to an all-powerful fate. Not so the middle classes, more especially the new petty *bourgeoisie*, who had no such background. Incompletely developed and frustrated, they did not know where to look, for neither the old nor the new offered them any hope. There was no adjustment to social purpose, no satisfaction of doing something worthwhile, even though suffering came in its train. Custom-ridden, they were born old, yet they were without the old culture. Modern thought attracted them, but they lacked its inner content, the modern social and scientific consciousness. Some tried to cling tenaciously to the dead forms of the past, seeking relief from present misery in them. But there could be no relief there, for, as Tagore has said, we must not nourish in our being what is dead, for the dead is death-dealing. Others made themselves pale and ineffectual copies of the west. So, like derelicts, frantically seeking some foothold of security for body and mind and finding none, they floated aimlessly in the murky waters of Indian life.

What could we do? How could we pull India out of this quagmire of poverty and defeatism which sucked her in? Not for a few years of excitement and agony and suspense, but for long generations our people had offered their 'blood and toil, tears and sweat.' And this process had eaten its way deep into the body and soul of India, poisoning every aspect of our corporate life, like that fell disease which consumes the tissues of the lungs and kill slowly but inevitably. Sometimes we thought that some swifter and more obvious process, resembling cholera or the bubonic plague, would have been better; but that was a passing thought, for adventurism leads nowhere, and the quack treatment of deep-seated diseases does not yield results.

And then Gandhi came. He was like a powerful current of fresh air that made us stretch ourselves and take deep breaths; like a beam of light that pierced the darkness and removed the scales from our eyes; like a whirlwind that upset many things, but most of all the working of people's minds. He did not descend from the top; he seemed to emerge from the millions of India, speaking their language and incessantly drawing attention to them and their appalling condition. Get off the backs of these peasants and workers, he told us, all you who live by their exploitation; get rid of the system that produces this poverty and misery. Political freedom took new shape then and acquired a new content. Much that he said we only partially accepted or sometimes did not accept at all. But all this was secondary. The essence of his teaching was fearlessness and truth, and action allied to these, always keeping the welfare of the masses in view. The greatest gift for an individual or a nation, so we had been told in our ancient books, was *abhaya* (fearlessness), not merely bodily courage but the absence of fear from the mind. Janaka and Yajnavalka had said, at the dawn of our history, that it was the function of the leaders of a people to make them fearless. But the dominant impulse in India under British rule was that of fear—pervasive, oppressing, strangling fear; fear of the army, the police, the widespread secret service; fear of the official class; fear of laws meant to suppress and of prison; fear of the landlord's agent; fear of the moneylender; fear of unemployment and starvation, which were always on the threshold. It was against this all-pervading fear that Gandhi's quiet and determined voice was raised: Be not afraid. Was it so simple as all that? Not quite. And yet fear builds its phantoms which are more fearsome than reality itself, and reality, when calmly analysed and its consequences willingly accepted, loses much of its terror.

So, suddenly, as it were, that black pall of fear was lifted from the people's shoulders, not wholly of course, but to an amazing degree. As fear is close companion to falsehood, so truth follows fearlessness. The Indian people did not become much more truthful than they were, nor did they change their essential nature overnight; nevertheless a sea-change was visible as the need for falsehood and furtive behaviour lessened. It was a psychological change, almost as if some expert in psycho-analytical methods had probed deep into the patient's past, found out the origins of his complexes, exposed them to his view, and thus rid him of that burden.

There was that psychological reaction also, a feeling of shame at our long submission to an alien rule that had degraded and humiliated us, and a desire to submit no longer whatever the consequences might be.

We did not grow much more truthful perhaps than we had been previously, but Gandhi was always there as a symbol of uncompromising truth to pull us up and shame us into truth. What is truth? I do not know for certain, and perhaps our truths are relative and absolute truth is beyond us. Different persons may and do take different views of truth, and each individual is powerfully influenced by his own background, training, and impulses. So also Gandhi. But truth is at least for an individual what he himself feels and knows to be true. According to this definition I do not know of any person who holds to the truth as Gandhi does. That is a dangerous quality in a politician, for he speaks out his mind and even lets the public see its changing phases.

Gandhi influenced millions of people in India in varying degrees. Some changed the whole texture of their lives, others were only partly affected, or the effect wore off; and yet not quite, for some part of it could not be wholly shaken off. Different people reacted differently and each will give his own answer to this question. Some might well say almost in the words of Alcibiades: 'Besides, when we listen to anyone else talking, however eloquent he is, we don't really care a damn what he says; but when we listen to you, or to someone else repeating what you've said, even if he puts it ever so badly, and never mind whether the person who is listening is man, woman, or child, we're absolutely staggered and bewitched. And speaking for myself, gentlemen, if I wasn't afraid you'd tell me I was completely bottled, I'd swear on oath what an extraordinary effect his words have had on me—and still do, if it comes to that. For the moment I hear him speak I am smitten by a kind of sacred rage, worse than any Corybant, and my heart jumps into my mouth and the tears start into my eyes—

Oh, and not only me, but lots of other men.

'And there is one thing I've never felt with anybody else—not the kind of thing you would expect to find in me, either—and that is a sense of shame. Socrates is the only man in the world that can make me feel ashamed. Because there's no getting away from it, I know I ought to do the things he tells me to; and yet the moment I'm out of his sight I don't care what I do to keep in with the mob. So I dash off like a runaway slave, and keep out of his way as long as I can: and the next time I meet him I remember all that I had to admit the time before, and naturally I feel ashamed....

'Yes, I have heard Pericles and all the other great orators, and very eloquent I thought they were; but they never affected me like that; they never turned my whole soul upside down and left me feeling as if I were the lowest of the low; but this latter day Maryas, here, has often left me in such a state of mind that I've felt I simply couldn't go on living the way I did....

'Only I've been bitten by something much more poisonous than a snake; in fact, mine is the most painful kind of bite there is. I've been bitten in the heart, or the mind or whatever you like to call it....'*

The Congress Becomes a Dynamic Organization under Gandhi's Leadership

Gandhi for the first time entered the Congress organization and immediately brought about a complete change in its constitution. He made it democratic and a mass organization. Democratic it had been previously also but it had so far been limited in franchise and restricted to the upper classes. Now the peasants rolled in and, in its new garb, it began to assume the look of a vast agrarian organization with a strong sprinkling of the middle classes. This agrarian character was to grow. Industrial workers also came in but as individuals and not in their separate organized capacity.

Action was to be the basis and, objective of this organization, action based on peaceful methods. Thus far the alternatives had been just talking and passing resolutions, or terroristic activity. Both of these were set aside and terrorism was especially condemned as opposed to the basic policy of the Congress. A new technique of action was evolved which, though perfectly peaceful, yet implied non-submission to what was considered wrong and, as a consequence, a willing acceptance of the pain and suffering involved in this. Gandhi was an odd kind of pacifist, for he was an activist full of dynamic energy. There was no submission in him to fate or anything that he considered evil; he was full of resistance, though this was peaceful and courteous.

*From 'The Five Dialogues of Plato', Everyman's Library.

The call of action was two-fold. There was, of course, the action involved in challenging and resisting foreign rule; there was also the action which led us to fight our own social evils. Apart from the fundamental objective of the Congress—the freedom of India— and the method of peaceful action, the principal planks of the Congress were national unity, which involved the solution of the minority problems, and the raising of the depressed classes and the ending of the curse of untouchability.

Realizing that the main props of British rule were fear, prestige, the co-operation, willing or unwilling, of the people, and certain classes whose vested interests were centred in British rule, Gandhi attacked these foundations. Titles were to be given up and though the title-holders responded to this only in small measure, the popular respect for these British-given titles disappeared and they became symbols of degradation. New standards and values were set up and the pomp and splendour of the viceregal court and the princes, which used to impress so much, suddenly appeared supremely ridiculous and vulgar and rather shameful, surrounded as they were by the poverty and misery of the people. Rich men were not so anxious to flaunt their riches; outwardly at least many of them adopted simpler ways, and in their dress, became almost indistinguishable from humbler folk.

The older leaders of the Congress, bred in a different and more quiescent tradition, did not take easily to these new ways and were disturbed by the upsurge of the masses. Yet so powerful was the wave of feeling and sentiment that swept through the country, that some of this intoxication filled them also. A very few fell away and among them was Mr. M. A. Jinnah. He left the Congress not because of any difference of opinion on the Hindu-Moslem question but because he could not adapt himself to the new and more advanced ideology, and even more so because he disliked the crowds of ill-dressed people, talking in Hindustani, who filled the Congress. His idea of politics was of a superior variety, more suited to the legislative chamber or to a committee-room. For some years he felt completely out of the picture and even decided to leave India for good. He settled down in England and spent several years there.

It is said, and I think with truth, that the Indian habit of mind is essentially one of quietism. Perhaps old races develop that attitude to life; a long tradition of philosophy also leads to it and yet Gandhi, a typical product of India, represents the very antithesis of quietism. He has been a demon of energy and action, a hustler, and a man who not only drives himself but drives others. He has done more than anyone I know to fight and change the quietism of the Indian people.

He sent us to the villages, and the countryside hummed with the activity of innumerable messengers of the new gospel of action. The peasant was shaken up and he began to emerge from his quiescent shell. The effect on us was different but equally far-reaching, for we saw, for the first time as it were, the villager in the intimacy of his mud-hut, and with the stark shadow of hunger always pursuing him. We learnt our Indian economics more from these visits than from books and learned discourses. The emotional experience we had already undergone was emphasized and confirmed and henceforward there could be no going back for us to our old life or our old standards, howsoever much our views might change subsequently.

Gandhi held strong views on economic, social, and other matters. He did not try to impose all of these on the Congress, though he continued to develop his ideas, and sometimes in the process varied them, through his writings. But some he tried to push into the Congress. He proceeded cautiously for he wanted to carry the people with him. Sometimes he went too far for the Congress and had to retrace his steps. Not many accepted his veiws in their entirety; some disagreed with that fundamental outlook. But many accepted them in the modified form in which they came to the Congress as being suited to the circumstances then existing. In two respects the background of his thought had a vague but considerable influence; the fundamental test of everything was how far it benefited the masses, and the means were always important and could not be ignored even though the end in view was right, for the means governed the end and varied it.

Gandhi was essentially a man of religion, a Hindu to the inner-most depths of his being, and yet his conception of religion had nothing to do with any dogma or custom or ritual.* It was basically concerned with his firm belief in the moral law, which he calls the law of truth or love. Truth and non-violence appear to him to be the same thing or different aspects of one and the same thing, and he uses these words almost interchangeably. Claiming to understand the spirit of Hinduism, he rejects every text or practice which does not fit in with his idealist interpretation of what it should be, calling it an interpolation or a subsequent accretion. 'I decline to be a slave,' he has said, 'to precedents or practice I cannot understand or defend on a moral basis.' And so in practice he is singularly free to take the path of his choice, to change and adapt himself, to develop his philosophy of life and action, subject only to the over-riding consideration of the moral law as he conceives this to be. Whether that philosophy is right

*Gandhi told the Federation of International Fellowships in January, 1928, that 'After long study and experience I have come to these conclusions that: (1) all religions are true, (2) all religions have some error in them, (3) all religions are almost as dear to me as my own Hinduism. My veneration for other faiths is the same as for my own faith. Consequently, the thought of conversion is impossible....Our prayer for others ought never to be: "God give them the light thou has given to me!" But: "Give them all the light and truth they need for their highest development!" '

or wrong, may be argued, but he insists on applying the same fundamental yard-stick to everything, and himself especially. In politics, as in other aspects of life, this creates difficulties for the average person, and often misunderstanding. But no difficulty makes him swerve from the straight line of his choosing, though within limits he is continually adapting himself to a changing situation. Every reform that he suggests, every advice that he gives to others, he straightway applies to himself. He is always beginning with himself and his words and actions fit into each other like a glove on the hand. And so, whatever happens, he never loses his integrity and there is always an organic completeness about his life and work. Even in his apparent failures he has seemed to grow in stature.

What was his idea of India which he was setting out to mould according to his own wishes and ideals? 'I shall work for an India in which the poorest shall feel that it is their country, in whose making they have an effective voice, an India in which there shall be no high class and low class of people, an India in which all communities shall live in perfect harmony....There can be no room in such an India for the curse of untouchability or the curse of intoxicating drinks and drugs....Women will enjoy the same right as men....This is the India of my dreams.' Proud of his Hindu inheritance as he was, he tried to give to Hinduism a kind of universal attire and included all religions within the fold of truth. He refused to narrow his cultural inheritance.

'Indian culture,' he wrote, 'is neither Hindu, Islamic, nor any other, wholly. It is a fusion of all.' Again he said: 'I want the culture of all lands to be blown about my house as freely as possible. But I refuse to be blown off my feet by any. I refuse to live in other peoples' houses as an interloper, a beggar, or a slave.' Influenced by modern thought currents, he never let go of his roots and clung to them tenaciously.

And so he set about to restore the spiritual unity of the people and to break the barrier between the small westernized group at the top and the masses, to discover the living elements in the old roots and to build upon them, to waken these masses out of their stupor and static condition and make them dynamic. In his single-track and yet many-sided nature the dominating impression that one gathered was his identification with the masses, a community of spirit with them, an amazing sense of unity with the dispossessed and poverty-stricken not only of India but of the world. Even religion, as everything else, took second place to his passion to raise these submerged people. 'A semi-starved nation can have neither religion, nor art nor organization.' 'Whatever can be useful to starving millions is beautiful to my mind. Let us give to-day first the vital things of life, and all the graces and ornaments of life will follow....I want art and literature that can speak to millions.' These unhappy dispossessed millions haunted him and everything seemed to revolve round them. 'For millions it is an eternal vigil or an eternal trance.' His ambition, he said, was 'to wipe every tear from every eye.'

It is not surprising that this astonishingly vital man, full of self-confidence and an unusual kind of power, standing for equality and freedom for each individual, but measuring all this in terms of the poorest, fascinated the masses of India and attracted them like a magnet. He seemed to them to link up the past with the future and to make the dismal present appear just as a stepping-stone to that future of life and hope. And not the masses only but intellectuals and others also, though their minds were often troubled and confused and the change-over for them from the habits of a lifetime was more difficult. Thus he effected a vast psychological revolution not only among those who followed his lead but also among his opponents and those many neutrals who could not make up their minds what to think and what to do.

Congress was dominated by Gandhi and yet it was a peculiar domination, for the Congress was an active, rebellious, many-sided organization, full of variety of opinion, and not easily led this way or that. Often Gandhi toned down his position to meet the wishes of others, sometimes he accepted even an adverse decision. On some vital matters for him, he was adamant, and on more than one occasion there came a break between him and the Congress. But always he was the symbol of India's independence and militant nationalism, the unyielding opponent of all those who sought to enslave her, and it was as such a symbol that people gathered to him and accepted his lead, even though they disagreed with him on other matters. They did not always accept that lead when there was no active struggle going on, but when the struggle was inevitable that symbol became all important, and everything else was secondary.

Thus in 1920 the National Congress, and to a large extent the country, took to this new and unexplored path and came into conflict repeatedly with the British power. The conflict was inherent both in these methods and in the new situation that had arisen, yet back of all this was not political tactics and manoeuvring but the desire to strengthen the Indian people, for by that strength alone could they achieve independence and retain it. Civil disobedience struggles came one after the other, involving enormous suffering, but that suffering was self-invited and therefore strength giving, not the kind which overwhelms the unwilling, leading to despair and defeatism. The unwilling also suffered, caught in the wide net of fierce governmental repression, and even the willing sometimes broke up and collapsed. But many remained true and steadfast, harder for all the experience they had undergone. At no time, even when its fortunes were low, did

Congress surrender to superior might or submit to foreign authority. It remained the symbol of India's passionate desire for independence and her will to resist alien domination. It was because of this that vast numbers of the Indian people sympathized with it and looked to it for leadership, even though many of them were so weak and feeble, or so circumstanced, as to be unable to do anything themselves. The Congress was a party in some ways; it has also been a joint platform for several parties; but essentially it was something much more, for it represented the innermost desire of vast numbers of our people. The number of members on its rolls, large as this was, was only a feeble reflection of its widespread representative character for membership depended not on the people's desire to join but on our capacity to reach remote villages. Often (as now) we have been an illegal organisation, not existing at all in the eyes of the law, and our books and papers have been taken away by the police.

Even when there was no civil disobedience struggle going on, the general attitude of non-co-operation with the British apparatus of government in India continued, though it lost its aggressive character. That did not mean, of course, non-co-operation with Englishmen as such. When Congress governments were installed in many provinces, there was inevitably much co-operation in official and governmental work. Even then, however, that background did not change much and instructions were issued regulating the conduct of Congressmen, apart from official duties. Between Indian nationalism and an alien imperialism there could be no final peace, though temporary compromises and adjustments were sometimes inevitable. Only a free India could co-operate with England on equal terms.

Congress Governments in the Provinces

The British Parliament, after some years of commissions, committees, and debates, passed a Government of India Act in 1935. This provided for some kind of provincial autonomy and a federal structure, but there were so many reservations and checks that both political and economic power continued to be concentrated in the hands of the British Government. Indeed in some ways it confirmed and enlarged the powers of an executive responsible solely to that Government. The federal structure was so envisaged as to make any real advance impossible, and no loophole was left for the representatives of the Indian people to interfere with or modify the system of British-controlled administration. Any change or relaxation of this could only come through the British Parliament. Thus, reactionary as this structure was, there were not even any seeds in it of self-growth, short of some kind of revolutionary action. The Act strengthened the alliance between the British

365

Government and the princes, landlords, and other reactionary elements in India; it added to the separate electorates, thus increasing the separatist tendencies; it consolidated the predominant position of British trade, industry, banking, and shipping and laid down statutory prohibitions against any interference with this position, any 'discrimination,' as it was called;* it retained in British hands complete control over Indian finance, military, and foreign affairs; it made the Viceroy even more powerful than he had been.

In the limited sphere of provincial autonomy the transfer of authority was, or appeared to be, much greater. Nevertheless, the position of a popular government was extraordinary. There were all the checks of viceregal powers and an irresponsible central authority, and even the Governor of the province, like the Viceroy, could intervene, veto, legislate on his own sole authority, and do almost anything he wanted even in direct opposition to the popular ministers and the provincial legislature. A great part of the revenues were mortgaged to various vested interests and could not be used. The superior services and the police were protected and could hardly be touched by the ministers. They were wholly authoritarian in outlook and looked, as of old, to the Governor for guidance and not to the ministers. And yet these were the very people through whom the popular government had to function. The whole complicated structure of government remained as it was, from the Governor down to the petty official and policeman; only somewhere in the middle a few ministers, responsible to a popularly elected legislature, were thrust in to carry on as best they could. If the Governor (who represented British authority) and the services under him agreed and fully co-operated with the ministers, the apparatus of government might function smoothly. Otherwise—and this was much more likely, as the policy and methods of a popular government differed entirely from the old authoritarian police-state ways—there was bound to be continuous friction. Even when the Governor or the services were not openly at variance with or disloyal to the policy of the popular government, they could obstruct, delay, pervert, and undo what that Government did or wished to do. In law there was nothing to prevent the Governor and the Viceroy from acting as they liked, even in active opposition to the ministry and the legislature; the

---

*The removal of these statutory prohibitions is still fiercely resisted by representatives of British industry and trade in India. In April, 1945, a resolution demanding this removal was passed in the Central Assembly in spite of British opposition. Indian nationalism, and indeed all Indian parties and groups are strongly in favour of this removal, and of course Indian industrialists are most anxious about it. And yet, it is significant to note that Indian businessmen in Ceylon are demanding exactly the same kind of protection in Ceylon which they rightly resent having been given to British business interests in India. Self-interest not only blinds one to justice and fair play but also to the simplest applications of logic and reason.

only real check was fear of conflict. The ministers might resign, no others could command a majority in the legislature, and popular upheavals might follow. It was the old constitutional conflict between an autocratic king and parliament which had so often taken place elsewhere, leading to revolutions and the suppression of the king. Here the king was in addition a foreign authority, supported by foreign military and economic power and the special interests and lap-dog breed it had created in the country.

About this time also Burma was separated from India. In Burma there had been a conflict between British and Indian and, to some extent, Chinese, economic and commerical interests. It had therefore been British policy to encourage anti-Indian and anti-Chinese sentiments among the Burmese people. This policy was helpful for sometimes, but when it was joined on to a denial of freedom to the Burmese, it resulted in creating the powerful pro-Japanese movements in Burma which came to the surface when the Japanese attacked in 1942.

The Act of 1935 was bitterly opposed by all sections of Indian opinion. While the part dealing with provincial autonomy was severely criticized for its many reservations and the powers given to the Governors and the Viceroy, the federal part was even more resented. Federation as such was not opposed and it was generally recognized that a federal structure was desirable for India, but the proposed federation petrified British rule and vested interests in India. Only the provincial autonomy part of it was applied and the Congress decided to contest elections. But the question whether responsibility for provincial governments should be undertaken, within the terms of the Act, led to fierce debate within the Congress. The success of the Congress in the elections was overwhelming in most of the provinces, but still there was hesitation in accepting ministerial responsibility unless it was made clear that there would be no interference by the Governor or Viceroy. After some months vague assurances were given to this effect and Congress governments were established in July, 1937. Ultimately there were such governments in eight of the eleven provinces, the three remaining ones being Sind, Bengal, and Punjab. Sind was a small, newly-created, and rather unstable province. In Bengal the Congress had the largest single party in the legislature, but as it was not in a majority, it did not participate in the Government. Bengal (or rather, Calcutta) being the principal headquarters of British capital in India, the European commercial element has been given astonishingly heavy representation. In numbers they are a mere handful (some thousands) and yet they have been given twenty-five seats as compared to the fifty seats for the general non-Moslem population consisting of about seventeen millions (apart from the scheduled castes) of the whole province. This British group in the legislature thus plays an important part

367

in Bengal politics and can make or unmake ministries.

The Congress could not possibly accept the Act of 1935 as even a temporary solution of the Indian problem. It was pledged to independence and to combat the Act. Yet a majority had decided to work provincial autonomy. It had thus a dual policy: to carry on the struggle for independence and at the same time to carry through the legislatures constructive measures of reform. The agrarian question especially demanded immediate attention.

The question of Congressmen joining other groups to form coalition governments was considered, although there was no necessity for this as the Congress had clear majorities. Still it was desirable to associate as many people as possible in the work of government. There was nothing inherently wrong about coalitions at all times, and indeed some form of coalition was agreed to in the Frontier Province and in Assam. As a matter of fact, the Congress itself was a kind of coalition or joint front of various groups tied together by the dominating urge for India's independence. In spite of this variety within its fold, it had developed a discipline, a social outlook, and a capacity to offer battle in its own peaceful way. A wider coalition meant a joining up with people whose entire political and social outlook was different, and who were chiefly interested in office and ministerships. Conflict was inherent in the situation, conflict with the representatives of British interests—the Viceroy, the Governor, the superior services; conflict also with vested interests in land and industry over agrarian questions and workers' conditions. The non-Congress elements were usually politically and socially conservative; some of them were pure careerists. If such elements entered government, they might tone down our whole social programme, or at any rate obstruct and delay it. There might even be intrigues with the Governor over the heads of the other ministers. A joint front against British authority was essential. Any breach in this would be harmful to our cause. There would have been no binding cement, no common loyalty, no united objective, and individual ministers would have looked and pulled in different directions.

Our public life naturally included many who could be called politicians and nothing more, careerists, both in the good and bad sense of the word. There were able, earnest, and patriotic men and women, as well as careerists, both in the Congress and in other organizations. But the Congress had been, ever since 1920, something much more than a constitutional political party, and the breath of revolutionary action, actual or potential, surrounded it and often put it outside the pale of the law. The fact that this action was not connected with violence, secret intrigue, and conspiracy, the usual accompaniments of revolutionary activity, did not make it any the less revolutionary. Whether it was right or wrong, effective or not, may be an arguable matter, but it is manifest that it involved cold-blooded courage and endurance of a high order. Perhaps it is easier to indulge in short violent spurts of courage, even unto death, than to give up, under the sole compulsion of one's own mind, almost everything that life offers and carry on in this way day after day, month after month, year after year. That is a test which few can survive anywhere and it is surprising that so many in India have stood it successfully.

The Congress parties in the legislatures were anxious to pass legislative measures in favour of the peasants and workers as soon as possible before some crisis overwhelmed them. That sense of impending crisis was always present; it was inherent in the situation. In nearly all the provinces there were second chambers elected on a very limited franchise and thus representing vested interests in land and industry. There were also other checks to progressive legislation. Coalition governments would add to all these difficulties and it was decided not to have them to begin with, except in Assam and the Frontier.

This decision was itself by no means final and the possibility of change was kept in view, but rapidly developing circumstances made any change more difficult and the Congress governments in the provinces became entangled in the numerous problems that urgently demanded solution. In subsequent years there has been much argument about the wisdom of that decsiion and opinions have differed. It is easy to be wise after the event, but I am still inclined to think that politically, and situated as we were then, it was a natural and logical decision for us. Nevertheless it is true that the consequences of it on the communal question were unfortunate and it led to a feeling of grievance and isolation among many Moslems. This played into the hands of reactionary elements who utilized it to strengthen their own position among certain groups.

Politically and constitutionally, the new Act and the establishment of Congress governments in the provinces made no vital difference to the British structure of government. Real power remained where it had so long been. But the psychological change was enormous and an electric current seemd to run through the countryside. This change was noticeable more in the rural areas than in the cities, though in the industrial centres the workers also reacted in the same way. There was a sense of immense relief as of the lifting of a weight which had been oppressing the people; there was a release of long-suppressed mass energy which was evident everywhere. The fear of the police and secret service vanished for a while at least and even the poorest peasant added to his feeling of self-respect and self-reliance. For the first time he felt that he counted and could not be ignored. Government was no longer an unknown and intangible monster, separated from him by innumerable layers of officials, whom he could not easily approach and much less influence, and who were bent on extracting as much out of him as possible. The seats of the mighty were now occupied by men he had often seen and heard and talked to; sometimes they had been in prison together and there was a feeling of comradeship between them.

At the headquarters of the provincial governments, in the very citadels of the old bureaucracy, many a symbolic scene was witnessed. These provincial secretariats, as they were called, where all the high offices were congregated, had been the holy of holies of government, and out of them issued mysterious orders which none could challenge. Policemen and red-liveried orderlies, with shining daggers thrust in their waistbands, guarded the precincts, and only those who were fortunate or greatly daring or had a long purse, could pass them. Now, suddenly, hordes of people, from the city and the village, entered these sacred precincts and roamed about almost at will. They were interested in everything; they went into the Assembly Chamber, where the sessions used to be held; they even peeped into the Ministers' rooms. It was difficult to stop them for they no longer felt as outsiders; they had a sense of ownership in all this, although it was all very complicated for them and difficult to understand. The policemen and orderlies with shining daggers were paralysed; the old standards had fallen; European dress, symbol of position and authority, no longer counted. It was difficult to distinguish between members of the legislatures and the peasants and townsmen who came in such large numbers. They were often dressed more or less alike, mostly in handspun cloth with the well-known Gandhi cap on their heads.

It had been very different in the Punjab and in Bengal where ministries had come into existence several months earlier. There had been no impasse there and the change-over had taken place quietly without ruffling the surface of life in any way. In the Punjab especially the old order continued and most of the ministers were not new. They had been high officials previously and they continued to be so. Between them and the British administration there was no conflict or sense of tension, for politically that administration was supreme.

This difference between the Congress provinces and Bengal and Punjab was immediately apparent in regard to civil liberties and political prisoners. In both Bengal and Punjab there was no relaxation of the police and secret service *raj*, and political prisoners were not released. In Bengal, where the ministry often depended on European votes, there were in addition thousands of *detenus*, that is, men and women kept indefinitely for years and years in prison without charge or trial. In the Congress provinces, however, the very first step taken was the release of political prisoners. In regard to some of these, who had been convicted for violent activities, there was delay because of the Governor's refusal to agree. Matters came to a head early in 1938 over this issue and two of the Congress Governments (United Provinces and Bihar) actually offered their resignations. Thereupon the Governor withdrew his objections and the prisoners were released.

Indian Dynamism versus British Conservatism in India

The new provincial assemblies had a much larger representation from the rural areas and this inevitably led to a demand in all of them for agrarian reforms. In Bengal, because of the permanent settlement and for other reasons, the condition of the tenantry was worst of all. Next came the other big zamindari (landlord) provinces, chiefly Bihar and the United Provinces, and thirdly the provinces where originally some kind of peasant proprietorship had been established (Madras, Bombay, Punjab, etc.), but where big landed estates had also grown up. The permanent settlement came in the way of any effective reform in Bengal. Almost everybody is agreed that this must go, and even an official commission has recommended it, but vested interests still manage to prevent or delay change. The Punjab was fortunate in having fresh land at its disposal.

For the Congress the agrarian question was the dominating social issue and much time had been given to its study and the formulation of policy. This varied in different provinces as conditions were different and also the class composition of the provincial Congress organizations, differed from one another. There was an all-India agrarian policy which had been formulated by the central organization and each province added to it and filled in the details. The United Provinces Congress was in this respect the most advanced and it had reached the conclusion that the zamindari (landlord) system should be abolished. This, however, was impossible under the Government of India Act of 1935, even apart from the special powers of the Viceroy and the Governor, and the second chamber which largely consisted of the landed class. Changes had thus to be made within the larger framework of this system, unless of course some revolutionary upheaval ended that system itself. This made reform difficult and terribly complicated and it took much longer than was anticipated.

However, substantial agrarian reforms were introduced and the problem of rural indebtedness was also attacked. So also labour conditions in factories, public health and sanitation, local self-government, education both in the lower stages and in the university, literacy, industry, rural development, and many other problems were tackled. All these social, cultural, and economic problems had been ignored and neglected by previous governments, their function had been to make the police and the revenue departments efficient and to allow the rest to take their own course. Occasionally some little effort had been made and commissions and inquiry committees had been appointed, which produced huge reports after years of labour and travelling about. Then the reports had been put away in their respective pigeon-holes and little was done. Even proper statistics had not been collected, in spite of insistent popular demand. This lack of statistics and surveys and necessary information had been a serious impediment in the way of progress in any direction. Thus the new provincial governments had, apart from the normal work of administration, to face a mountain of work, the result of years of neglect, and on every side urgent problems faced them. They had to change a police-state into a socially-guided state—never an easy job but made much more difficult by the limitation on their power, the poverty of the people, and the divergence of outlook between these provincial governments and the central authority, which was completely autocratic and authoritarian, under the Viceroy.

We knew all these limitations and barriers, we realized in our hearts that we could not do much till conditions were radically changed—hence our overwhelming desire for independence—and yet the passion for progress filled us and the wish to emulate other countries which had gone so far ahead in many ways. We thought of the United States of America and even of some eastern countries which were forging ahead. But most of all we had the example of the Soviet Union which in two brief decades, full of war and civil strife and in the face of what appeared to be insurmountable difficulties, had made tremendous progress. Some were attracted to communism, others were not, but all were fascinated by the advance of the Soviet Union in education and culture and medical care and physical fitness and in the solution of the problem of nationalities—by the amazing and prodigious effort to create a new world out of the dregs of the old. Even Rabindranath Tagore, highly individualistic as he was and not attracted towards some aspects of the communistic system, became an admirer of this new civilization and contrasted it with present conditions in his own country. In his last death-bed message he referred to the 'unsparing energy with which Russia has tried to fight disease and illiteracy, and has succeeded in steadily liquidating ignorance and poverty, wiping off the humiliation from the face of a vast continent. Her civilization is free from all invidious distinction between one class and another, between one sect and another. The rapid and astounding progress achieved by her made me happy and jealous at the same time. . . . When I see elsewhere some 200 nationalities—which only a few years ago were at vastly different stages of development—marching ahead in peaceful progress and amity, and when I look about my own country and see a very highly evolved and intellectual people drifting into the disorder of barbarism, I cannot help contrasting the two systems of governments, one based on co-operation, the other on exploitation, which have made such contrary conditions possible.'

If others could do it, why not we? We had faith in our capacity, our intelligence, our will to persevere, to endure and succeed. We knew the difficulties, our poverty and backwardness, our reactionary groups and classes, our divisions; yet we would face them and overcome them. We knew that the price was a heavy one, but we were prepared to pay it, for no price could be greater than what we paid from day to day in our present condition. But how were we to begin on our internal problems when the external problem of British rule and occupation faced us at every turn and nullified our every effort?

Yet since we had some opportunity, however limited and restricted, in these provincial governments, we wanted to take advantage of it in the fullest measure. But it was a heart-breaking job for our ministers, who were overwhelmed with work and responsibility, and could not even share this with the permanent services, because of the lack of harmony and the absence of a common outlook. Unfortunately also, the number of these ministers was much too small. They were supposed to set an example in plain living and economy in public expenditure. Their salaries were small, and we had the curious spectacle of a minister's secretary or some other subordinate belonging to the Indian Civil Service drawing a salary and allowances which were four or five times the minister's salary. We could not touch the emoluments of the Civil Service. Also the minister would travel second-class by railway train, or even third, while some subordinate of his might be travelling first or in a lordly saloon in the same train.

It has often been stated that the central Congress Executive continually interfered with the work of these provincial governments by issuing orders from above. This is entirely incorrect, and there was no interference with the internal administration. What the Congress Executive desired was that a common policy on all fundamental political matters should be followed by the provincial governments, and that the Congress programme, as laid down in the election manifesto, should be furthered in so far as this was possible. In particular, the policy vis-a-vis the governors and the Government of India had to be uniform.

The introduction of provincial autonomy without any change in the central government, which continued to be wholly irresponsible and authoritarian, was likely to lead to a growth of provincialism and diversity, and thus to a lessening of the sense of Indian unity. Probably the British Government had this in view in furtherance of its policy of encouraging disruptive elements and tendencies. The Government of India, irremovable, irresponsible, and unresponsive, still representing the old tradition of British imperialism, stood as solid as a rock, and, of course, pursued a uniform policy with all the provincial governments. The Governors, acting on instructions from New Delhi or Simla did likewise. If the Congress provincial governments had reacted differently from this, each in its own way, they could have been disposed of separately. It was essential, therefore, for these provincial governments to hold together and present a united front to the Government of India. The Government of India, on the other hand, was equally anxious to prevent this co-operation, and preferred to deal with each provincial government separately without reference to similar problems elsewhere.

In August, 1937, soon after the formation of the Congress provincial governments, the Congress Executive passed the following resolution:

'The Working Committee recommend to the Congress ministers the appointment of a committee of experts to consider urgent and vital problems, the solution of which is necessary to any scheme of national reconstruction and social planning. Such solution will require extensive surveys and the collection of data, as well as a clearly-defined social objective. Many of these problems cannot be dealt with efficiently on a provincial basis, and the interests of adjoining provinces are interlinked. Comprehensive river surveys are necessary for the formulation of a policy to prevent disastrous floods, to utilise the water for the purposes of irrigation, to consider the problem of soil erosion, to eradicate malaria, and for the development of hydro-electric and other schemes. For this purpose the whole river valley will have to be surveyed and investigated, and large-scale state planning resorted to. The development and control of industries require also joint and co-ordinate action on the part of several provinces. The Working Committee advise therefore that, to begin with, an inter-provincial committee of experts be appointed to consider the general nature of the problems to be faced, and to suggest how, and in what order, those should be tackled. This expert committee may suggest the formation of special committees or boards to consider each such problem separately, and to advise the provincial governments concerned as to the joint action to be undertaken.'

This resolution indicates the kind of advice that was sometimes tendered to the provincial governments. It shows also how desirous the Congress Executive was to encourage co-operation between provincial governments in the economic and industrial sphere. That co-operation was not limited to the Congress governments, although the advice was necessarily addressed to them. A comprehensive river survey overlapped provincial boundaries; a survey of the Gangetic valley and the setting up of a Ganga River Commission (a work of the highest importance which yet awaits to be done) could only take place with the co-operation of the three provincial governments—those of the United Provinces, Bihar, and Bengal.

The resolution also demonstrates the importance attached by the Congress to large-scale state planning. Such planning was impossible so long as the central government was not under popular control and the shackles on the provincial governments had not been removed. We hoped, however, that some essential preliminary work might be done and the foundations for future planning laid down. Unfortunately, the provincial governments were so busy with their own problems that there was delay in giving effect to this resolution. Late in 1938 a National Planning Committee was constituted, and I became chairman of it.

I was often critical of the work of the Congress Governments and fretted at the slowness of progress made; but, looking back, I am surprised at their achievements during a brief period of two years and a quarter, despite the innumerable difficulties that surrounded them. Unfortunately, some of their important work did not bear fruit, as it was on the point of completion when they resigned, and it was shelved afterwards by their successor—that is, the British Governor. Both the peasantry and industrial labour benefited and grew in strength. One of the most important and far-reaching achievements was the introduction of a system of mass education called basic education. This was not only based on the latest educational doctrine but was peculiarly suited to Indian conditions.

Every vested interest came in the way of progressive change. A committee appointed by the United Provinces Government to inquire into labour conditions in the Cawnpore textile industry was treated by the employers (chiefly Europeans but including some Indians) with the greatest discourtesy, and many of the facts and figures demanded were refused. Labour had long faced the organized opposition of both the employers and Government, and the police had always been at the disposal of the employers. The change in policy introduced by the Congress Governments was therefore resented by the employers. Of the tactics of employers in India, Mr. B. Shiva Rao, who has had long experience of the Labour movement in India and belongs to the moderate wing of it, writes: 'The amount of resourcefulness and lack of scruple exhibited on such occasions (strikes etc.) by the employers with the assistance of police would be incredible to one unacquainted with Indian conditions.' The government of most countries, constituted as it is, inclines towards the employers. In India, Mr. Shiva Rao points out, there is an additional reason for this. 'Apart from personal animosities, officials in India with rare exceptions have been obsessed with the fear that trade unions, if allowed to develop, would foster mass consciousness; and with the political struggle in India periodically flaring up into movements like non-co-operation and civil disobedience, they have felt presumably that no risks should be taken in regard to the organization of the masses.'*

Governments lay down policy, legislatures pass laws; but the actual working out of this policy and the application of these laws depend ultimately on the services and the administrative personnel. The provincial governments had thus inevitably to rely on the permanent services, especially the Indian civil service and the police. These services, bred in a different and authoritarian tradition, disliked the new atmosphere, the assertive attitude of the public, the lessening of their own importance, and their subordination to persons whom they had been in the habit of arresting and imprisoning. They had been rather apprehensive at first as to what might happen. But nothing very revolutionary happened and they gradually settled down to their old rountine. It was not easy for the ministers to interfere with the man on the spot and only in obvious cases could they do so. The services formed a close corporation and hung together, and if one man was transferred, his successor was likely to act in the same way. It was impossible to change suddenly the old reactionary and autocratic mentality of the services as a whole. A few individuals might change, some might make an effort to adapt themselves to the new conditions, but the vast majority of them thought differently and had always functioned differently; how could they undergo a sea-change and emerge as crusaders of a new order? At the most they could give a passive and heavy-moving loyalty; there could not, in the very nature of things, be a flaming enthusiasm for the new kind of work to be done, in which they did not believe and which undermined their own vested interests. Unfortunately even this passive loyalty was often lacking.

Among the higher members of the civil service, long accustomed to authoritarian methods and unchecked rule, there was a feeling that these ministers and legislators were intruders in a domain reserved for them. The old conception that they, the permanent services and especially the British element in them, were India and all others were unimportant appendages, died hard. It was not easy to suffer the new-comers, much less to take orders from them. They felt as an orthodox Hindu might feel if untouchables pushed their way into the sacred precincts of his own particular temple. The edifice of prestige and racial

*B. Shiva Rao: 'The Industrial Worker in India' (London, 1939).

superiority which had been built with so much labour, and which had almost become a religion to them, was cracking. The Chinese are said to be great believers in 'face,' and yet I doubt if any among them are so passionately attached to 'face' as the British in India. For the latter it is not only individual, racial, and national prestige; it is also intimately connected with their rule and vested interests.

Yet the intruders had to be tolerated, but the toleration grew progressively less as the sense of danger receded. This attitude permeated all departments of the administration, but it was especially in evidence away from headquarters, in the districts, and in matters relating to, what is called, Law and Order, which was the special preserve of the district magistrate and the police. The emphasis of the Congress governments on civil liberty gave the local officials and the police an excuse for allowing things to happen which, ordinarily, no government could have permitted. Indeed I am convinced that in some cases the initiative for these undesirable occurrences came from the local officials or the police. Many of the communal (religious) riots that took place were due to a variety of causes, but the magistrates and the police were certainly not always free from guilt. Experience showed that a quick and efficient handling of the situation put an end to the trouble. What we saw repeatedly was an astonishing slackness and a deliberate evasion of duty. It became obvious that the objective was to discredit the Congress governments. In the Provinces, the industrial city of Cawnpore offered the most glaring example of utter ineptitude and mismanagement on the part of the local officials, which could only be deliberate. Communal (religious) friction, leading sometimes to local riots, had been more in evidence in the late twenties and early thirties. After the Congress governments took office it was in many ways much less. It changed its nature and became definitely political and deliberately encouraged and organized.

The civil service had a reputation, chiefly self-propagated, for efficiency. But it became evident that outside the narrow sphere of work to which they had been accustomed, they were helpless and incompetent. They had no training to function democratically and could not gain the goodwill and co-operation of the people, whom they both feared and despised; they had no conception of big and fast-moving schemes of social progress and could only hamper them by their red-tape and lack of imagination. Apart from certain individuals, this applied to both British and Indian members of the higher services. It was extraordinary how unfitted they were for the new tasks that faced them.

There was, of course, a great deal of inefficiency and incompetence on the popular side. But it was counterbalanced by energy and enthusiasm, and close touch with masses, and a desire and capacity to learn from one's own mistakes. There was vitality there, a bubbling life, a sense of tension, a desire to get things done, all of which contrasted strangely with the apathy and conservatism of the British ruling class and their supporters. India, the land of tradition, thus offered a strange picture of reversal of roles. The British, who had come here as representatives of a dynamic society, were now the chief upholders of a static, unchanging tradition; among the Indians there were many who represented the new dynamic order and were eager for change, change not only political but also social and economic. Behind those Indians there were, of course, vast new forces at work which perhaps even they hardly realized. This reversal of roles was a demonstration of the fact that whatever creative or progressive role the British might have played in the past in India, they had long ceased to play it, and were now a hindrance and an obstruction to all progress. The tempo of their official life was slow and incapable of solving any of the vital problems before India. Even their utterances, which used to have some clarity and strength, became turgid, inept, and lacking any real content.

There has long been a legend, propagated by British authorities, that the British Government, through its higher services in India, was training us for the difficult and intricate art of self-government. We had managed to carry on, and with a considerable degree of success, for a few thousand years before the British came here and gave us the advantage of their training. No doubt we lack many of the good qualities that we should possess, and some misguided persons even say that this deficiency has grown under British rule. But whatever our failings might be, it seemed obvious to us that the permanent services here were totally incapable of leading India in any progressive direction. The very qualities they possessed made them unhelpful, for the qualities necessary in a police state are utterly different from those required in a progressive democratic community. Before they could presume to train others, it would be necessary for them to untrain themselves, and to bathe in the waters of Lethe so that they might forget what they had been.

The odd position of a popular provincial government with an autocratic central government over it brought out many strange contrasts. The Congress governments were anxious to preserve civil liberties and they checked the wide-flung activities of the provincial C.I.D. (Criminal Investigation Department) whose chief function had been to shadow politicians and all those who were suspected of anti-government sentiments. While these activities were checked, the Imperial C.I.D. continued to function, probably with greater energy. Not only were our letters censored, but even the ministers' correspondence was sometimes subjected to this, though it was done quietly and not officially admitted. During the last quarter of a century or more I have not written a single letter, which has been posted in India, either to an Indian or a foreign address, without realizing that it would be seen, and possibly copied, by some secret service censor. Nor have I spoken on the telephone without remembering that my conversation was likely to be tapped. The letters that have reached me also have had to pass some censor. This does not mean that every single letter is always censored; sometimes this has been done, at other times selected ones are examined. This has nothing to do with the war, when there is a double censorship.

Fortunately we have functioned in the open and there has been nothing to hide in our political activities. Nevertheless this feeling of being subjected to continuous censorship, to prying and tapping and overhearing, is not a pleasant one. It irritates and oppresses and even comes in the way of personal relationships. It is not easy to write as one would like to, with the censor peering over one's shoulder.

The ministers worked hard and many of them broke down under the strain. Their health deteriorated and all the freshness faded away, leaving them haggard and utterly weary. But a sense of purpose kept them going and they made their Indian civil service secretaries and their staffs work hard also; the lights in their offices were on till late in the evening. When the Congress governments resigned early in November, 1939, there was many a sigh of relief; the government offices were henceforth closed punctually at four in the afternoon, and reverted to their previous aspect of cloistered chambers where quiet prevailed and the public was not welcomed. Life went back to its old routine and slow tempo, and the afternoons and evenings were free for polo and tennis and bridge and the amenities of club life. A bad dream had faded and business and play could now be carried on as in the old days. True, there was a war on, thus far only in Europe, and Poland had been crushed by Hitler's legions. But all this was far away, and anyway it was a phoney war. While soldiers did their duty and fought and died, here also duty had to be performed and this duty was to bear the white man's burden worthily and with dignity.

The brief period during which the Congress governments functioned in the provinces confirmed our belief that the major obstruction to progress in India was the political and economic structure imposed by the British. It was perfectly true that many traditional habits and social forms and practices were barriers to progress and they had to go. Yet the inherent tendency of Indian economy to expand was not restricted so much by these forms and habits as by the political and economic stranglehold of the British. But for that steel framework, expansion was inevitable, bringing

379

in its wake many social changes and the ending of out-worn customs and ceremonial patterns. Hence attention had to be concentrated on the removal of that framework, and the energy spent on other matters bore little result and was often like ploughing the sands. That framework was itself based on and protected the semi-feudal land tenure system and many other relics of the past. Any kind of democracy in India was incompatible with the British political and economic structure, and conflict between the two was inevitable. Hence the partial democracy of 1937-39 was always on the verge of conflict. Hence also the official British view that democracy in India had not been successful, because they could only consider it in terms of maintaining the structure and values and vested interests they had built up. As the kind of tame and subservient democracy of which they could have approved was not forthcoming, and all manner of radical changes were aimed at, the only alternative left to the British power was to revert to a purely authoritarian régime and put an end to all pretensions of democracy. There is a marked similarity in the development of this outlook and the birth and growth of fascism in Europe. Even the rule of law on which the British had prided themselves in India gave place to something in the nature of a state of siege and rule by ordinance and decree.

The Question of Minorities
The Moslem League: Mr. M. A. Jinnah

The development and growth of the Moslem League during the last seven years has been an unusual phenomenon. Started in 1906 with British encouragement and in order to keep away the new generation of Moslems from the National Congress, it remained a small upper-class organization controlled by feudal elements. It had no influence on the Moslem masses and was hardly known by them. By its very constitution it was limited to a small group and a permanent leadership which perpetuated itself. Even so, events and the growing middle class among the Moslems pushed it in the direction of the Congress. World War I and the fate of the Turkish Khilafat (Caliphate) and the Moslem holy places produced a powerful impression on the Moslems of India and made them intensely anti-British. The Moslem League, constituted as it was, could not offer any guidance or leadership to these awakened and excited masses; indeed the League suffered from an attack of nerves and practically faded away. A new Moslem organization grew up in close co-operation with the Congress— the Khilafat Committee. Large numbers of Moslems also joined the Congress and worked through it. After the first non-co-operation movement of 1920-23, the Khilafat Committee also began to fade away as its very *raison d'être* had disappeared—the Turkish

Khilafat. The Moslem masses drifted away from political activity, as also the Hindu masses to a lesser extent. But a very considerable number of Moslems, chiefly of the middle classes, continued to function through the Congress.

During this period a number of petty Moslem organizations functioned spasmodically, often coming into conflict with each other. They had no mass affiliations, no political importance except such as was given to them by the British Government. Their chief function was to demand special privileges and protection for the Moslems in the legislatures and services. In this matter they did represent a definite Moslem viewpoint, for there was a background of resentment and fear among the Moslems at the superior position of the Hindus in education, services, and industry, as well as in numbers. Mr. M. A. Jinnah retired from Indian politics, and indeed from India, and settled down in England.

During the second Civil Disobedience movement of 1930 the response from the Moslems was very considerable, though less than in 1920-23. Among those who were jailed in connection with this movement there were at least 10,000 Moslems. The North-West Frontier Province, which is an almost entirely Moslem province (95 per cent Moslems) played a leading and remarkable part in this movement. This was largely due to the work and personality of Khan Abdul Ghaffar Khan, the unquestioned and beloved leader of the Pathans in this province. Of all the remarkable happenings in India in recent times, nothing is more astonishing than the way in which Abdul Ghaffar Khan made his turbulent and quarrelsome people accept peaceful methods of political action, involving enormous suffering. That suffering was indeed terrible and has left a trail of bitter memories; and yet their discipline and self-control were such that no act of violence was committed by the Pathans against the Government forces or others opposed to them. When it is remembered that a Pathan loves his gun more than his brother, is easily excited, and has long had a reputation for killing at the slightest provocation, this self-discipline appears little short of miraculous.

The Frontier Province, under Abdul Ghaffar Khan's leadership, stood firmly by the side of the National Congress, so also did a large number of the politically conscious middle-class Moslems elsewhere. Among the peasantry and workers, Congress influence was considerable, especially in provinces like the United Provinces, which had an advanced agrarian and workers programme. But it was none the less true that the Moslem masses as a whole were reverting vaguely to their old local and feudal leadership, which came to them in the guise of protectors of Moslem interests as against Hindus and others.

The communal problem, as it was called, was one of adjusting the claims of the minorities and giving them sufficient protection from majority action. Minorities in India, it must be remembered, are not racial or national minorities as in Europe; they are religious minorities. Racially India is a patchwork and a curious mixture, but no racial questions have arisen or can arise in India. Religion transcends these racial differences, which fade into one another and are often hard to distinguish. Religious barriers are obviously not permanent, as conversions can take place from one religion to another, and a person changing his religion does not thereby lose his racial background or his cultural and linguistic inheritance. Latterly religion, in any real sense of the word, has played little part in Indian political conflicts, though the word is often enough used and exploited. Religious differences, as such, do not come in the way, for there is a great deal of mutual tolerance for them. In political matters, religion has been displaced by what is called communalism, a narrow group mentality basing itself on a religious community but in reality concerned with political power and patronage for the interested group.

Repeated efforts were made by the Congress as well as other organizations to settle this communal problem with the consent of the various groups concerned. Some partial success was achieved but there was always a basic difficulty—the presence and policy of the British Government. Naturally the British did not favour any real settlement which would strengthen the political movement— now grown to mass proportions—against them. It was a triangle with the Government in a position to play off one side against the other, by giving special privileges. If the other parties had been wise enough, they could have overcome even this obstacle, but they lacked wisdom and foresight. Whenever a settlement was almost reached, the Government would take some step which upset the balance.

There was no dispute about the usual provisions for minority protection, such as the League of Nations used to lay down. All those were agreed to and much more. Religion, culture, language, the fundamental rights of the individual and the group, were all to be protected and assured by basic constitutional provisions in a democratic constitution applying equally to all. Apart from this, the whole history of India was witness of the toleration and even encouragement of minorities and of different racial groups. There is nothing in Indian history to compare with the bitter religious feuds and persecutions that prevailed in Europe. So we did not have to go abroad for ideas of religious and cultural toleration; these were inherent in Indian life. In regard to individual and political rights and civil liberties, we were influenced by the ideas of the French and American revolutions, as also by the constitutional history of the British Parliament. Socialistic ideas, and the influence of the Soviet revolution, came in later to give a powerful economic turn to our thoughts.

Apart from full protection of all such rights of the individual and the group, it was common ground that every effort should be made by the state as well as by private agencies to remove all invidious social and customary barriers which came in the way of the full development of the individual as well as any group, and that educationally and economically backward classes should be helped to get rid of their disabilities as rapidly as possible. This applied especially to the depressed classes. It was further laid down that women should share in every way with men in the privileges of citizenship.

What remained? Fear that bigger numbers might politically overwhelm a minority. Normally speaking, numbers meant the peasantry and the workers, the masses of all religious faiths, who had long been exploited not only by foreign rule but by their own upper classes. Having assured the protection of religion and culture, etc., the major problems that were bound to come up were economic ones which had nothing to do with a person's religion. Class conflicts there might well be but not religious conflicts, except in so far as religion itself represented some vested interest. Nevertheless people had grown so accustomed to think along lines of religious cleavage, and were continually being encouraged to do so by communal religious organizations and Government action, that the fear of the major religious community, that is the Hindus, swamping others continued to exercise the minds of many Moslems. It was not clear how even a majority could injure the interests of a huge minority like the Moslems, concentrated mostly in certain parts of the country, which would be autonomous. But fear is not reasonable.

Separate electorates for Moslems (and later for other and smaller groups) were introduced and additional seats were given to them in excess of their population. But even excess in representation in a popular assembly could not convert a minority into a majority. Indeed separate electorates made matters a little worse, for the protected group for the majority electorate lost interest in it, and there was little occasion for mutual consideration and adjustment which inevitably takes place in a joint electorate when a candidate has to appeal to every group. The Congress went further and declared that if there was any disagreement between the majority and a religious minority on any issue touching the special interests of that minority, it should not be decided by majority votes but should be referred to an impartial judicial tribunal, or even an international tribunal, whose decision should be final.

It is difficult to conceive what greater protection could be given to any religious minority or group under any democratic system. It must be remembered also that in some provinces Moslems were actually in a majority and as the provinces were autonomous, the Moslem majority was more or less free to function as it chose, subject only to certain all-India considerations. In the central government Moslems would also inevitably have an important share. In the Moslem majority provinces this communal-religious problem was reversed, for there protection was demanded by the other minority groups (such as Hindu and Sikh) as against the Moslem majority. Thus in the Punjab there was a Moslem-Hindu-Sikh triangle. If there was a separate electorate for Moslems then others claimed special protection for themselves also. Having once introduced separate electorates there was no end to the ramifications and compartments and difficulties that arose from them. Obviously the granting of weightage in representation to one group could only be done at the cost of some other group, which had its representation reduced below its population figures. This produced a fantastic result, especially in Bengal, where, chiefly because of excessive European representation, the seats allotted to the general electorate were absurdly reduced. Thus the intelligentsia of Bengal, which had played such a notable part in Indian politics and the struggle for freedom, suddenly realized that it had a very weak position in the provincial legislature fixed and limited by statute.

The Congress made many mistakes, but these were in relatively minor questions of approach or tactics. It was obvious that even for purely political reasons the Congress was eager and anxious to bring about a communal solution and thus remove a barrier to progress. There was no such eagerness in the purely communal organizations, for their chief reason for existence was to emphasize the particular demands of their respective groups, and this had led to a certain vested interest in the *status quo*. Though predominantly Hindu in membership, the Congress had large numbers of Moslems on its rolls, as well as all other religious groups like Sikhs, Christians, etc. It was thus forced to think in national terms. For it the dominating issue was national freedom and the establishment of an independent democratic state. It realized that in a vast and varied country like India, a simple type of democracy, giving full powers to a majority to curb or overrule minority groups in all matters, was not satisfactory or desirable, even if it could be established. It wanted unity, of course, and took it for granted, but it saw no reason why the richness and variety of India's cultural life should be regimented after a single pattern. Hence a large measure of autonomy was agreed to, as well as safeguards for cultural growth and individual and group freedom.

But on two fundamental questions the Congress stood firm: national unity and democracy. These were the foundations on which it had been founded and its very growth for half a century had emphasized these. The Congress organization is certainly one of the most democratic organizations that I know of anywhere in the world, both in theory and practice. Through its tens of thousands of local committees spread out all over the country, it had trained the people in democratic ways and achieved striking success in this. The fact that a dominating and very popular personality like Gandhi was connected with it, did not lessen that essential democracy of the Congress. In times of crisis and struggle there was an inevitable tendency to look to the leader for guidance, as in every country, and such crises were frequent. Nothing is more absurd than to call the Congress an authoritarian organization, and it is interesting to note that such charges are usually made by high representatives of British authority, which is the essence of autocracy and authoritarianism in India.

The British Government had also stood in the past, in theory at least, for Indian unity and democracy. It took pride in the fact that its rule had brought about the political unity of India, even though that unity was one of common subjection. It told us further that it was training us in the methods and processes of democracy. But curiously enough its policy has directly led to the denial of both unity and democracy. In August, 1940, the Congress Executive was compelled to declare that the policy of the British Government in India 'is a direct encouragement of and incitement to civil discord and strife.' Responsible spokesmen of the British Government began to tell us openly that perhaps the unity of India might have to be sacrificed in favour of some new arrangement, and that democracy was not suited to India. That was the only answer they had left to India's demand for independence and the establishment of a democratic state. That answer, incidentally, tells us that the British have failed, on their own showing, in the two major objectives they had set themselves in India. It took them a century and a half to realize this.

We failed in finding a solution for the communal problem agreeable to all parties concerned, and certainly we must share the blame as we have to shoulder the consequences for this failure. But how does one get everybody to agree to any important proposition or change? There are always feudal and reactionary elements who are opposed to all change, and there are those who want political, economic, and social change; in between these are varying groups. If a small group can exercise a veto on change then surely there can never be any change. When it is the policy of the ruling power to set up such groups and encourage them, even though they may represent an infinitesimal proportion of the population, then change can only come through successful revolution. It is obvious that there are any number of feudal and reactionary groups in India, some native to the soil and some created and nurtured by the British. In numbers they may be small but they have the backing of the British power.

Among the Moslems various organizations grew up, apart

from the Moslem League. One of the older and more important ones was the Jamiat-ul-Ulema which consisted of divines and old-fashioned scholars from all over India. Traditional and conservative in its general outlook, and necessarily religious, it was yet politically advanced and anti-imperialist. On the political plane it often co-operated with the Congress and many of its members were also members of the Congress and functioned through its organization. The Ahrar organization was founded later and was strongest in the Punjab. This represented chiefly lower middle-class Moslems and had considerable influence on the masses also in particular areas. The Momins (principally the weaver class), though large in numbers, were the poorest and most backward among the Moslems and were weak and badly organized. They were friendly to the Congress and opposed to the Moslem League. Being weak they avoided political action. In Bengal there was the Krishak (peasant) Sabha. Both the Jamiat-ul-Ulema and the Ahrars often co-operated with the Congress in its normal work and its more aggressive campaigns against the British Government, and suffered for it. The chief Moslem organization which has never come into conflict, other than verbal, with the British authorities, is the Moslem League, which throughout subsequent changes and developments and even when large numbers joined it, never shed its upper class feudal leadership.

There were also the Shia Moslems organized separately, but rather vaguely, chiefly for the purpose of making political demands. In the early days of Islam, in Arabia, a bitter dispute about the succession to the Khilafat led to a schism and two groups or sects emerged—the Sunnis and Shias. That quarrel perpetuated itself and still separates the two, though the schism ceased to have any political meaning. Sunnis are in a majority in India and in the Islamic countries, except in Iran, where Shias are in a majority. Religious conflicts have sometimes taken place between the two groups. The Shia organization in India as such kept apart and differed from the Moslem League. It was in favour of joint electorates for all. But there are many prominent Shias in the League.

All these Moslem organizations, as well as some others (but not including the Moslem League) joined hands to promote the Azad Muslim Conference, which was a kind of joint Moslem front opposed to the Moslem League. This conference held a very representative and successful first session in Delhi in 1940.

The chief Hindu communal organization is the Hindu Mahasabha, the counterpart of the Moslem League, but relatively less important. It is as aggressively communal as the League, but it tries to cover up its extreme narrowness of outlook by using some kind of vague national terminology, though its outlook is more revivalist than progressive. It is peculiarly unfortunate in some of its leaders who indulge in irresponsible and violent diatribes, as indeed do some of the Moslem League leaders also. This verbal warfare, indulged in on both sides, is a constant irritant. It takes the place of action.

The Moslem League's communal attitude was often difficult and unreasonable in the past, but no less unreasonable was the attitude of the Hindu Mahasabha. The Hindu minorities in the Punjab and Sind, and the dominant Sikh group in the Punjab, were often obstructive and came in the way of a settlement. British policy was to encourage and emphasize these differences and to give importance to communal organizations as against the Congress.

One test of the importance of a group or party, or at any rate of its hold on the people, is an election. During the general elections in India in 1937 the Hindu Mahasabha failed completely; it was nowhere in the picture. The Moslem League did better but on the whole its showing was poor, especially in the predominantly Moslem provinces. In the Punjab and Sind it failed completely, in Bengal it met with only partial success. In the North-West Frontier Province Congress formed a ministry later. In the Moslem minority provinces, the League met with greater success on the whole, but there were also independent Moslem groups as well as Moslems elected as Congressmen.

Then began a remarkable campaign on behalf of the Moslem League against the Congress governments in the provinces and the Congress organization itself. Day after day it was repeated that the governments were committing 'atrocities' on the Moslems. The governments contained Moslem ministers also but they were not members of the Moslem League. What these 'atrocities' were it was not usually stated, or some petty local incidents, which had nothing to do with the government, were distorted and magnified. Some minor errors of some departments, which were soon rectified, became 'atrocities'. Sometimes entirely false and baseless charges were made. Even a report was issued, fantastic in its contents and having little to do with any facts. Congress governments invited those who made the charges to supply particulars for investigation or to come and inquire themselves with government help. No one took advantage of these offers. But the campaign continued unchecked. Early in 1940, soon after the resignation of the Congress ministers, the then Congress president, Dr. Rajendra Prasad wrote to Mr. M. A. Jinnah and also made a public statement inviting the Moslem League to place any charges against the Congress governments before the federal court of inquiry and decision. Mr. Jinnah declined this offer and referred to the possibility of a Royal Commission being appointed for the purpose. There was no question of any such commission being appointed and only the British Government could do so. Some of the British governors, who had functioned during the régime of the Congress governments declared publicly that they had found nothing objectionable in the treatment of minorities. Under the Act of 1935 they had been especially empowered to protect minorities if any such need arose.

I had made a close study of nazi methods of propaganda since Hitler's rise to power and I was astonished to find something very similar taking place in India. A year later, in 1938, when Czechoslovakia had to face the Sudetenland crisis, the nazi methods employed there were studied and referred to with approval by Moslem League spokesmen. A comparison was drawn between the position of Sudetenland Germans and Indian Moslems. Violence and incitements in speeches and in some newspapers became marked. A Congress Moslem minister was stabbed and there was no condemnation of this from any Moslem League leader; in fact it was condoned. Other exhibitions of violence frequently took place.

I was terribly depressed by these developments and by the general lowering of the standards of public life. Violence, vulgarity, and irresponsibility were on the increase, and it appeared that they were approved of by responsible leaders of the Moslem League. I wrote to some of these leaders and begged them to check this tendency but with no success. So far as the Congress governments were concerned, it was obviously to their interest to win over every minority or other group and they tried hard to do so. Indeed complaints arose from some quarters that they were showing undue favour to the Moslems at the expense of other groups. But it was not a question of a particular grievance which could be remedied, or a reasonable consideration of any matter. There was a regular campaign on the part of members or sympathisers of the Moslem League to make the Moslem masses believe that something terrible was happening and that the Congress was to blame. What that terrible thing was nobody seemed to know. But surely there must be something behind all this shouting and cursing, if not here then elsewhere. During by-elections the cry raised was 'Islam in danger' and voters were asked to take their oaths on the holy book to vote for the Moslem League candidate.

All this had an undoubted effect on the Moslem masses. And yet it is surprising how many resisted it. The League won most by-elections, lost some; even when they won, there was a substantial minority of Moslem voters who went against them, being influenced more by the Congress agrarian programme. But for the first time in its history the Moslem League got a mass backing and began to develop into a mass organization. Much as I regretted what was happening, I welcomed this development in a way as I thought that it might lead ultimately to a change in the feudal leadership and that more progressive elements would come forward. The real difficulty thus far had been the extreme political and social backwardness of the Moslems which made them liable to exploitation by reactionary leaders.

Mr. M. A. Jinnah himself was more advanced than most of his colleagues of the Moslem League. Indeed he stood head and shoulders above them and had therefore become the indispensable leader. From public platforms he confessed his great dissatisfaction with the opportunism, and sometimes even worse failings, of his colleagues. He knew well that a great part of the advanced, selfless, and courageous element among the Moslems had joined and worked with the Congress. And yet some destiny or course of events had thrown him among the very people for whom he had no respect. He was their leader but he could only keep them together by becoming himself a prisoner to their reactionary ideologies. Not that he was an unwilling prisoner, so far as the ideologies were concerned, for despite his external modernism, he belonged to an older generation which was hardly aware of modern political thought or development. Of economics, which overshadow the world to-day, he appeared to be entirely ignorant. The extraordinary occurrences that had taken place all over the world since World War I had apparently had no effect on him. He had left the Congress when the organization had taken a political leap forward. The gap had widened as the Congress developed an economic and mass outlook. But Mr. Jinnah seemed to have remained ideologically in that identical place where he stood a generation ago, or rather he had gone further back, for now he condemned both India's unity and democracy. 'They would not live,' he has stated, 'under any system of government that was based on the nonsensical notion of western democracy.' It took him a long time to realize that what he had stood for throughout a fairly long life was nonsensical.

Mr. Jinnah is a lone figure even in the Moslem League, keeping apart from his closest co-workers, widely but distantly respected, more feared than liked. About his ability as a politician there is no doubt, but somehow that ability is tied up with the peculiar conditions of British rule in India to-day. He shines as a lawyer-politician, as a tactician, as one who thinks that he holds the balance between nationalist India and the British power. If conditions were different and he had to face real problems, political, and economic, it is difficult to say how far his ability would carry him. Perhaps he is himself doubtful of this, although he has no small opinion of himself. This may be an explanation for that subconscious urge in him against change, to keep things going as they are, and to avoid discussion and the calm consideration of problems with people who do not wholly agree with him. He fits into this present pattern; whether he or anybody else will fit into a new pattern it is difficult to say. What passion moves him, what objective does he strive for? Or is it that he has no dominating passion except the pleasure he has in playing a fascinating political game of chess in which he often has an opportunity to say 'check'? He seems to have a hatred for the Congress which has grown with the years. His aversions and dislikes are obvious, but what does he like? With all his strength and tenacity, he is a strangely negative person whose appropriate symbol might well be a 'no'. Hence all attempts to understand his positive aspect fail and one cannot come to grips with it.

Since British rule came to India, Moslems have produced few outstanding figures of the modern type. They have produced some remarkable men but, as a rule, these represented the continuation of the old culture and tradition and did not easily fit in with modern developments. This incapacity to march with the changing times and adapt themselves culturally and otherwise to a new environment was not of course due to any innate failing. It derived from certain historical causes, from the delay in the development of a new industrial middle class, and the excessively feudal background of the Moslems, which blocked up avenues of development and prevented the release of talent. In Bengal the backwardness of the Moslems was most marked, but this was obviously due to two causes: the destruction of their upper classes during the early days of British rule, and the fact that the vast majority were converts from the lowest class of Hindus, who had long been denied opportunities of growth and progress. In northern India the cultured upper-class Moslems were tied up with their old traditional ways as well as the land system. In recent years there has been a marked change and a fairly rapid development of a new middle class among Indian Moslems, but even now they lag far behind Hindus and others in science and industry. The Hindus are backward also, sometimes even more hide-bound and tied up with traditional ways of thought and practice than the Moslems, but nevertheless they have produced some very eminent men in science, industry, and other fields. The small Parsee community has also produced outstanding leaders of modern industry. Mr. Jinnah's family, it is interesting to note, was originally Hindu.

Both among Hindus and Moslems a good deal of talent and ability has in the past gone into government service, as that was the most attractive avenue open. With the growth of the political movement for freedom, that attraction became less, and able, earnest, and courageous persons were drawn into the Congress. Thus many of the best types of Moslems came in to it. In more recent years young Moslems joined the socialist and communist parties also. Apart from all these ardent and progressive persons, Moslems were very poor in the quality of their leaders and were inclined to look to government service alone for advancement. Mr. Jinnah was a different type. He was able, tenacious, and not open to the lure of office, which had been such a failing of so many others. His position in the Moslem League, therefore, became unique and he was able to command the respect which was denied to many others prominent in the League. Unfortunately his tenacity prevented him from opening his mind to any new ideas, and his unquestioned hold on his own organization made him intolerant both of his own dissidents and of other organizations. He became the Moslem League. But a question arose: As the League was becoming a mass organization, how long could this feudal leadership with outmoded ideas continue?

When I was Congress president, I wrote to Mr. Jinnah on several occasions and requested him to tell us exactly what he would like us to do. I asked him what the League wanted and what its definite objectives were. I also wanted to know what the grievances of the League were against the Congress governments. The idea was that we might clarify matters by correspondence and then discuss personally the important points that had arisen in it. Mr. Jinnah sent me long replies but failed to enlighten me. It was extraordinary how he avoided telling me, or anyone else, exactly what he wanted or what the grievances of the League were. Repeatedly we exchanged letters and yet always there was the same vagueness and inconclusiveness and I could get nothing definite. This surprised me very much and made me feel a little helpless. It seemed as if Mr. Jinnah did not want to commit himself in any way and was not at all eager for a settlement.

Subsequently Gandhiji and others amongst us met Mr. Jinnah, several times. They talked for hours but never got beyond a preliminary stage. Our proposal was that representatives of the Congress and the League should meet and discuss all their mutual problems. Mr. Jinnah said that this could only be done after we recognized publicly that the Moslem League was the sole representative organization of the Moslems of India, and the Congress should consider itself a purely Hindu organization. This created an obvious difficulty. We recognized of course the importance of the League and because of that we had approached it. But how could we ignore many other Moslem organizations in the country, some closely associated with us? Also there were large numbers of Moslems in the Congress itself and in our highest executive. To admit Mr Jinnah's claim meant in effect to push out our old Moslem colleagues from the Congress 'and declare that the Congress was not open to them. It was to change the fundamental character of the Congress, and from a national organization, open to all, convert it into a communal body. That was inconceivable for us. If the Congress had not already been there, we would have had to build up a new national organization open to every Indian. We could not understand Mr. Jinnah's insistence on this and refusal to discuss any other matter. Again we could only con-clude that he did not want any settlement, nor did he want to commit himself in any way. He was satisfied in letting matters drift and in expecting that he could get more out of the British Government this way.

Mr. Jinnah's demand was based on a new theory he had recently propounded—that India consisted of two nations, Hindu and Moslem. Why only two I do not know, for if nationality was based on religion, then there were many nations in India. Of two brothers one may be a Hindu, another a Moslem; they would belong to two different nations. These two nations existed in varying proportions in most of the villages of India. They were nations which had no boundaries; they overlapped. A Bengali Moslem and a Bengali Hindu living together, speaking the same language, and having much the same traditions and customs, belonged to different nations. All this was very difficult to grasp; it seemed a reversion to some medieval theory. What a nation is it is difficult to define. Possibly the essential characteristic of national consciousness is a sense of belonging together and of together facing the rest of mankind. How far that is present in India as a whole may be a debatable point. It may even be said that India developed in the past as a multi-national state and gradually acquired a national consciousness. But all these are theoretical abstractions which hardly concern us. To-day the most powerful states are multi-national, but at the same time developing a national consciousness, like the U.S.A. or the U.S.S.R.

From Mr. Jinnah's two-nation theory developed the concep-tion of Pakistan, or splitting up of India. That, of course, did not solve the problem of the 'two nations,' for they were all over the place. But that gave body to a metaphysical conception. This again gave rise to a passionate reaction among many in favour of the unity of India. Ordinarily national unity is taken for granted. Only when it is challenged or attacked, or attempts are made to disrupt it, is unity really appreciated, and a posi-tive reaction to maintain it takes place. Thus sometimes attempts at disruption actually help to weld that unity.

There was a fundamental difference between the outlook of the Congress and that of the religious-communal organizations. Of the latter the chief were the Moslem League and its Hindu counterpart, the Hindu Mahasabha. These communal organiza-tions, while in theory standing for India's independence, were more interested in claiming protection and special privileges for their respective groups. They had thus inevitably to look to the British Government for such privileges, and this led them to avoid conflict with it. The Congress outlook was so tied up with India's freedom as a united nation that everything else was secondary, and this meant ceaseless conflict or friction with the British power.

Indian nationalism, as represented by the Congress, opposed British imperialism. The Congress had further developed agrarian, economic, and social programmes. Neither the Moslem League nor the Hindu Mahasabha had ever considered any such question or attempted to frame a programme. Socialists and communists were, of course, intensely interested in such matters and had their own programmes, which they tried to push in the Congress as well as outside.

There was yet another marked difference between Congress policy and work and those of the religious-communal organizations. Quite apart from its agitational side and its legislative activity, when such existed, the Congress laid the greatest stress on certain constructive activities among the masses. These activities consisted in organizing and developing cottage industries, in raising the depressed classes, and later in the spread of basic education. Village work also included sanitation and some simple forms of medical relief. Separate organizations for carrying on these activities were created by the Congress, which functioned apart from the political plane, and which absorbed thousands of whole-time workers and a much larger number of part-time helpers. This quiet non-political, constructive work was carried on even when political activities were at a low ebb; but even this was suppressed by Government when there was open conflict with the Congress. The economic value of some of these activities was questioned by a few people, but there could be no doubt of their social importance. They trained a large body of whole-time workers in intimate touch with the masses, and produced a spirit of self-help and self-reliance among the people. Congressmen and women also played an important part in trade union and agrarian organizations, actually building up many of these. The largest and best-organized trade union—that of the Ahmedabad textile industry—was started by Congressmen and worked in close co-operation with them.

All these activities gave a solid background to Congress work, which was completely lacking in the religious-communal organizations. These latter functioned on the agitational plane only by fits and starts, or during elections. In them also was lacking that ever-present sense of risk and personal danger from government action which Congressmen had almost always to face. Thus, there was a far greater tendency for careerists and opportunists to enter these organizations. The two Moslem organizations, the Ahrars and the Jamiat-ul-Ulema, however, suffered greatly from governmental repression because politically they often followed the same line as the Congress.

The Congress represented not only the nationalist urge of India, which had grown with the growth of the new bourgeoisie, but also, to a large extent, proletarian urges for social change. In particular,

393

it stood for revolutionary agrarian changes. This sometimes produced inner conflicts within the Congress, and the landlord class and the big industrialists, though often nationalistic, kept aloof from it for fear of socialistic changes. Within the Congress, socialists and communists found a place and could influence Congress policy. The communal organizations, whether Hindu or Moslem, were closely associated with the feudal and conservative elements and were opposed to any revolutionary social change. The real conflict had, therefore, nothing to do with religion, though religion often masked the issue, but was essentially between those who stood for a nationalist—democratic—socially revolutionary policy and those who were concerned with preserving the relics of a feudal regime. In a crisis, the latter inevitably depend upon foreign support which is interested in preserving the *status quo*.

The beginning of World War II brought an internal crisis which resulted in the resignation of the Congress governments in the provinces. Before this occurred, however, the Congress made another attempt to approach Mr. M. A. Jinnah and the Moslem League. Mr. Jinnah was invited to attend the first meeting of the Congress Executive after the commencement of the war. He was unable to join us. We met him later and tried to evolve a common policy in view of the world crisis. Not much progress was made but nevertheless we decided to continue our talks. Meanwhile the Congress governments resigned on the political issue which had nothing to do with the Moslem League and the communal problem. Mr. Jinnah, however, chose that moment for a fierce attack on the Congress and a call on his League for the observance of a 'Day of Deliverance' from Congress rule in the provinces. He followed this up by very unbecoming remarks on Nationalist Moslems in the Congress and especially on the Congress president, Maulana Abul Kalam Azad, who was greatly respected among Hindus and Moslems alike. The 'Day of Deliverance' was rather a flop and counter demonstrations among Moslems took place in some parts of India. But it added to bitterness and confirmed the conviction that Mr. Jinnah and the Moslem League under his leadership had no intention whatever of coming to any settlement with the Congress, or of advancing the cause of Indian freedom. They preferred the existing situation.*

*After I had finished writing this book, I read a book by a Canadian scholar, *Wilfrid Cantwell Smith*, who has spent some years in Egypt and India. This book, which is called '*Modern Islam in India—A Social Analysis*, (Lahore, 1943), is an able analysis and careful survey of the development of ideas among Indian Moslems since the Indian Mutiny of 1857. He deals with the progressive and reactionary movements from Sir Syed Ahmad Khan's time onwards, and the different phases of the Moslem League.

The National Planning Committee

Towards the end of 1938 a National Planning Committee was constituted at the instance of the Congress. It consisted of fifteen members plus representatives of provincial governments and such Indian states as chose to collaborate with us. Among the members were well-known industrialists, financiers, economists, professors, scientists, as well as representatives of the Trade Union Congress and the Village Industries Association. The non-Congress Provincial Governments (Bengal, Punjab' and Sind), as well as some of the major states (Hyderabad, Mysore, Baroda, Travancore, Bhopal) co-operated with this committee. In a sense it was a remarkably representative committee cutting across political boundaries as well as the high barrier between official and non-official India—except for the fact that the Government of India was not represented and took up a non-co-operative attitude. Hard-headed big business was there as well as people who are called idealists and doctrinaires, and socialists and near-communists. Experts and directors of industries came from provincial governments and states.

It was a strange assortment of different types and it was not clear how such an odd mixture would work. I accepted the chairmanship of the committee not without hesitation and misgiving; the work was after my own heart and I could not keep out of it.

Difficulties faced us at every turn. There were not enough data for real planning and few statistics were available. The Government of India was not helpful. Even the provincial governments, though friendly and co-operative, did not seem to be particularly keen on all-India planning and took only a distant interest in our work. They were far too busy with their own problems and troubles. Important elements in the Congress, under whose auspices the committee had come into existence, rather looked upon it as an unwanted child, not knowing how it would grow up and rather suspicious of its future activities. Big business was definitely apprehensive and critical, and probably joined up because it felt that it could look after its interests better from inside the committee than from outside.

It was obvious also that any comprehensive planning could only take place under a free national government, strong enough and popular enough to be in a position to introduce fundamental changes in the social and economic structure. Thus the attainment of national freedom and the elimination of foreign control became an essential pre-requisite for planning. There were many other obstacles—our social backwardness, customs, traditional outlook, etc.—but they had in any event to be faced. Planning thus was not so much for the present, as for an unascertained future, and there was an air of unreality about it. Yet it had to be based on the present and we hoped that this future was not a distant one. If we could collect the available material, co-ordinate it, and draw up blue-prints, we would prepare the ground for the real effective future planning, meanwhile indicating to provincial governments and states the lines on which they should proceed and develop their resources. The attempt to plan and to see the various national activities—economic, social, cultural—fitting into each other, had also a highly educative value for ourselves and the general public. It made the people come out of their narrow grooves of thought and action, to think of problems in relation to one another, and develop to some extent at least a wider co-operative outlook.

The original idea behind the Planning Committee had been to further industrialization—'the problems of poverty and unemployment, of national defence and of economic regeneration in general cannot be solved without industrialization. As a step towards such industrialization, a comprehensive scheme of national planning should be formulated. This scheme should provide for the development of heavy key industries, medium scale industries, and cottage industries....' But no planning could possibly ignore agriculture, which was the main stay of the people; equally important were the social services. So one thing led to another and it was impossible to isolate anything or to progress in one direction without corresponding progress in another. The more we thought of this planning business, the vaster it grew in its sweep and range till it seemed to embrace almost every activity. That did not mean we intended regulating and regimenting everything, but we had to keep almost everything in view even in deciding about one particular sector of the plan. The fascination of this work grew upon me and, I think, upon the other members of our committee also. But at the same time certain vagueness and indefiniteness crept in; instead of concentrating on some major aspects of the plan we tended to become diffuse. This also led to delay in the work of many of our sub-committees which lacked the sense of urgency and of working for a definite objective within a stated time.

Constituted as we were, it was not easy for all of us to agree to any basic social policy or principles underlying social organization. Any attempt to discuss these principles in the abstract was bound to lead to fundamental differences of approach at the outset and possibly to a splitting up of the committee. Not to have such a guiding policy was a serious drawback, yet there was no help for it. We decided to consider the general problem of planning as well as each individual problem concretely and not in the abstract, and allow principles to develop out of such considerations. Broadly speaking, there were two approaches: the socialist one aiming at the elimination of the profit motive and emphasizing the importance of equitable distribution, and the big business one striving to retain free enterprise and the profit motive as far as possible, and laying greater stress on production. There was also a difference in outlook between those who favoured a rapid growth of heavy industry and others who wanted greater attention to be paid to the development of village and cottage industries, thus absorbing the vast number of the unemployed and partially employed. Ultimately there were bound to be differences in the final conclusions. It did not very much matter even if there were two or more reports, provided that all the available facts were collected and co-ordinated, the common ground mapped out, and the divergencies indicated. When the time came for giving effect to the Plan, the then existing democratic government would have to choose what basic policy to adopt. Meanwhile a great deal of essential preparation would have been made and the various aspects of the problem placed before the public and the various provincial and state governments.

Obviously we could not consider any problem, much less plan, without some definite aim and social objective. That aim was declared to be to ensure an adequate standard of living for the masses, in other words, to get rid of the appalling poverty of the people. The irreducible minimum, in terms of money, had been estimated by economists at figures varying from Rs. 15 to Rs. 25 *per capita* per month. (These are all pre-war figures.) Compared to western standards this was very low, and yet it meant an enormous increase in existing standards in India. An approximate estimate of the average annual income *per capita* was Rs. 65. This included the rich and the poor, the town-dweller, and the villager. In view of the great gulf between the rich and the poor and the concentration of wealth in the hands of a few, the average income of the villager was estimated to be far less, probably about Rs. 30 *per capita* per annum. These figures bring home the terrible poverty of the people and the destitute condition of the masses. There was lack of food, of clothing, of housing and of every other essential requirement of human existence. To remove this lack and ensure an irreducible minimum standard for everybody the national income had to be greatly increased, and in addition to this increased production there had to be a more equitable distribution of wealth. We calculated that a really progressive standard of living would necessitate the increase of the national wealth by 500 or 600 per cent. That was, however, too big a jump for us, and we aimed at a 200 to 300 per cent increase within ten years.

We fixed a ten-year period for the plan, with control figures for different periods and different sectors of economic life.

Certain objective tests were also suggested:

(1) The improvement of nutrition—a balanced diet having a calorific value of 2,400 to 2,800 units for an adult worker.

(2) Improvement in clothing from the then consumption of

about fifteen yards to at least thirty yards *per capita* per annum.

(3) Housing standards to reach at least 100 square feet *per capita*.

Further, certain indices of progress had to be kept in mind:

(i) Increase in agricultural production. (ii) Increase in industrial production. (iii) Diminution of unemployment. (iv) Increase in *per capita* income. (v) Liquidation of illiteracy. (vi) Increase in public utility services. (vii) Provision of medical aid on the basis of one unit for 1,000 population. (viii) Increase in the average expectation of life.

The objective for the country as a whole was the attainment, as far as possible, of national self-sufficiency. International trade was certainly not excluded, but we were anxious to avoid being drawn into the whirlpool of economic imperialism. We neither wanted to be victims of an imperialist power nor to develop such tendencies ourselves. The first charge on the country's produce should be to meet the domestic needs of food, raw materials, and manufactured goods. Surplus production would not be dumped abroad but used in exchange for such commodities as we might require. To base our national economy on export markets might lead to conflicts with other nations and to sudden upsets when those markets were closed to us.

So, though we did not start with a well-defined social theory, our social objectives were clear enough and afforded a common basis for planning. The very essence of this planning was a large measure of regulation and co-ordination. Thus, while free enterprise was not ruled out as such, its scope was severely restricted. In regard to defence industries it was decided that they must be owned and controlled by the state. Regarding other key industries, the majority were of opinion that they should be state-owned, but a substantial minority of the committee considered that state control would be sufficient. Such control, however, of these industries had to be rigid. Public utilities, it was also decided, should be owned by some organ of the state—either the Central Government, provincial government, or a local board. It was suggested that something of the nature of the London Transport Board might control public utilities. In regard to other important and vital industries, no special rule was laid down but it was made clear that the very nature of planning required control in some measure, which might vary with the industry.

In regard to the agency in state-owned industries it was suggested that as a general rule an autonomous public trust would be suitable. Such a trust would ensure public ownership and control and at the same time avoid the difficulties and inefficiency which sometimes creep in under direct democratic control. Co-operative ownership and control were also suggested for industries. Any planning would involve a close scrutiny of the development of

398

industry in all its branches and a periodical survey of the progress made. It would mean also the training of the technical staffs necessary for the further expansion of industry, and the state might call upon industries to train such staffs.

The general principles governing land policy were laid down: 'Agricultural land, mines, quarries, rivers, and forests are forms of national wealth, ownership of which must vest absolutely in the people of India collectively.' The co-operative principle should be applied to the exploitation of land by developing collective and co-operative farms. It was not proposed, however, to rule out peasant farming in small holdings, to begin with at any rate, but no intermediaries of the type of talukdars, zamindars, etc., should be recognized after the transition period was over. The rights and title possessed by these classes should be progressively bought out. Collective farms were to be started immediately by the state on culturable waste land. Co-operative farming could be combined either with individual or joint ownership. A certain latitude was allowed for various types to develop so that, with greater experience, particular types might be encouraged more than others.

We, or some of us at any rate, hoped to evolve a socialized system of credit. If banks, insurance, etc., were not to be nationalized they should at least be under the control of the state, thus leading to a state regulation of capital and credit. It was also desirable to control the export and import trade. By these various means a considerable measure of state control would be established in regard to land as well as in industry as a whole, though varying in particular instances, and allowing private initiative to continue in a restricted sphere.

Thus, through the consideration of special problems, we gradually developed our social objectives and policy. There were gaps in them and occasional vagueness and even some contradiction; it was far from a perfect scheme in theory. But I was agreeably surprised at the large measure of unanimity achieved by us in spite of the incongruous elements in our Committee. The big business element was the largest single group and its outlook on many matters, especially financial and commercial, was definitely conservative. Yet the urge for rapid progress, and the conviction that only thus could we solve our problems of poverty and unemployment, were so great that all of us were forced out of our grooves and compelled to think on new lines. We had avoided a theoretical approach, and as each practical problem was viewed in its larger context, it led us inevitably in a particular direction. To me the spirit of co-operation of the members of the Planning Committee was peculiarly soothing and gratifying, for I found it a pleasant contrast to the squabbles and conflicts of politics. We knew our differences and yet we tried and often succeeded, after discussing every point of view, in arriving at an integrated conclusion which was accepted by all of us, or most of us.

Constituted as we were, not only in our Committee but in the larger field of India, we could not then plan for socialism as such. Yet it became clear to me that our plan, as it developed, was inevitably leading us towards establishing some of the fundamentals of the socialist structure. It was limiting the acquisitive factor in society, removing many of the barriers to growth, and thus leading to a rapidly expanding social structure. It was based on planning for the benefit of the common man, raising his standards greatly, giving him opportunities of growth, and releasing an enormous amount of latent talent and capacity. And all this was to be attempted in the context of democratic freedom and with a large measure of co-operation of some at least of the groups who were normally opposed to socialistic doctrine. That co-operation seemed to me worth while even if it involved toning down or weakening the plan in some respects. Probably I was too optimistic. But so long as a big step in the right direction was taken, I felt that the very dynamics involved in the process of change would facilitate further adaptation and progress. If conflict was inevitable, it had to be faced; but if it could be avoided or minimized that was an obvious gain. Especially as in the political sphere there was conflict enough for us and, in the future, there might well be unstable conditions. A general consent for a plan was thus of great value. It was easy enough to draw up blue-prints based on some idealist conception. It was much more difficult to get behind them that measure of general consent and approval which was essential for the satisfactory working of any plan.

Planning, though inevitably bringing about a great deal of control and co-ordination and interfering in some measure with individual freedom, would, as a matter of fact, in the context of India to-day, lead to a vast increase of freedom. We have very little freedom to lose. We have only to gain freedom. If we adhered to the democratic state structure and encouraged co-operative enterprises, many of the dangers of regimentation and concentration of power might be avoided.

At our first sessions we had framed a formidable questionnaire which was issued to various governments and public bodies, universities, chambers of commerce, trade unions, research institutes, etc. Twenty-nine sub-committees were also appointed to investigate and report on specific problems. Eight of these sub-committees were for agricultural problems; several were for industry; five for commerce and finance; two for transport; two for education; two for public welfare; two for demographic relations; and one for women's role in planned economy. There were in all about 350 members of these sub-committees, some of them overlapping. Most of them were specialists or experts in their subjects—businessmen, government, state, and municipal employees, university professors or lecturers, technicians, scientists, trade unionists, and police-men. We collected in this way much of the talent available in the country. The only persons who were not permitted to co-operate with us, even when they were personally desirous of doing so, were the officials and employees of the Government of India. To have so many persons associated in our work was helpful in many ways. We had the advantage of their special knowledge and experi-ence, and they were led to think of their special subject in relation to the wider problem. It also led to a greater interest in planning all over the country. But these numbers were disadvantageous also, for there was inevitable delay when busy people spread out all over a vast country had to meet repeatedly.

I was heartened to come into touch with so much ability and earnestness in all departments of national activity, and these contacts added to my own education greatly. Our method of work was to have an interim report from each sub-committee, which the planning committee considered, approving of it or partly criticizing it, and then sending it back with its remarks to the sub-committee. A final report was then submitted out of which arose our decisions on that particular subject. An attempt was being made continually to co-ordinate the decisions on each sub-ject with those arrived at on other subjects. When all the final reports had been thus considered and disposed of, the Planning Committee was to review the whole problem in its vastness and intricacy and evolve its own comprehensive report, to which the sub-committees' reports would be added as appendices. As a matter of fact that final report was gradually taking shape in the course of our consideration of the sub-committees' reports.

There were irritating delays, chiefly due to some of the sub-committees not keeping to the time-table fixed for them, but on the whole we made good progress and got through an enormous amount of work. Two interesting decisions were made in connection with education. We suggested that definite norms of physical fitness for boys and girls be laid down for every stage of education. We also suggested establishment of a system of compulsory social or labour service, so as to make every young man and woman contri-bute one year of his or her life, between the ages of eighteen and twenty-two, to national utility, including agriculture, industry, public utilities, and public works of all kinds. No exemption was to be allowed except for physical or mental disability.

When World War II started in September, 1939, it was sug-gested that the National Planning Committee should suspend its activities. In November the Congress governments in the provinces resigned and this added to our difficulties, for under the absolute rule of the Governors in the provinces no interest was taken in our work. Business men were busier than ever making money out of war requirements and were not so much interested in planning.

The situation was changing from day to day. We decided, however, to continue and felt that the war made this even more necessary. It was bound to result in further industrialization, and the work we had already done and were engaged in doing could be of great help in this process. We were dealing then with our sub-committees' reports on engineering industries, transport, chemical industries, and manufacturing industries, all of the highest importance from the point of view of the war. But the Government was not interested in our work and in fact viewed it with great disfavour. During the early months of the war—the so-called 'phoney' period—their policy was not to encourage the growth of Indian industry. Afterwards, the pressure of events forced them to buy many of their requirements in India, but even so they disapproved of any heavy industries being started there. Disapproval meant virtual prohibition, for no machinery could be imported without government sanction.

The Planning Committee continued its work and had nearly finished dealing with its sub-committees' reports. We were to finish what little remained of this work and then proceed to the consideration of our own comprehensive report. I was, however, arrested in October, 1940, and sentenced to a long term of imprisonment. Several other members of the Planning Committee and its sub-committees were also arrested and sentenced. I was anxious that the Planning Committee should continue to function and requested my colleagues outside to do so. But they were not willing to work in the Committee in my absence. I tried to get the Planning Committee's papers and reports in prison so that I might study them and prepare a draft report. The Government of India intervened and stopped this. No such papers were allowed to reach me, nor were interviews on the subject permitted.

So the National Planning Committee languished, while I spent my days in jail. All the work we had done which, though incomplete, could be used to great advantage for war purposes, remained in the pigeon-holes of our office. I was released in December, 1941, and was out of prison for some months. But this period was a hectic one for me, as it was for others. All manner of new developments had taken place, the Pacific war was on, India was threatened with invasion, and it was not possible then to pick up the old threads and continue the unfinished work of the planning committee unless the political situation cleared up. And then I returned to prison.

The Congress and Industry:
Big Industry versus Cottage Industry

The Congress, under Gandhiji's leadership, had long championed the revival of village industries, especially hand-spinning and hand-weaving. At no time, however, had the Congress been opposed to the development of big industries, and whenever it had the chance, in the legislatures or elsewhere, it had encouraged this development. Congress provincial governments were eager to do so. In the twenties when the Tata Steel and Iron Works were in difficulties, it was largely due to the insistence of the Congress party in the Central Legislature that government aid was given to help to tide over a critical period. The development of Indian shipbuilding and shipping services had long been a sore point of conflict between nationalist opinion and government. The Congress, as all other sections of Indian opinion, was anxious that every assistance should be given to Indian shipping; the government was equally anxious to protect the vested interests of powerful British shipping companies. Indian shipping was thus prevented from growing by official discrimination against it, although it had both capital and technical and managerial ability at its disposal. This kind of discrimination worked all along the line whenever any British industrial, commercial, or financial interests were concerned.

That huge combine, the Imperial Chemical Industries, has been repeatedly favoured at the expenses of Indian industry. Some years ago it was given a long term lease for the exploitation of the minerals, etc., of the Punjab. The terms of this agreement were, so far as I know, not disclosed, presumably because it was not considered 'in the public interest' to do so.

The Congress provincial governments were anxious to develop a power alcohol industry. This was desirable from many points of view, but there was an additional reason in the United Provinces and Bihar. The large numbers of sugar factories there were producing as a by-product a vast quantity of molasses which was being treated as waste material. It was proposed to utilise this for the production of power alcohol. The process was simple, there was no difficulty, except one—the interests of the Shell and Burma Oil combine were affected. The Government of India championed these interests and refused to permit the manufacture of power alcohol. It was only in the third year of the present war, after Burma fell and the supplies of oil and petrol were cut off, that the realization came that power alcohol was necessary and must be produced in India. The American Grady Committee strongly urged this in 1942.

The Congress has thus always been in favour of the industrialization of India and, at the same time, has emphasized the development of cottage industries and worked for this. Is there a conflict between these two approaches? Possibly there is a difference in emphasis, a realization of certain human and economic factors which were overlooked previously in India. Indian industrialists and the politicians who supported them thought too much in terms of the nineteenth century development of capitalist industry in Europe and ignored many of the evil consequences that were obvious in the twentieth century. In India, because normal progress had been arrested for 100 years those consequences were likely to be more far-reaching. The kind of medium-scale industries that were being started in India, under the prevailing economic system, resulted not in absorbing labour, but in creating more unemployment. While capital accumulated at one end, poverty and unemployment increased at the other. Under a different system, with a stress on big scale industries absorbing labour, and with planned development this might well have been avoided.

This fact of increasing mass poverty influenced Gandhi powerfully. It is true, I think, that there is a fundamental difference between his outlook on life generally and what might be called the modern outlook. He is not enamoured of ever-increasing standards of living and the growth of luxury at the cost of spiritual and moral values. He does not favour the soft life; for him the straight way is the hard way, and the love of luxury leads to crookedness and loss of virtue. Above all he is shocked at the vast gulf that stretches between the rich and the poor, in their ways of living, and their opportunities of growth. For his own personal and psychological satisfaction, he crossed that gulf and went over to the side of the poor, adopting, with only such improvements as the poor themselves could afford, their ways of living, their dress or lack of dress. This vast difference between the few rich and the poverty-stricken masses seemed to him to be due to two principal causes: foreign rule and the exploitation that accompanied it, and the capitalist industrial civilization of the west as embodied in the big machine. He reacted against both. He looked back with yearning to the days of the old autonomous and more-or-less self-contained village community where there had been an automatic balance between production, distribution, and consumption; where political or economic power was spread out and not concentrated as it is to-day; where a kind of simple democracy prevailed; where the gulf between the rich and the poor was not so marked; where the evil of great cities were absent and people lived in contact with the life-giving soil and breathed the pure air of the open spaces.

There was all this basic difference in outlook as to the meaning of life itself between him and many others, and this difference coloured his language as well as his activities. His language, vivid and powerful as it often was, drew its inspiration from the religious and moral teachings of the ages, principally of India but also of other countries. Moral values must prevail, the ends can never justify unworthy means, or else the individual and the race perish.

And yet he was no dreamer living in some fantasy of his own creation, cut off from life and its problems. He came from Gujrat, the home of hard-headed businessmen, and he had an unrivalled knowledge of the Indian villages and the conditions of life that prevailed there. It was out of that personal experience that he evolved his programme of the spinning-wheel and village industry. If immediate relief was to be given to the vast numbers of the unemployed and partially employed, if the rot that was spreading throughout India and paralysing the masses was to be stopped, if the villagers' standards were to be raised, however, little *en masse*, if they were to be taught self-reliance instead of waiting helplessly like derelicts for relief from others, if all this was to be done without much capital, then there seemed no other way. Apart from the evils inherent in foreign rule and exploitation, and the lack of freedom to initiate and carry through big schemes of reform, the problem of India was one of scarcity of capital and abundance of labour—how to utilize that wasted labour, that manpower that was producing nothing. Foolish comparisons are made between manpower and machine-power; of course a big machine can do the work of a thousand or ten thousand persons. But if those ten thousand sit idly by or starve, the introduction of the machine is not a social gain, except in long perspective which envisages a change in social conditions. When the big machine is not there at all, then no question of comparison arises; it is a nett gain both from the individual and the national point of view to utilize manpower for production. There is no necessary conflict between this and the introduction of machinery on the largest scale, provided that machinery is used primarily for absorbing labour and not for creating fresh unemployment.

Comparisons between India and the small highly industrialized countries of the west, or big countries with relatively sparse populations, like the U.S.S.R. or the U.S.A., are misleading. In western Europe the process of industrialization has proceeded for 100 years, and gradually the population has adjusted itself to it; the population has grown rapidly, then stabilized itself, and is now declining. In the U.S.A. and the U.S.S.R. there are vast tracts with a small, though growing, population. A tractor is an absolute necessity there to exploit the land for agriculture. It is not so obvious that a tractor is equally necessary in the densely populated Gangetic valley, so long as vast numbers depend on the land alone for sustenance. Other problems arise, as they have arisen even in America. Agriculture has been carried on for thousands of years in India and the soil has been exploited to the utmost. Would the deep churning up of the soil by tractors lead to impoverishment of this soil as well as to soil erosion? When railways were built in India and high embankments put up for the purpose, no thought was given to the natural drainage of the country. The embankments interfered with this drainage system and, as a result, we have had repeated and ever-increasing floods and soil erosion, and malaria has spread.

I am all for tractors and big machinery, and I am convinced that the rapid industrialization of India is essential to relieve the pressure on land, to combat poverty and raise standards of living, for defence and a variety of other purposes. But I am equally convinced that the most careful planning and adjustment are necessary if we are to reap the full benefit of industrialization and avoid many of its dangers. This planning is necessary to-day in all countries of arrested growth, like China and India, which have strong traditions of their own.

In China I was greatly attracted to the Industrial Co-operatives—the Indusco movement—and it seems to me that some such movement is peculiarly suited to India. It would fit in with the Indian background, give a democratic basis to small industry, and develop the co-operative habit. It could be made to complement big industry. It must be remembered that, however rapid might be the development of heavy industry in India, a vas field will remain open to small and cottage industries. Even in Soviet Russia owner-producer co-operatives have played an important part in industrial growth.

The increasing use of electric power facilitates the growth of small industry and makes it economically capable of competing with large-scale industry. There is also a growing opinion in favour of decentralization, and even Henry Ford had advocated it. Scientists are pointing out the psychological and biological dangers of loss of contact with the soil which results from life in great industrial cities. Some have even said that human survival necessitates a going back to the soil and the village. Fortunately, science has made it possible to-day for populations to be spread out and remain near the soil and yet enjoy all the amenities of modern civilization and culture.

However that may be, the problem before us in India during recent decades has been how, in the existing circumstances and restricted as we were by alien rule and its attendant vested interests, we could relieve the poverty of the masses and produce a spirit of self-reliance among them. There are many arguments in favour of developing cottage industries at any time, but situated as we were that was certainly the most practical thing we could do. The methods adopted may not have been the best or the most suitable. The problem was vast, difficult, and intricate, and we had frequently to face suppression by government. We had to learn gradually by the process of trial and error. I think we should have encouraged co-operatives from the beginning, and relied more on expert technical and scientific knowledge for the improvement of small machines suitable for cottage and village use. The co-operation principle is now being introduced in these organizations.

G. D. H. Cole, the economist, has said that 'Gandhi's campaign for the development of the home-made cloth industry is no mere fad of a romantic eager to revive the past, but a practical attempt to relieve the poverty and uplift the standard of the village.' It was that undoubtedly, and it was much more. It forced India to think of the poor peasant in human terms, to realize that behind the glitter of a few cities lay this morass of misery and poverty, to grasp the fundamental fact that the true test of progress and freedom in India did not lie in the creation of a number of millionaires or prosperous lawyers and the like, or in the setting up of councils and assemblies, but in the change in the status and conditions of life of the peasant. The British had created a new caste or class in India, the English-educated class, which lived in a world of its own, cut off from the mass of the population, and looked always, even when protesting, towards its rulers. Gandhi bridged that gap to some extent and forced it to turn its head and look towards its own people.

Gandhiji's attitude to the use of machinery seemed to undergo a gradual change. 'What I object to,' he said, 'is the craze for machinery, not machinery as such.' 'If we could have electricity in every village home, I shall not mind villagers plying their implements and tools with electricity.' The big machines seemed to him to lead inevitably, at least in the circumstances of to-day, to the concentration of power and riches: 'I consider it a sin and injustice to use machinery for the purpose of concentration of power and riches in the hands of the few. To-day the machine is used in this way.' He even came to accept the necessity of many kinds of heavy industries and large-scale key industries and public utilities, provided they were state-owned and did not interfere with some kinds of cottage industries which he considered as essential. Referring to his own proposals, he said: 'The whole of this programme will be a structure on sand if it is not built on the solid foundation of economic equality.'

Thus even the enthusiastic advocates for cottage and small-scale industries recognize that big-scale industry is, to a certain extent, necessary and inevitable; only they would like to limit it as far as possible. Superficially then the question becomes one of emphasis and adjustment of the two forms of production and economy. It can hardly be challenged that, in the context of the modern world, no country can be politically and economically independent, even within the framework of international interdependence, unless it is highly industrialized and has developed its power resources to the utmost. Nor can it achieve or maintain high standards of living and liquidate poverty without the aid of modern technology in almost every sphere of life. An industrially backward country will continually upset the world equilibrium and encourage the aggressive tendencies of more developed countries. Even if it retains its political independence, this will be nominal only, and economic control will tend to pass to others. This control will inevitably upset its own small-scale economy which it has sought to preserve in pursuit of its own view of life. Thus an attempt to build up a country's economy largely on the basis of cottage and small-scale industries is doomed to failure. It will not solve the basic problems of the country or maintain freedom, nor will it fit in with the world framework, except as a colonial appendage.

Is it possible to have two entirely different kinds of economy in a country—one based on the big machine and industrialization, and the other mainly on cottage industries? This is hardly conceivable, for one must overcome the other, and there can be little doubt that the big machine will triumph unless it is forcibly prevented from doing so. Thus it is not a mere question of adjustment of the two forms of production and economy. One must be dominating and paramount, with the other as complementary to it, fitting in where it can. The economy based on the latest technical achievements of the day must necessarily be the dominating one. If technology demands the big machine, as it does to-day in a large measure, then the big machine with all its implications and consequences must be accepted. Where it is possible, in terms of that technology, to decentralize production, this would be desirable. But, in any event, the latest technique has to be followed, and to adhere to out-worn and out-of-date methods of production, except as a temporary and stop gap measure, is to arrest growth and development.

Any argument as to the relative merits of small-scale and large-scale industry seems strangely irrelevant to-day when the world, and the dominating facts of the situation that confront it, have decided in favour of the latter. Even in India the decision has been made by these facts themselves, and no one doubts that India will be rapidly industrialized in the near future. She has already gone a good way in that direction. The evils of unrestricted and unplanned industrialization are well recognized to-day. Whether these evils are necessary concomitants of big industry, or derived from the social and economic structure behind it, is another matter. If the economic structure is primarily responsible for them, then surely we should set about changing that structure, instead of blaming the inevitable and desirable development in technique.

The real question is not one of quantitative adjustment and balancing of various incongruous elements and methods of production, but a qualitative change-over to something different and new, from which various social consequences flow. The economic and political aspects of this qualitative change are important, but equally important are the social and psychological aspects. In India especially, where we have been wedded far too long to past forms and modes of thought and action, new experiences, new processes, leading to new ideas and new horizons, are necessary. Thus we will change the static character of our living and make it dynamic and vital, and our minds will become active and adventurous. New situations lead to new experiences, as the mind is compelled to deal with them and adapt itself to a changing environment.

It is well recognized now that a child's education should be intimately associated with some craft or manual activity. The mind is stimulated thereby and there is a co-ordination between the activities of the mind and the hands. So also the mind of a growing boy or girl is stimulated by the machine. It grows under the machine's impact (under proper conditions, of course, and not as an exploited and unhappy worker in a factory) and opens out new horizons. Simple scientific experiments, peeps into the microscope, and an explanation of the ordinary phenomena of nature bring excitement in their train, an understanding of some of life's processes, and a desire to experiment and find out instead of relying on set phrases and old formulæ. Self-confidence and the co-operative spirit grow, and frustration, arising out of the miasma of the past, lessens. A civilization based on ever-changing and advancing mechanical techniques leads to this. Such a civilization is a marked change, a jump almost from the older type, and is intimately connected with modern industrialization. Inevitably it gives rise to new problems and difficulties, but it also shows the way to overcome them.

I have a partiality for the literary aspects of education and I admire the classics, but I am quite sure that some elementary scientific training in physics and chemistry, and especially biology, as also in the application of science, is essential for all boys and girls. Only thus can they understand and fit into the modern world and develop, to some extent at least, the scientific temper. There is something very wonderful about the high achievements of science and modern technology (which no doubt will be bettered in the near future), in the superb ingenuity of scientific instruments, in the amazingly delicate and yet powerful machines, in all that has flowed from the adventurous inquiries of science and its applications, in the glimpses into the fascinating workshop and processes of nature, in the fine sweep of science, through its myriad workers, in the realms of thought and practice, and, above all, in the fact that all this has come out of the mind of man.

Government Checks Industrial Growth
War Production is Diversion from Normal Production

Heavy industry was represented in India by the Tata Iron and Steel Works at Jamshedpur. There was nothing else of the kind and the other engineering workshops were really jobbing shops. Even the development of Tatas had been slow because of Government policy. During World War I, when there was a shortage of locomotives and railway carriages and wagons, Tatas decided to make locomotives and, I think, even imported machinery for the purpose; but when the war ended, the Government of India and the Railway Board (which is a department of the central government) decided to continue their patronage of British locomotives. There is obviously no private market for locomotives, as the railways were either controlled by Government or owned by British companies, and so Tatas had to give up the idea of making locomotives.

The three fundamental requirements of India, if she is to develop industrially and otherwise, are a heavy engineering and machine-making industry, scientific research institutes, and electric power. These must be the foundations of all planning, and the national planning committee laid the greatest emphasis on them. We lacked all three, and bottlenecks in industrial expansion were always occurring. A forward policy could have rapidly removed these bottlenecks, but the government's policy was the reverse of forward and was obviously one of preventing the development of heavy industry in India. Even when World War II started, the necessary machinery was not allowed to be imported; later shipping difficulties were pleaded. There was neither lack of capital nor skilled personnel in India, only machinery was lacking, and industrialists were clamouring for it. If opportunities had been given for the importation of machinery, not only would the economic position of India have been infinitely better, but the whole aspect of the war in the far eastern theatres might have changed. Many of the essential articles which had to be brought over, usually by air and at great cost and under considerable difficulties, could have been manufactured in India. India would have really become an arsenal for China and the east, and her industrial progress might have matched that of Canada or Australia. But imperative as the needs of the war situation were, the future needs of British industry were always kept in view, and it was considered undesirable to develop any industries in India which might compete with British industries in the post-war years. This was no secret policy; public expression was given to it in British journals, and there was continuous reference to it and protests against it in India.

Jamshedji Tata, the far-sighted founder of Tata Steel, had vision enough to start the Indian Institute of Science in Bangalore. This research institute was one of the very few of its kind in India; the others were some government institutions with limited objectives. The vast field of scientific and industrial research, which has thousands of institutes, academies, and special stations in the U.S.A. and the Soviet Union, was thus almost wholly neglected in India, except for the Bangalore institute and some work done in the universities. An effort was made, sometime after World War II started, to encourage research and, though limited in scope, it has produced good results.

While shipbuilding and locomotive manufacture were discouraged and prevented, an effort to build up an automobile industry was also scotched. Some years before World War II, preparations were started for this and everything was worked out in co-operation with a famous American firm of automobile manufacturers. A number of assembly plants had already been functioning in India. It was now proposed to manufacture all the parts in India with Indian capital and management and Indian personnel. By arrangement with the American corporation their patents could be used and their skilled and technical supervision was available for the initial period. The provincial government of Bombay, which was then functioning under a Congress ministry, promised assistance in various ways. The planning committee was especially interested in this project. Everything in fact had been fixed up and all that remained was to import the machinery. The Secretary of State for India however did not approve and gave his fiat against the importation of the machinery. According to him 'any attempt to set up this industry now would divert both labour and machinery which are more urgently needed for the war.' This was in the early months of the war, during the so-called phoney period. It was pointed out that plenty of labour, even skilled labour, was available and in fact was idle. War necessity was also a curious argument, for that necessity itself demanded motor transport. But the Secretary of State for India, the final authority, sitting in London, was not moved by these arguments. It was reported also that a rival and powerful automobile corporation in America did not approve of the starting of an automobile industry in India under someone else's auspices.

Transport became one of the major problems of the war in India. There was the lack of motor trucks, of petroleum, of locomotives and railway wagons, even of coal. Almost all these difficulties would have been much easier of solution if the prewar proposals on behalf of India had not been turned down. Locomotives, railway cars, motor trucks, as well as armoured vehicles would have been manufactured in India. Power alcohol would have helped greatly in easing the strain caused by scarcity of petroleum. As for coal there was no scarcity in India; there were huge reserves but only very little was produced for use. Coal production has actually gone down during the war years in spite of increased demand. Conditions in coal mines were so bad and wages so low that workers were not attracted. Ultimately the bar on women working underground was removed as women were available at those wages. No attempt was made to overhaul the coal industry and improve conditions and wages so as to attract workers. Owing to lack of coal, the expansion of industry has suffered greatly and even existing factories have had to stop working.

Some hundreds of locomotives and many thousands of railway cars were shipped from India to the Middle East, thus adding to the transport difficulties in India. Even the permanent way was uprooted in some places for transfer elsewhere. The casual way in which all this was done, without any regard to future consequences, was amazing. There was a complete lack of planning and foresight, and the partial solution of one problem led immediately to more serious problems.

An attempt was made at the end of 1939 or the beginning of 1940 to start an aircraft manufacturing industry in India. Again everything was fixed up with an American firm and urgent cables were sent to the Government of India and army headquarters in India for their consent. There was no response. After repeated reminders a reply was forthcoming disapproving of the scheme. Why make aeroplanes in India when you could buy them in England and America?

In pre-war days a large number of medicines and drugs and vaccines used to come to India from Germany. War stopped this. It was immediately suggested that some of the more essential vaccines and medicines might be made in India. This could easily be done in some of the Government institutes. The Government of India did not approve and pointed out that everything that was necessary could now be obtained through Imperial Chemical Industries. When it was suggested that the same thing could be made in India at much less cost, and utilized for army as well as general public use without any private interest, high authority was indignant at the intrusion of such base considerations in matters of state policy. 'Government,' it was said, 'was not a commercial institution!'

Government was not a commercial institution but it was very much interested in commercial institutions, and one of these was Imperial Chemicals. This huge combine was given many facilities. Even without such facilities it had such enormous resources that no Indian firm, except to some extent Tatas, could possibly compete with it. Apart from these facilities it had powerful support both in India and England. A few months after leaving the viceroyalty of India, Lord Linlithgow appeared in a new role as a director of Imperial Chemicals. This demonstrates the very close connection between big business in England and the Government of India, and how this connection must necessarily affect policy. Lord Linlithgow may have been a substantial shareholder in Imperial Chemicals even when he was Viceroy of India. In any event he has now placed the prestige of his Indian connection and his special knowledge derived as Viceroy at the disposal of Imperial Chemicals.

Lord Linlithgow declared as Viceroy in December, 1942: 'We have achieved immense things in the field of supply. India has made a contribution of outstanding importance and value... for the first six months of the war the value of contracts placed was approximately 29 crores. For the next months from April to October, 1942, it was 137 crores. Over the whole period to the end of October, 1942, it was no less than 428 crores; and these figures exclude the value of work done in the ordnance factories which is in itself very considerable.'* This is perfectly true and India's contribution to the war effort has grown tremendously since this was said. One would imagine that this represents a vast increase in industrial activity and a much larger index of production. Yet, surprisingly, there has not been much change. The index of India's industrial activity in 1938-39 was 111.1 (taking 1935 as 100). In 1939-40 it was 114.0; in 1940-41 it varied between 112.1 to 127.0; in March, 1942, it was 118.9; it fell in April, 1942, to 109.2, and then gradually rose to 116.2 in July, 1942. These figures are not complete as they do not include munitions and some chemical industries. Nevertheless they are important and significant.

The amazing fact emerges that the total industrial activity of India in July, 1942, was, apart from munitions, etc., only slightly in excess of the pre-war period. There was a brief spurt in December, 1941, when the index figure went up to 127.0, and then declined. And yet the value of Government contracts placed with industries was progressively increasing. For the six months October to March, 1939-40, these contracts amounted to 290 million rupees, according to Lord Linlithgow, and for the six months April to October, 1942, they were for 1,370 million rupees.

All these tremendous war orders thus do not represent any increase in the total industrial activity, but indicate its large-scale diversion from normal production to production for specialized war purposes. For the moment they supplied war needs but at the cost of a terrific lowering of production for civilian needs. This inevitably had far-reaching consequences. While sterling balances in favour of India grew in London, and money accumulated in the hands of a few persons in India, the country as a whole was starved of essential needs, vast and ever-increasing quantities of paper money circulated, and prices went up and sometimes reached fantastic figures. Already by the middle of 1942 a food crisis was evident; in the autumn of 1943 famine killed its millions in Bengal and other parts of India. The burden

The figures are in rupees. A crore is ten millions.

of the war and of the official policy pursued in its connection fell on scores of millions in India who were least capable of shouldering it, and crushed out of existence vast numbers of people who died by the cruellest of deaths—slow starvation.

The figures I have given end with 1942; I have no later ones. Probably many changes have taken place since then and the index of India's industrial activity may be higher now.* But the picture they reveal has not changed in any fundamental aspect. The same processes are at work, the same crises follow one after the other, the same patchwork and temporary remedies are applied, the same lack of any planned and comprehensive outlook is evident, the same partiality for the present and future of British industry prevails—and meanwhile people continue to die from lack of food and from epidemics.

It is true that some of the existing industries, notably the textile, the iron and steel, and the jute industries, have prospered exceedingly. The number of millionaires among industrial magnates, war contractors, hoarders, and profiteers, has grown, and large sums have accumulated in the hands of small upper strata of India's people, in spite of a heavy super tax. But labour generally has not profited, and Mr. N. M. Joshi, the labour leader, declared in the Central Assembly that labour conditions in India had become worse during the war. Land owners and middle farmers, especially in the Punjab and Sind, have prospered, but the great majority of the agricultural population have been hard hit by war conditions and have suffered greatly. Consumers generally have been progressively ground down by inflation and the rise in prices.

In the middle of 1942 an American technical mission—the Grady Committee—came to India to inspect the existing industries and make suggestions for increased production. They were naturally concerned with production for war purposes only. Their report was never published, possibly because the Government of India vetoed publication. A few of their recommendations were, however, announced. They suggested the production of power alcohol, the expansion of the steel industry, more electric power, greater production of aluminium and refined sulphur, and rationalization in various industries. They also recommended the institution of high-powered control of production, independent of established Government agencies, on the American model.

**It is not so. The Calcutta journal, Capital, of March 9th, 1944, gives the following figures for the index of industrial activity in India.*

(1935-36=100): 1938-39: 111.1. 1939-40: 114.0. 1940-41: 117.3. 1941-42: 122.7. 1942-43: 108.8. 1943-44: 108.0 (approx.). 1944 (January): 111.7.

These do not include armament production. Thus, after more than four years of war, industrial activity as a whole in India was actually somewhat lower than in the pre-war period.

Evidently the Grady Committee was not filled with admiration for the leisurely, casual, and inefficient methods of the Government of India, on which even total war had produced little impression. They were struck, however, by the efficiency and organization of the Tata Steel Works, a vast organization run entirely by Indians. It was further stated in the preliminary report of the Grady Committee that 'the mission has been impressed with the good quality and excellent potentiality of Indian labour. The Indian is skilful with his hands, and given satisfactory working conditions and security of employment, is dependable and industrious.'*

During the last two or three years the chemical industry has grown in India, shipbuilding has made some advance, and an infant aircraft industry has been started. All war industries, including jute and textile mills, have made vast profits, in spite of the super tax, and a great deal of capital has accumulated. The Government of India had put a ban on capital issues for fresh industrial undertakings. Recently there has been some relaxation in this respect, though nothing definite may be done till after the war. Even this little relaxation has led to a burst of energy from big business and huge industrial schemes are taking shape. India, whose growth has so long been arrested, appears to be on the verge of large-scale industrialization.

*Commenting on the shelving of the Grady Committee's Report, Commerce (Bombay, November 28th, 1942) wrote: 'The fact remains that powerful interests are operating abroad for the purpose of throttling further industrialization of this country, so that in the post-war world there would not be any dangerous competition to the west from the east.'

CHAPTER NINE

THE LAST PHASE (3)

World War II

The Congress Develops a Foreign Policy

THE NATIONAL CONGRESS, LIKE ALL OTHER POLITICAL ORGANIZATIONS in India, was for long entirely engrossed in internal politics and paid little attention to foreign developments. In the nineteen-twenties it began to take some interest in foreign affairs. No other organization did so except the small groups of socialists and communists. Moslem organizations were interested in Palestine and occasionally passed resolutions of sympathy for the Moslem Arabs there. The intense nationalism of Turkey, Egypt, and Iran was watched by them but not without some apprehension, as it was secular, and was leading to reforms which were not wholly in keeping with their ideas of Islamic traditions. The Congress gradually developed a foreign policy which was based on the elimination of political and economic imperialism everywhere and the co-operation of free nations. This fitted in with the demand for Indian independence. As early as 1920 a resolution on foreign policy was passed by the Congress, in which our desire to co-operate with other nations and especially to develop friendly relations with all our neighbouring countries was emphasized. The possibility of another large-scale war was later considered, and in 1927, twelve years before World War II actually started, the Congress first declared its policy in regard to it.

This was five or six years before Hitler came into power and before Japanese aggression in Manchuria had begun. Mussolini was consolidating himself in Italy but did not then appear as a major threat to world peace. Fascist Italy was on friendly terms with England and British statesmen expressed their admiration for the Duce. There were a number of petty dictators in Europe, also usually on good terms with the British Government. Between England and Soviet Russia, however, there was a complete breach; there had been the Arcos raid and withdrawal of diplomatic representatives. In the League of Nations and the International Labour Office British and French policy was definitely conservative. In the interminable discussions on disarmament, when every other country represented in the League, as well as the U.S.A., were in favour of the total abolition of aerial bombardment, Britain made some vital reservations. For many years the British Government had used aircraft, for 'police purposes' it was called, for bombing towns and villages in Iraq and the North-West Frontier of India. This 'right' was insisted upon, thus preventing any general agreement on this subject in the League and later in the Disarmament Conference.

Germany—the Weimar republican Germany—had become a full member of the League of Nations, and Locarno had been hailed as a forerunner of perpetual peace in Europe and a triumph of British policy. Another view of all these developments was that Soviet Russia was being isolated and a joint front against her was being created in Europe. Russia had just celebrated the tenth anniversary of her revolution and had developed friendly ties with various eastern countries—Turkey, Iran, Afghanistan, and Mongolia.

The Chinese revolution had also advanced with great strides and the nationalist armies had taken possession of half of China, coming into conflict with foreign, and especially British, interests in the port towns and the interior. Subsequently there had been internal trouble and a break-up of the Kuomintang into rival groups.

The world situation seemed to be drifting towards a major conflict with England and France as heads of a European group of nations, and Soviet Russia associated with some eastern nations. The United States of America held aloof from both these groups; their intense dislike of communism kept them away from Russia, and their distrust of British policy and competition with British finance and industry, preventing them from associating themselves with the British group. Over and above these considerations was the isolationist sentiment of America and the fear of being embroiled in European quarrels.

In this setting Indian opinion inevitably sided with Soviet Russia and the eastern nations. This did not mean any widespread approval of communism, though a growing number were attracted to socialist thought. The triumphs of the Chinese revolution were hailed with enthusiasm as portents of the approaching freedom of India and of the elimination of European aggression in Asia. We developed an interest in nationalist movements in the Dutch East Indies and Indo-China, as well as the western Asiatic countries and Egypt. The conversion of Singapore into a great naval base and the development of Trincomalee harbour in Ceylon appeared as parts of the general preparations for the coming war, in which Britain would try to consolidate and strengthen her imperialist position and crush Soviet Russia and the rising nationalist movements of the east.

It was with this background that the National Congress began to develop its foreign policy in 1927. It declared that India could be no party to an imperialist war, and in no event should India be made to join any war without the consent of her people being obtained. In the years that followed, this declaration was frequently repeated and widespread propaganda was carried on in accordance with it. It became one of the foundations of Congress policy and, it was generally accepted, of Indian policy. No individual or organization in India opposed it.

Meanwhile changes were taking place in Europe, and Hitler and nazism had risen. The Congress immediately reacted against these changes and denounced them, for Hitler and his creed seemed the very embodiment and intensification of the imperialism and racialism against which the Congress was struggling. Japanese aggression in Manchuria produced even stronger reactions because of sympathy for China. Abyssinia, Spain, the Sino-Japanese war, Czechoslovakia, and Munich, added to this strength of feeling and the tension of approaching war.

But this coming war was likely to be different from the one that had been envisaged before Hitler had arisen. Even so, British policy had been almost continuously pro-fascist and pro-nazi and it was difficult to believe that it would suddenly change overnight and champion freedom and democracy. Its dominant imperialist outlook and desire to hold on to its empire would continue despite other developments; also its basic opposition to Russia and what Russia represented. But it became increasingly obvious that in spite of every desire to appease Hitler he was becoming a dominating power in Europe, entirely upsetting the old balance and menacing the vital interests of the British Empire. War between England and Germany became probable, and if this broke out what then would our policy be? How would we reconcile the two dominating trends of our policy: Opposition to British imperialism and opposition to fascism and nazism? How would we bring in line our nationalism and our internationalism? It was a difficult question in the existing circumstances, difficult for us, but offering no difficulty if the British Government took a step to demonstrate to us that they had given up their imperialist policy in India and wanted to rely on popular goodwill.

In a contest between nationalism and internationalism, nationalism was bound to win. That had happened in every country and in every crisis; in a country under foreign domination, with bitter memories of continuous struggle and suffering, that was an inevitable and unavoidable consequence, England and France had played false to republican Spain and betrayed Czechoslovakia, and thus sacrificed internationalism for what they considered, wrongly as events proved, their national interests. The United States of America had clung to isolationism, in spite of their evident sympathy with England, France, and China, and their hatred of nazism and Japanese militarism and aggression. It was Pearl Harbour that flung them headlong into war. Soviet Russia, the very emblem of internationalism, had followed a strictly national policy, bringing confusion to many of her friends and sympathizers. It was the sudden and un-announced attack by the German armies that brought war to the U.S.S.R. The Scandinavian countries and Holland and Belgium tried to avoid war and entanglement in the vain hope of saving themselves, and yet were overwhelmed by it. Turkey has sat precariously for five years on the thin edge of a varying neutrality, governed solely by national considerations. Egypt, still a semi-colonial country in spite of its apparent independ-ence, itself one of the major battle areas, occupies a curious and anomalous position. For all practical purposes it is a belligerent country completely under the control of the armed forces of the United Nations, and yet apparently it is not a belligerent.

There may be justification or excuse for all these policies adopted by various governments and countries. A democracy cannot easily jump into war without preparing its people and gaining their co-operation. Even an authoritarian state has to prepare the ground. But whatever the reason or justification may be, it is clear that whenever a crisis has occurred, national consi-derations, or what were considered to be such, have been para-mount and all others, which did not fit in with them, have been swept away. It was extraordinary how, during the Munich crises, the hundreds of international organizations, anti-fascist leagues, etc., in Europe were struck dumb and became powerless and ineffective. Individuals and small groups may become inter-nationally minded and may even be prepared to sacrifice personal and immediate national interests for a larger cause, but not so nations. It is only when international interests are believed to be in line with national interests that they arouse enthusiasm.

A few months ago the London *Economist*, discussing British foreign policy, wrote: 'The only foreign policy that has any hope of being consistently pursued is one in which national interests are fully and obviously safeguarded. No nation puts the interests of the international community before its own. It is only if the two can be seen to coincide that there is any possibility of effective internationalism.'

Internationalism can indeed only develop in a free country, for all the thought and energy of a subject country are directed towards the achievement of its own freedom. That subject con-dition is like a cancerous growth inside the body, which not only prevents any limb from becoming healthy but is a constant irritant to the mind and colours all thought and action. Conflict is inherent in it and such conflict leads to a concentration of thought on it and prevents a consideration of wider issues. The history of a long succession of past conflicts and suffering becomes the inseparable companion of both the individual and the national mind. It becomes an obsession, a dominating passion, which cannot be exorcised except by removing its root cause. And even then, when the sense of subjection has gone, the cure is slow, for the injuries of the mind take longer to heal than those of the body.

All this background we have long had in India, and yet Gandhi gave a turn to our nationalist movement which lessened the feelings of frustration and bitterness. Those feelings continued but I do not know of any other nationalist movement which has been so free from hatred. Gandhi was an intense nationalist; he was also, at the same time, a man who felt he had a message not only for India but for the world, and he ardently desired world peace. His nationalism, therefore, had a certain world outlook and was entirely free from any aggressive intent. Desiring the independence of India, he had come to believe that a world federation of interdependent states was the only right goal, however distant that might be. He had said: 'My idea of nationalism is that my country may become free, that if need be the whole of the country may die, so that the human race may live. There is no room for race hatred here. Let that be our nationalism.' And again: 'I do want to think in terms of the whole world. My patriotism includes the good of mankind in general. Therefore, my service of India includes the services of humanity....Isolated independence is not the goal of the world states. It is voluntary interdependence. The better mind of the world desires to-day not absolutely independent states, warring one against another, but a federation of friendly, inter-dependent states. The consummation of that event may be far off. I want to make no grand claims for our country. But I see nothing grand or impossible about our expressing our readiness for universal inter-dependence rather than independence. I desire the ability to be totally independent without asserting the independence.'

As the nationalist movement grew in strength and self-confidence, many people began to think in terms of a free India: what she would be like, what she would do, and what her relations with other countries would be. The very bigness and potential strength and resources of the country made them think in big terms. India could not be a mere hanger-on of any country or group of nations; her freedom and growth would make a vital difference to Asia and therefore to the world. That led inevitably to the conception of full independence and a severance of the bonds that tied her to England and her empire. Dominion status, even when that status approached independence, seemed an absurd limitation and a hindrance to full growth. The idea behind dominion status, of a mother country closely connected with her daughter nations, all of them having a common cultural background, seemed totally inapplicable to India. It meant certainly a wider sphere of international co-operation, which was desirable, but it also meant at the same time lesser co-operation with countries outside that empire or commonwealth group. It thus became a limiting factor, and our ideas, full of the promise of the future, overstepped these boundaries and looked to a wider co-operation. In particular, we thought of close relations with our neighbour countries in the east and west, with China, Afghanistan, Iran, and the Soviet Union. Even with distant America we wanted closer relations, for we could learn much from the United States as also from the Soviet Union. There was a feeling that we had exhausted our capacity for learning anything more from England, and in any event we could only profit by contact with each other after breaking the unhealthy bond that tied us and by meeting on equal terms.

The racial discrimination and treatment of Indians in some of the British dominions and colonies were powerful factors in our determination to break from that group. In particular, South Africa was a constant irritant, and East Africa and Kenya, directly under the British colonial policy. Curiously enough we got on well, as individuals, with Canadians, Australians, and New Zealanders, for they represent a new tradition and were free from many of the prejudices and the social conservatism of the British.

When we talked of the independence of India it was not in terms of isolation. We realized, perhaps more than many other countries, that the old type of complete national independence was doomed, and there must be a new era of world co-operation. We made it repeatedly clear, therefore, that we were perfectly agreeable to limit that independence, in common with other nations, within some international framework. That framework should preferably cover the world or as large a part of it as possible, or be regional. The British Commonwealth did not fit in with either of these conceptions, though it could be a part of the larger framework

It is surprising how internationally minded we grew in spite of our intense nationalism. No other nationalist movement of a subject country came anywhere near this, and the general tendency in such other countries was to keep clear of international commitments. In India also there were those who objected to our lining up with republican Spain and China, Abyssinia and Czechoslovakia. Why antagonize powerful nations like Italy, Germany, and Japan, they said; every enemy of Britain should be treated as a friend; idealism has no place in politics, which concerns itself with power and the opportune use of it. But these objectors were overwhelmed by the mass sentiment the Congress had created and hardly ever gave public expression to their views. The Moslem League remained throughout discreetly silent and never committed itself on any such international issue.

In 1938 the Congress sent a medical unit consisting of a number of doctors and necessary equipment and material to China. For several years this unit did good work there. When this was organized, Subhas Bose was president of the Congress. He did not approve of any step being taken by the Congress which was anti-Japanese or anti-German or anti-Italian. And yet such was the feeling in the Congress and the country that he did not oppose this or many other manifestations of Congress sympathy with China and the victims of fascist and nazi aggression. We passed many resolutions and organized many demonstrations of which he did not approve during the period of his presidentship, but he submitted to them without protest because he realized the strength of feeling behind them. There was a big difference in outlook between him and others in the Congress Executive, both in regard to foreign and internal matters. and this led to a break early in 1939. He then attacked Congress policy publicly and, early in August, 1939. the Congress Executive took the very unusual step of taking disciplinary action against him, one of its ex-presidents.

The Congress Approach to War

Thus the Congress laid down and frequently repeated a dual policy in regard to war. There was, on the one hand, opposition to fascism, nazism, and Japanese militarism, both because of their internal policies and their aggression against other countries; there was intense sympathy with the victims of that aggression; and there was a willingness to join up in any war or other attempt to stop this aggression. On the other hand, there was an emphasis on the freedom of India, not only because that was our fundamental objective for which we had continuously laboured, but also especially in relation to a possible war. For we reiterated that only a free India could take proper part in such a war; only through freedom could we overcome the bitter heritage of our past relations with Britain and arouse enthusiasm and mobilize our great resources. Without that freedom the war would be like any old war, a contest between rival imperialism, and an attempt to defend and perpetuate the British Empire as such. It seemed absurd and impossible for us to line up in defence of that very imperialism against which we had been struggling for so long. And even if a few of us, in view of larger considerations, considered that a lesser evil, it was utterly beyond our capacity to carry our people. Only freedom could release mass energy and convert bitterness into enthusiasm for a cause. There was no other way.

The Congress specially demanded that India should not be committed to any war without the consent of her people or their representatives, and that no Indian troops be sent for service abroad without such consent. The Central Legislative Assembly, consisting of various groups and parties, had also put forward this latter claim. It had long been a grievance of the Indian people that our armed forces were sent abroad for imperialist purposes and often to conquer or suppress other peoples with whom we had no quarrel whatever, and with whose efforts to regain their freedom we sympthized. Indian troops had been used as mercenaries for this purpose in Burma, China, Iran, and the Middle East, and parts of Africa. They have become symbols of British imperialism in all these countries and antagonized their peoples against India. I remember the bitter remark of an Egyptian: 'You have not only lost your own freedom but you help the British to enslave others.'

The two parts of this dual policy did not automatically fit into each other; there was an element of mutual contradiction in them. But that contradiction was not of our creation; it was inherent in the circumstances and was inevitably mirrored in any policy that arose from those circumstances. Repeatedly we pointed out the inconsistency of condemning fascism and nazism and maintaining imperialist domination. It was true that the former were indulging in horrid crimes whilst imperialism in India and elsewhere had stabilized itself. The difference was one of degree and of time, not of kind. The former also were far away, some thing which we read about; the latter was always at our doorstep, surrounding all of us and pervading the entire atmosphere. We emphasized the absurdity of holding aloft the banner of democracy elsewhere and denying it to us in India.

Whatever inconsistency there might have been in our dual policy, no question of the doctrine of non-violence coming in the way of armed conflict for defence or against aggression arose.

I was in England and on the continent of Europe in the summer of 1938 and in speech, writing, and private conversation I explained this policy of ours, and pointed out the dangers of allowing matters to drift or to remain as they were. At the height of the Sudetenland crisis, anxious Czechs asked me what India was likely to do in case of war. Danger was too near and terrible for them to consider fine points and old grievances, nevertheless they appreciated what I said and agreed with the logic of it.

About the middle of 1939 it became known that Indian troops had been despatched overseas, probably to Singapore and the Middle East. Immediately there was an outcry at this having been done without any reference to the representatives of the

people. It was recognized that troop movements during a period of crisis have often to be secret. Still there were many ways of taking representative leaders into confidence. There were the party leaders in the Central Assembly, and in every province there were popularly elected governments. In the normal course the Central Government had to consult and share confidence in many matters with these provincial ministers. But not even formal or nominal respect was shown to the people's representatives and the declared wishes of the nation. Steps were also being taken, through the British Parliament, to amend the Government of India Act of 1935 under which the provincial governments were functioning, with a view to concentrating all power, in the event of a war emergency, in the Central Government. Normally, in a democratic country, this might have been a natural and reasonable step, if taken with the consent of the parties concerned. It is well known that federating states, provinces, or autonomous units in a federation are very jealous of their rights and do not easily agree to give them up to a central administration even in a period of crisis and emergency. This tug-of-war is continuous in the U.S.A. and, as I write this, a referendum in Australia has rejected the proposal to add to the powers of the Commonwealth Government at the expense of the states even for the purposes and duration of the war. And yet both in the U.S.A. and Australia the Central Government and legislature are popularly elected and consist of representatives of those very states. In India the Central Government was, and is, wholly irresponsible and authoritarian, not elected and not in any way responsible to the people generally or to the provinces. It functioned completely as an agent of the British Government. To add to its power at the expense of the provincial governments and legislatures meant weakening still further these popular provincial governments and striking at the very basis of provincial autonomy. This was deeply resented. It was felt that this was contrary to the assurances under which Congress governments had been formed, and indicated that, as previously, war would be imposed upon India without any reference to her chosen representatives.

The Congress Executive expressed its strong dissent with this policy which it considered a deliberate flouting of the declarations both of the Congress and the Central Legislature. It declared that it must resist any imposition of this kind and could not agree to India being committed to far-reaching policies without the consent of her people. Again it stated (early in August 1939) that 'In this world crisis the sympathies of the Working Committee are entirely with the people who stand for democracy and freedom and the Congress has repeatedly condemned fascist aggression in Europe, Africa, and the far east of Asia, as well as the betrayal of democracy by British imperialism in Czechoslovakia and Spain.' But, it was added, 'The past policy of the British Government as well as recent developments, demonstrated abundantly that this government does not stand for freedom and democracy and may at any time betray these ideals. India cannot associate herself with such a government or be asked to give her resources for democratic freedom which is denied to her and which is likely to be betrayed.' As a first step in protest against this policy, the Congress members of the Central Legislative Assembly were asked to refrain from attending the next session of the Assembly.

This last resolution was passed three weeks before war actually broke out in Europe. It seemed that the Government of India, and the British Government behind it, were bent on ignoring completely Indian opinion, not only in regard to the major issues raised by the war crisis, but also on many minor matters. This policy was reflected in the attitudes of the Governors in the provinces and the civil service administration which became more non-co-operative with the Congress governments. The position of these Congress provincial governments was becoming increasingly difficult, and strong sections of public opinion were excited and apprehensive. They feared that the British Government would act as it had done a quarter of a century earlier in 1914, impose the war on India, ignoring the provincial governments and public opinion and everything that had happened during this period, and make the war a cloak for suppressing such limited freedom as India had obtained and exploiting her resources without check.

But much had happened during this quarter of a century and the mood of the people was very different. The idea of a great country like India being treated as a chattel and her people utterly and contemptuously ignored was bitterly resented. Was all the struggle and suffering of the past twenty years to count for nothing? Were the Indian people to shame the land from which they sprang by quietly submitting to this disgrace and humiliation? Many of them had learnt to resist what they considered evil, and not to submit when such submission was considered shameful. They had willingly accepted the consequences of such non-submission.

Then there were others, a younger generation, which had little personal experience of the nationalist struggle and what it had involved, and for whom even the civil disobedience movements of the twenties and early thirties were past history and nothing more. They had not been tested in the fire of experience and suffering and took many things for granted. They were critical of the older generation, considering it weak and compromising, and imagined that strong language was good substitute for action. They quarrelled amonsgst themselves over questions of personal leadership or fine points of political or economic doctrine. They discussed world affairs without knowing much about them; they were immature and lacked ballast. There was good material in them, much enthusiasm for good causes, but somehow the general effect produced by them was disappointing and discouraging. Perhaps it was a temporary phase, which they would outgrow, which they may have outgrown already after the bitter experiences which they have since had.

Whatever the other differences, all these groups within the nationalist ranks reacted in similar fashion to British policy towards India during the crisis. They were angered by it and called upon Congress to resist it. A proud and sensitive nationalism did not want to submit to this humiliation. All other considerations became secondary.

War was declared in Europe and immediately the Viceroy of India announced that India was also at war. One man, and he a foreigner and a representative of a hated system, could plunge four hundred millions of human beings into war without the slightest reference to them. There was something fundamentally wrong and rotten in a system under which the fate of these millions could be decided in this way. In the dominions the decision was taken by popular representatives after full debate and consideration of various points of view. Not so in India, and it hurt.

Reaction to War

I was in Chungking when the war began in Europe. The Congress President cabled me to return immediately, and I hurried back. A meeting of the Congress Executive was being held when I arrived, and to this meeting Mr. M. A. Jinnah was also invited, but he expressed his inability to come. The Viceroy had not only committed India formally to the war but had issued a number of ordinances; the British Parliament had also passed the Government of India Amending Act. All these enactments circumscribed and limited the powers and activities of the provincial governments and were resented, especially as no effort had been made to consult the people's representatives. Indeed, their oft-repeated wishes and declarations had been completely ignored.

On September 14th, 1939, after long deliberation, the Congress Working Committee issued a lengthy statement on the war crisis. The steps the Victory had taken and the new enactments and decrees were referred to and it was stated that 'the Working Committee must take the gravest view of these developments.' Fascism and nazism were condemned, and particularly 'the latest aggression of the nazi government in Germany against Poland,' and sympathy was expressed for those who resisted it.

While co-operation was offered it was added that 'any imposed decision...will necessarily have to be opposed by them. If co-operation is desired in a worthy cause, this cannot be obtained by compulsion and imposition, and the Committee cannot agree to the carrying out by the Indian people of orders issued by external authority. Co-operation must be between equals by mutual consent for a cause which both consider to be worthy. The people of India have, in the recent past, faced grave risks and willingly made great sacrifices to secure their own freedom and establish a free democratic state in India, and their sympathy is entirely on the side of democracy and freedom. But India cannot associate herself in a war said to be for democratic freedom when that very freedom is denied to her, and such limited freedom as she possesses taken away from her.

'Th e Committee are aware that the Governments of Great Britain and France have declared that they are fighting for democracy and freedom and to put an end to aggression. But the history of the recent past is full of examples showing the constant divergence between the spoken word, the ideals proclaimed, and the real motives and objectives.' Certain past events, during and after World War I, were referred to and then: 'Subsequent history has demonstrated afresh how even a seemingly fervent declaration of faith may be followed by an ignoble desertion....Again it is asserted that democracy is in danger and must be defended, and with this statement the Committee are in entire agreement. The Committee believe that the peoples of the west are moved by this ideal and objective, and for these they are prepared to make sacrifices; but again and again the ideals and sentiments of the people and of those who have sacrificed themselves in the struggle have been ignored and faith has not been kept with them.

'If the war is to defend the *status quo*, imperialist possessions, colonies, vested interests, and privilege, then India can have nothing to do with it. If, however, the issue is democracy and a world order based on democracy, then India is intensely interested in it. The Committee are convinced that the interests of Indian democracy do not conflict with the interests of British democracy or of world democracy; but there is an inherent and ineradicable conflict between democracy for India and elsewhere and imperialism and fascism. If Great Britain fights for the maintenance and extension of democracy, then she must necessarily end imperialism in her own possessions....A free democratic India will gladly associate herself with other free nations for mutual defence against aggression and for economic co-operation. She will work for the establishment of a real world order based on freedom and democracy, utilising the world's kowledge and resources for the progress and advancement of humanity.'

The Congress Executive, nationalist as it was, took an international view and considered the war as something much more than a conflict of armed forces. 'The crisis that has overtaken Europe is not of Europe only but of humanity, and will not pass like other crises or wars, leaving the essential strucure of the present-day world intact. It is likely to re-fashion the world for good or ill, politically, socially, and economically. This crisis is the inevitable consequence of the social and political conflicts and contradictions which have grown alarmingly since the last Great War, and it will not be finally resolved till these conflicts and contradictions are removed and a new equilibrium established. That equilibrium can only be based on the ending of the domination and exploitation of one country by another, and on a reorganization of economic relations on a more just basis for the common good of all. India is the crux of the problem, for India has been the outstanding example of modern imperialism, and no re-fashioning of the world can succeed which ignores this vital problem. With her vast resources she must play an important part in any scheme of world reorganization; but she can only do so as a free nation whose energies have been released to work for this great end. Freedom to-day is indivisible, and every attempt to retain imperialist domination in any part of the world will lead inevitably to fresh disaster.'

The Committee proceeded to refer to the offers of Rulers of Indian states to support the cause of democracy in Europe, and suggested that it would be fitting if they introduced democracy within their own states, where undiluted autocracy prevailed.

The Committee again stated their eagerness to help in every way but expressed their apprehension at the trend of British policy both in the past and present in which they failed 'to find any attempt to advance the cause of democracy or self-determination or any evidence that the present war declarations of the British Government are being, or are going to be, acted upon.' They added, however, that in view 'of the gravity of the occasion and the fact that the pace of events during the last few days has often been swifter than the working of men's minds, the Committee desire to take no final decision at this stage, so as to allow for full elucidation of the issues at stake, the real objectives aimed at, and the position of India in the present and in the future.' They invited therefore 'the British Government to declare in unequivocal terms what their war aims are in regard to democracy and imperialism and the new order that is envisaged, in particular, how these aims are going to apply to India and to be given effect to in the present. Do they include elimination of imperialism and the treatment of India as a free nation whose policy will be guided in accordance with the wishes of her people?....The real test of any declaration is its application in the present, for it is the present that will govern action to-day and give shape to the future....It will be infinite tragedy if even this terrible war is carried on in the spirit of imperialism and for the purpose of retaining this structure which is itself the cause of war and human degradation.'

This statement, issued after anxious deliberation, was an attempt to overcome the barriers that had arisen between India and England and poisoned their relations for a century and a half, to find some way to reconcile our eagerness to join in this world struggle with popular enthusiasm behind us, and our passionate desire for freedom. The assertion of India's right to freedom was no new thing; it was not the result of the war or the international crisis. It had long been the very basis for all our thoughts and activities, round which we had revolved for many generations. There was no difficulty whatever in making a clear declaration of India's freedom and then adapting this to existing circumstances, keeping the needs of the war in view. Indeed the very necessities of the war demanded it. If England had the desire and the will to acknowledge India's freedom, every major difficulty vanished and what remained was capable of adjustment with the consent of the parties concerned. In every province provincial governments were functioning. It was easy to evolve a popular central apparatus of government for the war period, which would organize the war effort on an efficient and popular basis, co-operate fully with the armed forces, and be a link between the people and the provincial governments on the one hand, and the British Government on the other. Other constitutional problems could be postponed till after the war, though of course it was desirable to attempt to solve them even earlier. After the war the elected representatives of the people would draw up the permanent constitution and enter into a treaty with England in regard to our mutual interests.

It was no easy matter for the Congress Executive to make this offer to England when most of our people had little appreciation of the international issues involved and were expressing their resentment at recent British policy. We knew that long-standing distrust and suspicion on both sides could not vanish away by some magic word. Yet we hoped that the very stress of events would induce England's leaders to come out of their imperialist grooves, take a long view and accept our offer, thus ending the long feud between England and India, and releasing India's enthusiasm and resources for the war.

But that was not to be, and their answer was a refusal of all we had asked for. It became clear to us that they did not want us as friends and colleagues but as a slave people to do their bidding. We used the same word 'co-operation,' but a different meaning was attached to it by either party. For us co-operation was to be between comrades and equals; for them it meant their

429

commanding and our obeying without demur. It was impossible for us to accept this position without abandoning and betraying everything we had stood for and that had given some meaning to our lives. And even if some of us had been willing to do so we could not have carried our people with us; we would have been stranded, isolated, and cut off from the living currents of nationalism, as well as from the internationalism that we envisaged.

The position of our provincial governments became difficult and the choice for them was submission to continuous interference by the Governor and the Viceroy or conflict with them. The superior services were wholly on the Governor's side and looked upon the ministers and the legislature, even more than before, as intruders. Again there was the old constitutional conflict between an autocratic king or his representatives and a parliament, with this addition, that the former were foreigners basing their rule on armed force. It was decided that the Congress governments in the eight provinces out of eleven (all except Bengal, Punjab, and Sind) should resign in protest. Some were of opinion that instead of resigning they should carry on and thus invite dismissal by the Governor. It was clear that in view of the inherent conflict, which was daily becoming more obvious, clashes between them and the governors were inevitable and if they did not resign, they would be dismissed from office. They took the strictly constitutional course of resigning and thus inviting a dissolution of the legislature and fresh elections. As big majorities were behind them in the lgislatures no other ministries could be formed. The governors, however, were anxious to avoid new elections as they knew well enough that these would result in the overwhelming triumph of the Congress. They did not dissolve the legislatures but merely suspended them, and assumed all the powers of the provincial governments and legislatures. They became completely autocratic heads of provinces, making laws, issuing decrees, and doing everything else they wanted to without the slightest reference to any elected body or to public opinion.

British spokesmen have often asserted that the Congress Executive acted in an authoritarian manner in calling upon the provincial governments to resign. This is an odd charge, coming from those who have been functioning in a more autocractic and authoritarian manner than anyone outside the fascist and nazi countries. As a matter of fact the very foundation of Congress policy, on which members of the legislatures had been elected and provincial governments had been formed after assurances from the Viceroy, was freedom of action in the provincial sphere and no interference by Governor or Viceroy. This interference was now a frequent occurrence and even the statutory powers of the provincial governments, given under the Government of India Act of 1935, had been further limited. These statutory powers of the provinces were now overridden for war purposes by an amendment of the Act by the British Parliament. The discretion when and where to interfere in the provinces was left entirely to the Government of India, which meant the Viceroy, and no statutory safeguards were left to protect the powers of the provincial governments, which could carry on only on sufferance. The Viceroy and Governor-General, with the assured co-operation of his nominated executive council, could override, under cloak of war necessity, every decision of the provincial governments and legislatures. No responsible ministry could function in these circumstances; it would either come into conflict with the Governor and the services or with the legislature and its constituents. Each legislature, where there was a Congress majority, formally adopted the demand of the Congress after the war began, and the rejection of this demand by the Viceroy, inevitably meant conflict or resignation. The general feeling among the rank and file was for launching a struggle with the British power. The Congress Executive was, however, anxious to avoid this as far as possible and took the milder course. It was easy for the British Government to test the feeling of the people generally or of the voters by having general elections. They avoided this because they had no doubt that elections would result in overwhelming Congress victories.

In the major provinces of Bengal and the Punjab and in the small province of Sind, there were no resignations. In both Bengal and Punjab the Governors and the superior services had all along played a dominant role and hence no conflict could arise. Even so, in Bengal on a later occasion the Governor did not like the Prime Minister and forced him and his ministry to resign. In Sind also, at a later stage, the Prime Minister addressed a letter to the Viceroy criticising the British Government's policy and, as a protest, gave up an honour conferred on him by that Government. He did not resign. The Viceroy, however, made the Governor dismiss him from the premiership because of this letter, which was not considered in keeping with the viceregal dignity.

It is nearly five years since the Congress provincial governments resigned. During this entire period there has been one-man rule, the Governor's in each of the provinces and we have gone back, under the pretext and in the fog of war, to the full-blooded autocracy of the middle-nineteenth century. The civil service and the police are supreme and if any of their number, English or Indian, shows the slightest disinclination to carry out the ruthless policy of the British Government, the gravest displeasure is visited on him. Much of the work done by the Congress governments has been undone and their schemes have been liquidated. Fortunately, some of the tenancy legislation has remained, but even this is often interpreted against the interests of the tenants.

During the last two years, in the three minor provinces of Assam, Orissa, and the North-West Frontier, provincial governments have been reconstituted by the very simple device of imprisoning a number of members of the legislatures, and thus converting a minority into a majority. In Bengal the existing ministry depends entirely on the support of the large European bloc. The Orissa ministry did not survive for long and that province reverted to the Governor's one-man rule. In the Frontier Province a ministry continued to function, though it had no majority to back it, and hence a meeting of the Legislature was avoided. In the Punjab and Sind special executive orders were passed on Congress members of the legislatures (those out of prison) preventing them from attending the sessions of the legislative assemblies or participating in any public activities.*

Another Congress Offer and its Rejection by the British Government. Mr. Winston Churchill

The change-over to autocratic and one-man rule in eight of the provinces was not a mere substitution of the people at the top, such as a change in ministries might indicate. It was a radical and organic change affecting the whole spirit, policy, and methods of the entire state organization. The legislatures and the various popular checks on the executive and the permanent services vanished, and the approach of the civil service, from the Governor downwards, and of the police service, towards the public became different. It was not merely a reversion and setback to the days before the Congress governments had come into power. It was much worse. In so-called law it was a going back to the unchecked autocracy of the nineteenth century. In practice it was harsher, as the old confidence and paternalism were absent, and all the fear and passion of a long-established vested interest which was breaking up, pervaded the British element in the administration. The two and a quarter years of Congress governments had been hard to bear, the carrying out of the policy and orders of those who could always be sent to prison if they gave trouble had not been pleasant. Now there was a desire not only to resume the old thread but also to put these trouble-makers in their proper places. Everyone, the peasant in the field, the worker in the factory, the artisans, and the shopkeepers, the industrialists, the professional classes, the young men and women in colleges, the subordinate services, and even those Indians in the higher ranks of the services who had

*Early in 1945 the Frontier Legislative Assembly had at last to meet for the budget session. The Ministry was defeated on a vote of confidence and resigned. A Congress Ministry, with Dr. Khan Sahib as Premier, then took office.

shown any enthusiasm for the popular governments, must be made to realize that British Raj still functioned and had to be reckoned with. It was that Raj that would determine their individual future and their chances of preferment, and not some temporary intruders from outside. Those who had functioned as the secretaries of the ministers were now the bosses, acting under the Governor, and spoke again in their old superior way; the district magistrates resumed their old functions of *gauleiters* for their respective areas; the police felt freer to revert to old habits, knowing well that they would be supported and protected from above even when they misbehaved. The fog of war could be made to cover everything.

Many even of the critics of Congress governments viewed this prospect with dismay. They remembered now many of the virtues of those governments and expressed their strong displeasure at their resignation. According to them, they should have held on whatever the consequences. Curiously enough even members of the Moslem League were apprehensive.

If this was the reaction of non-Congressmen and critics of the Congress governments, the reaction of the members and sympathisers of the Congress, and the members of the legislatures can well be imagined. The ministers had resigned from their offices but not from membership of the legislature, nor had the speakers and the members of these legislatures resigned. Nevertheless they were pushed aside and ignored, and no fresh elections were held. Even from a purely constitutional point of view this was not easy to tolerate and would have produced a crisis in any country. A powerful, semi-revolutionary organization like the Congress, representing the nationalist sentiment of the country, and with a long record of struggle for freedom behind it, could not passively accept this autocratic one-man rule It could not just be a spectator of what was happening, more especially as this was directed against it. There were strong and repeated demands for positive action to counter this suppression of the legislatures and of public activity generally and the whole policy of the British Government in regard to India.

After the refusal of the British Government to state their war aims or to make any advance in India, the Congress Working Committee had declared: 'The answer to this demand (of the Congress) has been entirely unsatisfactory and an attempt has been made on behalf of the British Government to create misunderstanding and to befog the main and moral issue....The Committee can only interpret this attempt to avoid a statement of war aims and Indian freedom, by taking shelter under irrelevant issues, as a desire to maintain imperialist domination of India in alliance with the reactionary elements in the country. The Congress has looked upon the war crisis and the problems

433

it raises as essentially a moral issue, and has not sought to profit by it in any spirit of bargaining. The moral and dominant issue of war aims and India's freedom has to be settled satisfactorily before any other subsidiary question can be considered. In no event can the Congress accept the responsibility of government, even in the transitional period, without real power being given to popular representatives.'

The Committee went on to say that because of the declarations made on behalf of the British Government, the Congress had been compelled to dissociate itself from British policy and, as a first step in non-co-operation, the Congress Governments in the provinces had resigned. The general policy of non-co-operation continued, and would have to continue unless the British Government revised its policy. 'The Working Committee would, however, remind Congressmen that it is inherent in every form of Satyagraha that no effort is spared to achieve an honourable settlement with the opponent....The Working Committee will, therefore, continue to explore the means of arriving at an honourable settlement, even though the British Government has banged the door in the face of the Congress.'

In view of the excitement prevailing in the country and the possibility of young men taking to violent courses, the Committee reminded the country of the basic policy of non-violence and warned it against any breach of it. Even if there was to be any civil resistance it must be wholly peaceful. Further that 'Satyagraha means goodwill towards all, especially towards opponents.' This reference to non-violence had no connection with the war or with the defence of the country against aggression; it was meant to apply to any action that might be taken in the cause of Indian freedom against British rule.

Those were the months when the war in Europe was in a quiescent state after the crushing of Poland. It was the so-called 'phoney' period, and in India especially war seemed very far off to the average person, and probably even more so to the British authorities in India, except in so far as material had to be supplied. The Communist Party in India then, and right upto the day when Germany attacked Russia in June, 1941, was wholly against any co-operation with the British war effort. Their organization had been banned. Their influence was inconsiderable, except among some groups of young men. But because they gave aggressive expression to a prevailing sentiment, they became a kind of ginger group.

It would have been easy during this period to have general elections both in the provinces and for the Central Assembly. The war certainly did not come in the way. Such elections would have cleared the atmosphere and brought the real situation in the country to the surface. But it was that reality itself which was feared by the British authorities, for it would have put an end to the many unreal arguments that they were continually advancing about the influence of various groups. But all elections were avoided. The provinces continued under one-man rule, and the Central Assembly, elected under a very restricted franchise for a three-year period, has now been in existence for ten years. Even when the war started in 1939 it was ancient and had exceeded its allotted span by two years. Year after year its life is extended, its members grow older and more venerable, and sometimes die, and even the memory of elections fades away. Elections are not liked by the British Government. They spoil the routine of life and blur the picture of an India of warring creeds and parties. Without elections it is much easier to give importance to any individual or group that is deserving of favour.

The situation in the country as a whole, and especially in the many provinces where one-man rule now flourished, became progressively more tense. Individual Congressmen were sent to prison for their normal activities; the peasantry cried loudly for relief from the renewed oppression of petty officials and police, who sought favour from their superiors by making all manner of exactions in the name of the war. The demand for some action to meet this situation became imperative, and the Congress, at its annual session held at Ramgarh, in Bihar, in March, 1940, under the presidentship of Maulana Abul Kalam Azad, decided that civil disobedience was the only course left. Even so it avoided taking any positive step then and asked people to prepare for it.

There was a sense of deepening internal crisis and it seemed that a conflict was inevitable. The Defence of India Act, passed as a war measure, was being used extensively to suppress normal activities and arrest and imprison people, many without trial.

The sudden change in the war situation, resulting in the invasion of Denmark and Norway, and a little later in the astonishing collapse of France, produced a profound impression. People's reactions naturally varied, but there was a powerful current of sympathy for France and for England immediately after Dunkirk and during the air blitz over England. Congress, which had been on the verge of civil disobedience, could not think in terms of any such movement while the very existence of free England hung in the balance. There were some people, of course, who thought that England's difficulty and peril were India's opportunity, but the leaders of the Congress were definitely opposed to any such advantage being taken of a situation full of disastrous foreboding for England, and declared so publicly. All talk of civil disobedience was given up for the time being.

Another attempt was made on behalf of the Congress to arrive at a settlement with the British Government. If the previous attempt had been far-reaching and asked for a declaration of war-aims in addition to changes in India, the present one was brief and concise and referred to India only. It asked for a recognition of Indian freedom and the establishment of a national government at the centre, which meant the co-operation of various parties. No fresh legislation by the British Parliament was envisaged at that stage. Within the legal framework then existing, Congress proposed that a national government be formed by the Viceroy. The changes proposed, important as they were, could be brought about by agreement and convention. Statutory and constitutional changes would of course have to follow, but they could await further discussion and a more favourable opportunity, provided that India's claim to complete freedom was recognized. Under these conditions, full co-operation in the war effort was offered.

These proposals, intiated by C. Rajagopalachari, toned down the oft-repeated Congress demand; they were much less than what we had long been claiming. They could be put into effect immediately without legal difficulty. They tried to meet the claims of other important groups and parties, for the national government would inevitably be a composite government. They even took into consideration the peculiar position of the British Government in India. The Viceroy was to continue, though it was presumed that he would not veto the decisions of the national government. But his presence as the head of the administration necessarily meant intimate contacts with that government. The war apparatus remained under the commander-in-chief; the whole complicated structure of civil administration built up by the British remained. Indeed the principal effect of the change would be to introduce a new spirit in the administration, a new outlook, a vigour, and increasing popular co-operation in the war effort as well as in tackling the serious problems that were facing the country. These changes, together with the definite assurance of India's independence after the war, would produce a new psychological background in India, leading to the fullest co-operation in the war.

It was no easy matter for the Congress to put forward this proposal after all its past declarations and experiences. It was felt that a national government built up and circumscribed in this way would be ineffective and rather helpless. There was considerable opposition in Congress circles, and it was only after much difficult and anxious thinking that I brought myself round to agree to it. I agreed chiefly because of larger international considerations and my desire that, if it was at all honourably possible, we should identify ourselves completely with the struggle against fascism and nazism.

But there was a much greater difficulty before us and that was

Gandhiji's opposition. This opposition was almost entirely due to his pacifism. He had not opposed our previous offers to help in the war effort, though no doubt he must have felt uncomfortable about them. Right at the beginning of the war he had told the Viceroy that Congress could give full moral help only, but that had not been the Congress position as subsequently and repeatedly defined. Now he expressed himself definitely against Congress agreeing to undertake responsibility for a violent war effort. He felt so strongly that he broke on this issue from his colleagues as well as the Congress organization. This was a painful wrench to all those associated with him, for the Congress of to-day was his creation. Nevertheless the Congress organization could not accept his application of the principle of non-violence to the war situation, and in its eagerness to bring about a settlement with the British Government, it went to the extreme length of breaking with its cherished and well-loved leader.

The situation in the country was deteriorating in many ways. Politically this was obvious. Even economically, while some among the peasantry and the workers were somewhat better off owing to war conditions, large numbers had been hit hard. The persons who were really prospering were the war profiteers, contractors, and a horde of officials, chiefly British, employed at fancy salaries for war work. The Government's idea apparently was that the war effort would be best promoted by encouraging the motive for excessive profit. Corruption and nepotism were rampant and there were no popular checks on them. Public criticism was considered a discouragement of war effort and hence to be put down by the all-embracing provisions of the Defence of India Act. It was a discouraging spectacle.

All these factors induced us to try our utmost once again to arrive at a settlement with the British Government. What were the chances? Not very promising. The whole organization of the permanent services was enjoying a freedom from control and criticism such as they had not had for more than two generations. They could clap in prison any person they disapproved of, with or without trial. The Governors enjoyed unrestrained power and authority over vast provinces. Why should they consent to a change unless they were forced to do so by circumstances? Over the top of the imperial structure sat the Viceroy, Lord Linlithgow, surrounded by all the pomp and ceremony befitting his high position. Heavy of body and slow of mind, solid as a rock and with almost a rock's lack of awareness, possessing the qualities and failings of an old-fashioned British aristocrat, he sought with integrity and honesty of purpose to find a way out of the tangle. But his limitations were too many; his mind worked in the old groove and shrank back from any innovations; his vision was limited by the traditions of the ruling class out of which he came; he saw and heard through the eyes and ears of the civil service and others who surrounded him; he distrusted people who talked of fundamental political and social changes; he disliked those who did not show a becoming appreciation of the high mission of the British Empire and its chief representative in India.

In England there had been a change during the dark days of the German *blitzkreig* over western Europe. Mr. Neville Chamberlain had gone and that was a relief from many points of view. The Marquess of Zetland, that ornament of his noble order, had also departed from the India Office without any tears being shed. In his place had come Mr. Amery, about whom little was known, but this little was significant. He had vigorously defended in the House of Commons Japanese aggression over China, giving as an argument that if they condemned what Japan had done in China, they would have to condemn equally what Britain had done in India and Egypt. A sound argument used perversely for a wrong purpose.

But the person who really counted was Mr. Winston Churchill, the new Prime Minister. Mr. Churchill's views on Indian freedom were clear and definite and had been frequently repeated. He stood out as an uncompromising opponent of that freedom. In January, 1930, he had said: 'Sooner or later you will have to crush Gandhi and the Indian Congress and all they stand for.' In December of that year he said: 'The British nation has no intention whatever of relinquishing control of Indian life and progress....We have no intention of casting away that most truly bright and precious jewel in the crown of the King, which, more than all our dominions and dependencies, constitutes the glory and strength of the British empire.'

Later he explained what those magic words 'Dominion status,' so frequently thrown at us, really meant in relation to India. In January, 1931, he said: 'We have always contemplated it (dominion status) as the ultimate goal, but no one has supposed, except in a purely ceremonious sense in the way in which representatives of India attend conferences during the war, that the principle and policy for India would be carried into effect in any time which it is reasonable or useful for us to foresee.' And, again, in December, 1931: 'Most of the leading public men—of whom I was one in those days—made speeches—I certainly did—about dominion status, but I did not contemplate India having the same constitutional rights and system as Canada in any period which we can foresee....England, apart from her empire in India, ceases for ever to exist as a great power.'

That was the crux of the question. India was the empire; it was her possession and exploitation that gave glory and strength to England and made her a great power. Mr. Churchill could not conceive of England except as the head and possessor of a vast empire, and so he could not conceive of India being free. And dominion status, which had so long been held out to us as something within our grasp, was explained to be a mere matter of words and ceremony, very far removed from freedom and power. Dominion status, even in its fullest sense, had been rejected by us and we claimed independence. The gulf between Mr. Churchill and us was vast indeed.

We remembered his words and knew him to be a stout and uncompromising person. We could hope for little from England under his leadership. For all his courage and great qualities of leadership, he represented the nineteenth century, conservative, imperialist England, and seemed to be incapable of understanding the new world with its complex problems and forces, and much less the future which was taking shape. And yet he was a big man who could take a big step. His offer of a union with France, though made at a time of dire peril, showed vision and adaptation to circumstances and had impressed India greatly. Perhaps the new position he occupied, with its vast responsibilities, had enlarged his vision and made him outgrow his earlier prejudices and conceptions. Perhaps the very needs of the war situation, which were paramount for him, would compel him to realize that India's freedom was not only inevitable but desirable from the point of view of the war. I remembered that when I was going to China in August, 1939, he had sent me, through a mutual friend, his good wishes for my visit to that war-racked country.

So we made that offer not without hope, though not hoping too much. The response of the British Government came soon after. It was a total rejection, and, what was more, it was couched in terms which convinced us that the British had no intention whatever of parting with power in India; they were bent on encouraging division and strengthening every mediæval and reactionary element. They seemed to prefer civil war and the ruin of India to a relaxation of their imperialist control.

Used though we were to this kind of treatment, it came as a shock and a feeling of depression grew. I remember writing an article just then to which I gave the title: 'The Parting of the Ways.' I had long stood for the independence of India, convinced that in no other way could we progress and develop as a people, or have normal friendly and co-operative relations with England. Yet I had looked forward to those friendly relations. Now suddenly I felt that unless England changed completely there was no common path for us. We must follow different ways.

Individual Civil Disobedience

So instead of the intoxication of the thought of freedom which would unleash our energies and throw us with a nation's enthusiasm into the world struggle, we experienced the aching frustration of its denial. And this denial was accompanied by an arrogance of language, a self-glorification of British rule and policy, and an enumeration of conditions which were said to be necessary before India could claim freedom, conditions some of which seemed impossible of realization. It became obvious that àll this talk and ritual of parliamentary debate in England, of rounded phrases and pompous utterance, was just political trickery, barely veiling the fixed intention to hold on to India as an imperial domain and possession for as long as this was possible. The claws of imperialism would continue deep in the living body of India. And that was the measure of that international order of freedom and democracy for which Britain claimed to be fighting.

There was yet another significant indication: Burma had put forward a modest claim that an assurance of dominion status *after* the war be given her. This was long before the Pacific War started, and in any event it did not interfere with the war in any way, for it was only intended to take effect after the conclusion of hostilities. She asked for dominion status only, not independence. As in the case of India, she had been told repeatedly that dominion status was the goal of British policy. Unlike India, she was a much more homogeneous country and all the objections, real or fancied, which were advanced by the British in the case of India, did not apply to her. Yet that unanimous demand was refused and no assurance was given. Dominion status was for some distant hereafter; it was a vague and shadowy metaphysical conception which applied to some other world, some different age from ours. It was, as Mr. Winston Churchill had indicated, empty verbiage and ceremony with no relation to the present or to the immediate future. So also the objections that were raised against India's independence, the absurd conditions that were laid down, were empty verbiage which everyone knew had no reality or substance. The only realities were Britain's determination to hold on to India at all costs and India's determination to break this hold. All else was quibbling, lawyer's talk, or diplomatic prevarication. Only the future could show the result of this conflict between incompatibles.

The future showed us soon enough the results of British policy in Burma. In India also that future slowly unrolled itself, bringing struggle and bitterness and suffering in its train.

To remain passive spectators of what was happening in India after the last insolent repulse from the British Government became impossible. If this was the attitude of that Government in the middle of a perilous war, when millions of people all over the world believed and faced enormous sacrifices in the cause of freedom, what would it be when the crisis was over and that popular pressure had subsided? Meanwhile, our people were being picked off all over India and sent to prison; our normal activities were interfered with and restricted. For it must be remembered that the British Government in India is always carrying on a war against the nationalist and labour movements; it does not wait for civil disobedience to take action. That war flares up occasionally and becomes an attack on all fronts, or it tones down a little, but always it has continued.* During the brief period of Congress governments in the provinces, it was in a quiescent stage, but soon after their resignation it started afresh, and the permanent services took peculiar pleasure in issuing orders to and imprisoning prominent Congressmen and members of the legislatures.

Positive action became inevitable, for sometimes the only failure is in failing to act. That action could only be, in accordance with our established policy, in the nature of civil disobedience. Yet care was taken not to have any popular upheavals, and civil disobedience was limited to chosen individuals. It was what is called individual civil disobedience as contrasted with the mass variety of it. It was really in the nature of a great moral protest. From a politician's point of view it seems odd that we should deliberately avoid any attempt to upset the administration and make it easy for it to put the trouble-makers in prison. That has not been the way of aggressive political action or revolution anywhere else. Yet that was Gandhi's way of combining morality with revolutionary politics, and he was always the inevitable leader when any such movement took place. It was his way of showing that while we refused to submit to British policy and showed our resentment and determination by voluntarily inviting suffering for ourselves, yet our object was not to create trouble.

This individual civil disobedience movement started in a very small way, each person having to pass some kind of a test and get permission before he or she could take part in it. Those who were chosen broke some formal order, were arrested, and sentenced to imprisonment. As is usual with us, men at the top were chosen first—members of the Congress Executive, ex-ministers of provincial governments, members of the legislatures, members of the All-India and Provincial Congress committees. Gradually the circle grew till between twenty-five to thirty thousand men and women were in prison. These included the speakers and a large number of members of our provincial legislative assemblies, which had been

*Many people have been in prison continuously from the pre-war period. Some young comrades of mine have now spent fifteen years in prison and are still there. They were boys when they were sentenced, barely out of their teens; now they are grey-haired and middle-aged. I have come across them during my repeated visits to the United Provinces prisons. I have come, stayed for a while, and then gone out; they have remained. Although they are United Provinces men and have been kept for some years in United Provinces prisons, they were sentenced in the Punjab and are therefore under the orders of the Punjab government. The Congress government in the Unitid Provinces recommended their release but the Punjab government did not agree.

suspended by the Government. Thus we demonstrated that if our elected assemblies were not allowed to function their members would not submit to autocratic rule and preferred prison to it.

Apart from those who offered formal civil disobedience, many thousands were arrested and sentenced for making speeches or for some other activity, or detained without trial. I was arrested at an early stage and sentenced to four years' imprisonment for a speech.

From October, 1940, for over a year, all these persons remained in prison. We tried to follow, with such material as we could obtain, the course of the war and of events in India and the world. We read of the Four Freedoms of President Roosevelt, we heard of the Atlantic Charter, and, soon after, of Mr. Churchill's qualification that this Charter had no application to India.

In June, 1941, we were stirred by Hitler's sudden attack on Soviet Russia, and followed with anxious interest the dramatic changes in the war situation.

On December 4th, 1941, many of us were discharged. Three days later came Pearl Harbour and the Pacific War.

After Pearl Harbour. Gandhi and Non-Violence

When we came out of prison the nationalist position, the question of India versus England, had in no way changed. Prison affects people in various ways; some break down or weaken, others grow harder and more confirmed in their convictions, and it is usually the latter whose influence is felt more by the mass of the people. But though nationally we remained where we were, Pearl Harbour and what followed it suddenly created a new tension and gave a new perspective. The Congress Working Committee met immediately after in this new atmosphere of tension. The Japanese had made no great advance till then, but major and stunning disasters had already taken place. The war ceased to be a distant spectacle and began to approach India and affect her intimately. Among Congressmen the desire to play an effective part in these perilous developments became strong, and the jail-going business seemed pointless in this new situation; but what could we do unless some door was open for honourable co-operation, and the people could be made to feel some positive inspiration for action? A negative fear of threatening danger was not enough.

In spite of past history and all that had happened, we were eager to offer our co-operation in the war and especially for the defence of India, subject necessarily to a national government which would enable us to function in co-operation with other elements in the country, and to make the people feel that it was really a national effort and not one imposed by outsiders who had enslaved us. There was no difference of opinion on this general approach among Congressmen and most others, but a vital difference of principle arose rather unexpectedly. Gandhiji found himself unable to give up his fundamental principle of non-violence even in regard to external war. The very nearness of that war became a challenge to him and a test of faith. If he failed at this critical moment, either non-violence was not the all-embracing and basic principle and course of action he had believed it to be, or else he was wrong in discarding it or compromising with it. He could not give up the faith of a lifetime on which he had based all his activities, and he felt that he must accept the necessary consequences and implications of that non-violence.

A similar difficulty and conflict had arisen for the first time about the time of the Munich crisis in 1938, when war seemed to be impending. I was in Europe then and was not present at the discussions that took place. But the difficulty passed with the passing of the crisis and the postponement of war. When war actually started in September, 1939, no such question arose or was discussed by us. It was only in the late summer of 1940 that Gandhiji again made it clear to us that he could not make himself a party to violent warfare and he would like the Congress to adopt the same attitude in regard to it. He was agreeable to giving moral and every other kind of help, short of actual assistance in armed and violent warfare. He wanted Congress to declare its adherence to the principle of non-violence even for a free India. He knew, of course, that there were many elements in the country, and even within the Congress, which did not have that faith in non-violence; he realized that a government of free India was likely to discard non-violence when questions of defence were concerned and to build up military, naval, and air power. But he wanted, if possible, for Congress at least to hold the banner of non-violence aloft and thus to train the minds of the people and make them think increasingly in terms of peaceful action. He had a horror of seeing India militarized. He dreamt of India becoming a symbol and example of non-violence, and by her example weaning the rest of the world from war and the ways of violence. Even if India as a whole had not accepted this idea, Congress should not discard it when the time for trial came.

The Congress had long ago accepted the principle and practice of non-violence in its application to our struggle for freedom and in building up unity in the nation. At no time had it gone beyond that position or applied the principle to defence from external aggression or internal disorder. Indeed it had taken an eager interest in the development of the Indian army and frequently demanded the indianization of its officer personnel. The Congress party in the Central Legislature had often moved or participated in resolutions on this subject. As the leader of that party in the 'twenties, my father had accepted membership of the Skeen Committee which had been formed for the indianization and reorganization of the

443

Indian army. He resigned subsequently from it, but that was for political reasons and had nothing to do with non-violence. In 1937-38 the Congress party had put forward in the Central Assembly, after consulting all the provincial governments, proposals for the expansion of the Indian army, its mechanization, the development of the absurdly small and almost non-existent naval and air arms, and the progressive replacement of the British army in India by the Indian army. As the cost of British troops in India was about four times that of the Indian troops, the latter could be mechanized and expanded without much additional cost, if they took the place of British troops. Again during the Munich period the importance of developing the air arm was emphasized, but Government said that expert opinion was not agreed about this. In 1940 the Congress Party especially attended the Central Assembly and repeated all this and pointed out how incompetent the Government and its military department were in making arrangements for India's defence.

At no time, so far as I am aware, was the question of non-violence considered in relation to the army, navy, or air forces, or the police. It was taken for granted that its application was confined to our struggle for freedom. It is true that it had a powerful effect on our thinking in many ways, and it made the Congress strongly favour world disarmament and a peaceful solution of all international, as well as national, disputes.

When the Congress governments were functioning in the provinces, many of them were eager to encourage some form of military training in the universities and colleges. It was the Government of India that disapproved of this and came in the way.

Gandhiji, no doubt, disapproved of these tendencies, but he did not interfere. He did not even like the use of the police as an armed force for the suppression of riots, and he expressed his distress at it. But he put up with it as a lesser evil, and hoped that his teaching would gradually sink into the mind of India. It was his disapproval of such tendencies within the Congress that led him to sever his formal membership connection with the Congress in the early 'thirties, though even so he continued as the undoubted leader and adviser of the Congress. It was an anomalous and unsatisfactory position for all of us, but perhaps it made him feel that thus he was not personally responsible for all the varied decisions which Congress took from time to time, which did not wholly conform to his principles and convictions. Always there has been that inner conflict within him and in our national politics, between Gandhi as a national leader and Gandhi as a man with a prophetic message, which was not confined to India but was for humanity and the world. It is never easy to reconcile a strict adherence to truth as one sees it, with the exigencies and expediencies of life, and especially of political life. Normally people do not even worry themselves over this problem. They keep truth apart in some corner of their minds, if they keep it at all anywhere, and accept expediency as the measure of action. In politics that has been the universal rule, not only because, unfortunately, politicians are a peculiar species of opportunists, but because they cannot act purely on the personal plane. They have to make others act, and so they have to consider the limitations of others and their understanding of, and receptivity to, truth. And because of this they have to make compromises with that truth and adapt it to the prevailing circumstances. That adaptation becomes inevitable, and yet there are always risks attending it; the tendency to ignore and abandon truth grows, and expediency becomes the sole criterion of action.

Gandhi, for all his rock-like adherence to certain principles, has shown a great capacity to adapt himself to others and to changing circumstances, to take into consideration the strength and weakness of those others, especially of the mass of the people, and how far they were capable of acting up to the truth as he saw it. But from time to time he pulls himself up, as if he were afraid that he had gone too far in his compromising, and returns to his moorings. In the midst of action, he seems to be in tune with the mass mind, responsive to its capacity and therefore adapting himself to it to some extent; at other times he becomes more theoretical and apparently less adaptable. There is also the same difference observable in his action and his writings. This is confusing to his own people, and more so to others who are ignorant of the background in India.

How far a single individual can influence a people's thought and ideology, it is difficult to say. Some people in history have exerted a powerful influence, and yet, it may be that they have emphasized and brought out something that already existed in the mind of the people, or have given clear and pointed expression to the vaguely felt ideas of the age. Gandhi's influence on India's mind has been profound in the present age; how long and in what form it will endure only the future can show. His influence is not limited to those who agree with him or accept him as a national leader; it extends to those also who disagree with him and criticize him. Very few persons in India accept in its entirety his doctrine of non-violence or his economic theories, yet very many have been influenced by them in some way or other. Usually speaking in terms of religion, he has emphasized the moral approach to political problems as well as those of everyday life. The religious background has affected those chiefly who were inclined that way, but the moral approach has influenced others also. Many have been appreciably raised to higher levels of moral and ethical action, many more have been forced to think at least in those terms, and that thought itself has some effect on action and behaviour. Politics cease to be just expediency and opportunism, as they usually have been everywhere, and there is a continuous moral tussle preceding thought and action. Expediency, or what appears to be immediately possible and desirable, can never be ignored, but it is toned down by other considerations and a longer view of more distant consequences.

Gandhi's influence in these various directions has pervaded India and left its mark. But it is not because of his non-violence or economic theories that he has become the foremost and most outstanding of India's leaders. To the vast majority of India's people he is the symbol of India determined to be free, of militant nationalism, of a refusal to submit to arrogant might, of never agreeing to anything involving national dishonour. Though many people in India may disagree with him on a hundred matters, though they may criticize him or even part company from him on some particular issue, at a time of action and struggle when India's freedom is at stake they flock to him again and look up to him as their inevitable leader.

When Gandhiji raised in 1940 the question of non-violence in relation to the war and the future of free India, the Congress Working Committee had to face the issue squarely. They made it clear to him that they were unable to go as far as he wanted them to go and could not possibly commit India or the Congress to future applications of this principle in the external domain. This led to a definite and public break with him on this issue. Two months later further discussions led to an agreed formula which was later adopted as part of a resolution by the All-India Congress Committee. That formula did not wholly represent Gandhiji's attitude; it represented what he agreed, perhaps unwillingly, that Congress should say on this subject. At that time the British Government had already rejected the latest offer made by the Congress for co-operation in the war on the basis of a national government. Some kind of conflict was approaching and, as was inevitable, both Gandhiji and Congress looked towards each other and were impelled by a desire to find a way out of the deadlock between them. The formula did not refer to the war, as just previously our offer of co-operation had been unceremoniously and utterly rejected. It dealt theoretically with the Congress policy in regard to non-violence, and for the first time stated how, in the opinion of the Congress, the free India of the future should apply it in its external relations. That part of the resolution ran thus:

The All-India Congress Committee 'firmly believes in the policy and practice of non-violence, not only in the struggle for Swaraj, but also, in so far as this may be possible of application, in free India. The Committee is convinced, and recent world events have demonstrated, that complete world disarmament is necessary an ' the establishment of a new and juster political and economic order, if the world is not to destroy itself and revert to barbarism. A free

446

India will, therefore, throw all her weight in favour of world disarmament and should herself be prepared to give a lead in this to the world. Such lead will inevitably depend on external factors and internal conditions, but the state would do its utmost to give effect to this policy of disarmament. Effective disarmament and the establishment of world peace by the ending of national wars depend ultimately on the removal of the causes of wars and national conflicts. These causes must be rooted out by the ending of the domination of one country over another and the exploitation of one people or group by another. To that end India will peacefully labour and it is with this objective in view that the people of India desire to attain the status of a free and independent nation. Such freedom will be the prelude to the close association with other countries within a comity of free nations for the peace and progress of the world.' This declaration, it will be noticed, while strongly affirming the Congress wish for peaceful action and disarmament, also emphasized a number of qualifications and limitations.

The internal crisis within the Congress was resolved in 1940 and then came a year of prison for large numbers of us. In December, 1941, however, the same crisis took shape again when Gandhiji insisted on complete non-violence. Again there was a split and public disagreement, and the president of the Congress, Maulana Abul Kalam Azad, and others were unable to accept Gandhiji's viewpoint. It became clear that the Congress as a whole, including some of the faithful followers of Gandhiji, disagreed with him in this matter. The force of circumstances and the rapid succession of dramatic events influenced all of us, including Gandhiji, and he refrained from pressing his viewpoint on the Congress, though he did not identify himself with the Congress view.

At no other time was this issue raised by Gandhiji in the Congress. When later Sir Stafford Cripps came with his proposals, there was no question of non-violence. His proposals were considered purely from the political point of view. In late months, leading up to August, 1942, Gandhiji's nationalism and intense desire for freedom made him even agree to Congress participation in the war if India could function as a free country. For him this was a remarkable and astonishing change, involving suffering of the mind and pain of the spirit. In the conflict between that principle of non-violence, which had become his very life-blood and meaning of existence, and India's freedom, which was a dominating and consuming passion for him, the scales inclined towards the latter. That did not mean, of course, that he weakened in his faith in non-violence. But it did mean that he was prepared to agree to the Congress not applying it in this war. The practical statesman took precedence over the uncompromising prophet.

As I have watched and thought over this frequent struggle in Gandhi's mind, which has led often to so many seeming contradictions—and which affected me and my activities so intimately—I have remembered a passage in one of Liddell Hart's books: 'The idea of the indirect approach is closely related to all problems of the influence of mind over mind—the most influencial factor in human history. Yet it is hard to reconcile with another lesson: that true conclusions can only be reached, or approached, by pursuing the truth without regard to where it may lead or what its effect may be—on different interests.

'History bears witness to the vital part that the "prophets" have played in human progress—which is evidence of the ultimate practical value of expressing unreservedly the truth as one sees it. Yet it also becomes clear that the acceptances and spreading of that vision has always depended on another class of men— "leaders" who had to be philosophical strategists, striking a compromise between truth and men's receptivity to it. Their effect has often depended on their own limitations in perceiving the truth as on their practical wisdom in proclaiming it.

'The prophets must be stoned; that is their lot, and the test of their self-fulfilment. But a leader who is stoned may merely prove that he has failed in his function through a deficiency of wisdom, or through confusing his function with that of a prophet. Time alone can tell whether the effect of such a sacrifice redeems the apparent failure as a leader that does honour to him as a man. At the least he avoids the more common fault of leaders—that of sacrificing the truth to expediency without ultimate advantage to the cause. For whoever habitually suppresses the truth in the interests of tact will produce a deformity from the womb of his thought.

'Is there a practical way of combining progress towards the attainment of truth with progress towards its acceptance? A possible solution of the problem is suggested by reflection on strategic principles—which point to the importance of maintaining an object consistently and, also, of pursuing it in a way adapted to circumstances. Opposition to the truth is inevitable, especially if it takes the form of a new idea, but the degree of resistance can be diminished—by giving thought not only to the aim but to the method of approach. Avoid a frontal attack on a long established position; instead seek to turn it by a flank movement, so that a more penetrable side is exposed to the thrust of truth. But, in any such indirect approach, take care not to diverge from the truth— for nothing is more fatal to its real advancement than to lapse into untruth.

'Looking back on the stages by which various fresh ideas gained acceptance, it can be seen that the process was eased when they could be presented, not as something radically new, but as the revival in modern terms of a time-honoured principle or practice that had been forgotten. This required not deception but care to trace the connection—since "there is nothing new under the sun." '*

Tension

In India tension grew in those early months of 1942. The theatre of war came ever nearer and there was now the probability of air raids over Indian cities. What was going to happen in those eastern countries where war was raging? What new development would take place in the relations between India and England? Were we going to carry on in the old way, glaring at each other, tied up and separated by the bitter memories of past history, victims of a tragic fate which none could avert? Or would common perils help us to bridge that chasm? Even the bazaars woke up from their normal lethargy, a wave of excitement passed over them and they buzzed with all manner of rumours. The monied classes were afraid of the future that was advancing so swiftly towards them, for that future, whatever else it might be, was likely to upset the social structure they were accustomed to and endanger their interests and special position. The peasant and the worker had no such fear for he had little to lose, and he looked forward to any change from his present unhappy condition.

In India there had all along been much sympathy for China and, as a consequence, a certain antipathy to Japan. The Pacific War, it was thought at first, would bring relief to China. For four and a half years China had fought single-handed against Japan; now she had powerful allies, and surely this must lighten her burden and lessen her danger. But those allies suffered blow after blow, and before the advancing Japanese armies the British colonial empire cracked up with amazing rapidity. Was this proud structure then just a house of cards with no foundations or inner strength? Inevitably, comparisons were made with China's long resistance to Japanese aggression in spite of her lack of almost everything required for modern war. China went up in people's estimation, and though Japan was not liked, there was a feeling of satisfaction at the collapse of old-established European colonial powers before the armed strength of an Asiatic power. That racial, Oriental-Asiatic, feeling was evident on the British side also. Defeat and disaster were bitter enough but the fact that an Oriental and Asiatic power had triumphed over them added to the bitterness and humiliation. An Englishman occupying a high position said that he would have preferred it if the *Prince of Wales* and the *Repulse* had been sunk by the Germans instead of by the yellow Japanese.

The visit of the Chinese leaders, Generalissimo and Madame Chiang Kai-shek, was a great event in India. Official conventions and the wishes of the Government of India prevented them from

Liddell Hart: 'The Strategy of Indirect Approach' (1941), Preface.

mixing with the people, but their presence in India itself at that critical stage and their manifest sympathy for India's freedom helped to bring India out of her national shell and increased her awareness of the international issues at stake. The bonds that tied India and China grew stronger, and so did the desire to line up with China and other nations against the common adversary. The peril to India helped to bring nationalism and internationalism close together, the only separating factor being the policy of the British Government.

The Government of India were no doubt very conscious of the approaching perils; there must have been anxiety in their minds and a sense of urgency. But such was the conventional existence of the British in India, so set were they in their established grooves, so wedded to the never-ending processes of bureaucratic red-tape, that no marked change was visible in their outlook or activities. There was no sense of hurry and speed, of tension and getting things done. The system they represented had been built up for another age and with other objectives. Whether it was their army or their civil services, the objective in view was the occupation of India and of suppression of any attempts of the Indian people to free themselves. It was sufficient enough for that purpose, but modern war against a powerful and ruthless adversary was a very different matter, and they found it exceedingly difficult to adapt themselves to it. They were not only mentally unfitted for this, but a great part of their energies was absorbed in keeping down nationalism in India. The collapse of the Burmese and Malayan administrations before new problems had been significant and revealing, yet it taught no lesson. Burma had been governed by the same kind of civil service as India; indeed till a few years ago, it had been part of the Indian administration. The ways of government there were identical with those of India, and Burma had demonstrated how moribund this system was. But the system continued without change and the Viceroy and his high officials functioned in the same way as before. They added to their number many of the higher officials who had failed so conspicuously in Burma; there was another Excellency sitting on the hill-top at Simla. Like the *émigré* governments in London, we were given the privilege of having in our midst *émigré* officials from British colonies. They fitted like a glove into the British structure in India.

Like shadows on a stage these high officials continued to function in their old way, trying to impress us with their elaborate imperial ritual, their court ceremonies, their durbars and investitures, their parades, their dinners and evening dresses, their pompous utterances. The Viceroy's house in New Delhi was the chief temple where the high priest officiated, but there were many other temples and priests. All this ceremonial and display of imperial pomp was designed to impress, and it had impressed our people in the old days, for Indians are also given to ceremonial observances. But new standards had arisen, different values had been created, and now this elaborate show was the subject of jest and ridicule. Indians are supposed to be a slow-moving people, disinclined to rush and hurry, but even they had developed a certain speed and vigour in their work, so strong was their desire to get things done. The Congress provincial governments, whatever their failings might have been, were anxious to achieve results and worked hard and continuously, disregarding many old-established routines. It was irritating to see the passivity and slowness of the Government of India and its many agents in the face of grave crisis and peril.

And then came the Americans. They were very much in a hurry, eager to get things done, ignorant of the ways and ceremonial of the Government of India and not particularly anxious to learn them. Intolerant of delay, they pushed aside obstructions and red-tape methods and upset the even tenor of life in New Delhi. They were not even careful of the dress they should wear on particular occasions, and sometimes offended against the rigid rules of protocol and official procedure. While the help they were bringing was very welcome, they were not liked in the highest official circles, and relations were strained. Indians liked them on the whole; their energy and enthusiasm for the work in hand were infectious, and contrasted with the lack of these qualities in British official circles in India. Their forthrightness and freedom from official constraints were appreciated. There was much silent amusement at the underlying friction between the newcomers and the official class, and many true or imagined stories of this were repeated.

The approach of the war to India disturbed Gandhi greatly. It was not easy to fit in his policy and programme of non-violence with this new development. Obviously civil disobedience was out of the question in the face of an invading army or between two opposing armies. Passivity or acceptance of invasion were equally out of the question. What then? His own colleagues, and the Congress generally, had rejected non-violence for such an occasion or as an alternative to armed resistance to invasion, and he had at last agreed that they had a right to do so; but he was nonetheless troubled and for his own part, as an individual, he could not join any violent course of action. But he was much more than an individual; whether he had any official status or not in the nationalist movement, he occupied an outstanding and dominating position and his word carried weight with large numbers of people.

Gandhiji knew India, and especially the Indian masses, as very few, if any, have known them in the past or the present. Not only had he widely travelled all over India and come into touch with millions of people, but there was something else which enabled him to come into emotional contact with those masses. He could merge himself with the masses and feel with them, and because they were conscious of this they gave him their devotion and loyalty. And yet his view of India was to some extent coloured by the outlook he had imbibed in his early days in Gujrat. The Gujratis were essentially a community of peaceful traders and merchants, influenced by the Jain doctrine of non-violence. Other parts of India had been influenced much less by this, and some not at all. The widespread Kshatriya class of warriors certainly did not allow it to interfere with war or hunting wild animals. Other classes also, including the Brahmins, had been as a whole little influenced by it. But Gandhiji took an eclectic view of the development of Indian thought and history, and believed that non-violence had been the basic principle underlying it, even though there had been many deviations from it. That view appeared to be far-fetched and many Indian thinkers and historians did not agree with it. This had nothing to do with the merits of non-violence in the present stage of human existence, but it did indicate a historical bias in Gandhiji's mind.

The accidents of geography have had a powerful effect on determining national character and history. The fact that India was cut off by the tremendous barrier of the Himalayas and by the sea produced a sense of unity in this wide area and at the same time bred exclusiveness. Over this vast territory a vivid and homogenous civilization grew up which had plenty of scope for expansion and development, and which continued to preserve a strong cultural unity. Yet within that unity geography again produced diversity. The huge northern and central plain differed from the hilly and variegated areas of the Deccan, and the people living in different geographical areas developed different characteristics. History also took a different course in the north and in the south, though often the two overlapped and joined hands. The flatness of the land, and the vast open spaces of the north, as in Russia, required powerful central governments for protection against external enemies. Empires flourished in the south as well as the north, but the north was really the centre of empire and often dominated the south. A strong central government in the old days inevitably meant autocracy. It was not a mere accident of history that the Mughal Empire was broken up, among other causes, by the Marathas. The Marathas came from the hilly tracts of the Deccan, and had preserved some spirit of independence when the great majority of the dwellers on the northern plains had grown servile and submissive. The British had an easy victory in Bengal, and the people of the fertile plains there submitted with extraordinary docility. Having established themselves there they spread elsewhere.

Geography counts still and must count in the future, but other factors play a more important role now. Mountains and seas are no longer barriers, but they still determine a people's character and a country's political and economic position. They cannot be ignored in considering new schemes of division, partition or re-merging, unless the planning is on a world scale.

Gandhiji's knowledge of India and the Indian people is profound. Though not greatly interested in history as such, and perhaps not possessing that feeling for history, that historical sense, which some people have, he is fully conscious and intimately aware of the historical roots of the Indian people. He is well informed about current events and follows them carefully, though inevitably he concentrates on present-day Indian problems. He has a capacity for picking out the essence of a problem or a situation, avoiding non-essentials. Judging everything by what he considers the moral aspect, he gets a certain grip and a longer perspective. Bernard Shaw has said that though he (Gandhi) may commit any number of tactical errors, his essential strategy continues to be right. Most people, however, are not much concerned with the long run; they are far more interested in the tactical advantage of the moment.

Sir Stafford Cripps comes to India

With the fall of Penang and Singapore, and as the Japanese advanced in Malaya, there was an exodus of Indians and others and they poured into India. They had to leave very suddenly, carrying nothing with them except the clothes they were in. Then followed the flood of refugees from Burma, hundreds of thousands of them, mostly Indians. The story of how they had been deserted by civil and other authorities and left to shift for themselves spread thoughout India. They trekked hundreds of miles across mountains and through dense forests, surrounded by enemies, many dying on the way, killed by dagger or disease or starvation. That was a horrible result of the war and had to be accepted. But it was not the war that caused discrimination in treatment between Indian and British refugees. The latter were cared for as far as possible and arrangements made for their transport and assistance. From one place in Burma, where vast numbers of refugees were gathering, there were two roads leading to India. The better one was reserved for Britishers or Europeans; it came to be known as the White Road.

Horrible stories of racial discrimination and suffering reached us, and as the famished survivors spread out all over India they carried these stories with them, creating a powerful effect on the Indian mind.

Just then Sir Stafford Cripps came to India with the proposals of the British War Cabinet. Those proposals have been discussed fully during the past two and a half years and they are past history already. It is a little difficult for one who took part in the negotiations that followed to deal with them in any detail without saying much that had better to be left unsaid till some future time. As a matter of fact all the relevant issues and considerations that arose have already been made public.

I remember that when I read those proposals for the first time I was profoundly depressed, and that depression was largely due to the fact that I had expected something more substantial from Sir Stafford Cripps as well as from the critical situation that had arisen. The more I read those proposals and considered their many implications, the greater was my feeling of depression. I could understand a person unacquainted with Indian affairs imagining that they went far to meet our demands. But, when analysed, there were so many limitations, and the very acceptance of the principle of self-determination was fettered and circumscribed in such a way as to imperil our future.

The proposals dealt essentially with the future, after the cessation of hostilities, though there was a final clause which vaguely invited co-operation in the present. That future, while asserting the principle of self-determination, gave the right to provinces not to join the Indian union, and to form separate independent states. Further, the same right of non-accession to the Indian union was given to the Indian states, and it should be remembered that there are nearly 600 such states in India, some major ones and the great majority tiny enclaves. These states, as well as the provinces, would all join in the constitution making, would influence that constitution, and then could walk out of it. The whole background would be of separatism and the real problems of the country, economic or political, would take secondary place. Reactionary elements, differing from each other in many ways, would unite to frustrate the evolution of a strong, progressive, unified national state. Under the constant threat of withdrawal, many undesirable provisions might be introduced into the constitution, the central government might be weakened and emasculated, and yet the withdrawal might still follow, and it would be difficult then to refashion the constitution and make it more workable for the remaining provinces and states. The elections in the provinces for the constitution-making body would take place under the existing system of separate religious electorates; that was unfortunate, as it would bring with it the old spirit of cleavage, and yet, in the circumstances, it was inevitable. But in the states there was no provision for elections and their ninety million inhabitants were completely ignored. The semi-feudal rulers of the states could nominate their own representatives in proportion to the population. These nominees might contain some able ministers but, as a whole, they would inevitably represent, not the people of the states, but the feudal and autocratic ruler. They would form nearly one quarter of the members of the constitution-making body, and would powerfully influence its decisions by their numbers, their socially backward attitude, and their threats of subsequent withdrawal. The constituent assembly or constitution-making body would be a curious mixture of elected and non-elected elements, the former chosen by separate religious electorates as well as by certain vested interests, the latter nominated by the rulers of the states. To this had to be added the fact that there would be no pressure to accept joint decision, and the sense of reality which comes from evolving integrates and final decisions would be lacking. The tendency for many of its members would be to act in a wholly irresponsible manner, for they would feel that they could always withdraw and refuse to accept the responsibility for carrying out those decisions.

Any proposal to cut up India into parts was a painful one to contemplate; it went against all those deeply-felt sentiments and convictions that move people so powerfully. The whole nationalist movement of India had been based on India's unity, but the sentiment was older and deeper than the present phase of nationalism; it went far back into the remote periods of Indian history. That belief and sentiment had been strengthened by modern developments till it had become an article of faith for vast numbers of people, something that could not be challenged or controverted. A challenge had come from the Moslem League but few took it seriously, and there were certainly large numbers of Moslems who did not agree with it. Even the basis of that challenge was not really territorial, though it suggested a vague undefined partition of territory. The basis was a mediæval conception of nations based on religious differences, and according to it, therefore, in every village in India there were two or more nations. Even a partition of India could not get over these widespread and overlapping religious divisions. A partition would in fact add to the difficulty and increase the very problems it was intended to solve.

Apart from sentiment, there were solid reasons against partition. The social and economic problems of India had reached a crisis, chiefly because of the policy of the British Government, which necessitated rapid and all-round progress if the gravest of disasters had to be averted. That progress could only take place with real and effective planning for the whole of India, for the various parts supplied each other's deficiencies. As a whole, India was to a large extent a powerful and self-sufficient unit, but each part by itself would be weak and dependent on others. If all these, and other, arguments were valid and sufficient in the past, they became doubly important through modern political and economic developments. Small states were disappearing everywhere as independent entities; they were becoming absorbed in, or economic appendages to, the larger states. There was an inevitable tendency for vast federations, or collections of many states functioning together, to grow up. The idea of the national state itself was giving place to the multi-national state, and in the distant future there appeared a vision of a world federation. To think of partitioning India at this stage went against the whole current of modern historical and economic development. It seemed to be fantastic in the extreme.

And yet under stress of dire necessity or some compelling disaster one has to agree to many undesirable things. Circumstances may force a partition of what logically and normally must not be divided. But the proposals put forward on behalf of the British Government did not deal with any definite and particular partition of India. They opened out a vista of an indefinite number of partitions both of provinces and states. They incited all the reactionary, feudal, and socially backward groups to claim partition. Probably none of them seriously wanted it because they could not stand by themselves. But they could give a lot of trouble and obstruct and delay the formation of a free Indian state. If they were backed by British policy, as they well might be, it meant no freedom at all for a long time. Our experience of that policy had been bitter and at every stage we had found that it encouraged fissiparous tendencies. What was the guarantee that it would not continue to do so, and then claim that it could not fulfil its promise because the conditions for it were lacking? Indeed the probability was that this policy would continue.

Thus this proposal was not a mere acceptance of Pakistan or a particular partition, bad as that would have been, but something much worse, opening the door to the possibility of an indefinite number of partitions. It was a continuing menace to the freedom of India and a barrier to the fulfilment of the very promise that had been made.

The decision about the future of the Indian states was not going to be made by the people of those states or their chosen representatives, but by their autocratic rulers. Our acceptance of this principle would have been a negation of our well-established and often repeated policy and a betrayal of the people of the states, who would have been condemned to autocratic rule for a much longer period. We were prepared to treat the princes as gently as possible so as to gain their co-operation in the change-over to democracy, and if there had been no third party, like the British power, we would no doubt have succeeded. But with the British Government supporting autocracy in the states, the princes were likely to keep out of the Indian Union and rely on British military support for protection against their own people. Indeed, we were told, that if such circumstances arose, foreign armed forces would be kept in the states. As these states were often likely to be isolated islands in the territory of the proposed Indian Union, the question arose how foreign forces could reach them or com-

municate with the forces in some other similar state. That necessitated a right of way for foreign forces over the territory of the
Indian Union.

Gandhiji had repeatedly declared that he was no enemy of the
princes. Indeed his attitude has been consistently a friendly one
towards them, though he had often criticized their methods of
government and their denial of even elementary rights to their
people. For many years he had prevented the Congress from interfering directly with the affairs of the states, believing as he did
that the people of the states should themselves take the initiative
and thus develop self-confidence and strength. Many of us had
disapproved of this attitude of his. Yet behind it lay one basic
conviction, as he put it himself: 'One fundamental element in
my attitude is that I shall never be a party to the sale of the
rights of the people of the states (even) for the sake of the freedom
of the people of British India.' Professor Berriedale Keith, the
eminent authority on the British Commonwealth and Indian
constitutions, supported Gandhiji's claim (which was the Congress claim) in regard to the states. Keith wrote: 'It is impossible
for the Crown's advisers to contend that the people of the states
shall be denied the rights of Indians in the provinces, and it is their
clear duty to advise the King-Emperor to use his authority to
secure that the princes shall enter into constitutional reforms
which will result at no distant date in securing responsible government therein. No federation can be deemed in the interest of India,
if in it representatives of the provinces are compelled to sit with
the nominees of irresponsible rulers. There is, in fact, no answer
to Mr. Gandhi's claim that the princes are bound to follow the
Crown in its transfer of authority to the people.' Professor Keith
had given this opinion in regard to the earlier proposal of the
British Government relating to federation, but it was even more
applicable to the proposals brought by Sir Stafford Cripps.

The more one thought of these proposals the more fantastic
they grew. India became a chequer-board containing scores of
nominally independent or semi-independent states, many of them
relying on Britain for military protection of autocratic rule. There
was to be neither political nor economic unity and Britain might
well continue to exercise dominating power, both politically and
economically, through the many petty states she controlled.*

What the British War Cabinet had in mind for the future I do
not know. I think Sir Stafford Cripps meant well for India and
hoped to see her free and united. But this was not a matter of

---

*The entire dependence of the Indian States on British power and protection is stressed by
Sir Geoffrey de Montmorency in his 'The Indian States and Indian Federation' (1942):
The states 'are still so numerous in India that they offer a grave conundrum in evolution to
which no solution is at present forthcoming. . . . Their disappearance and absorption would, of
course, be inevitable if Britain ever ceased to be the supreme power as regards India.'

individual views or opinions or personal goodwill. We had to consider a state document, carefully drafted in spite of its deliberate vagueness, and we were told that we had to accept it or reject it as a whole. And behind it lay the continuous, century-old policy of the British Government, creating division in India and encouraging every factor that came in the way of national growth and freedom. Every forward step that had been taken in the past had always been hedged in by qualifications and limitations, which seemed innocuous enough at the beginning, and yet which proved to be formidable checks and brakes.

It was possible, and even probable, that the dire consequences that seemed to flow from the proposals need not all take shape. Wisdom and patriotism, and a larger view of what was good for India and the world, would no doubt influence many people, including rulers and ministers of Indian states. Left to ourselves, we would have faced each other with confidence, considered all the complexities of the problem and the difficulties that faced each group, and after full deliberation hammered out an integrated solution. But we were not going to be left to ourselves in spite of the suggestion that we were going to exercise self-determination. The British Government was always there, occupying strategic points, in a position to hinder and interfere in many ways. It controlled not only the whole apparatus of government, services, etc., but, in the states, its residents and political agents occupied a dominating position. Indeed the princes, autocratic as they were as regards their people, were themselves completely subject to the control of the political department which was directly under the Viceroy. Many of their principal ministers had been imposed upon them and were members of British services.

Even if we escaped many of the possible consequences of the British proposals, enough remained to undermine Indian freedom, delay progress, and raise fresh and dangerous problems which would create enormous difficulties. The introduction of separate religious electorates a generation or more earlier had played enough mischief; now the door was opened to every obscurantist group giving trouble, and to the fear of continuing division and vivisection of India. We were asked to pledge ourselves to this arrangement for that undetermined future which was to emerge as the issue of the war. Not only the National Congress but politically the most moderate of our politicians, who had always co-operated with the British government, expressed their inability to do so. And yet the Congress, for all its passion for Indian unity, was anxious to win over the minority and other groups and even declared that a territorial unit could not be kept in the Indian Union against the declared will of its people. It accepted the principle even of partition, if this became unavoidable, but it did not want to encourage it in any way. The Working Committee of the Congress, in the course of its resolution on the Cripps proposals, said: 'The Congress has been wedded to Indian freedom and unity and any break in that unity, especially in the modern world, when people's minds inevitably think in terms of ever larger federations, would be injurious to all concerned and exceedingly painful to contemplate. Nevertheless the Committee cannot think in terms of compelling the people in any territorial unit to remain in an Indian Union against their declared and established will. While recognizing this principle, the Committee feel that every effort should be made to create conditions which would help the different units in developing a common and co-operative national life. The acceptance of the principle inevitably involves that no changes should be made which result in fresh problems being created and compulsion being exercised on other substantial groups within that area. Each territorial unit should have the fullest possible autonomy within the union, consistent with a strong national state. The proposal now made on the part of the British War Cabinet encourages and will lead to attempts at separation at the very inception of a union and thus create friction just when the utmost co-operation and goodwill are most needed. This proposal has been presumably made to meet a communal demand, but it will have other consequences also and lead politically reactionary and obscurantist groups among different communities to create trouble and divert public attention from the vital issues before the country.'

The Committee went on to say that 'in to-day's grave crisis, it is the present that counts, and even proposals for the future are important in so far as they affect the present. Although they had been unable to agree to the proposals made for the future, they were anxious to come to some settlement so that, as they said, India might shoulder the burden of her defence worthily. There was no question of non-violence involved and no mention of this was made at any stage. In fact one of the matters discussed was that there should be an Indian Minister of Defence.

The Congress position at this stage was that in view of the imminent war peril to India they were prepared to put aside questions about the future and concentrate on the formation of a national government which would co-operate fully in the war. They could not agree to the British Government's specific proposals for the future as these involved all manner of dangerous commitments. So far as they were concerned, these proposals could be withdrawn or might remain as an indication of British intention, it being clearly understood that the Congress did not accept them. But this need not come in the way of finding a method for present co-operation.

So far as the present was concerned, the British War Cabinet's proposals were vague and incomplete, except that they made it clear that the defence of India must remain the sole charge of the British Government. From Sir Stafford Cripps' repeated statements it appeared that except for defence all other subjects would be transferred to effective Indian control. There was even mention of the Viceroy functioning merely as a constitutional head, like the King of England. This led us to imagine that the only issue that remained for consideration was that of defence. Our position was that defence in war time might be made to cover, and to a large extent did cover, most other national activities and functions. If defence was wholly removed from the scope of the national government's work, very little might remain. It was agreed that the British Commander-in-Chief would continue to exercise full authority over the armed forces and military operations. It was also agreed that the general strategy would be directed by the Imperial staff. Apart from this, it was claimed that there should be a Defence Member of the national government.

After some discussion it was agreed by Sir Stafford that there might be a Defence Department under an Indian member, but the matters to be dealt with by this department were: public relations, petroleum, canteens, stationery and printing, social arrangements for foreign missions, amenities for troops, etc. This list was remarkable and made the position of an Indian Defence Member ludicrous. Further discussions led to a somewhat different approach. There still seemed to be a considerable gap between the two viewpoints, but we seemed to be moving towards one another. For the first time I felt, and so did others, that a settlement was probable. The deepening crisis in the war situation was a continuous spur to all of us to come to an agreement.

The peril of war and invasion was great and had in any event to be met. Yet there were different ways of meeting it, or rather there was only one really effective way of doing so in the present, and much more so for the future. We felt that the psychological moment might pass, not only bringing present dangers in its train but also adding to the greater dangers of the future. New weapons were necessary as well as old, new ways of using them, new enthusiasms, new horizons, a new faith in a future that was going to be essentially different from the past and the present, and the proof of it lay in a change in the present. Perhaps our eagerness fed our optimism and made us forget for a while or minimize the width and depth of the formidable chasm that separated us from Britain's rulers. It was not so easy for the centuries-old conflict to be resolved even in face of peril and disaster; it had never been easy for an imperial power to loosen its grip on its subject dominions unless forced to do so. Had circumstances produced that force, that conviction? We did not know, but we hoped it might be so.

And then, just when I was most hopeful, all manner of odd things began to happen. Lord Halifax, speaking somewhere in the U.S.A., made a violent attack on the National Congress. Why he should do so just then in far America was not obvious, but he could hardly speak in that manner, when he presented the views and policy of the British Government. In Delhi it was well known that the Viceroy, Lord Linlithgow, and the high officials of the Civil Service were strongly opposed to a settlement and to a lessening of their powers. Much happened which was only vaguely known.

When we met Sir Stafford Cripps again to discuss the latest formula about the functions of the Defence Minister, it transpired that all our previous talk was entirely beside the point, as there were going to be no ministers with any power. The existing Viceroy's Executive Council was to continue, and all that was contemplated was to appoint additional Indians, representing political parties, to this Council. The Council was in no sense a cabinet; it was just a group of heads of departments or secretaries, and all power was concentrated in the Viceroy's hands. We realized that legal changes take time and we had not therefore pressed for them, but we insisted that a convention should be observed that the Viceroy was to treat this Council as a cabinet and accept its decisions. We were now told that this was not possible and the Viceroy's powers must remain unaltered not only in theory but in practice. This was an astonishing development which we could hardly credit, for all our previous talks had taken place on a different basis.

We discussed how we could increase India's powers of resistance against invasion. We were anxious to make the Indian army feel that it was a national army and thus to introduce a patriotic element in the war. Also to build up new armies, militias, home guards, etc., rapidly for home defence in case of invasion. All these would of course function under the Commander-in-Chief. We were told that we could not do so. The Indian army was really a part and section of the British army and it could not be considered, or even referred to, as a national army. It was further doubtful if we could be allowed to raise any separate forces like militias or home guards.

So it all came to this, that the existing structure of government would continue exactly as before, the autocratic powers of the Viceroy would remain, and a few of us could become his liveried camp-followers and look after canteens and the like. There was not an atom of difference between this and what Mr. Amery had offered eighteen months earlier, which had seemed to us then an affront to India. It was true that there would be a psychological change after all that had happened, and individuals make a difference. Strong and capable men would function differently from the servile breed that usually surrounded the viceregal throne.

But it was inconceivable and impossible for us to accept this position at any time and more specially at that time. If we had ventured to do so we would have been disowned and rejected by our own people. As a matter of fact, when later the facts were known to the public, there was an outcry against the many concessions we had agreed to in the course of the negotiations.

In the whole course of our talks with Sir Stafford Cripps, the so-called minority or communal issue was at no time raised or considered. Indeed it did not arise at that stage. It was an important issue in considering future constitutional changes, but these had been deliberately put aside after our initial reaction to the British proposals. If the principle of an effective transfer of power to a national government had been agreed to, then the question would no doubt have arisen as to the relative strengths of the various groups represented in it. But as we never reached the stage of agreement on that principle, the other question did not arise and was not considered at all. So far as we were concerned, we were so anxious to have an effective national government enjoying the confidence of the principal parties, that we felt that the question of proportions would not give much trouble. Maulana Abul Kalam Azad, the Congress president, in a letter to Sir Stafford Cripps had said: 'We would point out to you that the suggestions we have put forward are not ours only but may be considered to be the unanimous demand of the Indian people. On these matters there is no difference of opinion among various groups and parties, and the difference is as between the Indian people as a whole and the British Government. Such differences as exist in India relate to constitutional changes in the future. We are agreeable to the postponement of this issue so that the largest possible measure of unity might be achieved in the present crisis for the defence of India. It would be a tragedy that even when there is this unanimity of opinion in India, the British Government should prevent a free national government from functioning and from serving the cause of India as well as the larger causes for which millions are suffering and dying to-day.'

In a subsequent and final letter of the Congress president it was stated: 'We are not interested in the Congress as such gaining power, but we are interested in the Indian people as a whole having freedom and power.... We are convinced that if the British Government did not pursue a policy of encouraging disruption, all of us, to whatever party or group we belonged, would be able to come together and find a common line of action. But, unhappily, even in this grave hour of peril, the British Government is unable to give up its wrecking policy. We are driven to the conclusion that it attaches more importance to holding on to its rule in India, as long as it can, and promoting discord and disruption here with that end in view, than to an effective defence of India against the aggression and invasion that overhang us. To us, and to all Indians, the dominant consideration is the defence and safety of India, and it is by that test that we judge.'

In this letter he also made clear our position in regard to defence. 'No one has suggested any restrictions on the normal powers of the Commander-in-Chief. Indeed we went beyond this and were prepared to agree to further powers being given to him as war minister. But it is clear that the British Government's conception and ours in regard to defence differ greatly. For us it means giving it a national character and calling upon every man and woman in India to participate in it. It means trusting our own people and seeking their full co-operation in this great effort. The British Government's view seems to be based on an utter lack of confidence in the Indian people and in withholding real power from them. You refer to the paramount duty and responsibility of His Majesty's Government in regard to defence. That duty and responsibility cannot be discharged effectively unless the Indian people are made to have and feel their responsibility, and the recent past stands witness to this. The Government of India do not realise that the war can only be fought on a popular basis.'

Almost immediately after this last letter of the Congress president, Sir Stafford Cripps returned to England by air. But before he did so, and on his return, he made certain statements to the public which were contrary to the facts and which were bitterly resented in India. In spite of contradiction by responsible persons in India, these statements were repeated by Sir Stafford and others.

The British proposals had been rejected, not by the Congress only, but by every single party or group in India. Even the most moderate of our politicians had expressed their disapproval of them. Apart from the Moslem League, the reasons for disapproval were more or less the same. The Moslem League, as has been its custom, waited for others to express their opinions and then, for its own reasons, rejected the proposals.

It was stated in the British Parliament and elsewhere that the rejection by the Congress was due to the uncompromising attitude of Gandhiji. This is wholly untrue. Gandhiji had strongly disapproved, in common with most others, of the indefinite and innumerable partitions that the proposals involved, and of the way in which the ninety million people of the Indian states had been allowed no say in their future. All the subsequent negotiations, which dealt with changes in the present and not with the future, took place in his absence, as he had to leave because of his wife's illness, and he had nothing whatever to do with them. The Congress Working Committee had, on several previous occasions, disagreed with him on the question of non-violence, and was anxious to have a National Government to co-operate in the war and especially in the defence of India.

The war was the dominant issue and thought in men's minds, and the invasion of India seemed imminent. And yet it was not the war that came in the way of agreement, for that war would inevitably have to be conducted by experts and not by laymen. On the conduct of the war itself it was easy to come to an agreement. The real question was the transfer of power to the National Government. It was the old issue of Indian nationalism versus British imperialism, and on that issue, war or no war, the British governing class in England and in India was determined to hold on to what it had. Behind them stood the imposing figure of Mr. Winston Churchill.

Frustration

The abrupt termination of the Cripps' negotiations and Sir Stafford's sudden departure came as a surprise. Was it to make this feeble offer, which turned out to be, so far as the present was concerned, a mere repetition of what had been repeatedly said before—was it for this that a member of the British War Cabinet had journeyed to India? Or had all this been done merely as a propaganda stunt for the people of the U.S.A.? The reaction was strong and bitter. There was no hope of a settlement with Britain; no chance was given to the people of India even to defend their country against invasion as they wanted to.

Meanwhile the chances of that invasion were growing and hordes of starving Indian refugees were pouring across the eastern frontiers of India. In eastern Bengal, in a panicky state of mind in anticipation of an invasion, tens of thousands of river boats were destroyed. (It was subsequently stated that this had been done by a mistaken interpretation of an official order.) That vast area was full of waterways and the only transport possible was by these boats. Their destruction isolated large communities, destroyed their means of livelihood and transport, and was one of the contributory causes of the Bengal famine. Preparations were made for large-scale withdrawals from Bengal, and a repetition of what had happened in Rangoon and Lower Burma seemed probable. In the city of Madras a vague and unconfirmed (and, as it turned out, a false) rumour of the approach of a Japanese fleet led to the sudden departure of high Government officials and even to a partial destruction of harbour facilities. It seemed that the civilian administration of India was suffering from a nervous breakdown. It was strong only in its suppression of Indian nationalism.

What were we to do? We could not tolerate any part of India submitting tamely to invasion. So far as armed resistance was concerned that was a matter for the army and air force, such as they were. American help was pouring in, especially in the shape of aircraft, and was slowly changing the military situation. The only way we could have helped was by changing the whole atmosphere of the home front, by creating enthusiasm in the people and a fierce desire to resist at all costs, by building up citizen forces for this purpose and home guards and the like. That had been made terribly difficult for us by British policy. Even on the eve of invasion no Indian outside the regular army could be trusted with a gun, and even our attempts to organize unarmed self-defence units in villages were disapproved and sometimes suppressed. Far from encouraging the organization of popular resistance the British authorities were afraid of this, for they had long been accustomed to look upon all popular self-defence organization as seditious and dangerous to British rule. They had to follow their old policy, for the only alternative was to accept a national government relying on the people and organizing them for defence. This alternative had been definitely rejected by them and there was no middle course or half-way house. Inevitably they were led to treat the people as chattels, who were to be allowed no initiative and were to be used and disposed of entirely according to their own wishes. The All-India Congress Committee, which met at the end of April, 1942, declared its deep resentment at this policy and treatment, and said that it could never accept a position which involved our functioning as slaves of foreign authority.

Nevertheless, we could not remain silent and inert spectators of the tragedy that seemed to be imminent. We had to advise the people, the vast masses of the civilian population, as to what they should do in case of invasion. We told them that in spite of their indignation against British policy they must not interfere in any way with the operations of the British or allied armed forces, as this would be giving indirect aid to the enemy aggressor. Further, that they must on no account submit to the invader, or obey his orders, or accept any favours from him. If the invading forces sought to take possession of the people's homes and fields they must be resisted even unto death. This resistance was to be peaceful; it was to be the completest form of non-co-operation with the enemy.

Many people criticized with considerable sarcasm what seemed to them the absurd notion of resisting an invading army with these methods of non-violent non-co-operation. Yet far from being absurd, it was the only method, and a very brave method, left to the people. The advice was not offered to the armed forces, nor was peaceful resistance put forward as an alternative to armed resistance. That advice was meant only for the unarmed civilian population, which almost invariably submits to the invader when its armed forces are defeated or withdrawn. Apart from the regular armed forces, it is possible to organize guerrilla units to harass the enemy. But this was not possible for us, for it requires training, arms, and the full co-operation of the regular army. And even if some guerrilla units could have been trained the rest of the population remained. Normally the civilian population is expected to submit to enemy occupation. Indeed, it was known that directions had been issued by British authorities in certain threatened areas advising submission, even by some of the petty officials, to the enemy when the army and the higher officials withdrew.

We knew perfectly well that peaceful non-cooperation could not stop an advancing enemy force. We knew also that most of the civilian inhabitants would find it difficult to resist even if they wanted to do so. Nevertheless we hoped that some leading personalities in the towns and villages occuped by the enemy would refuse to submit or carry out the enemy's orders or help in getting provisions or in any other way. That would have meant swift punishment for them, very probably death as well as reprisals. We expected this non-submission and resistance to death of even a limited number of persons to have a powerful effect on the general population, not only in the area concerned but in the rest of India. Thus we hoped that a national spirit of resistance might be built up.

For some months previously we had been organizing, often in the face of official opposition, food committees and self-defence units in towns and villages. The food problem was troubling us and we feared a crisis in view of the increasing difficulties of transport and other developments of the war situation. Government was doing next to nothing in regard to this. We tried to organize self-sufficient units, especially in the rural areas, and to encourage primitive methods of transport by bullock-cart in case modern methods failed. There was also the possibility of large numbers of refugees and evacuees suddenly marching west, as they had done in China, in case of invasion from the east. We tried to prepare ourselves to receive them and provide for them. All this was exceedingly difficult, indeed hardly possible, without the co-operation of the Government, yet we made such attempts as we could. The purpose of the self-defence units was to help in these tasks and to prevent panic and keep order in their respective areas. Air raids and the news of invasion, even in a distant area, 'might well cause panic in the civilian population, and it was important to stop this. The official measures taken in this behalf were totally insufficient and looked upon with distrust by the public. In the rural areas dacoities and robberies were on the increase.

We made these vast plans and in a small measure gave effect to them, but it was obvious that we were only scratching the surface of the tremendous problem which confronted us. A real solution could come only through complete co-operation between the governmental apparatus and the people, and that had been found to be impossible.

It was a heart-breaking situation, for while the crisis called to us and we were bubbling over with the desire to act, effective action was denied us. Catastrophe and disaster advanced with tremendous strides towards us while India lay helpless and inert, bitter and sullen, a battle ground for rival and foreign forces.

Much as I hated war, the prospect of a Japanese invasion of India had in no way frightened me. At the back of my mind I was in a sense attracted to this coming of war, horrible as it was, to India. For I wanted a tremendous shake-up, a personal experience for millions of people, which would drag them out of that peace of the grave that Britain had imposed upon us. Something that would force them to face the reality of to-day and to outgrow the past which clung to them so tenaciously, to get beyond the petty political squabbles and exaggerations of temporary problems which filled their minds. Not to break with the past, and yet not to live in it; realise the present and look to the future.... To change the rhythm of life and make it in tune with this present and future. The cost of war was heavy, and the consequences full of uncertainty. That war was not of our seeking, but since it had come, it could be made to harden the fibre of the nation and provide those vital experiences out of which a new life might blossom forth. Vast numbers would die, that was inevitable, but it is better to die in war than through famine; it is better to die than to live a miserable, hopeless life. Out of death, life is born afresh, and individuals and nations who do not know how to die, do not know also how to live. 'Only where there are graves are there resurrections.'

But though the war had come to India, it had brought no exhilaration of the spirit to us, no pouring out of our energies in some glad endeavour, when pain and death were forgotten and self itself ignored and only the cause of freedom counted and the vision of the future that lay beyond. Only the suffering and sorrow were for us, and an awareness of impending disaster which sharpened our perceptions and quickened pain, and which we could not even help to avert. A brooding sense of inevitable and ineluctable tragedy grew upon us, a tragedy that was both personal and national.

This had nothing to do with victory or defeat in the war, with who won and who lost. We did not want the Axis powers to win, for that led to certain disaster; we did not want the Japanese to enter or occupy any part of India. That had to be resisted anyhow, and we repeatedly impressed the public with this fact, but all this was a negative approach. What positive aim was there in this war, what future would emerge out of it? Was it just a repetition of past follies and disasters, a play of nature's blind forces which took no cognizance of man's wishes and ideals? What was going to be the fate of India?

We thought of Rabindranath Tagore's last testament, his death-bed message given the year before: '...the demon of barbarity has given up all pretence and has emerged with unconcealed fangs ready to tear up humanity in an orgy of devastation. From one end of the world to the other the poisonous fumes of hatred darken the atmosphere. The spirit of violence which perhaps lay dormant in the psychology of the west has at last roused itself and desecrated the spirit of man.

'The wheels of fate will some day compel the English to give up their Indian empire. But what kind of India will they leave behind, what stark misery? When the stream of their centuries' administration runs dry at last, what a waste of mud and filth they will leave behind! I had one time believed that the springs of civilization would issue out of the heart of Europe. But to-day when I am about to quit the world that faith has gone bankrupt altogether.

'As I look round I see the crumbling ruins of a proud civilization strewn like a vast heap of futility. And yet I shall not commit the grievous sin of losing faith in man. I would rather look forward to the opening of a new chapter in his history after the cataclysm is over and the atmosphere rendered clean with the spirit of service and sacrifice. Perhaps that dawn will come from this horizon, from the east where the sun rises. A day will come when unvanquished man will retrace his path of conquest, despite all barriers, to win back his lost human heritage.

'To-day we witness the perils which attend on the insolence of might; one day shall be borne out the full truth of what the sages have proclaimed: "By unrighteousness man prospers, gains what appears desirable, conquers enemies, but perishes at the root."'

No, one may not lose faith in man. God we may deny, but what hope is there for us if we deny man and thus reduce everything to futility? Yet it was difficult to have faith in anything or to believe that the triumph of righteousness is inevitable.

Weary of body and troubled in mind I sought escape from my surroundings and journeyed to Kulu in the inner valleys of the Himalayas.

The Challenge: Quit India Resolution

On my return from Kulu after a fortnight's absence I realized that the internal situation was changing rapidly. The reaction from the failure of the last attempt at a settlement had grown and there was a feeling that no hope lay in that direction. British official statements in Parliament and elsewhere had confirmed that view and angered the people. Official policy in India was definitely aiming at the suppression of our normal political and public activities and there was an all-round tightening of pressure. Many of our workers had remained in prison throughout the Cripps negotiations; now some of the nearest and most important of my friends and colleagues had been arrested and imprisoned under the Defence of India Act. Rafi Ahmad Kidwai was arrested early in May. Shri Krishnadat Palliwal, president of the United Provinces Provincial Congress committee, followed soon after, and so did many others. It seemed that most of us would be picked off in this way and removed from the scene of action, and our national movement prevented from functioning and gradually disintegrated. Could we submit to all this passively? We had not been trained that way, and both our personal and national pride rose in revolt against this treatment.

But what could we do in view of the grave war crisis and possibility of invasion? Yet inaction was no service even to this cause, for it was leading to the growth of sentiments which we viewed with anxiety and apprehension. There were many trends in public opinion, as was natural in such a vast country and at such a time of crisis. Actual pro-Japanese sentiment was practically nil, for no one wanted to change masters, and pro-Chinese feelings were strong and widespread. But there was a small group which was indirectly pro-Japanese in the sense that it imagined that it could take advantage of a Japanese invasion for Indian freedom. They were influenced by the broadcasts being made by Subhas Chandra Bose who had secretly escaped from India the year before. Most people were, of course, just passive, dumbly awaiting developments. If unfortunately circumstances so fashioned themselves that a part of India was under the invader's control, then there would undoubtedly be many collaborators, especially among the upper income groups, whose ruling passion was to save themselves and their property. That breed and mentality of collaborators had been cherished and encouraged by the British Government in India in the past for its own purposes, and they could adapt themselves to changing circumstances, always keeping their own personal interests in view. We had seen collaboration in full flood even in France and Belgium and Norway and many of the occupied countries of Europe, in spite of growing resistance movements. We had seen how the men of Vichy had (in Pertinax's words) 'racked their brains to palm off shame as honour, cowardice as courage, pusillanimity and ignorance as wisdom, humiliation as virtue, and wholehearted acceptance of the German victory as moral regeneration.' If that had been so in France, that country of revolution and fiery patriotism, it was certainly not unlikely among similar classes in India, where the mentality of collaboration had flourished for so long under British patronage and brought so many rewards. Indeed it was highly likely that chief among those who might collaborate with the invader would be many of the persons who had been collaborating with British rule and who proclaimed their loyalty to that rule from the house tops. They had perfected the art of collaboration and would find no difficulty in holding on to that basis even though the superstructure changed. And if subsequently there was yet another change of that superstructure, well they would readapt themselves again as others of their kind were doing in Europe. When necessity arose they could take advantage of the anti-British feelings that had grown more powerful than ever after the failure of the Cripps negotiations. So would others also, not for personal and opportunist reasons but pushed on by different motives, losing all perspective and forgetting the larger issues. These developments filled us with dismay and we felt that the growth of enforced and sullen submission to British policy in India would lead to all manner of dangerous consequences and the complete degradation of the people.

There was a fairly widespread feeling that in case of attempted invasion and occupation of some eastern areas, there would be a breakdown of the civil administration over larger areas elsewhere, leading to chaotic conditions. What had happened in Malaya and Burma was before us. Hardly anyone expected any considerable part of the country to be occupied by the enemy even if the chances of war favoured him. India was vast, and we had seen in China that space counts. But space counts only when there is a determination to take advantage of it and resist, and not to collapse and submit. Apparently well-founded reports stated that the Allied armed forces would probably withdraw to inner lines of defence, leaving wide areas open to enemy occupation, though probably the enemy, as in China, might not actually occupy them all. So questions arose as to how we should meet this situation both in these areas as well as in other areas where the civil administration might cease to function. We tried, as far as we could, to prepare mentally and otherwise for such crises by encouraging local organizations which could function and keep order, and at the same time by insisting that the invader had to be resisted at any cost.

Why had the Chinese fought so stoutly for many years? Why, above all others, had the Russians and other peoples of the Soviet Union fought with such courage, tenacity, and whole-heartedness? Elsewhere people fought bravely also because they were moved by love of country, fear of aggression, and desire to preserve their ways of life. And yet there appeared to be a difference in the whole-heartedness of the war effort between Russia and other countries. Others had fought magnificently as at the time of Dunkirk and after, but there had been some moral slackening of effort when the immediate crisis was past; it seemed as if there were some doubts about the future, though the war had anyhow to be won. In the Soviet Union, so far as one could judge from the material available, there seemed to be no doubt or debate (though it was true that debate was not encouraged), and there was a supreme confidence in both the present and the future.

In India? There was a deep-seated dislike of the present and the future seemed equally dark. No patriotic urge to action moved the people, only a desire to defend themselves against invasion and a worse fate. A few were moved by international considerations. Mixed up with all these feelings was resentment at being ordered about, suppressed and exploited by an alien and imperialist power. There was a fundamental wrongness in a system under which everything depended on the wishes and whims of an autocrat. Freedom is dear to all, but most of all to those who have been deprived of it, or those who are in danger of losing it. Freedom in the modern world is conditioned and limited in many ways but those who do not possess it, do not realize these limitations, and idealize the conception till it becomes a passionate craving and an overwhelming and consuming desire. If anything does not fit in with this longing or seems to go counter to it, that thing must inevitably suffer. The desire for freedom, for which so many in India had laboured and suffered, had not only received a check but it seemed that the prospect of it had receded into some dim and distant future. Instead of tacking that passion on to the world struggle that was going on, and drawing upon the vast reservoir of energy in the cause of Indian and world freedom and for India's defence, the war had been isolated from it, and no hope was centred in its issue. It is never wise to leave any people, even enemies, without hope.

There were some of course in India who looked upon the war as something far bigger and vaster than the petty ambitions of the statesmen of the various countries involved in it; some who felt its revolutionary significance in their bones and realized that its ultimate issue and the consequences that would flow from it would take the world far beyond military victories and the pacts and utterances of politicians. But the number of these people was inevitably limited and the great majority, as in other countries, took a narrower view, which they called realistic, and were governed by the considerations of the moment. Some, inclined to opportunism, adapted themselves to British policy and fitted themselves into it, as they would have collaborated with any other authority and policy. Some reacted strongly against this policy and felt that a submission to it was a betrayal not only of India's cause, but the world's cause. Most people became just passive, static, quiescent: the old failing of the Indian people against which we had struggled for so long.

While this struggle was going on in India's mind and a feeling of desperation was growing, Gandhiji wrote a number of articles which suddenly gave a new direction to people's thoughts, or, as often happens, gave shape to their vague ideas. Inaction at that critical stage and submission to all that was happening had become intolerable to him. The only way to meet that situation was for Indian freedom to be recognized and for a free India to meet aggression and invasion in co-operation with the allied nations. If this recognition was not forthcoming then some action must be taken to challenge the existing system and wake up the people from the lethargy that was paralysing them and making them easy prey to every kind of aggression.

There was nothing new in this demand, for it was a repetition of what we had been saying all along, but there was a new urgency and passion in his speech and writing. And there was the hint of action. There was no doubt that he represented at the moment the prevailing sentiment in India. In a conflict between the two, nationalism had triumphed over internationalism, and Gandhiji's new writings created a stir all over India. And yet that nationalism was at no time opposed to internationalism and indeed was trying its utmost to find some opening to fit in with that larger aspect, if only it could be given an opportunity to do so honourably and effectively. There was no necessary conflict between the two for, unlike the aggressive nationalisms of Europe, it did not seek to interfere with others but rather to co-operate with them to their common advantage. National freedom was seen as the essential basis of true internationalism and hence as the road to the latter, as well as the real foundation for co-operation in the common struggle against fascism and nazism. Meanwhile that internationalism, which was being so much talked about, was beginning to look suspiciously like the old policy of the imperialist powers, in a new, and yet not so new, attire; indeed it was itself an aggressive nationalism which, in the name of empire or commonwealth or mandatory, sought to impose its will on others.

Some of us were disturbed and upset by this new development, for action was futile unless it was effective action, and any such effective action must necessarily come in the way of the war effort at a time when India herself stood in peril of invasion. Gandhiji's general approach also seemed to ignore important international considerations and appeared to be based on a narrow view of nationalism. During the three years of war we had deliberately followed a policy of non-embarrassment, and such action as we had indulged in had been in the nature of symbolic protest. That symbolic protest had assumed huge dimensions when 30,000 of our leading men and women were sent to prison in 1940-41. And yet even the prison-going was a selected individual affair and avoided any mass upheaval or any direct interference with the governmental apparatus. We could not repeat that, and if we did something else it had to be of a different kind and on a more effective scale. Was this not bound to interfere with the war on India's borders and encourage the enemy?

These were obvious difficulties and we discussed them at length with Gandhiji without converting each other. The difficulties were there and risks and perils seemed to follow any course of action or inaction. It became a question of balancing them and choosing the lesser evil. Our mutual discussion led to a clarification of much that had been vague and cloudy, and to Gandhiji's appreciation of many international factors to which his attention was drawn. His subsequent writing underwent a change and he himself emphasized these international considerations and looked at India's problem in a wider perspective. But his fundamental attitude remained: his objection to a passive submission to British autocratic and repressive policy in India and his intense desire to do something to challenge this. Submission, according to him, meant that India would be broken in spirit and, whatever shape the war might take, whatever its end might be, her people would act in a servile way and their freedom would not be achieved for a long time. It would mean also submission to an invader and not continuing resistance to him regardless even of temporary military defeat or withdrawal. It would mean the complete demoralization of our people and their losing all the strength that they had built up during a quarter of a century's unceasing struggle for freedom. It would mean that the world would forget India's demand for freedom and the post-war settlement would be governed by the old imperialist urges and ambitions. Passionately desirous of India's freedom as he was, India was to him something more than his loved homeland; it was the symbol of all the colonial and exploited peoples of the world, the acid test whereby any world policy must be judged. If India remained unfree then also the other colonial countries and subject races would continue in their present enslaved condition and the war would have been fought in vain. It was essential to change the moral basis of the war. The armies and the navies and air forces would function in their respective spheres and they might win by superior methods of violence, but to what end was their victory? And even armed warfare requires the support of morale; had not Napoleon said that in war 'the moral is to the physical as three to one?' The moral factor of hundreds of millions of subject and exploited people all over the world realizing and believing that this war was really for their freedom was of immense importance even from the narrower viewpoint of the war, and much more so for the peace to come. The very fact that a crisis had risen in the fortunes of the war necessitated a change in outlook and policy and the conversion of these sullen and doubting millions into enthusiastic supporters. If this miracle could take place all the military might of the axis powers would be of little avail and their collapse was assured. Many of the peoples of the axis countries might themselves be affected by this powerful world sentiment.

In India it was better to convert the sullen passivity of the people into a spirit of non-submission and resistance. Though that non-submission would be, to begin with, to arbitrary orders of the British authorities, it could be turned into resistance to an invader. Submissiveness and servility to one would lead to the same attitude towards the other and thus to humiliation and degradation.

We were familiar with all these arguments; we believed them and had ourselves used them frequently. But the tragedy was that the policy of the British Government prevented that miracle from taking place; all our attempts to solve the Indian problem, even temporarily, during the course of the war had failed, and all our requests for a declaration of war aims had been turned down. It was certain that a further attempt of this kind would also fail. What then? If it was to be conflict, however much it might be justified on moral or other grounds, there could be no doubt that it would tend to interfere greatly with the war effort in India at a time when the danger of invasion was considerable. There was no getting away from that fact. And yet, oddly enough, it was that very danger that had brought this crisis in our minds, for we could not remain idle spectators of it and see our country mismanaged and ruined by people whom we considered incompetent and wholly incapable of shouldering the burden of a people's resistance which the occasion demanded. All our pent-up passion and energy sought some outlet, some way of action.

Gandhiji was getting on in years, he was in the seventies, and a long life of ceaseless activity, of hard toil, both physical and mental, had enfeebled his body; but he was still vigorous enough, and he felt that all his life work would be in vain if he submitted to circumstances then and took no action to vindicate what he prized most. His love of freedom for India and all other exploited nations and peoples overcame even his strong adherence to non-violence. He had previously given a grudging and rather reluctant consent to the Congress not adhering to this policy in regard to defence and the state's functions in an emergency, but he had kept himself aloof from this. He realized that his half-hearted attitude in this matter might well come in the way of a settlement with Britain and the United Nations. So he went further and himself sponsored a Congress resolution which declared that the primary function of the provisional government of free India would be to throw all her great resources in the struggle for freedom and against aggression, and to co-operate fully with the United Nations in the defence of India with all the armed as well as other forces at her command. It was no easy matter for him to commit himself in this way, but he swallowed the bitter pill, so overpowering was his desire that some settlement should be arrived at to enable India to resist the aggressor as a free nation.

Many of the theoretical and other differences that had often separated some of us from Gandhiji disappeared, but still that major difficulty remained—any action on our part must interfere with the war effort. Gandhiji, to our surprise, still clung to the belief that a settlement with the British Government was possible, and he said he would try his utmost to achieve it. And so, though he talked a great deal about action, he did not define it or indicate what he intended to do.

While we were doubting and debating, the mood of the country changed, and from a sullen passivity it rose to a pitch of excitement and expectation. Events were not waiting for a Congress decision or resolution; they had been pushed forward by Gandhiji's utterances, and now they were moving onwards with their own momentum. It was clear that, whether Gandhiji was right or wrong, he had crystallized the prevailing mood of the people. There was a desperateness in it, an emotional urge which gave second place to logic and reason and a calm consideration of the consequences of action. Those consequences were not ignored, and it was realized that whether anything was achieved or not the price paid in human suffering would be heavy. But the price that was being paid from day to day in torture of the mind was also heavy and there was no prospect of escape from it. It was better to jump into the uncharted seas of action and do something, rather than be the tame objects of a malign fate. It was not a politician's approach but that of a people grown desperate and reckless of consequences; yet there was always an appeal to reason, an attempt to rationalize conflicting emotions, to find some consistency in the fundamental inconsistencies of human character. The war was going to be a long one, to last many more years; there had been many disasters and there were likely to be more, but the war would continue in spite of them till it had tamed and exhausted the passions which gave rise to it and which it had itself encouraged. This time there would be no half-success which are often more painful than failures. It had taken a wrong turn not only in the field of military action but even more so in regard to the more fundamental objectives for which it was supposed to be fought. Perhaps such action as we might indulge in might draw forcible attention to this latter failure and help to give a new and more promising turn. And even if present success was lacking it might serve that saving purpose in the longer run, and thus help also in giving powerful support in the future to military action.

If the temper of the people rose, so also did the temper of the Government. No emotional or other urge was required for this, for it was its natural temper and its normal way of functioning —the way of an alien authority in occupation of a subject country. It seemed to welcome this opportunity of crushing once for all, as it thought, all the elements in the country which dared to oppose its will; and for this it prepared accordingly.

Events marched ahead, and yet, curiously, Gandhiji, who had said so much about action to protect the honour of India and affirm her right to freedom, and as a free nation to co-operate fully in the fight against aggression, said nothing at all about the nature of this action. Peaceful, of course, it had necessarily to be, but what more? He began to lay greater stress on the possibilities of an agreement with the British Government, of his intention to approach it again and try his utmost to find a way out. His final speech at the All-India Congress Committee expressed his earnest desire for a settlement and his determination to approach the Viceroy for this. Neither in public nor in private at the meetings of the Congress Working Committee did he hint at the nature of the action he had in mind, except in one particular. He had suggested privately that in the event of failure of all negotiations he would appeal for some kind of non-co-operation and a one-day protest *hartal*, or cessation of all work in the country, something in the nature of a one-day general strike, symbolic of a nation's protest. Even this was a vague suggestion which he did not particularize, for he did not want to make any further plans till he had made his attempt at a settlement. So neither he nor the Congress Working Committee issued any kind of directions, public or private, except that people should be prepared for all developments, and should in any event adhere to the policy of peaceful and non-violent action.

Though Gandhiji was still hopeful of finding some way out of the impasse, very few persons shared his hope. The course of events and all the development that had taken place pointed inevitably to a conflict, and when that stage is reached middle positions cease to have importance and each individual has to choose on which side he will range himself. For Congressmen, as for others who felt that way, there was no question of choice; it was inconceivable that the whole might of a powerful government should try to crush our people and that any of us should stand by and be passive spectators of a struggle in which India's freedom was involved. Many people of course do stand by in spite of their sympathies, but any such attempt to save himself from the consequences of his own previous acts would have been shameful and dishonourable for prominent Congressmen. But even apart from this there was no choice left for them. The whole of India's past history pursued them, as well as the agony of the present and the hope of the future, and all these drove them forward and conditioned their actions. 'The piling up of the past upon the past goes on without relaxation,' says Bergson in his 'Creative Evolution.' 'In reality the past is preserved by itself, automatically. In its entirety, probably, it follows us at every instant....Doubtless we think with only a small part of our past, but it is with our entire past, including the original bent of our soul, that we desire, will and act.'

On August 7th and 8th, in Bombay the All-India Congress Committee considered and debated in public the resolution, which has since come to be known as the 'Quit India Resolution.' That resolution was a long and comprehensive one, a reasoned argument for the immediate recognition of Indian freedom and the ending of British rule in India 'both for the sake of India and for the success of the cause of the United Nations. The continuation of that rule is degrading and enfeebling India and making her progressively less capable of defending herself and of contributing to the cause of world freedom.' 'The possession of empire, instead of adding to the strength of the ruling power, has become a burden and a curse. India, the classic land of modern imperialism, has become the crux of the question, for by the freedom of India will Britain and the United Nations be judged, and the peoples of Asia and Africa be filled with hope and enthusiasm.' The resolution went on to suggest the formation of a provisional government, which would be composite and would represent all important sections of the people and whose 'primary function must be to defend India and resist aggression with all the armed as well as the non-violent forces at its command, together with its allied powers.' This government would evolve a scheme for a constituent assembly which would prepare a constitution for India acceptable to all sections of the people. The constitution would be a federal one, with the largest measure of autonomy for the federating units and with the residuary powers vesting in those units. 'Freedom will enable India to resist aggression effectively with the people's united will and strength behind it.'

This freedom of India must be the symbol of the prelude to the freedom of all other Asiatic nations. Further, a world federation of free nations was proposed, of which a beginning should be made with United Nations.

The Committee stated that it was 'anxious not to embarrass in any way the defence of China and Russia, whose freedom is precious and must be preserved, or to jeopardize the defensive capacity of the United Nations.' (At that time the dangers to China and Russia were the greatest.) 'But the peril grows both to India and these nations, and inaction and submission to a foreign administration at this stage is not only degrading India and reducing her capacity to defend herself and resist aggression but is no answer to that growing peril and is no service to the peoples of the United Nations.'

The Committee again appealed to Britain and the United Nations 'in the interest of world freedom.' But—and there came the sting of the resolution—'the Committee is no longer justified in holding the nation back from endeavouring to assert its will against an imperialist and authoritarian Government which dominates over it and prevents it from functioning in its own interest and in the interest of humanity. The Committee resolves therefore to sanction, for the vindication of India's inalienable right to freedom and independence, the starting of a mass struggle on non-violent lines under the inevitable leadership of Gandhiji.' That sanction was to take effect only when Gandhiji so decided. Finally, it was stated that the Committee had 'no intention of gaining power for the Congress. The power, when it comes, will belong to the whole people of India.'

In their concluding speeches Maulana Abul Kalam Azad, the Congress president, and Gandhiji made it clear that their next steps would be to approach the Viceroy, as representing the British Government, and to appeal to the heads of the principal United Nations for an honourable settlement, which, while recognizing the freedom of India, would also advance the cause of the United Nations in the struggle against the aggressor Axis powers.

The resolution was finally passed late in the evening of August 8th, 1942. A few hours later, in the early morning of August 9th, a large number of arrests were made in Bombay and all over the country. And so to Ahmadnagar Fort.

CHAPTER TEN

AHMADNAGAR FORT AGAIN

The Chain of Happening

AHMADNAGAR FORT. AUGUST THIRTEENTH, NINETEEN FORTY-FOUR.
It is just over two years since we came here, two years of a dream
life rooted in one spot, with the same few individuals to see, the
same limited environment, the same routine from day to day.
Sometime in the future we shall wake up from this dream and
go out into the wider world of life and activity, finding it a changed world. There will be an air of unfamiliarity about the persons
and things we see; we shall remember them again and past
memories will crowd into our minds, and yet they will not be the
same, nor will we be the same, and we may find it difficult to fit
in with them. Sometimes we may wonder whether this renewed
experience of everyday living is not itself a sleep and a dream from
which we may suddenly wake up. Which is the dream and which
is the waking? Are they both real, for we experience and feel them
in all their intensity, or are they both unsubstantial and of the
nature of fleeting dreams which pass, leaving vague memories
behind?

Prison and its attendant solitude and passivity lead to thought
and an attempt to fill the vacuum of life with memories of past
living, of one's own life, and of the long chain of history of human activity. So during the past four months, in the course of this
writing, I have occupied my mind with India's past records and
experiences, and out of the multitude of ideas that came to me
I have selected some and made a book out of them. Looking back
at what I have written, it seems inadequate, disjointed and lacking
in unity, a mixture of many things, with the personal element
dominant and giving its colour even to what was intended to be
an objective record and analysis. That personal element has
pushed itself forward almost against my will; often I checked it
and held it back but sometimes I loosened the reins and allowed
it to flow out of my pen, and mirror, to some extent, my mind.

By writing of the past I have tried to rid myself of the burden
of the past. But the present remains with all its complexity and
irrationality and the dark future that lies beyond, and the burden
of these is no less than that of the past. The vagrant mind, finding

no haven, still wanders about restlessly, bringing discomfort to its possessor as well as to others. There is some envy for those virgin minds which have not been soiled or violated by thought's assault, and on which doubt has cast no shadow nor written a line. How easy is life for them in spite of its occasional shock and pain.

Events take place one after the other and the uninterrupted and unending stream of happenings goes on. We seek to understand a particular event by isolating it and looking at it by itself, as if it were the beginning and the end, the resultant of some cause immediately preceding it. Yet it has no beginning and is but a link in an unending chain, caused by all that has preceded it, and resulting from the wills, urges, and desires of innumerable human beings coalescing and conflicting with each other, and producing something different from that which any single individual intended to happen. Those wills, urges, and desires are themselves largely conditioned by previous events and experiences, and the new event in its turn becomes another conditioning factor for the future. The man of destiny, the leader who influences the multitude, undoubtedly plays an important part in this process, and yet he himself is the product of past events and forces and his influence is conditioned by them.

The Two Backgrounds: Indian and British

What happened in India in August, 1942, was no sudden development but a culmination of all that had gone before. Much has been written about it, in attack, criticism or defence, and many explanations given. And yet most of this writing misses the real meaning, for it applies purely political considerations to something that was deeper than politics. Behind it all lay an intense feeling that it was no longer possible to endure and live under foreign autocratic rule. All other questions became secondary—whether under that rule it was possible to make improvements or progress in some directions, or whether the consequences of a challenge might be more harmful still. Only the overwhelming desire to be rid of it and to pay any price for the riddance remained, only the feeling that whatever happened this could not be endured.

That feeling was no new sensation; it had been there for many years. But previously it had been restrained in many ways and disciplined to keep pace with events. The war itself was both a restraining and releasing factor. It opened out our minds to vast developments and revolutionary changes, to the possibility of the realization of our hopes in the near future; and it put a brake on much that we might otherwise have done because of our desire to help, and certainly not to hinder in any way, the struggle against the Axis powers.

But, as the war developed, it became ever clearer that the western democracies were fighting not for a change but for a perpetuation of the old order. Before the war they had appeased fascism, not only because of the fear of its consequences but also because of a certain ideological sympathy with it and an extreme dislike of some of the probable alternatives to it. Nazism and fascism were no sudden growths or accidents of history. They were the natural developments of the past course of events, of empire and racial discrimination, of national struggles, of the growing concentration of power, of technological growth which found no scope for its fulfilment within the existing framework of society, of the inherent conflict between the democratic ideal and a social structure opposed to it. Political democracy in western Europe and North America, opening the door to national and individual progress, had also released new forces and ideas, aiming inevitably at economic equality. Conflict was inherent in the situation; there would either be an enlargement of that political democracy or attempts to curb it and end it. Democracy grew in content and area, in spite of constant opposition, and became the accepted ideal of political organization. But a time came when a further expansion endangered the basis of the social structure, and then the upholders of that structure became clamant and aggressive and organized themselves to oppose change. In countries so circumstanced that the crisis developed more rapidly, democracy was openly and deliberately crushed and fascism and nazism appeared. In the democracies of western Europe and North America the same processes were at play though many other factors delayed the crisis and probably the much longer tradition of peaceful and democratic government also helped. Behind some of these democracies lay empires where there was no democracy at all and where the same kind of authoritarianism which is associated with fascism prevailed. There also, as in fascist countries, the governing class allied itself to reactionary and opportunist groups and feudal survivals in order to suppress the demand for freedom. And there also they began to assert that democracy, though good as an ideal and desirable in their own home lands, was not suited to the peculiar conditions prevailing in their colonial domains. So it was a natural consequence for these western democracies to feel some kind of an ideological bond with fascism, even when they disliked many of its more brutal and vulgar manifestations.

When they were forced to fight in self-defence, they looked forward to a restoration of that very structure which had failed so dismally. The war was looked upon and presented as a defensive war, and this was true enough in a way. But there was another aspect of the war, a moral aspect which went beyond military objectives and attacked aggressively the fascist creed and outlook. For it was a war, as has been said, for the soul of the peoples of the world. In it lay the seeds of change not only for the fascist countries but also for the United Nations. This moral aspect of the war was obscured by powerful propaganda, and emphasis was laid on defence and perpetuation of the past and not on creating a new future. There were many people in the west who ardently believed in this moral aspect and wanted to create a new world which would afford some guarantees against that utter failure of human society which the World War represented. There were vast numbers of people everywhere, including especially the men who fought and died on the field of battle, who vaguely but firmly hoped for this change. And there were those hundreds of millions of the dispossessed and exploited and racially discriminated against in Europe and America, and much more so in Asia and Africa, who could not isolate the war from their memories of the past and their present misery, and passionately hoped, even when hope was unreasonable, that the war would somehow lift the burdens that crushed them.

But the eyes of the leaders of the United Nations were turned elsewhere; they looked back to the past and not forward to the future. Sometimes they spoke eloquently of the future to appease the hunger of their people, but their policy had little to do with these fine phrases. For Mr. Winston Churchill it was a war of restoration and nothing more, a continuation, with minor changes, of both the social structure of England and the imperial structure of her empire. President Roosevelt spoke in terms of greater promise, but his policy had not been radically different. Still many people all over the world looked to him with hope as a man of vision and high statesmanship.

So the future for India and the rest of the world, in so far as the British ruling class could help it, would be in line with the past, and the present had necessarily to conform to it. In that very present the seeds of this future were being sown. The Cripps proposals, for all their seeming advance, created new and dangerous problems for us, which threatened to become insuperable barriers to freedom. To some extent they have already had this result. The all-pervading autocracy and authoritarianism of the British Government in India, and the widespread suppression of the most ordinary civil rights and liberties, had reached their further limits during, and under cover of, the war. No one in the present generation had experienced the like of these. They were constant reminders of our enslaved condition and continuing humiliation. They were also a presage of the future, of the shape of things to come, for out of this present, the future would grow. Anything seemed to be better than to submit to this degradation.

How many people out of India's millions felt this way is impossible to say. For most of those millions all conscious feeling has been deadened by poverty and misery. Among the others were those who had been corrupted by office or privilege or vested interest, or whose minds had been diverted by special claims. Yet the feeling was very widespread, varying in intensity and sometimes overlaid by other feelings. There were many gradations in it, from an intensity of belief and a desire to brave all hazards, which led inevitably to action, to a vague sympathy from a safe distance. Some, tragically inclined, felt suffocated and strangled at the lack of air to breathe in the oppressive atmosphere that surrounded them; others, living on the ordinary trivial plane, had more capacity to adapt themselves to conditions they disliked.

The background of the British governing personnel in India was entirely different. Indeed nothing is more striking than the vast gulf that separates the mind of the British and the Indians and, whoever may be right or wrong, this very fact demonstrates the utter incapacity of the British to function as a ruling class in India. For there must be some harmony, some common outlook, between the rulers and the ruled if there is to be any advance; otherwise there can only be conflict, actual or potential. The British in India have always represented the most conservative elements of Britain; between them and the liberal tradition in England there is little in common. The more years they spend in India, the more rigid they grow in outlook, and when they retire and go back to England, they become the experts who advise on Indian problems. They are convinced of their own rectitude, of the benefits and necessity of British rule in India, of their own high mission in being the representatives of the imperial tradition. Because the national Congress has challenged the whole basis of this rule and sought to rid India of it, it has become, in their eyes, Public Enemy No. 1. Sir Reginald Maxwell, the then Home Member of the Government of India, speaking in the Central Assemby in 1941, gave a revealing glimpse of his mind. He was defending himself against the charge that Congressmen and socialists and communists, detained without trial in prison, were subjected to inhuman treatment, far worse than that given to German and Italian prisoners of war. He said that Germans and Italians were, at any rate, fighting for their countries, but these others were enemies of society who wanted to subvert the existing order. Evidently, it seemed to him preposterous that an Indian should want freedom for his country or should want to change the economic structure of India. As between the two his sympathies were obviously for the Germans and Italians, though his own country was engaged in a bitter war against them. This was before Russia entered the war and it was safe then to condemn every attempt to change the social order. Before World War II began, admiration for the fascist régimes was frequently expressed. Had not Hitler himself said, in his 'Mein Kampf' and subsequently, that he wanted the British Empire to continue?

The Government of India certainly was anxious to help in every way in the war against the Axis powers. But in its mind that victory would be incomplete if it was not accompanied by another victory—the crushing of the nationalist movements in India as represented mainly by the Congress. The Cripps negotiations had perturbed it and it rejoiced at their failure. The way was now open to deal the final blow at the Congress and all those who sided with it. The moment was favourable, for at no previous time had there been such concentration of unlimited power, both at the centre and in the provinces, in the hands of the Viceroy and his principal subordinates. The war situation was a difficult one and it was a feasible argument that no opposition or trouble could be tolerated. Liberal elements in England and America, interested in India, had been quietened by the Cripps affair and the propaganda that followed. In England the ever-present feeling of self-righteousness in relation to India had grown. Indians, or many of them, it was felt there, were intransigent, troublesome persons, narrow in outlook, unable to appreciate the dangers of the situation, and probably in sympathy with the Japanese. Mr. Gandhi's articles and statements, it was said, had proved how impossible he was and the only way left open was to put an end to all this by crushing Gandhi and the Congress once for all.

Mass Upheavals and their Suppression

In the early morning of August 9th, 1942, numerous arrests were made all over India. What happened then? Only scraps of news trickled through to us after many weeks, and even now we can form only an incomplete picture of what took place. All the prominent leaders had been suddenly removed and no one seemed to know what should be done. Protests, of course, there had to be, and there were spontaneous demonstrations. These were broken up and fired upon, and tear-gas bombs were used; all the usual channels of giving expression to public feeling were stopped. And then all these suppressed emotions broke out and crowds gathered in cities and rural areas and came in conflict with the police and the military. They attacked especially what seemed to them the symbols of British authority and power, the police stations, post offices, and railway stations; they cut the telegraph and telephone wires. These unarmed and leaderless mobs faced police and military firing, according to official statements, on

538 occasions, and they were also machine-gunned from low-flying aircraft. For a month or two or more these disturbances continued in various parts of the country and then they dwindled away and gave place to sporadic occurrences. 'The disturbances,' said Mr. Churchill in the House of Commons, 'were crushed with all the weight of the Government,' and he praised 'the loyalty and steadfastness of the brave Indian police as well as the Indian official class generally whose behaviour has been deserving of the highest praise.' He added that 'larger reinforcements have reached India and the number of white troops in that country is larger than at any time in the British connection.' These foreign troops and the Indian police had won many a battle against the unarmed peasantry of India and crushed their rebellion; and that other main prop of the British Raj in India, the official class, had helped, actively or passively, in the process.

This reaction in the country was extraordinarily widespread, both in towns and villages. In almost all the provinces and in a large number of the Indian states there were innumerable demonstrations, in spite of official prohibition. There were *hartals*, closure of shops and markets and a stoppage of business everywhere, varying in duration from a number of days to some weeks and, in a few cases, to over a month. So also labour strikes. More organized and used to disciplined group action, industrial workers in many important centres spontaneously declared strikes in protest against Government action in arresting national leaders. A notable instance of this was at the vital steel city of Jamshedpur where the skilled workers, drawn from all over India, kept away from work for a fortnight and only agreed to return on the management promising that they would try their best to get the Congress leaders released and a national government formed. In the great textile centre of Ahmedabad also there was a sudden and complete stoppage of work in all the numerous factories without any special call from the trade union.* This general strike in Ahmedabad continued peacefully for over three months in

*It has been stated by high Government officials, and frequently repeated by others, that these strikes, especially in Jamshedpur and Ahmedabad, were encouraged by the employers and millowners. This is hardly credible for the strikes involved the employers in very heavy losses, and I have yet to know big industrialists who work against their own interests in this manner. It is true that many industrialists sympathise with and desire India's independence, but their conception of India's freedom is necessarily one in which they have a secure place. They dislike revolutionary action and any vital change in the social structure. It is possible, however, that influenced by the depth and widespread character of public feeling in August and September, 1942, they refrained from adopting that aggressive and punitive attitude, in co-operation with the police, which they usually indulge in when strikes take place.

Another frequent assertion, almost taken for granted in British circles and the British press, is that the Indian Congress is heavily financed by the big industrialists. This is wholly untrue, and I ought to know something about it as I have been general secretary and president of the Congress for many years. A few industrialists have financially helped from time to time in the social reform activities of Gandhiji and the Congress, such as, village industries,

485

spite of all attempts to break it. It was a purely political and spontaneous reaction of the workers, and they suffered greatly, for it was a time of relatively high wages. They received no financial help whatever from outside during this long period. At other centres the strikes were of briefer duration, lasting sometimes only for a few days. Cawnpore, another big textile centre, had, so far as I know, no major strike, chiefly because the communist leadership there succeeded in averting it. In the railways also, which are Government-owned, there was no marked or general stoppage of work, except such as was caused by the disturbances, and this latter was considerable.

Among the provinces, the Punjab was probably the least affected, but there were many *hartals* and strikes even there. The North-West Frontier Province, almost exclusively Moslem in population, occupied a peculiar position. To begin with, there were no mass arrests or other provocative action there on the part of the Government, as in the other provinces. This may have been partly due to the fact that the frontier people were considered inflammable material, but also partly to the policy of Government to show that Moslems were keeping apart from the nationalist upheaval. But when news of happenings in the rest of India reached the Frontier Province there were numerous demonstrations and even aggressive challenges to British authority. There was firing on the demonstrators and the usual methods of suppressing popular activities were adopted. Several thousands of people were arrested, and even the great Pathan leader Badshah Khan (as Abdul Ghaffar Khan is popularly known) was seriously injured by police blows. This was extreme provocation and yet, surprisingly enough, the excellent discipline, which Abdul Ghaffar Khan had established among his people, held, and there were no violent disturbances there of the kind that occurred in many parts of the country.

The sudden, unorganized demonstrations and outbreaks on the part of the people, culminating in violent conflicts and destruction, and continued against overwhelming and powerful

---

abolition of untouchability and raising of depressed classes, basic education, etc. But they have kept scrupulously aloof from the political work of the Congress, even in normal times, and much more so during periods of conflict with government. Whatever their occasional sympathies, they believe, like most sober and well-established individuals, in safety first. Congress work has been carried on almost entirely on the petty subscriptions and donations of its large membership. Most of the work has been voluntary and unpaid. Occasionally, in the cities, the merchants have helped a little. The only exception to this was probably during the general elections of 1937 when some big industrialists contributed to the central election fund. Even this fund, considering the scope of our activity, was inconsiderable. It is astonishing, and it will be incredible to westerners, with what little money we have carried on our work in the Congress during the last quarter of a century — a period when India has been convulsed repeatedly by political activity and direct action movements. In the United Provinces, one of our most active and well-organized provinces, and one with which I am best acquainted, almost our entire work was based on the four anna subscriptions of our members.

armed forces, were a measure of the intensity of their feelings. Those feelings had been there even before the arrest of their leaders, but the arrests, and the frequent firings that followed them, roused the people to anger and to the only course that an enraged mob can follow. For a time there seems to have been a sense of uncertainty as to what should be done. There was no direction, no programme. There was no well-known person to lead them or tell them what to do, and yet they were too excited and angry to remain quiescent. As often happens in these circumstances, local leaders sprang up and were followed for the moment. But even the guidance they gave was little; it was essentially a spontaneous mass upheaval. All over India, the younger generation, especially university students, played an important part in both the violent and peaceful activities of 1942. Many universities were closed. Some of the local leaders attempted even then to pursue peaceful methods of action and civil disobedience, but this was difficult in the prevailing atmosphere. The people forgot the lesson of non-violence which had been dinned into their ears for more than twenty years, and yet they were wholly unprepared, mentally or otherwise, for any effective violence. That very teaching of non-violent methods produced doubt and hesitation and came in the way of violent action. If the Congress, forgetful of its creed, had previously given even a hint of violent action, there is no doubt that the violence that actually took place would have increased a hundred-fold.

But no such hint had been given, and, indeed, the last message of the Congress had again emphasized the importance of non-violence in action. Yet perhaps one fact had some effect on the public mind. If, as we had said, armed defence was legitimate and desirable against an enemy aggressor, why should that not apply to other forms of existing aggression? The prohibition of violent methods of attack and defence once removed had unintended results, and it was not easy for most people to draw fine distinctions. All over the world extreme forms of violence were prevailing and incessant propaganda encouraged them. It became then a question of expediency and of intensity of feeling. Then there were also people, outside or in the Congress, who never had any belief in non-violence and who were troubled with no scruples in regard to violent action.

But in the excitement of the moment few people think; they act in accordance with their long-suppressed urges which drive them forward. And so, for the first time since the great revolt of 1857, vast numbers of people again rose to challenge by force (but a force without arms!) the fabric of British rule in India. It was a foolish and inopportune challenge, for all the organized and armed force was on the other side, and in greater measure indeed than at any previous time in history. However great the numbers of the crowd, it cannot prevail in a contest of force against armed forces. It had to fail unless those armed forces themselves changed their allegiance. But those crowds had not prepared for the contest or chosen the time for it. It came upon them unawares and in their immediate reaction to it, however unthinking and misdirected it was, they showed their love of India's freedom and their hatred of foreign domination.

Though the policy of non-violence went under, for the time being at least, the long training that the people had received under it had one important and desirable result. In spite of the passions aroused there was very little, if any, racial feeling, and, on the whole, there was a deliberate attempt on the part of the people to avoid causing bodily injury to their opponents. There was a great deal of destruction of communications and governmental property, but even in the midst of this destruction care was taken to avoid loss of life. This was not always possible or always attempted, especially in actual conflicts with the police or other armed forces. According to official reports, so far as I have been able to find them, about 100 persons were killed by mobs in the course of the disturbances all over India. This figure is very small considering the extent and area of the disturbances and the conflicts with the police. One particularly brutal and distressing case was the murder of two Canadian airmen by a mob somewhere in Bihar. But, generally speaking, the absence of racial feeling was very remarkable.*

Official estimates of the number of people killed and wounded by police or military firing in the 1942 disturbances are: 1,028 killed and 3,200 wounded. These figures are certainly gross under-estimates for it has been officially stated that such firing took place on at least 538 occasions, and besides this people were frequently shot at by the police or the military from moving lorries. It is very difficult to arrive at even an approximately correct figure. Popular estimates place the number of deaths at 25,000, but probably this is an exaggeration. Perhaps 10,000 may be nearer the mark.

It was extraordinary how British authority ceased to function

*A revealing incident is reported in 'British Soldier Looks at India,' being letters of Clive Branson. Branson was an artist and a communist. He served in the International Brigade in Spain, and in 1941 joined the Royal Armoured Corps, in which he was a sergeant. He was sent to India with his regiment in 1942. In February, 1944, he was killed in action in Arakan in Burma. He was in Bombay in August, 1942, after the arrest of the Congress leaders, and at a time when the people of Bombay were seething with anger and passion and were being shot down. Branson is reported to have said: 'What a clean healthy nationalism you have! I asked people the way to the Communist Party's office. I was in uniform. Men like me were shooting unarmed Indians, and naturally I was a little worried. I wondered how I would be treated. But everyone whom I asked was anxious to help—not one tried to insult or mislead me.'

over many areas, both rural and urban, and it took many days, and sometimes weeks, for a 'reconquest', as it was often termed. This happened particularly in Bihar, in the Midnapur district of Bengal and in the south-eastern districts of the United Provinces. It is note-worthy that in the district of Ballia in the United Provinces (which had to be 'reconquered') there have been no serious allegations of physical violence and injury to human beings caused by the crowds, so far as one can judge from the numerous subsequent trials by special tribunals. The ordinary police proved incapable of meeting the situation. Early in 1942, however, a new force called the Special Armed Constabulary (S.A.C.) had been created and this had been especially trained to deal with popular demonstrations and disturbances. This played an important part in curbing and suppressing the people and often functioned after the manner of the 'Black and Tans' in Ireland. The Indian army was not often used in this connection, except for certain groups and classes in it. British soldiers were more often employed, and also the Gurkhas. Sometimes Indian soldiers as well as the special police were sent to distant parts of the country where they functioned more or less as strangers, being unacquainted with the language.

If the reaction of the crowd was natural, so also, in the circumstances, was the reaction of the government. It had to crush both the impromptu frenzy of the mob and the peaceful demonstrations of other people and, in the interests of its own self-preservation, attempt to destroy those whom it considered its enemies. If it had had the capacity or desire to understand and appreciate what moved the people so powerfully, the crisis would not have risen at all and India's problem would have been nearer solution. The government had prepared carefully to crush once for all, as it thought, any challenge to its authority; it had taken the initiative and chosen the time for its first blow; it had removed to its prisons thousands of men and women who had played a prominent part in the nationalist, the labour, and the peasant movements. Yet it was surprised and taken aback by the upheaval that suddenly convulsed the country and, momentarily, its widespread apparatus of repression was disjoined. But it had enormous resources at its command and it utilized them to crush both the violent and non-violent manifestations of the rebellion. Many of the upper and richer classes, timidly nationalist, and sometimes even critical of government, were frightened by this exhibition of mass action on an All-India scale, which cared little for vested interests and smelt not only of political revolution but also of social change. As the success of the government in crushing the rebellion became apparent, the waverers and the opportunists lined up with it and began to curse all those who had dared to challenge authority.

The external evidences of rebellion having been crushed, its very roots had to be pulled out, and so the whole apparatus of government was turned in this direction in order to enforce complete submission to British domination. Laws could be produced over-night by the Viceroy's decree or ordinance, but even the formalities of these laws were reduced to a minimum. The decisions of the Federal Court and the High Courts, which were creations and emblems of British authority, were flouted and ignored by the executive, or a new ordinance was issued to override those decisions. Special tribunals (which were subsequently held by the courts to be illegal) were established, functioning without the trammels of the ordinary rules of procedure and evidence, and these sentenced thousands to long terms of imprisonment and many even to death. The police (and especially the Special Armed Constabulary) and the secret service were all powerful and became the chief organs of the state, and could indulge in any illegalities or brutalities without criticism or hindrance. Corruption grew to giant proportions. Vast numbers of students in schools and colleges were punished in various ways and thousands of young men were flogged. Public activity of all kinds was prohibited unless it was in favour of the government.

But the greatest sufferers were the simple-hearted, poverty-stricken villagers of the rural areas. Suffering, for many generations, had been the badge of their tribe; they had ventured to look up and hope, to dream of better times; they had even roused themselves to action; whether they had been foolish or mistaken or not, they had proved their loyalty to the cause of Indian freedom. Their effort had failed, and the burden had fallen on their bent shoulders and broken bodies. Cases were reported of whole villages being sentenced from flogging to death. It was stated on behalf of the Bengal Government that 'Government forces burnt 193 Congress camps and houses in the sub-divisions of Tamluk and Contai before and after the cyclone of 1942.' The cyclone had worked havoc in that area and created a wilderness but that made no difference to the official policy.

Huge sums were imposed on villages as a whole as punitive fines. According to Mr. Amery's statement in the House of Commons, the total collective fines amounted to rupees ninety lakhs (9,000,000), and out of this Rs. 7,850,000 were realized. How these vast sums were realized from starving wretches is another matter, and nothing that took place in 1942 or after, not the shooting and the burning by the police, caused such an intensity of suffering as this forcible realization. Not merely were the fines imposed realized, but often much more, the excess vanishing in the process of realization.

All the conventions and subterfuges that usually veil the activities of governments were torn aside and only naked force remained as the symbol of power and authority. There was no further need for subterfuge for the British power had succeeded, at least for the time being, in crushing both the non-violent and violent attempts made to replace it by a national authority and stood supreme in India. India had failed in that final test when strength and power only count and all else is mere quibbling and irrelevance. She had failed not only because of British armed might and the confusion produced by the war situation in people's minds, but also because many of her own people were not prepared for that last sacrifice which freedom requires. So the British felt they had firmly re-established their rule in India and they saw no reason to loosen their hold again.

Reactions Abroad

A strict censorship cast a heavy veil over the happenings in India. Even newspapers in India were not permitted to give publicity to much that was daily taking place, and messages to foreign countries were subject to an ever stricter surveillance. At the same time official propaganda was let loose abroad and false and tendentious accounts were circulated. The United States of America were especially flooded with this propaganda, for opinion there was held to count, and hundreds of lecturers and others, both English and Indian, were sent there to tour the country.

Even apart from this propaganda, it was natural in England, suffering the strain and anxiety of war, for resentment to be felt against Indians and especially those who were adding to their troubles in time of crisis. One-sided propaganda added to this and, even more so, the conviction of the British in their own righteousness. Their very lack of awareness of others' feelings had been their strength and it continued to justify actions taken on their behalf, and to cast the blame for any mishap on the iniquity of others who were so blind to the obvious virtues of the British. Those virtues had now been justified afresh by the success of British forces and the Indian police in crushing those in India who had ventured to doubt them. Empire had been justified and Mr. Winston Churchill declared, with special reference to India: 'I have not become the King's first minister in order to preside over the liquidation of the British Empire.' In saying so, Mr. Churchill undoubtedly represented the viewpoint of the vast majority of his people, and even of many who had previously criticized the theory and practice of imperialism. The leaders of the British Labour Party, anxious to demonstrate that they were behind no other group in their attachment to the imperial tradition, supported Mr. Churchill's statement and 'stressed the resolve of the British people to keep the empire together after the war.'

In America, opinion, in so far as it was interested in the far away problem of India, was divided, for people there were not equally convinced of the virtues of the British ruling class and looked with some disapproval on other peoples' empires. They were also anxious to gain India's goodwill and utilize her resources fully in the war against Japan. Yet one-sided and tendentious propaganda inevitably produced results, and there was a feeling that the Indian problem was far too complicated for them to tackle, and anyway it was difficult for them to interfere in the affairs of their British ally.

What those in authority, or people generally, in Russia thought about India it was impossible to say. They were far too busy with their stupendous war effort, and with driving the invader from their country, to think of matters of no immediate concern to them. Yet they were used to thinking far ahead and they were not likely to ignore India which touched their frontiers in Asia. What their future policy would be no one could say, except that it would be realistic and principally concerned with adding to the political and economic strength of the U.S.S.R. They had carefully avoided all reference to India, but Stalin had declared in November, 1942, on the occasion of the twenty-fifth anniversary of the Soviet Revolution, that their general policy was: 'Abolition of racial exclusiveness, equality of nations and integrity of their territories, liberation of the enslaved nations and restoration of their sovereign rights, the right of every nation to arrange its affairs as it wishes, economic aid to nations that have suffered and assistance to them in attaining their material welfare, restoration of democratic liberties, the destruction of the Hitlerite regime.'

In China, it was evident that, whatever the reaction of the people to any particular action of ours, their sympathies were entirely on the side of Indian freedom. That sympathy had historical roots, but, even more so, it was based on the realization that unless India was free, China's freedom might be endangered. It was not in China only but throughout Asia, Egypt, and the Middle East, Indian freedom had become a symbol of a larger freedom for other subject and dependent countries, a test in the present and a measuring rod for the future. Mr. Wendell Willkie in his book—'One World'—says: 'Many men and women I have talked with from Africa to Alaska asked me the question which has become almost a symbol all through Asia: What about India? ...From Cairo on, it confronted me at every turn. The wisest man in China said to me: "When the aspiration of India for freedom was put aside to some future date, it was not Great Britain that suffered in public esteem in the Far East. It was the United States."'

What had happened in India had compelled the world to look at India for a while, even in the midst of the war crisis, and to think of the basic problems of the east; it had stirred the mind and heart of every country of Asia. Even though, for the moment, the Indian people appeared helpless in the powerful grip of British imperialism, they had demonstrated that there would be no peace in India or Asia unless India was free.

Reactions in India

Foreign rule over a civilized community suffers from many disadvantages and many ills follow in its train. One of these disadvantages is that it has to rely on the less desirable elements in the population.. The idealists, the proud, the sensitive, the self-respecting, those who care sufficiently for freedom and are not prepared to degrade themselves by an enforced submission to an alien authority, keep aloof or come into conflict with it. The proportion of careerists and opportunists in its ranks is much higher than it would normally be in a free country. Even in an independent country with an autocratic form of government many sensitive people are unable to co-operate in governmental activities, and there are very few opportunities for the release of new talent.

An alien government, which must necessarily be authoritarian suffers from all these disadvantages and adds to them, for it has always to function in an atmosphere of hostility and suppression. Fear becomes the dominant motive of both the government and the people, and the most important services are the police and the secret service.

When there is an actual conflict between the Government and the people, this tendency to rely on and encourage the undesirable elements in the population becomes even more strongly marked. Many conscientious people, of course, through force of circumstances, have to continue functioning in the governmental structure, whether they like it or not. But those who come to the top and play the most important roles are chosen for their anti-nationalism, their subservience, their capacity to crush and humiliate their own countrymen. The highest merit is opposition, often the result of personal rivalries and disappointments, to the sentiments and feelings of the great majority of the people.

In this turgid and unwholesome atmosphere no idealism or noble sentiment has any place, and the prizes held out are high positions and big salaries. The incompetence or worse failings of the supporters of government have to be tolerated, for the measure of everything is the active support given to that government in crushing its opponents. This leads to government cohabiting with strange groups and very odd persons. Corruption, cruelty, callousness, and a complete disregard of the public welfare flourish and poison the air.*

*The Bengal Administrative Inquiry Committee, presided over by Sir Archibald R wlands,

While much that the Government does is bitterly resented, far greater resentment is caused by those Indian supporters of it who become more royalist than the king. The average Indian has a feeling of disgust and nausea at this behaviour, and to him such people are comparable to the men of Vichy or the puppet régimes set up by the German and Japanese governments. This feeling is not confined to Congress men but extends to members of the Moslem League and other organizations, and is expressed even by the most moderate of our politicians.*

The war afforded a sufficient excuse and was a cover for intense anti-national activities of the Government and novel forms of propaganda. Mushroom labour groups were financed to build up 'labour morale,' and newspapers containing scurrilous attacks on Gandhi and the Congress were started and subsidized, in spite of the paper shortage which came in the way of other newspapers functioning. Official advertisements, supposed to be connected with the war effort, were also utilized for this purpose. Information centres were opened in foreign countries to carry on continuous propaganda on behalf of the Government of India. Crowds of undistinguished and often unknown individuals were sent on officially organized deputations, especially to the U.S.A., despite the protest of the central assembly, to act as propaganda agents and stools of the British Government. Persons holding independent views or critical of Government policy had no chance of going abroad; they could neither get a passport nor transport facilities.

All these and many other devices have been employed by the Government during the last two years to create a semblance of what it considers 'public tranquillity.' Political and public life becomes dormant, as, indeed, it must in a country more or less under military occupation and rule. But this forcible suppres-

---

in their report, issued in May, 1945, say: 'So widespread has corruption become, and so defeatist is the attitude taken towards it, that we think that the most drastic steps should be taken to stamp out the evil which has corrupted the public service and public morals.' The Committee received, with surprise and regret, evidence that the attitude of some civil servants towards the public left much to be desired. It was stated that 'they adopt an attitude of aloof superiority, appear to pay greater regard to the mechanical operation of a soulless machine than to promoting the welfare of the people and look upon themselves rather as masters than as servants of the people.'

*Hitler, an expert in compelling others to submit to his yoke, says in 'Mein Kampf': 'We must not expect embodiments of characterless submission suddenly to repent in order, on the basis of intelligence and all human experience, to act otherwise than hitherto. On the contrary, these very people will hold every such lesson at a distance, until the notion is either once and for all accustomed to its slave's yoke, or until better forces push to the surface to wrest power from the infamous corrupters. In the first case these people continue to feel not at all badly since they not infrequently are entrusted by the victors with the office of slave overseer, which these characterless types then exercise over their own nation and that generally more heartlessly than any alien beast imposed by the enemy himself.'

sion of symptoms can only cause an aggravation of the disease, and India is very sick. Prominent Indian conservatives, who have always tried to co-operate with the Government, have been filled with anxiety at this volcano which has been temporarily sealed at its mouth, and they have stated that they have never known such bitterness against the British Government.

I do not know and cannot tell till I come into contact with my people how they have changed during these two years and what feelings stir in their hearts, but I have little doubt that these recent experiences have changed them in many ways. I have looked into my own mind from time to time and examined its almost involuntary reaction to events. I had always looked forward in the past to a visit to England, because I have many friends there and old memories draw me. But now I found that there was no such desire and the idea was distasteful. I wanted to keep as far away from England as possible, and I had no wish even to discuss India's problems with Englishmen. And then I remembered some friends and softened a little, and I told myself how wrong it was to judge a whole people in this way. I thought also of the terrible experiences that the English people had gone through in this war, of the continuous strain in which they had lived, of the loss of so many of their loved ones. All this helped to tone down my feelings, but that basic reaction remained. Probably time and the future will lessen it and give another perspective. But if I, with all my associations with England and the English, could feel that way, what of others who had lacked those contacts?

India's Sickness: Famine

India was very sick, both in mind and body. While some people had prospered during the war, the burden on others had reached breaking point, and as an awful reminder of this came famine, a famine of vast dimensions affecting Bengal and east and south India. It was the biggest and most devastating famine in India during the past 170 years of British dominion, comparable to those terrible famines which occurred from 1766 to 1770 in Bengal and Bihar as an early result of the establishment of British rule. Epidemics followed, especially cholera and malaria, and spread to other provinces, and even to-day they are taking their toll of scores of thousands of lives. Millions have died of famine and disease and yet that spectre hovers over India and claims its victims.*

*Estimates of the number of deaths by famine in Bengal in 1943-44 vary greatly. The Department of Anthropology of the Calcutta University carried out an extensive scientific survey of sample groups in the famine areas. They arrived at the figure of about 3,400,000 total deaths by famine in Bengal. It was also found that during 1943 and 1944, 46 per

This famine unveiled the picture of India as it was below the thin veneer of the prosperity of a small number of people at the top—a picture of poverty and ugliness of British rule. That was the culmination and fulfilment of British rule in India. It was no calamity of nature or play of the elements that brought this famine, nor was it caused by actual war operations and enemy blockade. Every competent observer is agreed that it was a man-made famine which could have been foreseen and avoided. Every one is agreed that there was amazing indifference, incompetence, and complacency shown by all the authorities concerned. Right up to the last moment, when thousands were dying daily in the public streets, famine was denied and references to it in the Press were suppressed by the censors. When the *Statesman*, newspaper of Calcutta, published gruesome and ghastly pictures of starving and dying women and children in the streets of Calcutta, a spokesman of the Government of India, speaking officially in the central assembly, protested against the 'dramatization' of the situation; to him apparently it was a normal occurrence for thousands to die daily from starvation in India. Mr. Amery, of the India Office in London, distinguished himself especially by his denials and statements. And then, when it became impossible to deny or cloak the existence of widespread famine, each group in authority blamed some other group for it. The Government of India said it was the fault of the provincial government, which itself was merely a puppet government functioning under the Governor and through the civil service. They were all to blame, but most of all inevitably that authoritarian government which the Viceroy represented in his person and which could do what it chose anywhere in India. In any democratic or semi-democratic country such a calamity would have swept away all the governments concerned with it. Not so in India where everything continued as before.

Considered even from the point of view of the war, this famine took place in the very region which stood nearest to the theatre of war and possible invasion. A widespread famine and collapse of the economic structure would inevitably injure the capacity for defence and even more so for offence. Thus did the Government of India discharge its responsibility for India's defence and the prosecution of the war against the Japanese aggressors. Not scorched earth but scorched and starved and dead human beings

cent *of the people of Bengal suffered from major diseases. Official figures of the Bengal Government, based largely on unreliable reports from village patwaris or headmen, gave a much lower figure. The official Famine Inquiry Commission, presided over by Sir John Woodhead, has come to the conclusion that about 1,500,000 deaths occurred in Bengal 'as a direct result of the famine and the epidemics which followed in its train.' All these figures relate to Bengal alone. Many other parts of the country also suffered from famine and epidemic diseases consequent upon it.*

by the million in this vital war area were the emblems of the policy that Government had pursued.

Indian non-official organizations from all over the country did good work in bringing relief, and so did those efficient humanitarians, the Quakers of England. The central and provincial governments also at last woke up and realized the immensity of the crisis and the army was utilized in the relief operations. For the moment something was done to check the spread of famine and mitigate its after-effects. But the relief was temporary and those after-effects continue, and no one knows when famine may not descend again on an even worse scale. Bengal is broken up, her social and economic life shattered, and an enfeebled generation left as survivors.

While all this was happening and the streets of Calcutta were strewn with corpses, the social life of the upper ten thousand of Calcutta underwent no change. There was dancing and feasting and a flaunting of luxury, and life was gay. There was no rationing even till a much later period. The horse races in Calcutta continued and attracted their usual fashionable throngs. Transport was lacking for food, but racehorses came in special boxes by rail from other parts of the country. In this gay life both Englishmen and Indians took part for both had prospered in the business of war and money was plentiful. Sometimes that money had been gained by profiteering in the very foodstuffs, the lack of which was killing tens of thousands daily.

India, it is often said, is a land of contrasts, of some very rich and many very poor, of modernism and mediævalism, of rulers and ruled, of the British and Indians. Never before had these contrasts been so much in evidence as in the city of Calcutta during those terrible months of famine in the latter half of 1943. The two worlds, normally living apart, almost ignorant of each other, were suddenly brought physically together and existed side by side. The contrast was startling, but even more startling was the fact that many people did not realize the horror and astonishing incongruity of it and continued to function in their old grooves. What they felt one cannot say; one can only judge them by their actions. For most Englishmen this was perhaps easier for they had lived their life apart and, caste-bound as they were, they could not vary their old routine, even if some individuals felt the urge to do so. But those Indians who functioned in this way showed the wide gulf that separated them from their own people, which no considerations even of decency and humanity could bridge.

The famine, like every great crisis, brought out both the good qualities and the failings of the Indian people. Large numbers of them, including the most vital elements, were in prison and unable to help in any way. Still the relief works, organized unofficially, drew men and women from every class who laboured hard under discouraging circumstances, displaying ability, the spirit of mutual help and co-operation and self-sacrifice. The failings were also evident in those who were too full of their petty rivalries and jealousies to co-operate together, those who remained passive and did nothing to help others, and those few who were so denationalized and dehumanized as to care little for what was happening.

The famine was a direct result of war conditions and the carelessness and complete lack of foresight of those in authority. The indifference of the authorities to the problem of the country's food passes comprehension when every intelligent man who gave thought to the matter knew that some such crisis was approaching. The famine could have been avoided, given proper handling of the food situation in the earlier years of the war. In every other country affected by the war full attention was paid to this vital aspect of war economy even before the war started.

In India, the Government of India started a food department three and a quarter years after the war began in Europe and over a year after the Japanese war started. And yet it was common knowledge that the Japanese occupation of Burma vitally affected Bengal's food supply. The Government of India had no policy at all in regard to food till the middle of 1943 when famine was already beginning its disastrous career. It is most extraordinary how inefficient the Government always is in every matter other than the suppression of those who challenge its administration. Or perhaps it is more correct to say that, constituted as it is, its mind is completely occupied in its primary task of ensuring its own continuance. Only an actual crisis forces it to think of other matters. That crisis again is accentuated by the ever-present crisis of want of confidence in the Government's ability and bona fides.*

*The Famine Inquiry Commission, presided over by Sir John Woodhead (Report published in May, 1945), reveal in restrained official language the tragic succession of official errors and private greed which led to the Bengal famine. 'It has been for us a sad task,' they say, 'to inquire into the course and causes of the Bengal famine. We have been haunted by a deep sense of tragedy. A million and a half of the poor of Bengal fell victims to circumstances for which they themselves were not responsible. Society, together with its organs, failed to protect its weaker members. Indeed there was a moral and social breakdown, as well as administrative breakdowns.' They refer to the low economic level of the province, to the increasing pressure on land not relieved by growth of industry, to the fact that a considerable section of the population was living on the margin of subsistence and was uncapable of standing any severe economic stress, to the very bad health conditions and low standards of nutrition, to the absence of a 'margin of safety' as regards either health or wealth. They consider the more immediate causes to be: the failure of the season's crop, the fall of Burma leading to stoppage of imports of Burma rice, to the 'denial' policy of Government which brought ruin to certain poorer classes, to the military demands on food and transport, and the lack of confidence in the Government. They condemn the policy, or often the lack of policy or the ever-changing policy, of both the Government of India and of the Bengal Government; their inability to think ahead and provide for coming events; their refusal to recognize and declare

Though the famine was undoubtedly due to war conditions and could have been prevented, it is equally true that its deeper causes lay in the basic policy which was impoverishing India and under which millions lived on the verge of starvation. In 1933 Major General Sir John Megaw, the Director-General of the Indian Medical Service, wrote in the course of a report on public health in India: 'Taking India as a whole the dispensary doctors regard 39 per cent of the people as being well nourished, 41 per cent as poorly nourished, and 20 per cent as very badly nourished. The most depressing picture is painted by the doctors of Bengal who regard only 22 per cent of the people of the province as being well nourished while 31 per cent are considered to be very badly nourished.'

The tragedy of Bengal and the famines of Orissa, Malabar, and other places are the final judgment on British rule in India. The British will certainly leave India, and their Indian Empire will become a memory, but what will they leave when they have to go, what human degradation and accumulated sorrow? Tagore saw this picture as he lay dying three years ago: 'But what kind of India will they leave behind, what stark misery? When the stream of their centuries' administration runs dry at last, what a waste of mud and filth they will leave behind them!'

India's Dynamic Capacity

The stream of life goes on in spite of famine and war, full of its inherent contradictions, and finding sustenance even in those contradictions and the disasters that follow in their train. Nature renews itself and covers yesterday's battlefield with flowers and

famine even when it had come; their totally inadequate measures to meet the situation. They go on to say: 'But often considering all the circumstances, we cannot avoid the conclusion that it lay in the power of the Government of Bengal, by bold, resolute and well-conceived measures at the right time to have largely prevented the tragedy of the famine as it actually took place. Further, that the Government of India failed to recognize at a sufficiently early date the need for a system of planned movement of food grains.... The Government of India must share with the Bengal Government responsibility for the decision to decontrol in March, 1943.... The subsequent proposal of the Government of India to introduce free trade throughout the greater part of India was quite unjustified and should not have been put forward. Its application, successfully resisted by many of the provinces and states...might have led to serious catastrophies in various parts of India.'

After referring to the apathy and mismanagement of the governmental apparatus both at the centre and in the province, the Commission say that 'the public in Bengal, or at least certain sections of it, have also their share of blame. We have referred to the atmosphere of fear and greed which, in the absence of control, was one of the causes of the rapid rise in the price level. Enormous profits were made out of the calamity, and in the circumstances profits for some meant death for others. A large part of the community lived in plenty while others starved, and there was much indifference in face of suffering. Corruption was widespread throughout the province and in many classes of society.' The total profit made in this traffic of starvation and death is estimated at 150 crores of rupees (Rs. 1,500 millions). Thus if there were a million and a half deaths by famine, each death was balanced by roughly a 1,000 rupees of excess profit!

green grass, and the blood that was shed feeds the soil and gives strength and colour to new life. Human beings with their unique quality of possessing memory live in their storied and remembered pasts and seldom catch up to the present in 'The worlde that neweth every daie.' And that present slips into the past before we are hardly aware of it; to-day, child of yesterday, yields place to its own offspring, to-morrow. Winged victory ends in a welter of blood and mud; and out of the heavy trials of seeming defeat the spirit emerges with new strength and wider vision. The weak in spirit yield and are eliminated, but others carry the torch forward and hand it to the standard-bearers of to-morrow.

The famine in India brought some realization of the terrible urgency of India's problems, of the overwhelming disaster that hung over the country. What people in England felt about it I do not know, but some of them, as is their way, cast the blame on India and her people. There was lack of food, lack of doctors, lack of sanitation and medical supplies, lack of transport, lack of everything except human beings, for the population had grown and seemed to be growing. This excessive population of an improvident race, growing without notice or warning and upsetting the plans or planlessness of a benevolent government, must be to blame. And so, economic problems suddenly assumed a new importance and we were told that politics and political problems had to be put aside, as if politics has any meaning at all unless it can solve the major problems of the day. The Government of India, one of the few representatives of the *laissez-faire* tradition in the world, began to talk of planning, but of organized planning it had no notion. It could only think in terms of preserving the existing structure and its own and allied vested interests.

The reaction on the people of India was deeper and more powerful, though it found little public expression owing to the widespread tentacles of the Defence of India Act and its rules. There had been a complete collapse of the economic structure of Bengal and tens of millions of people had been literally broken up. Bengal was an extreme example of what was happening in many parts of India and it seemed that there could be no going back to the old economy. Even the industrialists who had prospered so much during the war were shaken up and compelled to look beyond their narrow sphere. They were realists in their own way, rather afraid of the idealism of some of the politicians, but that realism itself led them to far-reaching conclusions. A number of Bombay industrialists, chiefly connected with the Tata enterprises, produced a fifteen-year plan for India's development. That plan is still not complete and there are many lacunæ in it. Inevitably it is conditioned by the ways of thinking of big industry and tries to avoid revolutionary changes as far as possible. Yet the very pressure of events in India has forced them to think in a big way and to go out of many of their accustomed grooves of thought. Revolutionary changes are inherent in the plan, though the authors may themselves not like some of them. Some of these authors of the plan were members of the national planning committee and they have taken advantage of a part of its work. This plan will undoubtedly have to be varied, added to and worked out in many ways, but, coming from conservative quarters, it is a welcome and encouraging sign of the way India must go. It is based on a free India and on the political and economic unity of India. The conservative banker's view of money is not allowed to dominate the scene, and it is emphasized that the real capital of the country consists of its resources in material and manpower. The success of this or any other plan must inevitably depend not merely on production but on a proper and equitable distribution of the national wealth created. Also, agrarian reform is a fundamental prerequisite.

The idea of planning and a planned society is accepted now in varying degrees by almost everyone. But planning by itself has little meaning and need not necessarily lead to good results. Everything depends on the objectives of the plan and on the controlling authority, as well as, of course, the government behind it. Does the plan aim definitely at the well-being and advancement of the people as a whole, at the opening out of opportunity to all and the growth of freedom and methods of co-operative organization and action? Increase of production is essential, but obviously by itself it does not take us far and may even add to the complexity of our problems. An attempt to preserve old-established privileges and vested interests cuts at the very root of planning. Real planning must recognize that no such special interests can be allowed to come in the way of any scheme designed to further the well-being of the community as a whole. The Congress governments in the provinces were hampered and restricted in all directions by the basic assumption of the Parliamentary statute that most of these vested interests must not be touched. Even their partial attempts to change the land tenure system and to impose an income-tax on incomes from land were challenged in the law courts.

If planning is largely controlled by big industrialists, it will naturally be envisaged within the framework of the system they are used to, and will be essentially based on the profit motive of an acquisitive society. However well-intentioned they might be, and some of them certainly are full of good intentions, it is difficult for them to think on new lines. Even when they talk of state control of industry they think of the state more or less as it is to-day.

We are sometimes told that the present Government of India, with its ownership and control of railways, and a growing control of and interference in industry, finance, and, indeed, life in general, is moving in a socialist direction. But this is something utterly different from democratic state control, apart from being essentially foreign control. Though there is a limitation of certain capitalist functions, the system is based on the protection of privilege. The old authoritarian colonial system ignored economic problems except in so far as certain special interests were concerned. Finding itself unable to meet the necessities of the new situation by its old *laissez-faire* methods, and yet bent on preserving its authoritarian character, it goes inevitably in a fascist direction. It tries to control economic operations by fascist methods, suppresses such civil liberties as exist, and adapts its own autocratic government as well as the capitalist system, with some variations, to the new conditions. Thus the endeavour is, as in fascist countries, to build up a monolithic state, with considerable control of industry and national life, and with many limitations on free enterprise, but based on the old foundations. This is very far from socialism; indeed, it is absurd to talk of socialism in a country dominated by an alien power. Whether such an attempt can succeed, even in a temporary sense, is very doubtful, for it only aggravates the existing problems; but war conditions certainly give it a favourable environment to work in. Even a complete nationalization (so-called) of industry unaccompanied by political democracy will lead only to a different kind of exploitation, for while industry will then belong to the state, the state itself will not belong to the people.

Our major difficulties in India are due to the fact that we consider our problems – economic, social, industrial, agricultural, communal, Indian states—within the framework of existing conditions. Within that framework, and retaining the privileges and special status that are part of it, they become impossible of solution. Even if some patchwork solution is arrived at under stress of circumstances, it does not and cannot last. The old problems continue and new problems, or new aspects of old problems, are added to them. This approach of ours is partly due to tradition and old habit, but essentially it is caused by the steel-frame of the British Government which holds together the ramshackle structure.

The war has accentuated the many contradictions existing in India—political, economic, and social. Politically, there is a great deal of talk of Indian freedom and independence, and yet her people have probably at no time in their long history been subjected to such authoritarian rule and intensive and widespread repression as exist to-day, and out of this to-day to-morrow will necessarily grow. Economically, British domination is also paramount, and yet the expansive tendency of Indian economy is continually straining at the leash. There is famine and widespread misery and, on the other hand, there is an accumulation of capital. Poverty and riches go side by side, decay and building up, disruption and unity, dead thought and new. Behind all the distressing features there is an inner vitality which cannot be suppressed.

Outwardly the war has encouraged India's industrial growth and production, and yet it is doubtful how far this has led to the establishment of new industries, or is merely an extension and diversion of old industries. The apparent stability of the index of India's industrial activity during war-time indicates that no fundamental advance has been made. Indeed, some competent observers are of the opinion that the war and British policy during it have actually had a hampering effect on India's industrial growth. Dr. John Mathai, an eminent economist and a director of Tata's, said recently: 'The general belief...that the war has tremendously accelerated India's industrial progress is a proposition which, to say the least, would need a lot of proving. While it is true that certain established industries have increased their production in response to the war demand, several new industries of fundamental importance to the country, which had been projected before the war have, under stress of war conditions, been either abandoned or been unable to reach completion. My personal view is that, on a careful balance of the various factors in the situation, it will be found that, unlike countries such as Canada and Australia, the war has been more a hampering than an accelerating influence in India. I agree, however...that India has sufficient potential capacity to supply her basic manufactured needs.' Such statistical evidence of industrial activity as is available supports this view, and indicates that if pre-war progress could have been maintained at the old rate it would have led not only to the establishment of new industries, but also to far greater production as a whole.*

What the war has demonstrated beyond a shadow of a doubt is India's capacity to convert this potential into actuality with remarkable speed, given the opportunity to do so. Functioning as an economic unit, she has accumulated large capital assets

*Mr. J. R. D. Tata, speaking in London on May 30th, 1945, also denied that the war had enabled India materially to expand her industries and industrial capacity. 'There may have been isolated cases of expansion, but on the whole, when armament factories and other specialized industries connected with the war have been excluded, there has been none. A number of projects would have been started if there had been no war. I can speak from personal experience of projects that have been abandoned because of the impossibility of obtaining bricks, steel, and machinery. Those who talk about industrial and economic progress in India during the war do not know the true position.' Again he said: 'I must prick this bubble. It is nonsense to say that India has materially advanced and gained by the war. For one reason or another there has been no important progress or development in India. Rather there has been considerable retardation. In fact what has happened is this. As a result of the war and India's contribution towards it, we have millions dead in Bengal owing to famine. We also have had famine of cloth. Thus, it is clear, that economic progress has been conspicuous by its absence.'

within five war years, in spite of all the obstructions placed in her way. These assets are in the form of sterling securities which are not available to her and which, it is stated, will be blocked in the future. These sterling securities represent the expenditure incurred by the Government of India on behalf of the British Government as well as the U.S.A. They also represent the hunger, famine, epidemics, emasculation, weakened resistance, stunted growth, and death by starvation and disease of vast numbers of human beings in India.

Because of the accumulation of capital assets, India has paid off her big debt to England and has become a creditor country. Owing to gross negligence and mismanagement, tremendous suffering has been caused to the people of India, but the fact remains that India can accumulate these huge sums in a short period of time. The actual expenditure on the war incurred by India in five years greatly exceeds the total British investments in India during more than 100 years. This fact brings into proper perspective how little the progress made in India has been during the past century of British administration—railways, irrigation works and the like of which we hear so much. It also demonstrates the enormous capacity of India to advance with rapidity on all fronts. If this striking effort can be made under discouraging conditions and under a foreign government which disapproves of industrial growth in India, it is obvious that planned development under a free national government would completely change the face of India within a few years.

There is a curious habit of the British of appraising their economic and social achievement in present-day India by criteria derived from social achievement here or elsewhere in the distant past. They compare, with evident satisfaction to themselves, what they have done in India during their régime with changes made some hundreds of years ago. The fact that the industrial revolution, and more especially the vast technological improvements of the past fifty years or so, have entirely changed the pace and *tempo* of life somehow escapes them when they think of India. They forget also that India was not a barren, sterile, and barbarous country when they came here, but a highly evolved and cultured nation which had temporarily become static and backward in technical achievements.

What values and standards are we to apply in making such comparisons? The Japanese made Manchukuo within eight years highly industrialized for their own purposes; more coal was being produced there than in India after many generations of British effort. Their material record in Korea compares well with other colonial empires.* And yet behind these records there

*Hallett Abend, who was the New York Times correspondent in the Far East for many years, says in his book 'Pacific Charter' (1943): 'In fairness to the Japanese it must be conceded

is slavery, cruelty, humiliation, exploitation, and the attempt to destroy the soul of a people. The nazis and the Japanese have created new records in the inhuman suppression of subject peoples and races. We are often reminded of this and told that the British have not treated us quite so badly. Is that to be the new measure and standard of comparison and judgement?

There is a great deal of pessimism in India to-day and a sense of frustration, and both can be understood, for events have dealt harshly with our people and the future is not promising. But there is also below the surface a stirring and a pushing, signs of a new life and vitality, and unknown forces are at work. Leaders function at the top but they are driven in particular directions by the anonymous and unthinking will of an awakening people, who seem to be outgrowing their past.

India's Growth Arrested

A nation, like an individual, has many personalities, many approaches to life. If there is a sufficiently strong organic bond between these different personalities, it is well; otherwise those personalities split up and lead to disintegration and trouble. Normally, there is a continuous process of adjustment going on and some kind of an equilibrium is established. If normal development is arrested, or sometimes if there is some rapid change which is not easily assimilated, then conflict arises between those different personalities. In the mind and spirit of India, below the surface of our superficial conflicts and divisions, there has been this fundamental conflict due to a long period of arrested growth. A society, if it is to be both stable and progressive, must have a certain more or less fixed foundation of principles as well as a dynamic outlook. Both appear to be necessary. Without the dynamic outlook there is stagntaion and decay, without some fixed basis of principle there is likely to be disintegration and destruction.

In India from the earliest days there was a search for those basic principles, for the unchanging, the universal, the absolute. Yet the dynamic outlook was also present and an appreciation of life and the changing world. On these two foundations a

that in a material sense they have done a magnificent job in Korea. When they took it over the country was filthy, unhealthy, and woefully poverty-stricken. The mountains had been denuded of their forests, the valleys were subject to recurrent floods, decent roads were nonexistent, illiteracy was prevalent, and typhoid, smallpox, cholera, dysentery, and the plague were epidemic annually. To-day the mountains are reafforested; railway, telephone, and telegraph systems are excellent; the public health service is highly efficient, good highways abound; flood-control and irrigation works have vastly increased the food production, and fine harbours have been developed and well managed. The country has become so prosperous and healthy that the 1905 population of 11,000,000 has risen to 24,000,000 and the average scale of living to-day is almost immeasurably higher than it was at the turn of the century.' But Mr. Abend points out that all this material improvement has not been instituted for the benefit of the Korean people but so that greater profits might go to the Japanese.

stable and progressive society was built up, though the stress was always more on stability and security and the survival of the race. In later years the dynamic aspect began to fade away, and in the name of eternal principles the social structure was made rigid and unchanging. It was, as a matter of fact, not wholly rigid and it did change gradually and continuously. But the ideology behind it and the general framework continued unchanged. The group idea as represented by more or less autonomous castes, the joint family and the communal self-governing life of the village were the main pillars of this system, and all these survived for so long because, in spite of their failings, they fulfilled some essential needs of human nature and society. They gave security, stability to each group and a sense of group freedom. Caste survived because it continued to represent the general power-relationships of society, and class privileges were maintained, not only because of the prevailing ideology, but also because they were supported by vigour, intelligence, and ability, as well as a capacity for self-sacrifice. That ideology was not based on a conflict of rights but on the individual's obligations to others and a satisfactory performance of his duties, on co-operation within the group and between different groups, and essentially on the idea of promoting peace rather than war. While the social system was rigid, no limit was placed on the freedom of the mind.

Indian civilization achieved much that it was aiming at, but, in that very achievement, life began to fade away, for it is too dynamic to exist for long in a rigid, unchanging environment. Even those basic principles, which are said to be unchanging, lose their freshness and reality when they are taken for granted and the search for them ceases. Ideas of truth, beauty, and freedom decay, and we become prisoners following a deadening routine.

The very thing India lacked, the modern West possessed and possessed to excess. It had the dynamic outlook. It was engrossed in the changing world, caring little for ultimate principles, the unchanging, the universal. It paid little attention to duties and obligations and emphasized rights. It was active, aggressive, acquisitive, seeking power and domination, living in the present and ignoring the future consequences of its actions. Because it was dynamic, it was progressive and full of life, but that life was a fevered one and the temperature kept on rising progressively.

If Indian civilization went to seed because it became static, self-absorbed and inclined to narcissism, the civilization of the modern West, with all its great and manifold achievements, does not appear to have been a conspicuous success or to have thus far solved the basic problems of life. Conflict is inherent in it and periodically it indulges in self-destruction on a colossal scale. It seems to lack something to give it stability, some basic principles to give meaning to life though what these are I cannot say. Yet because it is dynamic and full of life and curiosity, there is hope for it.

India, as well as China, must learn from the West, for the modern West has much to teach, and the spirit of the age is represented by the West. But the West is also obviously in need of learning much and its advances in technology will bring it little comfort if it does not learn some of the deeper lessons of life, which have absorbed the minds of thinkers in all ages and in all countries.

India has become static and yet it would be utterly wrong to imagine that she was unchanging. No change at all means death. Her very survival as a highly evolved nation shows that there was some process of continuous adaptation going on. When the British came to India, though technologically somewhat backward, she was still among the advanced commercial nations of the world. Technical changes would undoubtedly have come and changed India as they have changed some western countries. But her normal development was arrested by the British power. Industrial growth was checked and as a consequence social growth was also arrested. The normal power-relationships of society could not adjust themselves and find an equilibrium, as all power was concentrated in the alien authority, which based itself on force and encouraged groups and classes which had ceased to have any real significance. Indian life thus progressively became more artificial, for many of the individuals and groups who seemed to play an important role in it had no vital functions left and were there only because of the importance given to them by the alien power. They had long ago finished their role in history and would have been pushed aside by new forces if they had not been given foreign protection. They became straw-stuffed symbols of protégés of foreign authority, thereby cutting themselves still further away from the living currents of the nation. Normally, they would have been weeded out or diverted to some more appropriate function by revolution or democratic process. But so long as foreign authoritarian rule continued, no such development could take place. And so India was cluttered up with these emblems of the past and the real changes that were taking place were hidden behind an artificial façade. No true social balances or power-relationships within society could develop or become evident, and unreal problems assumed an undue importance.

Most of our problems to-day are due to this arrested growth and the prevention by British authority of normal adjustments taking place. The problem of the Indian princes is easily capable of solution if the external factor is removed. The minorities problem is utterly unlike any minority problem elsewhere;

507

indeed it is not a minority problem at all. There are many aspects of it and no doubt we are to blame for it in the past and in the present. And yet, at the back of these and other problems is the desire of the British Government to preserve, as far as possible, the existing economy and political organization of the Indian people, and, for this purpose, to encourage and preserve the socially backward groups in their present condition. Political and economic progress has not only been directly prevented, but also made dependent on the agreement of reactionary groups and vested interests, and this may be purchased only by confirming them in their privileged positions or giving them a dominating voice in future arrangement, and thus putting formidable obstacles in the way of real change and progress. A new constitution, in order to have strength and effectiveness behind it, should not only represent the wishes of the vast majority of the people but should also reflect the inter-relation of social forces and their power relationships at the time. The main difficulty in India has been that constitutional arrangements for the future suggested by the British, or even by many Indians, ingore present social forces, and much more so potential ones which have long been arrested and are now breaking out, and try to impose and make rigid an order based on a past and vanishing relationship which has no real relevance to-day.

The fundamental reality in India is British military occupation and the policy which it supports. That policy has been expressed in many ways and has often been cloaked in dubious phrases, but latterly, under a soldier Viceroy, it has been expressed with clarity. That military occupation is to continue so long as the British can help it. But there are certain limits to the application of force. It leads not only to the growth of opposing forces but to many other consequences unthought of by those who rely upon it too much.

We see the consequences of this enforced stunting of India's growth and this arresting of her progress. The most obvious fact is the sterility of British rule in India and the thwarting of Indian life by it. Alien rule is inevitably cut off from the creative energies of the people it dominates. When this alien rule has its own economic and cultural centre far from the subject country and is further backed by racialism, this divorce is complete, and leads to spiritual and cultural starvation of the subject peoples. The only real scope that the nation's creative energy finds is in some kind of opposition to that rule, and yet that scope itself is limited and the outlook becomes narrow and one-sided. That opposition represents the conscious or unconscious effort of the living and growing forces to break through the shell that confines them and is thus a progressive and inevitable tendency. But it is too single-track and negative to have full touch with many aspects of reality in our lives. Complexes and prejudices and phobias grow and darken the mind, mental idols of the group and the community take shape, and slogans and set phrases take the place of inquiry into real problems. Within the farmework of a sterile alien rule no effective solutions are possible, and national problems, unable to find solution, become even more acute. We have arrived in India at a stage when no half measures can solve our problems, no advance on one sector is enough. There has to be a big jump and advance all along the line, or the alternative may be overwhelming catastrophe.

As in the world as a whole, so in India, it is a race between the forces of peaceful progress and construction and those of disruption and disaster, with each succeeding disaster on a bigger scale than the previous one. We can view this prospect as optimists or as pessimists, according to our predilections and mental make-up. Those who have faith in a moral ordering of the universe and of the ultimate triumph of virtue can, fortunately for them, function as lookers on or as helpers, and cast the burden on God; others will have to carry that burden on their own weak shoulders, hoping for the best and preparing for the worst.

Religion, Philosophy, and Science

India must break with much of her past and not allow it to dominate the present. Our lives are encumbered with the dead wood of this past; all that is dead and has served its purpose has to go. But that does not mean a break with, or a forgetting of, the vital and life-giving in that past. We can never forget the ideals that have moved our race, the dreams of the Indian people through the ages, the wisdom of the ancients, the buoyant energy and love of life and nature of our forefathers, their spirit of curiosity and mental adventure, the daring of their thought, their splendid achievements in literature, art and culture, their love of truth and beauty and freedom, the basic values that they set up, their understanding of life's mysterious ways, their toleration of other ways than theirs, their capacity to absorb other peoples and their cultural accomplishments, to synthesize them and develop a varied and mixed culture; nor can we forget the myriad experiences which have built up our ancient race and lie embedded in our sub-conscious minds. We will never forget them or cease to take pride in that noble heritage of ours. If India forgets them she will no longer remain India and much that has made her our joy and pride will cease to be.

It is not this that we have to break with, but all the dust and dirt of ages that have covered her up and hidden her inner beauty and significance, the excrescences and abortions that

509

have twisted and petrified her spirit, set it in rigid frames, and stunted her growth. We have to cut away these excrescences and remember afresh the core of that ancient wisdom and adapt it to our present circumstances. We have to get out of traditional ways of thought and living which, for all the good they may have done in a past age, and there was much good in them, have ceased to have significance to-day. We have to make our own all the achievements of the human race and join up with others in the exciting adventure of man, more exciting to-day perhaps than in earlier ages, realizing that this has ceased to be governed by national boundaries or old divisions and is common to the race of man everywhere. We have to revive the passion for truth and beauty and freedom which gives meaning to life, and develop afresh that dynamic outlook and spirit of adventure which distinguished those of our race who, in ages past, built our house on these strong and enduring foundations. Old as we are, with memories stretching back to the early dawns of human history and endeavour, we have to grow young again, in tune with our present time, with the irrepressible spirit and joy of youth in the present and its faith in the future.

Truth as ultimate reality, if such there is, must be eternal, imperishable, unchanging. But that infinite, eternal and unchanging truth cannot be apprehended in its fullness by the finite mind of man which can only grasp, at most, some small aspect of it limited by time and space, and by the state of development of that mind and the prevailing ideology of the period. As the mind develops and enlarges its scope, as ideologies change and new symbols are used to express that truth, new aspects of it come to light, though the core of it may yet be the same. And so, truth has ever to be sought and renewed, reshaped, and developed, so that, as understood by man, it might keep in line with the growth of his thought and the development of human life. Only then does it become a living truth for humanity, supplying the essential need for which it craves, and offering guidance in the present and for the future.

But if some one aspect of the truth has been petrified by dogma in a past age, it ceases to grow and develop and adapt itself to the changing needs of humanity; other aspects of it remain hidden and it fails to answer the urgent questions of a succeeding age. It is no longer dynamic but static, no longer a life-giving impulse but dead thought and ceremonial and a hindrance to the growth of the mind and of humanity. Indeed, it is probably not even understood to the extent it was understood in that past age when it grew up and was clothed in the language and symbols of that age. For its context is different in a later age, the mental climate has changed, new social habits and customs have grown up, and it is often difficult to understand the sense, much less the spirit, of that ancient writing. Moreover, as Aurobindo Ghose has pointed out, every truth, however true in itself, yet taken apart from others which at once limit and complete it, becomes a snare to bind the intellect and a misleading dogma; for in reality each is one thread of a complex weft and no thread must be taken apart from the weft.

Religions have helped greatly in the development of humanity. They have laid down values and standards and have pointed out principles for the guidance of human life. But with all the good they have done, they have also tried to imprison truth in set forms and dogmas, and encouraged ceremonials and practices which soon lose all their original meaning and become mere routine. While impressing upon man the awe and mystery of the unknown that surrounds him on all sides, they have discouraged him from trying to understand not only the unknown but what might come in the way of social effort. Instead of encouraging curiosity and thought, they have preached a philosophy of submission to nature, to established churches, to the prevailing social order, and to everything that is. The belief in a supernatural agency which ordains everything has led to a certain irresponsibility on the social plane, and emotion and sentimentality have taken the place of reasoned thought and inquiry. Religion, though it has undoubtedly brought comfort to innumerable human beings and stabilized society by its values, has checked the tendency to change and progress inherent in human society.

Philosophy has avoided many of these pitfalls and encouraged thought and inquiry. But it has usually lived in its ivory tower cut off from life and its day-to-day problems, concentrating on ultimate purposes and failing to link them with the life of man. Logic and reason were its guides and they took it far in many directions, but that logic was too much the product of the mind and unconcerned with fact.

Science ignored the ultimate purposes and looked at fact alone. It made the world jump forward with a leap, built up a glittering civilization, opened up innumerable avenues for the growth of knowledge, and added to the power of man to such an extent that for the first time it was possible to conceive that man could triumph over and shape his physical environment. Man became almost a geological force, changing the face of the planet earth chemically, physically, and in many other ways. Yet when this sorry scheme of things entirely seemed to be in his grasp, to mould it nearer to the heart's desire, there was some essential lack and some vital element was missing. There was no knowledge of ultimate purposes and not even an understanding of the immediate purpose, for science had told us nothing about any purpose in life. Nor did man, so powerful in his control of nature, have the power to control himself, and the monster he had created ran amok. Perhaps new developments in biology, psychology, and similar sciences, and the interpretation of biology and physics, may help man to understand and control himself more than he has done in the past. Or, before any such advances influence human life sufficiently, man may destroy the civilization he has built and have to start anew.

There is no visible limit to the advance of science, if it is given the chance to advance. Yet it may be that the scientific method of observation is not always applicable to all the varieties of human experience and cannot cross the uncharted ocean that surrounds us. With the help of philosophy it may go a little further and venture even on these high seas. And when both science and philosophy fail us, we shall have to rely on such other powers of apprehension as we may possess. For there appears to be a definite stopping place beyond which reason, as the mind is at present constituted, cannot go. 'La derniere démarche de la raison,' says Pascal, 'c'est de connaitre qu'il y a une infinite de choses qui la surpassent. Elle est bien faible si elle ne va jusque-la.'

Realizing these limitations of reason and scientific method, we have still to hold on to them with all our strength, for without that firm basis and background we can have no grip on any kind of truth or reality. It is better to understand a part of truth and apply it to our lives, than to understand nothing at all and flounder helplessly in a vain attempt to pierce the mystery of existence. The applications of science are inevitable and unavoidable for all countries and peoples to-day. But something more than its application is necessary. It is the scientific approach, the adventurous and yet critical temper of science, the search for truth and new knowledge, the refusal to accept anything without testing and trial, the capacity to change previous conclusions in the face of new evidence, the reliance on observed fact and not on pre-conceived theory, the hard discipline of the mind—all this is necessary, not merely for the application of science but for life itself and the solution of its many problems. Too many scientists to-day, who swear by science, forget all about it outside their particular spheres. The scientific approach and temper are, or should be, a way of life, a process of thinking, a method of acting and associating with our fellowmen. That is a large order and undoubtedly very few of us, if any at all, can function in this way with even partial success. But this criticism applies in equal or even greater measure to all the injunctions which philosophy and religion have laid upon us. The scientific temper points out the way along which man should travel. It is the temper of a free man. We live in a scientific age, so we are told, but there is little evidence of this temper in the people anywhere or even in their leaders.

Science deals with the domain of positive knowledge but the

temper which it should produce goes beyond that domain. The ultimate purposes of man may be said to be to gain knowledge, to realize truth, to appreciate goodness and beauty. The scientific method of objective inquiry is not applicable to all these, and much that is vital in life seems to lie beyond its scope—the sensitiveness to art and poetry, the emotion that beauty produces, the inner recognition of goodness. The botanist and zoologist may never experience the charm and beauty of nature; the sociologist may be wholly lacking in love for humanity. But even when we go to the regions beyond the reach of the scientific method and visit the mountain tops where philosophy dwells and high emotions fill us, or gaze at the immensity beyond, that approach and temper are still necessary.

Very different is the method of religion. Concerned as it is principally with the regions beyond the reach of objective inquiry, it relies on emotion and intuition. And then it applies this method to everything in life, even to those things which are capable of intellectual inquiry and observation: Organized religion, allying itself to theology and often more concerned with its vested interests than with things of the spirit, encourages a temper which is the very opposite to that of science. It produces narrowness and intolerance, credulity and superstition, emotionalism and irrationalism. It tends to close and limit the mind of man, and to produce a temper of a dependent, unfree person.

Even if God did not exist, it would be necessary to invent Him, so Voltaire said—'si Dieu n'existait pas, il faudrait l'inventer.' Perhaps that is true, and indeed the mind of man has always been trying to fashion some such mental image or conception which grew with the mind's growth. But there is something also in the reverse proposition: even if God exists, it may be desirable not to look up to Him or to rely upon Him. Too much dependence on supernatural factors may lead, and has often led, to a loss of self-reliance in man and to a blunting of his capacity and creative ability. And yet some faith seems necessary in things of the spirit which are beyond the scope of our physical world, some reliance on moral, spiritual, and idealistic conceptions, or else we have no anchorage, no objectives or purpose in life. Whether we believe in God or not, it is impossible not to believe in something, whether we call it a creative life-giving force or vital energy inherent in matter which gives it its capacity for self-movement and change and growth, or by some other name, something that is as real, though elusive, as life is real when contrasted with death. Whether we are conscious of it or not most of us worship at the invisible altar of some unknown god and offer sacrifices to it— some ideal, personal, national or international; some distant objective that draws us on, though reason itself may find little substance in it; some vague conception of a perfect man and a better world. Perfection may be impossible of attainment, but the demon in us, some vital force, urges us on and we tread that path from generation to generation.

As knowledge advances, the domain of religion, in the narrow sense of the word, shrinks. The more we understand life and nature, the less we look for supernatural causes. Whatever we can understand and control ceases to be a mystery. The processes of agriculture, the food we eat, the clothes we wear, our social relations, were all at one time under the dominion of religion and its high priests. Gradually they have passed out of its control and become subjects for scientific study. Yet much of this is still powerfully affected by religious beliefs and the superstitions that accompany them. The final mysteries still remain far beyond the reach of the human mind and are likely to continue to remain so. But so many of life's mysteries are capable of and await solution, that an obsession with the final mystery seems hardly necessary or justified. Life still offers not only the loveliness of the world but also the exciting adventure of fresh and never ceasing discoveries, of new panoramas opening out and new ways of living, adding to its fullness and ever making it richer and more complete.

It is therefore with the temper and approach of science, allied to philosophy, and with reverence for all that lies beyond, that we must face life. Thus we may develop an integral vision of life which embraces in its wide scope the past and the present, with all their hights and depths, and look with serenity towards the future. The depths are there and cannot be ignored, and always by the side of the loveliness that surrounds us is the misery of the world. Man's journey through life is an odd mixture of joy and sorrow; thus only can he learn and advance. The travail of the soul is a tragic and lonely business. External events and their consequences affect us powerfully, and yet the greatest shocks come to our minds through inner fears and conflicts. While we advance on the external plane, as we must if we are to survive, we have also to win peace with ourselves and between ourselves and our environment, a peace which brings satisfaction not only to our physical and material needs but also to those inner imaginative urges and adventurous spirits that have distinguished man ever since he started on his troubled journey in the realms of thought and action. Whether that journey has any ultimate purpose or not we do not know, but it has its compensations, and it points to many a nearer objective which appears attainable and which may again become the starting point for a fresh advance.

Science has dominated the western world and everyone there pays tribute to it, and yet the west is still far from having developed the real temper of science. It has still to bring the spirit and the flesh into creative harmony. In India in many obvious ways we have a greater distance to travel. And yet there may be fewer major obstructions on our way, for the essential basis of Indian thought for ages past, though not its later manifestations, fits in with the scientific temper and approach, as well as with internationalism. It is based on a fearless search for truth, on the solidarity of man, even on the divinity of everything living, and on the free and co-operative development of the individual and the species, ever to greater freedom and higher stages of human growth.

The Importance of the National Idea. Changes Necessary in India

A blind reverence for the past is bad and so also is a contempt for it, for no future can be founded on either of these. The present and the future inevitably grow out of the past and bear its stamp, and to forget this is to build without foundations and to cut off the roots of national growth. It is to ignore one of the most powerful forces that influence people. Nationalism is essentially a group memory of past achievements, traditions, and experiences, and nationalism is stronger to-day than it has ever been. Many people thought that nationalism had had its day and must inevitably give place to the ever-growing international tendencies of the modern world. Socialism with its proletarian background derided national culture as something tied up with a decaying middle class. Capitalism itself became progressively international with its cartels and combines and overflowed national boundaries. Trade and commerce, easy communications and rapid transport, the radio and cinema, all helped to create an international atmosphere and to produce the delusion that nationalism was doomed.

Yet whenever a crisis has arisen nationalism has emerged again and dominated the scene, and people have sought comfort and strength in their old traditions. One of the remarkable developments of the present age has been the rediscovery of the past and of the nation. This going back to national traditions has been most marked in the ranks of labour and the proletarian elements, who were supposed to be the foremost champions of international action. War or similar crisis dissolves their internationalism and they become subject to nationalist hates and fears even more than other groups. The most striking example of this is the recent development of the Soviet Union. Without giving up in any way its essential social and economic structure, it has become more nationalist-minded and the appeal of the fatherland is now much greater than the appeal of the international proletariat. Famous figures in national history have again been revived and have become heroes of the Soviet people. The inspiring record of the Soviet people in this war, the strength and unity they have shown, are no doubt due to a social and economic structure which has resulted in social advances on a wide front, on planned production and consumption, on the development of science and its functions, and on the release of a vast quantity of new talent and capacity for leadership, as also on brilliant leadership. But it may also be partly due to a revival of national memories and traditions and a new awareness of the past, of which the present was felt to be a continuation. It would be wrong to imagine that this nationalist outlook of Russia is just a reversion to old-style nationalism. It is certainly not that. The tremendous experiences of the revolution and all that followed it cannot be forgotten, and the changes that resulted from it in social structure and mental adjustment must remain. That social structure leads inevitably to a certain international outlook. Nevertheless nationalism has reappeared in such a way as to fit in with the new environment and add to the strength of the people.

It is instructive to compare the development of the Soviet state with the varying fortunes of the Communist Parties in other countries. There was the first flush of enthusiasm among many people in all countries, and especially in proletarian ranks, soon after the Soviet Revolution. Out of this grew communist groups and parties. Then conflicts arose between these groups and national labour parties. During the Soviet five-year plans there was another wave of interest and enthusiasm, and this probably affected middle-class intellectuals even more than Labour. Again there was a reaction at the time of the purges in the Soviet Union. In some countries Communist Praties were suppressed, in others they made progress. But almost everywhere they came into conflict with organized national Labour. Partly this was due to the conservatism of Labour, but more so to a feeling that the Communist Party represented a foreign group and that they took their policies from Russia. The inherent nationalism of Labour came in the way of its accepting the co-operation of the Communist Party even when many were favourably inclined towards communism. The many changes in Soviet policy, which could be understood in relation to Russia, became totally incomprehensible as policies favoured by Communist Parties elsewhere. They could only be understood on the basis that what may be good for Russia must necessarily be good for the rest of the world. These Communist Parties, though they consisted of some able and very earnest men and women, lost contact with the nationalist sentiments of the people and weakened accordingly. While the Soviet Union was forging new links with national tradition, the Communist Parties of other countries were drifting further away from it.

I cannot speak with much knowledge of what happened elsewhere, but I know that in India the Communist Party is completely divorced from, and is ignorant of, the national traditions that fill the minds of the people. It believes that communism necessarily implies a contempt for the past. So far as it is concerned, the history of the world began in November, 1917, and everything that preceded this was preparatory and leading up to it. Normally speaking, in a country like India with large numbers of people on the verge of starvation and the economic structure cracking up, communism should have a wide appeal. In a sense there is that vague appeal, but the Communist Party cannot take advantage of it because it has cut itself off from the springs of national sentiment and speaks in a language which finds no echo in the hearts of the people. It remains an energetic, but small group, with no real roots.

It is not only the Communist Party in India that has failed in this respect. There are others who talk glibly of modernism and modern spirit and the essence of western culture, and are at the same time ignorant of their own culture. Unlike the communists, they have no ideal that moves them and no driving force that carries them forward. They take the external forms and outer trappings of the west (and often some of the less desirable features), and imagine that they are in the vanguard of an advancing civilization. Naïve and shallow and yet full of their own conceits, they live, chiefly in a few large cities, an artificial life which has no living contacts with the culture of the east or of the west.

National progress can, therefore, neither lie in a repetition of the past nor in its denial. New patterns must inevitably be adopted but they must be integrated with the old. Sometimes the new, though very different, appears in terms of pre-existing patterns, and thus creates a feeling of a continuous development from the past, a link in the long chain of the history of the race. Indian history is a striking record of changes introduced in this way, a continuous adaptation of old ideas to a changing environment, of old patterns to new. Because of this there is no sense of cultural break in it and there is that continuity, in spite of repeated change, from the far distant days of Mohenjodaro to our own age. There was a reverence for the past and for traditional forms, but there was also a freedom and flexibility of the mind and a tolerance of the spirit. So while forms often remained, the inner content continued to change. In no other way could that society have survived for thousands of years. Only a living and growing mind could overcome the rigidity of traditional forms, only those forms could give it continuity and stability.

Yet this balance may become precarious and one aspect may overshadow, and to some extent, suppress this other. In India there was an extraordinary freedom of the mind allied to certain rigid social forms. These forms ultimately influenced the freedom of the mind and made it in practice, if not in theory, more rigid and limited. In western Europe there was no such freedom of the mind and there was also much less rigidity in social forms. Europe had a long struggle for the freedom of the mind and, as a consequence, social forms also changed.

In China the flexibility of the mind was even greater than in India and for all her love of, and attachment to, tradition, that mind never lost its flexibility and essential tolerance. Tradition sometimes delayed changes but that mind was not afraid of change, though it retained the old patterns. Even more than in India, Chinese society built up a balance and an equilibrium which survived through many changes for thousands of years. Perhaps one of the great advantages that China has had over other countries is her entire freedom from dogma, from the narrow and limited religious outlook, and her reliance on reason and common sense. No other country has based its culture less on religion and more on morality and ethics and a deep understanding of the variety of human life.

In India, because of the recognized freedom of the mind, howsoever limited in practice, new ideas are not shut out. They are considered and can be accepted far more than in countries which have a more rigid and dogmatic outlook on life. The essential ideals of Indian culture are broad-based and can be adapted to almost any environment. The bitter conflict between science and religion which shook up Europe in the nineteenth century would have no reality in India, nor would change based on the applications of science bring any conflict with those ideals. Undoubtedly such changes would stir up, as they are stirring up, the mind of India, but instead of combating them or rejecting them it would rationalize them from its own ideological point of view and fit them into its mental framework. It is probable that in this process many vital changes may be introduced in the old outlook, but they will not be super-imposed from outside and will seem rather to grow naturally from the cultural background of the people. This is more difficult to-day than it might have been, because of the long period of arrested growth and the urgent necessity for big and qualitative changes.

Conflict, however, there will be, with much of the superstructure that has grown up round those basic ideals and which exist and stifles us to-day. That superstructure will inevitably have to go, because much of it is bad in itself and is contrary to the spirit of the age. Those who seek to retain it do an ill service to the basic ideals of Indian culture, for they mix up the good and the bad and thus endanger the former. It is no easy matter to separate the two or draw a hard and fast line between them, and here opinions will differ widely. But it is not necessary to draw any such theoretical and logical line; the logic of changing life and the march of events will gradually draw that line for us. Every kind of development—technological or philosophical—necessitates contact with life itself, with social needs, with the living movements of the world. Lack of this contact leads to stagnation and loss of vitality and creativeness. But if we maintain these contacts and are receptive to them, we shall adapt ourselves to the curve of life without losing the essential characteristic which we have valued.

Our approach to knowledge in the past was a synthetic one, but limited to India. That limitation continued and the synthetic approach gave place gradually to a more analytical one. We have now to lay greater stress on the synthetic aspect and make the whole world our field of study. This emphasis on synthesis is indeed necessary for every nation and individual if they are to grow out of the narrow grooves of thought and action in which most people have lived for so long. The development of science and its applications have made this possible for us, and yet the very excess of new knowledge has added to its difficulty. Specialization has led to a narrowing of individual life in a particular groove, and man's labour in industry is often confined to some infinitesimal part of the whole product. Specialization in knowledge and work will have to continue, but it seems more essential than ever that a synthetic view of human life and man's adventure through the ages should be encouraged. This view will have to take into consideration the past and the present, and include in its scope all countries and peoples. In this way perhaps we might develop, in addition to our own national backgrounds and cultures, an appreciation of others and a capacity to understand and co-operate with the peoples of other countries. Thus also we might succeed to some extent in building up integrated personalities instead of the lop-sided individuals of to-day. We might become, in Plato's words, 'spectators of all time and all being,' drawing sustenance from the rich treasures that humanity has accumulated, adding to them, and applying them in building for the future.

It is a curious and significant act that, in spite of all modern scientific progress and talk of internationalism, racialism and other separating factors are at least as much in evidence to-day, if not more so, than at any previous time in history. There is something lacking in all this progress, which can neither produce harmony between nations nor within the spirit of man. Perhaps more synthesis and a little humility towards the wisdom of the past, which, after all, is the accumulated experience of the human race, would help us to gain a new perspective and greater harmony. That is especially needed by those peoples who live a fevered life in the present only and have almost forgotten the past. But for countries like India a different emphasis is necessary, for we have too much of the past about us and have ignored the present. We have to get rid of that narrowing religious outlook, that obsession with the supernatural and metaphysical speculations, that loosening of the mind's discipline in religious ceremonial and mystical emotionalism, which come in the way of our understanding ourselves and the world. We have to come to grips with the present, this life, this world, this nature which surrounds us in its infinite variety. Some Hindus talk of going back to the Vedas; some Moslems dream of an Islamic theocracy. Idle fancies, for there is no going back to the past; there is no turning back even if this was thought desirable. There is only one-way traffic in Time.

India must therefore lessen her religiosity and turn to science. She must get rid of the exclusiveness in thought and social habit which has become life a prison to her, stunting her spirit and preventing growth. The idea of ceremonial purity has erected barriers against social intercourse and narrowed the sphere of social action. The day-to-day religion of the orthodox Hindu is more concerned with what to eat and what not to eat, who to eat with and from whom to keep away, than with spiritual values. The rules and regulations of the kitchen dominate his social life. The Moslem is fortunately free from these inhibitions, but he has his own narrow codes and ceremonials, a routine which he rigorously follows, forgetting the lesson of brotherhood which his religion taught him. His view of life is, perhaps, even more limited and sterile than the Hindu view, though the average Hindu to-day is a poor representative of the latter view, for he has lost that traditional freedom of thought and the background that enriches life in many ways.

Caste is the symbol and embodiment of this exclusiveness among the Hindus. It is sometimes said that the basic idea of caste might remain, but its subsequent harmful development and ramifications should go; that it should not depend on birth but on merit. This approach is irrelevant and merely confuses the issue. In a historical context a study of the growth of caste has some value, but we cannot obviously go back to the period when caste began; in the social organization of to-day it has no place left. If merit is the only criterion and opportunity is thrown open to everybody, then caste loses all its present-day distinguishing features and, in fact, ends. Caste has in the past not only led to the suppression of certain groups, but to a separation of theoretical and scholastic learning from craftsmanship, and a divorce of philosophy from actual life and its problems. It was an aristocratic approach based on traditionalism. This outlook has to change completely, for it is wholly opposed to modern conditions and the democratic ideal. The functional organization of social groups in India may continue, but even that will undergo a vast change as the nature of modern industry creates new functions and puts an end to many old ones. The tendency to-day everywhere is towards a functional organization of society, and the concept of abstract rights is giving place to that of functions. This is in harmony with the old Indian ideal.

The spirit of the age is in favour of equality, though practice denies it almost everywhere. We have got rid of slavery in the narrow sense of the word, that a man can be the property of another. But a new slavery, in some ways worse than the old, has taken its place all over the world. In the name of individual freedom, political and economic systems exploit human beings and treat them as commodities. And again, though an individual cannot be the property of another, a country and a nation can still be the property of another nation, and thus group slavery is tolerated. Racialism also is a distinguishing feature of our times, and we have not only master nations but also master races.

Yet the spirit of the age will triumph. In India, at any rate, we must aim at equality. That does not and cannot mean that everybody is physically or intellectually or spiritually equal or can be made so. But it does mean equal opportunities for all and no political, economic, or social barrier in the way of any individual or group. It means a faith in humanity and a belief that there is no race or group that cannot advance and make good in its own way, given the chance to do so. It means a realization of the fact that the backwardness or degradation of any group is not due to inherent failings in it, but principally to lack of opportunities and long suppression by other groups. It should mean an understanding of the modern world wherein real progress and advance, whether national or international, have become very much a joint affair and a backward group pulls back others. Therefore, not only must equal opportunities be given to all, but special opportunities for educational, economic and cultural growth must be given to backward groups so as to enable them to catch up to those who are ahead of them. Any such attempt to open the doors of opportunity to all in India will release enormous energy and ability and transform the country with amazing speed.

If the spirit of the age demands equality, it must necessarily also demand an economic system which fits in with it and encourages it. The present colonial system in India is the very antithesis of it. Absolutism is not only based on inequality but must perpetuate it in every sphere of life. It suppresses the creative and regenerative forces of a nation, bottles up talent and capacity, and discourages the spirit of responsibility. Those who have to suffer under it, lose their sense of dignity and self-reliance. The problems of India, complicated as they seem, are essentially due to an attempt to advance while preserving the political and economic structure more or less intact. Political advance is made subject to the preservation of this structure and existing vested interests. The two are incompatible.

Political change there must be, but economic change is equally necessary. That change will have to be in the direction of a democratically planned collectivism. 'The choice,' says R. H. Tawney, 'is not between competition and monopoly, but between monopoly which is irresponsible and private and a monopoly which is responsible and public.' Public monopolies are growing even in capitalist states and they will continue to grow. The conflict between the idea underlying them and private monopoly will continue till the latter is liquidated. A democratic collectivism need not mean an abolition of private property, but it will mean the public ownership of the basic and major industries. It will mean the co-operative or collective control of the land. In India especially it will be necessary to have, in addition to the big industries, co-operatively controlled small and village industries. Such a system of democratic collectivism will need careful and continuous planning and adaptation to the changing needs of the people. The aim should be the expansion of the productive capacity of the nation in every possible way, at the same time absorbing all the labour power of the nation in some activity or other and preventing unemployment. As far as possible there should be freedom to choose one's occupation. An equalization of income will not result from all this, but there will be far more equitable sharing and a progressive tendency towards equalization. In any event, the vast differences that exist to-day will disappear completely, and class distinctions, which are essentially based on differences in income, will begin to fade out.

Such a change would mean an upsetting of the present-day acquisitive society based primarily on the profit motive. The profit motive may still continue to some extent but it will not be the dominating urge, nor will it have the same scope as it has to-day. It would be absurd to say that the profit motive does not appeal to the average Indian, but it is nevertheless true that there is no such admiration for it in India as there is in the west. The possessor of money may be envied but he is not particularly respected or admired. Respect and admiration still go to the man or woman who is considered good and wise, and especially to those who sacrifice themselves or what they possess for the public good. The Indian outlook, even of the masses, has never approved of the spirit of acquisitiveness.

Collectivism involves communal undertakings and co-operative effort. This again is fully in harmony with old Indian social conceptions which were all based on the idea of the group. The decay of the group system under British rule, and especially of the self-governing village, has caused deep injury to the Indian masses, even more psychological than economic. Nothing positive came in its place, and they lost their spirit of independence, their sense of responsibility, and their capacity to co-operate together for common purposes. The village, which used to be an organic and vital unit, became progressively a derelict area, just a collection of mud huts and odd individuals. But still the village holds together by some invisible link and old memories revive. It should be easily possible to take advantage of these age-long traditions and to build up communal and co-operative concerns in the land and in small industry. The village can no longer be a self-contained economic unit (though it may often be intimately connected with a collective or co-operative farm), but it can very well be a governmental and electoral unit, each such unit functioning as a self-governing community within the larger political framework, and looking after the essential needs of the village. If it is treated to some extent as an electoral unit, this will simplify provincial and all-India elections considerably by reducing the number of direct electors. The village council, itself chosen by all the adult men and women of the village, could form these electors for the bigger elections. Indirect elections may have some disadvantages but, having regard to the background in India, I feel sure that the village should be treated as a unit. This will give a truer and more responsible representation.

In addition to this territorial representation, there should also be direct representation of the collectives and co-operatives on the land and in industry. Thus the democratic organization of the state will consist of both functional and territorial representatives, and will be based on local autonomy. Some such arrangement will be completely in harmony with India's past as well as with her present requirements. There will be no sense of break (except with the conditions created by British rule) and the mass mind will accept it as a continuation of the past which it still remembers and cherishes.

Such a development in India would be in tune with political and economic internationalism. It would breed no conflicts with other nations and would be a powerful factor for peace in Asia and the world. It would help in the realization of that one world towards which we are inevitably being driven, even though our passions delude us and our minds fail to understand it. The Indian people, freed from the terrible sense of oppression and frustration, will grow in stature again and lose their narrow nationalism and exclusiveness. Proud of their Indian heritage, they will open their minds and hearts to other peoples and other nations, and become citizens of this wide and fascinating world, marching onwards with others in that ancient quest in which their forefathers were the pioneers.

India: Partition or Strong National State or Centre of Supra-National State?

It is difficult to discover a just balance between one's hopes and fears or to prevent one's wishes colouring the thinking of one's mind. Our desires seek out supporting reasons and tend to ignore facts and arguments that do not fit in with them. I try to reach that balance so that I may be able to judge correctly and find out the true basis for action, and yet I know how far I am from success and how I cannot get rid of the multitude of thoughts and feelings which have gone to build me up and to fence me in with their invisible bars. So also others may err in different directions. An Indian's and an Englishman's view of India and her place in the world will inevitably diverge and differ, conditional as each is on a different individual and national past. The individual and the national group fashion their own destiny by their actions; these past actions lead to the present and what they do to-day forms the basis of their to-morrows. *Karma*, they have called this in India, the law of cause and effect, the destiny which our past activities create for us. It is not an invariable destiny and many other factors go to influence it, and the individual's will is itself supposed to have some play. If this freedom to vary the results of past action were not present, then indeed we would all be mere robots in the iron grip of an unavoidable fate. Yet that past *Karma* is a powerful factor in shaping the individual and the nation, and nationalism itself is a shadow of it with all its good and bad memories of the past.

Perhaps, this past inheritance influences the national group even more than the individual, for large numbers of human beirgs are driven more by unconscious and impersonal urges than the individual, and it is more difficult to divert them from their course. Moral considerations may influence an individual but their effect on a group is far less, and the larger the group the less is their effect on it. And it is easier, especially in the modern world, to influence the group by insidious propaganda. And yet sometimes, though rarely, the group itself rises to a height of moral behaviour, forcing the individual to forget his narrow and selfish ways. More often the group falls far below the individual standard.

War produces both these reactions, but the dominant tendency is a release from moral responsibility and the collapse of the standards that civilization has so laboriously built up. Successful war and aggression lead to a justification and continuance of this policy, to imperialist domination and ideas of a master race. Defeat results in frustration and the nursing of feelings of revenge. In either event, hatred and the habit of violence grow. There is ruthlessness and brutality, and a refusal even to try to understand the other's viewpoint. And thus the future is conditioned and more wars and conflicts follow with all their attendant consequences.

The last 200 years of enforced relationship between India and England have built up this *Karma*, this destiny, for both of them, and it continues to govern their relations to each other. Entangled in its meshes, we have thus far struggled in vain to rid ourselves of this past inheritance and start afresh on a different basis. The last five years of war have unhappily added to that past evil *Karma* and made reconciliation and a normal relationship more difficult. That record of 200 years, like all else, is a mixture of good and evil. To the Englishman the good outweighs the evil, to the Indian the evil is so overwhelming that it darkens the whole period. But whatever the balance of good and evil there might be, it is obvious that any relationship that is enforced produces hatred and a bitter dislike of each other, and out of these feelings only evil consequences can flow.

A revolutionary change, both political and economic, is not only needed in India but would appear to be inevitable. At the end of 1939, soon after the war started, and again in April, 1942, there seemed to be a faint possibility of such a change taking place by consent between India and England. But those possibilities and opportunities passed because every basic change was feared. But the change will come. Has the stage of consent passed? In the presence of common perils the past loses some of its obsessions and the present is viewed in terms of the future. Now the past has returned and has been grievously added to. The receptive mood has changed and become hard and bitter. Some settlement will come sooner or later, after more conflict or without it, but it is far less likely to be real, sincere, and co-operative. More probably it will be an unwilling submission on both sides to overriding circumstances with continuing ill-will and distrust. No attempted solution which assumes even in principle the retention of India as part of the British empire has the slightest chance of acceptance of adoption. No solution which retains feudal relics in India can possibly last.

Life is cheap in India and when this is so, life is empty and ugly and shoddy and all the horrid brood of poverty envelop it. There is an enervating atmosphere in India, due to many causes, imposed or inherent, but essentially the resultant of poverty and want. We have a terribly low standard of living and a very high rate of dying. Industrially developed and rich countries have a way of looking at undeveloped and poor countries just as the rich man looks on the poor and unfortunate.

The rich man, out of his abundant resources and opportunities, develops high standards and fastidious tastes and blames the poor for their habits and lack of culture. Having denied them the opportunity to better themselves, he makes their poverty and its attendant evils justifications for a further denial.

India is not a poor country. She is abundantly supplied with everything that makes a country rich, and yet her people are very poor. She has a noble heritage of culture-forms and her culture-potential is very great; but many new developments and the accessories of culture are lacking. This lack is due to many causes and largely to deliberate deprivation. When this is so, the vital energy of the people must overcome the obstacles in the way and fill the lack. That is happening in India to-day. Nothing can be clearer than the fact that India has the resources as well as the intelligence, skill, and capacity to advance rapidly. She has the accumulated cultural and spiritual experience of ages behind her. She can progress both in scientific theory and the applications of science and become a great industrial nation. Her scientific record is already noteworthy, in spite of the many limitations she suffers from and the lack of opportunity for her young men and women to do scientific work. That record is not great considering the size and possibilities of the country, but it is significant of what will happen when the energies of the nation are released ond opportunities are provided.

Only two factors may come in the way: international developments and external pressure on India, and lack of a common objective within the country. Ultimately it is the latter alone that will count. If India is split up into two or more parts and can no longer function as a political and economic unit, her progress will be seriously affected. There will be the direct weakening effect, but much worse will be the inner psychological conflict between those who wish to reunite her and those who oppose this. New vested interests will be created which will resist change and progress, a new evil *Karma* will pursue us in the future. One wrong step leads to another; so it has been in the past and so it may be in the future. And yet wrong steps have to be taken sometimes lest some worse peril befall us; that is the great paradox of politics, and no man can say with surety whether present wrong-doing is better and safer in the end than the possibility of that imagined peril. Unity is always better than disunity, but an enforced unity is a sham and dangerous affair, full of explosive possibilities. Unity must be of the mind and heart, a sense of belonging together and of facing together those who attack it. I am convinced that there is that basic unity in India, but it has been overlaid and hidden to some extent by other forces. These latter may be temporary and artificial and may pass off, but they count to-day and no man can ignore them.

It is our fault, of course, and we must suffer for our failings. But I cannot excuse or forgive the British authorities for the deliberate part they have played in creating disruption in India. All other injuries will pass, but this will continue to plague us for a much longer period. Often I am reminded of Ireland and China when I think of India. Both differ from India and from each other in their past and present problems, and yet there are many similarities. Shall we have to tread that same path in the future?

Jim Phelan in his 'Jail Journey' tells us of the effect of jail on human character, and everyone who has spent a long time in prison knows how true his statement is: The jail...acts as a magnifying glass on human character. Every tiny weakness is brought out, emphasized, wakened, until presently there is no more of the convict with the weakness but only a weakness wearing convict clothes.' Some such effect is produced on national character by foreign rule. That is not the only effect, for noble qualities also develop and strength is gradually built up through resistance. But foreign authority encourages the former and tries to suppress the latter. Just as we have convict warders in prison whose chief qualification is to spy on their fellow-convicts, so in a subject country there is no lack of puppets and sycophants who put on the livery of authority and act on its behalf. There are others also who do not consciously line up in this way but who are nevertheless influenced by the policies and intrigues of the dominant power.

To accept the principle of a division of India, or rather the principle that there should be no enforced unity, may lead to a calm and dispassionate consideration of its consequences and thus to a realization that unity is in the interest of all. Yet obviously there is the danger that once this wrong step is taken, other like ones may follow in its train. The attempt to solve one problem in the wrong way may well create new problems. If India is to be divided into two or more parts, then the amalgamation of the major Indian states into India becomes more difficult, for those states will find an additional reason, which they might not otherwise have, for keeping aloof and holding on to their authoritarian regimes.*

*It may be said that the Indian States as a whole, while anxious to maintain their internal autonomy, are equally desirous of having a strong federal India of which they are members with equal rights. The proposal to divide India has been vigorously opposed by some of the leading ministers and statesmen of the states, and they have made it clear that, if such a division takes place, the states might well prefer to keep to themselves and not tie up with either part of divided India. Sir C. P. Ramaswami Aiyar, the Dewan of Travancore and one of the ablest and most experienced of states' ministers (though with a reputation for autocratic methods and

Any division of India on a religious basis as between Hindus and Moslems, as envisaged by the Moslem League to-day, cannot separate the followers of these two principal religions of India, for they are spread out all over the country. Even if the areas in which each group is in a majority are separated, huge minorities belonging to the other group remain in each area. Thus instead of solving the minority problem, we create several in place of one. Other religious groups, like the Sikhs, are split up unfairly against their will and placed in two different states. In giving freedom to separate to one group, other groups, though in a minority, are denied that freedom and compelled to isolate themselves from the rest of India against their emphatic and deeply felt wishes. If it is said that the majority (religious) must prevail in each area, so far as the question of separation is concerned, there is no particular reason why the majority view should not decide the question for the whole of India. Or that each tiny area should not decide its independent status for itself and thus create a vast number of small states—an incredible and fantastic development. Even so it cannot be done with any logic, for religious groups are intermingled and overlap in the population all over the country.

It is difficult enough to solve such problems by separation

a suppression of those of whom he does not approve) is a strong advocate of the internal autonomy of the states. He is at the same time an aggressive and persistent opponent of 'Pakistan', or any other suggested division. In an address delivered on October 6th, 1944, before the Bombay branch of the Indian Council of World Affairs, he said: 'The states, in other words, should, and in my view would, come into a scheme whereby the various political and administrative units in India, while exercising a full measure of autonomy in local matters, would co-operate with other units in the composition and working of the central legislative and executive organizations. Such organizations will function effectively within and without the limits of India as national and co-ordinating as well as representative bodies. Within the limits of India the relationship between the units will be one of equality and there will be no question of paramountcy as such inter se, though the rights residual and otherwise of the centre will have to be firmly established and implemented.' He further says: 'My point is this, namely, that treaty rights or no treaty rights, no Indian state has a right to exist which does not come into any scheme by which there is created a central direction or central control of matters that appertain to the Indian states and British India alike, or which does not loyally conform to all political arrangements that may be arrived at for the governance of India and all ideologies that may be evolved as the result of free and equal discussion and resultant compromises.' 'I wish to emphasize strongly, though I know I shall evoke a certain amount of controversy, that no Indian state has the rigth to exist unless it is abreast of, if not ahead of, British India in the things that matter in relation to the well-being of the people'.

Another fact that Ramaswami Aiyar emphasizes is that there is no getting away from the fact that it is impossible to deal with 601 states on an equal footing. He thinks that in a new constitution for India these 601 states will have to be reduced to something like fifteen or twenty, the others being absorbed into the larger units, province or state.

Ramaswami Aiyar apparently does not attach very much importance to this internal political progress of the states, or at any rate considers this a secondary matter. Yet the lack of this, especially in the states otherwise advanced, inevitably leads to ceaseless conflict between the people and the state authorities.

where nationalities are concerned. But where the test becomes a religious one it becomes impossible of solution on any logical basis. It is a reversion to some medieval conception which cannot be fitted into the modern world.

If the economic aspects of separation are considered it is clear that India as a whole is a strong and more-or-less self-sufficient economic unit. Any division will naturally weaken her and one part will have to depend on the other. If the division is made so as to separate the predominantly Hindu and Moslem areas, the former will comprise far the greater part of the mineral resources and industrial areas. The Hindu areas will not be so hard hit from this point of view. The Moslem areas, on the other hand, will be the economically backward, and often deficit, areas which cannot exist without a great deal of outside assistance. Thus the odd fact emerges that those who to-day demand separation will be the greatest sufferers from it. Because of a partial realization of this fact, it is now stated on their behalf that separation should take place in such a way as to give them an economically balanced region. Whether this is possible under any circumstances I do not know, but I rather doubt it. In any event any such attempt means forcibly attaching other large areas with a predominantly Hindu and Sikh population to the separated area. That would be a curious way of giving effect to the principle of self-determination. I am reminded of the story of the man who killed his father and mother and then threw himself on the mercy of the court as an orphan.

Another very curious contradiction emerges. While the principle of self-determination is invoked, the idea of a plebiscite to decide this is not accepted, or at most, it is said that the plebiscite should be limited to Moslems only in the area. Thus in Bengal and the Punjab the Moslem population is about 54 per cent or less. It is suggested that if there is to be voting only this 54 per cent should vote and decide the fate of the remaining 46 per cent or more, who will have no say in the matter. This might result in 28 per cent deciding the fate of the remaining 72 per cent.

It is difficult to understand how any reasonable person can advance these propositions or expect them to be agreed to. I do not know, and nobody can know till an actual vote takes place on this issue, how many Moslems in the areas concerned would vote for partition. I imagine that a large number of them, possibly even a majority, would vote against it. Many Moslem organizations are opposed to it. Every non-Moslem, whether he is a Hindu, or Sikh, or Christian, or Parsee, is opposed to it. Essentially this sentiment in favour of partition has grown in the areas where Moslems are in a small minority—areas which in any event, would remain undetached from the rest of India. Moslems in provinces where they are in a majority have been less influenced by it; naturally, for they can stand on their own feet and have no reason to fear other groups. It is least in evidence in the North-West Frontier Province (95 per cent Moslem), where the Pathans are brave and self-reliant and have no fear complex. Thus, oddly enough, the Moslem League's proposal to partition India finds far less response in the Moslem areas sought to be partitioned than in the Moslem minority areas which are unaffected by it. Yet the fact remains that considerable numbers of Moslems have become sentimentally attached to this idea of separation without giving thought to its consequences. Indeed, the proposition has so far only been vaguely stated and no attempt has been made to define it, in spite of repeated requests.

I think this sentiment has been artificially created and has no roots in the Moslem mind. But even a temporary sentiment may be strong enough to influence events and create a new situation. Normally, adjustments would take place from time to time, but in the peculiar position in which India is situated to-day, with power concentrated in foreign hands, anything may happen. It is clear that any real settlement must be based on the goodwill of the constituent elements and on the desire of all parties to it to co-operate together for a common objective. In order to gain that any sacrifice in reason is worth while. Every group must not only be theoretically and actually free and have equal opportunities of growth, but should have the sensation of freedom and equality. It is not difficult, if passions and unreasoning emotions are set aside, to devise such freedom with the largest autonomy for provinces and states and yet a strong central bond. There could even be autonomous units within the larger provinces or states, as in Soviet Russia. In addition to this, every conceivable protection and safeguard for minority rights could be inserted into the constitution.

All this can be done, and yet I do not know how the future will take shape under the influence of various indeterminate factors and forces, the chief of these being British policy. It may be that some division of India is enforced, with some tenuous bond joining the divided parts. Even if this happens, I am convinced that the basic feeling of unity and world developments will later bring the divided parts nearer to each other and result in a real unity.

That unity is geographical, historical, and cultural, and all that; but the most powerful factor in its favour is the trend of world events. Many of us are of opinion that India is essentially a nation; Mr. Jinnah has advanced a two-nation theory and has lately added to it and to political phraseology by describing some religious groups as sub-nations, whatever these might be. His thought identifies a nation with religion. That is not the usual approach to-day. But whether India is properly to be described as one nation or two or more really does not matter, for the modern idea of nationality has been almost divorced from statehood. The national state is too small a unit to-day and small states can have no independent existence. It is doubtful if even many of the larger national states can have any real independence. The national state is thus giving place to the multi-national state or to large federations. The Soviet Union is typical of this development. The United States of America, though bound together by strong national ties, constitute essentially a multi-national state. Behind Hitler's march across Europe there was something more than the nazi lust for conquest. New forces were working towards the liquidation of the small states system in Europe. Hitler's armies are now rapidly rolling back or are being destroyed, but the conception of large federations remains.

Mr. H. G. Wells has been telling the world, with all the fire of an old prophet, that humanity is at the end of an age—an age of fragmentation in the management of its affairs, fragmentation politically among separate sovereign states and economically among unrestricted business organizations competing for profit. He tells us that it is the system of nationalist individualism and unco-ordinated enterprise that is the world's disease. We shall have to put an end to the national state and devise a collectivism which neither degrades nor enslaves. The prophets are ignored and sometimes even stoned by their generation. And so Mr. Wells' warnings, and those of many others, are voices in the wilderness so far as those in authority are concerned. Nevertheless, they point to inevitable trends. These trends can be hastened or delayed, or if those who have power are so blind, may even have to wait another and greater disaster before they take actual shape.

In India, as elsewhere, we are too much under the bondage of slogans and set phrases derived from past events, and ideologies which have little relevance to-day, and their chief function is to prevent reasoned thought and a dispassionate consideration of the situation as it exists. There is also the tendency towards abstractions and vague ideals, which arouse emotional responses and are often good in their way, but which also lead to a woolliness of the mind and unreality. In recent years a great deal has been written and said on the future of India, and especially on the partition or unity of India; and yet the astonishing fact remains that those who propose 'Pakistan' or partition have consistently refused to define what they mean or to consider the implications of such a division. They move on the emotional plane only, as also many of those who oppose them, a plane of imagination and vague desire, behind which lie imagined interests. Inevitably, between these two emotional and imaginative approaches there is no meeting ground. And so 'Pakistan' and 'Akhand Hindustan' (undivided India) are bandied about and hurled at each other. It is clear that group emotions and conscious or subconscious urges count and must be attended to. It is at least equally clear that facts and realities do not vanish by our ignoring them or covering them up by a film of emotion; they have a way of emerging at awkward moments and in unexpected ways. And decisions taken primarily on the basis of emotions, or when emotions are the dominating consideration, are likely to be wrong and to lead to dangerous developments.

It is obvious that whatever may be the future of India, and even if there is a regular partition, the different parts of India will have to co-operate with each other in a hundred different ways. Even independent nations have to co-operate with each other, much more so must Indian provinces or such parts as emerge from a partition, for these stand in an intimate relationship to each other and must hang together or deteriorate, disintegrate, and lose their freedom. Thus the very first practical question is: What are the essential common bonds which must bind and cement various parts of India if she is to progress and remain free, and which are equally necessary even for the autonomy and cultural growth of those parts. Defence is an obvious and outstanding consideration, and behind that defence lie the industries feeding it, transport and communications, and some measure at least of economic planning. Customs, currency, and exchange also, and the maintenance of the whole of India as an internally free-trade area, for any internal tariff barriers would be fatal barriers to growth. And so on; there are many other matters which would inevitably, both from the point of view of the whole and the parts, have to be jointly and centrally directed. There is no getting away from it whether we are in favour of Pakistan or not, unless we are blind to everything except a momentary passion. The vast growth of air services to-day has led to the demand for their internationalization, or to some form of international control. Whether various countries are wise enough to accept this is doubtful, but it is quite certain that air developments can only take place in India on an all-India basis; it is inconceivable for a partitioned India to make progress in regard to them in each part separately. This applies glso to many other activities which already tend to outgrow even national boundaries. India is big enough as a whole to give them scope for development, but not so partitioned India.

Thus we arrive at the inevitable and ineluctable conclusion that, whether Pakistan comes or not, a number of important and basic functions of the state must be exercised on an all-India basis if India is to survive as a free state and progress. The alternative is stagnation, decay, and disintegration, leading to loss of political and economic freedom, both for India as a whole and its various separated parts. As has been said by an eminent authority: 'The inexorable logic of the age presents the country with radically different alternatives: union plus independence or disunion plus dependence.' What form the union is to take, and whether it is called union or by some other name, is not so important, though names have their own significance and psychological value. The essential fact is that a number of varied activities can only be conducted effectively on a joint all-India basis. Probably many of these activities will soon be under the control of international bodies. The world shrinks and its problems overlap. It takes less than three days now to go right across the world by air, from any one place to another, and to-morrow, with the development of stratosphere navigation, it may take even less time. India must become a great world centre of air travel, India will also be linked by rail to western Asia and Europe on the one side, and to Burma and China on the other. Not far from India, across the Himalayas in the north, lies in Soviet Asia one of the highly developed industrial areas, with an enormous future potential. India will be affected by this and will react in many ways.

The way of approach, therefore, to the problem of unity or Pakistan, is not in the abstract and on the emotional level, but practically, and with our eyes on the present-day world. That approach leads us to certain obvious conclusions, that a binding cement in regard to certain important functions and matters is essential for the whole of India. Apart from them there may be and should be the fullest freedom to constituent units, and an intermediate sphere where there is both joint and separate functioning. There may be differences of opinion as to where one sphere ends, and the other begins, but such differences, when considered on a practical basis, are generally fairly easy of adjustment.

But all this must necessarily be based on a spirit of willing co-operation, on the absence of a feeling of compulsion, and on the sensation of freedom in each unit and individual. Old vested interest have to go; it is equally important that no new ones are created. Certain proposals, based on metaphysical conceptions of groups and forgetting the individuals who comprise them, make one individual politically equal to two or three others and thus create new vested interests. Any such arrangement can only lead to grave dissatisfaction and instability.

The right of any well-constituted area to secede from the Indian federation or union has often been put forward, and the argument of the U.S.S.R. advanced in support of it. That argument has little application, for conditions there are wholly different and the right has little practical value. In the emotional atmosphere in India to-day it may be desirable to agree to this for the future in order to give that sense of freedom from compulsion which is so necessary. The Congress has in effect agreed to it. But even the exercise of that right involves a pre-consideration of all those common problems to which reference has been made. Also there is grave danger in a possibility of partition and division to begin with, for such an attempt might well scotch the very beginnings of freedom and the formation of a free national state. Insuperable problems will rise and confuse all the real issues. Disintegration will be in the air and all manner of groups, who are otherwise agreeable to a joint and unified existence, will claim separate states for themselves, or special privileges which are encroachments on others. The problem of the Indian states will become far more difficult of solution, and the states system, as it is to-day, will get a new lease of life. The social and economic problems will be far harder to tackle. Indeed, it is difficult to conceive of any free state emerging from such a turmoil, and if something does emerge, it will be a pitiful caricature full of contradictions and insoluble problems.

Before any such right of secession is exercised there must be a properly constituted, functioning, free India. It may be possible then, when external influences have been removed and real problems face the country, to consider such questions objectively and in a spirit of relative detachment, far removed from the emotionalism of to-day, which can only lead to unfortunate consequences which we may all have to regret later. Thus it may be desirable to fix a period, say ten years after the establishment of the free Indian state, at the end of which the right to secede may be exercised through proper constitutional process and in accordance with the clearly expressed will of the inhabitants of the area concerned.

Many of us are utterly weary of present conditions in India and are passionately eager to find some way out. Some are even prepared to clutch at any straw that floats their way in the vague hope that it may afford some momentary relief, some breathing space to a system that has long felt strangled and suffocated. That is very natural. And yet there is danger in these rather hysterical and adventurist approaches to vital problems affecting the well-being of hundreds of millions and the future peace of the world. We live continually on the verge of disaster in India, and indeed the disaster sometimes overwhelms us, as we saw in Bengal and elsewhere in India last year. The Bengal famine, and all that followed it, were not tragic exceptions due to extraordinary and unlooked for causes which could not be controlled or provided for. They were vivid, frightful pictures of India as she is, suffering for generations past from a deep-seated organic disease which has eaten into her very vitals. That disease will take more and more dangerous and disastrous forms unless we divert all our joint energies to its uprooting and cure. A divided India, each part trying to help itself and not caring for, or co-operating with, the rest, will lead to an aggravation of the disease and to sinking into a welter of hopeless, helpless misery. It is terribly late already and we have to make up for lost time. Must even the lesson of the Bengal famine be lost upon us? There are still many people who can think only in terms of political percentages, of weightage, of balancing, of checks, of the preservation of privileged groups, of making new groups privileged, of preventing others from advancing because they themselves are not anxious to, or are incapable of, doing so, of vested interests, of avoiding major social and economic changes, of holding on to the present picture of India with only superficial alterations. That way lies supreme folly.

The problems of the moment seem big and engross our attention. And yet, in a longer perspective, they may have no great importance and, under the surface of superficial events, more vital forces may be at work. Forgetting present problems then for a while and looking ahead, India emerges as a strong united state, a federation of free units, intimately connected with her neighbours and playing an important part in world affairs. She is one of the very few countries which have the resources and capacity to stand on their own feet. To-day probably the only such countries are the United States of America and the Soviet Union. Great Britain can only be reckoned as one of these if the resources of her empire are added to her own, and even then a spread-out and disgruntled empire is a source of weakness. China and India are potentially capable of joining that group. Each of them is compact and homogeneous and full of natural wealth, manpower, and human skill and capacity; indeed India's potential industrial resources are probably even more varied and extensive than China's, and so also her exportable commodities which may be required for the imports she needs. No other country, taken singly, apart from these four, is actually or potentially in such a position. It is possible of course that large federations or groups of nations may emerge in Europe or elsewhere and form huge multi-national states.

The Pacific is likely to take the place of the Atlantic in the future as a nerve centre of the world. Though not directly a Pacific state, India will inevitably exercise an important influence there. India will also develop as the centre of economic and political activity in the Indian Ocean area, in south-east Asia and right up to the Middle East. Her position gives an economic and strategic importance in a part of the world which is going to develop rapidly in the future. If there is a regional grouping of the countries bordering on the Indian Ocean on either side of India—Iran, Iraq, Afghanistan, India, Ceylon, Burma, Malaya, Siam, Java, etc.—present day minority problems will disappear, or at any rate will have to be considered in an entirely different context.

Mr. G. D. H. Cole considers India to be itself a supra-national area, and he thinks that in the long run she is destined to be the centre of a mighty supra-national state covering the whole of the Middle East and lying between a Sino-Japanese Soviet Republic, a new state based on Egypt, Arabia, and Turkey, and the Soviet Union in the north. All this is pure conjecture and whether any such development will ever take place no man can say. For my part I have no liking for a division of the world into a few huge supra-national areas, unless these are tied together by some strong world bond. But if people are foolish enough to avoid world unity and some world organization, then these vast supra-national regions, each functioning as one huge state but with local autonomy, are very likely to take shape. For the small national state is doomed. It may survive as a culturally autonomous area but not as an independent political unit.

Whatever happens it will be well for the world if India can make her influence felt. For that influence will always be in favour of peace and co-operation and against aggression.

Realism and Geopolitics. World Conquest or World Association.
The U.S.A. and the U.S.S.R

The war has entered on its final stage in Europe and the nazi power collapses before the advancing armies in the east and west. Paris, that lovely and gracious city, so tied up with freedom's struggle, is itself free again. The problems of peace, more difficult than those of war, rise up to trouble men's minds and behind them lies the disturbing shadow of the great failure of the years that followed World War I. Never again, it is said. So they said also in 1918.

Fifteen years ago, in 1929, Mr. Winston Churchill said: 'It is a tale that is told, from which we may draw the knowledge and comprehension needed for the future. The disproportion between the quarrels of nations and the suffering which fighting out those quarrels involves; the poor and barren prizes which reward sublime endeavour on the battlefield; the fleeting triumph of war; the long, slow, rebuilding; the awful risks so hardily run; the doom missed by a hair's breadth, by the spin of a coin, by the accident of an accident—all this should make the prevention of another great war the main preoccupation of mankind.'

Mr. Churchill should know, for he has played a leading part in war and peace, led his country with extraordinary courage at a time of distress and peril and, in victory, nursed great ambitions on its behalf. After World War I, British armies occupied the whole of western Asia from the borders of India across Iran and Iraq and Palestine and Syria right up to Constantinople. Mr. Churchill saw then a vision of a new middle eastern empire for Britain, but fate decided otherwise. What dreams does he cherish now for the future? 'War is a strange alchemist,' so wrote a gallant and distinguished colleague of mine, now in prison, 'and in its hidden chambers are such forces and powers brewed and distilled that they tear down the plans of the victorious and vanquished alike. No peace conference at the end of the last war dicided that four mighty empires of Europe and Asia should fall into dust—the Russian, the German, the Austrian, and the Ottoman. Nor was the Russian, the German, the Turkish revolution decreed by Lloyd George, Clemenceau, or Wilson.'

What will the leaders of the victorious nations say when they meet together after success in war has crowned their efforts? How is the future taking shape in their minds, and how far do they agree or differ between themselves? What other reactions will there be when the passion of war subsides and people try to return to the scarce-remembered ways of peace? What of the underground resistance movements of Europe and the new forces they have released? What will the millions of war-hardened soldiers, returning home much older in mind and experience, say and do? How will they fit into the life which has gone on changing while they were away? What will happen to devastated and martyred Europe, and what to Asia and Africa? What of the 'overpowering surge for freedom of Asia's hundreds of millions,' as Mr. Wendell Willkie describes it? What of all this and more? And what, above all, of the strange trick that fate so often plays, upsetting the well-laid schemes of our leaders?

As the war has developed and the danger of a possible victory of the fascist powers has receded, there has been a progressive hardening and a greater conservatism in the leaders of the United

Nations. The four freedoms and the Atlantic charter, vague as they were and limited in scope, have faded into the background, and the future has been envisaged more and more as a retention of the past. The struggle has taken a purely military shape, of physical force against force, and has ceased to be an attack on the philosophy of the nazis and fascists. General Franco and petty or prospective authoritarian rulers in Europe have been encouraged. Mr. Churchill still glories in the conception of empire. George Bernard Shaw recently declgred that: 'There is no power in the world more completely imbued with the idea of its dominance than the British empire. Even the word "empire" sticks in Mr. Churchill's throat every time he tries to utter it.'*

There are many people in England, America and elsewhere who want the future to be different from the past and who fear that unless this is so, fresh wars and disasters, on a more colossal scale, will follow this present war. But those who have power and authority do not appear to be much influenced by these considerations, or are themselves in the grip of forces beyond their control. In England, America, and Russia we revert to the old game of power politics on a gigantic scale. That is considered realism and practical politics. An American authority on geo-politics, Professor N. J. Spykman, has written in a recent book: 'The statesman who conducts foreign policy can concern himself with the values of justice, fairness, and tolerance only to the extent that they contribute to, or do not interfere with, the power objective. They can be used instrumentally as moral justification for the power quest, but they must be discarded the moment their application brings weakness. The search for power is not made for the achievement of moral values: moral values are used to facilitate the attainment of power.'†

This may not be representative of American thought, but it certainly represents a powerful section of it. Mr. Walter Lipp-

*It is clear that the British ruling classes do not contemplate the ending of the era of imperialism; at the most they think in terms of modernizing their system of colonial rule. For them the possession of colonies is 'a necessity of greatness and wealth.' The London Economist, representing influential opinion in Britain, wrote on September 16th, 1944: 'The American prejudice against "imperialism"—British, French, or Dutch—has led many of the postwar planners to assume that the old sovereignties will not be re-established in south-east Asia and that some form of international control, or the transfer of the imperium to local peoples, will take the place of the old authority exercised by the western nations. Since this attitude exists and is even backed by the most widely distributed American journals and newspapers, it is time that the future intentions of the British, the French, and the Dutch were frankly and fully explained. Since none of them has any intention of abandoning its colonial empire, but on the contrary regards the restoration of Malaya to the British, the East Indies to the Dutch, and French Indo-China to the French as an essential part of the destruction of Japan's co-prosperity sphere, it would be inviting the worst sort of misunderstanding, and even accusation of bad faith, if the three nations allowed any doubt on the matter to continue in the mind of their American ally.'

†'America's Strategy in World Politics.'

man's vision of the three or four orbits encompassing the globe —the Atlantic community, the Russian, the Chinese, and later the Hindu-Moslem in South Asia—is a continuation of power politics on a vaster scale, and it is difficult to understand how he can see any world peace or co-operation emerging out of it. America is a curious mixture of what is considered hard-headed realism and a vague idealism and humanitarianism. Which of these will be the dominating tendency of the future, or what will result from their mixing together? Whatever the mass of the people may think, foreign policy remains a preserve for the experts in charge of it and they are usually wedded to a continuation of old traditions and fear any innovations which might involve their countries in new risks. Realism of course there must be, for no nation can base its domestic or foreign policy on mere good-will and flights of the imagination. But it is a curious realism that sticks to the empty shell of the past and ignores or refuses to understand the hard facts of the present, which are not only political and economic but also include the feelings and urges of vast numbers of people. Such realism is more imaginative and divorced from to-day's and to-morrow's problems than much of the so-called idealism of many people.

Geopolitics has now become the anchor of the realist and its jargon of 'heartland' and 'rimland' is supposed to throw light on the mystery of national growth and decay. Originating in England (or was it Scotland?), it became the guiding light of the nazis, fed their dreams and ambitions of world domination, and led them to disaster. A partial truth is sometimes more dangerous than a falsehood; a truth that has had its day blinds one to the reality of the present. H. J. Mackinder's theory of geopolitics, subsequently developed in Germany, was based on the growth of civilization on the oceanic fringes of the continents (Asia and Europe), which had to be defended from pressure from land invaders from the 'heartland,' which was supposed to be the centre of the Eurasian block. Control of this heartland meant world domination. But civilization is no longer confined to the oceanic fringes and tends to become universal in its scope and content. The growth of the Americas also does not fit in with a Eurasian heartland dominating the world. And air-power has brought a new factor which has upset the balance between sea-power and land-power.

Germany, nursing dreams of world conquest, was obsessed by fears of encirclement. Soviet Russia feared a combination of her enemies. England's national policy has long been based on a balance of power in Europe and opposition to any dominating power there. Always there has been fear of others, and that fear has led to aggression and tortuous intrigues. An entirely new situation will arise after the present war, with two dominating world powers—the U.S.A. and the U.S.S.R.—and the rest a good distance behind them, unless they form some kind of bloc. And now even the United States of America are told by Professor Spykman, in his last testament, that they are in danger of encirclement, that they should ally themselves with a 'rimland' nation, that in any event they should not prevent the 'heartland' (which means now the U.S.S.R.) from uniting with the rimland.

All this looks very clever and realistic and yet is supremely foolish, for it is based on the old policy of expansion and empire and the balance of power, which inevitably leads to conflict and war. Since the world happens to be round, every country is encircled by others. To avoid such encirclements by the methods of power politics, there must be alliances and counter-alliances, expansion, and conquest. But, however huge a country's domination or sphere of influence becomes, there is always the danger of encirclement by those who have been left out of it, and who, on their part, fear this abnormal growth of a rival power. The only way to get rid of this danger is by world conquest or by the eliminations of every possible rival. We are witnessing to-day the failure of the latest attempt at world domination. Will that lesson be learnt or will there be others, driven by ambition and pride of race and power, to try their fortunes on this fatal field?

There really seems no alternative between world conquest and world association; there is no choice of a middle course. The old divisions and the quest of power politics have little meaning to-day and do not fit in with our environment, yet they continue. The interests and activities of states overflow their boundaries and are world-wide. No nation can isolate itself or be indifferent to the political or economic fate of other nations. If there is no co-operation there is bound to be friction with its inevitable results. Co-operation can only be on a basis of equality and mutual welfare, on a pulling-up of the backward nations and peoples to a common level of well-being and cultural advancement, on an elimination of racialism and domination. No nation and no people are going to tolerate domination and exploitation by another, even though this is given some more pleasant name. Nor will they remain indifferent to their own poverty and misery when other parts of the world are flourishing. That was only possible when there was ignorance of what was happening elsewhere.

All this seems obvious, and yet the long record of past happenings tell us that the mind of man lags far behind the course of events and adjusts itself only slowly to them. Self-interest itself should drive every nation to this wider co-operation in order to escape disaster in the future and build its own free life on the basis of others' freedom. But the self-interest of the 'realist' is far too limited by past myths and dogmas, and regards ideas and social forms, suited to one age, as immutable and as unchanging parts of human nature and society, forgetting that nothing is so changeable as human nature and society. Religious forms and notions take permanent shape, social institutions become petrified, war is looked upon as a biological necessity, empire and expansion as the prerogatives of a dynamic and progressive people, the profit motive as the central fact dominating human relations, and ethnocentrism, a belief in racial superiority, becomes an article of faith and, even when not proclaimed, is taken for granted. Some of these ideas were common to the civilizations of east and west; many of them form the back-ground of modern western civilization out of which fascism and nazism grew. Ethically there is no great difference between them and the fascist creed, though the latter went much further in its contempt for human life and all that humanism stands for. Indeed, humanism, which coloured the outlook of Europe for so long, is a vanishing tradition there. The seeds of fascism were present in the political and economic structure of the west. Unless there is a break from this past ideology, success in war brings no great change. The old myths and fancies continue and, pursued as of old by the Furies, we go through the self-same cycle again.

The two outstanding facts emerging from the war are the growth in power and actual and potential wealth of the U.S.A. and the U.S.S.R. The Soviet Union actually is probably poorer than it was prior to the war, owing to enormous destruction, but its potential is tremendous and it will rapidly make good and go further ahead. In physical and economic power there will be none to challenge it on the Eurasian continent. Already it is showing an expansionist tendency and is extending its territories more or less on the basis of the Tsar's Empire. How far this process will go it is difficult to say. Its socialist economy does not necessarily lead to expansion for it can be made self-sufficient. But other forces and old suspicions are at play and again we notice the fear of so-called encirclement. In any event the U.S.S.R. will be busy for many years in repairing the ravages of war. Yet the tendency to expand, if not in territory then in other ways, is evident. No other country to-day presents such a politically solid and economically well-balanced picture as the Soviet Union, though some of the developments there in recent years have come as a shock to many of its old admirers. Its present leaders have an unchallengeable position, and everything depends on their outlook for the future.

The United States of America have astonished the world by their stupendous production and organizing capacity. They have thus not only played a leading part in the war but have accelerated a process inherent in American economy and produced a problem for themselves which will tax their wits and energies to the utmost. Indeed it is not easy to foresee how they will solve it within the limits of their existing economic structure without serious internal and external friction. It is said that America has ceased to be isolationist. Inevitably so, for she must now depend to an extent on her exports abroad. What was a marginal factor in her pre-war economy, which could almost be ignored, will now be a dominant consideration. Where will all these exports go to, without creating friction and conflict, when production for peace takes the pace of war production? And how will the millions of armed men returning home be absorbed? Every warring country will have to face this problem, but none to the same extent as the U.S.A. The vast technological changes that have taken place will lead to very great over-production or to mass unemployment, or possibly to both. Unemployment on any major scale will be bitterly resented and has been ruled out by the declared policy of the United States Government. Much thought is already being given to the absorption of the returning soldiers, etc., in gainful employment and to the prevention of unemployment. Whatever the domestic aspect of all this may be, and it will be serious enough unless basic changes take place, the international aspect is equally important.

Such is the curious nature of present-day economy in these days of mass production, that the U.S.A., the wealthiest and most powerful country in the world, becomes dependent on other countries absorbing its surplus production. For some years after the war there will be a big demand in Europe, China, and India for machinery as well as manufactured goods. This will be of considerable help to America to dispose of her surplus. But every country will rapidly develop its own capacity to manufacture most of its needs, and exports will tend to be limited to specialized goods not produced elsewhere. The consumption capacity will also be limited by the purchasing power of the masses, and to raise this fundamental economic changes will be needed. It is conceivable that with the substantial raising of the standard of living all over the world, international trade and exchange of goods will prosper and increase. But that raising itself requires a removal of political and economic fetters on production and distribution in the colonial and backward countries. That inevitably involves big changes with their consequent dislocation and adaptation to new systems.

England's economy has been based in the past on a big export business, on investments abroad, on the City of London's financial leadership, and on a vast maritime carrier trade. Before the war Britain depended on imports for nearly 50 per cent of her food supplies. Probably this dependence is less now owing to her intensive food-growing campaign. These imports of food as well as raw materials had to be paid for by exports of manufactured goods, investments, shipping, financial services, and what are called 'invisible' exports. Foreign trade and, in particular, a large volume of exports were thus an essential and vital feature of British economy. That economy was maintained by the exercise of monopoly controls in the colonial areas and special arrangements within the empire to maintain some kind of equilibrium. Those monopoly controls and arrangements were much to the disadvantage of the colonies and dependencies and it is hardly possible to maintain them in these old forms in future. Britain's foreign investments have disappeared and given place to huge debts, and London's financial supremacy has also gone. This means that in the post-war years Britain will have to depend even more on her export business and her carrier trade. And yet the possibilities of increasing exports, or even maintaining them at the old level, are strictly limited.

Great Britain's imports (*less* re-exports) in the pre-war years 1936-38 averaged £866,000,000. They were paid for as follows:

Exports	..	£478 million.
Income on foreign investments	..	£203 ,,
Shipping services	..	£105 ,,
Financial services	..	£40 ,,
Deficit	..	£40 ,,
		£866 million.

Instead of the substantial income from foreign investment there is going to be a heavy burden of external debt, due to borrowings in goods and services (apart from American Lend-Lease) from India, Egypt, Argentine, and other countries. Lord Keynes has estimated that, at the end of the war, these frozen sterling credits will amount to £3,000,000,000. At 5 per cent this will amount to £150 million per annum. Thus on a pre-war average basis Britain may have to face a deficit of considerably over £300 millions annually. Unless this is made good by additional income from exports and various services, it will lead to a marked reduction in living standards.

This appears to be the governing factor in Britain's post-war policy, and if she is to maintain her present economy, she feels she must retain her colonial empire, with only such minor changes as are unavoidable. only as the dominant partner of a group of countries, colonial and non-colonial, does she hope to play a leading role, and to balance, politically and economically, the vast resources of the two giant powers—the United States of America and the Soviet Union. Hence the desire to continue her empire, to hold on to what she has got, as well as to extend her sphere of influence over fresh territories, for instance over Thailand. Hence also the aim of British policy to bring about a closer integration with the Dominions, as well as some of the smaller countries of western Europe. French and Dutch colonial policy generally support the British view in regard to colonies and dependencies. The Dutch Empire is indeed very much a 'satellite empire' and it could not continue to exist without the British Empire.

It is easy to understand these trends of British policy, based, as they are, on past outlook and standards and formulated by men tied up with that past. Yet, within that past context of a nineteenth century economy, the difficulties facing Britain to-day are very great. In the long run, her position is weak, her economy unsuited to present-day conditions, her economic resources are limited, and her industrial and military strength cannot be maintained at the old level. There is an essential instability in the methods suggested to maintain that old economy, for they lead to unceasing conflict, to lack of security, and to the growth of ill-will in the dependencies, which may make the future still more perilous for Britain. The desire of the British, understandable enough, to maintain their living standards on the old level and even to raise them, is thus made dependent upon protected markets for British exports and controlled colonial and other areas for the supply of raw materials and cheap food. This means that British living standards must be kept up even at the cost of keeping down at subsistence level or less hundreds of millions of peoples in Asia and Africa. No one wants to reduce British standards, but it is obvious that the peoples of Asia and Africa are never going to agree to the maintenance of this colonial economy which keeps them at a sub-human level. The annual purchasing power (pre-war) in Britain is said to have been £97 *per capita* (in the U.S.A. it was much greater); in India it was less than £6. These vast differences cannot be tolerated, and indeed the diminishing returns of a colonial economy ultimately affect adversely even the dominating power. In the U.S.A. this is vividly realized, and hence their desire to raise the colonial peoples' purchasing power through industrialization and self-government. Even in Britain there is some realization of the necessity of Indian industrialization. and the Bengal famine made many people think furiously on this subject. But British policy aims at industrial development in India under British control with a privileged position for British industry. The industrialization of India, as of other countries in Asia, is bound to take place; the only question is one of pace. But it is very doubtful if it can be fitted in with any form of colonial economy or foreign control.

The British Empire, as it is to-day, is not of course a geographical unit; nor is it an effective economic or military unit. It is a historical and sentimental unit. Sentiment and old bonds count still, but they are not likely to override, in the long run, other more vital considerations. And even this sentiment applies only to certain areas containing populations racially similar to the people of Britain. It certainly does not apply to India or the rest of the dependent colonial empire, where it is the other way about. It does not even apply to South Africa, so far as the Boers are concerned. In the major Dominions subtle changes are taking place which tend to weaken their traditional links with Britain. Canada, which has grown greatly in industrial stature during the war, is an important power, closely tied up with the U.S.A. She has developed an expanding economy which will, in some repects, come in the way of British industry. Australia and New Zealand, also with expanding economics, are realizing that they are not in the European orbit of Great Britain but in the Asiatic-American orbit of the Pacific, where the United States are likely to play a dominant role. Culturally, both Canada and Australia are progressively drawn towards the U.S.A.

The British colonial outlook to-day does not fit in with American policy and expansionist tendencies. The United States want open markets for their exports and do not look with favour on attempts by other powers to limit or control them. They want rapid industrialization of Asia's millions and higher standards everywhere, not for sentimental reasons but to dispose of their surplus goods. Friction between American and British export businesses and maritime trade seems to be inevitable. America's desire to establish world air supremacy, for which she has at present abundant resources, is resented in England. America probably favours an independent Thailand while England would prefer to make it a semi-colony. These opposing approaches based, in each case, on the nature of the respective economy aimed at, run through the whole colonial sphere.

The aim of British policy to have a closer integration of the commonwealth and empire is understandable in the peculiar circumstances in which Britain is placed to-day. But against it is the logic of facts and world tendencies, as well as the growth of dominion nationalism and the disruptive tendencies of the colonial empire. To try to build on old foundations, to continue to think in terms of a vanished age, to dream and talk still of an empire and of monopolies spread out all over the globe, is for Britain an even more unwise and shortsighted policy than it might be for some other nations; for most of the reasons which made her a politically, industrially, and financially dominant nation have disappeared. Nevertheless Britain has had in the past, and has still, remarkable qualities — courage and the will to pull together, scientific and constructive ability and a capacity for adaptation. These qualities, and others which she possesses go a long way to make a nation great and enable it to overcome the dangers and perils that confront it. And so she may be able to face her vital and urgent problems by changing over to a different and more balanced economic structure. But it is highly unlikely that she will succeed if she tries to continue, as of old, with an empire tacked on to her and supporting her.

Much will inevitably depend on American and Soviet policy, and on the degree of co-ordination or conflict between the two and Britain. Everybody talks loudly about the necessity for the Big Three to pull together in the interests of world peace and co-operation, yet rifts and differences peep out at every stage, even during the course of the war. Whatever the future may hold, it is clear that the economy of the U.S.A. after the war will be powerfully expansionist and almost explosive in its consequences. Will this lead to some new kind of imperialism? It would be yet another tragedy if it did so, for America has the power and opportunity to set the pace for the future.

The future policy of the Soviet Union is yet shrouded in mystery, but there have been some revealing glimpses of it already. It aims at having as many friendly and dependent or semi-dependent countries near its borders as possible. Though working with other powers for the establishment of some world organization, it relies more on building up its own strength on an unassailable basis. So, presumably, do other nations also, in so far as they can. That is not a hopeful prelude to world co-operation. Between the Soviet Union and other countries there is not the same struggle for export markets as between Britain and the U.S.A. But the differences are deeper, their respective viewpoints further apart, and mutual suspicions have not been allayed even by joint effort in the war. If these differences grow, the U.S.A. and Britain will tend to seek each other's company and support as against the U.S.S.R. group of nations.

Where do the hundreds of millions of Asia and Africa come in this picture? They have become increasingly conscious of themselves and their destiny, and at the same time are also world conscious. Large numbers of them follow world events with interest. For them, inevitably, the test of each move or happening is this: Does it help towards our liberation? Does it end the domination of one country over another? Will it enable us to live freely the life of our choice in co-operation with others? Does it bring equality and equal opportunity for nations as well as groups within each nation? Does it hold forth the promise of an early liquidation of poverty and illiteracy and bring better living conditions? They are nationalistic but this nationalism seeks no dominion over, or interference with, others. They welcome all attempts at world co-operation and the establishment of an international order, but they wonder and suspect if this may not be another device for continuing the old domination. Large parts of Asia and Africa consist of an awakened, discontented, seething humanity, no longer prepared to tolerate existing conditions. Conditions and problems differ greatly in the various countries of Asia, but throughout this vast area, in China and India, in south-east Asia, in western Asia, and the Arab world run common threads of sentiment and invisible links which hold them together.

For a thousand years or more, while Europe was backward and often engulfed in its dark ages, Asia represented the advancing spirit of man. Epoch after epoch of a brilliant culture flourished there and great centres of civilization and power grew up. About five hundred years ago Europe revived and slowly spread eastward and westward till, in the course of centuries, it became the dominant continent of the world in power, wealth, and culture. Was there some cycle about this change and is that process now being reversed? Certainly, power and authority have shifted more to America in the far west and to eastern Europe, which was organically hardly a part of the European heritage. And in the east also there has been tremendous growth in Siberia, and other countries of the east are ripe for change and rapid advance. Will there be conflict in the future or a new equilibrium between the east and the west?

But only the distant future will decide that, and it serves little purpose to look so far ahead. For the present we have to carry the burden of the day and face the many problems which afflict us. Behind these problems in India, as in many other countries, lies the real issue, which is not merely the establishment of democracy of the nineteenth century European type but also of far-reaching social revolution. Democracy has itself become involved in that seemingly inevitable change, and hence among those who disapprove of the latter, doubts and denials arise about the feasibility of democracy, and this leads to fascist tendencies and the continuation of an imperialist outlook. All our present-day problems in India—the communal or minority problem, the Indian princes, vested interests of religious groups and the big landowners, and the entrenched interests of British authority and industry in India —ultimately resolve themselves into opposition to social change. And because any real democracy is likely to lead to such change, therefore democracy itself is objected to and considered as unsuited to the peculiar conditions of India. So the problems of India, for all their seeming variety and differences from others, are of the same essential nature as the problems of China or Spain or many other countries of Europe and elsewhere, which the war has brought to the surface. Many of the resistance movements of

Europe reflect these conflicts. Everywhere the old equilibrium of social forces has been upset, and till a new equilibrium is established there will be tension, trouble, and conflict. From these problems of the moment we are led to one of the central problems of our time: how to combine democracy with socialism, how to maintain individual freedom and initiative and yet have centralized social control and planning of the economics of the people, on the national as well as the international plane.

Freedom and Empire

The U.S.A. and the Soviet Union seem destined to play a vital part in the future. They differ from each other almost as much as any two advanced countries can differ and even their faults lie in opposite directions. All the evils of a purely political democracy are evident in the U.S.A.; the evils of the lack of political democracy are present in the U.S.S.R. And yet they have much in common—a dynamic outlook and vast resources, a social fluidity, an absence of a medieval background, a faith in science and its applications, and widespread education and opportunities for the people. In America, in spite of vast differences in income, there are no fixed classes as in most countries and there is a sense of equality. In Russia, the outstanding event of the past twenty years has been the tremendous educational and cultural achievements of the masses. Thus in both countries the essential basis for a progressive, democratic society is present, for no such society can be based on the rule of a small intellectual *élite* over an ignorant and apathetic people. Nor can such an *élite* long continue to dominate over an educationally and culturally advanced people.

A hundred years ago de Tocqueville, discussing the Americans of those days, said: 'If the democratic principle does not, on the one hand, induce men to cultivate science for its own sake, on the other, it does enormously increase the number of those who do cultivate it....Permanent inequality of conditions leads men to confine themselves to the arrogant and sterile researches of abstract truths, whilst the social condition and institutions of democracy prepare them to seek the immediate and useful practical results of the sciences. The tendency is natural and inevitable.' Since then America has developed and changed and become an amalgam of many races, but its essential characteristics continue.

Yet another common characteristic of both Americans and Russians is that they do not carry that heavy burden of the past which has oppressed Asia and Europe, and conditioned to a great extent their activities and conflicts. They cannot, of course, escape, as none of us can, the terrible burden of this generation. But they have a clearer past, so far as other people are concerned, and are less encumbered for their journey into the future.

As a result of this they can approach other peoples without that background of mutual distrust which always accompanies the contacts of well-established imperialist nations with others. Not that their past is free of spots and stains and suspicions. Americans have their negro problem which is a continuing reproach to their professions of democracy and equality. Russians have yet to wipe out memories of past hatreds in eastern Europe and the present war is adding to them. Still Americans make friends easily in other countries. Russians are almost totally devoid of racialism.

Most of the European nations are full of mutual hatreds and past conflicts and injustices. The imperialist powers have inevitably added to this the intense dislike for them of people over whom they have ruled. Because of England's long record of imperialist rule, her burden is the greatest. Because of this, or because of racial characteristics, Englishmen are reserved and exclusive and do not easily make friends with others. They are unfortunately judged abroad by their official representatives who are seldom the standard-bearers of their liberalism or culture, and who often combine snobbery with an apparent piety. These officials have a peculiar knack of antagonising others. Some months ago a secretary to the Government of India wrote an official letter to Mr. Gandhi (in detention) which was an example of studied insolence, and which was looked upon by large numbers of people as a deliberate insult to the Indian people. For Gandhi happens to be a symbol of India.

Another era of imperialism, or an age of international co-operation or world commonwealth, which is it going to be in the future? The scales incline towards the former and the old arguments are repeated but not with the old candour. The moral urges of mankind and its sacrifices are used for base ends, and rulers exploit the goodness and nobility of man for evil purposes and take advantage of the fears, hatreds, and false ambitions of the people. They used to be more frank about empire in the old days. Speaking of the Athenian empire, Thucydides wrote: 'We make no fine profession of having a right to our empire because we overthrew the Barbarian single-handed, or because we risked our existence for the sake of our dependents and of civilization. States, like men, cannot be blamed for providing for their proper safety. If we are now here in Sicily, it is in the interest of our own security....It is fear that forces us to cling to our empire in Greece, and it is fear that drives us hither, with the help of our friends, to order matters in Sicily.' And again when he referred to the tribute of the Athenian colonies: 'It may seem wickedness to have won it; but it is certainly folly to let it go.'

The history of Athens is full of lessons of the incompatibility of democracy with empire, of the tyranny of a democratic state over its colonies, and the swift deterioration and fall of that empire. No upholder of freedom and empire to-day could state his case so well and so eloquently as Thucydides did: 'We are the leaders of civilization, the pioneers of the human race. Our society and intercourse is the highest blessing man can confer. To be within the circle of our influence is not dependence but a privilege. Not all the wealth of the east can repay the riches we bestow. So we can work on cheerfully, using the means and the money that flow into us, confident that, try as they will, we shall still be creditors. For through effort and suffering and on many a stricken field we have found the secret of human power, which is the secret of happiness. Men have guessed at it under many names; but we alone have learnt to know it and to make it at home in our city. And the name we know it by is freedom, for it has taught us that to serve is to be free. Do you wonder why it is that alone among mankind we confer our benefits, not on conditions of self-interest, but in the fearless confidence of freedom?'

All this has a familiar ring in these days when freedom and democracy are so loudly proclaimed and yet limited to some only. There is truth in it and a denial of truth. Thucydides knew little of the rest of mankind and his vision was confined to the Mediterranean countries. Proud of the freedom of his famous city, praising this freedom as the secret of happiness and human power, yet he did not realize that others also aspired to this freedom. Athens, lover of freedom, sacked and destroyed Melos and put to death all the grown men there and sold the women and children as slaves. Even while Thucydides was writing of the empire and freedom of Athens, that empire had crumbled away and that freedom was no more.

For it is not possible for long to combine freedom with domination and slavery; one overcomes the other and only a little time divides the pride and glory of empire from its fall. To-day, much more than ever before, freedom is indivisible. The splendid eulogy of Pericles for his beloved city was followed soon after by its fall and the occupation of the Acropolis by a Spartan garrison. Yet his words move us still for their love of beauty, wisdom, freedom and courage, not merely in their application to the Athens of his day, but in the larger context of the world: 'We are lovers of beauty without extravagance, and lovers of wisdom without unmanliness. Wealth to us is not mere material for vainglory but an opportunity for achievement; and poverty we think it no disgrace to acknowledge but a real degradation to make no effort to overcome....Let us draw strength, not merely from twice-told arguments—how fair and noble a thing it is to show courage in battle—but from the busy spectacle of our great city's life as we have it before us day by day, falling in love with her as we see her, and remembering that all this greatness she owes to men with the fighter's daring, the wise man's understanding of his duty, and the good man's self-discipline in its performance—to men who, if they failed in any ordeal, disdained to deprive the city of their services, but sacrificed their lives as the best offerings on her behalf. So they gave their bodies to the commonwealth and received, each for his own memory, praise that will never die, and with it the grandest of all sepulchres, not that in which their mortal bones are laid, but a home in the minds of men, where their glory remains fresh to stir to speech or action as the occasion comes by. For the whole earth is a sepulchre of famous men; and their story is not graven only on stone over their native earth, but lives on far away, without visible symbol, woven into the stuff of other men's lives. For you now it remains to rival what they have done and, knowing the secret of happiness to be freedom and the secret of freedom a brave heart, not idly to stand aside from the enemy's onset.'*

The Problem of Population. Falling Birth-rates and National Decay

Five years of war have brought about enormous changes and displacements of population on a vaster scale probably than at any previous epoch of history. Apart from the scores of millions of war casualties, more especially in China, Russia, Poland, and Germany, masses of people have been uprooted from their homes and countries. There have been military requirements, labour demands and enforced evacuations, and swarms of refugees have fled before invading armies. Even before the war the refugee problem in Europe, due to nazi policy, had grown to formidable proportions. But these pale into insignificance when compared to war developments. Apart from the direct consequences of the war, the changes in Europe are largely due to a deliberate demographic policy pursued by the nazis. They have apparently killed off millions of Jews and broken up the population integrity of many countries occupied by them. In the Soviet Union many millions have moved east, forming new settlements on the other side of the Urals, which are likely to be permanent. In China it is estimated that fifty million people have been torn from their roots.

Attempts will, no doubt, be made to repatriate and rehabilitate these people, or such as survive after the war, though the task is one of prodigious complexity. Many will come back to

*The quotations from Thucydides have been taken from Alfred Zimmern's 'The Greek Commonwealth' (1924).

their old homes, many may choose to remain in their new environment. On the other hand, it seems also likely that, as a result of political changes in Europe, there will be further displacement and exchange of populations.

Of far deeper and more far-reaching significance are the changes, partly physiological and biological, that are rapidly changing the population of the world. The industrial revolution and the spread of modern technology resulted in a rapid growth of population in Europe, and more especially in north-western and central Europe. As this technology has spread eastwards to the Soviet Union, aided by a new economic structure and other factors, there has been an even more spectacular increase in population in these regions. This eastward sweep of technology, accompanied by education, sanitation, and better public health, is continuing and will cover many of the countries of Asia. Some of these countries, like India, far from needing a bigger population, would be better off with fewer people.

Meanwhile, in western Europe a reverse process has set in as regard population and the problem of a falling birth-rate is growing in importance.

This tendency appears to be widespread and affects most countries in the world, with some notable exceptions like China, India, Java, and the U.S.S.R. It is most marked in the industrially advanced countries. The population of France ceased to grow many years ago and is now slowly declining. In England a steady fall in the fertility rate has been noticeable since the eighties of the last century, and it is the lowest now in Europe, except for France. Hitler's and Mussolini's efforts to increase the birth-rate in Germany and Italy bore only temporary results. In northern, western, and central Europe the decline is more marked than in southern and eastern Europe (exclusive of U.S.S.R.), but similar tendencies are observable in all these regions. Europe, apart from Russia, reaches its maximum population, according to present trends, about 1955 and then begins to decline. This has nothing to do with war losses which will aggravate this downward tendency.

The Soviet Union, on the other hand, goes on rapidly increasing its population and is likely to reach a figure exceeding 250 millions by 1970. This does not include any additions due to territorial changes as a result of the war. This growth of population taken together with technological and other kinds of progress inevitably makes it the dominant power in Europe and Asia. In Asia much depends on the industrial development of China and India. Their huge populations are a burden and a weakness unless they are properly and productively organized. In Europe the great colonial powers of the past appear to have definitely passed the stage of expansion and aggression. Their economic and political organization and the skill and ability of their people may still give them an important place in world affairs, but they will progressively cease to count as major powers, unless they function as a group. 'It does not seem likely that any nation of north-western and central Europe will challenge the world again. Germany, like her western neighbours, has passed the period in which she could become a dominant world power, owing to the diffusion of technological civilization to peoples that are growing more rapidly.'*

Technological and industrial growth have brought power to a number of western peoples and countries. It is exceedingly unlikely that this source of power will remain the monopoly of a few nations. Hence the political and economic dominance of Europe over great parts of the world must inevitably decline rapidly and it will cease to be the nerve-centre of the Eurasian continent and Africa. Because of this basic reason the old European powers will think and act more in terms of peace and international co-operation and will avoid war in so far as they can. When aggression is almost certain to lead to disaster, it ceases to attract. But those world powers, that are still dominant, have not the same urge to co-operation with others, unless it is the moral urge, which is very seldom associated with power.

What is the cause of this widespread phenomenon of falling birth-rates? The increasing use of contraceptives and the desire to have small regulated families may have produced some effect, but it is generally recognized that this has not made any great difference. In Ireland, which is a catholic country and where contraceptives are presumably little used, a fall in the birth-rate started earlier than in other countries. Probably the increasing postponement of marriages in the west is one of the causes. Economic factors may have some influence but even that is hardly an important consideration. It is well known that as a rule fertility is higher among the poor than among the rich, as it is also higher in rural areas than in urban. A smaller group can maintain higher standards, and the growth of individualism lessens the importance of the group and the race. Professor J. B. S. Haldane tells us that it is a general rule that in a great many civilized societies those types which are regarded in the particular society in question as admirable are less fertile than the general run of the population. Thus those societies would appear to be biologically unstable. Large families are often associated with inferior intelligence. Economic success is also supposed to be the opposite of biological success.

*Frank W. Notestein in an article on 'Population and Power in Post-War Europe' in the American, Foreign Affairs' for April, 1944. (The I.L.O. have issued a study on 'The Displacement of Population in Europe' by E. M. Kulischer 1943).

Little seems to be known about the basic causes behind the falling birth-rate, though many subsidiary ones are suggested. It is possible, however, that certain physiological and biological reasons lie at the back of it—the kind of life industrialized communities lead and the environment in which they live. A deficient diet, alcoholism, neurotic conditions or poor health generally, mental or physical, affect reproduction. And yet disease-ridden and insufficiently fed communities, as in India, still reproduce themselves at a prodigious rate. Perhaps the strain and stress of modern life, the ceaseless competition and worry, lessen fertility. Probably the divorce from the life-giving soil is an important factor. Even in America the fertility of farm labourers is considerably more than double that of the professional classes.

It would seem that the kind of modern civilization that developed first in the west and spread elsewhere, and especially the metropolitan life that has been its chief feature, produces an unstable society which gradually loses its vitality. Life advances in many fields and yet it loses its grip; it becomes more artificial and slowly ebbs away. More and more stimulants are needed— drugs to enable us to sleep or to perform our other natural functions, foods and drinks that tickle the palate and produce a momentary exhilaration at the cost of weakening the system, and special devices to give us a temporary sensation of pleasure and excitement—and after the stimulation comes the reaction and a sense of emptiness. With all its splendid manifestations and real achievements, we have created a civilization which has something counterfeit about it. We eat ersatz foods produced with the help of ersatz fertilizers; we indulge in ersatz emotions and our human relations seldom go below the superficial plane. The advertiser is one of the symbols of our age with his continuous and raucous attempts to delude us and dull our powers of perception and induce us to buy unnecessary and even harmful products. I am not blaming others for this state of affairs. We are all products of this age with the characteristics of our generation, equally entitled to credit or blame. Certainly I am as much a part of this civilization, that I both appreciate and criticize, as any one else and my habits and ways of thought are conditioned by it.

What is wrong with modern civilization which produces at the roots these signs of sterility and racial decadence? But this is nothing new, it has happened before and history is full of examples of it. Imperial Rome in its decline was far worse. Is there a cycle governing this inner decay and can we seek out the causes and eliminate them? Modern industrialism and the capitalist structure of society cannot be the sole causes, for decadence has often occurred without them. It is probable, however, that in their present forms they do create an environment, a physical and mental climate, which is favourable for the functioning of those causes. If the basic cause is something spiritual, something affecting the mind and spirit of man, it is difficult to grasp though we may try to understand it or intuitively feel it. But one fact seems to stand out: that a divorce from the soil, from the good earth, is bad for the individual and the race.

The earth and the sun are the sources of life and if we keep away from them for long life begins to ebb away. Modern industrialized communities have lost touch with the soil and do not experience that joy which nature gives and the rich glow of health which comes from contact with mother earth. They talk of nature's beauty and go to seek it in occasional week-ends, littering the countryside with the product of their own artificial lives, but they cannot commune with nature or feel part of it. It is something to look at and admire, because they are told to do so, and then return with a sigh of relief to their normal haunts; just as they might try to admire some classic poet or writer and then, wearied by the attempt, return to their favourite novel or detective story, where no effort of mind is necessary. They are not children of nature, like the old Greeks or Indians, but strangers paying an embarrassing call on a scarce-known distant relative. And so they do not experience that joy in nature's rich life and infinite variety and that feeling of being intensely alive which came so naturally to our forefathers. Is it surprising then that nature treats them as unwanted step-children?

We cannot go back to that old pantheistic outlook and yet perhaps we may still sense the mystery of nature, listen to its song of life and beauty, and draw vitality from it. That song is not sung in the chosen spots only, and we can hear it, if we have the ears for it, almost everywhere. But there are some places where it charms even those who are unprepared for it and comes like the deep notes of a distant and powerful organ. Among these favoured spots is Kashmir where loveliness dwells and an enchantment steals over the senses. Writing about Kashmir, M. Foucher, the French savant, says: 'May I go further and say what I believe to be the true reason for this special charm of Kashmir, the charm which everybody seeks, even those who do not try to analyse it? It cannot be only because of its magnificent woods, the pure limpidity of its lakes, the splendour of its snowy mountain tops, or the happy murmur of its myriad brooks sounding in the cool soft air. Nor can it be only the grace or majesty of its ancient buildings, though the ruins of Martand rise at the prow of their Karewa as proudly as a Greek temple on a promontory, and the little shrine of Payar, carved out of ten stones, has the perfect proportions of the choragic monuments of Lysicrates. One cannot even say that it comes of the combination of art and landscape, for fine buildings in a romantic setting are to be found in many other countries. But what is found in Kashmir alone is the grouping of these two kinds of beauty in the midst of a nature still animated with a mysterious life, which knows how to whisper close to our ears and make the pagan depths of us quiver, which leads us back, consciously or unconsciously, to those past days lamented by the poet, when the world was young, when

le ciel sur la terre
*Marchait et respirait dans un peuple de dieux.**

But my purpose is not to praise Kashmir, though my partiality for it occasionally leads me astray, nor to advance an argument in favour of pantheism, though I am pagan enough to believe that a touch of paganism is good for the mind and body. I do think that life cut off completely from the soil will ultimately wither away. Of course there is seldom such a complete cutting off and the processes of nature take their time. But it is a weakness of modern civilization that it is progressively going further away from the life-giving elements. The competitive and acquisitive characteristics of modern capitalist society, the enthronement of wealth above everything else, the continuous strain and the lack of security for many, add to the ill-health of the mind and produce neurotic states. A saner and more balanced economic structure would lead to an improvement of these conditions. Even so it will be necessary to have greater and more living contacts with the land and nature. This does not mean a return to the land in the old and limited sense of the word, or to a going back to primitive ways of life. That remedy might well be worse than the disease. It should be possible to organize modern industry in such a way as to keep men and women, as far as possible, in touch with the land, and to raise the cultural level of the rural areas. The village and the city should approach each other in regard to life's amenities, so that in both there should be full opportunities for bodily and mental development and a full all-rounded life.

That this can be done I have little doubt, provided only that people want to do it. At present there is no such widespread desire and our energies are diverted (apart from killing each other) in producing ersatz products and ersatz amusements. I have no basic objection to most of these, and some I think are definitely desirable, but they absorb the time that might often be better employed and give a wrong perspective to life. Artificial fertilisers are in great demand to-day and I suppose they do good

*'L'art greco-bouddhique du Gandhara.'

in their own way. But it does seem odd to me that in their enthusiasm for the artificial product, people should forget natural manure and even waste it and throw it away. Only China, as a nation, has had the good sense to make full use of the natural stuff. Some experts say that artificial fertilisers, though producing quick results, weaken the soil by depriving it of some essential ingredients, and thus the land grows progressively more sterile. With the earth, as with our individual lives, there is far too much of burning the candle at both ends. We take her riches from her at a prodigious pace and give little or nothing back.

We are proud of our increasing ability to produce almost anything in the chemical laboratory. From the age of steam, we proceeded to that of electricity and now we are in an age of biotechnics and electronics. The age of social science, which we hope will solve many of the intimate problems that trouble us so much, looms ahead. We are also told that we are on the threshold of the magnesium-aluminium age and as both these metals are extremely abundant and universally distributed, there can be no lack for any one. The new chemistry is building a new life for mankind. We seem to be on the verge of increasing enormously the power resources of humanity and all manner of epoch-making discoveries hover over the near future.

All this is very comforting and yet a doubt creeps into my mind. It is not lack of power that we suffer from but a misuse of the power we possess or not a proper application of it. Science gives power but remains impersonal, purposeless, and almost unconcerned with our application of the knowledge it puts at our disposal. It may continue its triumphs and yet, if it ignores nature too much, nature may play a subtle revenge upon it. While life seems to grow in outward stature, it may ebb away inside for lack of something yet undiscovered by science.

The Modern Approach to an Old Problem

The modern mind, that is to say the better type of the modern mind, is practical and pragmatic, ethical and social, altruistic and humanitarian. It is governed by a practical idealism for social betterment. The ideals which move it represent the spirit of the age, the Zeitgist, the Yugadharma. It has discarded to a large extent the philosophic approach of the ancients, their search for ultimate reality, as well as the devotionalism and mysticism of the medieval period. Humanity is its god and social service its religion. This conception may be incomplete, as the mind of every age has been limited by its environment, and every age has considered some partial truth as the key to all truth. Every generation and every people suffer from the illusion that their way of looking at things is the only right way, or is, at any rate, the nearest approach to it. Every culture has certain values attached to it, limited and conditioned by that culture. The people governed by that culture take these values for granted and attribute a permanent validity to them. So the values of our present-day culture may not be permanent and final; nevertheless they have an essential importance for us for they represent the thought and spirit of the age we live in. A few seers and geniuses, looking into the future, may have a completer vision of humanity and the universe; they are of the vital stuff out of which all real advance comes. The vast majority of people do not even catch up to the present-day values, though they may talk about them in the jargon of the day, and they live imprisoned in the past.

We have therefore to function in line with the highest ideals of the age we live in, though we may add to them or seek to mould them in accordance with our national genius. Those ideals may be classed under two heads: humanism and the scientific spirit. Between these two there has been an apparent conflict but the great upheaval of thought to-day, with its questioning of all values, is removing the old boundaries between these two approaches, as well as between the external world of science and the internal world of introspection. There is a growing synthesis between humanism and the scientific spirit, resulting in a kind of scientific humanism. Science also, while holding on to fact, is on the verge of other domains, or at any rate, has ceased to deny them contemptuously. Our five senses and what they can perceive, obviously, do not exhaust the universe. During the past twenty-five years there has been a profound change in the scientist's picture of the physical world. Science used to look at nature as something almost apart from man. But now, Sir James Jeans tells us that the essence of science is that 'man no longer sees nature as something distinct from himself.' And then the old question arises which troubled the thinkers of the Upanishads: how can the knower be known? How can the eyes that can see external objects see themselves? And if the external is part and parcel of the internal, what we perceive or conceive is but a projection of our minds, and the universe and nature and the soul and mind and body, the transcendent and the immanent are all essentially one, how then are we, within the limited framework of our minds to understand this mighty scheme of things objectively? Science has begun to touch these problems and though they may elude it, still the earnest scientist of to-day is the prototype of the philosopher and the man of religion of earlier ages. 'In this materialistic age of ours,' says Professor Albert Einstein, 'the serious scientific workers are the only profoundly religious people.'*

*Fifty years ago, Vivekananda regarded modern science as a manifestation of the real religious spirit, for it sought to understand truth by sincere effort.

In all this there appears to be a firm belief in science and yet an apprehension that purely factual and purposeless science is not enough. Was science, in providing so much of life's furniture, ignoring life's significance? There is an attempt to find a harmony between the world of fact and the world of spirit, for it was becoming increasingly obvious that the over-emphasis on the former was crushing the spirit of man. The question that troubled the philosophers of old has come up again in a different form and context: How to reconcile the phenomenal life of the world with the inner spiritual life of the individual. The physicians have discovered that it is not enough to treat the body of the individual or of society as a whole. In recent years, medical men, familiar with the finding of modern psycho-pathology, have abandoned the antithesis between 'organic' and 'functional' diseases, and lay greater stress on the psychological factor. 'This is the greatest error in the treatment of sickness,' wrote Plato, 'that there are physicians for the body and physicians for the soul, and yet the two are one and indivisible.'

Einstein, most eminent among scientists, tells us that 'the fate of the human race was more than ever dependent on its moral strength to-day. The way to a joyful and happy state is through renunciation and self-limitation everywhere.' He takes us back suddenly from this proud age of science to the old philosophers, from the lust for power and the profit motive to the spirit of renunciation with which India has been so familiar. Probably most other scientists of to-day will not agree with him in this or when he says: 'I am absolutely convinced that no wealth in the world can help humanity forward, even in the hands of the most devoted worker in the cause. The example of great and pure characters is the only thing that can produce fine ideas of noble deeds. Money only appeals to selfishness and always tempts its owners irresistibly to abuse it.'

In facing this question, that is as old as civilization itself, modern science has many advantages denied to the old philosophers. It possesses stores of accumulated knowledge and a method which has abundantly justified itself. It has mapped and chartered many regions which were unknown to the ancients. As it has enlarged man's understanding and control over many things, they have ceased to be mysteries to be exploited by the priests of religion. But it has some disadvantages also. The very abundance of its accumulated knowledge has made it difficult for man to take a synthetic view of the whole, and he loses himself in some part of it, analyses it, studies it, partly understands it, and fails to see its connection with the whole. The vast forces science has released overwhelm him and carry him forward relentlessly, and often an unwilling victim, to unknown shores. The pace of modern life, the succession of crisis after crisis, comes in the way of a dispassionate search for truth. Wisdom itself is hustled and pushed about and cannot easily discover that calm and detached out-look which is so necessary for true understanding. 'For still are the ways of wisdom and her temper trembleth not.'

Perhaps we are living in one of the great ages of mankind and have to pay the price for that privilege. The great ages have been full of conflict and instability, of an attempt to change over from the old to something new. There is no permanent stability or security or changelessness; if there were life itself would cease. At the most we can seek a relative stability and a moving equilibrium. Life is a continuous struggle of man against man, of man against his surroundings, a struggle on the physical, intellectual, and moral plane out of which new things take shape and fresh ideas are born. Destruction and construction go side by side and both aspects of man and nature are ever evident. Life is a principle of growth, not of standing still, a continuous becoming, which does not permit static conditions.

To-day, in the world of politics and economics there is a search for power and yet when power is attained much else of value has gone. Political trickery and intrigue take the place of idealism, and cowardice and selfishness the place of disinterested courage. Form prevails over substance, and power, so eagerly sought after, somehow fails to achieve what it aimed at. For power has its limitations, and force recoils on itself. Neither can control the spirit, though they may harden and coarsen it. 'You can rob an army of its general,' says Confucius, 'but not the least of men of his will.'

John Stuart Mill wrote in his autobiography: 'I am now convinced that no great improvements in the lot of mankind are possible, until a great change takes place in the fundamental constitution of their modes of thought.' And yet that fundamental change in the modes of thought itself comes from a changing environment and the pain and suffering that accompany life's unceasing struggles. And so, though we may try to change those modes of thought directly, it is even more necessary to change the environment in which they grew and found sustenance. Each depends on and influences the other. There is an endless variety of men's minds. Each one sees the truth in his own way and is often unable to appreciate another's viewpoint. Out of this comes conflict. Out of this interaction also a fuller and more integrated truth emerges. For we have to realize that truth is many-sided and is not the monopoly of any group or nation. So also the way of doing things. There may be different ways for different people in different situations. India and China, as well as other nations, evolved their own ways of life and gave them an enduring foundation. They imagined, and many among them vainly imagine still, that their way is the only way. To-day, Europe and America have evolved their own way of life, which is dominant in the world, and which, their people imagine, is the only way. But probably none of these ways is the one and only desirable way and each may learn something from the other. Certainly India and China must learn a great deal, for they had become static and the west not only represents the spirit of the age but is dynamic and changing and has the capacity for growth in it, even though this functions through self-destruction and periodical human sacrifice.

In India, and perhaps in other countries also, there are alternating tendencies for self-glorification and self-pity. Both are undesirable and ignoble. It is not through sentimentality and emotional approaches that we can understand life, but by a frank and courageous facing of realities. We cannot lose ourselves in aimless and romantic quests unconnected with life's problems, for destiny marches on and does not wait for our leisure. Nor can we concern ourselves with externals only, forgetting the significance of the inner life of man. There has to be a balance, an attempt at harmony between them. 'The greatest good,' wrote Spinoza in the seventeenth century, 'is the knowledge of the union which the mind has with the whole of nature....The more the mind knows the better it understands its forces and the order of nature; the more it undrestands its forces or strength, the better it will be able to direct itself and lay down rules for itself; and the more it understands the order of nature the more easily it will be able to liberate itself from useless things; this is the whole method.'

In our individual lives also we have to discover a balance between the body and the spirit, and between man as part of nature and man as part of society. 'For our perfection,' says Tagore, 'we have to be vitally savage and mentally civilized; we should have the gift to be natural with nature and human with human society.' Perfection is beyond us for it means the end, and we are always journeying, trying to approach something that is ever receding. And in each one of us are many different human beings with their inconsistencies and contradictions, each pulling in a different direction. There is the love of life and the disgust with life, the acceptance of all that life involves and the rejection of much of it. It is difficult to harmonize these contrary tendencies, and sometimes one of them is dominant and sometimes another.

'Oftentimes,' says Lao Tzu:

Oftentimes, one strips oneself of passion
In order to see the Secret of Life;

561

Oftentimes, one regards life with passion,
In order to see its manifold results.

For all our powers of reason and understanding and all our accumulated knowledge and experience, we know little enough about life's secrets, and can only guess at its mysterious processes. But we can always admire its beauty and, through art, exercise the god-like function of creation. Though we may be weak and erring mortals, living a brief and uncertain span of life, yet there is something of the stuff of the immortal gods in us. 'We must not,' therefore, says Aristotle, 'obey those who urge us, because we are human and mortal, to think human and mortal thoughts; in so far as we may we should practise immortality, and omit no effort to live in accordance with the best that is in us.'

Epilogue

Nearly five months have gone by since I took to this writing and I have covered a thousand hand-written pages with this jumble of ideas in my mind. For five months I have travelled in the past and peeped into the future and sometimes tried to balance myself on that 'point of intersection of the timeless with time.' These months have been full of happenings in the world and the war has advanced rapidly towards a triumphant conclusion, so far as military victories go. In my own country also much has happened of which I could be only a distant spectator, and waves of unhappiness have sometimes temporarily swept over me and passed on. Because of this business of thinking and trying to give some expression to my thoughts, I have drawn myself away from the piercing edge of the present and moved along the wider expanses of the past and the future.

But there must be an end to this wandering. If there was no other sufficient reason for it, there is a very practical consideration which cannot be ignored. I have almost exhausted the supply of paper that I had managed to secure after considerable difficulty and it is not easy to get more of it.

The discovery of India—what have I discovered? It was presumptuous of me to imagine that I could unveil her and find out what she is to-day and what she was in the long past. To-day she is four hundred million separate individual men and women, each differing from the other, each living in a private universe of thought and feeling. If this is so in the present, how much more difficult is it to grasp that multitudinous past of innumerable successions of human beings. Yet something has bound them together and binds them still. India is a geographical and economic entity, a cultural unity amidst diversity, a bundle of contradictions held together by strong but invisible threads.

Overwhelmed again and again, her spirit was never conquered, and to-day when she appears to be the plaything of a proud conqueror, she remains unsubdued and unconquered. About her there is the elusive quality of a legend of long ago; some enchantment seems to have held her mind. She is a myth and an idea, a dream and a vision, and yet very real and present and pervasive. There are terrifying glimpses of dark corridors which seem to lead back to primeval night, but also there is the fullness and warmth of the day about her. Shameful and repellent she is occasionally, perverse and obstinate, sometimes even a little hysteric, this lady with a past. But she is very lovable, and none of her children can forget her wherever they go or whatever strange fate befalls them. For she is part of them in her greatness as well as her failings, and they are mirrored in those deep eyes of hers that have seen so much of life's passion and joy and folly, and looked down into wisdom's well. Each one of them is drawn to her, though perhaps each has a different reason for that attraction or can point to no reason at all, and each sees some different aspect of her many-sided personality. From age to age she has produced great men and women, carrying on the old tradition and yet ever adapting it to changing times. Rabindranath Tagore, in line with that great succession, was full of the temper and urges of the modern age and yet was rooted in India's past, and in his own self built up a synthesis of the old and the new. 'I love India,' he said, 'not because I cultivate the idolatry of geography, not because I have had the chance to be born in her soil but because she has saved through tumultuous ages the living words that have issued from the illuminated consciousness of her great ones.' So many will say, while others will explain their love for her in some different way.

The old enchantment seems to be breaking to-day and she is looking around and waking up to the present. But however she changes, as change she must, that old witchery will continue and hold the hearts of her people. Though her attire may change, she will continue as of old, and her store of wisdom will help her to hold on to what is true and beautiful and good in this harsh, vindictive, and grasping world.

The world of to-day has achieved much, but for all its declared love for humanity, it has based itself far more on hatred and violence than on the virtues that make man human. War is the negation of truth and humanity. War may be unavoidable sometimes, but its progeny are terrible to contemplate. Not mere killing, for man must die, but the deliberate and persistent propagation of hatred and falsehood, which gradually become the normal habits of the people. It is dangerous and harmful to be guided in our life's course by hatreds and aversions, for they are wasteful of energy and limit and twist the mind and prevent it from perceiving the truth. Unhappily there is hatred to-day in India and strong aversions, for the past pursues us and the present does not differ from it. It is not easy to forget repeated affronts to the dignity of a proud race. Yet, fortunately, Indians do not nourish hatred for long; they recover easily a more benevolent mood.

India will find herself again when freedom opens out new horizons, and the future will then fascinate her far more than the immediate past of frustration and humiliation. She will go forward with confidence, rooted in herself and yet eager to learn from others and co-operate with them. To-day she swings between a blind adherence to her old customs and a slavish imitation of foreign ways. In neither of these can she find relief or life or growth. It is obvious that she has to come out of her shell and take full part in the life and activities of the modern age. It should be equally obvious that there can be no real cultural or spiritual growth based on imitation. Such imitation can only be confined to a small number which cuts itself off from the masses and the springs of national life. True culture derives its inspiration from every corner of the world but it is home-grown and has to be based on the wide mass of the people. Art and literature remain lifeless if they are continually thinking of foreign models. The day of a narrow culture confined to a small fastidious group is past. We have to think in terms of the people generally, and their culture must be a continuation and development of past trends, and must also represent their new urges and creative tendencies.

Emerson, over 100 years ago, warned his countrymen in America not to imitate or depend too much culturally on Europe. A new people as they were, he wanted them not to look back on their European past but to draw inspiration from the abounding life of their new country. 'Our day of dependence, our long apprenticeship to the learning of other lands, draws to a close. The millions that around us are rushing into life cannot always be fed on the sere remains of foreign harvests. Events, actions arise, that must be sung, that will sing themselves...there are creative manners, there are creative actions and creative words...that is, indicative of no custom or authority, but springing spontaneous from the mind's own sense of good and fair.' And again in his essay on self-reliance: 'It is for want of self-culture that the superstition of travelling, whose idols are Italy, England, Egypt, retains its fascination for all educated Americans. They who made England, Italy, or Greece venerable in the imagination did so by sticking fast where they were, like an axis of the earth. In manly hours we feel that duty is our place. The soul is no traveller; the wise man stays at home, and when his necessities, his duties, on any occasion call him from his house, or into foreign fields, he is at home still, and shall make men sensible by the expression of his countenance that he goes the missionary of wisdom and virtue, and visits cities and men like a sovereign and not like an interloper or a valet.'

'I have no churlish objection,' continues Emerson, 'to the cir-cum-navigation of the globe, for the purposes of art, of study, and benevolence, so that man is first domesticated, or does not go abroad with the hope of finding something greater than he knows. He who travels to be amused, or to get somewhat which he does not carry, travels away from himself, and grows old even in youth among old things. In Thebes, in Palmyra, his will and mind have become old and dilapidated as they. He carries ruins to ruins.

'But the rage for travelling is a symptom of a deeper unsound-ness affecting the whole intellectual action....We imitate.... Our houses are built with foreign taste; our shelves are garnished with foreign ornaments; our opinions, our tastes, our faculties, lean on and follow the past and the distant. The soul created the arts wherever they have flourished. It was in his own mind that the artist sought his model. It was an application of his own thought to the thing to be done and the conditions to be observed....Insist on yourself; never imitate. Your own gift you can present every moment with the cumulative force of a whole life's cultivation; but of the adopted talent of another you have only an extemporaneous half possession.'

We in India do not have to go abroad in search of the past and the distant. We have them here in abundance. If we go to foreign countries it is in search of the present. That search is necessary, for isolation from it means backwardness and decay. The world of Emerson's time has changed and old barriers are breaking down; life becomes more international. We have to play our part in this coming internationalism and, for this pur-pose, to travel, meet others, learn from them and understand them. But a real internationalism is not something in the air without roots or anchorage. It has to grow out of national cultures and can only flourish to-day on a basis of freedom and equality and true internationalism. Nevertheless Emerson's warn-ing holds to-day as it did in the past, and our search can only be fruitful in the conditions mentioned by him. Not to go any-where as interlopers, but only if we are welcomed as equals and as comrades in a common quest. There are countries, notably in the British dominions, which try to humiliate our countrymen. They are not for us. We may, for the present, have to suffer the enforced subjection to an alien yoke and to carry the grievous burdens that this involves, but the day of our liberation cannot be distant. We are citizens of no mean country and we are proud of the land of our birth, of our people, our culture and traditions. That pride should not be for a romanticised past to which we want to cling; nor should it encourage exclusiveness or a want of appreciation of other ways than ours. It must never allow us to forget our many weaknesses and failings or blunt our longing to be rid of them. We have a long way to go and much leeway to make up before we can take our proper station with others in the van of human civilization and progress. And we have to hurry, for the time at our disposal is limited and the pace of the world grows ever swifter. It was India's way in the past to welcome and absorb other cultures. That is much more necessary to-day, for we march to the one world of to-morrow where national cultures will be intermingled with the international culture of the human race. We shall therefore seek wisdom and knowledge and friendship and comradeship wherever we can find them, and co-operate with others in common tasks, but we are no suppliants for others' favours and patronage. Thus we shall remain true Indians and Asiatics, and become at the same time good internationalists and world citizens.

My generation has been a troubled one in India and the world. We may carry on for a little while longer, but our day will be over and we shall give place to others, and they will live their lives and carry their burdens to the next stage of the journey. How have we played our part in this brief interlude that draws to a close? I do not know. Others of a later age will judge. By what standards do we measure success or failure? That too I do not know. We can make no complaint that life has treated us harshly, for ours has been a willing choice, and perhaps life has not been so bad to us after all. For only they can sense life who stand often on the verge of it, only they whose lives are not governed by the fear of death. In spite of all the mistakes that we may have made, we have saved ourselves from triviality and an inner shame and cowardice. That, for our individual selves, has been some achievement. 'Man's dearest possession is life, and since it is given to him to live but once, he must so live as not to be seared with the shame of a cowardly and trivial past, so live as not to be tortured for years without purpose, so live that dying he can say: "All my life and my strength were given to the first cause of the world—the liberation of mankind." '*

*Nicoli Ostrovsky.

566

POSTSCRIPT

Allahabad 29th December 1945

DURING MARCH AND APRIL, 1945, THE MEMBERS OF THE CONGRESS Working Committee, interned in Ahmadnagar Fort prison camp, were dispersed and sent to their respective provinces. The camp jail was wound up and presumably reverted to the military authorities. Three of us—Govind Ballabh Pant, Narendra Deva, and I—left Ahmadnagar Fort on March 28th and were brought to Naini Central Prison where we met a number of our old colleagues, among whom was Rafi Ahmad Kidwai. For the first time since our arrest in August, 1942, we had an opportunity of having first-hand accounts of some of the occurrences of 1942, for many of those in Naini Prison had been arrested some time after us. From Naini we three were taken to Izatnagar Central Prison, near Bareilly. Govind Ballabh Pant was released on account of ill-health. Narendra Deva and I lived together in a barrack in this prison for over two months. Early in June we were transferred to the mountain prison of Almora, which I had known so intimately ten years earlier. On June 15th we were both discharged, 1,041 days after our arrest in August, 1942. Thus ended my ninth and longest term of imprisonment.

Since then six months and a half have passed. I came from the long seclusion of prison to crowds, intense activity and continuous travelling. I spent only a night at home and then hurried to Bombay for a meeting of the Congress Working Committee. And then to the Simla Conference convened by the Viceroy. I found it a little difficult to adjust myself to the new and changing environment and could not easily fit in. Though everything was familiar and it was good to meet old friends and colleagues, I felt somewhat as a stranger and an outsider, and my mind wandered to mountains and snow-covered peaks. As soon as the Simla business was over I hurried to Kashmir. I did not stay in the valley, but almost immediately started on a trek to the higher regions and passes. For a month I was in Kashmir and then I came back to the crowds and the excitements and boredoms of everyday life.

Gradually some picture of the past three years formed itself in my mind. I found, as others did, that what had taken place was far more than we had imagined. These three years had been a time of heavy travail for our people and each person we met bore the mark of it on his face. India had changed and under the seeming quiet of the surface there was doubt and questioning, frustration and anger, and a suppressed passion. With our release and the turn events took, a change came over the scene. The smooth surface was ruffled and cracks appeared. Waves of exitement passed across the country; after three years of suppression, the people broke through that shell. I had not previously seen such crowds, such frenzied excitement, such a passionate desire on the part of masses of people to free themselves. Young men and women, boys and girls, were afire with the urge to do something, though what they should do was not clear to them.

The War ended and the atom bomb became the symbol of the new age. The use of this bomb and the tortuous ways of power politics brought further disillusion. The old imperialisms still functioned, and events in Indonesia and Indo-China added to the horror of the scene. The use of Indian troops in both these countries against people struggling to be free brought shame to us at our helplessness and an abiding anger and bitterness. The temper of the country continued to rise.

The story of the Indian National Army, formed in Burma and Malaya during war years, spread suddenly throughout the country and evoked an astonishing enthusiasm. The trial by court martial of some of its officers aroused the country as nothing else had done, and they became the symbols of India fighting for her freedom. They became also the symbol of unity among the various religious groups in India, for Hindu and Moslem and Sikh and Christian were all represented in that army. They had solved the communal problem amongst themselves, and so why should we not do so?

We are on the eve of general elections in India and these elections absorb attention. But the elections will be over soon— and then? The coming year is likely to be one of storm and trouble, of conflict and turmoil. There is going to be no peace in India or elsewhere except on the basis of freedom.

INDEX

A

Abbasiya Khalifas, 229
Abdul Hamid, Sultan, 346
Abdul Rahim Khankhana, 260, 269
Abend, Hallet, 504n
Abdur-Razzak, 240
Abhidharmakosa, 173n
Abu Nasr Farabi, 233
Abyssinia, 18, 47, 418, 421
Adams, Brooke, quoted, 297-98
Adil Sha, Ibrahim, 161
Advaita Ashrama, 339n
Advaita Vedanta, 28, 32, 189-90, 337
Afghan(istan), 141, 142, 213, 227, 229, 234, 237-39, 241-43, 248, 258-59, 264, 417, 421, 536
Afghan Period, 147, 160, 167, 198, 237-39, 241-43, 249
Africa, 227, 228, 332, 421
Africa, future of, 537, 544, 546-47
Aga Khan, 346, 354,
Agra, 51, 58, 258
Agra, battle of, 276
Agriculture, ancient, 111, 299-301
 National Congress, and, 371
Ahimsa, 108, 187
Ahmad, Dr. Nazir, 346
Ahmadnagar Fort, 15, 35, 240, 478-79, 567
Ahmad Nizam Shah, 240
Ahmad Shah Durrani, 274
Ahmedabad, 331, 485
Ahrars, 386, 393
Aibak, Qutb-ud-Din, 238
Aiterya Brahmana, 91
Aiyar, Sir C. P. Ramaswami, quoted, 527-28n
Ajanta frescoes, 153, 203, 213

Akbar, Emperor, 35, 52, 142, 242, 257-61, 263-65, 269-71, 344
Akhand Hindustan, 532
Akkad, 70
Al Ahzar University, Cairo, 347
Alaric, the Goth, 215
Al-Balagh, 349
Alberuni, 156, 234-35
Albuquerque, 207, 260
Alcestis, 163n
Alcibiades, quoted, 359-60
Alexander the Great, 98, 114-15, 122-23
Alexandria, 154, 216
Al-Hilal, 347-50
Alice in Wonderland, 100
Aligarh College, 345, 348, 354
Ali, Maulana Mohammad, 349
Ali, Munshi Karamat, 346
Ali, Shaukat, 349
Ali, Syed Chirag, 346
Al Khwarismi, 232
Allahabad, 39, 42, 51, 325
Al-Mansur, Khalif, 220, 232
Almora Jail, 39, 567
Amarji, Ranchodji, 235n
Amarnath Cave, 192
Ambala, 70
Americans in India, see U.S.A.
Amery, Leopold, 438, 461, 490, 496
Amaravati University, 223
Amritsar massacre, 325, 340
Ananda, 130
Ananga, 101
Ancient Indian Colonies, 201n
Andhra(s), 61, 132
Angkor, 51, 201, 204, 205, 208-09
Annam, 205
Ansari, Dr. M.A., 347
Antigonus, 115

vital energy of, 55; Vivekananda on, 337

Universities, 117-18, 132, 223; Moslem; 343, 345, 347, 348-49; strikes in, 487; under English rule, 316-17

Untouchables, 253-54

Upanishads, 77, 89-94, 96, 98, 108, 119, 173, 176, 179, 189, 339, 558; Chhandogya, 93n, 177

Urdu, 168, 317

Urwick, 155

V

Vaishesika system, 184

Vaishnavaism, 314

Vaishyas, 85, 253, 332

Vallabhi University, 223

Vasanta, 101

Vasubandhu, 173n

Vedānta, system, 28, 32, 93, 187, 335, 337; *Advaita*, 28, 32, 189, 337

Vedas, 76-77, 79-80, 335, 520

Vedic dharma, 74

Vedic religion, 77, 146, 156

Viceroy's Council, 293

Vijayanagar, 240-41, 258

Vikram Samvant calendar, 103

Vikramshila University, 223

Village autonomy, 247, 523

Village industries, 303; distribution of, 402-03, 407-09

Vindhya Mountains, 107

Virgil, 160

Vishaka-datta, 160

Vishnu, 208

Vivekananda, Swami, 92, 187-88, 336-39, 341, 343, 558n

W

Wales, Dr. H.G. Quaritch, 201

Waley, Arthur, 199

Warfare, 141, 230-31, 246, 260

Watt, 298

Wells, H. G., quoted, 135, 531

Western Culture, 291-92, 314, 317

White Huns, 120, 139, 222

White India, 148

White Road, 453

Willkie, Wendell, 537; quoted, 492

Wilson, Woodrow, 537

Winternitz, Prof. 76

Women, position of 41, 118, 242-43, 267-68; rights of, 383; suttee, 315; underground, 357, 412

Woodhead, Sir John, 496n, 498n

Working Committee, 374, 426-7, 433-34, 442, 446, 476-78, 567

World War I, 347, 349, 353, 357, 389, 410, 427, 536

World War II, 18-19, 394, 401, 410, 411, 416-68, 481-84, 536-48

Writings, Hindu, 115-16

Y

Yajnavalkya, 118, 122, 358

Yarkand, 194

Yashovarman, 205

Yaswant Rao, Holkar, 278

Yavanas, 155

Yemen, 228

Yi-Tsing (I-Tsing), 193

Yoga system, 184-88, 337

Young Turk Movement, 346

Yuan-Chwang (*see* Huan Tsang), 139, 180

Yueh Chih, 74, 136, 143

Z

Zainulabdin, 244

Zakaullah, Munshi, 346

Zamindari system, 371

Zetland, Marquis of, quoted, 256, 438

Zoroastrianism, 137, 146, 147, 170